lonely planet

Austria

Upper Austria
p151

Vienna
p56

The
Salzkammergut
p198

Lower Austria &
Burgenland
p113

Tyrol & Vorarlberg
p284

Salzburg &
Salzburgerland
p216

Styria
p172

Carinthia
p261

THIS

Ken

04989018

Contents

HALLSTÄTTER SEE, P202

SCHLOSS MIRABELL,
SALZBURG P225

Contents

First Time Austria

Welcome to Austria

Austria is a contrast of spectacular natural landscapes and elegant urban sleeves. One day you're plunging into an alpine lake, the next you're exploring a narrow backstreet of Vienna.

Culture in Many Disguises

The cultural contours of the Habsburg empire can be felt everywhere in Austria today, whether it's while taking in a performance of Lipizzaner stallions, or crossing the Hofburg to admire a Rubens masterpiece in the Kunsthistorisches Museum. Beyond this grand historical face, the classical works of composer Arnold Schönberg, inspired by Mozart, echo atonally across the country; music festivals like Bregenzer Festspiele are staged against spectacular lakeside or mountain backdrops, and artists like Klimt, Schiele and the radical Actionists feature in Vienna's extraordinary MuseumsQuartier.

Landscapes & the Outdoors

Travel in Austria is often a meandering journey through deeply carved valleys, along roads and railways cut improbably into the rocky flanks of mountains, and around picturesque lakes. But often the landscape is simply too rugged for road or rail: hiking and mountain biking is then the best way to reach isolated alpine meadows. Sometimes cable cars or dizzying chair-lifts offer an alternative way up, and come winter they bundle skiers and snowboarders onto the slopes. Austria's plentiful lakes are ideal for summer swimming, and in winter many freeze over for skating.

Architecture

Austria is best known for its sugar-cake baroque church interiors, its historic palaces such as Schloss Belvedere and its Gothic masterpieces such as Stephansdom, but we don't often imagine it as a country with impressive contemporary architectural contours. A visit to Vienna's MuseumsQuartier, to Ars Electronica in Linz, or a stroll alongside the illuminated 'slug-like' Kunsthaus Graz casts Austria in a different light.

Food & Wine Experiences

You can taste countries – their food, their wines, their customs of years gone by. Vienna's traditional coffee houses are perfect for breathing in the dark aromas of coffee in a homely atmosphere. Traditional *Beisln* (bistro pubs) are laced with the smell of goulash and other traditional dishes. Outside Vienna, regions such as the Waldviertel, the Danube Valley and southern Styria are places for rustic food and wine experiences in picturesque landscapes. Traditional *Heurigen* (wine taverns) abound almost everywhere – places to explore local specialities while on on trips through Austria's character-filled gourmet and wine regions.

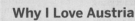

Why I Love Austria

By Anthony Haywood, Author

One day you're riding a forestry track in Carinthia, stopping to wash down a *Brettljause* (cold platter) with a cool beer in a meadow hut, the next you're combing the atmospheric alleys of the capital. The contrasts are what I love most about Austria. It's small, but the landscape changes quickly and dramatically, offsetting one experience of a place against another – the boondocks in contrast to a large city like Vienna, or a cool alpine lake like Weissensee with the shallow-steppe Neusiedler See. And in Vienna itself, there's a stark contrast between the historic centre and the Vorstädte (inner suburbs), which I love exploring on walks at night.

For more about our authors, see page 416

Above: Zillertal Alps (p301), Tyrol

Austria

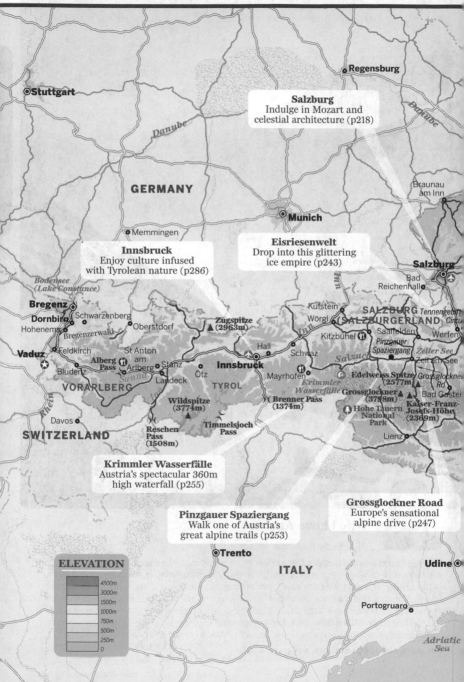

Salzburg
Indulge in Mozart and celestial architecture (p218)

Innsbruck
Enjoy culture infused with Tyrolean nature (p286)

Eisriesenwelt
Drop into this glittering ice empire (p243)

Krimmler Wasserfälle
Austria's spectacular 360m high waterfall (p255)

Pinzgauer Spaziergang
Walk one of Austria's great alpine trails (p253)

Grossglockner Road
Europe's sensational alpine drive (p247)

Stuttgart

Regensburg

GERMANY

Memmingen

Munich

Braunau
am Inn

Salzburg

Bad
Reichenhall

Bodensee
(Lake Constance)

Bregenz
Dornbirn
Hohenems
Schwarzenberg
Oberstdorf
Bregenzerwald

Zugspitze
▲(2963m)

Kufstein
Wörgl

SALZBURG
SALZBURGERLAND
Tennengebirge
Circu

Saalfelden
Pinzgauer
Spaziergang

Werfen

Vaduz
Feldkirch
St Anton
am
Alberg
Pass
Arlberg Stanz
Bludenz
Landeck
VORARLBERG
Sanna

Hall

Schwaz

Kitzbühel

Zeller See

Zell am See

Innsbruck

Ötz
TYROL
Mayrhofen

Inn

Salzach

Krimmler
Wasserfälle

Edelweiss Spitze
▲(2577m)
Grossglockne
Rd

Grossglockner
▲(3798m)
▲
Bad Gastei

Kaiser-Franz-
Josefs-Höhe
(2369m)

Davos

Wildspitze
(3774m)
▲

Reschen
Pass
(1508m)

Timmelsjoch
Pass

Brenner Pass
(1374m)

Hohe Tauern
National
Park

Rhein

SWITZERLAND

Lienz

Trento

ITALY

Udine

Portogruaro

Adriatic
Sea

Stuttgart

Danube

Danube

ELEVATION

4500m
3000m
1500m
1000m
750m
500m
250m
0

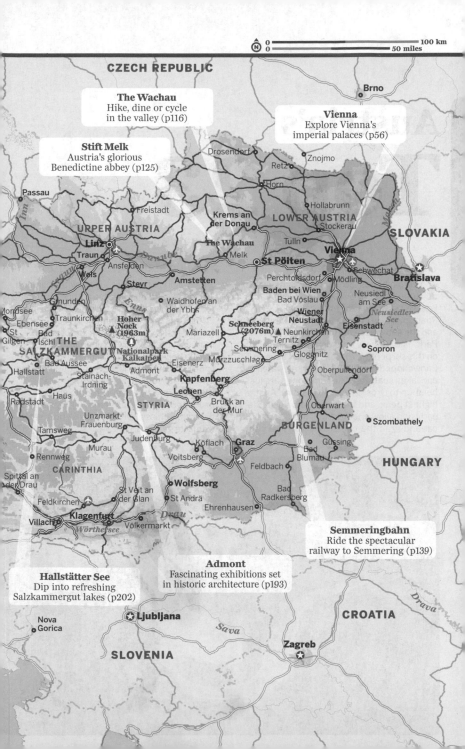

CZECH REPUBLIC

0 ──── 100 km
0 ──── 50 miles

The Wachau
Hike, dine or cycle
in the valley (p116)

Vienna
Explore Vienna's
imperial palaces (p56)

Stift Melk
Austria's glorious
Benedictine abbey (p125)

Brno

Drosendorf

Znojmo

Retz

Passau

Horn

Freistadt

Hollabrunn

UPPER AUSTRIA

Krems an
der Donau

LOWER AUSTRIA

Stockerau

SLOVAKIA

Linz

The Wachau

Tulln

Traun

Melk

St Pölten

Vienna

Ansfelden

Schwechat

Wels

Perchtoldsdorf

Mödling

Bratislava

Steyr

Amstetten

Baden bei Wien

Neusiedl
am See

Bad Vöslau

Gmunden

Waidhofen an
der Ybbs

Wiener
Neustadt

Neusiedler
See

Mondsee

Traunkirchen

Hoher
Nock
(1963m)

Mariazell

Schneeberg
(2076m)

Neunkirchen

Eisenstadt

Ebensee

St
Gilgen

Bad
Ischl

Ternitz

Sopron

**THE
SALZKAMMERGUT**

**Nationalpark
Kalkalpen**

Semmering

Bad Aussee

Eisenerz

Mürzzuschlag

Gloggnitz

Oberpullendorf

Hallstatt

Admont

Stainach-
Irdning

Kapfenberg

Radstadt

Haus

Leoben

Bruck an
der Mur

Oberwart

Unzmarkt-
Frauenburg

STYRIA

BURGENLAND

Tamsweg

Judenburg

Köflach

Graz

Szombathely

Murau

Gössing

Voitsberg

Murau

Bad
Blumau

Rennweg

CARINTHIA

Feldbach

HUNGARY

Spittal an
der Drau

Wolfsberg

Bad
Radkersberg

Feldkirchen

St Veit an
der Glan

St Andrä

Villach

Klagenfurt

Ehrenhausen

Wörthersee

Völkermarkt

Drau

Semmeringbahn
Ride the spectacular
railway to Semmering (p139)

Admont
Fascinating exhibitions set
in historic architecture (p193)

Hallstätter See
Dip into refreshing
Salzkammergut lakes (p202)

Nova
Gorica

Ljubljana

CROATIA

Sava

Drava

SLOVENIA

Zagreb

Austria's
Top 23

Grossglockner Road

1 Hairpin bends: 36. Length: 48km. Average slope gradient: 9%. Highest viewpoint: Edelweiss Spitze (2571m). Grossglockner Road (p246) is one of Europe's greatest drives and the showpiece of Hohe Tauern National Park. The scenery unfolds as you climb higher on this serpentine road. And what scenery! Snowcapped mountains, plunging waterfalls and lakes scattered like gemstones are just the build-up to Grossglockner (3798m), Austria's highest peak, and the Pasterze Glacier. Start early and allow enough time, there's a stop-the-car-and-grab-the-camera view on every corner.

Imperial Palaces of Vienna

2 Imagine what you could do with unlimited riches and Austria's top architects at hand for 640 years and you'll have the Vienna of the Habsburgs. The monumentally graceful Hofburg (p65) whisks you back to the age of empires; marvel at the treasury's imperial crowns, the equine ballet of the Spanische Hofreitschule (p66) and the chandelier-lit apartments fit for Empress Elisabeth. The palace is rivalled in grandeur only by the 1441-room Schloss Schönbrunn (p82), a Unesco World Heritage site, and baroque Schloss Belvedere (p78), both set in exquisite gardens. Right: Schloss Schönbrunn (p82)

Skiing

3 In a country where three-year-olds can snowplough, 70-year-olds still slalom and the tiniest village has its own lift system, skiing is more than just a sport – it's a way of life. Why? Just look around you. There's St Anton am Arlberg for off-piste and après-ski, Mayrhofen for freestyle boarding and its epic Harakiri, Kitzbühel for its perfect mix – the scope is limitless and the terrain fantastic. Cross-country or back-country, downhill or glacier, whatever your ski style, Austria has a piste with your name on it.

Top: Skiing in St Anton am Arlberg (p320)

Festung Hohensalzburg

4 Work up a sweat on the steep walk or step into the funicular and sway up to Salzburg's glorious fortress, Festung Hohensalzburg (p219), beckoning on a forested peak above the city. As you make your way through Europe's best-preserved fortress, glide through the Golden Hall, with its celestial ceiling capturing the star-lit heavens. After all this beauty, you will find yourself cast among a chilling array of medieval torture instruments in the Fortress Museum. Don't miss the 360-degree views from the tower.

Invigorating Spas

5 Austria's crisp mountain air and thermal springs radiate good health. Drift off in flying-saucer-shaped pools at crystalline Aqua Dome (p314), or in the fantastical hot springs of Hundertwasser's technicolor Rogner-Bad Blumau (p196). History bubbles to the surface in the Wienerwald's Römertherme (p136), where beauty-conscious Romans once took the sulphuric waters. The Victorians favoured Bad Gastein (p259), whose radon-laced springs reputedly cure a multitude of ills.

Top: Alpen Therme spa (p260), Bad Hofgastein

The Wachau

6 When Strauss composed 'The Blue Danube', he surely had the Wachau in mind. Granted Unesco World Heritage status for its natural and cultural beauty, this stretch of the Danube Valley waltzes you through landscapes of terraced vineyards, forested slopes and apricot orchards. Beyond the Stift Melk, Dürnstein's Kuenringerburg (p121) begs exploration. This hilltop castle is where the troubadour Blondel attempted to rescue Richard the Lionheart from the clutches of Duke Leopold V. Bottom: Krems an der Donau (p116), Danube Valley

Outdoor Adventure in Tyrol

7 Anywhere where there's foaming water, a tall mountain or a sheer ravine, there are heart-pumping outdoor escapades in Austria. For a summertime buzz, you can't beat throwing yourself down raging rivers such as the Inn and Sanna in Tyrol, Austria's rafting mecca. Or strap into your harness and be blown away by the alpine scenery paragliding in the Zillertal. Cyclists use the cable-car network to access the many high-altitude and downhill routes. Below: Hiking in Tyrol (p286)

The Sound of Music

8 Salzburg is a celebrity for those who have never even set foot in the city, thanks to its star appearance in *The Sound of Music*. The sculpture-dotted Mirabellgarten (p225) of 'Do-Re-Mi' fame, the Benedictine nunnery Stift Nonnberg (p225), the 'Sixteen Going on Seventeen' pavilion in Hellbrunn Park (p241) – it's enough to make you yodel out loud. For the truth behind the celluloid legend, stay the night at the original Villa Trapp (p231), a 19th-century mansion in the Aigen district. Below: View of Stift Nonnberg (p225), Salzburg

WESTEND61/ GETTY IMAGES ©

Hiking the Pinzgauer Spaziergang

9 You're on the Pinzgauer Spaziergang, a crisp blue sky overhead, snowy peaks crowding the horizon. You're waking up to a rose-tinted sunrise in the Dolomites. You're thanking your lucky stars you packed your walking boots... Locals delight in telling you that the best – no, no, the only – way to see the Austrian Alps is on foot. And they're right. Here a peerless network of trails and alpine huts brings you that bit closer to nature.

Cafe Culture in Vienna

10 A pianist plays and bow-tied waiters bustle to and fro . Ahhh, this is what the Viennese mean by *Gemütlichkeit* (cosiness), you realise, as you sip your *Melange* (milky coffee), rustle your newspaper and watch life go decadently by. Café Sacher (p99) for the richest of chocolate cakes, Café Jelinek (p103) for its quirky vibe, Café Leopold Hawelka (p99) for bohemian flavour. Indulge, talk, read and dream; just as Trotsky and Freud, Hundertwasser and Warhol once did. Top: Café Leopold Hawelka (p99)

MuseumsQuartier

11 Once the imperial stables, now one of the world's biggest exhibition spaces, Vienna's 60,000-sq-metre Museums-Quartier (p67) contains more art than some small countries. Emotive works by Klimt and Schiele hang out in the Leopold Museum (p72), while the basalt MUMOK (p72) highlights provocative Viennese Actionists, and the Kunsthalle (p72) new media. Progressive boutiques, workshops and cafes take creativity beyond the canvas. On warm days, Viennese gather in the huge courtyard to chat, drink and watch the world go by.

Stift Melk

12 Austria's greatest works of art are those wrought for God, some say. Gazing up at the golden glory of Stift Melk (p125), Austria's must-see Benedictine abbey-fortress, you can't help but agree. The twin-spired monastery church is a baroque tour de force, swirling with prancing angels, gilt flourishes and Johann Michael Rottmayr's ceiling paintings. Such opulence continues in the library and marble hall, both embellished with illusionary *trompe l'oeil* tiers by Paul Troger. If you can, stay to see the monarch of monasteries strikingly lit by night. Below: Stift Melk's spiral staircase

STEPHEN SAKS / GETTY IMAGES ©

Salzburg Festival

13 No country can outshine Austria when it comes to classical music. The country was a production line of great composers in the 18th and 19th centuries. And there's always a reason to celebrate that heritage, especially at the much-lauded Salzburg Festival (p230). Held late July to August, and staged for the first time in 1920, today it is a highlight of Austria's cultural calendar. As well as concerts featuring illustrious composers such as home-grown Mozart, make sure you catch an opera and a theatre performance or two.

Eisriesenwelt

14 The twinkling chambers and passageways of Eisriesenwelt (p243) are like something out of Narnia under the White Witch. Sculpted drip by drip over millenniums, the icy underworld of the limestone Tennengebirge range is billed as the world's largest accessible ice cave. Otherworldly sculptures, shimmering lakes and a cavernous *Eispalast* (ice palace) appear as you venture deep into the frozen heart of the mountain, carbide lamp in hand. Even in summer, temperatures down here are subzero, so wrap up warm.

Admont's Benedictine Abbey

15 Situated deep in the rifts of the Gesäuse mountains in Styria, Admont's Benedictine Abbey (p193) is a remarkable fusion of landscape, architecture and museum space. The baroque library, with its ceiling frescoes from the 18th century, should be sufficient to lure you into this remote region. But take the time to stroll around the museums, which bring together the region's natural history with contemporary art and works from past ages. From a glass staircase you can revel in the spectacular view to the Nationalpark Gesäuse. Top: Ceiling frescoes

Lakes of the Salzkammergut

16 With its jewel-coloured alpine lakes, the Salzkammergut is a great place to escape the hustle and bustle of the city. The Hallstätter See (p202), set at the foot of the abrupt and monumentally rugged Dachstein Mountains, is a spectacular place to enjoy the lakes. While Hallstatt draws the crowds, across the lake in Obertraun (p204) the lake shore retains a sleepy air. A stroll around the warmer and gentler Wolfgangsee (p211) is within easy reach of small towns like Bad Aussee and Bad Ischl, or unfurl the sails and let the breeze carry you along on the Mondsee (p214). Bottom: Hallstatt, Hallstätter See

15

16

WESTEND61 / GETTY IMAGES ©

GETTY IMAGES / GETTY IMAGES ©

Krimmler Wasserfälle

17 No doubt you'll hear the thunderous roar of the 380m-high Krimmler Wasserfälle (p255), Europe's highest waterfall, before you see it. You can't help but feel insignificant when confronted with the sheer force and scale of this cataract, which thrashes immense boulders and produces the most photogenic of rainbows. It looks best from certain angles, namely from the Wasserfallweg (Waterfall Trail). The path zigzags up through moist, misty forest to viewpoints that afford close-ups of the three-tiered falls and a shower in its fine spray.

Graz

18 Austria's largest city after Vienna is also one the country's most relaxed. After you have visited Schloss Eggenberg (p176) and climbed the Schlossberg (p175) for magnificent views of town – perhaps sipping a long drink or two on a warm afternoon at the Aiola Upstairs (p180) – set your sights upon the south Styrian wine roads. This winegrowing region about 50km south of Graz is a treat to the tastebuds as well as to the eyes: rolling, verdant hills and picturesque vineyards unfolding to the Slovenian border.Graz. Top right: Uhrturm (p175), Schlossberg Hill, Graz

Semmeringbahn

19 The monumental Semmeringbahn (p139; Semmering Railway) is a panoramic journey through the eastern Alps and a nostalgic trip back to early rail travel. Some 20,000 workers toiled to create the railway, an alpine first, in a feat of 19th-century engineering that is now a Unesco World Heritage site. Though steam has been replaced by electricity, you can still imagine the wonder of the first passengers as the train curves around 16 viaducts, burrows through 15 tunnels and glides across 100 stone bridges. The grandeur of the railway and landscapes is timeless.

DANITA DELIMONT / ALAMY ©

Wine Tasting in Heurigen

20 If you see an ever-green branch hanging on a door in Vienna's outskirts and around the Neusiedler See, you've probably stumbled across a traditional *Heuriger*. Pull up a chair in one of these wine taverns to taste the local vintage of crisp white Grüner Veltliner and spicy Blaufränkisch wines. The experience is partly to do with the wine and partly what surrounds it – the atmosphere, the scenery, the chatty locals, the hearty food. September is the month for new wine and vineyard strolls. Top Left: *Heurigen* in Grinzing (p98), Vienna

Mozart's Salzburg

21 Mozart's spiritual home may have been Vienna, but the musical prodigy was born and bred in Salzburg. You can see where the 18th-century superstar lived, loved and composed (p224). Orchestras wish the late Amadeus a happy birthday at Mozartwoche (p227). There are concerts of Mozart's music in the surrounds of the Marmorsaal (Marble Hall) at Schloss Mirabell (p225) year-round and marionettes bring his operas magically to life at the nearby Salzburger Marionettentheater (p236). Top Right: Schloss Mirabell (p225), Salzburg

Innsbruck

22 Set against an impressive backdrop of the Nordkette Alps, Tyrol's capital is the kind of place where at one moment you are celebrating cultural achievement in elegant state apartments (p288) or the Gothic Hofkirche (p287), and the next whizzing up into the Alps inside Zaha Zadid's futuristic funicular (p291) or heading out for the ski pistes. If clinging to a fixed rope on the Innsbrucker Klettersteig (p291) while you make your way across seven peaks sounds too head-swirling, try the marginally less vertiginous Nordkette Singletrail (p291) mountain-bike track.

Vienna's Naschmarkt

23 Austrians pride themselves on mouthwatering, home-grown flavours and many of these find their way to Vienna's largest and most famous market, the Naschmarkt (p97) – fresh cheeses from the Kemptal in Lower Austria or the Bregenzerwald, or Thum ham from the Mangalitza breed. The markets take you not only through the culinary regions of Austria, but also into a sensory world of exotic spices. Drop into the food stalls where you can fill up on some of the capital's best food.

Right: Naschmarkt in Vienna

RICK GERHARTER / GETTY IMAGES ©

23

Need to Know

For more information, see Survival Guide (p381)

Currency
Euro (€)

Language
German

Visas
Austria is part of the Schengen Agreement. Generally, for stays of up to three months a visa is not necessary, but some nationalities need a Schengen visa.

Money
ATMs widely available. Maestro direct debit and Visa and MasterCard credit cards accepted in most hotels and in midrange restaurants.

Mobile Phones
Travellers from outside Europe will need a tri or quad band (world) mobile phone for roaming. Local SIM cards (about €15) are easily purchased for 'unlocked' phones.

Time
Central European Time (GMT/UTC plus one hour)

When to Go

Mild to hot summers, cold winters
Warm to hot summers, mild winters
Mild year-round
Cold climate

Vienna
GO Late Mar–Oct

Kitzbühel
GO Jun–Sep &
Dec–Mar

Salzburg
GO Jul & Aug

Innsbruck
GO Jun–Sep &
Dec–Mar

Graz
GO Apr–Oct

High Season
(Apr–Oct)

➡ High season peaks from July to August.

➡ In lake areas the peak is June to September.

➡ Prices rise over Christmas and Easter.

➡ Salzburg is busiest in July and August for the Salzburg Festival.

Shoulder
(Apr–May & late Sep–Oct)

➡ The weather's changeable, the lakes are chilly and the hiking's excellent.

➡ Sights are open and less crowded.

Low Season
(Nov–Mar)

➡ Many sights are closed at this time of year.

➡ There's a cultural focus in Vienna and the regional capitals.

➡ Ski resorts open from mid-December.

➡ High season for skiing is mid-December to March.

Useful Websites

Lonely Planet (www.lonely-planet.com/austria) Destination information, hotel bookings, traveller forum and more.

Österreich Werbung (www.austria.info) National tourism authority.

Tiscover (www.tiscover.com) Information and hotel bookings.

Embassy of Austria (www.austria.org) US-based website with current affairs and information.

Important Numbers

To dial listings from outside Austria, dial your international access code, the country code, the city code and then the number.

Country code	☑643
International access code	☑00
International operator & information (inland, EU & neighbouring countries)	☑118 877
International operator & information (other countries)	☑090 011 88 77
Mountain rescue	☑140
Emergency (police, fire, ambulance)	☑112

Exchange Rates

Australia	A$1	€0.67
Canada	C$1	€0.69
Japan	¥100	€0.72
New Zealand	NZ$1	€0.60
Russia	RUB1	€0.02
UK	UK£1	€1.21
USA	US$1	€0.74
Switzerland	CHF1	€0.81

For current exchange rates see www.xe.com.

Daily Costs

**Budget:
Less than €80**

➡ Dorm beds or cheap doubles: about €25 per person

➡ Self-catering or lunch specials: €6–€12

➡ Cheap museums: €4

**Midrange:
€80–€160**

➡ Hotel singles: €60–90 per person

➡ Two-course meal with glass of wine: €30

➡ High-profile museums: €12

**Top end:
More than €160**

➡ Luxury suites and doubles in large cities: from €200

➡ Pampering at wellness facilities: €40–€100

➡ Superb meals with fine wine: €70

Opening Hours

Opening hours vary throughout the year. We've provided high-season opening hours, generally from April to October, peaking June to August, with April/May and September/October shoulder seasons. Winter resorts peak December to March.

Banks 8am or 9am to 3pm weekdays, to 5.30pm Thursday

Shops 9am to 6.30pm Monday to Friday and until 5pm Saturday, earlier in small towns

Restaurants 11am to 2.30pm or 3pm and 6pm to 11pm or midnight, kitchen in some open all day

Supermarkets 7.15am to 7.30pm Monday to Friday, to 6pm Saturday

Pubs and clubs See listings. Opening times vary; closing is normally between midnight and 4am throughout the week

Arriving in Austria

Vienna International Airport (p110)The City Airport Train (CAT) runs to Wien-Mitte every 30 minutes from 6.06am to 11.36pm and takes 16 minutes. A bus runs every 30 minutes 24/7; it takes 22 minutes to Schwedenplatz (central Vienna).

Graz Airport (p183) Trains depart at least hourly from 4.47am to 10.47pm Monday to Friday, 5.17am to 10.47pm Saturday and 5.17am to 9.47pm Sunday and take 18 minutes. Buses to the Hauptbahnhof are less frequent but convenient between trains.

Vienna Hauptbahnhof (p394) Due to be fully completed in January 2015. Until finished, many services arrive in Wien-Meidling and Westbahnhof.

Getting Around

Public transport is excellent for reaching even remote regions, but it takes longer.

Car Small towns and even small cities often have limited or no car-hire services, so reserve ahead from major cities.

Train and bus Austria's national railway system is integrated with the Postbus bus services. Plan your route using the Österreiche Bundesbahn (Austrian Federal Railway; ÖBB, www.oebb.at) or Postbus (www.postbus.at) websites.

For much more on **getting around**, see p392

First Time Austria

For more information, see Survival Guide (p381)

Checklist

⇒ Make sure your passport is valid for at least six months from your arrival date

⇒ Make sure you have a visa if you need one (p390)

⇒ Arrange travel insurance, and medical insurance if needed (p387)

⇒ Check credit/debit card can be used with ATMs internationally

⇒ Make copies of all important documents and cards (store online or in hard copy)

⇒ Turn off data roaming on mobile phone

What to Pack

⇒ Hiking boots, plus one pair of dress shoes (with profile for snow)

⇒ Waterproof jacket (summer) or winter jacket

⇒ Day pack

⇒ Electrical adapter if needed (p386)

Top Tips for Your Trip

⇒ Explore towns like Vienna also at night; consider an easy night hike on a forestry track – it gives a different feel.

⇒ Choose a convenient city, small town or village as a regional hub and explore on day trips – it can save time and lugging bags.

⇒ Build time into your day for coffee house or *Beisl* (bistro pub) visits in Vienna and Salzburg between sights, or for sitting around in a park or square to soak up the 'feel' of Austria.

⇒ On one day combine big sights with small ones, and those involving a lot of leg-work with 'lazybones' sights.

What to Wear

Winter can be cold and the ground icy, so several layers of warm clothing and good shoes are essential, along with gloves, scarf and a woollen cap or a hat. In summer wear layers you can peel off and make sure you have something for occasional rain showers. Especially in larger cities, Austrians tend to dress up well in the evening or for good restaurants, but fashion jeans are fine even for upmarket clubs and restaurants if combined with a good shirt or blouse and a men's sports coat *(Sakko)* or women's summer jacket.

Sleeping

From October to March often you won't need to book ahead except during the ski period in resorts. Book three days to a week ahead in May, June and September and for Friday and Saturday nights, earlier for July and August.

⇒ **Hotels** Anything from basic places with cheap laminate woods to stylish five-star resorts. Occasionally breakfast costs extra.

⇒ **Pensionen** Smaller, usually not purpose-built but family-run establishments, many virtually indistinguishable from hotels. Breakfast always included.

⇒ **Private rooms** Tourist offices keep brochures with lists of these, or see tourist-office websites. Similar to a low-budget B&B.

Money

ATMs are located in even the smallest towns, but not all are open 24 hours. Travellers cheques are not accepted; expect to pay cash in many restaurants. Most Austrian ATMs – including Bank of Austria and BAWAG P.S.K. (Postsparkasse) – accept Amex credit cards as well as Visa and MasterCard for cash withdrawals.

For more information, see p388.

Bargaining

Bargaining in shops is not really part of Austrian culture. Flea markets are the exception, or when negotiating a longer-than-usual period of rental for, say, a kayak or a bicycle. Ask whether there's a cheaper rate for that period.

Tipping

➡ **Hotels** One or two euros per bag for bellboys is sufficient. The same in top-flight hotels for valet parking. Leaving loose change behind for cleaners is not expected but appreciated.

➡ **Restaurants** Tip unless the service is abominable. About 10% is common, done by rounding up the bill (eg by saying *zwanzig euro, bitte*) or, if the bill comes in a leather folder, either by stating the amount as you hand it over or leaving the tip in the folder when you leave.

➡ **Bars** About 5% at the bar and 10% at a table.

➡ **Taxis** About 10%.

RUTH EASTHAM & MAX PAOLI / GETTY IMAGES ©

Spittal an der Drau (p275), Carinthia

Etiquette

Austrians are fairly formal and use irony to alleviate social rules and constraints rather than debunk or break them obviously.

➡ **Telephone** Always give your name at the start of a telephone call, especially when making reservations. When completing the call, say *auf Wiederhören* ('goodbye'; customary form on phone).

➡ **Greetings** Use the *Sie* (formal 'you') form unless you're young-ish (in your 20s) and among peers, or your counterpart starts using *du* (informal 'you'). Acknowledge fellow hikers on trails with a *Servus, Grüss di* (or the informal *Grüss dich*) or *Grüss Gott* (all ways of saying 'hello!').

➡ **Eating and Drinking** Bring chocolate or flowers as a gift if invited into a home. Before starting to eat, say *Guten Appetit*. To toast say *Zum Wohl* (if drinking wine) or *Prost!* (beer), and look your counterpart in the eye – not to do so is impolite and reputedly brings seven years of bad sex.

Language

In Vienna, regional capitals and tourist areas such as around lakes or in resorts you'll find a lot of people speak English, especially in restaurants and hotels. In much of the countryside it's a slightly different picture, where you should equip yourself with a few necessary phrases. Conductors on trains and many bus drivers know enough English to help with necessities. See Language (p401) for more information.

If You Like...

Museums & Palaces

MuseumsQuartier Where baroque stables have morphed into Europe's finest modern museum quarter. (p67)

Vienna's Hofburg Home to the Habsburgs for over 600 years and now hosting magnificent museums. (p65)

Schloss Belvedere Prince Eugene's Viennese masterpiece, with sensational art collections. (p78)

Schloss Schönbrunn Vienna's premier palace and gardens where the Habsburg story is told. (p82)

Schloss Eggenberg Graz' magnificent Renaissance palace, with museums and gardens. (p176)

Festung Hohensalzburg Salzburg's mighty 900-year-old fortress, complete with torture chamber. (p219)

Salzburg's Residenz Opulence coupled with European grand masters. (p224)

Hiking

Pinzgauer Spaziergang An alpine walk affording mesmerising views of the snowcapped Hohe Tauern National Park and Kitzbühel Alps. (p253)

Llama trekking A guided walk with gentle-natured camelids. (p40)

Zillertal Circuit A classic alpine day hike starting at a jewel-coloured reservoir and offering fantastic views of the Zillertal Alps. (p301)

Radsattel Circuit One of Vorarlberg's most spectacular hikes, through valleys and high into the realms of glaciers and 3000m mountains. (p338)

Contemporary Eating & Drinking

Café Drechsler Classic goulash in a designer coffee house with DJs. (p101)

Wachau Dine in a restaurant or pack a picnic and head for the picturesque woods and vineyards. (p116)

Der Steirer Wine and the art of goulash. (p180)

Burgenland wines Reds galore. (p141)

South Styrian wine roads Mostly white wine and some excellent food. (p186)

Viennese Beisln & Heurigen Eat at least once in a traditional bistro pub or wine tavern.(p98)

Winter Sports

Major resorts Downhill skiing and snowboarding in Kitzbühel (p306), St Anton am Arlberg (p320) and Mayrhofen (p303).

Schladming Alpine skiing on pistes and on a glacier, plus gripping spectator events.(p195)

Epic descents Streif in Kitzbühel (p306) and Harakiri in Mayrhofen (p303) will test your mettle.

Igloo dreams Spend the night in an igloo at the Kitzsteinhorn Glacier. (p254)

Après-ski Best in St Anton (p320) and Ischgl (p318).

Low key Snowshoeing, sledding and cross-country skiing in Seefeld. (p312)

IF YOU LIKE... THE WIDE OPEN ROAD

Grossglockner Road is one of Austria's greatest mountain drives, with 48km of spectacular views to glistening lakes and into glaciers. (p246)

Lookouts & High Rides

Dachstein Eispalast and Skywalk Dangle precariously

at the vertical rock face before reaching the viewing platform at the top. (p195)

Hintertuxer Gletscher A cable-car ride to the glacier with views to die for. (p303)

Riesenrad Vienna's iconic Ferris wheel combines a great ride with fantastic city views. (p85)

Festung Hohensalzburg Views over the spires, domes and rooftops of Salzburg. (p219)

Edelweiss Spitze On the Grossglockner Road; 360-degree views of more than 30 peaks over 3000m. (p247)

Balthazar im Rudolfsturm Fantastic views over the Hallstätter See and a great place to sip on a long drink. (p204)

Kaisergebirge Kufstein's retro-ride cable car – angst at its most satisfying. (p310)

Mountain Biking & Cycling

Danube cycle path The quintessential path, from the German border via the Wachau and Vienna to Slovakia. (p42)

Schladming With 900km of bike trails and some challenging mountain-bike runs. (p195)

Bodensee cycle path Highly scenic trail circumnavigating Europe's third-largest lake. (p328)

Tauernradweg A 310km trail of mountain landscapes in Hohe Tauern National Park. (p255)

Dachsteinrunde (Dachstein Tour) Fab three-day mountain-bike trail. (p43)

Nordkette Singletrail Innsbruck's tough trail, one of the most exhilarating downhill rides in the country. (p291)

(Above) Danube cycle path (p42), Upper Austria.
(Below) Riesenrad (p85), Vienna's iconic Ferris wheel

Month by Month

January

The ski season is revving. One of the coldest months of the year, this is the time to hit the peaks for downhill or cross-country skiing, or for snowshoe hikes.

☆ New Year Concerts

On 1 January the new year is welcomed with classical concerts. The Vienna Philharmonic's performance in Vienna's Staatsoper is the most celebrated. (p104)

✱✲ Perchtenlaufen

Locals dress as *Perchten* (spirits crowned with elaborate headdresses) and parade through the streets across much of western Austria in a celebration to bring good fortune and bountiful harvests for the year.

☆ Mozartwoche

Held in Salzburg in late January, the Mozart Week celebrates the city's most famous son in a series of concerts. (p227)

February

The winter months are freezing, but in Vienna the museums and cultural scene are in full swing. Crowds are down. On the slopes the skiing is usually still excellent.

March

The sun is thawing the public squares. Hiking and cycling are becoming possible from late March, but many sights outside Vienna are still dormant.

✱✲ Easter

Easter is when families come together to celebrate. Salzburg celebrates with Osterfestspiele (p227), Vienna with OsterKlang Festival (p86).

May

Cities such as Vienna, Salzburg and Graz are a delight on bright days – uncrowded and often warm. A hike to a mountain *Alm* (meadow) becomes a romp through flowers, and since April all sights and activities have opened on a summer schedule.

☆ Wiener Festwochen

In Vienna arts from around the world hit the stages until mid-June. (p86)

☆ Musikwochen Millstatt

In Millstatt in Carinthia a string of concerts is held between May and September, mostly in the medieval abbey. (p277)

June

Mountain lakes are still very chilly, but the Wörthersee and others have soaked up the summer weather. Hiking and kayaking are excellent. Big-hitting sights in Vienna and Salzburg start to get crowded.

☆ Donauinselfest

Vienna gets down for a three-day festival of rock, pop, hardcore, folk and country music on the Donauinsel. (p86)

☆ Tanzsommer

A selection of top international contemporary dance

groups takes to the stage for a month during the Tanzsommer in June and July. (p292)

☆ Sommerszene

Salzburg's cutting-edge dance, theatre and music bash ignites from mid-June to mid-July. (p227)

☆ Styriarte

Graz' most important cultural festival offers almost continuous classical concerts in June and July. (p178)

July

School holidays begin in July, the time when families enjoy the warm weather on lakes and in the mountains. Cities can be sweltering and crowded, but restaurant dining is at its alfresco best.

☆ ImPuls Tanz

Vienna's premier avant-garde, five-week dance festival takes place from mid-July to mid-August, with the participation of dancers, choreographers and academics. (p87)

☆ Salzburg Festival

World-class opera, classical music and drama take the stage across Salzburg from late July to August. (p230)

☆ Spectaculum

On the last Saturday in July electric lights are extinguished and the town of Friesach returns to the Middle Ages. (p273)

August

School holidays continue to propel families into the resorts, making things a bit crowded. Hit some isolated spots in the fine weather – seek out a *Heuriger* (wine tavern) on a vineyard.

☆ Bregenzer Festspiele

Beginning in late July and continuing until late August, this is Vorarlberg's top-class cultural event, with classical music and performances on a floating, open-air stage. (p329)

September

The temperatures are beginning a gradual descent and crowds are tailing off. Museums and most of the activities are still in season, however, and a couple of top-class festivals are revving into action.

☆ Brucknerfest

Linz stages its most celebrated festival, a series of classical concerts based on composer Anton Bruckner. (p156)

☆ Internationale Haydntage

International and Austrian performers take the audience through the range of works by Josef Haydn throughout much of September in his home town of Eisenstadt. (p143)

October

Goldener Oktober – the light reflects the golden browns of autumn, the mountains are growing chilly at night, the wine harvest is in and some museums are preparing to close for winter.

☆ Steirischer Herbst

Held in Graz each year, this avant-garde festival has a program of music, theatre, film and more. (p178)

☆ Viennale

For two weeks from mid-October, city cinemas host screenings from fringe films through documentaries to short and feature films. (p87)

November

Many museums outside the capital have gone into winter hibernation, the days are getting short and the weather can be poor. Cafes, pubs and restaurants become the focal point.

December

Cold has set in, ski resorts are filling and in Vienna and other capitals winter programs are staged in theatres and classical-music venues – often the best performances are during the coldest months.

🔒 Christmas Markets

Christkindlmärkte (Christmas markets) spring up around the country from early December until the 24th and Austrians sip mulled wine on public squares.

☆ Silvester

Book early for the night of 31 December, celebrated with fireworks and a blaze of crackers and rockets on the crowded streets.

Itineraries

2 WEEKS : **Vienna to Salzburg via Graz**

This itinerary is ideal for getting a taste of classic Austria. It begins with three days in **Vienna** soaking up the atmosphere of coffee houses and taking in the top sights.

Board the train on day four and cross the Semmering Pass on one of Europe's finest railway journeys. If you like spa hotels and summer hiking (or winter skiing), alight in **Semmering** for an overnight stop. In summer take in the picturesque surroundings and fresh air on a walk before setting off for **Graz** late on day five or early on day six. In winter in Graz immerse yourself in the cultural scene, catching a performance or visiting a museum or two, and enjoying the local cuisine and nightlife. In summer don't miss Schloss Eggenberg.

After exploring Graz, the **wine roads** in the south or one of the surrounding sights, board the train by day nine for **Schladming**. In Schladming, visit the Skywalk and glacier, staying overnight (longer in winter for snow sports) before finishing the classic trip in **Salzburg** and (in summer) the nearby **Wolfgangsee**.

Vienna to Innsbruck

This trip brings together cities with spectacular scenery. Begin a trip with three days of exploring **Vienna**, making sure you take in either Schloss Belvedere or Schloss Schönbrunn, before heading west along the Danube Valley to **Krems an der Donau**, where you can enjoy good food, visit a couple of museums and tour the region. Don't miss the abbey in **Melk**, also a good place for easy hiking in summer.

On day seven (a day or two earlier in winter), continue the trip to **Linz** for an overnight stay in this industrial city with exciting museums such as the Lentos Kunstmuseum. The trail to **Hallstatt** and the lakes of the Salzkammergut on day eight will restore the feel for the picturesque landscape after Linz.

From Hallstatt you have a choice of travelling to **Salzburg** for the many cultural sights and crossing through Germany to Innsbruck, or bypassing Salzburg and stopping over in picturesque **Zell am See** before continuing to **Innsbruck**, where you can choose between culture, hiking trails (summer) or skiing (winter).

Salzburgerland & Salzkammergut

Get a taste of Mozart's Salzburg combined with magnificent lakes on this itinerary. Begin the trip in **Salzburg** and spend three days exploring the city, taking in big draws like the Festung Hohensalzburg. Make an excursion to the Italianate Schloss Hellbrunn and another to Salzwelten Salzburg in **Hallein** for a taste of the historic salt works.

From Salzburg the road goes south to the most popular and gently picturesque of the lakes in the Salzkammergut, the **Wolfgangsee**, where the summertime swimming, walking and cycling are splendid. Explore the lesser-known towns on hikes or rides over the next three to four days.

From St Wolfgang or St Gilgen on the lake it's a short bus hop to **Bad Ischl**, an excellent base for exploring other lakes in the Salzkammergut over the next three days. The most spectacular of these is the Hallstätter See, with **Hallstatt** or the quieter (but less historic) **Obertraun** perfect for overnighting. Near Obertraun, take in the ice caves on a cable-car ride and do one of the hikes in the area. Around Hallstatt you can visit another of the excellent salt works.

10 DAYS Styria & Carinthia

Consider combining this short itinerary with other adventures to put together a longer trip. Begin the trip in **Graz** and plan three or four days to get to know the city, its sights and its culinary delights. Explore the lively eating and drinking scenes or the formal cultural scene. On the fourth day take an excursion along the south **Styrian wine roads**, a Tuscan-like landscape hugging the Slovenian border with vineyards at every bend. You might like to spend a fifth day at one of the places easily accessible from Graz.

A train takes you to Klagenfurt via **Leoben** where you can break the journey for a few hours and check out its Museums-Centre Leoben. The remaining five days can be divided between the Carinthian towns of **Klagenfurt** and **Wörthersee**, **Villach** or **Spittal an der Drau**, all towns with a sprinkling of sights and good opportunities for activities nearby. Towns such as **Hermagor** in the Gail Valley have great cycling, hiking and (in winter) skiing possibilities at Nassfeld.

For a food, wine and culture focus, plan more time around Graz in Styria. For swimming and other activities, plan more time for Carinthia.

2 WEEKS Tyrol

Kick off with a few days in laid-back **Innsbruck**. Stroll the lanes of the historic Altstadt (old town), taking in its galleries, Habsburg treasures and upbeat nightlife. On the third day, you might opt to take the futuristic funicular to the Nordkette, or head out to Olympic ski jump, Bergisel. From Innsbruck, go south for scenic skiing in the **Stubai Glacier** or west to the exquisite baroque abbey in **Stams**.

Day five leads you further west to the spectacularly rugged **Ötztal**, where you can dip into prehistory at Ötzi Dorf and thermal waters at Aqua Dome spa. Spend the next couple of days rafting near **Landeck**, exploring the Rosengartenschlucht gorge at **Imst**, or hiking and skiing in **St Anton am Arlberg**.

In week two, retrace your steps to Innsbruck and swing east. Factor in a day to tour the pristine medieval town of **Hall in Tirol** and Swarovski Kristallwelten, the heart of the Swarovski crystal empire in **Wattens**. The alpine scenery of the **Zillertal** will keep you occupied with outdoor activities for a few days. Finish your adventure in fortress-topped **Kufstein** and the legendary mountains of **Kitzbühel**.

Plan Your Trip
Austria Outdoors

One look at a map of Austria says it all: jagged peaks and glacier-gouged valleys, mighty rivers and lakes cover almost every last lovely inch of the country. Be it hiking in wildflower-strewn pastures, schussing down Tyrol's mythical slopes or free-wheeling along the Danube, Austria will elevate, invigorate and amaze you.

Skiing & Snowboarding

No matter whether you're a slalom expert, a fearless free rider or a beginner, there's a slope with your name on it in Austria. And, oh, what slopes! Granted, the Swiss and French Alps may have the height edge, but Austria remains Europe's best skiing all-rounder. This land is the origin of modern skiing (thanks to Hannes Schneider's dashing Arlberg technique), the birthplace of Olympic legends and the spiritual home of après-ski. Here you'll find intermediate cruising, knee-trembling black runs and summertime glacier skiing – in short, powdery perfection for every taste and ability.

Ski-Run Classifications

Piste maps are available on most tourist office websites and at the valley stations of ski lifts; runs are colour-coded according to difficulty as follows:

➡ **Blue** Indicates easy, well-groomed runs that are suitable for beginners.

➡ **Red** Indicates intermediate runs, which are groomed but often steeper and narrower than blue runs. Skiers should have a medium level of ability.

➡ **Black** For expert skiers with polished technique and skills. The runs are mostly steep, not always groomed and may have moguls and steep vertical drops.

Best Outdoors

Best Skiing
St Anton am Arlberg (p34) is a holy grail for adventurous skiers, with varied terrain, exhilarating off-piste opportunities, an impeccable snow record and the hottest après-ski in the Austrian Alps.

Best Cycling
The smooth-as-silk Danube Cycle Path shadows the Danube. Take in story-book castles, vineyards and majestic abbeys as you pedal gently along.

Best Climbing
Sheer granite cliffs, bizarre rock formations and boulders make the Zillertal Alps a wonderland for the ardent climber.

Best Rafting
Landeck is a handy base for tackling the swirling waters of the Inn and Sanna Rivers.

Austria Outdoors

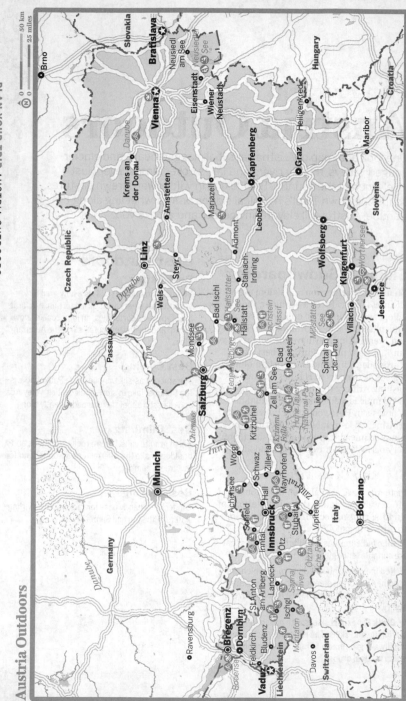

Safety

➡ Avalanches are a serious danger in snowbound areas and can be fatal.

➡ If you're skiing off-piste, never go alone and take an avalanche pole (a collapsible pole used to determine the location of an avalanche victim), a transceiver and a shovel and – most importantly – a professional guide.

➡ See www.lawine.at (in German) for the avalanche risk and snow coverage by region.

➡ UV rays are stronger at high altitudes and intensified by snow glare; wear ski goggles and sunscreen.

➡ Get in good shape before hitting the slopes and build up gradually.

➡ Wear layers to adapt to the constant change in body temperature; make sure your head, wrists and knees are protected (preferably padded).

➡ Before you hurtle down that black run, make sure you're properly insured and read the small print: mountain-rescue costs, medical treatment and repatriation can quickly add up.

Resources

Books

Alpine Ski Mountaineering: Central and Eastern Alps (Bill O'Connor) Great guide detailing ski tours through the Silvretta, Ötztal, Stubai and Ortler ranges.

Where to Ski and Snowboard (Chris Gill and Dave Watts) Updated annually, this is an indispensable guide to the slopes, covering everything from terrain to lift passes.

Which Ski Resort – Europe: Our Top 50 Recommendations (Pat Sharples and Vanessa Webb) Written by a freestyle champ and a ski coach, this handy guide has tips on everything from off-piste to après-ski.

Websites

Bergfex (www.bergfex.com) A great website with piste maps, snow forecasts of the Alps and details of every ski resort in Austria.

If You Ski (www.ifyouski.com) Resort guides, ski deals and info on ski hire and schools. You can beat the slopeside queues by prebooking your lift pass online.

MadDog Ski (www.maddogski.com) Fun skiing website full of insider tips on everything from slopes to where to stay and après-ski.

On the Snow (www.onthesnow.co.uk) Reviews of Austria's ski resorts, plus snow reports, webcams and lift pass details.

Where to Ski & Snowboard (www.where-toskiandsnowboard.com) Key facts on resorts, which are ranked according to their upsides and downsides, plus user reviews.

World Snowboard Guide (www.worldsnowboardguide.com) Snowboarder central, with comprehensive information on most Austrian resorts.

Lift Passes

Costing around €250 or thereabouts for a week, lift passes are a big chunk out of your budget. The passes give access to one or more ski sectors and nearly always include ski buses between the different areas. Lift passes for lesser-known places may be as little as half that charged in the jet-set resorts. Count on around €35 to €50 for a one-day ski pass, with substantial reductions for longer-term passes. Children usually pay half-price, while under-fives ski for free (bring a passport as proof of age).

Most lift passes are now 'hands-free', with a built-in chip that barriers detect automatically, and many can be prebooked online.

Equipment Hire

Skis (downhill, cross-country, telemark), snowboards, boots, poles and helmets can be rented at sport shops like **Intersport** (www.intersport.at) in every resort. Ski, snowboard or cross-country ski rental costs around €28/127 per day/week, or €34/158 for top-of-the-range gear. Boot hire is around €16/61 per day/week. With Intersport, children 14 and under pay half-

---

SOS SIX

The standard alpine distress signal is six whistles, six calls, six smoke puffs, six yodels – that is, six of whatever sign or sound you can make – repeated every 10 seconds for one minute. If you have a mobile phone, make sure you take it with you. **Mountain rescue** (☎140) in the Alps is very efficient but extremely expensive, so make sure you have adequate insurance (read the fine print).

price, under-10s get free ski hire when both parents rent equipment, and you can ski seven days for the price of six.

Ski Tuition

Most ski resorts have one or more ski schools; for a list of regional ski schools, visit www.skilehrer.at (in German) and click on 'Landesverbände'. Group lessons for both adults and children typically cost €70 per day (two hours in the morning, two hours in the afternoon), €200 for four days and €260 for six days. The more days you take, the cheaper it gets. Private instruction is available on request. Kids can start learning from the age of four.

Regions

Ski Amadé

Salzburgerland's **Ski Amadé** (www.skiamade.com; Salzburgerland; full-region 6-day pass €218) is Austria's biggest ski area, covering a whopping 860km of pistes in 25 resorts divided into five snow-sure regions. Among them are low-key Radstadt (p245) and family-friendly Filzmoos (p244). Such a vast area means that truly every level is catered for: from gentle cruising on tree-lined runs to off-piste touring.

Ski Arlberg

With 340km of slopes, **Ski Arlberg** (www.skiarlberg.at; Tyrol/Vorarlberg; 6-day pass €235) is one of Austria's most famous skiing regions and deservedly so. After all, this is the home of St Anton am Arlberg (p320), a mecca to expert skiers and boarders, with its great snow record, challenging terrain and terrific off-piste; not to mention the most happening après-ski in Austria, if not Europe. Its over-the-valley neighbours are the resorts of Lech and Zürs (p339) in Vorarlberg.

Kitzbühel (Tyrol)

The legendary Hahnenkamm, 170km of groomed slopes, a car-free medieval town centre and upbeat nightlife all make Kitzbühel (p306) one of Austria's most popular resorts. Critics may grumble about unreliable snow – with a base elevation of 762m, Kitzbühel is fairly low by alpine standards – but that doesn't stop skiers who come for the varied downhill, snowboarding and off-piste. A six-day KitzAlps AllStarCard for Kitzbühel and nine other resorts in the region (a total 1087km of slopes) costs €241.

Zillertal Arena

Mayrhofen (p303) is the showpiece of the **Zillertal Arena** (www.zillertalarena.at; Tyrol; 6-day Zillertal Superskipass €224), which covers 166km of slopes and 49 lifts (some pretty hi-tech) in the highly scenic Zillertal. As well as being intermediate heaven, Mayrhofen has Austria's steepest black run, the kamikaze-like Harakiri with a 78% gradient, and appeals to freestylers for its fantastic terrain park. Even if snow

---

TOP SLOPES

Cruise, carve, party and quake in your boots at some of these top spots:

➡ **Top descents** The Streif (p307), part of the epic Hahnenkamm, is Kitzbühel's king of scary skiing. Mayrhofen's Harakiri (p303) is Austria's steepest run, with a gradient of 78%. It's pitch-black and there's no turning baaaaaack...

➡ **Top family skiing** Filzmoos (p244) for its uncrowded nursery slopes, chocolate-box charm and jagged Dachstein mountains. Heiligenblut (p248) is refreshingly low-key and has a ski kindergarten.

➡ **Top snowboarding** Mayrhofen (p303) is a mecca to free riders, and some say it has Austria's most *awesome* terrain park, Vans Penken.

➡ **Top après-ski** Join the singing, swinging, Jägermeister-fuelled fun in St Anton am Arlberg (p320), Austria's après-ski king. Wild inebriation and all-night clubbing are the winter norm in raucous rival Ischgl (p318).

➡ **Top glacier skiing** The Stubai Glacier (p312) has snow-sure pistes within easy reach of Innsbruck. Head to the Kitzsteinhorn Glacier (p249) for pre- and post-season skiing at 3203m, with arresting views of the snowy Hohe Tauern range.

SLOPE SAVERS

It's worth checking websites like www.igluski.com, www.skiingaustria.co.uk, www.ifyouski.com and www.j2ski.com for last-minute ski deals and packages. Local tourist offices and www.austria.info might also have offers.

You can save time and euros by prebooking ski and snowboard hire online at **Snowbrainer** (www.snowbrainer.com), which gives a discount of up to 50% on shop rental prices.

lies thin in the valley, it's guaranteed at the nearby Hintertux Glacier (p303).

Zell am See–Kaprun

The lakeside resort of Zell am See (p249) and its twin **Kaprun** (www.zellamsee-kaprun.com; Zell am See–Kaprun, Hohe Tauern National Park; 6-day pass €225) share 138km of sunny slopes. Pistes tend to be more of the tree-lined and scenic kind, making this a sound choice for novices and families. Even if the snow coverage is thin on the lower slopes, there's fresh powder and a terrain park at the Kitzsteinhorn Glacier to play in. The après-ski in Zell am See's car-free old town is lively but not rowdy. The entire region affords gorgeous views of the glacier-capped Hohe Tauern range.

Silvretta-Montafon

The iconic arrow-shaped peak of Piz Buin (3312m) dominates the **Silvretta-Montafon** (http://winter.silvretta-montafon.at; Vorarlberg; 6-day pass €212.50) ski area. Tucked away in the southeast corner of Vorarlberg, this serene and beautiful valley's low-key resorts appeal to families, cruisers and ski tourers. Besides 246km of slopes to play on, there is off-piste fun from sledding to winter hiking.

Silvretta Arena

Ischgl (p318) is the centrepiece of the **Silvretta Arena** (www.silvretta.at; Tyrol; full-region 6-day pass €257), comprising 238km of prepared slopes and 71 ultramodern lifts. High slopes above 2000m mean guaranteed snow, mostly geared towards confident intermediates, off-piste fans and boarders. The resort has carved a name for itself as a party hot spot, with big-name season opening and closing concerts, and pumping (borderline sleazy) après-ski. For those seeking a quieter vibe, Galtür, Kappl and Samnaun (Switzerland) are nearby.

Sölden

The Ötztal (p313) is defined by some of the wildest and highest mountains in Austria. Its main ski resort is snow-sure **Sölden** (www.soelden.com; Tyrol; 6-day pass €246), with 150km of slopes between 1350m and 3340m, a state-of-the-art lift network and a crazy après-ski scene. The terrain is intermediate heaven, but presents more of a challenge on long runs such as the 50km Big 3 Rally and off-piste. A bonus to skiing here is the snow reliability on two glaciers (Rettenbach and Tiefenbach), making this a great pre- or late-season choice.

Cross-Country Skiing

Cross-country skiing (Langlauf) in Austria is considerably greener and cheaper than skiing (a day pass costs as little as €3 with a guest card). The two main techniques are the classic lift-and-glide method on prepared cross-country tracks (Loipen) and the more energetic 'skating' technique. The basics are easy to master at a cross-country school and tracks are graded from blue to black according to difficulty.

Seefeld (p312) features among Austria's top cross-country skiing destinations, with 279km of Loipen criss-crossing the region, including a floodlit track. Zell am See (p249) is another hot spot, with 40km of groomed trails providing panoramic views of the Hohe Tauern mountains. Other great resorts to test your stamina and stride include the Bad Gastein (p256) region, with 90km of well-marked

SUMMER SNOW

If the thought of pounding the powder in summer appeals, hightail it to glaciers such as the Stubai Glacier, Hintertux Glacier and Kitzsteinhorn Glacier, where, weather permitting, there's fine downhill skiing year-round.

cross-country trails. To search for cross-country regions and packages, see www.langlauf-urlaub.at (in German).

Walking & Hiking

Der Berg ruft (the mountain calls) is what Austrians say as they gallivant off to the hills at the weekend, and what shopkeepers post on closed doors in summer. And what more excuse do you need?

For Austrians, *Wandern* (walking) is not a sport, it's second nature. Kids frolicking in alpine pastures, nuns Nordic-walking in the hills, superfit 70-somethings trekking over windswept 2000m passes – such universal wanderlust is bound to rub off on you sooner or later.

With its towering peaks, forest-cloaked slopes and luxuriantly green valleys, the country's landscapes are perfectly etched and the walking opportunities are endless. Strike into Austria's spectacularly rugged backyard, listen closely and you too will hear those mountains calling...

Weather

If there's one rule of thumb in the Austrian Alps, it's to never take the weather for granted. It may *look* sunny but conditions can change at the drop of a hat – hail, lightning, fog, torrential rain, you name it.

Check the forecast before embarking on long hikes at high altitudes. Tourist offices also display and/or provide mountain-weather forecasts.

Österreichischer Alpenverein (ÖAV, Austrian Alpine Club; www.alpenverein.at) A reliable web source for weather forecasts for the alpine regions.

Snow Forecast (www.snow-forecast.com) Up-to-date snow forecasts for major Austrian ski resorts.

Wetter Österreich (www.wetter.at) Day and three-day weather forecasts, plus up-to-date weather warnings.

Walk Designations

Austria is criss-crossed with well-maintained *Wanderwege* (walking trails), which are waymarked with red-white-red stripes (often on a handy rock or tree) and yellow

---

HIKING EQUIPMENT CHECKLIST

Clothing
- ☐ windproof and waterproof jacket
- ☐ breathable fleece
- ☐ loose-fitting walking trousers, preferably with zip-off legs
- ☐ hiking shorts
- ☐ T-shirts or long-sleeved shirts
- ☐ socks (polypropylene)
- ☐ sun hat
- ☐ sunglasses
- ☐ swimwear (optional)

Footwear
- ☐ walking boots with a good grip
- ☐ trekking sandals or thongs
- ☐ socks

Other Equipment
- ☐ backpack or daypack
- ☐ sleeping bag
- ☐ water bottle
- ☐ map
- ☐ compass
- ☐ Swiss Army knife

For Emergencies
- ☐ emergency food rations
- ☐ first-aid kit
- ☐ torch (flashlight) with batteries and bulbs
- ☐ whistle
- ☐ mobile phone
- ☐ transceiver
- ☐ shovel
- ☐ avalanche pole

Miscellaneous Items
- ☐ camera and lenses
- ☐ umbrella
- ☐ insect repellent
- ☐ sunscreen (SPF15+)
- ☐ high-energy food (eg nuts, dried fruit, bread, cured meat)
- ☐ at least 1L of water per person, per day
- ☐ toiletries, toilet paper and towel
- ☐ stuff sacks

For Hikes above 2000m
- ☐ thermal underwear
- ☐ extra clothing
- ☐ gaiters
- ☐ gloves and warm hat
- ☐ walking sticks

TOP HIKES

Grab your rucksack and get out and stride on the following trails:

➡ **Top day hikes** The Zillertal Circuit (p301) is especially beautiful in early summer, when the alpine roses are in bloom. A moderately challenging hike in the Silvretta Alps is the Radsattel Circuit (p301), taking in glaciers, jewel-coloured lakes and the iconic peak of Piz Buin.

➡ **Top high-alpine hike** A classic high-level trail is the Pinzgauer Spaziergang (p253), affording mesmerising views of the snowcapped Hohe Tauern and Kitzbühel Alps with little real effort.

➡ **Top short hike** Take a photogenic forest stroll for close-ups of the 380m-high Krimmler Wasserfälle (p255), Europe's highest waterfall. The Rosengartenschlucht Circuit (p316) is an easygoing hike through Imst's dramatic gorge.

➡ **Top kid-friendly hike** Kids in tow? Rent a gentle-natured llama for the day to explore the rugged splendour of the Dolomites near Lienz (p278). Or skip up to a meadow hut from the shores of Weissensee (p280) in Carinthia.

signposts. Bear in mind, though, that these are no substitute for a decent map and/or compass in the Alps. Like ski runs, trails are colour-coded according to difficulty:

➡ **Blue** The blue routes (alternatively with no colour) are suitable for everyone; paths are well marked, mostly flat and easy to follow.

➡ **Red** The red routes require a good level of fitness, sure-footedness and basic mountain experience. They are sometimes steep and narrow, and may involve scrambling and/or short fixed-rope sections.

➡ **Black** For experienced mountain hikers with a head for heights, black routes are mostly steep, require proper equipment and can be dangerous in bad weather.

Walk Descriptions In This Guide

➡ The times and distances for walks are provided only as a guide.

➡ Times are based on the actual walking time and do not include stops for snacks, taking photos, rests or side trips. Be sure to factor these in when planning your walk.

➡ Distances should be read in conjunction with altitudes – significant elevation can make a greater difference to your walking time than lateral distance.

Safety

Most walker injuries are directly attributable to fatigue, heat exhaustion and inadequate clothing or footwear. Falling as a result of sliding on grass, scree or iced-over paths is a common hazard; watch out for black ice. On high-alpine routes, avalanches and rock falls can be a problem. A few common-sense rules will help you stay safe when walking:

➡ Always stick to the marked and/or signposted route, particularly in foggy conditions. With some care, most walking routes can be followed in fog, but otherwise wait by the path until visibility is clear enough to proceed.

➡ Study the weather forecast before you go and remember that weather patterns change suddenly in the mountains.

➡ Increase the length and elevation of your walks gradually, until you are acclimatised to the

SNOWSHOEING

Tired of the crowded slopes? Snowshoeing is a great alternative for nonskiers. On a sunny day, there's little that beats making enormous tracks through deep powder and twinkling forests in quiet exhilaration. If you imagine snowshoes as old-fashioned, tennis-racquet-like contraptions, think again: the new ones are lightweight and pretty easy to get the hang of.

Many resorts in the Austrian Alps have marked trails and some offer guided tours for a small charge. It costs roughly €15 to €20 to hire a set of snowshoes and poles for the day.

vast alpine scale; this will help prevent altitude sickness and fatigue.

➡ Where possible, don't walk in the mountains alone. Two is considered the minimum number for safe walking, and having at least one additional person in the party will mean someone can stay with an injured walker while the other seeks help.

➡ Inform a responsible person, such as a family member, hut warden or hotel receptionist, of your plans, and let them know when you return.

Resources

Books

Consider investing in a dedicated walking guide if you're planning on doing a lot of hiking. Here are a few to get you started:

100 Mountain Walks in Austria (Kev Reynolds, Cicerone) A useful guide, listing more than 100 walks in 10 regions (mostly in the Alps).

Alpine Flowers-Alpenblumen (NF 1300; Kompass) Become well-versed in the local flora with this handy pocket guide complete with colour illustrations.

Walking Austria's Alps Hut to Hut (Jonathan Hurdle) An informative and inspirational guide covering multiday routes and Austria's alpine huts.

Walking Easy in the Swiss & Austrian Alps (Chet Lipton) Covers gentle two- to six-hour hikes in the most popular areas.

Walking in Austria (Kev Reynolds, Cicerone) Gives the inside scoop on 102 routes, from day walks to multiday, hut-to-hut hikes.

Websites

Get planning with the routes, maps and GPS downloads on the following websites:

Austria Info (www.austria.info) Excellent information on walking in Austria, from themed day hikes to long-distance treks. Also has details on national parks and nature reserves, hiking villages and special walking packages. Region-specific brochures are available for downloading.

Bergfex (www.bergfex.comPlan your dream hike with detailed route descriptions (many are in German) and maps, searchable by region, fitness level and length. Free GPS downloads.

Naturfreunde Österreich (NFÖ, Friends of Nature Austria; www.naturfreunde.at) Hundreds of walking routes, walk descriptions, maps and GPS downloads, including Nordic walking and snowshoeing routes. Also information on NFÖ huts, tips on mountain safety and up-to-date weather reports.

ÖAV (www.alpenverein.at) Search for alpine huts and find information on events, tours, hiking

TOP FIVE LONG-DISTANCE HIKES

NAME	START	FINISH	DISTANCE	DURATION
Adlerweg	St Johann in Tyrol near Kitzbühel	St Anton am Arlberg	300km	3-4 weeks
Arnoweg	Salzburg	Salzburg	1200km	months
Berliner Höhenweg	Finkenberg near Mayrhofen	Mayrhofen	70km	8 days
Salzburger Almenweg	Pfarrwerfen near Werfen	Pfarrwerfen	350km	1 month
Stubai Höhenweg	Neustift im Stubaital	Neustift im Stubaital	120km	8 days

villages and conservation. There's a section on the country's 10 *Weitwanderwege* (long-distance trails), which stretch from 430km to 1400km and showcase different areas of Austria's stunning landscape.

On Tour (www.on-tour.at) Short and sweet walks searchable by region and graded according to difficulty. The site is in German but easy to navigate.

Maps

The best place to stock up on maps is a *Tabak* (tobacconist), newsagent or bookshop. Usually they only have local maps, although bookshops in the major cities offer a wider selection. Outdoor-activities shops usually sell a limited variety of walking maps. Many local tourist offices hand out basic maps that may be sufficient for short, easy walks.

A great overview map of Austria is Michelin's 1:400,000 national map No 730 *Austria*. Alternatively, the **ANTO** (www. austria.info) can send you a free copy of its 1:800,000 country map. Visit www.austrianmap.at for a zoomable topographic country map. High-quality walking maps can be purchased online:

Freytag & Berndt (www.freytagberndt. at) Publishes a wide selection of reliable 1:50,000-scale walking maps.

Kompass (www.kompass.at) Has a good series of 1:50,000 walking maps and includes a small booklet with contact details for mountain huts and background information on trails.

ÖAV (www.alpenverein.at) Produces large-scale (1:25,000) walking maps that are clear, detailed and accurate.

Regions

In a land where even the tiniest of villages can have scores of fabulous walks, the question is not *where* you can walk in Austria, but *how*. For purists, that means the high-alpine trails which dominate in the mountainous west of the country, but lowland areas such as the vine-strewn Wachau can be just as atmospheric. Tourist offices are usually well armed with brochures, maps and information on local guides.

In summer lots of places run themed guided hikes, which are sometimes free with a guest card; for instance in Innsbruck and Kitzbühel. Other regions such as Hohe Tauern National Park and Naturpark Zillertaler Alpen charge a small fee (usually around €5). The walks can range from herb trails to wildlife spotting, half-day hikes to photo excursions.

LEVEL	HIGHLIGHTS	RESOURCES
moderate	Classic alpine landscapes from the Kaisergebirge's limestone peaks to the Arlberg region's rugged mountainscapes	See www.adlerweg.tirol.at for maps, brochures and route descriptions
demanding	Epic circular tour of the Austrian Alps, taking in gorges, valleys and Hohe Tauern National Park's glacial landscapes	Rother's walking guide to Arnoweg covers the trail in detail, or see www.arnoweg. com
demanding	High-alpine, hut-to-hut route taking in the beautiful lakes, glaciers and mountains of the Zillertal Alps	See www.naturpark-zillertal.at for a detailed route description in German; Alpenvereinskarte 1:25,000 map No 35 *Zillertaler Alpen* covers the route
moderate	A hut-to-hut route taking in Salzburgerland's fertile *Almen* (alpine pastures), karst scenery and the eternally ice-capped peaks of Hohe Tauern	See www.salzburger-almenweg.at for detailed route descriptions, maps and a virtual tour
moderate-demanding	A classic circular hut-to-hut route passing glaciers, rocky peaks and wild alpine lakes	Download maps and route descriptions at www.stubaier-hoehenweg.at; Cicerone's *Trekking in the Stubai Alps* is a reliable guide

MODERN-DAY SHERPAS

If you love long-distance hiking but find carrying a rucksack a drag, you might want to consider *Wandern ohne Gepäck* (literally 'walking without luggage'). Many regions in Austria now offer this clever scheme, where hotels transport your luggage to the next hotel for a small extra charge. Visit www.austria.info or www.wanderhotels.com for more details.

If you would prefer your Sherpa to be of the cute and woolly kind, llama trekking could be just the thing. Many towns, including Lienz in the Dolomites (p281), now offer this family favourite. Nothing motivates kids to walk quite like these hikes, which reach from two-hour forest strolls to two-week treks on pilgrimage routes. The llamas carry your luggage and leave you free to enjoy the scenery. Contact local tourist offices for more options.

Accommodation

Hiking Hotels

Gone are the days when hiking meant a clammy tent and week-old socks. Austria has seriously upped the ante in comfort with its so-called *Wanderhotels* (hiking hotels). These hotels are run by walking specialists who offer guided walks from leisurely strolls to high-alpine hikes, help you map out your route and have equipment (eg poles, flasks and rucksacks) available for hire. Most establishments are family-run, serve up regional cuisine and have a sauna or whirlpool where you can rest your weary feet. See www.wanderhotels.com for something to suit every taste and pocket, from farmstays to plush spa hotels.

Going a step further are Austria's **Wanderdörfe** (www.wanderdoerfer.at), a countrywide network of 43 hiker-friendly villages and regions. Here, you can expect well-marked short and long-distance walks, beautiful scenery and alpine huts, good infrastructure (eg trains and/or hiking buses) and hosts geared up for walkers. You can order a free brochure online.

Hut-to-Hut Hiking

One of the joys of hiking in Austria is spending the night in a mountain hut. These trailside refuges give you the freedom to tackle multiday treks in the Alps with no more than a daypack. The highly evolved system means you're hardly ever further than a five- to six-hour walk from the next hut, so there's no need to lug a tent, camping stove and other gear that weighs hikers down. Huts generally open from mid-June to mid-September, when the trails are free of snow; the busiest months are July and August, when advance bookings are highly recommended. Consult the **ÖAV** (www.alpenverein.at) for hut contact details and opening times.

Accommodation is in multibed dorms called *Matratzenlager*, or in the *Notlager* (emergency shelter – wherever there's space) if all beds have been taken. Blankets and pillows are provided but you might need to bring your own sleeping sheet. In popular areas, huts are more like mountain inns, with drying rooms and even hot showers (normally at an extra charge).

Most huts have a convivial *Gaststube* (common room), where you can socialise and compare trekking tales over drinks and a bite to eat. ÖAV members can order the *Bergsteigeressen* – literally 'mountaineer's meal' – which is low in price but high in calories, though not necessarily a gastronomic treat! It's worth bringing your own tea or coffee, as *Teewasser* (boiled water) can be purchased from the hut warden.

Cycling & Mountain Biking

Austria is one of Europe's most bike-friendly lands. It is interlaced with well-marked cycling trails that showcase the mountains, valleys and cities from their best angles. Whether you want to test your stamina on hairpin bends and leg-aching mountain passes, blaze downhill on a mountain bike in the Alps, or free-wheel leisurely around the country's glorious lakes – Austria has routes that will take your breath away.

When to Go

Warmer temperatures from May to October beckon cyclists, while downhill mountain bikers head to the Alps from late June to mid-September. Snow rules out cycling at higher elevations in winter, but this can be a quiet time to explore Austria's low-lying valleys. Pedalling up alpine passes in July and August can be a hot, tiring, thirsty business; take ample sunscreen and water, and factor in time for breaks.

Resources

Websites

Bike Holidays (http://bike-holidays.at) Search by region for mountain-bike (MTB) trails, cycling routes, free-ride parks and bike hotels in Austria.

Biken (http://bike-holidays.at) Handy source for information on cycling and mountain biking in Salzkammergut and Upper Austria. You can order free brochures including *Cycling Country Austria*.

Radfahren (www.radfahren.at) Easy-to-navigate website with descriptions on cycling trails (including long distance routes), bike-friendly hotels, bike rental and transport throughout Austria. Has interactive maps.

Radtouren (www.radtouren.at) An excellent site listing Austria's major cycling routes and hotels.

Maps & Guides

Local tourist offices usually stock brochures and maps on cycling and mountain biking. Cycle clubs are another good source of information. For more detailed maps and guides try the following:

Esterbauer (www.esterbauer.com) Produces the Bikeline series of cycling and mountain-biking maps and guides which give comprehensive coverage on Austria's major trails.

Freytag & Berndt (www.freytagberndt.at) Stocks a good selection of cycling maps and produces the *Austria Cycling Atlas* detailing 160 day tours.

Kompass (www.kompass.at) For cycle tour maps at scales between 1:125,000 and 1:50,000. Covers long-distance routes, including those along the Bodensee, Danube and Inntal.

Rentals

City and mountain bikes are available for hire in most Austrian towns and resorts. **Intersport** (www.intersport.at) has a near monopoly on rental equipment, offering a selection of quality bikes in 250 stores throughout Austria. Day rates range from around €18 for standard to €25 for e-bikes (electric bikes). All prices include bicycle helmets and there's a 50% reduction on children's bikes. Those who want to plan their route can search by region and reserve a bike online.

Transport

Look for the bike symbol at the top of timetables or on the **Österreiche Bundesbahn** website (Austrian Federal Railway; ÖBB, www.oebb.at) to find trains where you can take your bike. A day ticket for your bike on regional and S-Bahn trains costs €5, for InterCity (IC) and EuroCity (EC) trains €10.

Many of Austria's leading resorts have cottoned onto the popularity of downhill mountain biking and allow cyclists to take their bikes on the cable cars for free or for a nominal charge in summer, so you can enjoy the downhill rush without the uphill slog!

Accommodation

Throughout Austria you'll find hotels and *Pensionen* (guesthouses) geared up for

---

ÖAV MEMBERSHIP

Before you hit the trail in the Austrian Alps, you might want to consider becoming a member of the **Österreichischer Alpenverein** (ÖAV, Austrian Alpine Club; www.alpenverein.at). Adult membership costs €52 per year and there are significant discounts for students and people aged under 25 or over 61. Membership gets you an up to 50% reduction at Austrian (ÖAV) and German (DAV) alpine huts, plus other benefits including insurance, workshops, access to climbing walls countrywide and discounts on maps. The club also organises walks. There is an arm of the club in England, the **Austrian Alpine Club** (www.aacuk.org.uk). You should allow at least two months for your application to be processed.

Of the 1000-odd huts in the Austrian Alps, 241 are maintained by the ÖAV.

cyclists, particularly in the Alps. So-called *Radhotels* go a step further with everything from storage facilities to bike repairs and staff well informed on local routes. You can browse for bike-friendly hotels by region on www.bike-holidays.com and www.radtouren.at. Local tourist offices can also point you in the right direction and sometimes offer special packages.

Cycling Routes

There's more to cycling in Austria than the exhilarating extremes of the Alps, as you'll discover pedalling through little-explored countryside with the breeze in your hair and the chain singing. There are plenty of silky-smooth cycling trails that avoid the slog without sacrificing the grandeur; many of them circumnavigate lakes or shadow rivers.

Danube Cycle Path

Shadowing the mighty Danube for 380km from Passau to Bratislava, this cycle route takes in some lyrical landscapes. Wending its way through woodlands, deep valleys and orchards, the trail is marked by green-and-white signs on both sides of the river. Esterbauer's Bikeline *Danube Bike Trail* is useful for maps and route descriptions. See www.donauradweg.at (in German) for details on the route and an interactive map, and www.donau-radweg.info for tours.

Inn Trail

Starting in Innsbruck (p286) and travelling 302km through Austria to Schärding, the Inn Trail (www.inn-radweg.com) sticks close to the turquoise Inn River. It's basically downhill all the way, passing through fertile farmland, alpine valleys and castle-topped towns in Tyrol, Bavaria and Upper Austria. The final stretch zips through bucolic villages and countryside to Schärding (p170). The route is well marked, but signage varies between regions.

Bodensee Cycle Path

Touching base with Bregenz (p325) in Vorarlberg, this 270km cycleway encircles the Bodensee (Lake Constance), Europe's third-largest lake. Marked with red-and-white signs, the mostly easygoing trail zips through Austria, Germany and Switzerland, passing through woodlands, marshes, orchards, vineyards and historic towns. Come in early autumn for fewer crowds, new wine and views of the Alps on clear days. Visit www.bodensee-radweg. com for details.

GOING TO EXTREMES

➡ **Go ahead, jump** The 152m-high platform of the capital's needle-thin Donauturm (p79) is one of the world's highest bungee jumps from a tower. Yo-yo-ing at speeds of 90km/h from this landmark sure is an original way to see Vienna. Daredevils also leap into oblivion from the 192m Europabrücke bridge above the Sill River, a thrilling upside-down bounce.

➡ **Get a grip** If you thought regular climbing was slippery, try ice climbing! Scaling frozen walls and waterfalls is pure adventure, but you'll need a decent pair of crampons and a good instructor. The Stubai Glacier (p312) and Lech (p339) are among the places where you can give it a go. Experts can search for ice-climbing locations countrywide on www.bergsteigen.at (in German).

➡ **Going down...** For a real heart-stopping moment, you can't beat rolling out of a plane at 4000m and freefalling for 60 seconds before your parachute opens. Tandem skydiving jumps are available all over Austria – from Vienna to Salzburg; see www.skydiveworld.com for details.

➡ **Alpine rush** Speed is of the essence in Tyrol, particularly on Igls' hair-raising Olympic bob run (p291). Add altitude to the equation by ziplining over incredible scenery on the flying fox at Area 47 (p314).

➡ **Snow crazy** Swap your skis for a more novel way of whizzing down the mountains. Most resorts in the Austrian Alps, including Sölden (p314) and Mayrhofen (p303), offer snow tubing. Other snow-sports crazes to look out for include airboarding and snowbiking.

Salzkammergut Trail

This 345km circular trail explores the pristine alpine lakes of the Salzkammergut, including Hallstätter See (p202), Attersee and Wolfgangsee. Though not exactly flat, the trail is well signposted (R2) and only moderate fitness is required. To explore in greater depth, pick up Esterbauer's Bikeline *Radatlas Salzkammergut*.

Tauern Trail

Rolling through some of Austria's most spectacular alpine scenery on the fringes of the Hohe Tauern National Park (p246), the 310km Tauern Trail is not technically difficult, but cycling at high altitude requires stamina. It begins at Krimml, then snakes along the Salzach River to Salzburg, then further onto the Saalach Valley and Passau. The trail is marked with green-and-white signs in both directions. For maps and GPS tracks, see www.tauernradweg.com.

Mountain Biking

The Austrian Alps are an MTB mecca, with hairpin bends, back-breaking inclines and heart-pumping descents. The country is criss-crossed with mountain-bike routes, with the most challenging terrain in Tyrol, Salzburgerland, Vorarlberg and Carinthia. Following is a sample of the tours and regions that attract two-wheeled speed demons.

Dachstein Tour

Hailed as one of the country's top mountain-bike routes; this three-day tour circles the rugged limestone pinnacles of the Dachstein massif and blazes through three provinces: Salzburgerland, Upper Austria and Styria. You'll need a good level of fitness to tackle the 182km trail that starts and finishes in Bad Goisern, pausing en route near Filzmoos (p244). For details, see the website www.dachsteinrunde.at.

Salzburger Almentour

On this 146km trail, bikers pedal through 30 *Almen* (mountain pastures) in three days. While the name conjures up visions of gentle meadows, the route involves some strenuous climbs up to tremendous viewpoints like Zwölferhorn peak. Green-and-white signs indicate the trail from

> ### GPS FREE-WHEELING
>
> It's easier to navigate Austria's backcountry and find little-known bike trails with a GPS tour. Check www.bike-gps.com for downloadable cycling and mountain-biking tours. Alternatively, head to www.gps-tour.info for hundreds of tours in Austria.

Annaberg to Edtalm via Wolfgangsee (p211). Route details and highlights are given online (www.almentour.com, in German).

Silvretta Mountain Bike Arena

Sidling up to Switzerland, the Silvretta Mountain Bike Arena (p318) in the Patznauntal is among the biggest in the Alps, with 1000km of trails; some climbing to almost 3000m. Ischgl makes an excellent base, with a technique park and plenty of trail information available at the tourist office. The 15 free-ride trails for speed freaks include the Velill Trail, involving 1300m of descent. Tour details are available at www.silvretta-bikeacademy.at, in German.

Kitzbühel

Covering 800km of mountain-bike trails, the Kitzbühel region (p306) ranks as one of Austria's top free-wheeling spots. Routes range from 700m to 2300m in elevation and encompass trial circuits, downhill runs and bike parks. The must-experience rides include the Hahnenkamm Bike Safari from Kitzbühel to Pass Thurn, affording far-reaching views of Grossglockner and Wilder Kaiser.

Stubaital & Zillertal

These two broad valleys running south from the Inn River in Tyrol are flanked by high peaks crisscrossed with 800km of mountain-bike trails. The terrain is varied and the landscape splendid, with gorges, waterfalls and glaciers constantly drifting into view. Highlights include the alpine route from Mayrhofen (p303) to Hintertux Glacier and the dizzying roads that twist up from Ginzling (p305) to the Schlegeisspeicher.

Adventure & Water Sports

Rock Climbing & Via Ferrate

Synonymous with mountaineering legends like Peter Habeler and South Tyrolean Reinhold Messner, Austria is a summertime paradise for ardent *Kletterer* (rock climbers). In the Alps there's a multitude of climbs ranking all grades of difficulty. Equipment rental (around €10) and guided tours are widely available.

If you are not quite ready to tackle the three-thousanders yet, nearly every major resort in the Austrian Alps now has a *Klettersteig* (via ferrata). These fixed-rope routes, often involving vertical ladders, ziplines and bridges, are great for getting a feel for climbing; all you'll need is a harness, helmet and a head for heights.

Resources

Bergsteigen (www.bergsteigen.at) Search by region or difficulty for climbing routes, via ferrate and ice-climbing walls.

ÖAV (www.alpenverein.at)

Rock Climbing (www.rockclimbing.com) Rock Climbing gives details on more than 1000 climbing tours in Austria, many with climbing grades and photos.

Regions

For serious mountaineers, the ascent of Grossglockner (3798m), Austria's highest peak, is the climb of a lifetime. Profes-sional guides can take you up into the wild heights of the Hohe Tauern National Park (p246), a veritable climbing nirvana.

Sheer granite cliffs, bizarre rock formations and boulders make the Zillertal Alps (p299) another hot spot, particularly Ginzling and Mayrhofen.

Other climbing magnets include Pelstein in Lower Austria, the limestone peaks of the Dachstein and the Tennengebirge in Salzburgerland.

Water Sports

Austria may be landlocked but it offers plenty of watery action on its lakes and rivers in summer. You can windsurf on Neusiedler See, white-water raft in Tyrol or scuba dive in Wörthersee (p268). Zipping across lakes by wind power is the most popular water sport in the country, and if Olympic medals are anything to go by, the locals aren't bad at it either.

Rafting & Canoeing

Rafting, canoeing or kayaking the swirling white waters of Austria's alpine rivers are much-loved summertime escapades. Big rivers that support these fast-paced sports include the Enns and Salza in Styria; the Inn, Sanna and Ötztaler Ache in Tyrol; and the Isel in East Tyrol. Tours start from around €30 and usually include transport and equipment.

Well-known rafting centres include Landeck (p316), Innsbruck (p286) for adventures on the Inn, Zell am Ziller (p300) and St Anton am Arlberg (p320).

Windsurfing & Sailing

Sailing, windsurfing and kitesurfing are all extremely popular pursuits on Austria's lakes.

Close to Vienna lies Neusiedler See (p144), one of the few steppe lakes in Central Europe and the number-one place for windsurfing and kitesurfing thanks to its stiff winds. It hosts a heat of the Surf World Cup from late April to early May.

St Gilgen (p213) and Mondsee (p214) in Salzkammergut are highly scenic lakes for water sports; the latter harbours Austria's largest sailing school. Millstätter See (p277) in Carinthia, Achensee (p306) in Tyrol and the vast Bodensee (p327) in Vorarlberg are other popular spots to set sail.

ON THE BEACH

There's no sea for miles, but nearly all of Austria's major lakes are fringed with *Strandbäder* (lidos) for an invigorating dip, many of which have beaches, outdoor pools and barbecue areas. Some are free, while others charge a nominal fee of around €3 per day. If you dare to bare all, *Frei Körper Kultur* (FKK; nudist) beaches, including those at Hard (p328) on Bodensee, Hallstätter See, Milstätter See and even the **Donauinsel** (Danube Island; ⓂDonauinsel) in Vienna, welcome skinny-dippers.

Kitesurfing (www.kitesurfing.at) For the low-down on kitesurfing on Neusiedler See.

Österreichischer Segelverband (Austrian Sailing Federation; www.segelverband.at) Can provide a list of clubs and locations in the country.

Segelkurs (www.segelkurs.at) Has contact details for sailing schools in Austria.

Swimming & Diving

Bath-warm or invigoratingly cold? Alpine or palm-fringed? Much of Austria is pristine lake country and there are scores of swimming sports to choose from. Carinthia is famed for its pure waters, which can heat up to a pleasantly warm 28°C in summer; Millstätter See (p277) and Wörthersee (p268) offer open-water swimming and scuba diving with great visibility. You can also make a splash in lakes such as Hallstätter See (p202) and Attersee (p210) in Salzkammergut, and Bodensee (p327) in Vorarlberg.

Paragliding

Wherever there's a mountain and a steady breeze, you'll find paragliding and hang-gliding in Austria. On a bright day in the Alps, look up to see the sky dotted with people catching thermals to soar above peaks and forests. In many alpine resorts,

you can hire the gear, get a lesson or go as a passenger on a tandem flight; prices for the latter start at around €100. Most people fly in summer, but a crystal-clear winter's day can be equally beautiful.

Tyrol is traditionally a centre for paragliding, with narrow valleys and plenty of cable cars. A good place to head is Zell am Ziller (p300). Another scenic paragliding base is Zell am See (p249) in the rugged Hohe Tauern National Park.

Find the best place to spread your wings at www.flugschulen.at, giving a regional rundown of flight schools offering paragliding and hang-gliding.

Canyoning

For a buzz, little beats scrambling down a ravine and abseiling down a waterfall while canyoning. This wet, wild sport has become one of the most popular activities in the Austrian Alps. Guided tours costing between €50 and €80 for half a day abound. Most companies provide all the gear you need, but you'll need to bring swimwear, sturdy shoes, a towel and a head for heights. A good level of fitness is also recommended.

Top locations for canyoning include Mayrhofen (p303) in the Zillertal, the Ötztal (p313) and Lienz (p278).

Plan Your Trip

Eat & Drink Like a Local

Schnitzel with noodles may have been Maria's favourite, but there's way more to Austrian food nowadays thanks to a generation of new-wave chefs adding a pinch of imagination to seasonal, locally grown ingredients. Worldly markets, well-stocked wineries and a rising taste for organic, foraged flavours are all making Austria a culinary destination to watch.

The Year in Food

Spring (Mar–May)
Chefs add springtime oomph to dishes with *Spargel* (asparagus) and *Bärlauch* (wild garlic). *Maibock* (strong beer) is rolled out for beer festivals in May.

Summer (Jun–Aug)
It's time for *Marille* (apricot) madness in the Wachau, touring dairies in Tyrol and the Bregenzerwald and eating freshwater fish by lake shores. Bludenz reaches melting point in July with its Milka Chocolate Festival. Every village gets into the summer groove with beer festivals and thigh-slapping folk music.

Autumn (Sep–Nov)
Misty autumn days dish up a forest feast of mushrooms and game, and *Sturm* (young wine) brings fizz to *Heuriger* (tavern) tables. Sip new *Most* (perry and cider) in the Mostviertel's orchards. Goose lands on tables for St Martin's Day (11 November).

Winter (Dec–Feb)
Try *Vanillekipferl* (crescent-shaped biscuits) and mulled wine at twinkling Christmas markets. Vienna's coffee houses are the perfect winter warmer.

Food Experiences

Though Austria can't be put on the same culinary pedestal as France or Italy, food is still likely to be integral to your travels here, whether you're sipping tangy cider in the apple orchards of the Mostviertel, sampling creamy alpine cheeses in the Bregenzerwald or eating local fish on the shores of the Salzkammergut's looking-glass lakes.

Meals of a Lifetime

➡ **Magazin** (p234) At the foot of Mönchsberg's cliffs, this Salzburg gastro trailblazer combines a deli, season-focused restaurant and cookery school.

➡ **Obauer** (p244) The Obauer brothers believe in careful sourcing at this address of foodist rigour in the Alps.

➡ **Mayer's** (p254) Michelin-starred dining with a dash of romance at this lake-front palace in Zell am See.

➡ **Die Wilderin** (p294) A welcome Innsbruck newcomer with foraged flavours, live jazz and a bistro buzz.

➡ **Waldgasthaus Triendlsäge** (p313) Hop in a horse-drawn sleigh to reach this woody winter wonderland of a restaurant, hidden in the forest above Seefeld.

➡ **Meierei im Stadtpark** (p93) Lots of style, a bright ambience and Vienna's finest goulash.

➡ **Der Steirer** (p180) Graz' top address for affordable mouth-watering Styrian regional dishes washed down by local wines.

➡ **Tom am Kochen** (p186) Thomas Riederer whips up idiosyncratic delights in the bucolic landscape of the south Styrian wine roads.

➡ **Hermagorer Bodenalm** (p280) Quell a rustic hunger and thirst with a *Brettljause* (cold platter) at this alpine meadow hut above Weissensee.

➡ **Aiola Upstairs** (p180) Good food enjoyed with a sensational view over Graz' historic centre.

Cheap Treats

It's not all about fine dining: some of your most memorable food experiences are likely to be on the hoof. Vienna's *Würstelstände* (sausage stands) are the stuff of snack legend, but there's more to street food here. Falafel, bagels, organic burgers, healthy wraps, salads and sushi to go – you'll find it all in the mix in Austria's worldly cities.

On almost every high street there is a *Bäckerei* (bakery), where you can grab a freshly made roll, and a *Konditorei* for a pastry or oven-fresh *Krapfen* (doughnut). Many *Metzgereien* (butchers) have stand-up counters where you can sink your teeth into a wurst, schnitzel or *Leberkässemmel* (meatloaf roll), often with change from €5.

Top Five Snack Spots

➡ **Bitzinger Würstelstand am Albertinaplatz** (p91) Join opera-goers and late-night nibblers to bite into a cheesy *Käsekrainer* or spicy *Bosna* bratwurst at the king of Vienna's sausage stands.

➡ **Kröll** (p293) Strudels sweet and savoury at this busy-as-a-beehive cafe in Innsbruck's Altstadt.

➡ **Tongues** (p95) Hip and wholesome Vienna deli-cum-record store. Stop by for bargain lunches and electro on vinyl.

➡ **Cafesito** (p329) Pair deliciously chewy bagels with smoothies and fair-trade coffee at this boho cafe in Bregenz.

➡ **IceZeit** (p232) Salzburg's best ice cream. Enough said.

Dare to Try

➡ **Graukäse** The Zillertal's grey, mouldy, sour-milk cheese is tastier than it sounds, honest!

➡ **Rindfleischsulz** Jellied beef brawn, often drizzled in pumpkin-seed-oil vinaigrette.

➡ **Käsekrainer** A fat cheese-filled sausage, way off the calorie-counting Richter scale. It's a popular wee-hour, beer-mopping snack at Vienna's sausage stands.

➡ **Leberknödelsuppe** Dig into liver dumpling soup, the entrée that gets meals off to a hearty start all over Austria.

➡ **Zillertaler Bauernschmaus** We dare you to try this farmer's feast of cold cuts, sauerkraut and dumplings. Not because of the ingredients, but because pronouncing it will surely get your tongue in a twist!

➡ **Waldviertel Mohn** Poppy dumplings, desserts, strudels and noodles add a floral addition to menus in the Waldviertel.

➡ **Schnecken** Escargots to the French, snails to English-speakers, these gastropods are slithering onto many of the top menus in the country.

EIN BIER, BITTE!

Some common beer-glass sizes and types of beer:

➡ *Pfiff* (0.125L)

➡ *Seidl, ein Glas* (0.3L)

➡ *Krügerl* or *Krügel, ein Grosses* (0.5L)

➡ *Eine Flasche*, a bottle

➡ *Zwickl*, unfiltered beer

➡ *Märzen*, a lager

➡ *Weizen/Weissbier*, wheat beer

➡ *Dunkel*, dark beer or stout

➡ *Pils*, pilsener

➡ *Radler*, lemonade shandy

➡ *Vom Fass*, draught beer

AUSTRIAN WINE

Austrian wine is having something of a moment, with wine bars popping up all over the country and quality continuing to rise. Austrian wine hails from 16 winegrowing areas, mostly situated in Lower Austria and Burgenland (known as the Weinland Österreich region), Styria (Steierland) and the vine-strewn fringes of Vienna.

A wine that is typical of the region is labelled DAC (Districtus Austriae Controllatus), which is similar to the French AOC and the Italian DOC or DOCG, and if it is labelled reserve then the wine has been made for cellaring. Well-known varieties to look out for include crisp *Grüner Veltliner* and *Weissburgunder* (Pinot blanc) whites, fruity *Blauburgunder* (Pinot noir) and full-bodied *Zweigelt* reds, and sweet *Eiswein*, made from grapes that have frozen on the vines.

In winegrowing regions, many vintners open their doors for tasting and rustic *Heurigen* (wine taverns) pair wine with hearty grub like roast pork, blood sausage and pickled vegetables. Often identified by a *Busch'n* (green wreath or branch) hanging over the door, these simple establishments date back to the Middle Ages and have the right to sell their wine directly from their own premises in winegrowing regions.

Because they are seasonal and are open on a roster, the easiest thing to do when in a winegrowing region is to pick up the local *Heurigenkalendar* (*Heurigen* calendar) from the tourist office. September to mid-October, following the harvest, is when the new wines are sold, and this is the time to indulge in *Sturm* (literally 'storm' for its cloudy appearance and chaotic effects on drinkers).

Picnic Perfect

Fill your picnic baskets with fixings from these five favourites:

➡ **Naschmarkt** (p97) Global grazing for olives, cheese, wine, spices and more at Vienna's must-shop food market.

➡ **No Solo Vino** (p157) Deli delight in Linz for a picnic beside the Danube.

➡ **Kaslöchl** (p232) Two at a time please at Salzburg's mouse-hole of a shop, stocked with 150 kinds of cheese.

➡ **s'Speckladele** (p294) Go for regional hams and chilli-spiked sausages made from 'happy pigs'.

➡ **Stiftsbäckerei St Peter** (p232) Pick up an oven-warm sourdough loaf at Salzburg's 700-year-old bakery.

Local Specialities

Locavore is huge in Austria, where locals take genuine pride in their home-grown produce. Bright and early Saturday morning, you'll see them combing farmers markets, baskets and jute bags in hand, for whatever is seasonal. It's as much a matter of ethics as taste: Austrians believe firmly in supporting their farmers, cheese-makers and vintners, many going out of their way to buy organic, regionally sourced goods.

Chefs often make the most of seasonal, regional ingredients too, and many have been quick to piggyback on the Slow Food trend (look for the snail symbol) in recent years. Piquant *Bergkäse* mountain cheese in Bregenzerwald, lake fish on the shores of Neusiedlersee, dark, nutty pumkin-seed oil in Styria and tangy Rieslings from the Wachau never taste better than at the source.

Vienna

Nothing says classic Austrian grub like the classic Wiener schnitzel, a breaded veal cutlet, often as big as a boot, which is fried to golden perfection. Imperial favourites with a Hungarian flavour – paprika-spiced *Fiakergulasch* and *Tafelspitz mit Kren* (boiled beef with horseradish) are big. Wines produced on the city's fringes are served at rustic *Heurigen* (wine taverns) with hunks of dark bread topped with creamy, spicy Liptauer fresh cheese. Regionally grown *Suppengemüse* (soup vegetables such as carrots, celery, radish and root vegetables) pop up at markets and on menus.

Vienna is naturally also king of Austria's *Kaffeehaus* (coffee-house) scene.

Lower Austria

If one fruit could sum up this region, the Wachau's tiny, juicy *Marille* (apricot), made into jam, schnapps and desserts, would rise to the challenge. Spreading north of the Danube Valley, the rural Waldviertel peps up everything from pasta to desserts with poppy seeds, while the orchard-wealthy Mostviertel to the south is cider and perry country. Some of Austria's finest wines are produced in the vines that march up the hillsides here, including tangy Grüner Veltiner and Riesling whites, fruity Zweigelt and medium-bodied *Blauburgunder* (Pinot noir) reds. Trout, carp and asparagus are also fished and grown locally.

Burgenland

Like Lower Austria, Burgenland is one of Austria's premier wine regions, but it is also famous for its Neusiedlersee fish – species like perch-pike, pike, carp and catfish. Toss in nuts, orchard produce and ham from a species of woolly pig called the Mangalitza and the region makes for a mouth-watering trip.

Styria

Styria is also a producer of Mangalitza ham, as well as beef locally produced from *Almochsen* (meadow beef) raised on mountain meadows in the region about 30km northeast of Graz. What the visitor to Styria, however, will immediately notice is that pumpkin oil is used to dress everything from salads to meats. This healthy, dark oil has a nutty flavour and here it often stands on tables alongside the salt and pepper.

Carinthia

Cheese, hams and salamis, game, lamb and beef count among the regional produce in mountainous Carinthia. Wherever there are lakes you'll also find trout and other freshwater fish on menus. On meat-free Fridays, some Carinthians dig into local pasta known as *Kärntner Nudel*, filled with potato, cheese, mint, wild parsley-like chervil, mushrooms and any number of combinations of these.

Upper Austria

With Bavaria in Germany and Bohemia in the Czech Republic just over the border, it's unsurprising that Upper Austria is one of the country's *Knödel* (dumpling) strongholds. Sweet tooth? Well, you won't want to miss *Linzer Torte*, a crumbly tart with a lattice pastry top, filled with almonds, spices and redcurrant jam.

Salzburg & Salzburgerland

Salzburg's *Mozartkugel* is a chocolate-coated pistachio marzipan and nougat confection that ungraciously translates as 'Mozart's Ball'. Like Upper Austrians, Salzburgers lean heavily towards noodle and dumpling dishes like cheese and onion-topped *Pinzgauer Kasnocken*, but this gives way to fish in the lakeside Salzkammergut. *Salzburger Nockerln*, the town's favourite desserts, are massive soufflé-like baked concoctions (don't ask how many egg whites are in them!) sprinkled with icing sugar.

LOOK INTO MY EYES

Every drink bought deserves a *Prost* (cheers) and eye contact with your fellow drinkers; not following this custom is thought of as rude. Even worse, it's believed to result in bad sex for the next seven years.

WHEN IN... TRY...

➡ **Vienna** Wiener schnitzel or *Tafelspitz* (boiled beef)

➡ **Lower Austria** Waldviertel beef, lamb, game or fish

➡ **Burgenland** Neusiedler See fish, local beef

➡ **Styria** *Steirischer Backhendl* (Styrian chicken) with *Kürbisöl* (pumpkin oil)

➡ **Carinthia** *Kärntner Nudel* (Carinthian noodle)

➡ **Upper Austria** *Knödel* (dumpling) – what else?

➡ **Salzburg** *Salzburger Nockerln*, *Mozartkugeln* (sweets)

➡ **Tyrol** *Tiroler Gröstl* (fry-up), cheese and hams

➡ **Vorarlberg** *Heumilch* (hay milk) dairy products

Tyrol & Vorarlberg

These two regions have one thing in common – cheese, most notably what is called locally *Heumilchkäse* (hay-milk cheese), which aficionados claim is the purest form of milk you can find. *Gröstl*, or *Gröstel* in some other regions, is a fry-up from leftovers, usually potato, pork and onions, topped with a fried egg, but there are sausage varieties and the *Innsbrucker Gröstl* or *Gröstl Kalb* has veal.

How to Eat & Drink

Clicking into the Austrians' culinary groove is easier than you might think. Read on to find out why breakfast is big, lunch is great value and coffee and cake are the perfect afternoon pick-me-up.

When to Eat & Drink

➡ **Frühstuck (breakfast)** Austrians are the first to reel off the old adage about breakfast being the most important meal of the day. During the week, the locals may just grab a jam-spread *Semmel* (roll) and a coffee or a bowl of muesli, but at the weekend breakfast is often a leisurely, all-morning affair. A rising number of coffee houses and cafes have Sunday brunch buffets for around €15 to €20, with everything from sunny-side-up eggs to salmon, antipasti, cereals, fresh-pressed juices and *Sekt* (sparkling wine). You won't need to eat again until dinner.

➡ **Mittagessen (lunch)** Another meal locals rarely skip, lunch is often a soup or salad followed by a main course. Standard hours are 11.30am to 2.30pm.

➡ **Kaffee und Kuchen (coffee and cake)** The exception to not snacking between mealtimes is this three o'clock ritual. Indulge at a local *Konditorei* (cake shop) or coffee house.

➡ **Apéritif** The trend for predinner drinks is on the rise. The pavement terrace tipple of choice? Aperol spritz.

➡ **Abendessen (dinner)** Late-night city dining aside, Austrians tend to dine somewhat earlier than their European counterparts, with kitchens open from 7pm to 9pm or 9.30pm. Many places have a *Kleine Karte* (snack menu) outside of these hours.

Where to Eat

➡ **Beisln/Gasthäuser** Rural inns often with wood-panelled, homely interiors and menus packed with *gutbürgerliche Küche* (home cooking) – Tafelspitz, schnitzel, goulash and the like.

➡ **Neo-Beisln** New-wave Beisln often with retro-cool decor and a creative, market-fresh take on Austrian classics. Typically found in the cities (especially Vienna).

➡ **Cafes** These can range from bakery-cafes for a quick coffee and sandwich to all-organic delis and *Eiscafés* (ice-cream parlours).

COOKING CLASSES

Cooking courses have really taken off in the past couple of years and are popping up all over the place in the cities. Besides learning how to bread a schnitzel the Austrian way or roll the perfect *Knödel* (dumpling), many focus on specific ingredients, fish and cookery styles, from Asian to French, Easter desserts to autumn game. Here are a few worth checking out:

➡ **Babettes** (Map p76; www.babettes.at; 04, Schleifmühlgasse 17; ◷10am-7pm Mon-Fri, to 5pm Sat; ⓂKettenbrückengasse) Brush up your kitchen skills with cookery courses from finger food to nice-and-spicy curries.

➡ **Hollerei** (☑01-892 33 56; www.hollerei.at; Hollergasse 9, 15, Klosterneuburg; 1½hr course €25) Here you cook with the chef and eat the result.

➡ **Mayer's** (p254) Andreas Mayer runs seasonal, ingredient-focused courses (from asparagus to lake fish) at this Michelin-starred castle restaurant.

➡ **Magazin** (p234) Hands-on cookery courses in Salzburg, focused on everything from the perfect pasta to 'erotic food'.

➡ **Deuring-Schlössle** (p329) Heino Huber runs cookery classes at this high-on-a-hill castle. Feast on the fruits of your labours with wine pairing.

➡ **Restaurants** Cover a broad spectrum, from pizzeria bites to Michelin-starred finery.

➡ **Heurigen** Going strong since medieval times, Austria's cosy wine taverns are often identified by a *Busch'n* (green wreath or branch) hanging over the door.

➡ **Konditoreien** Traditional cake-shop cafes; many do a sideline in confectionery.

➡ **Kaffeehäuser** Vienna's 'living rooms' are not only famous for their delectable tortes, cakes and arm-long coffee menus. Many also serve inexpensive breakfasts, lunches and snacks around the clock.

➡ **Imbiss** Any kind of snack or takeaway joint, the most famous being the *Würstelstand*.

➡ **Brauereien** Many microbreweries and brewpubs serve meaty grub too. Their beer gardens are popular gathering spots in summer.

Menu Decoder

➡ **Degustationsmenü** Gourmet tasting menu.

➡ **Hauptspeise** Main course or entree – fish, meat or vegetarisch (vegetarian).

➡ **Kindermenü** Two-or three-course kids' menu; sometimes includes a soft drink.

➡ **Laktosefrei/Glutenfrei** Lactose /gluten free.

➡ **Mittagstisch/Mittagsmenü** Fixed lunch menu; usually two courses, with a soup or salad followed by a main.

➡ **Nachtisch** Dessert, sometimes followed by coffee or a glass of schnapps.

➡ **Speisekarte** À la carte menu.

➡ **Tagesteller** Good-value dish of the day; generally only served at lunchtime.

➡ **Vorspeise** Starter, appetiser.

➡ **Weinkarte** Wine list.

LUNCHTIME SAVER

Take the lead of locals and save euros by making lunch your main meal of the day. Most restaurants offer an inexpensive *Tagesteller* (day special) or *Mittagsmenü* (lunch menu), which can cost as little as €6.50 for two courses.

Etiquette

➡ **Table reservations** Booking is highly advisable to snag a table at popular and top-end restaurants, especially in peak season. Call around a week in advance.

➡ **Menus** English menus are not a given, though you'll often find them in city hot spots like Salzburg and Vienna and in ski resorts. If in doubt, there's usually a waiter/waitress who can translate.

➡ **Bon appétit** Dining with a group of Austrians? It's polite to wish them *guten Appetit* or *Mahlzeit* before digging in.

➡ **Water** You can try your luck by asking for complimentary tap water (*Leitungswasser*), but it's not really the done thing, especially in upmarket places. Go local and order *stilles* (still) or *prickelndes* (sparkling) *Mineralwasser* (mineral water).

➡ **Dress** Smart casual is the way to go in fancier establishments, where the locals dress up for dinner. In more relaxed places, jeans, trainers (sneakers) and T-shirts are fine.

➡ **Paying** *Zahlen, bitte* or *die Rechnung, bitte* are the magic words if you want to pay.

➡ **Tipping** Around 10% is customary if you were satisfied with the service. Add the bill and tip together and hand it over waiter/waitress by saying *stimmt so* (keep the change).

Regions at a Glance

Vienna

Art & Architecture
Music
Drinking in Style

Palaces, Churches & Galleries

Palaces, churches and art spaces such as the Hofburg, Schloss Schönbrunn, Schloss Belvedere, Stephansdom, the MuseumsQuartier and Albertina make it literally impossible to turn a corner in Austria's capital without bumping into an architectural or artistic masterpiece.

Opera & Mozart

Listen to the music of Mozart at palatial venues across town, visit Mozart's former home, embrace decadence and operatic greats at the Staatsoper or head to the Klangforum where the up-and-coming composers perform.

Coffee Houses & Heurigen

Viennese coffee houses are legendary: sip, read, pause in palatial surrounds like Café Gloriette or at hip modern renditions such as Café Drechsler. Grab a cocktail in Secessionist architect Adolf Loos' miniscule bar or visit a *Heuriger* (wine tavern).

p56

Lower Austria & Burgenland

Food & Wine
Culture
Outdoor Pursuits

Local Produce

The Wachau region of the Danube Valley has top-class restaurants and local produce such as beef, cheeses and Waldviertel poppy seed, whereas Burgenland around the Neusiedler See is famous for wine, especially reds, and *Heurigen* where nothing beats a glass of Austria's finest to wash down a cold platter.

Venues with Flair

Stift Melk in the Wachau region is the monarch among abbeys, Schloss Grafenegg is a top-class venue for outdoor music and opera, Krems and Schloss Schallaburg host great exhibitions, and Eisenstadt has its splendid Schloss Esterházy.

Cycling & Water Sports

The most popular cycling path in Lower Austria is along the Danube River in the beautiful Wachau region, and for lakeside cycling and water sports don't miss the Neusiedler See in Burgenland.

p113

Upper Austria

Culture
Architecture
Rural Retreats

Art & Technology

Linz' strikingly lit Ars Electronica Center propels visitors into the future with robotic wizardry and virtual voyages, while the rectangular Lentos gallery hosts cutting-edge art exhibitions. Modern art and sculpture also hang out in the Landesgalerie.

Churches & Abbeys

Kremsmünster's Benedictine abbey and St Florian's baroque Augustinian abbey hide ecclesiastical treasures. Linz has neo-Gothic Neuer Dom and opulent Alter Dom, while Kefermarkt is known for the Gothic altar in its church.

Spas & Farmstays

Rolling countryside is scattered with story-book towns like Steyr and spa retreats like Bad Hall. Farmstays in the Mühlviertel and Traunviertel offer total peace. Hike in the limestone wilderness of the Nationalpark Kalkalpen.

p151

Styria

Culture
Outdoor Pursuits
Food & Wine

Graz Festivals

Famous for its festivals throughout the year, the capital, Graz, makes up for its small size with some big cultural hits and an ensemble of top-rate museums, including Schloss Eggenberg.

Hiking & Skiing

Hiking trails abound in Styria – some easy, others challenging – and some good hikes and mountain-bike rides can be had in the cleaved valleys of the remote Nationalpark Gesäuse, or in the more popular Schladming area. Here, the mountains soar to dizzying heights and the pistes rev to life in winter.

Styrian Wine Roads

Graz has some of the best food in the country. The wine at the tables often comes from the vineyards hugging the nearby Slovenian border. Fantastic whites are complemented by excellent restaurants on the south Styrian wine roads.

p172

The Salzkammergut

Lake Swimming
Outdoor Pursuits
Culture

Mountain Lakes

With its contrast of soaring mountains and deep lakes nestled in steeply walled valleys, the Salzkammergut is the best place to slip into lake waters. Some of these are cold – very cold – but others such as the Hallstätter See, the Wolfgangsee or Mondsee are perfect for challenging open-water swimming or quick dips.

Hiking & Cycling

Hallstatt and Obertraun are centres for lakeside hiking, forays into the heights of the Dachstein mountains by cable car or on foot, and winter ski hikes. The cycling is excellent in the Salzkammergut region too – the mountain variety or easier touring.

Salt Mining

Salt – the 'white gold' – is what has given the region its name, and above Hallstatt is Austria's best exhibition salt mine, tracing mining back to ancient times.

p198

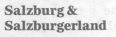

Salzburg & Salzburgerland

Culture
Wilderness
Food

Palaces & Spas

Salzburg's regal Residenz, the magnificent baroque Altstadt, and the Festung Hohensalzburg are highlights. The city hosts the world-renowned Salzburg Festival, whereas belle époque Bad Gastein is renowned for its radon-laced springs.

Ice Caves & Waterfalls

Hikers are mesmerised by the landscapes of the Tennengebirge. Underground lies Eisriesenwelt, the world's largest accessible ice caves, near the precipitous Liechtensteinklamm gorge. Hohe Tauern National Park is a 'greatest hits' of alpine scenery, with wondrous glaciers and 380m-high Krimmler Wasserfälle.

Coffee Houses & Brewpubs

Drink in history at grand coffee houses such as Bazar and Sacher, or at monk-run brewpubs such as Augustiner Bräustübl. The renowned Obauer in Werfen serves regional cuisine in refined surrounds.

p216

Carinthia

Lake Swimming
Winter Sports
Cycling

Lakes Warm or Cool

The Wörthersee is a summer playground for the rich, the famous and the rest of us. This is warm in summer and convenient to Klagenfurt, but those who like their waters cooler can head for Weissensee, Austria's highest alpine swimming lake.

Remote Skiing

At the far-flung but popular Nassfeld ski field near Hermagor-skiers take the 6km-long Millennium-Express cable car up to the slopes for some top skiing. Nordic skiing, ski hikes and ice skating are also excellent, especially in some of the province's rugged and remote regions.

Mountain Biking & Touring

Eleven kilometres downhill on one mighty run – mountain biking is a favourite pastime in Carinthia, but so too is touring on the trails and routes around Hermagor, Weissensee or outside Villach.

p261

Tyrol & Vorarlberg

Winter Sports
Outdoor Pursuits
Culture

Top-Flight Skiing

Tyrol has Austria's finest slopes – quite some feat in this starkly mountainous country. Alpine resorts such as St Anton am Arlberg, Kitzbühel, Mayrhofen and Ischgl excel in downhill, off-piste and upbeat après-ski. Seefeld has cross-country runs of Olympic fame.

Hiking & Cycling

Tyrol has some of the most scenic alpine hiking and cycling in Austria. Summer calls high-altitude walkers and mountain bikers to the valleys and peaks of the ruggedly beautiful Zillertal, Ötztal and Patznauntal. In Vorarlberg cyclists and beachgoers descend on glittering Bodensee.

Palaces & Dairies

Palatial Hofburg, Renaissance Schloss Ambras and galleries of Old Masters beckon in Innsbruck. In Vorarlberg, soak up the back-to-nature feel in the dairy country of the Bregenzerwald, sprinkled with farmstays and chocolate-box villages like Schwarzenberg.

p284

On the Road

Upper Austria
p151

Vienna
p56

The Salzkammergut
p198

Lower Austria & Burgenland
p113

Tyrol & Vorarlberg
p284

Salzburg & Salzburgerland
p216

Styria
p172

Carinthia
p261

Vienna

♪1 / POP 1.7 MILLION

Best Places to Eat with a Drink

➡ Halle (p93)

➡ Griechenbeisl (p92)

➡ Café Drechsler (p101)

➡ Café Sperl (p101)

➡ Motto am Fluss (p91)

Best Places to Stay

➡ Schweizer Pension (p87)

➡ Radisson Blu Style Hotel (p88)

➡ 25hours Hotel (p89)

➡ my MOjO vie (p89)

➡ DO & CO (p88)

Why Go?

Few cities in the world glide as effortlessly between the present and the past as Vienna. Its splendid historical face is easily recognised: grand imperial palaces and bombastic baroque interiors, museums flanking magnificent squares.

But Vienna is also one of Europe's most dynamic urban spaces. A stone's throw from Hofburg, the MuseumsQuartier houses some of the world's most provocative contemporary art behind a striking basalt facade. Outside, a courtyard buzzes on summer evenings with throngs of Viennese drinking and chatting.

The city of Mozart is also the Vienna of Falco (Hans Hölzel), who immortalised its urban textures in song. In this Vienna, it's OK to mention poetry slam and Stephansdom in one breath.

Throw in an abundance of green space within the city limits and the 'blue' Danube cutting a path east of the historical centre and this is a capital that is distinctly Austrian.

When to Go

➡ Vienna has such a strong range of sights and activities that anytime – summer or winter – is a good time to go.

➡ July, August and holidays such as Easter, Christmas and New Year are the most crowded.

➡ Crowds are down in spring and autumn, but weather can be changeable.

➡ In summer catch some rays on the Danube and loll about drinking made-on-the-premises wine in the outdoor gardens of the *Heurigen* (wine taverns).

➡ Hiking among the Vienna woods in October yields a spectacular autumn view of the capital.

➡ In December go ice skating in front of the Rathaus (town hall) or sip *Glühwein* (mulled wine) at one of the capital's atmospheric Christmas markets.

Vienna For Free

Simply walk or catch a tram around the Ringstrasse, or stroll through the Innere Stadt. The best of the Ringstrasse is around the Parlament and University Main Building; beyond these also check out the Altes AKH and Bethaus, especially the Christmas market, and the charming Servitenviertel. The northern side-aisle of Stephansdom (p60) is free, and the Justizpalast (Map p74; ☎ 521 52-0; www.ogh.gv.at; 01, Schmerlingplatz 11; ⊙ 7.30am-4pm Mon-Fri; Ⓜ Volkstheater, ⓓ D, 1, 2 Burgring) is great for a visit if you're not on trial (views are good from the canteen). The Hofburg (p65) is the most magnificent of the free highlights. Most churches are free and the Rathaus (p73) has free guided tours.

DON'T MISS

The Riesenrad (p85), the world's most iconic Ferris wheel, is in the centre of the Würstelprater, Vienna's favourite old-school amusement park. Step into the gargantuan containers and spin slowly around, taking in sweeping views of the city, the neighbouring hills and the Danube.

One of Vienna's most convivial markets, the Naschmarkt (p97) boasts stalls and stalls of international food, a cacophony of vendors urging you to try their goodies and a slew of top-notch restaurants, many housed in modern glass cubes along the river.

Be sure to hit one of the area's *Heurigen* (wine taverns), but take note of their (notoriously unpredictable) opening hours and call in advance. Don't fret if one is closed, as another will surely be open.

Before You Arrive

➡ **Six months ahead** Reserve your tickets for the Spanish Riding School, Spanische Hofreitschule (p66).

➡ **Two to three months ahead** Check the calendar for concert performances at the Staatsoper (p104) and the Musikverein (p104), and secure your seats to whatever looks appealing.

➡ **Four weeks ahead** Book your hotel of choice to make sure you get a room in a busy period.

➡ **One week ahead** Decide which day you'll visit Schloss Schönbrunn (p82) and book your tickets in advance online.

TRANSPORT PLANNING

For information about fares and routes around Vienna, consult www.wienerlineien. at. During clement weather, consider using Vienna's excellent city-bike scheme: www. citybikewien.at.

VIENNA

Fast Facts

➡ Number of districts: 23

➡ Percentage foreigners: 20%

➡ Green space: over 50%

Best Views

Climb the Südturm (p61) of Stephansdom for stunning views over Vienna from the small platform.

Relax with a Zombie on the terrace of Dachboden (p100) by moonlight, with views to the Innere Stadt.

Resources

➡ **Vienna Tourist Board** (www.wien.info) First port of call for any visitor.

➡ **Falter** (www.falter.at) Weekly entertainment, eating and drinking guide, with political commentary to boot. Listings are Friday to Thursday (€3.20 from newsagents, kiosks and sellers around town).

➡ **Austria Today (**www. austriatoday.at) News and opinion.

➡ **Austrian Times** (www. austriantimes.at) News and opinion.

Vienna Highlights

1 Scaling **Stephansdom** (p60), Vienna's glorious Gothic cathedral and beloved icon.

2 Savouring the bombastic pomp of **Schloss Schönbrunn** (p82) and the views from its gardens.

3 Hanging out in the **MuseumsQuartier** (p67), an art space spiked with bars and alive with urban energy.

4 Being provoked by naked bodies smeared with salad (among other modern-art flourishes) at Vienna's **MUMOK** (p72).

5 Slowing down and indulging in cake and coffee at one of Vienna's legendary coffee houses, such as **Café Sperl** (p101).

6 Immersing yourself a Viennese *Heuriger* (wine tavern), such as **Esterházykeller** (p99), on a ramble.

7 Spinning around in the giant rectangles dangling off the **Riesenrad** (p85), Vienna's oversized Ferris wheel, in the Prater outdoor area.

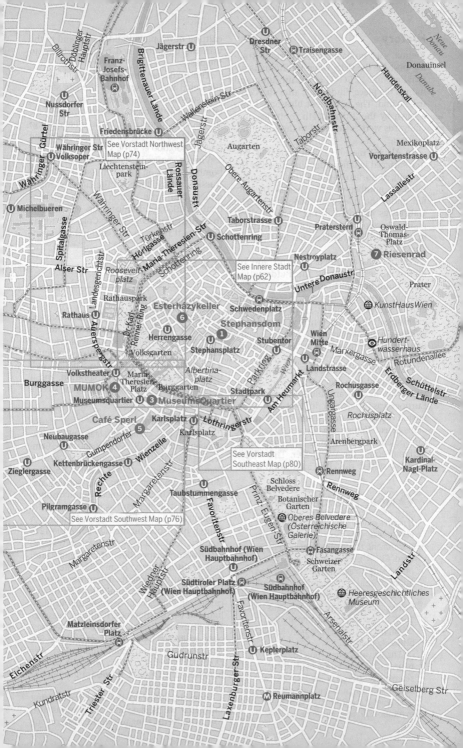

History

Vienna was probably an important trading post for the Celts when the Romans arrived around 15 BC. They set up camp and named the place Vindobona, after the Celtic tribe Vinid. The settlement blossomed into a town by the 3rd and 4th centuries, and vineyards were introduced to the surrounding area.

In AD 881 the town, then known as Wenia, surfaced in official documents. Over the ensuing centuries control of Vienna changed hands a number of times before the city fell under the rule of the Babenburgs. The Habsburgs inherited it, but none of them resided here permanently until Ferdinand I in 1533; the city was besieged by Ottoman Turks in 1529.

Vienna was a hotbed of revolt and religious bickering during the Reformation and Counter-Reformation and suffered terribly through plague and siege at the end of the 17th century. However, the beginning of the 18th century heralded a golden age for the city, with baroque architecture, civil reform and a classical-music revolution.

Things turned sour at the beginning of the 19th century – Napoleon occupied the city twice, in 1805 and 1809. His reign over Europe was brief, and in 1814–15 Vienna hosted the Congress of Vienna in celebration of his defeat. Vienna grew in post-Napoleonic Europe and in 1873 hosted its second international event, the World Fair. The advent of WWI stalled the city's architectural and cultural development and, by the end of the war, the monarchy had been consigned to the past.

The 1920s saw the rise of fascism, and in 1934 civil war broke out in the city streets. The socialists were defeated and Vienna's city council dissolved. Austria was ripe for the picking, and Hitler came a-harvesting; on 15 March 1938 he entered the city to the cries of 200,000 ecstatic Viennese.

Vienna suffered heavily under Allied bombing, and on 11 April 1945 advancing Russian troops liberated the city. The Allies joined them until Vienna became independent in 1955, and since then it has gone from the razor's edge of the Cold War to the focal point between new and old EU member nations.

⊙ Sights

⊙ Innere Stadt

The Innere Stadt is a timeless and magical place where Vienna's past swirls and eddies in narrow ways and atmospheric cobblestone streets. The city-centre district is a Unesco World Heritage site. Though well trodden, it rewards close exploration, and if crowds distract then try exploring the streets at night.

★**Stephansdom**   CHURCH
(St Stephan's Cathedral; Map p62; www.stephanskirche.at; 01, Stephansplatz; ◷6am-10pm Mon-Sat, from 7am Sun, main nave & Domschatz audio tours 9-11.30am & 1-5.30pm Mon-Sat, 1-5.30pm Sun; Ⓜ Stephansplatz) Vienna's Gothic masterpiece Stephansdom, or Steffl (Little Stephan) as it's locally called, symbolises Vienna like no other building. A church has stood on this site since the 12th century, and today reminders of this are the **Romanesque Riesentor** (Giant Gate) and **Heidentürme**. From 1359 Stephansdom began receiving its magnificent Gothic makeover, laying the foundations for today's cathedral. One section is dedicated to highlights of the **Domschatz** (Cathedral Treasures; Map p62; www.stephanskirche.at; 01, Stephansplatz; adult/child €4/1.50; ◷10am-6pm Mon-Sat; Ⓜ Stephansplatz), an exhibition called *Der Domschatz kehrt zurück,* which is located here until the Dom- & Diözesanmuseum undergoes restoration.

From the outside of the cathedral, the first thing that will strike you is the glorious tiled roof, with its dazzling row of chevrons on one

---

❶ MORE FOR YOUR MONEY

If you're planning on doing a lot of sightseeing in a short period, consider purchasing the **Wien-Karte** (Vienna Card; €19.90), which provides 72 hours of unlimited travel on the U-Bahn, bus and tram, plus a discount on the airport train. It also gets you discounts at selected museums, attractions, cafes and shops. It comes with an information brochure and is available from hotels and ticket offices.

The City of Vienna runs some 20 **municipal museums** (www.wienmuseum.at) scattered around the city, all of which are included in a free booklet available at the Rathaus. Permanent exhibitions in all are free on Sunday.

VIENNA IN...

Two Days

Jump on tram 1 at Schwedenplatz and circle the **Ringstrasse** for a brief but reward-ing informal tour of the boulevard's buildings. Get out at Kärntner Strasse and wander towards the heart of the city, where the glorious Gothic **Stephansdom** (p60) awaits. Make your way to the **Hofburg** (p65) before crossing the Ringstrasse to the **Kunsthistorisches Museum** (p70), home to a breathtaking art collection. Recharge your batteries at one of the many Innere Stadt restaurants before attending a performance at the **Staatsoper** (p104).

On day two visit imperial palace **Schönbrunn** (p82) before heading to the **Leopold Museum** (p72), a treasure chest of Austrian artists. Take an early dinner at Vienna's celebrated **Naschmarkt** (p97), then cross the city for a ride on the **Riesenrad** (p85) Ferris wheel. Finish the day with local food and a drink in a traditional *Beisl* (bistro pub).

Four Days

Start the third day with an exploration of the **Schloss Belvedere** (p78), an unequalled baroque palace, before lunching at **Steiereck im Stadtpark** (p93). See Klimt's sumptuous *Beethoven Frieze* in the **Secession** (p72), then end the night in a bar like **Dachboden** (p100).

The fourth day is best dedicated to your special interests. Read up on the sights and cobble together your itinerary. You might focus on music, dropping into the Sammlung Alter Musik Instrumente in the **Neue Burg Museums** (p67), taking in the other collections too, repose in a coffee house, then spend the afternoon visiting the **Haus der Musik** (p65) or **Mozarthaus** (p64). After that, cap off the visit with music in a club or in a classical venue like the **Musikverein** (p104) to experience the music of Beethoven or Mozart where it was originally played.

---

end and the Austrian eagle on the other; a good perspective of this is from the northeast of Stephansplatz. Inside the cathedral, the magnificent Gothic **stone pulpit** takes pride of place in the main nave, fashioned in 1515 with handrailing adorned with salamanders and toads fighting an eternal battle of good versus evil up and down its length. The baroque **high altar**, at the very far end of the main nave, shows the stoning of St Stephen. The chancel to its left has the winged **Wiener Neustadt altarpiece**, dating from 1447; the right chancel has the Renaissance red-marble **tomb of Friedrich III**. Under his guidance the city became a bishopric (and the church a cathedral) in 1469.

Entrance to the main nave with an audio guide costs adult/child €4.50/1.50, all-inclusive entrance to the cathedral, catacombs and towers with audio guide is €16 per adult (and an accompanying child). Note that the main nave is closed during Mass, held up to eight times a day.

➜ Stephansdom Katakomben

(Catacombs; Map p62; ☑ 515 52 3054; www.stephanskirche.at; 01, Stephansplatz; tours adult/child €5/2.50; ⊙ 10-11.30am & 1.30-4.30pm Mon-Sat, 1.30-4.30pm Sun; Ⓜ Stephansplatz) The cathedral's Katakomben house the remains of plague victims, kept in a mass grave and a bone house. Also on display are rows of urns containing the internal organs of the Habsburgs. One of the many privileges of being a Habsburg was to be dismembered and dispersed after death: their hearts are in the Augustinerkirche in the Hofburg and their bodies are in the Kaisergruft. You can only enter on tours.

➜ Cathedral South Tower

(Südturm; Map p62; ☑ 515 52 3054; www.stephanskirche.at; 01, Stephansplatz; adult/child €4/1.50; ⊙ 9am-5.30pm; Ⓜ Stephansplatz) When the foundation stone for the cathedral south tower was laid in 1359, Rudolf IV is said to have used a trowel and spade made of silver. Two towers were originally envisaged, but the Südturm grew so high that little space remained for the second. In 1433 the tower reached its final height of 136.7m, and today you can ascend the 343 steps to a cramped platform for one of Vienna's most spectacular views over the rooftops of the Innere Stadt.

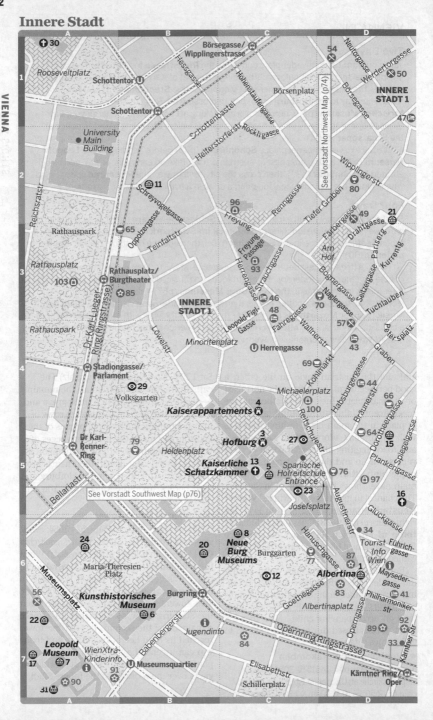

See Vorstadt Northwest Map (p74)

INNERE STADT 1

Rooseveltplatz

Schottentor

Schottentor

University Main Building

Rathauspark

Rathausplatz

Rathauspark

Dr Karl-Lueger-Ring (Ringstrasse)

Rathausplatz/ Burgtheater

Stadiongasse/ Parlament

Volksgarten

Dr Karl-Renner-Ring

Bellariastr

Börsegasse/ Wipplingerstrasse

Börsenplatz

Schottenbastei

Freyung

Freyung Passage

INNERE STADT 1

Minoritenplatz

Herrengasse

Michaelerplatz

Kaiserappartements

Hofburg

Kaiserliche Schatzkammer

Spanische Hofreitschule Entrance

Heldenplatz

Josefsplatz

See Vorstadt Southwest Map (p76)

Museumsplatz

Maria-Theresien-Platz

Kunsthistorisches Museum

Leopold Museum

WienXtra-Kinderinfo

Neue Burg Museums

Burggarten

Burgring

Jugendinfo

Museumsquartier

Schillerplatz

Albertina

Albertinaplatz

Opernring (Ringstrasse)

Elisabethstr

Kärntner Ring/ Oper

Werdertorgasse

Neutorgasse

Wipplingerstr

Tiefer Graben

Am Hof

Renngasse

Naglergasse

Tuchlauben

Graben

Kohlmarkt

Habsburgergasse

Bräunerstr

Dorotheergasse

Spiegelgasse

Plankengasse

Augustinerstr

Gluckgasse

Führich-gasse

Mayseder-gasse

Philharmoniker-str

Kärntner Str

Tourist Info Wien

Hanuschgasse

Goethegasse

Opernring

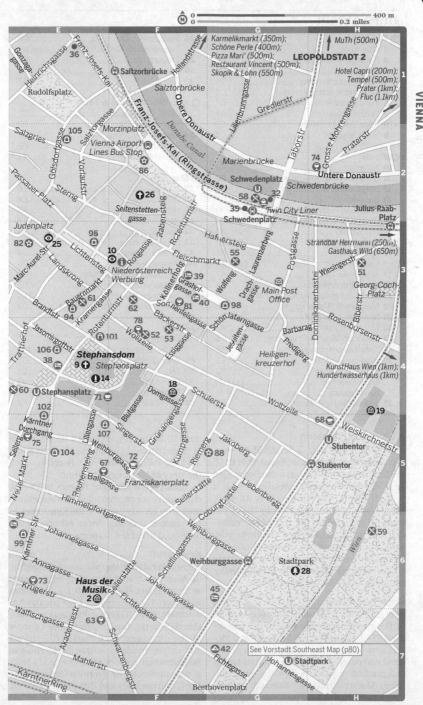

VIENNA

N 0 — 400 m
0 — 0.2 miles

36
Saltzorbrücke
Franz-Josefs-Kai
Gonzaga gasse
Heinrichsgasse
Rudolfsplatz
Salzorbrücke
Obere Donaustr.
Hollandstrasse

Karmelikmarkt (350m);
Schöne Perle (400m);
Pizza Mari' (500m);
Restaurant Vincent (500m);
Skopik & Lohn (550m)

LEOPOLDSTADT 2

↑ MuTh (500m)

Hotel Capri (200m);
Tempel (500m);
Prater (1km);
Fluc (1.1km)

Salzgries
Morzinplatz
105
Salztorgasse
Vienna Airport
Lines Bus Stop
86
Franz-Josefs-Kai (Ringstrasse)
Danube Canal
Gredlerstr
Lilienbrunngasse
Taborstr
Grosse Mohrengasse
Praterstr

Passauer Platz
Gölsdorfgasse
Sterng
Vorlaufstr
26
Seitenstetten-gasse
Rabensteig
Marienbrücke
74
Untere Donaustr.

Schwedenplatz
58 32
35
Twin City Liner
Schwedenbrücke
Julius-Raab-Platz

Judenplatz
82 25
10
Lichtensteg
Landskron
Marc-Aurel-Str
95
Rotenturmstr
Rotgasse
Haftersteig
Fleischmarkt
55
Laurenzerberg
Wolfeng
Postgasse
Wiesingerstr
51
Strandbar Herrmann (250m);
Gasthaus Wild (650m)
Georg-Coch-Platz

Bauermarkt
Brandtstr
Jasomirgottstr
94
61
Kramergasse
Rotenturmstr
62
Köllnerhof
39
Grashof gasse
40
Sonnenfelsgasse
81
98
Drach gasse
Schönlaterngasse
Main Post Office
Biberstr
Rosenbursenstr
Dominikanerbastei

78
101
52 53
Bäckerstr
Essigasse
Jesuiten gasse
Barbarag
Predigerg
Heiligen-kreuzerhof

Trattnerhof
106
38
Stephansdom
9 Stephansplatz
14
KunstHaus Wien (1km);
Hundertwasserhaus (1km)

60 Stephansplatz
71
18
Domgasse
Schulerstr
Wollzeile
Wollzeile
68
19
Weiskirchnerstr
Stubentor
Stubentor

102
Kärntner Durchgang
75
104
107
Singerstr
Grünangergasse
Kumpgasse
Riemerg
88
Jakoberg
Liebenberg
Wien

37
99
Kärntner Str
Johannesgasse
Annagasse
72
67
Ballgasse
Franziskanerplatz
Seilerstätte
Coburgbastei
Weihburggasse
59

73
Haus der Musik
2
Krugerstr
Walfischgasse
63
Himmelpfortgasse
Weihburggasse
Schellinggasse
Johannesgasse
Fichtegasse
45
Weihburggasse
Stadtpark
28

Seilergasse
Neuer Markt
Akademiestr
Mahlerstr
42
Fichtegasse
Johannesgasse
Stadtpark
Schwarzenbergstr

Kärntner Ring
Beethovenplatz

See Vorstadt Southeast Map (p80)

Innere Stadt

➡ Cathedral Pummerin

(Boomer Bell; Map p62; ☎515 52 3520; www.stephanskirche.at; Stephansplatz; adult/child €5/2; ◷8.15am-4.30pm mid-Jan–Jun & Sep-Dec, to 6pm Jul & Aug; Ⓜ Stephansplatz) Weighing in at a hefty 21 tonnes, the Pummerin is Austria's largest bell and was installed in the north tower in 1952. While the rest of the cathedral was rising up in its new Gothic format, work was interrupted on this tower due to a lack of cash and the fading allure of Gothic architecture; it's accessible by lift only today, without a ticket for the main nave.

Mozarthaus Vienna   MUSEUM

(Map p62; ☎512 17 91; www.mozarthausvienna.at; 01, Domgasse 5; adult/child €10/3, with Haus der Musik €17/7; ◷10am-7pm; Ⓜ Stephansplatz) Mozarthaus Vienna, the residence where the great composer spent two and a half happy and productive years, is now the city's premiere Mozart attraction. Although the exhibits in themselves are not startling (they

tend to be mainly copies of music scores or based around paintings), the free audio guide is indispensable and re-creates well the story of Mozart and his time.

Mozart spent a total of 11 years in Vienna, changing residence frequently and sometimes setting up his home outside the Ringstrasse in the cheaper Vorstädte (inner suburbs) when he needed to tighten his purse.

Kaisergruft   CHURCH

(Imperial Burial Vault; Map p62; www.kaisergruft.at; 01, Neuer Markt; adult/child €5/2; ◷10am-6pm; Ⓜ Stephansplatz, Karlsplatz, ⊠D, 1, 2, 71 Kärntner Ring/Oper) The Kaisergruft beneath the **Kapuzinerkirche** (Church of the Capuchin Friars; Map p62) is the final resting place of most of the Habsburg royal family (the hearts and organs reside in Augustinerkirche and Stephansdom, respectively). Opened in 1633, it was instigated by Empress Anna (1585–1618), and her body and that of her husband,

Emperor Matthias (1557–1619), were the first entombed in this impressive vault.

Only three Habsburgs are notable through their absence here. The last emperor, Karl I, was buried in exile in Madeira, and Marie Antoinette (daughter of Maria Theresia) still lies in Paris. The third in the triumvirate is Duc de Reichstadt, son of Napoleon's second wife, Marie Louise, transferred to Paris as a publicity stunt by the Nazis in 1940.

★ Haus der Musik   MUSEUM
(Map p62; 📞513 48 50; www.hdm.at; 01, Seilerstätte 30; adult/child €12/5.50, with Mozarthaus Vienna €17/7; ⏰10am-10pm; 🚼; Ⓜ Karlsplatz, 🚊 D, 1, 2 Kärntner Ring/Oper) The Haus der Musik is an interesting and unusual museum that explains the world of sound in an amusing and highly interactive way (in English and German) for both children and adults. Exhibits are spread over four floors and cover everything from how sound is created, through to Vienna's Philharmonic Orchestra and street noises.

Floor 1 hosts the **Museum of the Vienna Philharmonic**, which has a tool for composing your own waltz by rolling dice. Floor 2, called the **Sonosphere**, is packed with engaging instruments, interactive toys and touch screens. Here you can play around with sampled sounds to record your own CD (€7). Floor 3 covers Vienna's classical composers and is polished off with an amusing interactive video in which you conduct the Vienna Philharmonic Orchestra. The last floor has the so-called **virto|stage** in which your own body language shapes the music to create an opera.

★ Hofburg   PALACE
(Imperial Palace; Map p62; www.hofburg-wien.at; 01, Michaelerkuppel; 🚌1A, 2A Michaelerplatz, Ⓜ Herrengasse, 🚊 D, 1, 2, 71, 46, 49 Burgring) **FREE** Nothing symbolises the culture and heritage of Austria more than its Hofburg. The Habsburgs were based here for over six centuries, from the first emperor (Rudolf I in 1273) to the last (Karl I in 1918). The Hofburg

owes its size and architectural diversity to plain old one-upmanship; new sections were added by the new rulers, including the early baroque **Leopold Wing**, the 18th-century **Imperial Chancery Wing**, the 16th-century **Amalia Wing** and the Gothic **Burgkapelle** (Royal Chapel). The oldest section is the 13th-century **Schweizerhof** (Swiss Courtyard), named after the Swiss guards who used to protect its precincts. The Renaissance Swiss gate dates from 1553. The courtyard adjoins a larger courtyard, **In der Burg**, with a **monument to Emperor Franz II** adorning its centre. The palace now houses the offices of the Austrian president and a raft of museums.

★**Kaiserappartements** PALACE
(Imperial Apartments; Map p62; www.hofburg-wien.at; 01, Michaelerplatz; adult/child €10.50/6.50, with guided tour €13/7.50; ☺9am-5.30pm; Ⓜ Herrengasse) The Kaiserappartements were once the formal living quarters of Franz Josef I and Empress Elisabeth (or Sisi as she was affectionately named) and are extraordinary

for their opulence, fine furniture and bulbous crystal chandeliers. One section, known as the **Sisi Museum**, is devoted to Austria's most beloved empress, focusing strongly on the clothing and jewellery of Austria's monarch. The adjoining **Silberkammer** (Silver Depot; Map p62) collection is included in the entry price. The largest silver service here can take care of 140 dinner guests.

Audio guides – available in 11 languages – are also included in the admission price, and admission on **guided tours** includes the Kaiserappartements plus either the Silberkammer or the Sisi Museum.

Spanische Hofreitschule HISTORIC SHOW
(Map p62; ☑533 90 31; www.srs.at; Michaelerplatz 1, 01; tickets €23-143; ☺performances 11am Sat & Sun mid-Feb–Jun & late Aug-Dec, visitor centre 9am-4pm Tue-Fri, to 7pm Fri performance days; ☐1A, 2A Michaelerplatz, Ⓜ Herrengasse) The world-famous Spanish Riding School is a Viennese institution truly reminiscent of the imperial Habsburg era. This unequalled equestrian show is performed by Lipizzaner

---

THE WHITE HORSE IN HISTORY

The Lipizzaner stallion breed dates back to the 1520s, when Ferdinand I imported the first horses from Spain for the imperial palace. His son Maximilian II imported new stock in the 1560s, and in 1580 Archduke Charles II established the imperial stud in Lipizza (Lipica, today in Slovenia), giving the horse its name. Austria's nobility had good reason for looking to Spain for its horses: the Spanish were considered the last word in equine breeding at the time, thanks to Moors from the 7th century who had brought their elegant horses to the Iberian Peninsula. Italian horses were added to the stock around the mid-1700s (these too had Spanish blood) and by the mid-18th century the Lipizzaner had a reputation for being Europe's finest horses.

Over the centuries, natural catastrophe, but more often war, caused the Lipizzaner to be evacuated from their original stud in Slovenia on numerous occasions. One of their periods of exile from the stud in Lipica was in 1915 due to the outbreak of WWI. Some of the horses went to Laxemburg (just outside Vienna), and others to Bohemia in today's Czech Republic (at the time part of the Austro-Hungarian Empire).

When the Austrian monarchy collapsed in 1918, Lipica passed into Italian hands and the horses were divided between Austria and Italy. The Italians ran the stud in Slovenia, while the Austrians transferred their horses to Piber, near Graz, which had been breeding military horses for the empire since 1798 – at that time stallions were mostly crossed with English breeds.

The fortunes of our pirouetting equine friends rose and fell with the collapse of the Habsburg empire and advent of two world wars. When WWII broke out, Hitler's cohorts goose-stepped in and requisitioned the Piber stud in Austria and started breeding military horses and – spare the thought! – pack mules there. They also decided to bring the different studs in their occupied regions together under one roof, and Piber's Lipizzaner wound up in Hostau, situated in Bohemia. Fearing the Lipizzaner would fall into the hands of the Russian army as it advanced towards the region in 1945 (and amid rather odd fears that the stallions would be eaten), American forces seized the Lipizzaner and other horses in Hostau and transferred them back to Austria.

Today, Piber still supplies the Spanish Riding School with its white stallions.

ⓘ MUSEUMSQUARTIER TICKETS

The **MuseumsQuartier** (Museum Quarter; Map p62; www.mqw.at; 07, Museumsplatz; ⊗ info & ticket centre 10am-7pm; Ⓜ Museumsquartier, Volkstheater) is a remarkable ensemble of museums, cafes, restaurants and bars inside former imperial stables designed by Fischer von Erlach. This breeding ground of Viennese cultural life is the perfect place to hang out and watch or meet people on warm evenings, or to sup mulled wine in the weeks before Christmas. With over 60,000 sq metres of exhibition space, the complex is one of the world's most ambitious cultural spaces.

Of the combined tickets on offer, the MQ Kombi Ticket (€25) includes entry into every museum except Zoom (p79) and a 30% discount on performances in the TanzQuartier Wien (p105); MQ Art Ticket (€21.50) gives admission into the Leopold Museum, MUMOK, Kunsthalle and reduced entry into Zoom and the TanzQuartier Wien; MQ Duo Ticket (€17) covers the Leopold Museum and MUMOK and has Zoom and TanzQuartier reductions (a flexible version allows you to choose two from any of the museums); and the MQ Family Ticket (two adults and two children under 13; €29) offers entry to MUMOK and the Leopold Museum, with the Zoom and Tanzquartier reductions.

stallions formerly bred at an imperial stud established in Slovenia at Lipizza (hence 'Lipizzaner'). Visitors to the **Morgenarbeit** (Morning Training; adult/child €14/7; ⊗ 10am-noon Tue-Fri Jan-Jun & mid-Aug–Dec) sessions can drop in for part of a session and leave whenever they want to though, check website for exact dates. **Guided tours** (☑ 533 90 31; www srs at; adult/child €16/8; ⊗ 2pm, 3pm & 4pm, closed Mon late Jan & Feb) held in English and German take you into the performance hall, stables and other facilities, and a **combined morning training & tour** (adult/child €28/14) is another option. Tickets can be bought on the website. The visitor centre on Michaelerplatz sells all tickets, and morning training tickets can also be bought at Gate 2 on Josefsplatz during training sessions.

★ **Kaiserliche Schatzkammer** MUSEUM
(Imperial Treasury; Map p62; www.kaiserlicheschatzkammer.at; 01, Schweizerhof; adult/under 19yr €12/free; ⊗ 9am-5.30pm Wed-Mon; Ⓜ Herrengasse) The Schatzkammer contains secular and ecclesiastical treasures of priceless value and splendour – the sheer wealth of this collection of crown jewels is staggering. As you walk through the rooms you see magnificent treasures such as a golden rose, diamond-studded Turkish sabres, a 2680-carat Colombian emerald and, the highlight of the treasury, the imperial crown. The wood-panelled **Sacred Treasury** has a collection of rare religious relics, some of which can be taken with a grain of salt: fragments of the True Cross, one of the nails from the Crucifixion, a thorn from Christ's crown and a piece of tablecloth from the Last Supper.

Audio guides in German, English, Italian, French, Japanese, Russian and Spanish cost €4 (the shorter highlight audio tour is free) and are very worthwhile. A combined 'Treasures of the Habsburgs' ticket, which includes the Kunsthistorisches Museum (p70), costs €20. Allow anything from 30 minutes to two hours for the Schatzkammer.

★ **Neue Burg Museums** MUSEUM
(Map p62; ☑ 525 240; www.khm.at; 01, Heldenplatz; adult/under 19yr €14/free; ⊗ 10am-6pm Wed-Sun; Ⓜ Herrengasse, Museumsquartier, ⬜ D, 1, 2, 71 Burgring) The Neue Burg is home to the three Neue Burg Museums. The **Sammlung Alter Musik Instrumente** (Collection of Ancient Musical Instruments) contains instruments in all shapes, sizes and tones. The **Ephesos Museum** features artefacts from Ephesus and Samothrace donated (some say 'lifted') by the sultan in 1900 after a team of Austrian archaeologists excavated Ephesus in Turkey. Last but not least is the **Hofjägd und Rüstkammer** (Arms and Armour) museum, with a fine collection of ancient armour dating mainly from the 15th and 16th centuries. Admission includes both the Kunsthistorisches Museum (p70) and the Neue Burg museums. An audio guide costs €4.

Museum für Völkerkunde MUSEUM
(Museum of Ethnology; Map p62; ☑ 525 240; www.ethno-museum.ac.at; 01, Heldenplatz; adult/under 19yr €8/free; ⊗ 10am-6pm Wed-Mon; ⬜; Ⓜ Herrengasse, Museumsquartier, ⬜ D, 1, 2 Burgring) You can impress your children by taking them to this museum. Revamped a few years ago, it exudes a lightness of mood and has a thoughtful use of space that adults

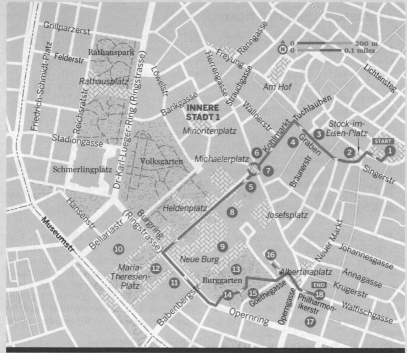

🏃 City Walk
The Historic Centre

START STEPHANSDOM
END HOTEL SACHER
LENGTH 2KM, 1½ HOURS

This walk takes you past recognisable sights that dominate this quarter of the Innere Stadt. Start at Vienna's cathedral, the Gothic **1 Stephansdom** (p60), offset by the unashamedly modern **2 Haas Haus**. Many Viennese were unhappy about the silver structure crowding their cathedral, but tourists seem happy to snap the reflections of Stephansdom's spire in its windows.

Leading northwest from Stock-im-Eisen-Platz is the broad pedestrian thoroughfare of plush shopping street **3 Graben**. It's dominated by the knobbly outline of the **4 Pestsäule**, completed in 1693 to commemorate the 75,000 victims of the Black Death. Turn left into Kohlmarkt and the arresting sight of **5 Michaelertor**, the Hofburg's northeastern gate, comes into view.

At Michaelerplatz, look out for the **6 Loos Haus**, a perfect example of the clean lines of Loos' work. Franz Josef hated it and described the windows, which lack lintels, as 'windows without eyebrows'. **7 Michaelerkirche** on the square portrays 500 years of architectural styles.

Pass through the imposing Michaelertor and past the **8 Schweizertor** to Heldenplatz and the impressive **9 Neue Burg** (p67). Continue, noting the Gothic spire of the Rathaus to the right. On the far side of the Ring stand rival identical twins the **10 Naturhistorisches Museum** (p70) and the **11 Kunsthistorisches Museum** (p70); between them is a **12 statue of Maria Theresia**.

Turn left onto the Ring and, once past the Neue Burg, turn left again into the peaceful **13 Burggarten** (p70), formerly reserved for the imperial family and high-ranking officials. It contains **14 statues of Mozart** and **15 Franz Josef** and cafe-bar **16 Palmenhaus** (p100). Not far down Philharmonikerstrasse is the grand **17 Staatsoper** (p104) and **18 Hotel Sacher** (p89), a perfect spot to rest those weary legs.

will appreciate too. Exhibits are on non-European cultures and divided into regions and nationalities, covering such countries as China, Japan and Korea, and also the Polynesian, Native American and Inuit cultures.

Nationalbibliothek Prunksaal   LIBRARY
(Grand Hall; Map p62; 534 10-394; www.onb. ac.at; 01, Josefsplatz 1; adult/under 19yr €7/free; ⊙10am-6pm Tue-Sun, to 9pm Thu; M Herrengasse, D, 1, 2, 71 Burgring) Austria's flagship library, the Nationalbibliothek contains an astounding collection of literature, maps, globes of the world and other cultural relics; its highlight, though, is the Prunksaal, a majestic baroque hall built between 1723 and 1726, with a fresco by Daniel Gran. Commissioned by Karl VI (whose statue is under the central dome), the library holds some 200,000 leather-bound scholarly tomes.

★ **Albertina**   GALLERY
(Map p62; www.albertina.at; 01, Albertinaplatz 3; adult/child €11/free; ⊙10am-6pm Thu-Tue, to 9pm Wed; ; M Karlsplatz, Stephansplatz, D, 1, 2, 71 Kärntner Ring/Oper) Once used as the Habsburg's imperial apartments for guests (you can walk through these), the Albertina is now a repository for the greatest collection of graphic art in the world. A very small selection of copies is on display, but the permanent **Batliner Collection** – with paintings covering the period from Monet to Picasso – and the high quality of changing exhibitions are what really make the Albertina so worthwhile visiting.

French Impressionism and post-Impressionism, as well as the works of the Swiss Alberto Giacometti, were the original focus of the Batliner Collection, but over time it has become a who's who of 20th-century and contemporary art: Monet, Picasso, Degas, Cézanne, Matisse, Chagal, Nolde, Jawlensky and many more.

This is augmented by the top-notch changing exhibitions. Multilingual audio guides (€4) cover all exhibition sections and tell the story behind the apartments and works you see. Tickets (but not the audio guides) are valid for the whole day, so you can retire to lunch somewhere and return later to finish off a visit.

The Österreichisches Filmmuseum (p107) is located in the Albertina.

Jüdisches Museum   MUSEUM
(Jewish Museum; Map p62; 535 04 31; www. jmw.at; 01, Dorotheergasse 11; adult/child incl Mu-

seum Judenplatz €10/free; ⊙10am-6pm Sun-Fri; M Stephansplatz) Housed inside Palais Eskeles, Vienna's Jüdisches Museum showcases the history of Jews in Vienna, from the first settlements at Judenplatz in the 13th century to the present. A new permanent exhibition on Jewry in the 21st century opened in 2013, complementing spaces mostly devoted to changing exhibitions, and the exhibition highlight, a startling collection of ceremonial art on the top floor. The admission ticket is valid for 48 hours for both Jewish museums.

Museum Judenplatz   MUSEUM
(Map p62; 535 04 31; www.jmw.at; 01, Judenplatz 8; adult/child incl Jüdisches Museum €10/free; ⊙10am-6pm Sun-Thu, to 2pm Fri; M Stephansplatz, Herrengasse) The main focus of Museum Judenplatz is on the excavated remains of a medieval synagogue that once stood on Judenplatz, with a film and numerous exhibits to elucidate Jewish history. It was built in the Middle Ages, but Duke Albrecht V's 'hatred and misconception' led him to order its destruction in 1421. The basic outline of the synagogue can still be seen here. Exhibits include a 12-minute video on Judaism, the synagogue and the Jewish quarter, the excavations, and glass cases containing fragments, such as documents from Jewish history in Vienna. An audio guide costs €2 (in German and English, with a special children's version too). Free **tours**, generally on the first Sunday in the month (in German), are conducted at 3pm from the Jüdisches Museum and 4.30pm from Museum Judenplatz, covering all exhibitions.

Neidhart-Fresken   MURAL
(Map p62; 535 90 65; 01, Tuchlauben 19; ⊙10am-1pm & 2 6pm Tue-Sun; M Stephansplatz) FREE An unassuming house on Tuchlauben hides quite a remarkable decoration: the oldest extant secular murals in Vienna. The small frescos, dating from 1398, tell the story of the minstrel Neidhart von Reuental (1180–1240) and life in the Middle Ages in lively and jolly scenes.

Ankeruhr   CLOCK
(Anker Clock; Map p62; 01, Hoher Markt 10-11; M Stephansplatz, Schwedenplatz) Hoher Markt is Vienna's oldest square and was once the centre of the Roman outpost; today it is also home to the Ankeruhr, an art nouveau masterpiece created by Franz von Matsch in 1911 and named after the Anker Insurance Co, which commissioned it. Over a

12-hour period, figures slowly pass across the clock face, indicating the time against a static measure showing the minutes. People flock here at noon, when all the figures trundle past in succession to the tune of organ music.

Ruprechtskirche CHURCH
(St Rupert's Church; Map p62; ☑ 535 60 03; www.ruprechtskirche.at; 01, Seitenstettengasse 5; ☺ 10am-noon & 3-5pm Mon, Wed & Fri, 10am-noon Tue & Thu; Ⓜ Schwedenplatz, ▣ 1, 2 Schwedenplatz) Located a few steps north of Ruprechtsplatz, the picturesque, ivy-clad Ruprechtskirche dates from about 1137 or earlier, giving it the honour of being the oldest church in Vienna. The interior is sleek and worth a quick viewing, with a Romanesque nave from the 12th century.

Beethoven Pasqualatihaus HOUSE MUSEUM
(Map p62; www.wienmuseum.at; 01, Mölker Bastei 8; adult/under 19yr €4/free; ☺ 10am-1pm & 2-6pm Tue-Sun; Ⓜ Schottentor, ▣ D, 1, 2 Schottentor) Beethoven made the 4th floor of this house his residence from 1804 to 1814 (he apparently occupied around 80 places in his 35 years in Vienna, but thankfully not all of them are museums!) and during that time composed Symphonies 4, 5 and 7 and the opera *Fidelio*, among other works. The museum is lightly filled with photos, articles and a handful of his personal belongings.

◉ Ringstrasse

Emperor Franz Josef was largely responsible for the monumental architecture around the Ringstrasse, a wide, tree-lined boulevard encircling much of the Innere Stadt. In 1857 he decided to tear down the redundant military fortifications and exercise grounds and replace them with grandiose public buildings in a variety of historical styles. Work began

---

ⓘ KUNSTHISTORISCHES MUSEUM TOURS

For insight into the Kunsthistorisches Museum (KHM), pick up a multilingual audio guide (€4) near the entrance. The KHM runs free guided tours in German, from 30-minute lunchtime tours (12.30pm Tuesday and Thursday) to hour-long tours focusing on a particular artist or period (4pm Wednesday, 10.15am Friday). See www.khm.at for more details.

---

the following year and reached a peak in the 1870s. The stock-market crash in 1873 put a major dampener on plans, and other grand schemes were shelved due to lack of money and the outbreak of WWI. The Ring is easily explored on foot or bicycle; if you've not the time, jump on tram 1 or 2, both of which run sections of the boulevard and offer a snapshot of the impressive architecture.

After all of the museums, take a relaxing walk in one the local gardens. **Burggarten** (Map p62; www.bundesgaerten.at; 01, Burgring; ☺ 6am-10pm Apr-Oct, 6.30am-7pm Nov-Mar; Ⓜ Museumsquartier, ▣ D, 1, 2, 71, 46, 49 Burgring) **FREE** and **Volksgarten** (Map p62; www.bundesgaerten.at; Dr-Karl-Renner-Ring; ☺ 6am-10pm Apr-Oct, 6.30am-7pm Nov-Mar; Ⓜ Volkstheater, Herrengasse, ▣ D, 1, 2, 71, 46, 49 Dr-Karl-Renner-Ring) **FREE** are both good places to chill out, and **Stadtpark** (City Park; Map p62; Ⓜ Stadtpark, ▣ 2 Weihburggasse) **FREE** has a gold statue of Johann Strauss.

★ Kunsthistorisches Museum MUSEUM
(Museum of Art History, KHM; Map p62; www.khm.at; 01, Maria-Theresien-Platz; adult/under 19yr incl Neue Burg museums €14/free; ☺ 10am-6pm Tue-Sun, to 9pm Thu; ♿; Ⓜ Museumsquartier, Volkstheater) One of the unforgettable experiences of being in Vienna will be a visit to the Kunsthistorisches Museum, brimming with works by Europe's finest painters, sculptors and artisans. The main building of the museum houses the **Picture Gallery**, a breathtaking window into mainly Flemish, Dutch, Italian, Spanish, French and German works from the 16th and 17th centuries – the time when the Habsburgs went on a collecting frenzy.

The **Kunstkammer** contains a stunning collection of art and curiosities that once belonged to the Habsburgs. This is augmented by the equally interesting **Egyptian and Near-Eastern Collection**, the **Collection of Greek and Roman Antiquities**, and the **Coin Collection**. Plan on spending a good three hours admiring all of these.

Naturhistorisches Museum MUSEUM
(Museum of Natural History; Map p62; www.nhm-wien.ac.at; 01, Maria-Theresien-Platz; adult/under 19yr €10/free; ☺ 9am-6.30pm Thu-Mon, to 9pm Wed; Ⓜ Museumsquartier, Volkstheater) This is the scientific counterpart to the Kunsthistorisches Museum, with a vast collection that spans minerals, meteorites and geology, fossils and dinosaurs, anthropology and all manner of other creatures, including hu-

mans. Show stoppers are the 25,000-year-old *Venus of Willendorf* statuette and her older sister, the 32,000 BC statuette *Venus of Galgenberg* (the oldest figurative sculpture in the world). The anthropology section is another highlight, giving you the chance to be remodelled in a photograph as one of many different types of early human, with

EXPLORING THE KHM PICTURE GALLERY

Features of the Kunsthistorisches Museum (KHM) building itself are highlights in their own rights, bringing together visual arts with architecture into one artistic whole.

As you climb the ornate main staircase, your gaze is drawn to the ever-decreasing circles of the cupola; marble columns guide the eye to delicately frescoed vaults, roaring lions and Antonio Canova's mighty statue of *Theseus Defeating the Centaur* (1805). Austrian legends Hans Makart and the brothers Klimt have left their hallmark between the columns and above the arcades – the former with lunette paintings, the latter with gold-kissed depictions of women inspired by Greco-Roman and Egyptian art.

After admiring the staircase and its lunettes, make a beeline for the Picture Gallery on the 1st floor.

Dutch, Flemish & German Painting

First up is the German Renaissance, where Lucas Cranach the Elder stages an appearance with engaging Genesis tableaux like *Paradise* (1530) and *Adam and Eve* (1520). The key focus, though, is the prized Dürer collection, with masterful pieces like *Portrait of a Venetian Lady* (1505), the spirit-soaring *Adoration of the Trinity* (1511) and the macabre *Martyrdom of the Ten Thousand* (1508).

Rubens throws you in the deep end of Flemish baroque painting next, with paintings rich in Counter-Reformation themes and mythological symbolism. The monumental *Miracle of St Francis Xavier* (1617), the celestial *Annunciation* (1610), the *Miracles of St Ignatius* (1615) and the *Triptych of St Ildefonso* (1630) all reveal the iridescent quality and linear clarity that underscored Rubens' style.

In 16th- and 17th-century Dutch Golden Age paintings, Rembrandt's lucid *Self-Portrait* (1652), showing the artist in a humble painter's smock, Van Ruisdael's palpable vision of nature in the *Large Forest* (1655) and Vermeer's seductively allegorical *Art of Painting* (1665), showing Clio, Greek muse of history, are all emblematic of the age.

The final three rooms are an ode to the art of Flemish baroque master Van Dyck and Flemish Renaissance painter Pieter Bruegel the Elder. Van Dyck's keenly felt devotional works include the *Vision of the Blessed Herman* (1630) and *Madonna and Child with St Rosalie, Peter and Paul* (1629). An entire room is given over to Pieter Bruegel the Elder's vivid depictions of Flemish life and landscapes, alongside his biblical star attraction – *The Tower of Babel* (1563).

Italian, Spanish & French Painting

The first three rooms here are given over to key exponents of the 16th-century Venetian style: Titian, Veronese and Tintoretto. High on your artistic agenda should be Titian's *Nymph and Shepherd* (1570). Veronese's dramatic depiction of the suicidal Roman heroine *Lucretia* (1583), with a dagger drawn to her chest, and Tintoretto's *Susanna at her Bath* (1556), watched by two lustful elders, are other highlights.

Devotion is central to Raphael's *Madonna of the Meadow* (1506) in room 4, one of the masterpieces of the High Renaissance, just as it is to the *Madonna of the Rosary* (1603), a stirring Counter-Reformation altarpiece by Italian baroque artist Caravaggio in the next room. Room 7 is also a delight, with compelling works like Giuseppe Arcimboldo's anthropomorphic paintings inspired by the seasons and elements. Look out, too, for Venetian landscape painter Canaletto's *Schönbrunn* (1761), meticulously capturing the palace back in its imperial heyday.

Of the artists represented in the final rooms dedicated to Spanish, French and English painting, the undoubted star is Spanish court painter Velázquez. Particularly entrancing is his almost 3D portrait of *Infanta Margarita Teresa in a Blue Dress* (1673), a vision of voluminous silk and eight-year-old innocence.

the free option of emailing the result (very impressive if you leave your glasses on). At a CSI table you can determine the gender, age and cause of death of a virtual skeleton.

★ Leopold Museum   MUSEUM

(Map p62; www.leopoldmuseum.org; 07, Museumsplatz 1; adult/child €12/7, audio guide €3; ☺ 10am-6pm Wed-Mon, to 9pm Thu; German guided tours 3pm Sun; Ⓜ Museumsquartier, Volkstheater) This museum is named after Rudolf Leopold, a Viennese ophthalmologist who, on buying his first Egon Schiele (1890–1918) for a song as a young student in 1950, started to amass a huge private collection of 19th-century and modernist Austrian artworks. In 1994 he sold the lot (5266 paintings) to the Austrian government for €160 million and the Leopold Museum was born.

The building itself has an attractive white, limestone exterior, contains plenty of open space (the 21m-high glass-covered atrium is lovely) and allows natural light to flood most rooms. Considering Rudolf Leopold's love of Schiele, it's no surprise it also contains the largest collection of the painter's work in the world: 41 paintings and 188 drawings and graphics. Among the standouts are the ghostly *Self Seer II Death and Man* (1911), the mournful *Mother with Two Children* (1915) and the caught-in-the-act *Cardinal and Nun* (1912).

Other artists well represented include Albin Egger-Lienz, with his unforgiving depictions of pastoral life, Richard Gerstl and Austria's third-greatest expressionist, Kokoschka. Of the handful of works on display by Klimt, the unmissable one is the allegorical *Death and Life* (1910), a swirling fusion of people juxtaposed by a skeletal grim reaper. Works by Loos, Hoffmann, (Otto) Wagner, Waldmüller and Romako are also on display.

★ MUMOK   GALLERY

(Museum Moderner Kunst, Museum of Modern Art; Map p76; www.mumok.at; 07, Museumsplatz 1; adult/child €10/free, 1hr tour free; ☺ 2-7pm Mon, 10am-7pm Tue-Sun, to 9pm Thu; free guided tours 1pm Fri, 2pm & 4pm Sat & Sun, 7pm Thu; Ⓜ Museumsquartier, Volkstheater, 🚋 49 Volkstheater) The dark basalt edifice and sharp corners of the Museum Moderner Kunst are a complete contrast to the MuseumsQuartier's historical sleeve. Inside, MUMOK is crawling with Vienna's finest collection of 20th-century art, centred on fluxus, nouveau realism, pop art and photorealism.

The best of expressionism, cubism, minimal art and Viennese Actionism is represented in a collection of 9000 works that are rotated and exhibited by theme – but take note that sometimes all this Actionism is packed away to make room for other exhibition pieces. On any visit you might glimpse: a wearily slumped attendant (not part of any exhibit), photos of horribly deformed babies, a video piece of a man being led by a beautiful woman across a pedestrian crossing on a dog leash, naked bodies smeared with salad and other delights, a man parting his own buttocks, flagellation in a lecture hall, and an ultra close-up of a urinating penis. The heavy stuff comes later. Other well-known artists represented throughout the museum – Picasso, Paul Klee, René Magritte, Max Ernst and Alberto Giacometti – are positively tame in comparison.

Kunsthalle Wien   MUSEUM

(Arts Hall; Map p62; ☎ 521 890; www.kunsthallewien.at; 07, Museumsplatz 1; both halls adult/child €12/2; ☺ 10am-7pm Fri-Wed, to 9pm Thu; Ⓜ Museumsquartier, Volkstheater, 🚋 49 Volkstheater) The Kunsthalle showcases Austrian and international contemporary art in two halls in the MuseumsQuartier. Programs, which run for three to six months, tend to focus mainly on photography, video, film, installation and new media.

Akademie der Bildenden Künste   MUSEUM

(Academy of Fine Arts; Map p76; www.akademiegalerie.at; 01, Schillerplatz 3; adult/under 19 yr €8/free; ☺ 10am-6pm Tue-Sun; Ⓜ Museumsquartier, Karlsplatz, 🚋 D, 1, 2 Kärntner Ring/Oper) The Akademie der Bildenden Künste, with an attractive facade designed by Theophil Hansen (1813–91), is an often underrated art space. Its gallery concentrates on the classic Flemish, Dutch and German painters, and includes important figures such as Hieronymus Bosch, Rembrandt, Van Dyck, Rubens, Titian, Francesco Guardi and Cranach the Elder, to mention a handful. The supreme highlight is Bosch's impressive and gruesome *Triptych of the Last Judgement* altarpiece (1504–08). The academy is the art school famous for having turned down Adolf Hitler twice. Hour-long tours (€3, in German only) take place at 10.30am every Sunday. Audio guides cost €2.

Secession   LANDMARK, GALLERY

(Map p76; www.secession.at; 01, Friedrichstrasse 12; adult/child €8.50/5, audio guide €3; ☺ 10am-6pm Tue-Sun; Ⓜ Karlsplatz) In 1897, 19 progressive

VIENNESE ACTIONISM

Viennese Actionism spanned the period from 1957 to 1968 and was one of the most extreme of all modern-art movements. It was linked to the Vienna Group (formed in the 1950s by HC Artmann), whose members experimented with surrealism and Dadaism in their sound compositions and textual montages. Actionism sought access to the unconscious through the frenzy of an extreme and very direct art; the Actionists quickly moved from pouring paint over the canvas and slashing it with knives to using bodies (live people, dead animals) as 'brushes' and using blood, excrement, eggs, mud and whatever came to hand as 'paint'. The traditional canvas was soon dispensed with altogether and the artist's body instead became the canvas. This turned the site of art into a deliberated event (a scripted 'action', staged both privately and publicly) and even merged art with reality.

It was a short step from self-painting to inflicting wounds upon the body, and engaging in physical and psychological endurance tests. For 10 years the Actionists scandalised the press and public, inciting violence and panic – but they got plenty of publicity. Often poetic, humorous and aggressive, the actions became increasingly politicised, addressing the sexual and social repression that pervaded the Austrian state. The press release for *Art in Revolution* (1968) gives the low down on what could be expected at a typical action: '[Günter] Brus undressed, cut himself with a razor, urinated in a glass and drank his urine, smeared his body with faeces and sang the Austrian national anthem while masturbating (for which he was arrested for degrading state symbols and sentenced to six months' detention)'. This was, not entirely surprisingly, the last action staged in Vienna. For more, see p370.

artists swam away from the mainstream Künstlerhaus artistic establishment to form the Vienna Secession *(Sezession)*. Among their number were Klimt, Josef Hoffman, Kolo Moser and Joseph M Olbrich. Olbrich designed the new exhibition centre of the Secessionists, which combined sparse functionality with stylistic motifs. Its biggest draw is Klimt's exquisitely gilded *Beethoven Frieze*.

The 14th exhibition (1902) held in the building featured the famous frieze by Klimt. This 34m-long work was intended as a temporary display, little more than an elaborate poster for the main exhibit, Max Klinger's Beethoven monument. Since 1983 it has been on display in the basement. Multilingual brochures explain the various graphic elements, which are based on Richard Wagner's interpretation of Beethoven's ninth symphony. The small room you enter before viewing the frieze tells the story of the building. It served as a hospital during WWI and was torched by the retreating Germans during WWII (the gold dome survived the fire). The ground floor is still used as it was originally intended: presenting temporary exhibitions of contemporary art.

The building is certainly a move away from the Ringstrasse architectural throw-backs. Its most striking feature is a delicate **golden dome** rising from a turret on the roof that deserves better than the description 'golden cabbage' accorded it by some Viennese.

Parlament LANDMARK
(☑ 401 10 2400; www.parlament.gv.at; 01, Dr-Karl-Renner-Ring 3; tours adult/under 19yr €5/free, visitor centre free; ☺ guided tours hourly 11am-4pm Mon-Sat, visitor centre 8.30am-6.30pm Mon-Fri, 9.30am-4.30pm Sat; Ⓜ Rathaus, Volkstheater, Ⓓ D, 1, 2 Stadiongasse/Parlament) The Parlament building opposite the Volksgarten strikes a governing pose over the Ringstrasse. Its neo-classical facade and Greek pillars, designed by Theophil Hansen in 1883, are impressive, and the beautiful **Athena Fountain**, sculpted by Karl Kundmann, which guards the building, offsets it magnificently. The visitor centre has exhibitions on political and parliamentary themes.

Rathaus LANDMARK
(City Hall; Map p74; ☑ 525 50; www.wien.gv.at; 01, Rathausplatz 1; ☺ guided tours 1pm Mon, Wed & Fri; Ⓜ Rathaus, Ⓓ D, 1, 2 Rathaus) **FREE** The crowning glory of the Ringstrasse boulevard's 19th-century architectural ensemble, Vienna's neo-Gothic City Hall was completed in 1883 by Friedrich von Schmidt of Cologne Cathedral fame and modelled on Flemish city

Vorstadt Northwest

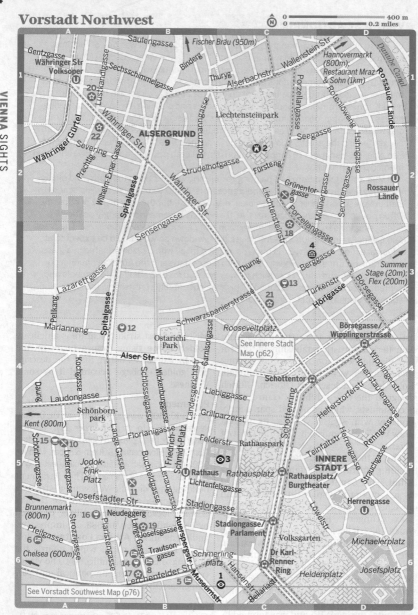

halls. From Rathauspark, where fountains dance and Josef Lanner and Johann Strauss I, fathers of the Viennese waltz, are immortalised in bronze, you get the full-on effect of its facade of lacy stonework, pointed-arch windows and spindly turrets. The main spire is 102m high if you include the pennant held by the medieval knight, or Rathausmann, guarding its tip. Tours are quite interesting, taking you through the building to see highlights like the enormous arcaded inner courtyard and elegant banquet hall.

Vorstadt Northwest

Votivkirche CHURCH
(Votive Church; Map p62; www.votivkirche.at; 09, Rooseveltplatz; ⊙9am-1pm & 4-6pm Tue-Sat, to 1pm Sun; Ⓜ Schottentor, Ⓓ D, 1, 2 Schottentor) In 1853 Franz Josef I survived an assassination attempt when a knife-wielding Hungarian failed to find the emperor's neck through his collar. The Votivkirche was commissioned in thanks for his lucky escape; in stepped Heinrich von Ferstel with a twin-towered, mosaic-roofed, neo-Gothic construction, completed in 1879. The rather bleak interior is bedecked with frescoes and bulbous chandeliers; the Antwerp Altar from 1460 is a prize exhibit in the small church **museum**.

Museum für Angewandte Kunst MUSEUM
(MAK, Museum of Applied Arts; Map p62; www.mak.at; 01, Stubenring 5; adult/under 19yr €7.90/free, 6-10pm Tue free, tours €2; ⊙10am-6pm Wed-Sun, to 10pm Tue, English tours noon Sun; Ⓜ Stubentor, Ⓓ 2 Stubentor) MAK is devoted to craftsmanship and art forms in everyday life. Each exhibition room showcases a different style, which includes Renaissance, baroque, ori-entalism, historicism, empire, art deco and the distinctive metalwork of the Wiener Werkstätte. Contemporary artists were invited to present the rooms in ways they felt were appropriate, resulting in eye-catching and unique displays. The 20th-century design and architecture room is one of the most fascinating, and Frank Gehry's cardboard chair is a gem. The collection encompasses tapestries, lace, furniture, glassware and ornaments; Klimt's *Stoclet Frieze* is upstairs.

The basement **Study Collection** has exhibits based on types of materials: glass and ceramics, metal, wood and textiles. Here you'll find anything from ancient oriental statues to unusual sofas (note the red-lips sofa).

◉ Across the Danube Canal

The districts across the Danube Canal from the Innere Stadt are predominantly residential neighbourhoods, largely void of individual sights of interest to the average visitor. But this is Vienna's outdoor playground.

★ Prater PARK
(www.wiener-prater.at; Ⓜ Praterstern) The Prater describes two distinct areas of parkland, which together comprise the city's favourite outdoor playground. First up, as you enter, is the **Würstelprater** (rides €1–€5), with all the roller-coaster-looping, dodgem-bashing fun of the fair, where the iconic Riesenrad (p85) turns. The **Unterer Prater** is a vast swath of woodland park, where Habsburgs once went hunting. Today, it is perfect for gentle bike rides, walks and warm-day picnics.

Madame Tussauds Vienna MUSEUM
(www.madametussauds.com/wien; 02, Riesenradplatz 1; adult/child €18.50/14.50; ⊙10am-6pm; Ⓜ Praterstern) This waxwork wonderland in the Würstelprater is a stage for a host of sculpted celebrities – Nicole Kidman, Michael Jackson and Johnny Depp star among them. Other figures such as Emperor Franz Joseph and his beloved Sisi, Klimt, Freud and Falco give the experience a distinctly Austrian edge.

Donauinsel & Alte Donau RECREATION AREA
(🚇) Dividing the Danube from the Neue Donau is the svelte Donauinsel, which stretches some 21.5km from opposite Klosterneuburg in the north to the Nationalpark Donau-Auen in the south. The island features long sections of swimming areas,

Vorstadt Southwest

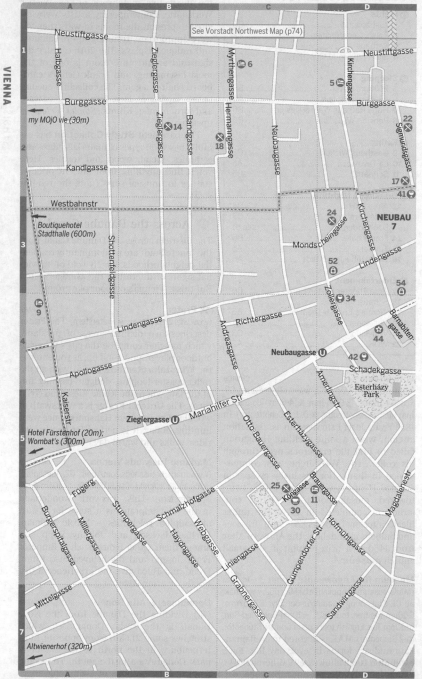

See Vorstadt Northwest Map (p74)

NEUBAU
7

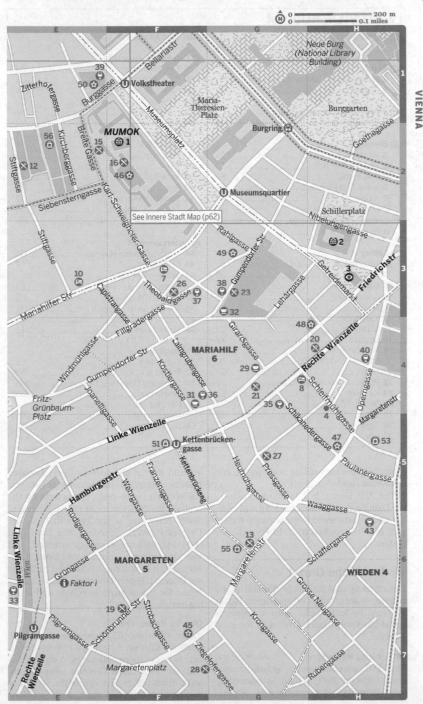

0   200 m
0   0.1 miles

Neue Burg
(National Library
Building)

Bellariastr

Volkstheater

Maria-
Theresien-
Platz

Burggarten

Zitterhofergasse

Burggasse

Museumsstr

MUMOK

Goethegasse

Burgring

Kirchberggasse

Breite Gasse

Karl-Schweighofer-Gasse

Stiftgasse

Museumsquartier

Schillerplatz

Siebensterngasse

Nibelungengasse

See Innere Stadt Map (p62)

Gumpendorfer Str

Friedrichstr

Getreidemarkt

Mariahilfer Str

Capistrangasse

Theobaldgasse

Filgradergasse

Girardgasse

Lehárgasse

Rechte Wienzeile

Windmühlgasse

Gumpendorfer Str

Köstlergasse

Königsklostergasse

MARIAHILF
6

Schleifmühlgasse

Operngasse

Margaretenstr

Fritz-
Grünbaum-
Platz

Joanelligasse

Schikanedergasse

Linke Wienzeile

Kettenbrücken-
gasse

Linke Wienzeile

Wien

Hamburgerstr

Franzensgasse

Kettenbrückeng

Heumühlgasse

Pressgasse

Paulanergasse

Waaggasse

Rüdigergasse

Wehrgasse

MARGARETEN
5

Grüngasse

Faktor i

Margaretenstr

Schäffergasse

WIEDEN 4

Grosse Neugasse

Pilgramgasse

Pilgramgasse

Schönbrunner Str

Strobachgasse

Krongasse

Rechte
Wienzeile

Margaretenplatz

Ziegelofengasse

Rubengasse

Vorstadt Southwest

concrete paths for walking and cycling, and restaurants and snack bars.

The Alte Donau is a landlocked arm of the Danube, a favourite of sailing and boating enthusiasts, swimmers, walkers, fishers and, in winter (when it's cold enough), ice skaters.

◉ Inside the Gürtel

The districts that lie inside the Gürtel are a dense concentration of apartment blocks pocketed by leafy parks, with a couple of grand baroque palaces thrown in for good measure.

★**Schloss Belvedere**   PALACE, GALLERY
(Map p80; www.belvedere.at; Ⓜ Taubstummengasse, Südtiroler Platz, ⓉⒹ 71 Schwarzenbergplatz) Belvedere is a masterpiece of total art and one of the world's finest baroque palaces. Designed by Johann Lukas von Hildebrandt (1668–1745), it was built for the brilliant military strategist Prince Eugene of Savoy, conqueror of the Turks in 1718. The Unteres (Lower) Belvedere was built first (1714–16), with an orangery attached, and was the prince's summer residence. Connected to it by a long, landscaped garden is the Oberes (Upper) Belvedere (1721–23), the venue for the prince's banquets and other big bashes.

Oberes Belvedere   GALLERY
(Upper Belvedere; 03, Prinz-Eugen-Strasse 27; adult/child €11/free; ⊙10am-6pm) Oberes Belvedere is one of those 'must sees'. A visit begins with the ornate **Sala Terrena**, with four colossal Atlas pillars supporting the weight of its delicately stuccoed vault. A ground-floor

section on **Medieval Art** leads you through the artistic development of the Middle Ages, with an exceptional portfolio of Gothic sculpture and altar pieces, many from Austrian abbeys and monasteries. The space devoted to **Modern Art & the Interwar Period** includes works by Oskar Kokoschka, Egon Schiele and Max Oppenheimer.

The 1st-floor **Vienna 1880–1914** collection is a holy grail for Klimt fans, with an entire room devoted to erotic golden wonders like *Judith* (1901), *Salome* (1909), *Adam and Eve* (1917) and *The Kiss* (1908). **Neoclassicism, Romanticism & Biedermeier Art** is strong on works by Georg Waldmüller and Caspar David Friedrich, whereas in the **Realism & Impressionism** section French masters share the limelight with their Austrian and German contemporaries.

Unteres Belvedere PALACE, MUSEUM
(Lower Belvedere; Map p80; 03, Rennweg 6; adult/child €11/free; ⊙10am-6pm Thu-Tue, to 9pm Wed; ⓓD) Built between 1712 and 1716, Lower Belvedere is a treat of baroque delights. Highlights include Prince Eugene's former residential apartment and ceremonial rooms, the **Groteskensaal** (Hall of the Grotesque; now the museum shop), a second **Marmorsaal** (Marble Hall), the **Marmorgalerie** (Marble Gallery) and the **Goldenes Zimmer** (Golden Room). Temporary exhibitions are held in the **Orangery** (Österreichishe Galerie; Map p80), with a walkway gazing grandly over Prince Eugene's private garden. Attached to the Orangery is the **Prunkstall** (⊙10am-noon), the former royal stables, where you can now trot through a 150-piece collection of Austrian medieval art, including religious scenes, altarpieces, sculpture and Gothic triptychs.

Belvedere Gardens GARDEN
(03, Rennweg/Prinz-Eugen-Strasse; ⓓD) The long garden between the two Belvederes was laid out in classical French style and has sphinxes and other mythical beasts along its borders. South of the Oberes Belvedere is the small **alpine garden** (www.bundesgaerten.at; 03, Prinz-Eugen-Strasse 27; adult/child €3.50/2.50;

VIENNA FOR CHILDREN

It was once said the Viennese love dogs more than they love children, and while this might be true for some folk, Vienna is actually quite child friendly. Its museums, attractions and theatres, such as the Kunsthistorisches Museum (p70) and the Albertina (p69), arrange children's programs over the summer months.

The Prater, with its wide playing fields, giant Ferris wheel (p85), playgrounds and funfair, is ideal for children. There are good combined tickets (see boxed text p85) for a magic show on Riesenradplatz known as Miraculum, Austria's highest structure, **Donauturm** (www.donauturm.at; 22, Donauturmstrasse 4; adult/child €7.40/5.20, combined ticket incl Riesenrad €13/7.4; ⊙10am-midnight ; ⓂKaisermühlen Vienna International Centre), and the **Liliputbahn** (www.liliputbahn.com; complete circuit adult/child €4/2.50), a miniature railway connecting the Würstelprater with Ernst-Happel-Stadion, see p85. Just as fascinating for adults as for kids – and adults can also relax here over a drink and sausage while the kids see the animals – is the Tirolerhof, inside the Tiergarten (p84) at Schloss Schönbrunn. Actually a historic farmhouse from Tyrol deconstructed and rebuilt inside the zoo, it holds ancient Noric horses, as well as goats, bulls, chickens and other farm animals. The Donauinsel (p75) is another place where kids can run off their energy. Swimming pools, located here and throughout Vienna, are free to children under 15 over the summer school holidays.

Two museums are aimed directly at kids. **Zoom** (Map p62; ☑524 79 08; www.kindermuseum.at; 07, Museumsplatz 1; exhibition adult/child €4/free, activities child €4-6, accompanying adult free; ⊙8.45am-4pm Tue-Fri, 9.45am-4pm Sat & Sun, activity times vary; ⓐ; ⓂMuseumsquartier, Volkstheater), next door to the WienXtra-Kinderinfo (p110) in the MuseumsQuartier, is a bonanza for kids, with a craft studio and ocean, lab, and science and exhibition sections (some of these multimedia) for exciting sessions of about 1½ or two hours aimed at kids up to the age of 14; book ahead.

Schönbrunn's **Kindermuseum** (Map p83; www.schoenbrunn.at; 13, Schloss Schönbrunn; adult/child €7/5.50; ⊙10am-5pm Sat & Sun; ⓐ) focuses quite understandably on the 16 children of Maria Theresia, and the kids dress up in costume. But it's not all hobnobbing – they'll also find out what aspects of life made the right royal Habsburgs different from mere low-life mortals. The obvious – fortune, fame, pets you can ride – are a start.

Vorstadt Southeast

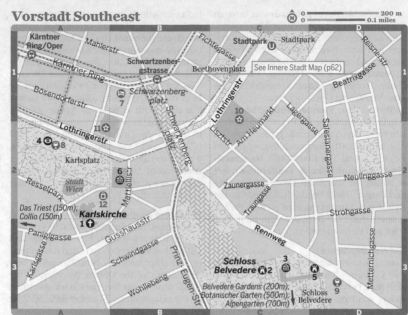

Vorstadt Southeast

⊙10am-6pm late Mar-early Aug; Ⓜ Südtiroler Platz, 🚆D, O, 18), which has 3500 plant species and a bonsai section. North of here is the much larger **Botanischer Gärten** (www.botanik.uni-vie.ac.at; 03, Rennweg 14; ⊙10am-1hr before dusk; 🚆71, O) **FREE** belonging to Vienna University.

Heeresgeschichtliches Museum MUSEUM (Museum of Military History; www.hgm.or.at; 03, Arsenal; adult/under 19yr €5.10/free, 1st Sun of month free; ⊙9am-5pm; Ⓜ Südtiroler Platz) The superb Heeresgeschichtliches Museum is housed in the Arsenal, a large neo-Byzantine barracks and munitions depot.

Spread over two floors, the museum works its way from the Thirty Years' War (1618–48) to WWII, taking in the Hungarian Uprising and the Austro-Prussian War (ending in 1866), the Napoleonic and Turkish Wars, and WWI. Highlights on the 1st floor include the Great Seal of Mustafa Pasha, which fell to Prince Eugene of Savoy in the Battle of Zenta in 1697.

On the ground floor, the room on the assassination of Archduke Franz Ferdinand in Sarajevo in 1914 – which set off a chain of events culminating in the start of WWI – steals the show. The car he was shot in (complete with bullet holes), the sofa he bled to death on and his rather grisly blood-stained coat are on show. The eastern wing covers the republic years after WWI up until the *Anschluss* (annexation into Germany) in 1938; the excellent displays include propaganda posters and Nazi paraphernalia, plus video footage of Hitler hypnotising the masses.

★ **Karlskirche** CHURCH
(St Charles Church; Map p80; www.karlskirche.
at; Karlsplatz; adult/child €8/4; ☉9am-5.30pm
Mon-Sat, 11.30am-5.30pm Sun; Ⓜ Karlsplatz)
Karlskirche rises at the southeast corner of
Resselpark and is the finest of Vienna's baroque churches. This dramatic structure was
built between 1716 and 1739, after a vow by
Karl VI at the end of the 1713 plague. It was
designed and commenced by Johann Bernhard Fischer von Erlach and completed by
his son Joseph.

The enormous twin columns at the front
are modelled on Trajan's Column in Rome
and show scenes from the life of St Charles
Borromeo (who helped plague victims in
Italy), to whom the church is dedicated. The
huge oval dome reaches 72m. The admission
price includes entrance to **Museo Borromeo**
and a small **museum** with a handful of religious art and clothing purportedly from the
saint, but the highlight is the lift to the **dome**
for a close-up view of the intricate frescoes
by Johann Michael Rottmayr. The high altar panel shows the ascension of St Charles
Borromeo. In front of the church is a pond,
replete with a Henry Moore sculpture from
1978.

Wien Museum MUSEUM
(Map p80; www.wienmuseum.at; 04, Karlsplatz
8; adult/under 19yr €8/free, 1st Sun of month
free; ☉10am-6pm Tue-Sun; Ⓜ Karlsplatz) The
Wien Museum presents a fascinating romp
through Vienna's history, from Neolithic
times to the mid-20th century, putting the
city and its personalities in a meaningful
context. Exhibits are spread over three
floors, including spaces for two temporary
exhibitions. Top billing goes to the 2nd
floor, which zooms in on Vienna's fin de
siécle artistic heyday. On show is the intact
modernist living room Adolf Loos designed
for his nearby apartment in 1903, replete
with mahogany and marble, alongside
stellar Secessionist works such as Klimt's
mythology-inspired, gold-encrusted *Pallas
Athene* (1898) and Egon Schiele's *Young
Mother* (1914).

Stadtbahn Pavillons LANDMARK
(Map p80; www.wienmuseum.at; 04, Karlsplatz;
adult/under 19yr €4/free; ☉10am-6pm Tue-Sun
Apr-Oct; Ⓜ Karlsplatz) Peeking above the
Resselpark at Karlsplatz are two of Otto
Wagner's finest designs, the Stadtbahn Pa-
villons. Built in 1898 at a time when Wagner
was assembling Vienna's first public trans-

VIENNA'S CITY WALLS

The Ringstrasse runs along the line of
the former 16th-century city walls. These
walls originally had the extra protection
of a ditch or moat, beyond which a wide,
sloped clearing allowed defenders to hurl
the heavy stuff at their exposed invaders. Anyone living in the Vorstädte (inner
suburbs) outside the fortress was expected to flee inside it as invading forces
approached – or take their chances.

port system (1893–1902), the pavilions are
gorgeous examples of *Jugendstil* (art nouveau), with floral motifs and gold trim on a
structure of steel and marble.

The west pavilion now holds an exhibit on
Wagner's most famous works, the Kirche am
Steinhof (p84) – situated in the grounds of a
psychiatric hospital and completed in 1907 –
and Postsparkasse, which fans of *Jugendstil*
will love. The eastern pavilion is now home
to **Club U** (Map p80; www.club-u.at; 04, Künstler-
hauspassage; ☉9pm-4am; Ⓜ Karlsplatz).

KunstHausWien MUSEUM
(Art House Vienna; www.kunsthauswien.com;
03, Untere Weissgerberstrasse 13; adult/child
€10/5; ☉10am-7pm; ☐1, O Radetzkyplatz) The
KunstHausWien, with its bulging ceramics, wonky surfaces, checkerboard facade,
technicolor mosaic tilework and rooftop
sprouting plants and trees, bears the inimitable hallmark of eccentric Viennese
artist and ecowarrior Hundertwasser
(1928–2000), who famously called the
straight line 'godless'. It is an ode to his
playful, boldly creative work, as well as to
his green politics.

Besides quality temporary exhibitions
featuring other artists, the gallery is something of a paean in honour of Hundertwasser, illustrating his paintings, graphics,
tapestry, philosophy, ecology and architecture. Monday is half-price day (unless it's a
holiday) and guided tours in German of the
permanent exhibition leave at noon on Sundays and are included in the price. Audio
guides cost €3.

Hundertwasserhaus LANDMARK
(03, cnr Löwengasse & Kegelgasse; ☐1 Hetzgasse)
This residential block of flats bears all the
wackily creative hallmarks of Hundertwasser, Vienna's radical architect and lover of

uneven surfaces, with its curvy lines, crayon-bright colours and mosaic detail.

It's not possible to see inside, but you can cross the road to visit the **Kalke Village** (www.kalke-village.at; 03, Kegelgasse 37-39; ☺9am-6pm; 🚇1 Hetzgasse) **FREE**, also the handiwork of Hundertwasser, created from an old Michelin factory. It contains overpriced cafes, souvenir shops and art shops, all in typical Hundertwasser fashion with colourful ceramics and a distinct absence of straight lines.

Palais Liechtenstein PALACE
(Map p74; ☎319 57 67; www.liechtensteinmuseum.at; 09, Fürstengasse 1; tours €20; ☺guided tours 3pm 1st & 3rd Fri of month; 🚇Rossauer Lände, 🚊D, 1 Seegasse) Once the muse of Italian landscape painter Canaletto, Palais Liechtenstein is a sublime baroque palace, which sits in beautifully landscaped, sculpture-dotted grounds. The palace containing the private collection of Prince Hans-Adam II of Liechtenstein, with around 200 paintings and 50 sculptures dating from 1500 to 1700, can be visited twice monthly on hour-long **guided tours** (in German only). Book ahead.

Sigmund Freud Museum HOUSE MUSEUM
(Map p74; www.freud-museum.at; 09, Berggasse 19; adult/child €8/3.50; ☺9am-6pm; 🚇Schottentor, Schottenring, 🚊D Schlickgasse) Sigmund Freud is a bit like the telephone – once he happened, there was no going back. This is where Freud spent his most prolific years and developed his groundbreaking theories;

moving here with his family in 1891 and staying until he was forced into exile by the Nazis in 1938. Pivotal to the permanent collection in this museum is the waiting room, where the Wednesday Psychological Society first met in 1902, the consulting room that once contained Freud's famous couch (now in London) and Freud's study. An audio guide gives background on exhibits and interview excerpts, including one where Freud talks about psychoanalytic theory.

◉ Outside the Gürtel

The districts that fall outside the Gürtel are quite an unusual blend. Parts are rather dull and uninviting (by Viennese standards) – in particular towards the south – while others are beautiful beyond belief and home to some of Vienna's greatest treasures.

★**Schloss Schönbrunn** PALACE
(Map p83; www.schoenbrunn.at; 13, Schönbrunner Schlossstrasse 47; Imperial Tour with audio guide adult/child €11.50/8.50, Grand Tour €14.50/9.50; ☺8.30am-5.30pm; 🚇Hietzing) In contrast to Schloss Belvedere, which is mostly about art in an imperial surrounding, Schloss Schönbrunn focuses on the palace itself, giving you a chance to see the lavish and exotically furnished rooms, soak up the atmosphere and learn more about the former inhabitants. Of the palace's 1441 rooms, 40 are open to the public; the **Imperial Tour**, which you do with an audio guide, takes you into 22 of these. The east wing of the

---

❶ TICKETS FOR SCHLOSS SCHÖNBRUNN

If you plan to see several sights at Schönbrunn, purchase one of the combined tickets. Prices vary according to whether it's summer season (April to October) or winter. The best way to get a ticket is to buy it in advance online. Print the ticket yourself and present it when you enter.

➡ **Summer Classic Pass** (adult/under 19 years €18/11) Valid for the Grand Tour of Schloss Schönbrunn and Kronprinzengarten (Crown Prince Garden), Irrgarten (Maze) and Labyrinth, Gloriette with viewing terrace, and Hofbackstube Schönbrunn (Court Bakery) with the chance to watch apple strudel being made and enjoy the result with a cup of coffee.

➡ **Summer Classic Pass 'light'** (adult/under 19 years €13.90/9.50) Excludes the apple strudel show. The Court Bakery Schönbrunn can be viewed separately (it's inside Café Residenz).

➡ **Summer Gold Pass** (adult/under 19 years €36/18) Includes the Grand Tour, Kronprinzengarten, Tiergarten, Palmenhaus, Wüstenhaus, Wagenburg, Gloriette, Maze and Labyrinth, and Hofbackstube Schönbrunn.

➡ **Winter Pass** (adult/under 19 years €25/12) includes the Grand Tour, Tiergarten, Palmenhaus, Wüstenhaus, Wagenburg, Gloriette and Maze and Labyrinth.

Schönbrunn

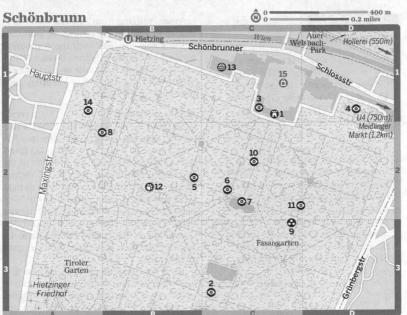

palace is accessible on the Grand Tour, with well-worthwhile extras like the **Napoleon Room**, where Europe's diminutive reformer and conqueror resided when he occupied Vienna in 1805 and 1809, and the chance to venture into the bedroom of Maria Theresia. The Habsburgs' overwhelmingly opulent summer palace and surrounding gardens are now a Unesco World Heritage site.

Schloss Schönbrunn Gardens   GARDEN
(Map p83; 13, Schloss Schönbrunn; ☉6am-dusk Apr-Oct, 6.30am-dusk Nov-Mar; MHietzing) **FREE** The beautifully tended formal gardens of the palace, arranged in the French style, are a symphony of colour in summer and a combination of greys and browns in winter; all seasons are appealing in their own right. The grounds, which were opened to the public by Joseph II in 1779, hide a number of attractions in the tree-lined avenues (arranged according to a grid and star-shaped system between 1750 and 1755). From 1772 to 1780 Ferdinand Hetzendorf added some of the final touches to the park under the instructions of Joseph II: fake **Roman ruins** (Map p83) in 1778; the **Neptunbrunnen** (Neptune Fountain; Map p83), a riotous ensemble from Greek mythology, in 1781; and the crowning glory, the **Gloriette** (Map p83; adult/child €3/2.20; ☉9am-5pm, closed early Nov-late Mar)

in 1775. The view from the Gloriette, looking back towards the palace with Vienna shimmering in the distance, ranks among the best in the city. It's possible to venture onto its roof for marginally better views alfresco.

> **WORTH A TRIP**
>
> ## THERME WIEN
>
> Rest museum-weary feet or escape the city for a day at **Therme Wien** (☑680 09; www.thermewien.at; 11, Kurbadstrasse 14; adult/child 3-hour ticket €16/10, day ticket €23/14; ⊙9am-10pm Mon-Sat, 8am-10pm Sun; ⓜ; ⓠ67 Oberlaa-Therme Wien). In Austria's largest thermal baths the water bubbles pleasantly at 27°C to 36°C and jets, whirlpools, waterfalls and grottolike pools pummel and swirl you into relaxation. Besides a jigsaw of indoor and outdoor pools, there is an area for kids, a sauna complex, as well as gardens with sun loungers, outdoor massage and games like volleyball and boules for warm-weather days. The best way to reach the thermal baths is by taking U1 to Reumannplatz, then catching tram 67 to Oberlaa-Therme Wien.

The original **Schöner Brunnen** (Fountain; Map p83), from which the palace gained its name, now pours through the stone pitcher of a nymph near the Roman ruins.

The garden's 630m-long **maze** (Map p83; adult/child €3.50/2.20; ⊙9am-6pm) is a classic hedge design based on the original maze that occupied its place from 1720 to 1892; adjoining this is the **labyrinth** (Map p83), a playground with games, climbing equipment and a giant mirror kaleidoscope.

To the east of the palace is the **Kronprinzengarten** (Crown Prince Garden; Map p83; adult/child €3/2.20; ⊙9am-5pm, closed early Nov-late Mar), a replica of the baroque garden that occupied the space around 1750. The gardens also harbour the world's oldest zoo, the **Tiergarten** (Map p83; www.zoovienna.at; adult/child €15/7; ⊙9am-6.30pm; ⓜ), founded in 1752, a **Wüstenhaus** (Desert House; Map p83; ☑877 92 940; 13, Maxingstrasse 13b; adult/child & student & senior €4/2.50; ⊙9am-6pm May-Sep, to 5pm Oct-Apr; ⓜHietzing) and **Palmenhaus** (Palm House; Map p83; 13, Maxingstrasse 13b; admission €4; ⊙9.30am-6pm May-Sep, to 5pm Oct-Apr; ⓜHietzing; ⓠ10, 58, 60).

Wagenburg   MUSEUM
(Imperial Coach Collection; Map p83; www.kaiserliche-wagenburg.at; 13, Schloss Schönbrunn; adult/under 19yr €6/free; ⊙9am-6pm Apr-Oct, 10am-4pm Nov-Mar) The Wagenburg displays carriages ranging from tiny children's wagons up to sumptuous vehicles of state, but nothing can compete with the coronation carriage of Emperor Franz Stephan (1708–65). Weighing in at 4000kg and dripping in ornate gold plating, it has Venetian glass panes and painted cherubs.

Kirche am Steinhof   CHURCH
(☑910 60-11 204; 14, Baumgartner Höhe 1; admission €2, tours €8; ⊙4-5pm Sat, noon-4pm Sun, tours 3-4pm Sat, 4-5pm Sun; ⓠ47A, 48A Baumgartner Höhe) Situated in the grounds of the Psychiatric Hospital of the City of Vienna, Kirche am Steinhof, built from 1904 to 1907, is the remarkable achievement of Otto Wagner. Kolo Moser chipped in with the mosaic windows, and the roof is topped by a copper-covered dome that earned the nickname Limoniberg (Lemon Mountain) for its original golden colour.

It's a bold statement in an asylum that has other art nouveau buildings, and it could only be pushed through by Wagner because the grounds were far from the public gaze.

Lainzer Tiergarten   PARK
(www.lainzer-tiergarten.at; 13, Hermesstrasse; ⊙8am-dusk; ⓠ60B Hermesstrasse, ⓠ60 Hermesstrasse) **FREE** At 25 sq km, the Lainzer Zoo is the largest (and wildest) of Vienna's city parks. The 'zoo' refers to the abundant wild boar, deer, woodpeckers and squirrels that freely inhabit the park, and the famous Lipizzaner horses that summer here.

Zentralfriedhof   CEMETERY
(www.friedhoefewien.at; 11, Simmeringer Hauptstrasse 232-244; ⊙7am-8pm, shorter hours in winter; ⓠ6, 71 Zentralfriedhof) **FREE** The cemetery's mammoth scale (2.4 sq km, more than three million resting residents) makes it one of Europe's biggest cemeteries. The cemetery has three gates; the information centre and map of the cemetery are at Gate Two. Just beyond Gate Two are the all-star **Ehrengräber** (Tombs of Honour). Besides the clump of big-name composers such as Beethoven, Brahms, Johann Strauss Father and Son, and Schubert, lie Austrian luminaries including artist Hans Makart, sculptor Fritz Wotruba, architect Adolf Loos, and 1980s pop icon Falco. Mozart has a monument here, but he is buried in an unmarked grave in the St Marxer Friedhof.

🏃 Activities

The Alte Donau is the main boating and sailing centre, but the Neue Donau also provides opportunities for boating, windsurfing and water skiing. Just opposite the Donauinsel (p75) is **Copa Cagrana Rad und Skateverleih** (📞 263 52 42; www.fahrradverleih. at; 22, Am Kaisermühlendamm 1; per hour/half-/full day from €5/15/25; ⊙ 9am-6pm Mar-Oct, to 9pm May-Aug; Ⓜ Kaisermühlen Vienna International Centre), with bike rental, and also skates (from €6 per hour).

Vienna's layout and well-marked cycle lanes make cycling a pleasant and popular pastime, especially along the banks of the Danube, in the Prater and around the Ringstrasse. The Wienerwald (Vienna Woods) is popular for mountain biking; check the websites www.mbike.at and www.mtbwienerwald.at (both in German) for ideas and trails.

The Donauinsel, Alte Donau and Lobau (all free bathing) are hugely popular places for taking a dip on steamy hot summer days. Topless sunbathing is quite the norm, as is nude sunbathing, but only in designated areas; much of Lobau and both tips of the Donauinsel are *Frei Körper Kultur* (FKK, nude-bathing areas).

⭐ Riesenrad
FERRIS WHEEL

(www.wienerriesenrad.com; 02, Prater 90; adult/child €9/4; ⊙ 9am-11.45pm, shorter hours in winter; 🚻; Ⓜ Praterstern) The Riesenrad is a towering, modern symbol of Vienna. Built in 1897 by Englishman Walter B Basset, the Ferris wheel rises to 65m and takes about 20 minutes to rotate its 430-tonne weight one complete circle – giving you ample time to snap some fantastic shots of the city spread out at your feet. It survived bombing in 1945 and has had dramatic lighting and a cafe at its base added. This icon achieved celluloid fame in *The Third Man*, in the scene where Holly Martins confronts Harry Lime, and also featured in the James Bond flick *The Living Daylights*, and *Before Sunrise*, directed by Richard Linklater.

Sailing School Hofbauer
BOATING

(📞 204 34 35; www.hofbauer.at; 22, An der Obere Alte Donau 191; ⊙ Apr-Oct; Ⓜ Alte Donau) Hofbauer rents sailing boats (from €14.80 per hour) and row boats (€8.40 per hour) on the eastern bank of the Alte Donau and can provide lessons (in English) for those wishing to learn or brush up on their skills. Pedal boats (€11.80 per hour) are also available for hire.

Wienerwald
WALKING

(Vienna Woods; www.wienerwald.info) To the west of the city, the rolling hills and marked trails of the Wienerwald are perfect for walkers. A good trail heading in the woods to the north of Vienna starts in Nussdorf (take tram D from the Ring) and climbs **Kahlenberg** (484m), a hill offering views of the city. On your return to Nussdorf you can undo all that exercise by imbibing at a *Heuriger*. The round trip is around 11km, or you can spare yourself the leg-work by taking the Nussdorf-Kahlenberg 38A bus in one or both directions.

Strandbad Gänsehäufel
SWIMMING

(www.gaensehaeufel.at; 22, Moissigasse 21; adult/child €5/1.70; ⊙ 9am-7pm May–mid-Sep; Ⓜ Kaisermühlen Vienna International Centre) Gänsehäufel occupies half an island in the Alte Donau. There's a swimming pool and FKK (read: nudist) area, playground, minigolf, tennis and volleyball court, and a climbing zone.

Prater
WALKING

Forest and parkland walking trails crisscross the Prater (p75).

👉 Tours

Vienna has everything from bus tours to horse-drawn carriage rides. Bus tours are good if you're very short on time, while the walking tours are perfect if you're interested in learning more on a specific topic.

Fiaker
HORSE & CARRIAGE TOUR

(20min/40min tour €55/80) More of a tourist novelty than anything else, a *Fiaker* is a traditional-style open carriage drawn by a pair of horses. Drivers generally speak English and point out places of interest en

---

ℹ️ RIESENRAD COMBINED TICKETS

The various combination tickets for the giant Ferris wheel, the Miraculum magic show, Donauturm, the Liliputbahn miniature railway, and Schönbrunn's Tiergarten can be good value, especially if you have kids (see p79). The Riesenrad plus Miraculum show costs adult/child €11.50/7, Riesenrad plus Liliputbahn costs €9.90/4.20, Riesenrad plus Tiergarten costs €16.50/7, and Riesenrad plus Donauturm costs €11/6.10.

route. Lines of horses, carriages and bowler-hatted drivers can be found at Stephansplatz, Albertinaplatz and Heldenplatz at the Hofburg. Short tours take you through the old town, while long tours include the Ringstrasse.

Ring Tram
TRAM TOUR

(Map p62; ☑ 790 91 00; www.wienerlinien.at; adult/child €7/4; ☺ 10am-6pm) Continuous hop-on, hop-off guided tour of the Ringstrasse with video screens and commentary on a clockwise route stopping at 13 stations. You can get on and off at any stop on a tour that lasts 25 minutes without stops. The first tour leaves Kärntner Ring-Oper at 10am, the last from Schwarzenbergplatz at 5.28pm.

City Segway Tours/Pedal Power
CYCLING

(☑ 729 72 34; www.pedalpower.at; Ausstellungsstrasse 3, 02; hired bike half-/full day €24/32; Ⓜ Praterstern) Pedal Power offers 'City Segway' and guided bike tours, which start at €70 and €29 respectively for a three-hour spin; visit the website for further details. You can also pick up city and mountain bikes here or, for an extra €5, arrange for the two wheels to be conveniently dropped off and picked up at your hotel.

Vienna Tour Guides
WALKING TOUR

(www.wienguide.at; adult/child €14/7) A collection of highly knowledgable guides who conduct over 60 different guided walking tours, some of which are in English. The monthly Wiener Spaziergänge (Vienna's Walking Tours) leaflet from tourist offices details all tours, departure points and tour languages. Also see the official city website www.wien. info/en/sightseeing/tours-guides for other options.

DDSG Blue Danube
BOAT TOUR

(Map p62; ☑ 588 80; www.ddsg-blue-danube.at; 01, Schwedenbrücke; adult/child from €19/9.50, under 10yr free; ☺ tours 11am & 3pm Apr-Oct; Ⓜ Schwedenplatz) Some of the most popular tours include circumnavigating the Leopoldstadt and Brigittenau districts along the Danube Canal and the Danube or through the historic Nussdorf locks (built by Otto Wagner around 1900). Tour length starts from 1½ hours.

Hop On Hop Off
BUS TOUR

(Vienna Sightseeing Tours; Map p62; ☑ 712 46 830; www.viennasightseeingtours.com; 01, Opernring; 1hr/2hr/all-day ticket €13/16/20; ☺ 10am-5pm; Ⓜ Karlsplatz, Ⓓ D, 1, 2, 71 Kärntner Ring/Oper) Buses stop at 15 sights around Vienna. Tickets range from one hour to two days, and you can hop on and off as often as you wish. Buses circle the Innere Stadt, with detours to Stephansplatz. Others take you east of the Danube Canal, and to Schönbrunn and Schloss Belvedere. See the website for details. All buses depart from directly outside the Staatsoper.

Redbus City Tours
BUS

(Map p62; ☑ 512 48 63; www.redbuscitytours.at; 01, Führichgasse 12; tours adult €14-24, child €7-12; ☺ 10am-7pm; Ⓜ Karlsplatz, Ⓓ D, 1, 2 Kärntner Ring/Oper) One-and-a-half-hour tours of the main sights in and around the Innere Stadt and 2½-hour tours of the city's big sights. Buses leave from outside the Albertina.

✩ Festivals & Events

Regardless of the time of year, there will be something special happening in Vienna; pick up a copy of the monthly booklet of events from the tourist office. Tickets for many events are available to personal callers at Wien-Ticket Pavillon (p106) in the hut by the Staatsoper.

Opernball
BALL

(☺ Jan/Feb) Of the 300 or so balls held in January and February, the Opernball (Opera Ball) is number one. Held in the Staatsoper (p104), it's a supremely lavish affair, with the men in tails and women in shining white gowns.

OsterKlang Festival
MUSIC

(Sound of Easter festival; ☑ 427 17; www.osterklang. at; ☺ Easter) Orchestral and chamber music recitals fill some of Vienna's best music halls. The highlight is the opening concert, which features the Vienna Philharmonic.

Wiener Festwochen
ARTS

(www.festwochen.at; ☺ May–mid-June) Wide-ranging program of arts from around the world.

Donauinselfest
MUSIC

(https://donauinselfest.at; ☺ late Jun) FREE For the younger generation, the Donauinselfest on the Donauinsel (p75) occupies the top spot on the year's events calendar. Held over three days, it features a feast of rock, pop, folk and country performers, and attracts almost three million onlookers. Best of all, it's free!

Jazz Fest Wien JAZZ
(📞408 60 30; www.viennajazz.org; ☉late Jun–mid-July,) Vienna relaxes to the smooth sound of jazz, blues and soul flowing from the Staatsoper and a number of clubs across town.

Musikfilm Festival FILM
(01, Rathausplatz; ☉Jul & Aug) Screenings of operettas, operas and concerts outside the Rathaus.

ImPuls Tanz PERFORMING ARTS
(📞523 55 58; www.impulstanz.com; ☉mid-Jul–mid-Aug) Vienna's premiere avant-garde dance festival attracts an array of internationally renowned troupes and newcomers at theatres across Vienna.

Lange Nacht der Museen CULTURE
(langenacht.orf.at; adult/child €12/10; ☉1st Sat Oct) Around 500 museums nationwide open their doors to visitors between 6pm and 1am. One ticket (available at museums) allows entry to all of them, including 90-plus museums in Vienna, and includes public transport around town.

Viennale Film Festival FILM
(📞526 59 47; www.viennale.at; ☉Oct) The country's best film festival features fringe and independent films from around the world with screenings at numerous locations around the city.

Christkindlmärkte CHRISTMAS MARKET
(www.christkindlmarkt.at; ☉mid-Nov–Christmas Day) Vienna's much-loved Christmas market season. See p108 for details on the various markets.

Silvester NEW YEAR'
The Innere Stadt becomes one big party zone for Silvester, which features loads of alcohol and far too many fireworks in crowded streets.

🛏 Sleeping

From palatial abodes to swanky minimalism, from youth hostels to luxury establishments like the Hotel Imperial and Hotel Sacher, where chandeliers, antique furniture and original 19th-century oil paintings are the norm rather than the exception, Vienna's lodgings cover it all. In between are homely *Pensionen* (B&B/guesthouses) and less ostentatious hotels, plus a small but smart range of apartments, many of which can be rented for only a few nights.

THE VIENNALE

Vienna's annual international film festival, the 'fringe-like' Viennale, is the highlight of the city's celluloid calendar. For two weeks from mid-October public cinemas screen works ranging from documentaries to short and feature films. Ticket sales commence on the Saturday before the festival begins. You can book by credit card, online or via a special hotline number that is published on the website www.viennale.at once sales begin. Tickets can be picked up at any of the booths set up around town, such as the **Viennale main booth** (Map p62; MuseumsQuartier, cnr Mariahilfer Strasse; ☉10am-8pm; M Museumsquartier), once sales begin.

Standards remain high, and generally so do prices; bargains are few and far between. A private bathroom and breakfast (normally a continental buffet) are invariably included in the price, but parking isn't, costing anything between €6 and €30 per 24 hours.

🛏 Innere Stadt

⭐**Schweizer Pension** PENSION €
(Map p62; 📞533 81 56; www.schweizerpension.com; 01, Heinrichsgasse 2; s €56-75, d €75-98; M Schottentor, 🚊1 Salztorbrücke) 🚲 Rooms at this pleasant little *Pension* are super clean, and while not flush with the most up-to-date amenities, everything you find inside – from big, comfy beds to ornamental ceramic stoves – has a cosy, homely feel to it. The feeling of well-being extends to low-allergy rooms and bio-breakfasts. The 11 rooms fill up quickly, so book ahead.

⭐**Hollmann Beletage** PENSION €€
(Map p62; 📞961 19 60; www.hollmann-beletage.at; 01, Köllnerhofgasse 6; d €159-230, tr €179-279, q €199-300, ste from €390; @🛜; M Schwedenplatz, 🚊1, 2 Schwedenplatz) This minimalist establishment offers style and clean lines throughout. Rooms are slick units, with natural wood floors, bare walls, simple, classic furniture and designer lamps and door handles. A terrace and lounge where you can enjoy free snacks at 2.30pm and 6pm are bonuses, as are the small hotel cinema and free use of an iPad.

Pension Nossek
PENSION €€

(Map p62; ☑ 533 70 41-0; www.pension-nossek.at; 01, Graben 17; s €80-100, d €125; ❄ @ ☎; Ⓜ Herrengasse, Stephansplatz) This *Pension* offers a prime location close to the Innere Stadt sights, coupled with typical Viennese service (professional and polite, if a little stiff); rooms are spotless, generally spacious and enhanced with baroque-style furnishings. The hotel does not accept credit cards. WLAN (wi-fi) costs €5 per stay.

Pension Pertschy
PENSION €€

(Map p62; ☑ 534 49-0; www.pertschy.com; 01, Habsburgergasse 5; s €83-119, d €91-228; ☎ ⓘ; Ⓜ Herrengasse, Stephansplatz) It's hard to find fault with Pension Pertschy. Its quiet yet central location, just off the Graben, is hard to beat, staff are exceedingly able, willing and friendly, and children are welcomed with gusto (toys for toddlers and high chairs for tots are available). Rooms are not only spacious but filled with a potpourri of period pieces and a rainbow of colours.

Aviano
PENSION €€

(Map p62; ☑ 512 83 30; www.secrethomes.at; 01, Marco-d'Aviano-Gasse 1; s €87-112, d €127-187; ☎; Ⓜ Stephansplatz) Aviano offers a supremely central position, high standards and all-round value for money. Rooms are small (there are no bathtubs) without being claustrophobic and feature high ceilings, decorative moulding and whitewashed antique furnishings; corner rooms have a charming alcove and bay window. The breakfast room is sunny and bright, and in summer utilises a small balcony on the courtyard.

★ Steigenberger Hotel Herrenhof
HOTEL €€€

(Map p62; ☑ 534 040; www.steigenberger.com/en/wien; 01, Herrengasse 10; r without breakfast €189-209, ste €600-700; ❄ @ ☎; Ⓜ Herrengasse) Decorated throughout in subtle and subdued aubergine colours, Steigenberger Hotel Herrenhof offers style and great value in 24- to 28-sq-metre superior rooms and 35-sq-metre deluxe rooms, complemented by free use of the spacious wellness area extending over two floors with sauna, steam bath and fully equipped gym. Corner deluxe rooms have extralarge windows.

★ Radisson Blu Style Hotel
DESIGN HOTEL €€€

(Map p62; ☑ 227 800; www.radissonblu.com/stylehotel-vienna; 01, Herrengasse 12; r €185-255, ste €310; ❄ ☎; Ⓜ Herrengasse) This elegant hotel is decorated throughout in demure grey shades. The 78 rooms have a contemporary and cosy atmosphere, and extras include use of the excellent wellness and fitness facilities. The least expensive rooms don't include breakfast (€23 per person). Rates can be lower, depending on demand.

★ DO & CO
LUXURY HOTEL €€€

(Map p62; ☑ 241 88; www.doco.com; 01, Stephansplatz 12; r without breakfast €350-370; @ ☎; Ⓜ Stephansplatz) In the heart of the historic centre, this hotel has superb views of Stephansdom in a selection of exquisite rooms with quality sound and entertainment systems. Several rooms have their own Jacuzzi, but guests should be aware that bathrooms (but not the toilets) have transparent glass walls.

HITLER IN VIENNA

Born in Braunau am Inn, Upper Austria, in 1889, with the name Adolf Schicklgruber (his father changed the family name when they moved to Germany in 1893), Adolf Hitler moved to Vienna when he was just 17. Six unsettled, unsuccessful, poverty-stricken years later he abandoned the city and moved to Munich to make a name for himself. He later wrote in *Mein Kampf* that his Vienna years were 'a time of the greatest transformation that I have ever been through. From a weak citizen of the world I became a fanatical anti-Semite'. Whether this had anything to do with being twice rejected by the Akademie der bildenden Künste (Academy of Fine Arts), who dismissed his work as 'inadequate', he did not say. Even though he was convinced that proper training would have made him into a very successful artist, these rejections caused Hitler to write to a friend that perhaps fate may have reserved for him 'some other purpose'. This 'purpose' became all too clear to everyone over time.

Hitler briefly returned to Vienna in 1938 at the head of the German army and was greeted by enthusiastic crowds on Heldenplatz. He left a day later.

Hotel Sacher LUXURY HOTEL €€€
(Map p62; 514 560; www.sacher.com; 01, Philharmonikerstrasse 4; r €480-1350, ste €1600-2900; ❄ @ 📶; Ⓜ Karlsplatz, 🚋 D, 1, 2, 71 Kärntner Ring/Oper) Walking into the Sacher is like turning back the clocks 100 years. The reception, with its dark-wood panelling, deep red shades and heavy gold chandelier, is reminiscent of an expensive fin de siècle bordello. There's a hi-tech spa complex, with herbal sauna, ice fountain and fitness room.

🛏 Ringstrasse

Pension Wild PENSION €
(Map p74; 406 51 74; www.pension-wild.com; 08, Lange Gasse 10; s €41-69, d €53-90, tr €114; Ⓜ Rathaus, Volkstheater) Wild is one of the few openly gay-friendly *Pensionen* in Vienna, but the warm welcome extends to all walks of life. The top-floor 'luxury' rooms are simple yet appealing, with light-wood furniture and private bathrooms, and are a big advantage over Wild's other two categories. All, however, are spotlessly clean and kitchens are there for guests to use.

★ 25hours Hotel DESIGN HOTEL €€
(Map p74; 521 51; www.25hours-hotels.com; 07, Lerchenfelder Strasse 1-3; r €100-130, ste €150-190; 📶 🚲; Ⓜ Volkstheater) You're not going to find trapeze artists at this circus-themed highrise hotel, but you will find groovy Dreimetadesigned rooms decked out in bold colours, with big-top-style murals, pod-shaped rugs and welcome touches like iPod docking systems. The Dachboden (p100) rooftop bar, Mermaid's Cave sauna area and free use of electric bikes (e-bikes) are bonuses.

Hotel Kärntnerhof HOTEL €€
(Map p62; 512 19 23; www.karntnerhof.com; 01, Grashofgasse 4; s €99-129, d €135-195, tr €199-235, ste €279-299; @ 📶; Ⓜ Stephansplatz) This tall treasure fuses old Vienna charm with cosy ambience, from the period paintings lining the walls to the wood- and frosted-glass panelled lift to the surprising roof terrace.

★ Hotel Imperial HOTEL €€€
(Map p80; 501 100; www.luxurycollection.com/imperial; 01, Kärntner Ring 16; r from €350; @ 📶; Ⓜ Karlsplatz, 🚋 D, 2 Karlsplatz) This former palace, with all the marble and majesty of the Habsburg era, has service as polished as its crystal. Suites are filled with 19th-century paintings and genuine antique furniture (and come with butler service), while 4th- and 5th-floor rooms in Biedermeier style

are far cosier and may come with balcony. The famous Fürsten Stiege, cloaked in rich red carpet, leads from the reception to the Royal suite.

Radisson Blu Palais Hotel LUXURY HOTEL €€€
(Map p62; 515 17-0; www.radissonblu.com; 01, Parkring 16; s without breakfast from €109, r from €139; 📶; Ⓜ Stubentor, Stadtpark, 🚋 2 Weihburggasse) Spread across two historic palace buildings, this is one of the top addresses in town and a preferred option among visiting state dignitaries. Single and doubles as well as suites and maisonettes are tastefully furnished with hints of the fin de siècle epoch, with maisonettes that are vast and span two levels (from about €239). Prices vary considerably according to demand, so check the internet.

🛏 Across the Danube Canal

Gal Apartments APARTMENT €
(0650-561 19 42; www.apartmentsvienna.net; 02, Grosse Mohrengasse 29; d/tr/q apt €89/99/119; @ 📶; Ⓜ Nestroyplatz, Taborstrasse) For a superb home away from home, check into these roomy apartments smack in the action of up-and-coming Leopoldstadt. Occupying a renovated Biedermeier house, the apartments are dressed in modern furniture and *Jugendstil*-inspired paintings. It's a short walk to the Karmelitermarkt, the Prater and the Augarten, and the subway whips you to the centre of town in less than 10 minutes.

Hotel Capri HOTEL €€
(214 84 04; www.hotelcapri.at; 02, Praterstrasse 44-46; s €75-105, d €109-149, tr €119-168, q €139-199; 🅿 📶 🚲; Ⓜ Nestroyplatz) This midranger looks nondescript on the face of things, but its merits are many: it's five minutes' walk from Prater, two U-Bahn stops from Stephansplatz, and staff bend over backwards to please. Done up in pastel colours, rooms are streamlined and immaculate, all with flat-screen TVs and kettles. Breakfast is a wholesome spread of fruit, cereals, cold cuts and eggs.

🛏 Inside the Gürtel

★ my MOjO vie HOSTEL €
(0676-551 11 55; http://mymojovie.at; 07, Kaiserstrasse 77; dm/d/tr/q €26/58/84/108; @ 📶; Ⓜ Burggasse Stadthalle) An old-fashioned cage lift rattles up to these incredible backpacker digs. Everything you could wish for

is here – design-focused dorms complete with dressing tables and snug-as-a-bug rugs, a kitchen with free supplies, netbooks for surfing, guidebooks for browsing and even musical instruments for your own jam session.

Believe It Or Not
HOSTEL €
(Map p76; ☎ 0676-550 00 55; www.believe-it-or-not-vienna.at; 07, Myrthengasse 10; dm €25-30; @ ⓢ; Ⓜ Volkstheater) It may seem nondescript on the face of things, but you really won't believe what a cosy, homely hostel this is. We love the dorms with mezzanine-style beds, laid-back lounge, kitchen with free basics and laptops for guest use. Lily, your South African host, puts on a great spread at breakfast.

Pension Kraml
PENSION €
(Map p76; ☎ 587 85 88; www.pensionkraml.at; 06, Brauergasse 5; s €35, d €56-76, tr €78-87, q €120; @ ⓢ; Ⓜ Zieglergasse) Tucked peacefully down a backstreet five minutes' walk south of Mariahilfer Strasse, this family-run *Pension* looks back on 150 years of history and prides itself on old-school hospitality and comfort. Rooms are surprisingly large, accommodating twin beds, bedside tables and a solid wardrobe, while leaving plenty of room for a close waltz. Internet is only available in the common areas.

Kaiser 23
HOSTEL, GUESTHOUSE €
(Map p76; ☎ 523 41 81; www.kaiser23.at; Kaiserstrasse 23, 07; s €37, d €47-52, tr €60; @ ⓢ; Ⓜ Westbahnhof) Though just a two-minute walk from Mariahilfer Strasse, the vibe is delightfully mellow at this hostel-guesthouse, part of a 19th-century convent. You might well bump into a friendly nun on your way to one of the bright, parquet-floored rooms, with pared-down furniture and splashes of lime adding a contemporary touch. Breakfast costs an extra €8.

Hotel Fürstenhof
HOTEL €€
(☎ 523 32 67; www.hotel-fuerstenhof.com; 07, Neubaugürtel 4; s €79-89, d €89-170, tr €148-185, q €159-200; ⓢ; Ⓜ Westbahnhof) This family-run affair overflowing with personality has been the choice of touring alternative bands for years – see the reception for proof. Rooms are basic, with blood red carpets, full-length curtains and deep colours creating a warm feel.

Hotel Drei Kronen
PENSION €€
(Map p76; ☎ 587 32 89; www.hotel3kronen.at; 04, Schleifmühlegasse 25; s/d €79/109; @ ⓢ; Ⓜ Kettenbrückengasse) Within stumbling distance of the Naschmarkt (some rooms overlook it), this family-owned abode is one of Vienna's best-kept secrets. Tiny palatial touches (shiny marble, polished brass, white-and-gold wallpaper) are distinctly Viennese, but nonetheless a casual feel prevails. Rooms are fitted with *Jugendstil* furniture and art (including many prints by Klimt).

Das Tyrol
HOTEL €€
(Map p76; ☎ 587 54 15; www.das-tyrol.at; 06, Mariahilfer Strasse 15; s €109-229, d €149-259; ✱ ⓢ; Ⓜ Museumsquartier) Design is the word at Das Tyrol. Done out in zesty yellow and green hues, the spacious rooms feature original artworks, such as Dieter Koch's playful Donald and Daisy Duck paintings, and Nespresso machines. Corner rooms have small balconies overlooking Mariahilfer Strasse. Breakfast, with eggs cooked to order and Prosecco, will keep you going all morning.

The gold-tiled spa has a sauna and a 'light therapy' shower where you can watch fish blub in the aquarium.

Altstadt
PENSION €€
(Map p76; ☎ 522 66 66; www.altstadt.at; 07, Kirchengasse 41; s €125-175, d €145-215, ste €195-350; @ ⓢ; Ⓜ Volkstheater) Otto Ernst Wiesenthal has poured his passion and impeccable taste into creating one of Vienna's most outstanding guesthouses in Spittelberg. Design elements by Vitra and Philippe Starck merge seamlessly with original art from the likes of Andy Warhol and Prachensky. The individually decorated rooms are charming and quirky (without being overcooked), with high ceilings, plenty of space and natural light.

Hotel Rathaus Wein & Design
BOUTIQUE HOTEL €€
(Map p74; ☎ 400 11 22; www.hotel-rathaus-wien.at; 08, Lange Gasse 13; s/d/tr €150/210/240; ✱ @ ⓢ;

Ⓜ Rathaus, Volkstheater) Each stylish room in this boutique hotel is dedicated to an Austrian winemaker and the minibar is stocked with premium wines from the growers themselves. The open-plan, minimalist-chic rooms reveal a razor-sharp eye for design and clever backlighting. The hotel offers wine tastings in its chandelier-lit bar, and excursions to Austria's nearby winegrowing regions.

Das Triest　　　　　　　　　HOTEL €€€
(☑ 589 18; www.dastriest.at; 04, Wiedner Hauptstrasse 12; s/d €229/296; ◙ 🛜; Ⓜ Karlsplatz, Kettenbrückengasse) This Sir Terence Conran creation is a symbiosis of history and modern design. The 300-year-old former stable is cutting edge, with an overall nautical theme; portholes replace spy holes and windows, and stairwell railings would be at home on the *Queen Mary 2*. Rooms reveal a clean aesthetic and muted tones, with little touches like fresh flowers polishing the scene off.

🛏 Outside the Gürtel

Wombat's　　　　　　　　　　HOSTEL €
(☑ 897 23 36; www.wombats-hostels.com; 15, Mariahilfer Strasse 137; dm €22-25, d €72-76; P◙🛜; Ⓜ Westbahnhof) For a dash of Aussie charm in Vienna, Wombat's is where savvy backpackers gravitate. The interior is a rainbow of colours, common areas include a bar, pool tables, music and comfy leather sofas, and the modern dorms have en suites. The relaxed staff hand you a drink and a useful city map on arrival, and bike hire can be arranged.

Altwienerhof　　　　　　　　HOTEL €€
(☑ 892 60 00; www.altwienerhof.at; 15, Herklotzgasse 6; s €50 65, d €89-99, q €125; ◙ 🛗; Ⓜ Gumpendorfer Strasse) This pseudo-plush family-run hotel, just outside the Gürtel ring, offers ridiculously romantic abodes that hark back to a bygone era. Miniature chandeliers, antique pieces, floral bed covers and couches, and lace tablecloths do a fine job of adding a touch of old-fashioned romance.

Boutiquehotel Stadthalle　　　HOTEL €€
(☑ 982 42 72; www.hotelstadthalle.at; 15, Hackengasse 20; s €78-138, d €118-198; 🛜 🛗; Ⓜ Schweglerstrasse) 🌱 Welcome to Vienna's most eco-aware hotel, which makes the most of solar power, rainwater collection and LED lighting, and has a roof fragrantly planted with lavender. Bursts of purple, pink and

peach enliven rooms that are a blend of the modern with polished antiques. An organic breakfast is served in the ivy-draped courtyard garden.

🍴 Eating

Vienna has thousands of restaurants and cafes covering all budgets and styles of cuisine, but dining doesn't stop there. *Kaffeehäuser* (coffee houses) and *Heurigen* are almost defining elements of the city, and just as fine for a good meal. *Beisln*, the Austrian cross between a bistro and pub, is normally a simple restaurant serving the best of Viennese cuisine.

🍴 Innere Stadt

Trzesniewski　　　　　　　SANDWICHES €
(Map p62; www.trzesniewski.at; 01, Dorotheergasse 1; bread & spread €1.10, glass of wine €2.10; ◷ 8.30am-7.30pm Mon-Fri, 9am-5pm Sat; Ⓜ Stephansplatz) Possibly the finest sandwich shop in Austria, Trzesniewski has been serving spreads and breads to the entire spectrum of munchers (Kafka was a regular here) for over 100 years. Choose from 22 delectably thick spreads. Plan on sampling a few; two bites and they're gone. This branch is one of seven in Vienna.

**Bitzinger Würstelstand am
Albertinaplatz**　　　　　　SAUSAGE STAND €
(Map p62; 01, Albertinaplatz; sausages €3.70-4.10; ◷ 9.30am-5am, drinks from 8am; Ⓜ Karlsplatz, Stephansplatz, 🚃 Kärntner Ring/Oper) Vienna has very many sausage stands but this one located behind the Staatsoper offers the contrasting spectacle of ladies and gents dressed to the nines, sipping beer, wine or champagne while enjoying sausage at outdoor tables or the heated counter after performances. You'll find Joseph Perrier champagne (€19.90 for 0.2L), and for the less well-heeled, there's house wine (€3.20).

★ Motto am Fluss　　　　INTERNATIONAL €€
(Map p62; ☑ 25 255; www.motto.at/mottoamfluss; 01, Franz-Josefs-Kai, btwn Marien- & Schwedenbrücke; mains €19-26; ◷ 11.30am-2.30pm & 6pm-2am, bar 6pm-4am, cafe 8am-12am; 🛜; Ⓜ Schwedenplatz, 🚃 1, 2 Schwedenplatz) Exuding an inviting glow from inside the Wien-City ferry terminal on the Danube Canal, Motto am Fluss (affiliated with Motto in Margareten) is one of Vienna's better midrange restaurants, with a stylish lounge feel throughout the bar and restaurant areas,

A SLICE OF ITALY IN THE INNERE STADT

One of the most useful places to know about in the Innere Stadt is **Zanoni & Zanoni** (Map p62; ☑512 79 79; www.zanoni.co.at; 01, Lugeck 7; ice creams from €1.30; ⊙7am-midnight; MStephansplatz). This Italian *gelataria* and *pasticceria* has some of the most civilised opening times around (365 days a year) and is just right when you realise you'd like a late-night dessert – there are about 35 varieties of gelati, with more cream than usual. It does breakfast and some great cakes with cream, but best of all it's a buzzing place on a Sunday where you can linger over a coffee and plan your moves for the day.

topped off by a cafe upstairs – and all of this is with fantastic views over the Danube Canal. After 10pm smoking is allowed, but it rarely gets smoky.

★**Expedit**   ITALIAN €€
(Map p62; ☑ 512 33 1323; www.xpedit.at; 01, Wiesingerstrasse 6; pasta €10.50-12.50, mains €18.50; ⊙11am-2am Mon-Fri, 8pm-2am Sat; 🚊2 Julius-Raab-Platz) Expedit successfully moulds itself on a Ligurian *osteria*. The warehouse decor helps lend an informal atmosphere along with a clean, smart look. Every day brings a new selection of seasonal dishes to the small menu. Reservations are recommended and you can take food away to eat in your hotel if you like.

★**Brezl Gwölb**   AUSTRIAN €€
(Map p62; ☑ 533 88 11; www.brezl.at; 01, Ledererhof 9; mains €9-16; ⊙11.30am-1am; 🖉; MSchottentor, Herrengasse) Brezl Gwölb has won a loyal following for its winningly fresh Austrian home cooking, served with smiles and a generous dollop of Gothic charm. Heart-warming dishes like beef broth with noodles, schnitzel and cheesy Pinzgauer Kasnocken dumplings are matched with some terrific wines from Lower Austria. The *Brezl* (pretzels) here are precisely as they should be – chewy, fluffy and fresh from the oven.

★**Griechenbeisl**   BISTRO PUB €€
(Map p62; ☑ 533 19 77; www.griechenbeisl.at; 01, Fleischmarkt 11; mains €11.60-25; ⊙11am-1am; MSchwedenplatz, 🚊1, 2 Schwedenplatz) As the oldest guesthouse in Vienna (dating from

1447), and once frequented by the likes of Ludwig van Beethoven, Franz Schubert and Johannes Brahms, Griechenbeisl is a lovely haunt popular among locals and tourists alike, with vaulted rooms, age-old wood panelling and a figure of Augustin trapped at the bottom of a well just inside the front door.

Figlmüller   BISTRO PUB €€
(Map p62; ☑ 512 61 77; www.figlmueller.at; 01, Wollzeile 5; mains €13-23; ⊙11am-10.30pm; 🛜; MStephansplatz) This famous *Beisl* has some of the biggest and best schnitzels in the business. The rural decor is contrived for its inner-city location and beer isn't served (wine is from the owner's vineyard), but it's a fun *Beisl* eating experience. The kitchen closes at 9.30pm, but the kitchen of the **Bäckerstrasse 6** (Map p62; ☑ 512 17 60; www.figlmueller.at; 01, Bäckerstrasse 6; ⊙11.45am-midnight) section, which does have beer, is open till 11pm.

Gasthaus Flosz   AUSTRIAN €€
(Map p62; ☑533 89 58; www.flosz.at; 01, Börseplatz 3; mains €15-20; ⊙11am-midnight Mon-Fri, from 5pm Sat; MSchottenring, 🚊1 Börsegasse) The chef uses a minimum of excellent locally sourced ingredients to produce regional food with real depth of flavour at this high-ceilinged brasserie. The season-driven menu might include dishes such as risotto with chanterelles and butter-soft organic Styrian beef with dill sauce, and there are 100 different Austrian wines to choose from. The three-course lunch is a snip at €10.90.

EN   JAPANESE €€
(Map p62; ☑532 44 90; www.restaurant-en.at; 01, Werdertorgasse 8; lunch menus €8.50-9.70, mains €9-25.50; ⊙11.30am-2.30pm & 5.30-10.30pm Mon-Sat; 🖉; MSchottenring) A Tokyo chef and Hokkaido staff banded together to create this exceptionally relaxed Japanese restaurant in a quiet corner of the Innere Stadt. The many different varieties of sushi are among the best in Vienna. The *gyoza* is delightful and warm sake or *genmaicha* (green tea with roasted rice) makes a perfect accompaniment.

Wrenkh   VEGETARIAN €€
(Map p62; ☑533 15 26; www.wiener-kochsalon.at; 01, Bauernmarkt 10; mains €8.80-26.50; ⊙noon-10pm Mon-Sat; 🖉; MStephansplatz) This long-standing vegetarian restaurant also serves a handful of meat and fish dishes. Choose from the vibrant front section with its glass

walls and chatty customers, or the quieter back room with its intimate booths. Vegetarian dishes cost less than €15, the lunch menu about €10.

★ **Meinl's Restaurant**   INTERNATIONAL €€€
(Map p62; ☑ 532 33 34-6000; www.meinlamgraben.at; 01, Graben 19; mains €26-45, 3- to 6-course menus €47-93; ⊙ lunch & dinner Mon-Sat; ⊕ ⊘; Ⓜ Stephansplatz) Meinl's combines cuisine of superlative quality with an unrivalled wine list and views of Graben. The freshest of ingredients are used to create inviting dishes, often integrating delicate Mediterranean sauces and sweet aromas. There is a quality **providore** (Map p62; ⊙ 8am-7.30pm Mon-Fri, 9am-6pm Sat) on-site, a cellar **wine bar** (Map p62; ⊙ 11am-midnight Mon-Sat) with good lunch menus (€9.90 to €12.90), as well as a cafe and sushi bar (€8.60 oto €18).

✕ **Ringstrasse**

Kantine   CAFE €
(Map p62; ☑ 523 82 39; www.mq-kantine.at; 07, Museumsplatz 1; mains €7-10; ⊙ 9am-2am Mon-Sun; ⊕ ⊘; Ⓜ Museumsquartier) This upbeat cafe-bar housed in the former stable of the emperor's personal steeds is the most laidback spot to eat in the MuseumsQuartier. Lit by a disco ball, the vaulted interior has comfy chairs for lounging, surfing and refuelling over a salad, pita wrap or cocktail. In summer folk spill out onto the patio on MuseumsQuartier's main square.

★ **Meierei im Stadtpark**   AUSTRIAN €€
(Map p62; ☑ 713 31 68; http://steirereck.at; 03, Am Heumarkt 2a; set breakfasts €19.50-23.50, mains €10.50-19, 6-cheese selection €8.90; ⊙ 8am-11pm Mon-Fri, 9am-7pm Sat & Sun; ⊘; Ⓜ Stadtpark) Attached to Steirereck im Stadtpark, Meierei im Stadtpark serves a bountiful breakfast until noon, with gastronomic show-stoppers such as poached egg with parsnip and Périgord truffle, gammon with fresh horseradish and panini, and warm curd-cheese strudel with elderberry compote. It also rolls out Viennese classic fare with unusual twists. The goulash is acknowledged to be Vienna's finest.

★ **Halle**   INTERNATIONAL €€
(Map p76; ☑ 523 70 01; ww2.diehalle.at; 07, Museumsplatz 1; midday menus €8.50-9.50, mains €9-20; ⊙ 10am-2am Mon-Sun; ⊕ ⊘; Ⓜ Museumsquartier) Halle is the versatile resident eatery of the Kunsthalle, with a good buzz and optical tricks like cylindrical lamps and low

tables. The chefs churn out antipastos, risottos, pastas, salads, plus several Austrian allrounders like goulash and pan-Asian dishes. On steamy summer days it's usually a fight for an outside table between the Kunsthalle and MUMOK.

Österreicher im MAK   AUSTRIAN €€
(Map p62; ☑ 714 01 21; www.oesterreicherimmak.at; 01, Stubenring 5; 2-course lunch €9.80, mains €16-22; ⊙ 10am-1am; Ⓜ Stubentor, ☒ 2 Stubentor) Located in the MAK, Österreicher im MAK is the brainchild of Helmut Österreicher, one of the country's leading chefs and a force behind the movement towards back-to-the-roots Austrian flavours. Using strictly seasonal, high-quality ingredients, the menu seesaws between classic and contemporary, with dishes like *Tafelspitz* (prime boiled beef) and sea bass on rocket noodles and beetroot.

★ **Steirereck im Stadtpark**   GASTRONOMIC €€€
(Map p62; ☑ 713 31 68; http://steirereck.at; 03, Am Heumarkt 2a; lunch mains €21-39, mains €44-48, 6-/7-course menus €125/135; ⊙ 11.30am-2.30pm & 6.30pm-midnight Mon-Fri; Ⓜ Stadtpark) Heinz Reitbauer is at the culinary helm of this two-starred Michelin restaurant, beautifully lodged in a 20th-century former dairy building in the leafy Stadtpark. His tasting menus are an exuberant feast, fizzing with natural, integral flavours that speak of a chef with exacting standards. Wine pairing is an additional €69/75 (six/seven courses).

> **DON'T MISS**
>
> ## TICHY ICE CREAM
>
> It only takes one lick of **Tichy** (☑ 604 44 46; 10, Reumannplatz 13; ⊙ 10am-11pm mid-Mar–Sep; Ⓜ U1 Reumannplatz) ice cream and you're hooked. In addition to the usual creamy suspects, this legendary *Eissalon* (ice-cream parlour) is known for pioneering *Eismarillenknödel* (ball of vanilla ice cream with apricot centre). It's a mere cone's throw away from the U-Bahn station – just look for Tichy's loyal patrons scattered around on park benches, grinning and enjoying their sweet treats. And be prepared to shove your way through crowds to reach the counter – it's all part of the fun.

Schnattl INTERNATIONAL €€€
(Map p74; ☑ 405 34 00; www.schnattl.com; 08, Lange Gasse 40; mains €21-26, 3-course menus €33-38; ⊙ 6pm-midnight Mon-Fri; ✐; Ⓜ Rathaus, ☒ 2 Rathaus, Josefstädter Strasse) Despite its weekday-only opening hours, Schnattl is a culinary institution in Josefstadt, particularly beloved of actors and arty types. The inner courtyard is perfect for summer dining, while bottle green wood panelling creates a cosy mood inside. The chef plays up seasonal specialities like creamy chestnut soup and meltingly tender organic beef, matured on the bone and served with green-pepper gnocchi.

Across the Danube Canal

Schöne Perle BISTRO €
(☑ 0664-243 35 93; www.schoene-perle.at; 02, Grosse Pfarrgasse 2; midday menus €7.20-8.50, mains €6-16; ⊙ noon-11pm Mon-Fri, 10am-11pm Sat & Sun; ✐ ⊞; Ⓜ Taborstrasse) UFO-shaped lights cast a contemporary glow over minimalist Schöne Perle (beautiful pearl), which serves everything from lentil soups through *Tafelspitz* to vegetarian and fish mains, all of which are created with organic produce.

Wines are from Austria, as are the large array of juices.

Pizza Mari' PIZZERIA €
(☑ 0676-687 49 94; www.pizzamari.at; 02, Leopoldgasse 23a; pizzas €6-9; ⊙ noon-midnight Tue-Sat, to 11pm Sun; ✐; Ⓜ Taborstrasse) Pizza Mari' serves some of the best pizzas this side of the canal, the inexpensive salads as side dishes are fresh and Mari' has a friendly, comfortable feel that makes you feel at home. The kitchen closes between 3pm and 6pm.

★ **Skopik & Lohn** MODERN EUROPEAN €€
(☑ 219 89 77; www.skopikundlohn.at; 02, Leopoldsgasse 17; mains €11-26; ⊙ 6pm-1am Tue-Sat; Ⓜ Taborstrasse) The spidery web of scrawl that creeps across the ceiling at Skopik & Lohn gives an avant-garde edge to an otherwise French-style brasserie – all wainscoting, globe lights, cheek-by-jowl tables and white-jacketed waiters. The menu is modern European, but sways heavily towards French.

Tempel INTERNATIONAL €€
(☑ 214 01 79; www.restaurant-tempel.at; 02, Praterstrasse 56; 2-/3-course lunch €12.50/16, mains €15-22; ⊙ noon-3pm & 6pm-midnight Tue-Fri; Ⓜ Nestroyplatz) Rudi runs a tight ship at this

---

FARMERS MARKETS

Unless noted, all the markets below are open 6am to 7.30pm Monday to Friday and 6am to 5pm Saturday.

Brunnenmarkt (16, Brunnengasse; Ⓜ Josefstädter Strasse, ☒ 2 Neulerchenfelder Strasse) West of the centre; one of Vienna's best produce and food markets, with lots of Turkish stands and some organic produce stalls.

Hannovermarkt (20, Hannovergasse; Ⓜ Jägerstrasse) In Brigittenau, north of the centre.

Karmelitermarkt (02, Karmelitermarkt; Ⓜ Taborstrasse, ☒ 2 Karmeliterplatz) North of the centre, with lots of eating options on and around Karmeliterplatz.

Naschmarkt (Map p76; www.wienernaschmarkt.eu; 06, Linke & Rechte Wienzeile; ⊙ 6am-7.30pm Mon-Fri, to 6pm Sat; Ⓜ Kettenbrückengasse) Vienna's top market. See p97 for more information.

Flohmarkt (Flea Market; Map p76; 05, Kettenbrückengasse; ⊙ dawn-4pm Sat; Ⓢ U4 Kettenbrückengasse) The atmospheric Flohmarkt, in the mould of an Eastern European market, shouldn't be missed, with goods piled up in apparent chaos on the walkway.

Meidlinger Markt (12, Niederhofstrasse; Ⓜ Niederhofstrasse) In Meidling, southwest of the centre.

Volkertmarkt (02, Volkertplatz; Ⓜ Praterstern) Northeast of the centre.

Vorgartenmarkt (02, Ennsgasse; Ⓜ Vorgartenstrasse) Between the Danube Canal and the Danube River.

Bio-Markt Freyung (Map p62; 01, Freyung; ⊙ 9am-6pm Fri & Sat; Ⓜ Herrengasse, Schottentor) Great for picnic fixings, this low-key market exclusively sells organic produce from farmers. Find everything from wood-oven bread to fruit, fish, meat, honey, cheese, wine and pumpkin-seed oil here.

intimate bistro, hidden in a courtyard off Praterstrasse. Presented with an eye for detail, dishes such as braised veal shank with caper-lemon sauce and chilli polenta reveal true depth of flavour and creativity. The selection of Austrian wines is excellent, as is the outdoor seating on warm summer evenings.

Restaurant Vincent INTERNATIONAL €€€
(🖉214 15 16; www.restaurant-vincent.at; 02, Grosse Pfarrgasse 7; mains €20-30, 10-course menu €110; ☺5.30pm-midnight Tue-Sat; Ⓜ Taborstrasse) Art-slung walls and candlelight set the scene in Vincent, which has evolved from a humble student place into its higher calling as one of Vienna's top gourmet addresses. Courses vary with the seasons but the focus is on classic produce such as lamb, beef and pheasant prepared expertly, but locally produced snails also feature.

Restaurant Mraz & Sohn INTERNATIONAL €€€
(🖉330 45 94; www.mraz-sohn.at; 20, Wallenstein Strasse 59; mains €40-48, set course menus €49-99; ☺7pm-midnight Mon-Fri; Ⓜ Jägerstrasse, 🚊5 Rauscherstrasse) Mraz & Sohn is not only a snappy name, it really is a family-owned-and-run restaurant. The *chef de cuisine*, Markus Mraz, is the creative force behind the Michelin star, chef hats and other accolades awarded for innovative dishes. The menu changes frequently.

✖ Inside the Gürtel

Tongues DELI €
(Map p76; www.tongues.at; 06, Theobaldgasse 16; lunch mains €3.60; ☺11am-8pm Mon-Fri, to 6pm Sat; ✐; Ⓜ Museumsquartier) ❂ DJs can sometimes be found on the decks at this groovy record-shop-cum-deli, where you can pop in for a healthy, organic lunch, electro on vinyl or some locally sourced cheese, salami, honey and wood-oven bread. Wholesome day specials range from homemade pizza to veggie dishes like zucchini-feta pasta bakes.

Pizzeria-Osteria Da Giovanni ITALIAN €
(Map p76; 🖉523 77 78; www.giovanniwien.com; 07, Sigmundsgasse 14; pizza s€4.60-10.70, mains €16-19; ☺6-11.30pm Mon-Thu, noon-3pm & 6-11.30pm Fri & Sat; 🖈; Ⓜ Volkstheater, 🚊49 Stiftgasse) A genuine slice of the south in the cobbled heart of Spittelberg, this homely Italian job rolls out pizzas just as they ought to be: thin, crisp and topped with mozzarella. The pasta is homemade; the handful of tables fills in a flash, so it's worth booking.

Aromat INTERNATIONAL €
(Map p76; 🖉913 24 53; 04, Margaretenstrasse 52; menus €7.90, mains €10-15; ☺5-11pm Tue-Sun; Ⓜ Kettenbrückengasse) This funky little eatery serves fusion cooking with a strong emphasis on Upper Austrian and Vietnamese cuisine. It has an open kitchen and often caters for those with an intolerance to wheat and gluten. The charming surroundings feature simple Formica tables, 1950s fixtures, a blackboard menu, and one huge glass frontage. Personable staff help to create a convivial, barlike atmosphere.

St Josef VEGETARIAN €
(Map p76; 🖉526 68 18; 07, Mondscheingasse 10; plates small/large €6.80/8.20; ☺8am-5pm Mon-Fri, to 4pm Sat; ✐; Ⓜ Neubaugasse, 🚊49 Siebensterngasse) St Josef is a canteenlike vegetarian place that cooks to a theme each day (Indian, for instance) and gives you the choice of a small or large plate filled with the various delights. It has a sparse, industrial character, which is part of its charm, a young and arty vibe and superfriendly staff.

★ Kulinarium 7 INTERNATIONAL €€
(Map p76; 🖉522 33 77; www.kulinarium7.at; 07, Sigmundsgasse 1; menus lunch €10-13, dinner €36-55, mains €20-22; ☺11.30am-2.30pm & 6pm-midnight Tue-Sat; ✐; Ⓜ Volkstheater, 🚊49 Stiftgasse) All sharp contours and modern buzz – you would never guess there was a 17th-century vaulted cellar hiding below this contemporary bistro. The chef elevates clean, bright seasonal flavours to gourmet heights. Wafer-thin beef carpaccio with beetroot might be followed, for instance, by beautifully cooked John Dory with leek, orange and vanilla.

Zum Alten Fassl AUSTRIAN €€
(Map p76; 🖉544 42 98; www.zum-alten-fassl.at; 05, Ziegelofengasse 37; midday menus €5.70-7.30, mains €7.50-18.50; ☺11.30am-3pm & 5pm-1am Mon-Fri, 5pm-1am Sat, noon-3pm & 5pm-1am Sun; Ⓜ Pilgramgasse) With its private garden amid residential houses and polished wooden interior (typical of a well-kept *Beisl*), Zum Alten Fassl is worth the trip south of the centre just for a drink. But while here sample the Viennese favourites and regional specialities, like *Eierschwammerl* (chanterelles) and *Blunzengröstl* (a potato, bacon, onion and blood sausage fry-up). When it's in season, *Zanderfilet* (fillet of zander) is the chef's favourite. Between 1974 and 1982 the singer Falco lived upstairs in this building – a plaque marks the spot.

Ra'mien ASIAN €€

(Map p76; ☑585 47 98; www.ramien.at; 06, Gumpendorfer Strasse 9; mains €7-17.50; ☺11am-midnight Tue-Sun; ☑; Ⓜ Museumsquartier) Picture a minimalist grey-white room and lots of bright, young hip things bent over piping-hot Thai, Japanese, Chinese and Vietnamese noodle soups and rice dishes and you have Ra'mien. Ra'mien fills up quickly at night, so it's worth booking ahead; the lounge bar downstairs has regular DJs and stays open until at least 2am.

Gasthaus Wild AUSTRIAN €€

(☑920 94 77; 03, Radetzkyplatz 1; 2-course lunch menus €7.50-8.50, mains €9-17.50; ☺9am-1am; ☑; ☒1, O Radetzkyplatz) Gasthaus Wild, formerly a dive of a *Beisl*, has in recent years morphed into a great *neo-Beisl*. Its dark, wood-panelled interior retains a traditional look, and the menu includes flavoursome favourites like goulash, schnitzel with potato salad, and paprika chicken with *Spätzle* (egg noodles). The menu changes regularly, the vibe is relaxed, the staff welcoming and the wine selection good.

La Tavolozza ITALIAN €€

(Map p74; ☑406 37 57; www.latavolozza.at; 08, Florianigasse 37; pizza €7-13.50, mains €12.50-22; ☺5pm-midnight Mon-Fri, from noon Sat & Sun; Ⓜ Rathaus, ☒2 Lederergasse) You'll feel part of the *famiglia* at this friendly neighbourhood Italian, where tightly packed tables are lit by candlelight. The food is superb: bread crisp from a wood oven is followed by generous, well-seasoned portions of grilled fish and meat, washed down with beefy Chianti reds. Seasonal specialities like truffles often star on the menu.

Motto FUSION €€

(Map p76; ☑587 06 72; www.motto.at; 05, Schönbrunner Strasse 30; mains €9-29; ☺6pm-2am Mon-Thu & Sun, to 4am Fri & Sat; Ⓜ Pilgramgasse) The darling of Margareten's dining scene is this theatrical lounge-style restaurant, which is all clever backlighting, high banquettes and DJ beats. Asian, Austrian and Mediterranean flavours are all in the mix, with well-executed dishes from red Thai curry to the signature fillet steak with chocolate-chilli sauce. Motto is very popular, particularly with the gay crowd; reservations are recommended. Entrance is through the forbidding chrome door on Rüdigergasse.

Steman AUSTRIAN €€

(Map p76; ☑597 85 09; www.steman.at; 06, Otto-Bauer-Gasse 7; mains €6-14.50; ☺11am-midnight Mon-Fri; Ⓜ Zieglergasse) Run by the same folk as Café Jelinek (p103), Steman serves good, honest Austrian food in a nicely restored, high-ceilinged interior, with a few tables outside in summer. The mood is laid-back, the service friendly and the menu packed with classics like goulash and *Käsespätzle* (cheese noodles). The €7.10 two-course lunch is a bargain.

Glacis Beisl BISTRO PUB €€

(Map p76; ☑526 56 60; www.glacisbeisl.at; 07, Breite Gasse 4; mains €7.50-17.50; ☺11am-2am Mon-Sun; ☑; Ⓜ Volkstheater) Hidden downstairs along Breite Gasse (follow the signs from MUMOK) in the MuseumsQuartier, Glacis Beisl does an authentic goulash, an accomplished Wiener Schnitzel and some other very decent Austrian classics, which you can wash down with excellent Austrian reds and whites.

Gasthaus Wickerl AUSTRIAN €€

(Map p74; ☑317 74 89; 09, Porzellangasse 24a; mains €9-midnight Mon-Fri, from 10am Sat, 10am-4pm Sun; Ⓜ Rossauer Lände) Wickerl is a beautiful *Beisl* with an all-wood finish and a warm, welcoming mood. Seasonal fare, such as *Kürbisgulasch* (pumpkin goulash) in autumn, *Marillenknödel* (apricot dumplings) in summer and *Spargel* (asparagus) in spring are mixed in with the usual Viennese offerings of *Tafelspitz*, *Zwiebelrostbraten* (steak with onions) and veal and pork schnitzel.

M Lounge INTERNATIONAL €€

(Map p76; ☑524 93 16; http://hackl-gastro.at; 07, Hermanngasse 31; tapas €3-4.50; ☺4pm-1am Mon-Thu, to 2am Fri & Sat; Ⓜ Neubaugasse) This contemporary lounge-style restaurant is quite the gourmet globetrotter, whisking you around the world in mini portions. The inventive tapas-style concept means you can try dishes like Thai tom yum soup, potato puree with veal schnitzel, Indian butter chicken and risotto with pesto all in the same sitting. Bartenders mix up a mean cocktail at the strikingly lit bar.

Amerlingbeisl AUSTRIAN €€

(Map p76; ☑526 16 60; www.amerlingbeisl.at; 07, Stiftgasse 8; mains €7-14; ☺9am-2am; ☑; Ⓜ Volkstheater, ☒49 Stiftgasse) Wiener whisper quietly about this tucked-away Spittelberg *Beisl*, an enchanting summer choice for its cobbled, lantern-lit courtyard swathed in ivy and vines. The seasonally inspired food hits the mark too, whether you opt for pasta like fettuccine with wild garlic or light mains like salad with smoked trout fillet. Sunday brunch (€10.90) is popular, as is the weekly cocktail special (€4.10).

Ubl
AUSTRIAN €€

(Map p76; ☎ 587 64 37; 04, Pressgasse 26; mains €9.50-18; ⊙ noon-2pm & 6pm-midnight Wed-Sun; Ⓜ Kettenbrückengasse) This much-loved *Beisl* is a favourite of the Wieden crowd. Its menu is heavily loaded with Viennese classics, such as *Schinkenfleckerl*, *Schweinsbraten* (roast pork) and four types of schnitzel, and is enhanced with seasonal cuisine throughout the year. You could do worse than finish the hefty meal off with a stomach-settling plum schnapps. The tree-shaded garden is wonderful in summer.

Gaumenspiel
INTERNATIONAL €€€

(Map p76; ☎ 526 11 08; www.gaumenspiel.at; 07, Zieglergasse 54; mains €19.50-25, menus €38-48; ⊙ 6pm-midnight Mon-Sat; ☑; Ⓜ Burggasse Stadthalle, ☒ 49 Westbahnstrasse/Zieglergasse) There's a real neighbourly feel to this *Beisl*, where a red-walled, wood-floored interior and tiny courtyard garden create a pleasantly low-key backdrop for fine dining. The menu changes regularly and Mediterranean-Austrian specialities reveal an attentive eye for quality, detail and presentation – be it goat's cheese soufflé with dates or wild duck with rose hip–red cabbage and mandarin polenta.

Collio
ITALIAN €€€

(☑ 589 18 133; www.dastriest.at; 04, Wiedner Hauptstrasse 12; mains €18-28, 2-course lunch menus €14.80, 5-course menus €49.80; ⊙ noon-2.30pm & 6-10pm Mon-Fri, 6-10pm Sat; ☑; Ⓜ Kettenbrückengasse, Karlsplatz) On the ground floor of Das Triest, this restaurant serves Italian food and is centered on a pretty inner courtyard.

✕ Outside the Gürtel

Kent
TURKISH €

(☑ 405 91 73; www.kent-restaurant.at; 16, Brunnengasse 67; mains €7-13; ⊙ 6am-2am; ☑; Ⓜ Josefstädter Strasse) Kent means 'small town' in Turkish, an appropriate name considering the hordes that frequent this ever-expanding restaurant. In summer the tree-shaded garden is one of the prettiest in the city, and the food is consistently top-notch. Menu highlights include shish kebab and *Ispanakli Pide* (long Turkish pizza with sheep's cheese, egg and spinach). Everything is available to take away.

Hollerei
VEGETARIAN €€

(☑ 892 33 56; www.hollerei.at; 15, Hollergasse 9; lunch menus €7.50-11, mains €14-15.50; ⊙ 11.30am-3pm & 6-11pm Mon-Sat, 11.30am-3pm Sun; ☑; Ⓜ Meidling Hauptstrasse, Schönbrunn) A 10-minute walk from Schloss Schönbrunn,

---

NASCHING AT THE NASCHMARKT

The **Naschmarkt** (Map p76; 06, Linke & Rechte Wienzeile; ⊙ 6am-7.30pm Mon-Fri, to 6pm Sat; Ⓜ Karlsplatz, Kettenbrückengasse) – to *nasch* means to 'snack' in German – is Vienna's biggest and boldest market and a food lover's dream come true. Not only are there food stalls selling meats, fruits, vegetables, cheeses and spices, but there's also a wide variety of restaurants. Here're a couple:

Neni (Map p76; ☑ 585 20 20; www.neni.at; 06, Naschmarkt 510; breakfasts €5-9, salads & snacks €4.50-10.50, mains €10.50-15; ⊙ 8am-midnight Mon-Sat; ☑; Ⓜ Kettenbrückengasse) This industro-cool glass cube combines a cafe, bar, and restaurant where food has mostly a Middle Eastern focus. Dishes such as caramelised aubergine with ginger and chilli are served alongside tuna steaks in a seasame-pepper crust with wasabi mash. Tables fill up fast most nights, so reserve ahead or drop by outside prime time. Breakast is served until 2pm.

Naschmarkt Deli (Map p76; www.naschmarkt-deli.at; 04, Naschmarkt 421; snacks €4-9, breakfast €7-9, mains €8-13.50; ⊙ 8am-midnight Mon-Sat; Ⓜ Kettenbrückengasse) Among the enticing stands along the Vienna River, Naschmarkt Deli has an edge on the others for its delicious snacks. Sandwiches, felafel, big baguettes and chunky lentil soups fill the menu, but much space is dedicated to a heady array of breakfasts. Come Saturday morning this glass box overflows with punters waiting in anticipation for the Turkish or English breakfast.

this wood-panelled, all-vegetarian bistro does a fine line in seasonal salads, soups and pasta dishes. It also holds a monthly cookery course for €25 (p50).

🍷 Drinking & Nightlife

Vienna is riddled with late-night drinking dens, but you will find concentrations of pulsating bars north and south of the Naschmarkt, around Spittelberg (many of these double as restaurants) and along the Gürtel (mainly around the U6 stops of Josefstädter Strasse and Nussdorfer Strasse). The Bermuda Dreieck (Bermuda Triangle), near the Danube Canal in the Innere Stadt, also has many bars, but they are more touristy.

Also during the summer months, party-goers congregate at Copa Kagrana and Sunken City, an area around the U1 Don-auinsel U-Bahn station. It's quite a tacky affair, but it can be a lot of fun. **Summer Stage** (☑315 52 02; Rossauer Lände, 09; ⊙5pm-1am Mon-Sat, 3pm-1am Sun May-Sep; Ⓜ Schottenring, Rossauer Lände) and the **Altes AKH** (Map p74; ☑87 05 04; cnr Alser Strasse & Spitalgasse; 🚋5, 33, 43, 44 Lange Gasse) also wage war against the threat of melting indoors.

Vienna's coffee houses are wonderful places for sipping tea or coffee, imbibing beer or wine, and catching up on gossip or news of the world. Most serve light meals, while most cafes have a good cake range.

Identified by a *Busch'n* (a green wreath or branch) hanging over the door, *Heurigen* nearly always have outside tables in large gardens or courtyards, while inside the atmosphere is rustic. Some serve light meals, which in Vienna can be a hot or cold buffet.

Concentrations of *Heurigen* can be found in the wine-growing suburbs to the north, southwest, west and northwest of the city. Grinzing, in the northwest, is the best-known *Heurigen* area, but it is also the most touristy. It's generally avoided by the Viennese, but if you like loud music and busloads of rowdy tourists, then it's the place for you.

🍺 Innere Stadt

★ Kruger's American Bar   BAR
(Map p62; www.krugers.at; 01, Krugerstrasse 5; ⊙from 6pm Mon-Sat; Ⓜ Stephansplatz, 🚋D, 1, 2, 71 Kärntner Ring/Oper) This wood-panelled American-style bar is a legend in Vienna, re-

taining some of its original furnishings from the 1930s and complete with a separate cigar and smoker's lounge.

★ Loos American Bar   COCKTAIL BAR
(Map p62; www.loosbar.at; 01, Kärntner Durchgang 10; ⊙noon-5am Thu-Sat, to 4am Sun-Wed; Ⓜ Stephansplatz) *The* spot for a classic cocktail in the Innere Stadt, expertly whipped up by talented mixologists. Designed by Adolf Loos in 1908, this tiny box (seating no more than about 20) is bedecked from head to toe in onyx and polished brass.

★ Palffy Club   CLUB
(Map p62; www.palais-palffy.at; 01, Josefsplatz 6; cover €12; ⊙from 10pm Fri & Sat; 🚌1A, 2A Michaelerplatz, Ⓜ Herrengasse, 🚋D, 1, 2, 71 Burgring) This 550-sq-metre club occupies two floors (right as you enter) of an illustrious old building used for live-music performances. The 1st-floor lounge bar is set with thousands of miniature gemstones below a 12m chandelier with 80,000 Swarovski crystals. The 1st floor has R&B and '70s and '80s, while the 2nd floor opens at 1am with house and techno beats.

Cafe Neko   JAPANESE
(Map p62; www.cafeneko.at; 01, Blumenstockgasse 5, cnr Ballgasse; hot drinks, nibbles under €5, nibble for cat €1; Ⓜ Stephansplatz) At Vienna's only 'cat cafe' (no dogs allowed) you can stroke and play with the feline friends or watch them walk or repose high up on a walkway. Owner Ishimitsu Takako is active in the local animal-protection society. Many of her guests, she says, are people who don't have cats themselves because they're not permitted to keep them in their flats, or they love cats but have a cat allergy. These people drop by and stay until their allergy gets the better of them.

Kleines Café   CAFE
(Map p62; 01, Franziskanerplatz 3; ⊙10am-2am Mon-Sat, 1pm-2am Sun; Ⓜ Stubentor, 🚋2 Weihburggasse) Designed by architect Hermann Czech in the 1970s, Kleines Café exudes a Bohemian atmosphere reminiscent of Vienna's heady *Jugendstil* days. It's tiny inside, but the wonderful summer outdoor seating on Franziskanerplatz is arguably the best in the Innere Stadt.

Vis-à-vis   WINE BAR
(Map p62; ☑512 93 50; www.weibel.at; 01, Wollzeile 5; ⊙4.30-10.30pm Tue-Sat; Ⓜ Stephansplatz) Hidden down a narrow, atmospheric passage is this wee wine bar seating only

GAY & LESBIAN VIENNA

Vienna is reasonably tolerant towards gays and lesbians. The Vienna Tourist Board (p110) has an excellent *Queer Guide* booklet and PDF download with listings of bars, restaurants, hotels, festivals and contact organisations.

Events to look out for on the gay and lesbian calendar include the **Regenbogen Parade** (Rainbow Parade; www.hosiwien.at/regenbogenparade; ☺ late Jun), a colourful parade that takes over the Ring and MuseumsQuartier, the **Life Ball** (www.lifeball.org; ☺ mid-May), an AIDS-charity event, and **Identities – Queer Film Festival** (www.identities.at; ☺ Jun odd years), a film festival showcasing queer movies.

Good gay-friendly cafes and bars are Why Not? (p100), Café Savoy (p102), Mango Bar (p103) and Café Berg (p103). Unfortunately there isn't much in the way of accommodation aimed specifically at gay and lesbians; Hotel-Pension Wild (p89) is one option.

10, but it makes up for it with over 350 wines on offer (with a strong emphasis on Austrian faves). It's a perfect spot to escape after a packed day of sightseeing – tapas, antipasto and gourmet olives round out the selection.

Haas & Haas
CAFE

(Map p62; ☎512 26 66; www.haas-haas.at; 01, Stephansplatz 4; ☺8am-8pm Mon-Sat, 9am-6pm Sun; Ⓜ Stephansplatz) The fragrance of tea from around the world greets customers on entry to Haas & Hass, Vienna's prime tearoom (coffee is also served). Green, herbal, aromatic, Assam, Ceylon, Darjeeling – the selection seems endless. The rear garden is a shaded retreat from the wind, rain, sun and tourist bustle, while the front parlour sports comfy cushioned booths and views of Stephansdom.

Café Bräunerhof
COFFEE HOUSE

(Map p62; ☎512 38 93; 01, Stallburggasse 2; ☺8am-9pm Mon-Fri, to 7pm Sat, 10am-7pm Sun; Ⓜ Herengasse, Stephansplatz) Little has changed in Bräunerhof from the days when Austria's seminal writer Thomas Bernhard frequented the premises: staff can be standoffish, the mood is somewhat stuffy and the newspaper selection good. For all this, it's a coffee house with traditional Viennese flavour. Classical music features from 3pm to 6pm on weekends.

Café Leopold Hawelka
COFFEE HOUSE

(Map p62; www.hawelka.at; 01, Dorotheergasse 6; ☺8am-1am Mon-Sat, 10am-1am Sun; Ⓜ Stephansplatz) This classic coffee house has a relaxed and convivial vibe with orange wallpaper and decorative tones. Nothing much has changed at Hawelka since it opened in the late 1930s. Friedensreich Hundertwasser, Elias Canetti, Arthur Miller and Andy Warhol, to just name a few, are among the artists and writers who have hung out here.

Café Sacher
CAFE

(Map p62; 01, Philharmonikerstrasse 4; ☺8am-midnight; Ⓜ Karlsplatz, ◫D, 1, 2, 71 Kärntner Ring/Oper) Sacher is the cafe every second tourist wants to visit. Why? Because of the celebrated Sacher Torte (€4), a rich chocolate cake with apricot jam once favoured by Emperor Franz Josef. Truth be told, as cafes go Sacher doesn't rate highly for authenticity, but it pleases the masses with its opulent furnishings, battalion of waiters and air of nobility.

Demel
COFFEE HOUSE

(Map p62; www.demel.at; 01, Kohlmarkt 14; ☺9am-7pm; ◫1A, 2A Michaelerplatz, Ⓜ Herengasse, Stephansplatz) An elegant and regal cafe within sight of the Hofburg, Demel was once the talk of the town but now mainly caters to tourists. The quality of the cakes hasn't dropped however, and it wins marks for the sheer creativity of its sweets. Demel's speciality is the Ana Demel Torte, a calorie-bomb of chocolate and nougat.

Esterházykeller
WINE TAVERN

(Map p62; ☎533 34 82; www.esterhazykeller.at; 01, Haarhof 1; ☺11am-11pm; Ⓜ Stephansplatz, Herengasse) Esterházykeller, tucked away on a quiet courtyard just off Kohlmarkt, has an enormous cellar – rustic decor, complete with medieval weaponry and farming tools – where excellent wine is served direct from the Esterházy Palace wine estate in Eisenstadt. Unlike most *Heurigen*, Esterházykeller offers beer.

Zwölf Apostelkeller
WINE TAVERN

(Twelve Apostle Cellar; Map p62; ☎512 67 77; www.zwoelf-apostelkeller.at; 01, Sonnenfelsgasse 3; ☺11am-midnight; Ⓜ Stephansplatz) Even though Zwölf Apostelkeller plays it up for the tourists, it still retains plenty of charm, dignity and authenticity. This is mostly due to the premises themselves: a vast, dimly lit multilevel cellar. The atmosphere is often lively and rowdy, helped along by traditional *Heuriger* music from 7pm daily.

Why Not?

GAY

(Map p62; www.why-not.at; 01, Tiefer Graben 22; cover after midnight €7; ⊙10pm-4am Fri & Sat; 🐭; MHerrengasse, 🚋1 Salztorbrücke) Why Not? is one of the few clubs focusing its attention solely on the gay scene. The small club quickly fills up with mainly young guys out for as much fun as possible.

Ringstrasse

★Dachboden

BAR

(Map p74; http://25hours-hotels.com; 07, Lerchenfelder Strasse 1-3; ⊙2pm-1am Tue-Sat, to 10pm Sun; 🐭; MVolkstheater) Housed in the circus-themed 25hours Hotel (p89), Dachboden has big-top views of Vienna's skyline from its decked terrace. Inside, the decor is retro-playful. Besides Fritz cola and an array of wines, beers and specialty teas, there are tapas-style snacks in case you get the munchies.

Café Prückel

COFFEE HOUSE

(Map p62; www.prueckel.at; 01, Stubenring 24; ⊙8.30am-10pm; 🐭; MStubentor, 🚋2 Stubentor) Prückel's unique mould is a little different from other Viennese cafes: instead of a sumptuous interior, it features an intact 1950s design. Intimate booths, aloof waiters, strong coffee, diet-destroying cakes and Prückel's speciality, its delicious apple strudel, are all big attractions. Live piano music tinkles across the room from 7pm to 10pm on Monday, Wednesday and Friday.

Volksgarten ClubDiskothek

CLUB

(Map p62; www.volksgarten.at; 01, Burgring 1; cover from €6; ⊙10pm-4am or later Tue & Thu-Sat; MMuseumsquartier, Volkstheater, 🚋D, 1, 2, 71 Dr-Karl-Renner-Ring) A hugely popular club superbly located near the Hofburg, Volksgarten serves a clientele eager to see and be seen. The long cocktail bar is perfect for people-watching and the music is an ever-rotating mix of hip-hop, house and hits. Opening hours are variable so check the website. Dress well to glide past the bouncers.

Palmenhaus

BAR, CAFE

(Map p62; www.palmenhaus.at; 01, Burggarten; ⊙10am-2am; MKarlsplatz, Museumsquartier, 🚋D, 1, 2, 71 Burgring) Housed in a beautifully restored Victorian palm house, complete with high-arched ceilings, glass walls and steel beams, Palmenhaus occupies one of the most attractive locations in Vienna. The crowd is generally well-to-do, but the ambience is relaxed and welcoming, making it ideal for a glass of wine or cup of coffee. The outdoor seating in summer is a must; it serves food (mains €16.80 to €27) and there are occasional club nights.

Volksgarten Pavillon

BAR

(Map p62; www.volksgarten-pavillon.at; 01, Burgring 1; ⊙11am-2am Apr–mid-Sep; 🐭; MVolkstheater, 🚋D, 1, 2, 71 Dr-Karl-Renner-Ring) Volksgarten Pavillon is a lovely 1950s-style pavilion with views of Heldenplatz. During the day and very early evening it's a cafe and restaurant, but its highlight is the legendary Tuesday night Techno Cafe, when its ever-popular garden is packed to the gunnels. Entrance some nights is free; for the Techno Cafe it's around €4.

Café Landtmann

COFFEE HOUSE

(Map p62; www.landtmann.at; 01, Dr-Karl-Lueger-Ring 4; ⊙7.30am-midnight; 🐭; MRathaus, 🚋D, 1, 2 Rathausplatz) Freud, Mahler and Marlene Dietrich all had a soft spot for this coffee house, which opened its doors in 1873. Today, it attracts both politicians and theatre-goers with its elegant interior and close proximity to the Burgtheater, Rathaus and Parlament. The dessert menu features Sacher Torte, and there's free live piano music from 8pm to 11pm Sunday to Tuesday.

Across the Danube Canal

★Le Loft

BAR

(Map p62; 02, Praterstrasse 1; ⊙10am-2am; MSchwedenplatz, 🚋2 Gredlerstrasse) In this slinky, glass-walled lounge on the 18th floor of the Sofitel you can pick out landmarks such as the Stephansdom and the Hofburg over a pomegranate martini or mojito. By night, the backlit ceiling swirls with an Impressionist painter's palette of colours.

Fluc

CLUB

(www.fluc.at; 02, Praterstern 5; ⊙6pm-4am; MPraterstern) Located on the wrong side of the tracks (Praterstern can be rough around the edges at times) and looking for all the world like a prefab schoolroom, Fluc is where black-clad students, alcoholics and the occasional TV celebrity all share the stripped-back venue without any hassle; DJs or live acts play every night (electronica features heavily).

Pratersauna CLUB
(www.pratersauna.tv; 02, Waldsteingartenstrasse 135; ⊗ club 9pm-6am Wed-Sun, pool 1-9pm Fri & Sat Jun-Sep; ⊠ Messe-Prater) Pool, cafe, bistro and club converge in a former sauna – these days, you'll sweat it up on the dance floor any given night. Pratersauna hosts light installations and performance art to check out before or after you groove to electronica played by international DJs. On warm nights it all spills out onto the terrace, gardens and illuminated pool.

🍷 Inside the Gürtel

★ Café Sperl COFFEE HOUSE
(Map p76; www.cafesperl.at; 06, Gumpendorfer Strasse 11; ⊗ 7am-11pm Mon-Sat, 11am-8pm Sun; ⊠; ⊠ Museumsquartier, Kettenbrückengasse) With its gorgeous *Jugendstil* fittings, grand dimensions, cosy booths and unhurried air, Sperl is one of the finest coffee houses in Vi-

enna. And that's to say nothing of a menu that features Sperl Torte, a mouth-watering mix of almonds and chocolate cream. Grab a slice and a newspaper, order a strong coffee, and join the rest of the patrons people-watching and daydreaming.

The food is good too, with snacks and hearty Austrian mains (€7 to €11) staving off hunger.

★ Strandbar Herrmann BAR
(www.strandbarherrmann.at; 03, Herrmannpark; ⊗ 10am-2am Apr-early Oct; ⊠; ⊠ Schwedenplatz, ⊠ O Hintere Zollamstrasse) You'd swear you're by the sea at this hopping canalside beach bar, with beach chairs, sand, DJ beats and hordes of Viennese livin' it up on hot summer evenings. Films occasionally feature, blankets are available and if you get bored of lounging, you can have a go at a game of boules.

★ Café Drechsler COFFEE HOUSE
(Map p76; www.cafedrechsler.at; Linke Wienzeile 22; ⊗ open 23hr, closed 2-3am; ⊠; ⊠ Kettenbrückengasse) One of the liveliest coffee houses in town, Drechsler reopened with a smash after extensive renovations (Sir Terence Conran worked his magic with polished marble bar and table tops, Bauhaus light fixtures and whitewashed timber panels – stylish yet

---

VIENNA'S MICROBREWERIES

1516 Brewing Company (Map p62; ☑ 961 15 16; www.1516brewingcompany.com; 01, Schwarzenbergstrasse 2; ⊗ 11am-2am; ⊠ Karlsplatz, ⊠ 2 Schwarzenbergstrasse) Unfiltered beers and a few unusual varieties, such as Heidi's Blueberry Ale, plus a large choice of cigars. Frequented by city workers, expats and UN staff.

Fischer Bräu (☑ 369 59 49; www.fischerbraeu.at; Billrothstrasse 17, 19; ⊗ 4pm-1am; ⊠ Nussdorfer Strasse) A new beer every four to six weeks, and a *Helles* (light) lager all year-round. The large garden is a local fave and and its live jazz on Sundays is perennially packed.

Salm Bräu (Map p80; www.salmbraeu.com; 03, Rennweg 8; ⊗ 11am-midnight; ⊠ Karlsplatz, ⊠ 71 Unteres Belvedere) Salm Bräu brews its own *Helles*, *Pils* (pilsner), *Märzen* (red-coloured beer with a strong malt taste), *G'mischt* (half *Dunkel* – dark – and half *Helles*), and *Weizen* (full-bodied wheat beer, slightly sweet in taste). Smack next to Schloss Belvedere and hugely popular.

Siebensternbräu (Map p76; www.7stern.at; 07, Siebensterngasse 19; ⊗ 11am-midnight; ⊠ Neubaugasse) Besides hoppy lagers and malty ales, there are unusual varieties like hemp, chilli and wood-smoked beer. The courtyard garden fills quickly with Wiener beer-lovers in the warmer months.

Wieden Bräu (Map p76; www.wieden-braeu.at; 04, Waaggasse 5; ⊗ 11.30am-midnight, from 4pm Jul & Aug; ⊠; ⊠ Taubstummengasse) *Helles*, *Märzen* and hemp beers are brewed year-round at this upbeat microbrewery, and there are a few seasonal choices, including a ginger beer. Tipples are matched with Austrian pub grub like schnitzel and goulash. Retreat to the garden in summer.

still distinctly Viennese). As well as the usual coffee-house suspects, its *Gulasch* (goulash) is legendary. In the evening the tunes the DJ spins seemingly change every few hours and always keep the vibe upbeat and hip.

Tanzcafé Jenseits
BAR, CLUB

(Map p76; www.tanzcafe-jenseits.com; 06, Nelkengasse 3; ☺8pm-4am Tue-Sat; ⓂNeubaugasse) Bordello meets Bohemian at this brothel-turned-bar, where soft lighting, red velvet and gilt mirrors keep the mood intimate. Jenseits has left its insalubrious past behind and today packs in media and arty types, who jostle for space on its tiny dance floor. The mercurial DJs flick from soul to trashy pop tunes in the blink of an eye.

Rote Bar
BAR

(Map p76; www.rotebar.at; 07, Neustiftgasse 1; ☺10pm-2am; ⓂVolkstheater) This marble-, chandelier- and thick-red-velvet-curtain-bedecked space in the nether regions of the Volkstheater is a gorgeous space for cocktails or a glass of wine with antipastos. It hosts regular events.

Chelsea
BAR, CLUB

(www.chelsea.co.at; 08, Lerchenfelder Gürtel 29-32; ☺6pm-4am; ⓂJosefstädter Strasse, Thaliastrasse, ☐2 Josefstädter Strasse) Chelsea is the old, ratty dog on the Gürtel and is very much a favourite of the student/alternative scene. DJs spin loud sounds (usually indie, sometimes techno) when live acts aren't playing. British and Irish beers are on tap.

Café Savoy
CAFE

(Map p76; www.savoy.at; 06, Linke Wienzeile 36; ☺noon-2am Sun-Thu, to 3am Fri & Sat; ☏; ⓂKettenbrückengasse) Café Savoy is an established gay haunt that has a more traditional cafe feel to it. The clientele is generally very mixed on a Saturday – mainly due to the proximity of the Naschmarkt – but at other times it's filled with men of all ages.

Phil
BAR, CAFE

(Map p76; www.phil.info; 06, Gumpendorfer Strasse 10-12; ☺5pm-1am Mon, 9am-1am Tue-Sun; ⓂMuseumsquartier, Kettenbrückengasse) Phil attracts a Bohemian crowd happy to squat on kitsch furniture your grandma used to own. Half the establishment is store rather than bar; TVs from the '70s, DVDs, records and books are for sale, as is all the furniture.

Weinstube Josefstadt
WINE BAR

(Map p74; 08, Piaristengasse 27; ☺4pm-midnight, closed Jan-Mar; ⓂRathaus) Weinstube Josef-

stadt is one of the loveliest *Stadtheurigen* (city wine taverns) in the city. Its garden is a barely controlled green oasis among concrete residential blocks, and tables are squeezed in between the trees and shrubs. Food is typical, with a buffet-style selection and plenty of cheap meats. The friendly, well-liquored locals come free of charge.

The location is not well signposted; the only sign of its existence is a metal *Busch'n* hanging from a doorway.

Europa
BAR, CAFE

(Map p76; 07, Zollergasse 8; ☺9am-5am; ☏; ⓂNeubaugasse) A long-standing fixture of the 7th district, Europa is a chilled spot any time day or night. During the sunny hours, join the relaxed set at a window table for coffee and food, and in the evening take a pew at the bar and enjoy the DJ's tunes. Its breakfast, served between 9am and 3pm daily, caters to a hungover clientele; Sunday features a sumptuous breakfast buffet.

Flex
CLUB

(www.flex.at; 01, Augartenbrücke; ☺9pm-6am Mon-Sat; ⓂSchottenring, ☐1, 2 Schottenring) Flex has been attracting a more mainstream crowd than it did in its early days but it still manages to retain a semblance of its former edginess. The sound system is without equal in Vienna, entry price generally reasonable and dress code unheard of. The monthly DJ line-up features local legends and international names, and live acts are commonplace.

Tunnel
CAFE

(Map p74; www.tunnel-vienna-live.at; 08, Florianigasse 39; ☺10am-1am, to 2am Fri & Sat; ☏🚻; ⓂRathaus, ☐2 Lederergasse) This laid-back, boho-flavoured cafe attracts students, arty types and all-comers. By day it's a relaxed spot to grab one of the worn wooden tables and flick through the papers over a coffee or €5 lunch special. By night the mood cranks up a notch with (mostly free) gigs at 9pm, skipping from rock to indie, Latin to contemporary jazz.

U4
CLUB

(www.u-4.at; 12, Schönbrunner Strasse 222; ☺8pm-late Mon, from 10pm Tue-Sun; ⓂMeidling Hauptstrasse) U4 was the birthplace of techno clubbing in Vienna way back when, and its longevity is a testament to its ability to roll with the times. A fairly young, studenty crowd are its current regulars, and while the music isn't as cutting edge as it used to be, it still manages to please the masses.

Roxy CLUB
(Map p76; www.roxyclub.org; 04, Operngasse 24; ⏰11pm-4am Thu-Sat; MKarlsplatz, 🚋D, 1, 2 Kärntner Ring/Oper) A seminal club for years, Roxy still manages to run with the clubbing pack, and sometimes leads the way. DJs from Vienna's electronica scene regularly guest on the turntables and most nights it's hard to find a space on the small dance floor. Expect a crowded, but very good, night out here.

Mon Ami BAR
(Map p76; www.monami.at; 06, Theobaldgasse 9; ⏰6pm-2am Wed-Sat; MMuseumsquartier) This former pet-grooming salon has morphed into a lovely '60s-style bar. It mixes excellent cocktails, serves a short but decent beer, has a wine and snacks list, and attracts a laid-back and unpretentious crowd. DJ Roman Schöny regularly works the decks.

Café Jelinek COFFEE HOUSE
(Map p76; www.steman.at; 06, Otto-Bauer-Gasse 5; ⏰9am-9pm; MZieglergasse) With none of the polish, airs and graces of some other coffee houses, this shabbily grand cafe is Viennese through and through. The wood-burning stove, picture-plastered walls and faded velvet armchairs draw people from all walks of life with their cocoonlike warmth.

Goodmann CLUB
(Map p76; www.goodmann.at; 04, Rechte Wienzeile 23; ⏰3am-10am Mon-Sat; MKettenbrückengasse) A tiny club attracting clubbers who want to boogie till breakfast, Goodmann serves food upstairs (until 8am) and hides its night owls, who are an eclectic mix of old and young (but always in a merry state), downstairs.

Mango Bar GAY, BAR
(Map p76; 06, Laimgrubengasse 3; ⏰9pm-4am; MKettenbrückengasse) Mango attracts a young, often men-only, gay crowd with good music, friendly staff and plenty of mirrors to check out yourself and others. It usually serves as a kick-start for a big night out on the town.

Café Berg GAY, CAFE
(Map p74; www.cafe-berg.at; 09, Berggasse 8; ⏰10am-midnight Mon-Sat, to 11pm Sun; 🔁; MSchottentor, 🚋D, 1 Schottentor) Café Berg is Vienna's leading gay bar, although it's welcoming to all walks of life. Its staff are some of the nicest in town, the layout sleek and smart, and the vibe chilled. Its bookshop,

Löwenherz (⏰10am-7pm Mon-Fri, to 5pm Sat), stocks a grand collection of gay magazines and books.

Frauencafé LESBIAN, CAFE
(Map p74; http://frauencafe.com; 08, Lange Gasse 11; ⏰6pm-midnight Thu & Fri, plus special events; MRathaus, Volkstheater) A strictly women-, lesbian- and transgendered-only cafe-bar, Frauencafé has long been a favourite of Vienna's lesbian scene, partly because of its homely, relaxed feel.

Café Willendorf GAY & LESBIAN, CAFE
(Map p76; http://cafe-willendorf.at; 06, Linke Wienzeile 102; ⏰6pm-2am Thu-Sat, to 1am Sun-Wed; MPilgramgasse) This is one of Vienna's seminal gay and lesbian bars. Housed in the pink **Rosa Lila Villa** (📞586 8150; www.villa.at), it's a very popular place to meet for a chat, a drink or a meal. The lovely inner courtyard garden opens for the summer months.

☕ Outside the Gürtel

This is where you find most of Vienna's *Heuriger*, atmospheric wine taverns serving a selection of meats and traditional accompaniments to the young wine.

Café Gloriette COFFEE
(Map p83; www.gloriette-cafe.at; 13, Gloriette; ⏰9am-dusk; MSchönbrunn, Hietzing) Café Gloriette occupies the neoclassical Gloriette, high on a hill behind Schloss Schönbrunn, built for the pleasure of Maria Theresia in 1775. With sweeping views of the Schloss, its magnificent gardens and the districts to the north, Gloriette has arguably one of the best vistas in all of Vienna. It's a welcome pit stop after the short climb up the hill.

10er Marie WINE TAVERN
(16, Ottakringerstrasse 222-224; ⏰3pm-midnight Mon-Sat; MOttakring, 🚋2, 10, 46 Ottakring) Vienna's oldest *Heuriger* is family run, rustic and attracts locals and visitors alike.

Hirt WINE TAVERN
(📞318 96 41; www.heuriger-hirt.at; 19, Eisernenhandgasse 165, Kahlenberg; ⏰3-11pm Wed-Fri, noon-11pm Sat & Sun, closed Wed-Fri Nov-Mar; 🚌38A Kahlenberg) Hidden among the vineyards on the eastern slopes of Kahlenberg, this is a simple *Heuriger* with few frills and pleasant views.

Mayer am Pfarrplatz WINE TAVERN
(📞370 12 87; www.pfarrplatz.at; 19, Pfarrplatz 2, Nussdorf; ⏰4pm-midnight Mon-Sat, from noon

Sun; ✦; 🚊D Nussdorf) Caters to tour groups but retains an authentic air. Beethoven lived here in 1817. There's a children's play area and live music from 7pm.

Zawodsky WINE TAVERN
(☎320 79 78; www.zawodsky.at; 19, Reinischgasse 3, Döbling; ⊙5pm-midnight Mon-Fri, from 2pm Sat & Sun, closed Mon-Wed Apr & Oct-Nov; 🚌38 An den langen Lüssen) This *Heuriger* has a stripped-back interior and picnic tables surrounded by apple trees and vineyards.

Edlmoser WINE TAVERN
(☎889 86 80; www.edlmoser.at; 23, Maurer Lange Gasse, Maurer; ⊙2.30pm-midnight; 🚌60 Maurer-Lange-Gasse) A *Heuriger* run by dynamic young winemaker Michael Edlmoser in a four-centuries-old house. Check the website for opening months.

☆ Entertainment

Vienna is, and probably will be till the end of time, the European capital of opera and classical music. The program of music events is never-ending, and as a visitor in the centre you'll continually be accosted by people in Mozart-era costume trying to sell you tickets for concerts or ballets. Even the city's buskers are often classically trained musicians.

The city also sports a number of great clubs, jazz bars and live-music venues. The tourist office produces a handy monthly listing of concerts and other events.

Opera & Classical Music

Outside of the main venues, many churches and cafes are fine places to catch a classical concert.

Staatsoper OPERA
(Map p62; ☎514 44 7880; www.wiener-staatsoper.at; 01, Opernring 2; 🚇Karlsplatz, 🚊D 1, 2 Kärntner Ring/Oper) The Staatsoper is *the* premiere opera and classical-music venue in Vienna. Productions are lavish affairs: the Viennese take their opera very seriously and dress up

accordingly. In the interval, be sure to wander around the foyer and refreshment rooms to fully appreciate the gold and crystal interior. Opera is not performed here in July and August (tours, however, still take place), but its repertoire still includes more than 70 different productions. Tickets can usually be purchased up to two months in advance.

Musikverein CONCERT VENUE
(Map p80; ☎505 81 90; www.musikverein.at; 01, Bösendorferstrasse 12; seats €25-89, standing room €4-6; ⊙box office 9am-8pm Mon-Fri, to 1pm Sat; 🚇Karlsplatz) The Musikverein holds the proud title of the best acoustics of any concert hall in Austria and is ranked among the top 10 in the world. The interior is suitably lavish and befitting the Vienna Philharmonic Orchestra, which often plays here. Tickets are available online, by phone or at the box office. All tickets are available up to seven weeks in advance.

Konzerthaus CONCERT VENUE
(Map p80; ☎242 002; www.konzerthaus.at; 03, Lothringerstrasse 20; ⊙box office 9am-7.45pm Mon-Fri, to 1pm Sat, plus 45 min before performance; 🚇Stadtpark, 🚊D Gusshausstrasse) The Konzerthaus is a major venue in classical-music circles, but throughout the year ethnic music, rock, pop or jazz can also be heard in its hallowed halls. Students can pick up €14 tickets 30 minutes before performances; children receive a 50% discount.

Theater an der Wien THEATRE
(Map p76; ☎588 85; www.theater-wien.at; 06, Linke Wienzeile 6; seats €10-160, standing room €7, student rush €10-15; ⊙box office 10am-7pm Mon-Sat; 🚇Karlsplatz) The Theater an der Wien has hosted some monumental premiere performances, such as Beethoven's *Fidelo*, Mozart's *Die Zauberflöte* and Strauss Jnr's *Die Fledermaus*, and has reestablished its reputation for high-quality opera, premiering a new opera each month. Unlike the Staatsoper, it has opera performances in

MOZART IN THE MAKING

Klangforum Wien (☎521 670; www.klangforum.at), an ensemble of 24 artists from nine countries, celebrates a unique collaboration between conductors, composers and interpreters who produce a wide range of musical styles, from improv to edgy jazz to classical notes. Many up-and-coming composers are represented here in what is often a sneak peek at the next best thing. The Klangforum performs at various venues in the city – check the website for dates and details.

VIENNA BOYS' CHOIR

As with Manner Schnitten, Stephansdom, Lipizzaner stallions and sausage stands, Vienna wouldn't be Vienna without the **Vienna Boys' Choir** (Wiener Sängerknaben; www.wienersaengerknaben.at). Founded over five centuries ago by Maximilian I as the imperial choir, its members over the ages have included famed composers Schubert and Gallus and conductors Richter and Krauss; Mozart composed for them in his day; Haydn was a member of another local choir, but he occasionally stepped in to sing with them. Today, it's the most famous boys' choir in the world. It now consists of four separate choirs – hand selected each year and mainly Austrian – who share the demanding global tour schedule.

The choir sings during Sunday mass in the **Burgkapelle** (Royal Chapel; Map p62; 📞 533 99 27; www.hofburgkapelle.at; 01, Schweizer Hof; ⏰ 10am-2pm Mon & Tue, 11am-1pm Fri; 🚌 2A Heldenplatz, Ⓜ Herrengasse, 🚋 D, 1, 2 Burgring) in the Hofburg from mid-September to June at 9.15am. For a free *Stehplatz* (standing-room space) in the Burgkapelle, simply show up by 8.30am. Uncollected tickets for the Burgkapelle are also resold on the day but arrive at least one hour earlier for a chance of getting one.

Other performances are held in the Volksoper and in **MuTh** (📞 347 80 80; www.muth.at; 02, Obere Augartenstrasse 1e, Vienna Boys' Choir Fri performance €39-89; ⏰ 4-6pm Mon-Fri & 1hr before performances; Ⓜ Taborstrasse), the choir's dedicated hall in Augarten. Regular two-hour Friday performances are usually held at 5.30pm in MuTH and last two hours. See the Vienna Boys' Choir website for links to the various venues with the performance date.

July and August. All tickets (standard and standing) are available online, by phone or from the box office. Student rush is 30 minutes before start, and standing tickets one hour before start.

Volksoper
CONCERT VENUE

(People's Opera; Map p74; 📞 514 44 3670; www.volksoper.at; 09, Währinger Strasse 78; Ⓜ Währinger Strasse) Offering a more intimate experience than the Staatsoper, the Volksoper specialises in operettas, dance performances, musicals and a handful of standard, heavier operas. Standing tickets go for €2 to €7 and, like many venues, there are a plethora of discounts and reduced tickets for sale 30 minutes before performances. The Volksoper closes for July and August.

Theatre & Dance

★ Burgtheater
THEATRE

(National Theatre; Map p62; 📞 514 44 4440; www.burgtheater.at; 01, Universitätsring 2; seats €5-51, standing room €2.50, students €8; ⏰ box office 9am-5pm Mon-Fri; Ⓜ Rathaus, 🚋 D, 1, 2 Rathaus) The Burgtheater is one of the foremost theatres in the German-speaking world, staging some 800 performances a year, which reach from Shakespeare to Woody Allen plays. The theatre also runs the 500-seater Akademietheater, which was built between 1911 and 1913. There's a 25% reduction on tickets one hour before the show.

Vienna's English Theatre
THEATRE

(Map p74; 📞 402 12 60; www.englishtheatre.at; 08, Josefsgasse 12; tickets €22-42; ⏰ box office 10am-7.30pm Mon-Fri, 5-7.30pm Sat performance days; Ⓜ Rathaus, 🚋 2 Rathaus/Josefstädter Strasse) Founded in 1963, Vienna's English Theatre is the oldest foreign-language theatre in Vienna (with the occasional show in French or Italian). Standby tickets for €9 go on sale 15 minutes before start.

Tanzquartier Wien
DANCE

(Map p62; 📞 581 35 91; www.tqw.at; 07, Museumsplatz 1; tickets €11-62; ⏰ box office 9am-8pm Mon-Fri, from 10am Sat; Ⓜ Museumsquartier, Volkstheater) Tanzquartier Wien, located in the MuseumsQuartier, hosts an array of local and international performances with a strong experimental nature. Students receive advance tickets at 30% or €7 for unsold seats 15 minutes before showtime.

Schauspielhaus
THEATRE

(Map p74; 📞 317 01 0111; www.schauspielhaus.at; 09, Porzellangasse 19; tickets €19; ⏰ box office 4-6pm Mon-Sat, 2hr before performance; Ⓜ Rossauer Lände) Performances in German. Student tickets cost €10.

Volkstheater
THEATRE

(Map p76; 📞 521 11-400; www.volkstheater.at; 07, Neustiftgasse 1; tickets €11-50; ⏰ box office 10am-7.30pm Mon-Sat; Ⓜ Volkstheater) Performances

ℹ️ SHOW TICKETS

Tickets for the Akademietheater, Burgtheater, Staatsoper and Volksoper can be purchased from the state ticket office, **Bundestheaterkassen** (Map p62; 📞 514 44-7880; www.bundestheater.at; 01, Operngasse 2; ⊙ 8am-6pm Mon-Fri, 9am-noon Sat & Sun; Ⓜ Stephansplatz). Tickets for the Staatsoper are available here two months prior to performance dates. Credit-card purchases can be made online or by telephone. For online bookings go to the Bundestheaterkassen website and click on the desired venue. Tourist Info Wien (p110) has an events calendar and all booking information. Places to buy tickets for most venues other than for Staatoper performances:

Wien-Ticket Pavillon (Map p62; 📞 588 85; www.wien-ticket.at; Herbert-von-Karajan-Platz; ⊙ 10am-7pm; Ⓜ Karlsplatz, 🚊 D, 1, 2 Kärntner Ring/Oper) Outside the Staatsoper.

Jirsa Theater Karten Büro (Map p74; 📞 400 600; www.viennaticket.at; 08, Lerchenfelder Strasse 12; ⊙ 9.30am-5.30pm Mon-Fri Sep-Jun, 10am-1pm Jul & Aug; 🚊 46 Auerspergstrasse) Covers most venues in town.

oeticket Center Museumsquartier (Map p76; www.oeticket.com; 07, Museumsplatz 1, Halle E+G; ⊙ 10am-1pm & 2-7pm ; Ⓜ Museumsquartier, Volkstheater) Online sales for events as well as ticket sales and pick up in oeticket Center MuseumsQuartier.

in German, with a strong focus on popular theatre but also some classics with a new flavour. Student rush tickets are available for €4 one hour before the start.

Live Music

Porgy & Bess
JAZZ

(Map p62; 📞 512 88 11; www.porgy.at; 01, Riemergasse 11; concerts around €18; ⊙ concerts 7pm or 8pm; Ⓜ Stubentor, 🚊 2 Stubentor) Quality is the cornerstone of Porgy & Bess' continuing popularity. Its program is loaded with modern jazz acts from around the globe, including many from the USA and nearby Balkan countries. The interior is dim and the vibe velvety and very grown-up.

WUK
CULTURAL CENTRE

(Workshop & Culture House; Map p74; 📞 401 21-0; www.wuk.at; 09, Währinger Strasse 59; Ⓜ Währinger Strasse) WUK is many things to many people. Basically a space for art, it hosts plenty of events in its concert hall. International and local rock acts vie with clubbing nights, classical concerts, film evenings, theatre and even children's shows. Its cafe has a fabulous cobbled courtyard.

Arena
LIVE MUSIC

(www.arena.co.at; 03, Baumgasse 80; Ⓜ Erdberg, Gasometer) A former slaughterhouse turned music and film venue, Arena is one of the city's quirkier places to see live acts. Hard rock, rock, metal, reggae and soul (along with cinema) can be seen on its outdoor stage from May to September; over winter bands are presented in one of its two indoor halls.

Jazzland
LIVE MUSIC

(Map p62; 📞 533 25 75; www.jazzland.at; 01, Franz-Josefs-Kai 29; cover €11-20; ⊙ from 7pm Mon-Sat, live music from 9pm; Ⓜ Schwedenplatz, 🚊 1, 2 Schwedenplatz) Jazzland has been an institution of Vienna's jazz scene for over 30 years. The music covers the whole jazz spectrum, and the brick venue features a grand mixture of both international and local acts.

Cinemas

Vienna has a fine mix of cinemas featuring Hollywood blockbusters and art-house films in both German and English. Falter (p110), *City* and *Der Standard* (daily newspapers) all contain film listings. Monday is *Kinomontag*, when many seats are discounted. Expect to pay about €8 to €12 for tickets.

Schikaneder
CINEMA

(Map p76; 📞 585 28 67; www.schikaneder.at; 04, Margaretenstrasse 24; Ⓜ Kettenbrückengasse) Located next to the bar of the same name, Schikaneder is the darling of Vienna's alternative-cinema scene. The film subject range is quite broad but also highly selective, and art house through and through.

Artis International
CINEMA

(Map p62; 📞 535 65 70; www.cineplexx.at; 01, Schultergasse 5; tickets €8.50; Ⓜ Stephansplatz, Schwedenplatz) Artis has six small cinemas in the heart of the Innere Stadt. It only shows English-language films, of the Hollywood blockbuster variety, often in original English without subtitles.

Burg Kino
CINEMA
(Map p62; ☑ 587 84 06; www.burgkino.at; 01, Opernring 19; Ⓜ Museumsquartier, ⓓ D, 1, 2 Burgring) The Burg Kino is a central cinema that shows only English-language films. It has regular screenings of the *The Third Man*, Orson Welles' timeless classic set in post-WWII Vienna. See the website for times.

English Cinema Haydn
CINEMA
(Map p76; ☑ 587 22 62; www.haydnkino.at; 06, Mariahilfer Strasse 57; Ⓜ Neubaugasse) The Haydn is a comfortable cinema screening mainly mainstream Hollywood-style films in their original language, on three separate screens.

Filmcasino
CINEMA
(Map p76; ☑ 581 39 00-10; www.filmcasino.at; 05, Margaretenstrasse 78; Ⓜ Kettenbrückengasse) An art-house cinema of some distinction, Filmcasino screens an excellent mix of Asian and European docos and avant-garde short films, along with independent feature-length films from around the world. Its '50s-style foyer is particularly impressive.

Österreichisches Filmmuseum
CINEMA
(Austrian Film Museum; Map p62; ☑ 533 70 54; www.filmmuseum.at; 01, Auginerstrasse 1; adult/child €10/5.80; Ⓜ Karlsplatz, ⓓ D, 1, 2, 71 Kärntner Ring/Oper) Situated inside the Albertina, the Austrian Film Museum shows a range of films with and without subtitles in the original language, featuring a director, group of directors or a certain theme from around the world in programs generally lasting a couple of weeks. Screenings are generally at 6.30pm; check the website for other times.

Top Kino
CINEMA
(Map p76; ☑ 208 30 00; www.topkino.at; 06, Rahlgasse 1; Ⓜ Museumsquartier) Top Kino offers an ever-changing array of European films and documentaries, generally in their original language with German subtitles. Top Kino also holds a variety of themed film festivals

Votivkino
CINEMA
(Map p74; ☑ 317 35 71; www.votivkino.at; 09, Währinger Strasse 12; ⓓ; Ⓜ Schottentor) Built in 1912, the Votiv is one of the oldest cinemas in Vienna. It's been extensively updated since then and is now among the best cinemas in the city. Its three screens feature a mix of Hollywood's more quirky ventures and art-house films in their original language.

The 11am Tuesday screening is reserved for mothers, fathers and babies, and weekend afternoons feature special matinées for kids.

🔒 Shopping

Vienna is one place where the glitz and glamour of shops selling high-end brands stand in stark contrast to some weird and idiosyncratic local stores. Specialities include porcelain, ceramics, handmade dolls, wrought-iron work and leather goods, and there are many shops selling *Briefmarken* (stamps), *Münze* (coins) and *Altwaren* (secondhand odds and ends).

Art Up
FASHION, ACCESSORIES
(Map p62; www.artup.at; 01, Bauernmarkt 8; ⊙ 11am-6.30pm Mon-Fri, to 5pm Sat; Ⓜ Stephansplatz) Take the temperature of Vienna's contemporary design scene at Art Up, offering space for young designers to get a foothold in the fashion world. The model makes for an eclectic collection – elegant fashion pieces rub against quirky accessories (Astroturf tie or handbag, anyone?) as well as ceramics and bigger art pieces.

Freaks & Icons
FASHION, ACCESSORIES
(Map p76; www.freaksandicons.com; 07, Zollergasse 12; ⊙ 11am-7pm Tue-Fri, to 5pm Sat; Ⓜ Neubaugasse) Freaks & Icons showcases individually tailored, figure-hugging clothing for women; smooth lines and quality fabrics (raw silk, delicate wool, flowing-yet-structured cotton) dominate, yet most items sell for less than €200.

Unger und Klein
WINE
(Map p62; ☑ 532 13 23; www.ungerundklein.at; 01, Gölsdorfgasse 2; ⊙ 3pm-midnight Mon-Fri, from 5pm Sat; Ⓜ Schwedenplatz, ⓓ 1 Salztorbrücke) Unger und Klein's small but knowledgable wine collection spans the globe, but the majority of its labels come from Europe. The

best of Austrian wines – from expensive boutique varieties to bargain-bin bottles – are available. It's also a small, laid-back wine bar, with a reasonable selection of wines by the glass, which gets crowded on Friday and Saturday evenings.

Henzls Ernte
FOOD

(Map p76; www.henzls.at; 05, Kettenbrückengasse 3; ☉1-6pm Tue-Fri, 9am-5pm Sat; Ⓜ Kettenbrückengasse) ✐ If you're lucky, you'll see the Henzl family drying, grinding and blending their home-grown and foraged herbs and spices together with sugar and salt at delightfully old-school Henzls Ernte.

Gabarage Upcycling Design
DESIGN STORE

(Map p76; www.gabarage.at; 06, Schleifmühlgasse 6; ☉10am-6pm Mon-Thu, to 7pm Fri, 11am-5pm Sat; Ⓜ Taubstummengasse) ✐ Recycled design, ecology and social responsibility underpin the quirky designs at Gabarage. Old bowling pins become vases, rubbish bins get a new life as tables and chairs, advertising tarpaulins morph into bags, and traffic lights are transformed into funky lights.

Austrian Delights
FOOD

(Map p62; ☏532 16 61; www.austriandelights.at; 01, Judengasse 1a; ☉11am-7pm Mon-Fri, to 6pm Sat; Ⓜ Stephansplatz) Stocking Austrian-made items by mainly small producers, at Austrian Delights you'll find regional specialities – fine confectionery, local wine, schnapps and cognac, jams, jellies, chutneys, honey, vinegars and oils – that you can't find anywhere else in the capital.

Manner
CONFECTIONERY

(Map p62; www.manner.com; 01, Stephansplatz 7; ☉10am-9pm; Ⓜ Stephansplatz) Even *Manner* (a glorious concoction of wafers and hazelnut cream), Vienna's favourite sweet since 1898, has its own concept store now, decked out in the biscuit's signature peachy pink.

Loden-Plankl
CLOTHING

(Map p62; ☏533 80 32; www.loden-plankl.at; 01, Michaelerplatz 6; ☉10am-6pm Mon-Sat; ☐1A, 2A Michaelerplatz, Ⓜ Herrengasse) Kit yourself out von Trapp–family style at this 180-year-old institution full of handmade embroidered *Dirndls* (women's traditional dress), blouses, capes, high-collared jackets, and deersuede and *loden* (a traditional fabric made from boiled and combed wool) coats.

Wein & Co
WINE

(Map p62; ☏535 09 16; www.weinco.at; 01, Jasomirgottstrasse 3-5; ☉10am-2am Mon-Sat, 3pm-midnight Sun; ☎; Ⓜ Stephansplatz) With a wide selection of quality European and New World wines, and a huge variety of local bottles, Wein & Co is probably your best bet for wine shopping – you should be able to pick up a bargain, as the specials here are always great. You can also buy cigars, and the wine bar has a terrace with a view of Stephansdom.

CHRISTMAS MARKETS

From mid-November, *Christkindlmärkte* (Christmas markets) start to pop up all over Vienna. Ranging from kitsch to quaint in style and atmosphere, the markets all have a few things in common: plenty of people, loads of Christmas gifts to purchase, mugs of *Glühwein* (mulled wine) and hotplates loaded with *Kartoffelpuffer* (hot potato patties) and *Maroni* (roasted chestnuts). Most close a day or two before Christmas Day. Some of the best:

Altwiener Christkindlmarkt auf der Freyung (Map p62; Freyung, 01; Ⓜ Herrengasse, Schottentor) Austrian arts and crafts and an old-world feel.

Heiligenkreuzerhof (Map p62; 01; Ⓜ Schwedenplatz, ☐2 Stubentor) Oft-forgotten market which is arguably the most authentic and quaint of all the *Christkindlmärkte*.

Karlsplatz (Map p80; Ⓜ Karlsplatz) Mainly sells arty gifts and is situated close to the Karlskirche.

Rathausplatz (Map p62; Ⓜ Rathaus, ☐D, 1, 2 Rathaus) Easily the biggest and most touristy Christmas market in Vienna but kitschy.

Schönbrunn Christmas Market (Map p83; ☐1A, Ⓜ Schönbrunn) Circle of upmarket stalls, loads of events for the kids and daily classical concerts at 6pm (more on weekends).

Spittelberg (Map p76; ☐48A, Ⓜ Volkstheater, ☐49) Traditional market occupying the charming cobblestone streets of the Spittelberg quarter. Stalls sell quality arts and crafts, but not at the cheapest prices.

SHOPPING STREETS

Kärntner Strasse The Innere Stadt's main shopping street and a real crowd-puller.

Kohlmarkt A river of high-end glitz.

Neubau The city's hottest designers along boutique-clogged streets like Kirchengasse, Lindengasse and Neubaugasse.

Mariahilfer Strasse Vienna's mile of high-street style, with big names and even bigger crowds.

Freihausviertel Lanes packed with home-grown fashion, design and speciality food stores, south of Naschmarkt around Schleifmühlgasse.

Theobaldgasse Just off Mariahilfer Strasse, Theobaldgasse's hole-in-the-wall shops purvey everything from fair-trade fashion to organic food.

Gumpendorferstrasse Retro fashion, up-market cosmetics, designer lighting – it's all on this funky 6th-district street.

Josefstädter Strasse An old-fashioned shopping street filled with idiosyncratic shops selling anything from *Altwaren* (old wares) to gemstones.

Woka HOMEWARES
(Map p62; www.woka.at; 01, Singerstrasse 16; ◉10am-6pm Mon-Fri, to 5pm Sat; Ⓜ Stephansplatz) Get a feel for the spectacular Wiener Werkstätte aesthetic and Bauhaus, art deco and Secessionist design, with its accurate reproductions of lamps designed by the likes of Adolf Loos, Kolo Moser and Josef Hoffmann.

Österreichische Werkstätten GLASS, CERAMICS
(Map p62; ✆ 512 24 18; www.austrianarts.com; 01, Kärntner Strasse 6; ◉10am-6.30pm Mon-Fri, to 6pm Sat; Ⓜ Stephansplatz) Österreichische Werkstätten is dedicated to selling work made by Austrian companies and designed by Austrian designers. Look out for Kisslinger, a family glassware company since 1946, with Klimt- and Hundertwasser-styled designs; Peter Wolfe's more traditional Tirolstyle designed glassware; and of course the world-renowned Riedel wine glasses.

J&L Lobmeyr Vienna CERAMICS
(Map p62; ✆ 512 05 08; www.lobmeyr.at; 01, Kärntner Strasse 26; ◉9am-5pm Mon-Fri; Ⓜ Stephansplatz) Sweep up the beautifully ornate wrought-iron staircase to one of Vienna's most lavish retail experiences. The collection of Biedermeier pieces, Loos-designed sets, fine or arty glassware and porcelain on display here glitters from the lights of the chandelier-festooned atrium. Production is focused towards pieces inspired by the Wiener Werkstätte artists from the early 20th century.

ℹ Orientation

Vienna occupies 415 sq km in the Danube Valley, with the Wienerwald (Vienna Woods) forming a natural border to the north and west. The Danube (Donau) River flows northeast to southwest through the city. Vienna's heart, the Innere Stadt (inner city; first district), is south of the river on a diversion of the Danube, the Danube Canal (Donaukanal).

It's encircled on three sides by the Ringstrasse, or Ring, a series of broad roads sporting an extravaganza of architectural delights. The Ring is at a distance of between 1.75km and 3km from the Gürtel (literally, 'belt'), a larger traffic artery that is fed by the flow of vehicles from outlying autobahn.

Stephansdom (St Stephen's Cathedral), with its slender spire, is in the heart of the Innere Stadt and is Vienna's principal landmark. Leading south from Stephansplatz station is Kärntner Strasse, an important pedestrian street that terminates at Karlsplatz, a major public-transport hub.

The Danube runs down a long, straight channel, built between 1870 and 1875 to eliminate flooding. This was supplemented 100 years later by the building of a parallel channel, the Neue Donau (New Danube), creating the Donauinsel (Danube Island) recreational area. The original Alte Donau (Old Danube) loops north of the Neue Donau to enclose the Donaupark, Vienna International Center (UNO City, home to the UN), beaches and water-sports centres. Squeezed between the Danube Canal and the Danube is the Prater, a large park and playground of the Viennese.

In terms of addresses, Vienna is divided into 23 *Bezirke* (districts), fanning out in approximate numerical order clockwise around the Innere Stadt. Note when reading addresses that the number of a building within a street *follows* the street name. The middle two digits of postcodes correspond to the district. Thus a postcode of 1010 means the place is in district one, and 1230 refers to district 23.

ℹ Information

EMERGENCY

Emergency number (☎112; ⊙24 hr) European emergency number. The deaf can send an SMS to ☎0800 133 133 (☎0043 800 133 133 if roaming) with a message.

Police station (☎313 10; 10, Deutschmeisterplatz 3; ⊙24hr)

Women's Emergency Line (Frauennotruf; ☎71 719; ⊙24hr)

MEDIA

Falter (www.falter.at) This weekly magazine is the best resource for political commentary and entertainment listings in every genre imaginable, with an online version and lots of specialised publications, such as the *Wien, wie es isst* eating guide. Listings are from Friday to Thursday. You can buy the print edition for €3.20 from newsagents, kiosks and sellers around town.

MEDICAL SERVICES

For medical advice for visitors, call ☎0800 633 49 46. If you require a *Zahnarzt* (dentist) after hours, call ☎512 20 78 (recorded message in German only); likewise if you need an *Apotheken* (pharmacy) outside shop hours, dial ☎1455 (in German only).

Allgemeines Krankenhaus (☎404 000; www.akhwien.at; 09, Währinger Gürtel 18-20) Hospital – emergency rooms open 24 hours a day, seven days a week.

MONEY

Banks and currency-exchange offices are located around town, but compare commission rates before changing money. *Bankomats* (ATMs) are found everywhere, including at the train stations and airport; those not located in foyers usually shut down at midnight.

POST

Main post office (Map p62; Fleischmarkt 19, 01; ⊙7am-10pm Mon-Fri, 9am-10pm Sat & Sun; Ⓜ Schwedenplatz, 🚋1, 2 Schwedenplatz)

TOURIST INFORMATION

Airport Information Office (⊙6am-11pm) Full services, with maps, Vienna Card and walk-in hotel booking. Located in the Vienna International Airport arrival hall.

Jugendinfo (Vienna Youth Information; Map p62; ☎4000 84 100; www.jugendinfowien.at; 01, Babenbergerstrasse 1; ⊙2-7pm Mon-Wed, 1-6pm Thu-Sat; Ⓜ Museumsquartier, 🚋 Burgring) Jugendinfo is tailored to those aged between 14 and 26, and has tickets for a variety of events at reduced rates for this age group. Staff can tell you about events around town, and places to log onto the internet.

Tourist Info Wien (Map p62; ☎245 55; www.wien.info; 01, Albertinaplatz; ⊙9am-7pm; ☎; Ⓜ Stephansplatz, 🚋D, 1, 2, 71 Kärntner Ring/Oper) Vienna's main tourist office, with a ticket agency, hotel booking service, free maps and every brochure under the sun.

WienXtra-Kinderinfo (Map p62; ☎4000 84 400; www.kinderinfowien.at; 07, Museumsplatz 1; ⊙2-6pm Tue-Fri, 10am-5pm Sat & Sun; 🚻; Ⓜ Museumsquartier) Marketed firstly at children (check out the knee-high display cases), then their parents, this child-friendly tourist office has loads of information on kids activities and a small indoor playground.

WEBSITES

About Vienna (www.aboutvienna.org) Cultural and sightseeing information.

City of Vienna (www.wien.gv.at) Comprehensive government-run website.

Lonely Planet (www.lonelyplanet.com/austria/vienna)

Vienna Online (www.vienna.at) Site with info on parties, festivals and news.

Vienna Tourist Board (www.wien.info) One of the first ports of call for any visitor.

ℹ Getting There & Away

AIR

Vienna is the main centre in Austria for international flights. Flying domestic routes offers few benefits over trains. Although there are frequent flights to Graz, Klagenfurt, Salzburg and Linz with Austrian Airlines from Vienna, Innsbruck in Tyrol is the one place where flying (one hour, five to seven times daily) is considerably faster than the train. Book early for the cheapest fares.

BOAT

Steamers head west (mostly from Krems, p116) and fast hydrofoils head east to Bratislava and Budapest (p394).

BUS

Vienna currently has no central bus station and national Bundesbuses arrive and depart from several different locations, depending on the destination. Bus lines serving Vienna include **Eurolines** (☎798 29 00; www.eurolines.com; Erdbergstrasse 200; ⊙6.30am-9pm; Ⓜ Erdberg).

TRAIN

Vienna is one of central Europe's main rail hubs. **Österreichische Bundesbahnen** (ÖBB; www.oebb.at; Austrian Federal Railway) is the main operator, providing direct services and connections to many European cities.

See p394 for information on Vienna's Hauptbahnhof and train departures and arrival points.

At press there were three main arrival and departure points: Wien Hauptbahnhof (in partial service, goes into full service early 2015), Wien-Meidling (Meidling-Philadelphiabrücke, not Meidling Hauptstrasse) and Westbahnhof.

Further stations include Franz-Josefs-Bahnhof (north of the centre; handles trains to/from the Danube Valley), Wien-Mitte and Praterstern.

🛈 Getting Around

TO/FROM THE AIRPORT

A standard taxi to/from the airport costs about €36 if you call ahead or go directly to the yellow **Taxi 40100** (☑ 40 100; www.taxi40100.at) service in the arrival hall (near the bookshop). Otherwise expect to pay about €50.

City Airport Train (CAT; www.cityairporttrain.com; return adult/child €19/free; ⊘ departs airport 6.06am-11.36pm, departs city 5.36am-11.06pm) Departs from Wien-Mitte; has luggage check-in facilities and boarding-card-issuing service.

Schnellbahn 7 (☑ 05 17 17; www.oebb.at) This train is the cheapest way (€3.80, 30 minutes) to get to the airport; departs from Wien-Mitte.

Vienna Airport Lines (☑ 700 732 300; www.postbus.at/en; ⊘ 8am-7.30pm Mon-Sat) Vienna Airport Lines has three services connecting different parts of Vienna with the airport. The most central is to/from the Vienna Airport Lines bus stop at Morzinplatz/Schwedenplatz (bus 1185; one way €8, 20 minutes), running via Wien-Mitte. A service also runs to/from Wien Westbahnhof via Wien Dörfelstrasse (Wien-Meidling Bahnhof) while the Hauptbahnhof is being completed.

BICYCLE

Cycling is an excellent way to get around and explore the city – over 800km of cycle tracks criss-cross the capital. Popular cycling areas include the 7km path around the Ringstrasse, the Donauinsel, the Prater and along the Danube Canal. There are a number of options for keen cyclists.

Citybike Wien (www.citybikewien.at; 1st hour free, 2nd/3rd hour €1/2, per hourr thereafter €4) Stands are scattered throughout the city. A credit card and €1 registration fee is required to hire bikes; just swipe your card in the machine and follow the instructions (provided in a number of languages). They can only be locked

---

MOVING ON?

For tips, recommendations and reviews, head to shop.lonelyplanet.com. If you're headed for Slovakia you can purchase a downloadable PDF of the Slovakia chapter from Lonely Planet's Western Europe guide.

up at a bike station, unless you have your own bike chain. A lost bike will set you back €600.

Vienna Explorer (Map p62; ☑ 890 96 82; www.viennaexplorer.com; Franz-Josefs-Kai 45; ⊘ 8.30am-7pm, tours Apr-Oct; Ⓜ Schwedenplatz, ⓐ 1 Salztorbrücke) Rents out bikes suitable for city cycling (from €14 per day) and excursions out of town (from €19 per day); it also does tours of the Wachau.

CAR & MOTORCYCLE

Due to a system of one-way streets and expensive parking, you're better off using Vienna's excellent public transport. If you do plan to drive in the city, take special care of the trams; they always have priority and vehicles must wait behind trams when they stop to pick up or set down passengers.

PUBLIC TRANSPORT

Vienna has an efficient, unified public-transport network. Flat-fare tickets are valid for trains, trams, buses, the underground (U-Bahn) and the S-Bahn regional trains. Services are frequent and you rarely have to wait more than 10 minutes. Sunday through Thursday, public transport starts around 5am or 6am; buses (with the exception of night buses) and trams finish between 11pm and midnight and S-Bahn and U-Bahn services between 12.30am and 1am. On Friday and Saturday nights the U-Bahn runs through the following morning at a reduced schedule. Free maps and information pamphlets are available from **Wiener Linien** (☑ 7909-100; www.wienerlinien.at).

Tickets and passes for Wiener Linien services (U-Bahn, trams and buses) can be purchased at U-Bahn stations and on trams and buses, in a *Tabakladen* (*Trafik*; tobacco kiosk), as well as from a few staffed ticket offices. They must be validated as you enter the station or board a tram or bus. If you're caught without a ticket you'll be fined €100.

Single ticket (*Einzelfahrschein*) – €2.10; good for one journey, with line changes; costs €2.20 if purchased on trams and buses (correct change required).

Children – For one, two or four trips for children between six and 15 years (ID or passport required). Tickets cost €1.10, €2.20 and €4.40 respectively.

24-/48-/72-hour tickets *(24-/48-/72-Stundenkarten)* – €7.10, €12.40 and €15.40 respectively. Require validation.

Weekly ticket *(Wochenkarte)* – €15.80; valid 12.01am Monday to 9am Monday of following week.

Monthly ticket *(Monatskarte)* – €47; valid from the 1st of the month to the last day of the month.

Vienna Card *(Die Wien-Karte)* – €19.90; 72 hours of unlimited travel from time of validation plus discounts.

Senior citizens – Those over 60 years of age can buy a €2.60 ticket that is valid for two trips; enquire at transport information offices.

TAXI & PEDAL TAXI

Taxis are reliable and relatively cheap by Western European standards. City journeys are metered; the minimum charge is roughly €3.80 from 6am to 11pm Monday to Saturday and €4.30 at any other time, plus a small per-kilometre fee.

A telephone reservation costs an additional €2.80. A small tip of 10% is expected. Taxis are easily found at train stations and taxi stands all over the city, or just flag them down in the street. To order one, call ☏ 40 100 or ☏ 60 160. These accept common credit and debit cards (check before hopping in, though).

Pedal taxis, known as *Faxis*, cost €5 for 2km or five minutes, or €10 for any longer or further ride within the Innere Stadt.

Lower Austria & Burgenland

Best Places to Eat

➡ Weingut Gabriel (p145)

➡ Zur Dankbarkeit (p148)

➡ Zum Kaiser von Österreich (p120)

➡ Mörwald Kloster Und (p120)

➡ Restaurant Loibnerhof (p122)

Best Places to Stay

➡ Weingut & Weingasthof Kloster am Spitz (p146)

➡ St Martins Therme & Lodge (p148)

➡ Restaurant & Hotel Schloss Grafenegg (p121)

➡ Hotel Schloss Dürnstein (p121)

Why Go?

Surrounding Vienna on all sides, Lower Austria is a cradle of Austrian civilisation and a region offering visitors one of the country's most lively cultural landscapes. Outdoor activities, some great museums, wine, food and a glimpse into the age of the Romans at Carnuntum make leaving the capital for a day or longer an attractive prospect.

And naturally everyone's heard of the Danube River which cuts a picturesque valley, the Wachau, through the region's northwest. A place of magnificent natural beauty, this is truly a European highlight for its vineyards, castles, abbeys and medieval villages.

To the south of the capital, undervisited Burgenland is all but the typical Austria of the holiday brochures; you won't find soaring mountains, glacial lakes and bombastic architecture here, just bucolic flatlands spread like a well-tenderised schnitzel around the jewel in its crown – Neusiedler See – a shallow mecca for extreme-water-sports fans and paddling toddlers alike.

When to Go

➡ Vist Burgenland, especially the Neusiedler See region in the north, between April and October.

➡ From November to March Burgenland goes into low-season hibernation and its prime attraction – the outdoors – becomes cold, grey and windswept.

➡ Visit Lower Austria during the April to October warm season, when the Wachau is often bathed in a soft light and you can make the most of the Danube River and its sights and activities.

➡ Autumn is the best time to enjoy wine in the Wachau, and from 11 November (St Martin's Day) each year young wine is sold.

Lower Austria & Burgenland Highlights

1 Wandering the cultural landscape of the Wachau in the **Danube Valley** (p116).

2 Sipping wines in one of the pretty *Heurigen* (wine taverns) in towns like **Rust** (p144).

3 Going baroque at Stift Melk, a magnificent monastery in **Melk** (p124), on the banks of the Danube.

4 Making a splash in the **Neusiedler See** (p144), Austria's slurping steppe lake.

5 Riding the footplate of the Semmeringbahn, a remarkable engineering feat in **Semmering** (p139).

6 Twitching at your leisure at Neusiedler See-Seewinkel National Park, a haven for bird life in **Seewinkel** (p148).

7 Taking in the thermal waters in **Frauenkirchen** (p148) at St Martins Therme & Lodge.

8 Scrambling through the cobbled streets of **Krems an der Donau** (p116).

9 Hiking or catching the train up **Schneeberg** (p140), Lower Austria's highest peak.

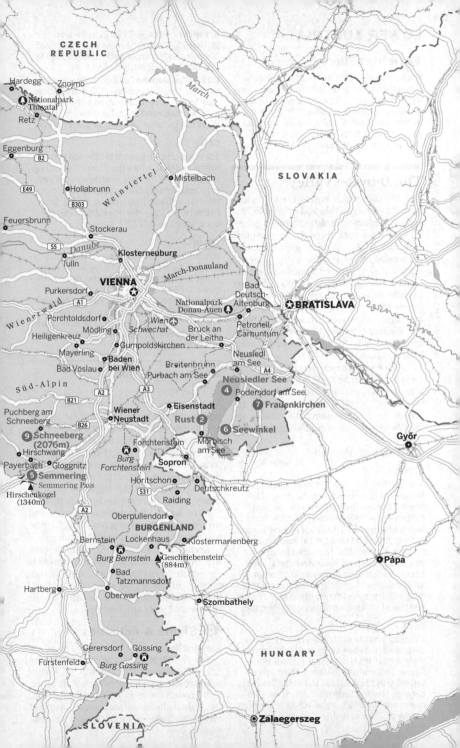

LOWER AUSTRIA

❶ Getting There & Around

Much of Lower Austria has excellent autobahn, rail and bus connections to the rest of the country. Travelling through the province can be done mostly by rail, but the Waldviertel north of the Danube and the Mostviertel south of the Danube have limited train connections. So it's better to have your own set of wheels, or use local buses.

The Danube Valley

The Danube, which enters Lower Austria from the west near Ybbs and exits in the east near Bratislava, Slovakia's capital, carves a picturesque path through the province's hills and fields. Austria's most spectacular section of the Danube is the dramatic stretch of river between Krems and der Donau and Melk, known as the Wachau. Here the landscape is characterised by vineyards, forested slopes, wine-producing villages and imposing fortresses at nearly every bend. The Wachau is today a Unesco World Heritage ite, due to its harmonious blend of natural and cultural beauty.

Tourismusverband Wachau Nibelungengau (🖉 02713-300 60 60; www.wachau.at; Schlossgasse 3, Spitz an der Donau; ⊙ 9am-4.30pm Mon-Thu, to 2.30pm Fri) are the people to approach for comprehensive information on the Wachau and the surrounding area.

❶ Getting Around

BICYCLE

A wonderfully flat cycle path runs along both sides of the Danube between Krems and Melk, passing through Krems, Dürnstein, Weissenkirchen and Spitz on the northern bank. Many hotels and *Pensionen* (B&Bs) are geared towards cyclists and most towns have at least one bikerental and repair shop. For more information, pick up a free copy of *The Donauradweg – Von Passau bis Bratislava* (from tourist offices or as a PDF download from http://brochures.austria.info), which provides details of distances, hotels and tourist information offices along the route.

BOAT

A popular way of exploring the region is by boat, particularly between Krems and Melk (through the Wachau); it's also possible to travel from Passau (in Germany) to Vienna. The most convenient time to take a boat trip on the Danube is between May and September, when boat companies operate on a summer schedule. Children receive a 50% discount.

Brandner (🖉 07433-25 90 21; www.brandner. at; Ufer 15, Wallsee) Services the Krems–Melk route one to two times daily from mid-April to late October; stops include Spitz.

DDSG Blue Danube (🖉 01-58 880; www.ddsg-blue-danube.at; Handelskai 265, Vienna) Operates boats between Krems and Melk, stopping in at Dürnstein and Spitz, from April to October. Bikes can be taken on board all boats for free.

CAR

The roads on both sides of the Danube between Krems and Melk, where the B3 and the B33 hug the contours of the river, lend themselves well to touring. Bridges taking motor vehicles cross the river at Krems (two crossing points), Melk, Pöchlarn and Ybbs. For a beautiful route, see our driving tour (p122).

TRAIN

Direct trains from Franz-Josefs-Bahnhof in Vienna to Krems are the easiest way into the valley. Trains from Vienna's Westbahnhof direct to Melk go via St Pölten and don't follow the Danube Valley. There is a seasonal rail service between Krems and Dürnstein but this doesn't run often enough to be of much use. Most take the hourly buses between the two towns that hug the Danube all the way.

Krems an der Donau

🖉 02732 / POP 23,900

Krems, as it's known to its friends, is the prettiest of the larger towns on the Danube and marks the beginning of the Wachau. Enjoyable eating and drinking, an atmospheric historical centre, rivers of top-quality wine from local vineyards and a couple of unexpected museums attract the summer tourist crowds, but the rest of the year things can be pretty quiet. Aimless wandering is the best plan of attack, dipping into churches and museums, strolling the banks of the Danube and sampling the local tipples as you go.

Krems has three parts: Krems to the east, the smaller settlement of Stein (formerly a separate town) to the west, and the connecting suburb of Und. Hence the local witticism: *Krems und Stein sind drei Städte* (Krems and Stein are three towns).

◉ Sights & Activities

Kunsthalle   GALLERY
(www.kunsthalle.at; Franz-Zeller-Platz 3; admission €10; ⊙ 10am-6pm) The flagship of Krems' **Kunstmeile** (www.kunstmeile-krems.at), an eclectic collection of galleries and museums, the Kunsthalle has a program of small but excellent changing exhibitions, which can

home in on anything from mid-19th-century landscapes to today's concept art. Guided **tours** run on Sundays at 2pm.

Karikaturmuseum
MUSEUM
(www.karikaturmuseum.at; Steiner Landstrasse 3a; admission €10; ☉10am-6pm) Austria's only caricature museum occupies a suitably tongue-in-cheek chunk of purpose-built architecture opposite the Kunsthalle. Changing exhibitions and a large permanent collection of caricatures of prominent Austrian and international figures make for a fun diversion.

Museum Krems
MUSEUM
(www.museumkrems.at; Körnermarkt 14; adult/child €5/3; ☉11am-6pm Wed-Sun Apr & May, daily Jun-Oct) Housed in a former Dominican monastery, the town's museum has collections of religious and modern art (including works by Kremser Schmidt, who painted the frescoes in Pfarrkirche St Veit), as well as winemaking artefacts and a section on the famous Krems mustard.

Pfarrkirche St Veit
CHURCH
(Pfarrplatz 5; ☉dawn-dusk) Known as the 'Cathedral of the Wachau', the large baroque parish church boasts colourful frescoes by Martin Johann Schmidt, an 18th-century local artist who was also known as Kremser Schmidt and occupied a house from 1756 near the Linzer Tor in Stein. The baroque building is the work of Cipriano Biasino who worked on several churches in the Wachau, including the abbey church at Stift Göttweig.

Piaristenkirche
CHURCH
(Frauenbergplatz; ☉dawn-dusk) Reached by a covered stairway from the Pfarrkirche, Krems' most impressive church has a wonderful webbed Gothic ceiling and huge, austerely plain windows. It's most atmospheric after dark when you can best imagine the effect the massive baroque altar would have had on 18th-century people.

Weingut der Stadt Krems
WINERY
(www.weingutstadtkrems.at; Stadtgraben 11; ☉9am-noon & 1-5pm Mon-Fri, 9am-noon Sat) This city-owned vineyard yielding 200,000 bottles per year (90% is Grüner Veltliner and Riesling) offers a variety of wine for sampling (and purchase).

🛏 Sleeping

Krems has plenty of places to kip but booking ahead is advised in summer. Stein has a good selection of private rooms and small guesthouses.

Gästehaus Einzinger
GUESTHOUSE $
(☑823 16; www.gaestehaus-einzinger.at; Steiner Landstrasse 82; s €38, d €58-70; ☎) The courtyard in this 16th-century guesthouse will blow away even the most history-hardened: blackbirds buzz and chirp, budgies taunt them from a cage, and one portico after another opens up around a courtyard spilling with foliage. The five singles and seven doubles are a little basic but some have views to night-lit Stift Göttweig.

Kolpinghaus
UNIVERSITY DORMS $
(☑835 41; www.kolpingkrems.at; Alauntalstrasse 95 & 97; s/d €38/71; ☉reception 8am-5pm Mon-Fri, to noon Sat & Sun; ℗☎) These superb student quarters are let out to travellers any time of year and are a great deal if you don't mind the slog up to the university. Some of the basic but comfortable rooms are huge and have bathrooms the size of some hotel singles, plus their own kitchens. Breakfast is included but don't get caught out by the early check-out time (10am). Outside of reception hours keys are left in a 'DigiSafe' outside if you've booked ahead – the code is emailed to you beforehand.

ÖAMTC Donaupark Camping
CAMPGROUND $
(☑844 55; www.donauparkcamping-krems.at; Yachthafenstrasse 19; camp sites per adult/child/car/tent €4.50/2.70/3.90/5; ☉Easter–mid-Oct; ℗) Well-maintained camping ground alongside the Danube with cycle hire and a snack bar.

Hotel-Garni Schauhuber
HOTEL $
(☑851 69; www.gaestehaus-schauhuber.at; Steiner Landstrasse 16; s/d €40/72; ☎) The Schauhuber is bright and tastefully furnished, with

---

WALKING KREMS

A walk through the cobblestone streets of Krems and Stein, especially at night, is one of the delights of a visit. Some of the most atmospheric parts to explore are on and behind **Schürerplatz** and **Rathausplatz** in Stein (don't miss these two wonderful squares), dominated by the baroque Mazzettihaus and the 18th-century Steiner Rathaus respectively; here you could be forgiven for thinking you had stumbled upon an isolated Adriatic village.

Krems an der Donau

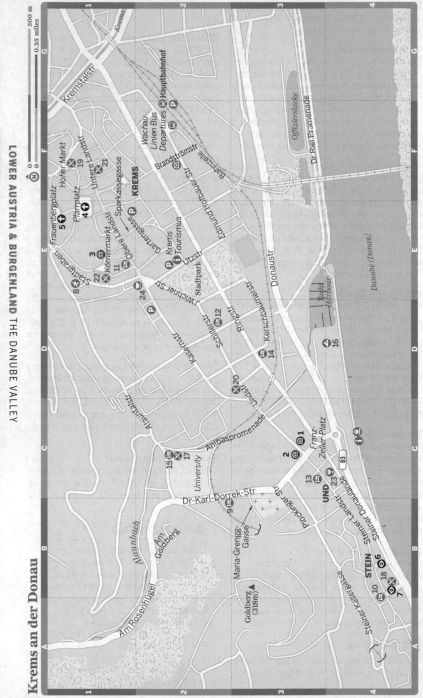

Krems an der Donau

sparkling tiled surfaces, whitewashed walls and large rooms. Breakfast is hearty enough for even the most ambitious Wachau explorer.

Hotel Alte Poste   HOTEL $
(☑822 76; www.altepost-krems.at; Obere Landstrasse 32; s €34-49, d €75-89; ℗) This guesthouse located in a historic 500-year-old house has an enchanting courtyard and 23 cosy rooms.

Jugendherberge   HOSTEL $
(☑834 52; oejhv.noe.krems@aon.at; Ringstrasse 77; dm €18; ⊙closed Nov-Mar; ℗) This popular Hostelling International (HI) hostel close to the tourist office is well geared for cyclists; it features a garage, an on-site bicycle-repair service and packed lunches.

★ **Arte Hotel Krems**   HOTEL $$
(☑71 123; www.arte-hotel.at; Dr-Karl-Dorrek-Strasse 23; s/d from €109/159; ℗⛷) This cutting-edge art hotel has 91 large, well-designed rooms scattered with big retro prints and patterns complementing the funky '60s-style furniture. The bathrooms (not the toilets) are open plan and aren't divided from the sleeping area, so you'd better be travelling with someone you know well. There's a separately owned wellness studio in the building, and a decent grill restaurant in the complex.

Hotel Unter den Linden   HOTEL $$
(☑82 115; www.udl.at; Schillerstrasse 5; s/d from €62/82; ⛷) This big, family-run hotel has knowledgable and helpful owners, 39 bright, welcoming rooms and a convenient location in Krems itself. The mix of historic and contemporary works well throughout and

breakfast is taken in the folksy dining room. Book ahead.

✕ Eating & Drinking

Don't omit a *Heuriger* visit; most are out of the centre and provide an authentic eating and drinking experience. They're only open for two- or three-week bursts during the year; pick up the schedule from the tourist office.

Filmbar im Kesselhaus   INTERNATIONAL $
(www.filmbar.at; Dr-Karl-Dorreck-Strasse 30; mains €6-12; ⊙10am-midnight Wed-Sun; ⛷) This sleek student restaurant and bar injects at least a bit of life into the otherwise very quiet university campus and has become *the* place in the area to meet up for a drink. There are regular art-house films and dishes contain organic, local ingredients.

Schwarze Kuchl   AUSTRIAN $
(Untere Landstrasse 8; mains €7-13; ⊙8.30am-7.30pm Mon-Fri, to 5pm Sat) For some good, honest local grub, head to this daytime tavern on the main drag through town where you can enjoy veal goulash, apricot-filled pancakes and Waldviertel *Gröstl* (potato-and-beef hotpot) while warming your toes on the huge tiled oven.

Gasthaus zum Elefanten   AUSTRIAN $
(www.zum-elefanten.at; Schürerplatz 10; mains €9.50-16.50; ⊙lunch & dinner Mon-Sat) Located on Stein's most romantic baroque piazza, the Elephant serves up local treats such as crayfish in spicy apricot sauce as well as gourmet burgers in an upmarket setting that won't threaten your budget. Bag a seat outside on summer evenings.

★**Zum Kaiser von Österreich** AUSTRIAN **$$**
(www.kaiser-von-oesterreich.at; Körnermarkt 9;
set dinner menu €36-48; ⊘dinner Tue-Sat) The
'Emperor of Austria' is one of Krems's best
gourmet eating spots and has a front door
of stickers to prove it. The inside is suitably
timber-rich and huntsman friendly, reflect-
ing the local fare you'll find on the set dinner
menus (which include a vegetarian option).
Local ingredients such as Wachau apples
and apricots, wild herbs and mushrooms,
Waldviertel fish and Weinviertel pumpkins
are used in the finely crafted, imaginative
dishes as much as possible.

Jell AUSTRIAN **$$**
(www.amon-jell.at; Hoher Markt 8-9; mains €12.50-
21; ⊘lunch & dinner Tue-Fri, lunch Sat & Sun) Occupying a gorgeous stone house, Jell is hard
to beat for a rustic atmosphere and fine
wine from its own vineyard. Its friendly staff
also adds to a great regional experience; located just east of Pfarrkirche St Veit.

★**Mörwald Kloster Und** AUSTRIAN **$$$**
(⊘70 493; www.moerwald.at; Undstrasse 6; mains
€35-41; ⊘lunch & dinner Tue-Sat) Mörwald is
the most central of a crop of restaurants run
by Toni Mörwald outside Vienna. It offers
exquisite delights ranging from roast pigeon
breast to beef, poultry and fish dishes with
French angles. A lovely yard and an impres-
sive wine selection round off one of the best
restaurants in the Wachau.

Stadtcafe Ulrich CAFE
(www.stadtcafe-ulrich.at; Südtirolerplatz 7; ⊘7am-
11pm Mon-Thu, to midnight Sat, 9am-11pm Sun)
Krems' busiest cafe is this elegantly high-
ceilinged Viennese job next to the Steinertor
(the medieval gateway into the Old Town),
good for your first and last cuppa of the day,
and everything in between as well.

Piano BAR
(www.piano-krems.at; Steiner Landstrasse 21;
⊘5pm-2am Mon-Thu, to 3am Fri & Sat, to midnight
Sun) A crossover crowd of students, young
workers and mellow jazz types pack in
tightly at this lively and offbeat pub. It does
a couple of local sausage snacks and sand-
wiches to go with its expertly assembled se-
lection of beers.

ⓘ Information

Krems Tourismus (⊘82 676; www.krems.
info; Utzstrasse 1; ⊘9am-6pm Mon-Fri) Helpful
office with another branch (⊘75 146; Steiner

Donaulände; ⊘9.30am-6pm Mon-Sat, to 4pm
Sun) at the boat quay.
Main post office (Brandströmstrasse 4-6)

ⓘ Getting There & Around

For boats, the river station is near Donaustrasse,
about 1.5km west of the train station.
Autovermietung Becker (⊘82 433; www.
rent.becker.at; Wachauer Strasse 30) rents cars
from €65 per day.

Frequent daily trains connect Krems with
Vienna's Franz-Josefs-Bahnhof (€14, one hour).
Wachau Linien (⊘0810 222 324; www.vor.
at) runs buses along the Danube Valley as far
as Melk (hourly, one hour). The Wachau Ticket
(€10) is available from the driver and gives one
day's unlimited travel on all buses (including
Krems city buses) and the Danube ferries.

Stift Göttweig

Brooding from its hilltop opposite Krems,
Stift Göttweig (Göttweig Abbey; ⊘02732-8558
1231; www.stiftgoettweig.at; Furth bei Göttweig;
adult/child €7/3.50; ⊘9am-6pm) was founded
in 1083 and restored after a devastating
fire in the early 18th century. Aside from
the grand view back across the Danube Val-
ley from its garden terrace and restaurant,
the abbey's highlights include the **Imperial
Staircase**, with a heavenly ceiling fresco
painted by Paul Troger in 1739, and the over-
the-top baroque interior of the **Stiftskirche**
(Abbey Church), with a Kremser Schmidt
work in the crypt. Guided **tours** at 11am and
3pm take in the abbey's **Imperial Wing** (per
person €2); the church can be viewed with-
out a tour.

The best way to reach Göttweig is by train
from Krems, though it's a steep walk uphill
from the Klein Wien station (€2.20, 10 min-
utes, every two hours).

Schloss Grafenegg

About 10km east of Krems near the road
to Tulln stands **Schloss Grafenegg** (www.
grafenegg.com; Grafenegg 10; adult/child €5/3;
⊘10am-5pm Tue-Sat, mid-Apr–Oct), a castle
with the look and feel of an ornate Tudor
mansion set in English woods. Built in a re-
vivalist (neo-Gothic) style by Leopold Ernst
in the mid-19th century, it is now a venue
for exhibitions and concerts but you can ex-
plore the interior, which includes a chapel
and decadent state rooms. The castle is
complemented by the addition of the inno-
vative, modern **Wolkenturm** (Cloud Tower),

which is used for concerts in the parkland in fine weather.

The wine bar **Vinothegg** (⊘ 11am-6pm Tue-Sat, 10am-6pm Sun Mar–mid-Dec) here has over 130 wines from the Kamptal. The castle's manicured gardens are perfect for a picnic, but for fine dining don't pass up **Restaurant & Hotel Schloss Grafenegg** (☑ 02735-2616-0; www.moerwald.at; Grafenegg 12; s €89-118, d €118-188; ⊘ 10am-10pm Wed-Sun Easter-Dec; ☑), owned by celebrity chef and winemaker Toni Mörwald. Two kilometres away in Feuersbrunn is Mörwald's **Hotel Villa Katharina** (☑ 02738-229 80; www.moerwald.at; Kleine Zeile 10; s €89-104, d €118-138; P �)), with its **Restaurant zur Traube** (☑ 02738-229 80; Kleine Zeile 13-17; mains €16.50-24.50; ⊘ lunch & dinner, closed Mon-Wed Jul & Aug; ☑).

To reach Schloss Grafenegg, take the train to nearby Wagram-Grafenegg (€3.80, 20 minutes, around nine daily) and walk 2km northeast to the castle.

Dürnstein

☑ 02711 / POP 970

The pretty town of Dürnstein, on a supple curve in the Danube, is not only known for its beautiful buildings but also for the castle above the town where Richard I (the Lionheart) of England was once imprisoned.

Busy with visitors in summer, Dürnstein completely shuts up shop over the winter.

⊙ Sights

Kuenringerburg   CASTLE

FREE Kuenringerburg, the castle high on the hill above the town, is where Richard the Lionheart was incarcerated from 1192 to 1193. His crime was to have insulted Leopold V; his misfortune was to be recognised despite his disguise when journeying through Austria on his way home from the Holy Lands. His liberty was achieved only upon the payment of an enormous ransom of 35,000kg of silver (which partly funded the building of Wiener Neustadt). It was also here that the singing minstrel Blondel attempted to rescue his sovereign.

An easy, yellow path starts at the Kremser Gate (marked 'Burgruine'); a more difficult route begins in the Altstadt (old town). It takes about 25 minutes to walk up to the ruins whichever path you follow. The ruins are great for scrambling around and there's an open-air exhibition of sorts

giving background on the castle's history and the personalities associated with it.

Chorherrenstift   ABBEY

(www.stiftduernstein.at; Stiftshof; adult/child €2.80/1.50; ⊘ 9am-6pm Apr-Oct) Of the picturesque 16th-century houses and other prominent buildings lining Dürnstein's streets, the meticulously restored Chorherrenstift is the most impressive. It's all that remains of the former Augustinian monastery originally founded in 1410; it received its baroque facelift in the 18th century (overseen by Josef Munggenast, among others). Kremser Schmidt did many of the ceiling and altar paintings. Entry includes access to the porch overlooking the Danube and an exhibition on the Augustinian monks who once ruled the roost here (up until the monastery was dissolved by Joseph II in 1788).

🛏 Sleeping & Eating

Pension Böhmer   GUESTHOUSE $

(☑ 239; Hauptstrasse 22; s €42, d €52-62; P) This small *Pension* in the heart of town has comfortable rooms that won't cost you a king's ransom. It's only a hop, step and a crawl to the castle from here.

★**Hotel Schloss Dürnstein**   HOTEL $$

(☑ 212; www.schloss.at; Dürnstein 2; s €139-169, d €185-225; ⊘ Apr-mid-Oct; P @ �) This castle is the last word in luxury in town and also boasts a high-end restaurant. Most rooms are tastefully furnished in antiques, a massage can be arranged for your arrival, and there's a sauna and steam bath. The terrace restaurant enjoys staggering views over the river. Stay 10 nights and you get a night on the house (which might be useful if you happen to be broke by that stage). Closed over the winter.

A HIKE FROM DÜRNSTEIN

After visiting the Kuenringerburg, where Richard the Lionheart was incarcerated, hike the Schlossbergweg (marked green) from there to **Fesselhütte** (www.fesslhuette.at; Dürsteiner Waldhütten 23; ⊘ 9.30am-6pm Wed-Sun Easter-Oct), about one hour by foot from the castle, to enjoy sausage, soup or wine at this forest tavern. A road also leads up here from Weissenkirchen.

Hotel Sänger Blondel HOTEL $$

(☑ 253; www.saengerblondel.at; Klosterplatz/Dürnstein 64; s €75, d €101-121; P @ 🖬) One of the best options in town, this hotel has generously cut rooms furnished in light woods, some with sofas. A couple have views to the Danube and others look out onto the castle or garden.

Weinschenke Altes Presshaus CAFE $

(Dürnstein 10; snacks & mains €3.50-9.50; ⊙ 2pm-late Tue-Sat, from 11am Sun Apr-Oct) Centrally located *Heuriger*-style place selling local wine (mainly Veltliner), snacks and more filling meals such as goulash, schnitzel and wild boar steaks. Very popular among visitors and locals alike.

★ Restaurant Loibnerhof AUSTRIAN $$

(☑ 82 890; www.loibnerhof.at; Unterloiben 7; mains €15-26; ⊙ 11.30am-midnight Wed-Sun) Situated 1.5km east of Dürnstein's centre, this family-run restaurant inside a 400-year-old building has a lovely garden where you can sample some delectable seasonal fare.

❶ Information

High visitor numbers didn't stop Dürnstein scrapping its tourist office in 2013 – try the **Rathaus** (town hall; ☑ 219; www.duernstein.at; Hauptstrasse 25; ⊙ 8am-noon Mon-Fri, plus 1-4pm Mon, 1-7pm Tue), which also has some information.

❶ Getting There & Away

Brandner (www.brandner.at) boats connect Dürnstein with Krems (20 to 30 minutes) once or twice daily from mid-April to late October. The landing station is near Chorherrenstift.

Dürnstein is linked to Melk (45 minutes, hourly) and Krems (25 minutes, 18 daily) by bus. This is by far the most convenient way to travel.

Dürnstein's train station is called Dürnstein-Oberloiben, with connections to Krems (17 minutes, three daily) and Weissenkirchen (seven minutes, three daily).

Weissenkirchen

☑ 02715 / POP 1440

In Weissenkirchen, 12km from Krems, the main attraction is the pretty hilltop **fortified parish church**, the front doors of which are approached along a labyrinth of covered pathways. This Gothic church was built in the 15th century and has a baroque altar and a garden terrace with good views of the Danube. Below the church is the

🏃 Driving & Cycling Tour
The Danube Valley

START KREMS
END KREMS
LENGTH 150KM, ONE DAY

From the Krems-Stein roundabout in ❶ **Krems an der Donau** (p116) take the B3 southwest towards Spitz. About 3km from Krems-Stein you approach the small settlement of Unterloiben, where on the right you can see the ❷ **Franzosendenkmal** (French Monument), erected in 1805 to celebrate the victory of Austrian and Russian troops here over Napoleon. Shortly afterwards the lovely town of ❸ **Dürnstein** (p121), 6km from Krems, comes into view with its blue-towered Chorherrenstift backed by Kuenringerburg, the castle where Richard the Lionheart was imprisoned in 1192.

The valley is punctuated by picturesque terraced vineyards as you enter the heart of the Wachau. In ❹ **Weissenkirchen** (p122), 12km from Krems, you'll find a pretty fortified parish church on the hilltop. The Wachau Museum here houses work by artists of the Danube school.

A couple of kilometres on, just after Wösendorf, you find the church of ❺ **St Michael**, in a hamlet with 13 houses. If the kids are along for this ride, now's the time to ask them to count the terracotta hares on the roof of the church (seven, in case they're not reading this!).

Some 17km from Krems, the pretty town of ❻ **Spitz** (p124) swings into view, surrounded by vineyards and lined with quiet cobblestone streets. Some good trails lead across hills and to *Heurigen* (wine taverns) here (start from the church).

Turn right at Spitz onto the B217 (Ottenschläger Strasse). The terraced hill on your right is ❼ **1000-Eimer-Berg**, so-named for its reputed ability to yield 1000 buckets of wine each season. On your left, high above the valley opening, is the castle ruin ❽ **Burgruine Hinterhaus**. Continue along the B217 to the mill wheel and turn right towards ❾ **Burg Oberranna** (p124), 6km west of Spitz in Mühldorf. Surrounded by woods, this castle and hotel overlooking the valley is furnished with period pieces and has a refreshing old-worldly feel.

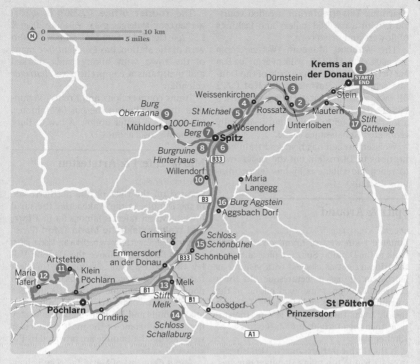

From here, backtrack down to the B3 and continue the circuit. The valley opens up and on the left, across the Danube, you glimpse the ruins of Burg Aggstein.

10 Willendorf, located 21km from Krems, is where a 25,000-year-old figurine of Venus was discovered. The original is today housed in the Naturhistorisches Museum in Vienna. Continuing along the B3, the majestic Stift Melk rises up across the river. There's some decent swimming in the backwaters here if you're game to dip into the Danube.

At Klein Pöchlarn a sign indicates a first turn-off on Artstettner Strasse (L7255); follow it for 5km to **11 Artstetten**, (p124) unusual for its many onion domes. From here, the minor road L7257 winds 6.5km through a sweeping green landscape to **12 Maria Taferl** (p124) high above the Danube Valley.

Head 6km down towards the B3. Turn left at the B3 towards Krems and follow the ramp veering off to the left and across the river at the Klein Pöchlarn bridge. Follow the road straight ahead to the B1 (Austria's longest road) and turn left onto this towards Melk.

This first section along the south bank is uninteresting, but it soon improves. Unless the weather isn't playing along, across the river you can make out Artstetten in the distance, and shortly **13 Stift Melk** (p125), will rise up ahead in a golden shimmering heap.

From Stift Melk, a 7km detour leads south to the splendid Renaissance castle of **14 Schloss Schallaburg** (p125). To reach the castle from the abbey in Melk, follow the signs to the *Bahnhof* (train station) and Lindestrasse east, turn right into Hummelstrasse/Kirschengraben (L5340) and follow the signs to the castle.

Backtrack to the B33. Be careful to stay on the south side of the river. When you reach the corner of Abt-Karl-Strasse and Bahnhofstrasse, go right and right again at the river. Follow the B1 for 4km to **15 Schloss Schönbühel**, a 12th-century castle standing high on a rock some 5km northeast of Melk. Continue along this lovely stretch of the B33 in the direction of Krems. About 10km from Schloss Schönbühel the ruins of **16 Burg Aggstein** swing into view. This 12th-century hilltop castle was built by the Kuenringer family and now offers a grand vista of the Danube.

About 27km from Melk some pretty cliffs rise up above the road. From Mautern it's a detour of about 6km to **17 Stift Göttweig** (p120).

charming **Teisenhoferhof** arcaded court-yard, with a covered gallery and lashings of flowers and dried corn.

The **Wachau Museum** (Weissenkirchen 32; adult/child €5/2.50; ⏲10am-5pm Tue-Sun Apr-Oct) houses works by artists of the Danube school. The **Raffelsberger Hof** (⏰22 01; www.raffelsbergerhof.at; Freisingerplatz 54; s €88-112, d €122-142; ⏲mid-Apr–Nov; P@🖥) is a four-star hotel in a small but beautifully renovated Renaissance castle.

Weissenkirchen has boat and train connections to Dürnstein but the easiest way to reach the village is by bus (eight minutes, 18 daily).

Spitz & Around

☎ 02713 / POP 1700

Situated 17km west of Krems on the north bank of the Danube, Spitz is a pleasant town that doesn't get as clogged with visitors as Dürnstein. It has a picturesque old town centre, and offers some good hiking in the surrounding forests and vineyards. To reach the old town, turn left after leaving the station then head right up Marktstrasse to Kirchenplatz.

If the Gothic **parish church** (Marktstrasse) in Spitz is one too many Danube churches, pick up some maps from the tourist office and hike up to **Burgruine Hinterhaus** (Hinterhaus castle ruin) on the bluff for fantastic views of the valley; other trails run through the forests of the **Jauerling Naturpark** (Jauerling Nature Reserve) behind the castle ruin. Hikes offering picturesque views also begin from **Rotes Tor** (Red Gate, 15 minutes walk from the church), a remnant of the town's gates and the last one to be taken by the Swedes in the Thirty Years' War in 1618–48 – it was reputedly red from the blood of battle. It's a nice spot for a picnic with gobsmacking Wachau views all about.

Six kilometres west of Spitz, **Mühldorf** is home to the castle and hotel **Burg Oberranna** (⏰8221; www.burg-oberranna.at; s/d €88/148; P🅿). Surrounded by woods and overlooking the valley, it is furnished with period pieces and has a refreshing old-world feel.

If you decide to stay in Spitz, the tourist office can help with accommodation, or you can look for signs advertising private rooms. **Hotel Wachauer Hof** (⏰2303; www.wachauerhof-spitz.at; Hauptstrasse 15; s €46-52 d €76-88; P) is very central, with comfortable rooms and a restaurant with outside seating in summer.

The **tourist office** (⏰2363; www.spitz-wachau.com; Mittergasse 3a; ⏲9am-12.30pm & 1.30-7pm Mon-Sat, 2-6pm Sun), situated 400m west of the station, has excellent free maps of the town with hiking trails marked and maintains a comprehensive *Heuriger* calendar.

Trains connect Spitz and Krems (35 minutes, three daily) but the bus (35 minutes, 20 daily) is a better option. A taxi to Burg Oberanna costs about €17.

Maria Taferl & Artstetten

☎ 07413 / POP 850

Located off the river on the northern side of the Danube in the Waldviertel, the small town of Maria Taferl is famous for its **Pfarr-und Wallfahrtskirche Maria Taferl** (Parish & Pilgrimage Church; www.basilika.at; Maria Taferl 1; ⏲7am-8pm) high above the Danube Valley. Created by Jakob Prandtauer (of Melk fame), this baroque church has two onion domes and dark dome-frescoes. Its altar is a complex array of figures in gold. You'll find lots of hotels and B&Bs if you decide to stay in town, and some of the most spectacular views across the Danube are provided by the village's location.

About 6km east of Maria Taferl and about the same distance off the Danube is **Artstetten**, where there's also a castle. This was created out of a 13th-century medieval castle and has seen modifications over the past 700 years, including Renaissance features. It gained fame and glory after passing into the hands of the Habsburgs in the early 19th century, winding up in the possession of Archduke Franz Ferdinand. Inside is a **museum** (www.schloss-artstetten.at; Artstetten 1; adult/child €8/5; ⏲9am-5.30pm Apr-Oct) devoted to the luckless heir, displaying photos and stories of his and his wife's time at the castle and their fateful trip to Sarajevo where his murder kicked off WWI. Their tomb is in the church.

You'll probably need your own wheels to visit Maria Taferl and Artstetten as no trains and very few buses go there.

Melk & Around

☎ 02752 / POP 5200

With its blockbuster abbey-fortress set high above the valley, Melk is a high point of any visit to the Danube Valley. Separated from the river by a stretch of woodland, this pretty town makes for an easy and rewarding day trip from Krems or even Vienna. Combine a visit with nearby Renaissance Schloss Schallaburg, 6km south of town, and you have yourself a day packed with architectural bliss.

Melk is one of the most popular destinations in Austria so you certainly won't be alone on its cobbled streets. It's also one of the few places in the Wachau that has a pulse in winter, making it a year-round option.

◎ Sights

Stift Melk
ABBEY

(Benedictine Abbey of Melk; ☑555 232; www.stift-melk.at; Abt Berthold Dietmayr Strasse 1; adult/child €10/5.50, with guided tour €12/7.50; ◎9am-5.30pm May-Sep, tours 11am & 2pm Oct-Apr) Of the many abbeys in Austria, Stift Melk is the most famous. Historically, Melk was of great importance to the Romans and later to the Babenbergs, who built a castle here. In 1089 the Babenberg margrave Leopold II donated the castle to Benedictine monks, who converted it into a fortified abbey. Fire destroyed the original edifice, which was completely baroque-ified between 1702 and 1738 according to plans by Jakob Prandtauer and his disciple, Josef Munggenast. It's claimed nine million bricks were used to create the 500 rooms – don't worry though, you don't have to visit them all! (Most of the complex is taken up by a school, monks' quarters and offices.)

Possibly Lower Austria's finest, the huge monastery **church** is enclosed by the buildings, but dominates the complex with its twin spires and high octagonal dome. The interior is baroque gone barmy, with regiments of smirking cherubs, gilt twirls and polished faux marble. The theatrical high-altar scene, depicting St Peter and St Paul (the two patron saints of the church), is by Peter Widerin. Johann Michael Rottmayr created most of the ceiling paintings, including those in the dome.

Other highlights include the **bibliothek** (library) and the **Marmorsaal** (Marble Hall); both have amazing *trompe l'œil*–painted tiers on the ceiling (by Paul Troger) to give the illusion of greater height, and ceilings are slightly curved to aid the effect. Eleven of the imperial rooms, where dignitaries (including Napoleon) stayed, are now used as a somewhat overcooked concept **museum.**

Before or after a tour of the main complex, take a spin around the **Nordbastei** where you'll discover some quirky temporary exhibitions, a viewing terrace and the *Stift's* gift shop.

A combined ticket with Schloss Schallaburg is €17.50. From around November to March, the monastery can only be visited by guided **tour** (◎11am & 2pm daily). Always phone or email ahead, even in summer, to ensure you get an English-language tour.

Schloss Schallaburg
PALACE

(☑02754-6317; www.schallaburg.at; Schallaburg 1; adult/child €10/3.50; ◎9am-5pm Mon-Fri, to 6pm Sat & Sun Apr-early Nov) This Renaissance palace set in lovely gardens is famous not only for its stunning architecture but also for the innovative exhibitions it houses. Architecturally, it boasts some 400 terracotta sculptures, completed between 1572 and 1573, the largest of which support the upper-storey arches of the palace. Every year the building hosts a prestigious exhibition based on a chosen cultural theme – shows in recent years have focused on The Beatles, Venice and Byzantium. Combined tickets with Stift Melk cost €17.50. To reach Schallaburg, take the shuttle bus (€4) which leaves Melk train station at 10.40am, 1.15pm and 4.45pm.

🛏 Sleeping & Eating

The tourist office maintains a comprehensive list of private rooms. Otherwise there's no shortage of places to lay your head in Melk.

Hotel Restaurant zur Post
HOTEL $$

(☑523 45; www.post-melk.at; Linzer Strasse 1; s €63-85, d €103-120; 🅿@🛜) A bright and pleasant hotel in the heart of town offering 25 large, comfortable rooms in plush colours with additional fancy touches such as brass bed lamps. There's a sauna, facilities for massages and free bike use for guests. The understatedly stylish restaurant cooks up mainly solid Austrian classics.

Hotel Wachau
HOTEL $$

(☑525 31; www.hotel-wachau.at; Am Wachberg 3; s €62-82, d €95-135; 🅿🛜) For 21st-century comfort, try this hotel 2km southeast of the train station. The restaurant here specialises in well-prepared regional cuisine.

Zum Fürsten INTERNATIONAL $

(☑523 43; Rathausplatz 3; mains €3.70-9.60; ⊙10.30am-11pm) Right at the foot of the Stift.After a tour relax on faux velvet 1970s seating at this popular cafe serving pastas, strudel, chilli con carne and other international favourites.

❶ Information

Melk Tourist Office (☑511 60; www.stadt-melk.at; Kremser Strasse 5; ⊙9.30am-6pm Mon-Sat, to 4pm Sun Apr-Oct, 9am-5pm Mon-Thu, to 2.30pm Fri Nov-Mar)

❶ Getting There & Away

Boats leave from the canal by Pionierstrasse, 400m north of the abbey. Wachau Linien (p120) runs buses along the Danube valley between Melk and Krems (hourly, one hour).

Wachau Touristik Bernhardt (☑02713-2222; www.wachau-touristik.at; per day €12) rents out bicycles from the ferry station in Melk and from the train station in Spitz.

Melk has the following train connections:
Salzburg €38.80, at least hourly, 2½ hours (change in St Pölten or Amstetten).
St Pölten €4.80, at least hourly, 20 minutes.
Vienna Westbahnhof €15.90, hourly, one hour 20 minutes.

Tulln

☑02272 / POP 15,200

Tulln, the home town of painter Egon Schiele and situated 30km northwest of Vienna on the Danube, has a couple of interesting museums and can be easily visited on a day trip from Vienna or Krems.

◉ Sights

Egon Schiele Museum MUSEUM
(www.egon-schiele.eu; Donaulände 28; adult/child €5/3; ⊙10am-5pm Wed-Sun Apr-Oct) The Egon Schiele Museum, housed in a former jail near the Danube, vividly presents the story of the life of the Tulln-born artist. It presents around 100 of his paintings and sketches, and a mock-up of the cell where he was briefly imprisoned. He fell foul of the law in 1912 when 125 of his erotic drawings were seized; some were of pubescent girls, and Schiele was also in trouble for allowing children to view his explicit works. Since 2013 hard-core Schiele fans have been able to visit his **birthplace** (Hauptbahnhof Tulln, Bahnhofstrasse 69; admission €2; ⊙9am-8pm) at Tulln's train station.

Museum im Minoritenkloster MUSEUM

(Minoritenplatz 1) This city-promoted museum space features some excellent changing exhibitions based around mostly Austrian artists. Recent shows have featured Schiele (surprise, surprise), Wilhelm Kaufmann and Paschek. Admission prices vary with the exhibition. It adjoins the Minorite church.

Minoritenkirche CHURCH

(Minoritenplatz 1; ⊙8am-7pm) Alongside the tourist office, the rococo Minorite church from 1739 is decorated with magnificent ceiling frescoes dedicated to St Johannes Nepomuk.

Pfarrkirche St Stephan CHURCH

(Wiener Strasse 20; ⊙7.30am-7.30pm) This parish church combines Gothic and baroque elements, along with the wonderful 13th-century frescoed Romanesque funerary chapel.

🛏 Sleeping & Eating

Junges Hotel Tulln HOSTEL $
(☑651 65 10; www.tulln.noejhw.at; Marc-Aurel-Park 1; dm/s/d €22/32/54; P) Youth hostel near the Danube catering for seminar guests as well as tourists. Dorms sleep between four and eight guests.

Donaupark Camping CAMPGROUND $
(☑652 00; www.campingtulln.at; Donaulände 76; camp sites per adult/tent & car €7/5; ⊙Apr-Oct; 🛜) This campground is located just east of the centre on the river and alongside a pretty forest.

Hotel Nibelungenhof HOTEL $$
(☑626 58; www.nibelungenhof.info; Donaulände 34; s €48-69, d €98; 🛜) Situated alongside the Danube River with a lovely terrace garden and cafe-restaurant downstairs, Hotel Nibelungenhof has individually furnished rooms in bright and attractive colours. The lounge has a large library of books and a real fire.

Gasthaus zur Sonne AUSTRIAN $$
(☑646 16; Bahnhofstrasse 48; mains €9-25; ⊙lunch & dinner Tue-Sat) This traditional restaurant serves excellent dishes such as goulash and veal liver in a balsamic vinegar. Reserve ahead as it's popular.

❶ Information

Tourist office (☑675 66; www.tullner-donauraum.at; Minoritenplatz 2; ⊙9am-7pm Mon-Fri, 10am-7pm Sat & Sun, closed Sat & Sun Oct-Apr) One block north of Hauptplatz from the fountain end.

ℹ Getting There & Around

Several regional and S-Bahn trains each hour connect Tulln with Vienna's Franz-Josefs-Bahnhof (€7.80, 30 to 45 minutes) and hourly trains go to Krems (€10, 35 minutes).

Tulln and its tourist office are well set up for cyclists, as the Danube cycleway runs alongside the river on the town's northern border. Tulln has numerous Leihradl stations where you can hire a bicycle.

Waldviertel & Weinviertel

Forming a broad swath across Lower Austria north of the Danube, the undervisited Waldviertel (Woods Quarter) begins near Krems and the Kamptal in the east (the latter borders the largely agricultural and winemaking region, the Weinviertel or 'Wine Quarter') and ends at the Czech border in the north and west. The Waldviertel is a picturesque region of rolling hills and rural villages, and while there isn't actually much forest to speak of, there are a number of fine attractions and retreats. The Kamptal in particular is a great place for escaping the tourist crowds.

The Waldviertel's **tourism website** (www.waldviertel.at) is a good place to start for information and planning.

ℹ Getting There & Away

Zwettl is best reached by frequent buses from Krems (€10, 45 minutes to 1¼ hours). From Horn, regular buses run to Altenburg (€2.60, 11 minutes).

Several direct trains run from Krems to Horn daily (€10, 70 minutes), stopping at Rosenburg (€7.80, one hour). Eggenburg has plenty of daily train connections to Tulln (€10, 40 minutes).

Drosendorf

☏ 02915 / POP 1200

Situated on the extreme northern fringe of the Waldviertel, hard on the Czech border, the lovely fortressed town of Drosendorf is often overlooked by the Viennese – it's simply too far-flung. Yet, with a completely intact town wall, it is a unique and beautiful town and one well worth the trouble it takes to reach it.

An **information service** (☏232 10; ⊘8am-4.30pm Mon-Thu, to 12.30pm Fri) is located inside the castle, and an information stand with a useful walk-by-numbers brochure (in German) as well as an accommodation list is situated on Hauptplatz, inside

the walls. The fortress walk also begins here; it passes the **castle**, a mostly baroque structure on top of Romanesque foundations, and exits through the **Hornertor**, the main gate in the southeast dating from the 13th to 15th centuries. Cross the moat and follow the wall clockwise.

For overnight stays, the best option is **Schloss Drosendorf** (☏232 10; www.schloss-drosendorf.at; Schlossplatz 1; s €38-44 d €68; **P@**). Poppies – or rather poppy-seed specialities – are a big local industry in the Waldviertel. **MOKA** (☏22 27; www.moka.at; Hauptplatz 5; ⊘9am-6pm Thu-Mon Apr-Oct) does a delicious poppy-seed cake and coffee, and also has a few comfortable rooms right on Hauptplatz (singles and doubles €70 to €120).

To reach Drosendorf from Vienna (Praterstern station), take the train leaving every two hours to Retz (€15.80, 70 minutes), making sure it connects with one of several buses on weekdays (€6.80, one hour). The only way into the Czech Republic from here is to backtrack to Retz from where there are trains to Znojmo, or hike (or take a taxi) 6km to the first village (Vratěnín) on the other side of the border, from where there are buses further into Moravia.

Nationalpark Thayatal

Tight against the border of Austria and the Czech Republic (a stretch of the old Iron Curtain) in the northwestern reaches of the Weinviertel is Austria's smallest national park, the Thayatal. This unique piece of landscape is actually two parks; its other half, Podyjí National Park, is located across the border. Of the 3000 plant species found in Austria, about 1300 occur in Thayatal. The landscape consists of a deep canyon cut by the Thaya river (the Dyje in Czech), numerous rock formations and steep slopes. Walking is by far the most popular activity in the park, with trails sometimes crossing from one country into the next.

The **Nationalparkhaus** (☏02949-7005-0; www.np-thayatal.at; exhibition adult/child €4/2.50; ⊘9am-6pm mid-Mar–Sep, 10am-4pm Oct), near Hardegg, has loads of information and also has an exhibition on the park's ecology. Hardegg is the natural jump-off point for the park, and is not easy to get to without your own transport; it's best approached by train from Vienna to Retz (€15.80, one hour), from where you take a bus to Pleising, then another to Hardegg.

WALDVIERTEL ROAD TRIP

The Kamptal, immediately northeast of Krems towards Langenlois, is a major centre of winegrowing and one of the most picturesque entry points into the Waldviertel. This route, which can be done by train between Krems (or Hadersdorf) train station and Schloss Rosenburg (€7.80, one hour, hourly), combines traditional *Heurigen* (wine taverns) with a castle, top-class dining, wellness and wine.

From Krems the Weinstrasse Kremstal (Krems Valley Wine Rd; B35) leads northeast. About 2km past Gedersdorf – just before Hadersdorf train station – veer right under the railway line and immediately left to Diendorf, where you find **Hofkäserei Robert Paget** (www.mozzaundjazz.at; Kirchenweg 2, Diendorf am Kamp; ⊙10am-6pm Fri & Sat). Here Robert Paget produces Austria's finest buffalo mozzarella cheese, as well as goat's cheese that you can buy from the shop. Cyclists and walkers can continue along the tiny Diendorfer Weg about another 1.5km to Hadersdorf's Hauptplatz, the magnificent central town square with Renaissance and baroque buildings, some of them *Heurigen* (by car take the B43).

In Hadersdorf, visit **Eat Art** (www.spoerri.at; Hauptlatz 23; mains €9-17; ⊙5-10pm Thu, 11am-10pm Fri, 9am-10pm Sat, 10am-5pm Sun; 🚗), part of the food and museum concept, **Eat Art & Ab Art** (Hauptlatz 23), by Romanian-born Swiss artist Daniel Spoerri.

About 6km south of Diendorf is Schloss Grafenegg (p120), the castle with the look and feel of an ornate Tudor mansion set in English woods.

Continuing north, the wine-focused **Loisium Hotel** (☎02734-77 100-0; www.loisium-hotel.at; Loisium Allee 2, Langenlois; s €134-150, d €188-205, mains €16-30, 4-course menu €49; ⊙lunch & dinner; 🅿@🛜🏊) is a useful stopover. Highlights are massages and wine treatments (some using sparkling wine or grape-seed oil), large spa facilities and the 20m heated outdoor pool that's open all year. Alongside the hotel is the **Loisium Weinwelt** (www.loisium.at; Loisium Allee 1; 90min audio tour adult/child €11.50/6.30; ⊙10am-7pm), an aluminium cube designed by the New York architect Steven Holl that slopes to the south. Multilingual audio tours here set off every 30 minutes and lead you through the 1.5km network of ancient tunnels. Bring a pullover as it's chilly. You can also taste several vintages.

Further north from Langelois, the B34 passes through the picturesque Naturpark Kamptal-Schönberg to **Schloss Rosenburg** (www.rosenburg.at; Rosenburg am Kamp; tours & falconry adult/child €14.50/8.50; ⊙9.30am-4.30pm Wed-Sun Apr & Oct, 9.30am-5pm Tue-Sun May-Sep), a Renaissance castle 50km north of Krems where falconry shows take place at 11am and 3pm.

From Rosenburg, the B34 and later B2 lead on an 18km detour east to the quaint town of **Eggenburg**. It's still surrounded by much of its original defensive walls.

Back in Rosenburg, follow the L53 and B38 5km to the Benedictine **Stift Altenburg** (www.stift-altenburg.at; Stift 1; adult/child €9/4.50, audio guide €2; ⊙10am-5pm Apr-Oct), which can trace its foundations back to 1144. The **abbey library** (which has ceiling frescoes by Paul Troger) and the crypt (with frescoes by Troger's pupils) are definite highlights.

By continuing along the B38 you pass Peygarten-Ottenstein on the **Ottensteiner Stausee**, one of several dams in the Waldviertel, and finish the tour near Zwettl at the baroque Cistercian abbey **Stift Zwettl** (www.stift-zwettl.at; Stift Zwettl 1; admission & audio guide adult/child €9.90/4.50; ⊙10am-4pm Easter-Oct, library tours 11am & 2pm). The B36 leads you 25km south back to the Danube Valley.

St Pölten

🚗 02742 / POP 51,900

A destination few may notice as they scream through on their way from Vienna to Salzburg, St Pölten may be Lower Austria's capital but it retains a very drowsy atmosphere. Though no beauty, it has a quaint-ish Altstadt contrasted by the new, oh-so-21st-century Landhausviertel (Landhaus Quarter).

History

The borders of Lower Austria were drawn by the Babenberg rulers in the 13th century, but in 1278 the region and empire-to-be fell to the Habsburgs. In a strange twist of fate – an ailing economy in the 1920s stalled the decision to give Lower Austria its own capital, and later the Nazis favoured making Krems the capital – St Pölten became capital of Lower Austria only in 1986, ending a long-running situation in which Lower Austria was administered geographically from Vienna, but was in fact a separate province. Ironically, it happens to have the oldest known municipal charter – granted in 1159. The Altstadt is noted for its baroque buildings: baroque master Jakob Prandtauer lived and died in the city.

◉ Sights

Rathausplatz SQUARE
Situated in the heart of St Pölten, Rathausplatz is a pretty town square lined with cafes and eye-catching pastel-coloured buildings. It is dominated by the **Rathaus** on its southern side, which has a baroque facade (1727) designed by Joseph Munggenast. On the northern fringe is the **Franziskanerkirche** (Rathausplatz 12; ☉ dawn-dusk), completed in 1770 with a grandiose altar offset by side altar paintings by Kremser Schmidt. Between the two is the tall **Dreifaltigkeitssäule** (Trinity Column; Rathausplatz) dating from 1782, a captivating white, oversized swirl of motifs, built partly as a religious vow following the passing of the plague.

Stadtmuseum MUSEUM
(www.stadtmuseum-stpoelten.at; Prandtauerstrasse 2; adult/child €5/2; ☉10am-5pm Wed-Sun) Although it obviously can't compete with the best of the bunch in Vienna, the City Museum is excellent and well worth a visit. Its permanent collection focusing on art nouveau in St Pölten is on the 1st floor, and a section on the ground floor is devoted to local archaeological treasures. Admission includes usually worthwhile temporary exhibitions.

Dom CATHEDRAL
(Domplatz 1; ☉ dawn-dusk) Jakob Prandtauer was one of the most important architects of the baroque epoch, and the cathedral, his masterpiece of baroque rebuilding in St Pölten, has an impressive interior with lashings of fake marble and gold, augmented by frescoes by Daniel Gran. While exploring the cathedral, be sure to visit the cloister with its old gravestones.

Synagoge SYNAGOGUE
(Dr-Karl-Renner-Promenade 22; ☉9am-3pm Mon-Fri) St Pölten's main synagogue dates from 1912 and has attractive art nouveau features. The Nazis laid it to waste during the pogroms of 1938, and during the Hitler years the building wound up in the hands of the city council, which used it as a camp

for Russian forced labour victims before the Red Army arrived and turned it into a grain store. It was restored and today houses an institute for Jewish history.

🛏 Sleeping

Jugendherberge St Pölten HOSTEL $
(☎321 96; www.oejhv.at; Bahnhofplatz 1a; dm/s/d €22/29/44; @ ☎) The youth hostel is about as convenient to the train station as it gets – it's all but in the same building.

Stadthotel Hauser Eck HOTEL $$
(☎733 36; www.hausereck.at; Schulgasse 2; s €43-60, d €80-150; ☎) This newly renovated hotel inside a rambling art nouveau building offers excellent value in the historic part of town. Rooms are well appointed if sometimes on the snug side and bathrooms are kept sparklingly clean. The restaurant downstairs offers Austrian and Italian staples.

Gasthof Graf HOTEL $$
(☎352 757; www.hotel-graf.at; Bahnhofplatz 7; s/d from €69/98; P☎) Opposite the train station, this 30-room hotel has no-frills rooms with cheapo furniture and brightly coloured walls as well as more expensive quarters with a touch trendier retro-design feel. The downstairs restaurant has affordable mains served with second-hand cigarette smoke.

Metropol HOTEL $$$
(☎707 00-0; www.austria-trend.at/met; Schillerplatz 1; s €200-220, d €250-270; P☎) Cosy, upmarket and aimed at a business and culture clientele, the Metropol is not cheap (low season prices are 20% less), but for these prices you do get free use of the sauna, steam bath and infrared lamps. Its restaurant serves up steak and good business-type meals.

✕ Eating & Drinking

Lilli's Gastwirtschaft AUSTRIAN $
(Rathausplatz 15/Marktgasse; mains €7-13; ☉9am-8pm Mon-Fri, to 2pm Sat; ☎) ✿ This homely restaurant does a lunch menu for €6.30 and often uses organic beef from the Waldviertel region. Expect to find classics well prepared, including *Tafelspitz* (prime boiled beef) and apricot-filled dumplings.

Landhaus Stüberl AUSTRIAN $
(www.landhausstueberl.at; Landhausboulevard 27; breakfast €4-6, lunch menu €7, mains €8.50-12; ☉7am-7pm Mon-Thu, to 5pm Fri) The name suggests a traditional tavern, but this

St Pölten

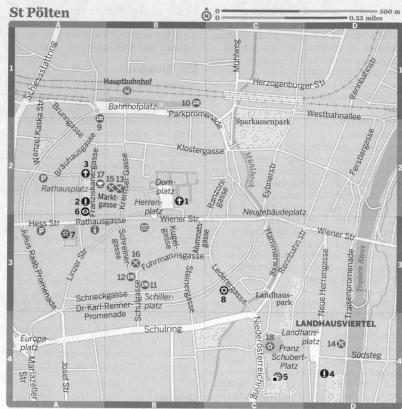

St Pölten

◉ Sights
1 Dom..B2
2 Dreifaltigkeitssäule............................A2
3 Franziskanerkirche............................A2
4 Klangturm..D4
5 Landesmuseum..................................C4
6 Rathausplatz....................................A2
7 Stadtmuseum....................................A3
8 Synagoge...C3

🛏 Sleeping
9 Gasthof Graf.....................................A2
10 Jugendherberge St Pölten................B1
11 Metropol..B3

12 Stadthotel Hauser Eck......................B3

✖ Eating
13 Backwerk...B2
14 Landhaus Stüberl..............................D4
15 Lilli's Gastwirtschaft.........................B2
16 Restaurant Galerie............................B3

⚲ Drinking & Nightlife
17 Cinema Paradiso...............................A2

✪ Entertainment
18 FestSpielHaus..................................C4

postmillenium eatery in the Landhausviertel is anything but, and is aimed firmly at bureaucrats from the nearby Landtag and culture managers who come here to finger their devices and 'touch base'. The food is Italo-Austrian and can be picked at indoors or on the terrace overlooking the Traisen River.

Backwerk BAKERY $
(Kremser Gasse 19; snacks €0.79-2.50; ⊙ 7am-6pm Mon-Fri, 8am-3pm Sat) The St Pölten branch of

this German bakery is the place to put together a euro-watching lunch on the run.

Restaurant Galerie AUSTRIAN $$
(Fuhrmannsgasse 1; mains €18.50-28.50, 4-course menu €35.50-57.50; ☺lunch & dinner Mon-Fri) Galerie serves delicious, if exceedingly pricey, Viennese cuisine and has a great wine list, especially for Italian and French vintages. Although Wiener Schnitzel isn't on the menu, it's always available if you ask nicely.

Cinema Paradiso CAFE
(Rathausplatz 14; ☺9am-1am) Supercentral trendoid spot for mulling over a paper or something heart-pumping. True to its name, it's also an art-house cinema.

❶ Information

Post office (Wiener Strasse 12)
Tourist office (🗗353 354; www.st-poelten. gv.at; Rathausplatz 1; ☺8am-5pm Mon-Fri, 9am-5pm Sat, 10am-5pm Sun, closed Sat & Sun Nov-Mar)

❶ Getting There & Away

St Pölten has good road connections: the east–west A1/E60 passes a few kilometres south of the city and the S33 branches north from there, bypassing St Pölten to the east, and continuing to Krems.

Trains run around three times an hour from Vienna Westbahnhof to St Pölten (€12, 30 minutes). There are also hourly direct trains to Krems (€7.60, 45 minutes), twice hourly departures for Melk (€5.80, 20 minutes) and at least four a day to Mariazell (€14.10, 2½ hours).

Herzogenburg

Although the region around Lower Austria's capital won't bowl you over, the baroque Augustinian abbey **Stift Herzogenburg** (🗗02782-831 12; www.stift-herzogenburg.at; Herzogenburg; adult/child €9/7; ☺tours 9.30am, 11am, 1.30pm, 3pm & 4.30pm Apr-Oct) is a highlight. Admission is with a guided tour (in English at 9.30am and 11am Tuesday, Thursday and Friday), which includes the **Stiftskirche** and a late-Gothic collection of paintings by the Danube school of artists.

Herzogenburg lies on the main train line between Krems (€3.80, 30 minutes) and St Pölten (€3.70, 15 minutes); at least a dozen trains pass through the town's train station (which is 10 minutes' walk from the abbey) daily.

Mostviertel

The Mostviertel, in Lower Austria's southwestern corner, takes its name from apple cider which is produced and consumed in the area. By Lower Austrian standards, the landscape is spectacular, with the eastern Alps ever-present in its southern reaches. It's largely ignored by international tourists and is certainly an area off the beaten track.

One town not to be missed is **Waidhofen an der Ybbs**, with historic gabled houses, arcaded courtyards and dramatic onion domes. Staff at its **tourist office** (🗗07442-511 255; www.waidhofen.at; Schlossweg 2; ☺9am-6pm Tue-Fri, to 5pm Sat) have information on the town and the numerous **mountain bike trails** of varying degrees of difficulty around Waidhofen. The tourist office rents road bicycles and mountain bikes for €12 per day for a maximum of one week. It also has useful maps of the region and can point you towards the mountain-bike trails.

From Gstadt, Bundesstrasse 31 leads through some lovely mountainous country and a string of pretty little villages such as **Göstling**, **Lunz am See** and **Gaming**.

In the eastern fringes of the Mostviertel, and only 23km south of St Pölten, is the **Cistercian monastery** (www.stift-lilienfeld. at; Klosterrotte 1; adult/child €3/1, incl tour €7/4; ☺8am-noon & 1-5pm, tours 10am & 2pm Mon-Sat, 2pm Sun) of Lilienfeld. Founded in 1202, the foundations of the monastery are Romanesque, but have received Gothic and baroque makeovers over the centuries.

❶ Getting There & Away

From St Pölten frequent daily trains go to Waidhofen an der Ybbs (€17.20, one hour, change at Amstetten). To Lilienfeld (€5.80, 40 minutes) the train service has been discontinued and replaced by a twice-hourly bus service. You are better off using a car or bicycle for Göstling, Lunz and for Gaming, which is 30km from Waidhofen.

March-Donauland

The March-Donauland, stretching from the eastern border of Vienna to the Slovakian border, is dominated by the Danube and its natural flood plains. Carnuntum, an important Roman camp during the days of the Roman Empire, and the Nationalpark Donau-Auen are found here.

DON'T MISS

LANDHAUSVIERTEL

The Landhausviertel (State Parliament Quarter) to the southeast of the historical core of St Pölten (p128), is a contemporary conflux of state buildings and cultural institutions strung out in a statement-making jumble of glass and steel alongside the river. To get your bearings, first head to the **Klangturm** (Landhausplatz; ⊙8am-6pm Mon-Sat, 9am-5pm Sun) **FREE**, from the top of which (reached by lift) there are 360-degree views not just of the neighbourhood but of almost all of St Pölten. There's a small gallery at the base of the tower and an information centre. A few steps from the tower stands the **Landesmuseum** (www.landesmuseum.net; Franz-Schubert-Platz 5; adult/child €8/4; ⊙9am-5pm Tue-Sun) housing an engaging collection on the history, art and environment of the region. The new-millenium feel of the quarter is reflected in the program of the nearby **FestSpielHaus** (☑90 80 80-222; www.festspielhaus.at; Kulturbezirk 2), which attracts an impressive list of musicians, orchestras, theatre companies and dance ensembles from both Austria and beyond.

Petronell-Carnuntum & Around

☑ 02165 / POP 1240

The Roman town of Carnuntum was the most important political and military centre in the empire's northeast; with a population of 50,000 people at its peak, it made Vienna look like a village in comparison. The town developed around AD 40 and was abandoned some 400 years later. Today it exists as a relic of Roman civilisation in Upper Pannonia. The main sights are spread between the modern-day settlement Petronell-Carnuntum, the larger spa town of Bad Deutsch-Altenburg about 4km away, and Hainburg, another 4km east of this.

◉ Sights

All four Roman attractions and the Kulturfabrik are covered by one ticket (adult/child €10/5) including transport in the archaeological park bus on weekends. Note that the months the sites open change slightly each year (check the website).

Freilichtmuseum Petronell   RUIN

(www.carnuntum.co.at; Hauptstrasse 1a, Petronell-Carnuntum; ⊙9am-5pm mid-Mar–mid-Nov) The open-air museum is the major attraction in Petronell-Carnuntum itself and lies on the site of the old civilian town. It includes ruins of the public baths and a reconstructed temple of Diana. Hunky young actors lead tours in kitsch tunics and togas, and you can buy replicas of Roman sandals and clothing here for your next toga party. The museum is enclosed and very touristy, but nevertheless interesting and good fun; descriptions everywhere are in *linguam anglicus*.

Ampitheatre   RUIN

(Wienerstrasse 52, Petronell-Carnuntum; ⊙9am-5pm mid-Mar–mid-Nov) Situated about 2km on from Freilichtmuseum Petronell towards Bad Deutsch-Altenburg, the grass-covered amphitheatre formerly seated 15,000. It now hosts a theatre festival over summer.

Museum Carnuntinum   MUSEUM

(Badgasse 40-46, Bad Deutsch-Altenburg; ⊙10am-5pm mid-Mar–mid-Nov) This museum of archaeological finds is the largest of its kind in Austria, having amassed over 3300 Roman treasures in its 100-year existence. The museum's highlight, *Tanzende Mänade* (Dancing Maenad), a marble figure with a perfect bum, is usually displayed here. While in Bad Deutsch-Altenburg, take a stroll around the *Kurpark* (spa gardens), situated alongside the Danube.

Kulturfabrik   MUSEUM

(www.kulturfabrik-hainburg.at; Kulturplatz 1; ⊙10am-5pm mid-Mar–mid-Nov) Situated 3.8km east of Bad Deutsch-Altenburg, this 'Culture Factory' is a museum depot for the archaeological riches of the region. It stages changing exhibitions mostly based on its own collection; see the website for details about what's currently on show.

The building in which the depot is housed is an interesting landmark in itself. It dates back to 1847 and was erected on the Danube to manufacture cigarettes and cigars, doing so until the local industry ran out of puff here in the 1990s. Today it has been refurbished with a glass wall fronting the river, offering magnificent views. Entry is via a glass and mirrored lift from street level. The **fenestra** (Latin for 'window') cafe offers fantastic views over the river, best enjoyed sipping coffee or nibbling a snack.

🛏 Sleeping & Eating

Bad Deutsch-Altenburg, with its pretty *Kurpark,* spa facilities and location near the Danube, is far more appealing than Petronell-Carnuntum.

Gasthof Hotel zum Amphitheater   HOTEL $
(📞627 37; www.zum-amphitheater.at; Wienerstrasse 51, Bad Deutsch-Altenburg; s/d €35/60; 🅿@🛜) Rising up opposite the amphitheatre, this friendly, family-run hotel is packed with local atmosphere; rooms are spacious and some have views over the fields or amphitheatre.

Pension Riedmüller   HOTEL $
(📞624 73-0; www.tiscover.at/riedmueller.hotels; Badgasse 28, Bad Deutsch-Altenburg; s/d €30/60; 🅿) This basic hotel has massage facilities, free bike use for guests and organises tours or helps with bike tours to Bratislava (€50 each way). The rooms are fine, but the delicious apple strudel downstairs in the cafe is even better.

Hotel-Gasthof Stöckl   HOTEL $
(📞623 37; www.gasthof-stoeckl.at; Hauptplatz 3, Bad Deutsch-Altenburg; s/d €46/70; 🅿❄🛜🏊) Comfortable, centrally located hotel with a solar-heated outdoor pool, and a sauna and steam bath.

Gasthaus Durkowitsch   AUSTRIAN $$
(Wiener Strasse 7, Bad Deutsch-Altenburg; mains €9-18; ⊙10am-11pm Wed-Sun) Family inn serving classics for under €15, along with more-expensive seasonal or game dishes such as venison ragout or duck. A room for smokers has a rustic, hunter atmosphere.

ⓘ Information

Bad Deutsch-Altenburg Tourist Office
(📞629 00; www.bad-deutsch-altenburg.gv.at; Erhardgasse 2; ⊙8am-noon & 1-7pm Mon, to 4pm Tue-Thu, 8am-1pm Fri)
Petronell-Carnuntum Tourist Office
(📞02163-337 70; www.carnuntum.co.at; Hauptstrasse 1a; ⊙9am-5pm mid-Mar–mid-Nov) At the open-air museum.

ⓘ Getting There & Around

There are hourly S-Bahn departures from Wien-Mitte for Petronell-Carnuntum, Bad Deutsch-Altenburg (both €9.90, one hour) and Hainburg (€11.50, 70 minutes).

The cycle path from Vienna goes along the north bank of the Danube, crosses to the south near Bad Deutsch-Altenburg, and continues into Slovakia.

Nationalpark Donau-Auen

Nationalpark Donau-Auen is a thin strip of natural flood plain on either side of the Danube, running from Vienna to the Slovak border. Established as a national park in 1997, it was the culmination of 13 years of protest and environmentalist action against the building of a hydroelectric power station in Hainburg. You'll find plentiful flora and fauna, including 700 species of fern and flowering plants, and a high density of kingfishers (feeding off the 50 species of fish). Guided tours by foot or boat are available; for more information contact **Nationalpark Donau-Auen** (www.donauauen.at; Schlossplatz 1, Orth an der Donau; adult/child €9.90/5.50; ⊙9am-6pm mid-Mar–Sep, to 5pm Oct).

From Vienna, the Nationalpark Donau-Auen is best explored either by bicycle or on one of the Nationalpark-run summer tours. Contact the **park office** (📞01-4000-49495; www.donauauen.at; Dechantweg 8, Vienna; ⊙10am-6pm Wed-Sun Mar-Oct) in Vienna for more details.

Wienerwald

The Wienerwald encompasses gentle wooded hills to the west and southwest of Vienna, and the wine-growing region directly south of the capital. For the Viennese, it's a place for walking, climbing and mountain biking. Numerous walking and cycling trails in the area are covered in the *Wienerwald Wander-und Radkarte,* available free from local tourist offices and the region's main office, **Wienerwald Tourismus** (📞02231-621 76; www.wienerwald.info; Hauptplatz 11, Purkersdorf; ⊙9am-5pm Mon-Fri)

Attractive settlements, such as the grape-growing towns of **Perchtoldsdorf** and **Gumpoldskirchen**, speckle the Wienerwald. Picturesque **Mödling**, only 15km south of Vienna, was once favoured by the artistically inclined: Beethoven's itchy feet took him to Hauptstrasse 79 from 1818 to 1820, and Austrian composer Arnold Schönberg stayed at Bernhardgasse 6 from 1918 to 1925. More information is available from the **Tourismus Information Mödling** (📞02236-267 27; www.moedling.at; Kaiserin Elisabeth-Strasse 2; ⊙9am-12.30pm & 1.30-5pm Mon-Fri).

About 20km from Mödling is **Heiligenkreuz** and the 12th-century Cistercian abbey **Stift Heiligenkreuz** (☑02258-8703; www.stift-heiligenkreuz.at; Heiligenkreuz 1; adult/child €7.50/3.80; ☉tours 10am, 11am, 2pm, 3pm & 4pm Mon-Sat, 11am, 2pm, 3pm & 4pm Sun). The chapter house is the final resting place of most of the Babenberg dynasty, which ruled Austria until 1246. The abbey museum contains 150 clay models by Giovanni Giuliani (1663–1744), a Venetian sculptor who also created the Trinity column in the courtyard. Note that tours in English are by advance request only.

Mayerling, which lies 6km southwest of Heiligenkreuz, has little to show now, but the bloody event that occurred here in 1889 still draws visitors to the site. The **Carmelite convent** (☑02258-2275; http://karmel-mayerling.org; Mayerling 1; admission €2.80; ☉9am-6pm) can be visited if you want to get a feel for events and see a few mementos. The altar in the chapel was built exactly where the bodies of Archduke Rudolf and Maria were found.

Between Mayerling and Weissenbach-Neuhaus, situated about 5km from both on the L4004 and accessible from the Schwarzensee parking area and bus stop, is **Peilstein** (716m), with rock climbing on the **Peilstein Klettersteig**. This is one of the most picturesque climbs in the region and a favourite among the Viennese. **Peilsteinhaus** (www.peilsteinhaus.gebirgsverein.at; Schwarzensee 15; ☉Wed-Sun; ▣), a hut and restaurant with a kids' playground, can be reached by hiking trails (01/06) via Mayerling from Heiligenkreuz (16km, 4½ hours to Peilstein). From the Schwarzensee/Peilstein bus stop, it's a half-hour hike and from Weisenbach it takes 1½ hours.

❶ Getting There & Away

To really get under the skin of this region, it's best to have your own bicycle or car, but trains and buses will carry you to the main centres. The main road through the area is the A21 that loops down from Vienna, passes by Heiligenkreuz, then curves north to join the A1 just east of Altlengbach.

Bus connections are from Baden bei Wien to Heiligenkreuz (€2, 20 to 30 minutes, seven daily on weekdays) or from Baden to Schwarzensee (€5.70, one hour, six daily Monday to Saturday).

To get here by train, take the S1 or S2 from Wien-Meidling via Perchtoldsdorf (€2.20, 11 minutes, four hourly) to Gumpoldskirchen (€3.80, 27 minutes, hourly) and the S50 from Wien-Meidling (or S60 from the Westbahnhof) to Purkersdorf (€3.80, 20 minutes, hourly). Indirect trains from Baden bei Wien to Weissenbach-Neuhaus (€5.80, 50 minutes, seven daily Monday to Saturday) require a change in Leobersdorf.

Baden bei Wien

☑02252 / POP 25,100

With its sulphurous mineral springs (lending it an egglike smell in parts) and its lush green parks, gardens and woods, this spa town on the eastern fringes of the Wienerwald is a picturesque anomaly. Baden has a long history of receiving notable visitors; the Romans came here to wallow in the medicinal waters, Beethoven blew into town in the hope of a cure for his deafness, and in the early 19th century it flourished as the favourite summer retreat of the Habsburgs. Much of the town centre is in the 19th-century Biedermeier style. Note that Baden goes into partial hibernation between October and March.

The centre is about 15 minutes by foot from the train station. Follow Kaiser-Franz-Joseph-Ring west and turn right into Wassergasse.

⊙ Sights & Activities

Arnulf Rainer Museum   MUSEUM
(www.arnulf-rainer-museum.at; Josefsplatz 5; adult/child €6/3; ☉10am-5pm) Located inside the former Frauenbad (Women's Bathhouse) near the tram terminus, this interesting museum showcases the work of its namesake Arnulf Rainer, who was born in Baden in 1929 and studied for one day at the School of Applied Arts in Vienna. He also went to the Academy of the Fine Arts but left after three days, only to return as a respected artist and become a professor there. He began painting in a surrealist style before developing his characteristic multimedia works, some of them (like painting with chimpanzees) idiosyncratic and bizarre. The museum has retained the delightful marble features of the Biedermeier bathhouse from 1815, making it all the more worth a visit. Exhibitions change twice a year.

Kurpark   PARK
The *Kurpark* is a magnificent setting for a stroll or as a place to repose on the benches in front of the **bandstand**, where free concerts are held from May to September. The tourist office can tell you about these and

others held in winter in the **Haus der Kunst** (prices and exhibitions vary); an **operetta festival** takes place from June to September. Attractive flower beds complement monuments to famous artists (Mozart, Beethoven, Strauss, Grillparzer etc). Near the southern entrance to the park, the **Undine-Brunnen** (fountain) is a fine amalgam of human and fish images.

Rollett Museum MUSEUM

(Weikersdorfer Platz 1; adult/child €3.50/2; ☺3-6pm Wed-Mon) The Rollett Museum, southwest of the town centre and just off Weilburgstrasse (a five-minute walk southeast of the Thermalstrandbad), covers important aspects of the town's history. The most unusual exhib-

it is the collection of skulls, busts and death masks amassed by the founder of phrenology, Josef Gall (1752–1828), who sparked the craze of inferring criminal characteristics from the shape of one's cranium. Keep your hat on.

Dreifaltigkeitssäule MONUMENT

This monument on Hauptplatz to the Holy Trinity, dating from 1714, is one of Austria's wierdest, the whole thing looking like icing dribbled over stacked meringue.

Mineral Spas & Springs SPA

Baden's prime attraction is its 14 hot springs that emerge at a temperature of 36°C and are enriched with sulphates. Its largest pool complex, the Thermalstrandbad (p136), is

MYSTERY AT MAYERLING

It's the stuff of lurid pulp fiction: the heir to the throne found dead in a hunting lodge with his teenage mistress. It became fact in Mayerling on 30 January 1889, yet for years the details of the case were shrouded in secrecy and denial. Even now a definitive picture has yet to be established – the 100th anniversary of the tragedy saw a flurry of books published on the subject.

The heir was Archduke Rudolf, 30-year-old son of Emperor Franz Josef, husband of Stephanie of Coburg, and something of a libertine who was fond of drinking and womanising. Rudolf's marriage was little more than a public facade by the time he met the 17-year-old Baroness Maria Vetsera in the autumn of 1888. The attraction was immediate, but it wasn't until 13 January the following year that the affair was consummated, an event commemorated by an inscribed cigarette case, a gift from Maria to Rudolf.

On 28 January, Rudolf secretly took Maria with him on a shooting trip to his hunting lodge in Mayerling. His other guests arrived a day later; Maria's presence, however, remained unknown to them. On the night of 29 January, the valet, Loschek, heard the couple talking until the early hours, and at about 5.30am a fully dressed Rudolf appeared and instructed him to get a horse and carriage ready. As he was doing his master's bidding, Loschek reportedly heard two gun shots; racing back, he discovered Rudolf lifeless on his bed, with a revolver by his side. Maria was on her bed, also fully clothed, also dead. Just two days earlier Rudolf had discussed a suicide pact with his long-term mistress Mizzi Caspar. Apparently he hadn't been joking.

The official line was proffered by Empress Elisabeth, who claimed Rudolf died of heart failure. The newspapers swallowed the heart failure story, though a few speculated about a hunting accident. Then the rumours began: some believed Maria had poisoned her lover, that Rudolf had contracted an incurable venereal disease, or that he had been assassinated by Austrian secret police because of his liberal politics. Even as late as 1982, Empress Zita claimed the heir to the throne had been killed by French secret agents. Numerous books have been written on the subject, but no one can say what exactly occurred on that ill-fated morning.

Through all the intrigue, the real victim remains Maria. How much of a willing party she was to the apparent suicide will never be known. What has become clear is that Maria, after her death, represented not a tragically curtailed young life but an embarrassing scandal that had to be discreetly disposed of. Her body was left untouched for 38 hours, after which it was loaded into a carriage in such a manner as to imply that it was a living person being aided rather than a corpse beyond help. Her subsequent burial was a rude, secretive affair, during which she was consigned to the ground in an unmarked grave (her body was later moved to Heiligenkreuz). Today the hunting lodge is no more – a Carmelite nunnery stands in its place.

EGGS BENEDICT IN THE BATH

Because of the sulphur content in its healing waters, Baden bei Wien has a distinctive 'poached egg' smell in parts of town. But it's more unusual when an outdoor swimming pool has the ubiquitous 'eggy' scent. If you've got a finely tuned nose, the egg smell is very in-your-face at the **Thermalstrandbad** (Helenenstrasse 19-21; all-day entry €6.90-9.40, child €3.50; ⏲ 8.30am-7.30pm May–mid-Sep). With its dubious brownish stretch of sand backed by a functionalist building from 1926, the pool complex is a sulphurous Hades-meets-Majorca. Originally, the designers wanted to import sand from the Adriatic (not exactly known for sandy beaches, but anyway); in the end they settled for sand from Melk in the Danube Valley.

actually dedicated to good old-fashioned fun. The **Römertherme** (☑ 450 30; www.roemertherme.at; Brusattiplatz 4; 3hr/all-day €12.10/15.30; ⏲ 10am-10pm) is all about health and relaxation. Admission weekdays is slightly cheaper.

Kronprinz-Rudolf-Weg CYCLING

Though interesting, the museums won't knock you over if you have seen those in Vienna, so cycling or hiking the 12-km long Kronprinz-Rudolf-Weg along the Schwechat River to Mayerling is a good summer alternative. The tourist office has a free trail description (in German) and bikes can be hired in town. The trail can be combined with a 6km return northern branch trail to Heiligenkreuz.

🛏 Sleeping

Baden is best tackled as a day trip from Vienna as in summer the hotels can get very full. The tourist office can help out with accommodation if you do decide to sleep over.

Villa Inge PENSION $

(☑ 431 71; Weilburgstrasse 24-26; s/d from €38/66; ⏲ Apr-Oct; P ❄ @) This large villa is set alongside the river close to the Thermalstrandbad. Rooms are spacious and the breakfast room is lovely and bright, looking out to the garden. It offers good value for Baden, especially for its family apartment (from €100).

★ Hotel Schloss Weikersdorf HOTEL $$

(☑ 48 301-0; www.hotelschlossweikersdorf.at; Schlossgasse 9-11; s €90-140, d €140-180; P @ ❄ ⛱) For a weekend of pampering, look no further than this luxurious hotel set in beautiful gardens. Rooms are up-to-the-minute affairs and there are massage services, relaxation coves, lounges and other wellness facilities. It also has three places to eat, including the Rosenkavalier restaurant, one of Baden's best.

Hotel Herzoghof HOTEL $$

(☑ 872 97; www.hotel-herzoghof.at; Kaiser-Franz-Ring 10; s €90-130, d €120-200; P ❄) This central hotel opposite the *Kurpark* offers good value for money for those with cash to splash. There's a sauna and steam bath on-site and a whole list of scary wellness procedures on offer. Things get significantly cheaper here in the low season.

🍴 Eating & Drinking

Despite its visitor numbers, Baden has relatively few places to fill the hole.

Cafe Damals AUSTRIAN $$

(Rathausgasse 3; mains €9-14; ⏲ 10am-11pm) Baden's most personality-packed feeding point takes diners way back to the days of the Habsburgs in unashamedly nostalgic fashion. A moustachioed Franz Joseph I plus various other monarchs glower down disapprovingly as you munch on well-prepared Austrian favourites.

Cafe Central CAFE

(Hauptplatz 19; ⏲ 7am-8pm Tue-Sat, 8am-8pm Sun) The town's epicentral cafe has an apt name, positioned as it is on Hauptplatz. The interior is a real kick up the '80s (or is it '70s?) with blue leather seating and faux veneer panelling.

Weinkult WINE BAR

(www.weinkult.at; Pfarrgasse 7; antipasto €10; ⏲ 11.30am-8pm Tue-Fri, 10.30am-5pm Sat) This wine shop sells almost 150 Austrian wines and serves 10 (mostly) Austrian wines by the glass, rotating the selection on a weekly basis. Antipasto is served to prime the palate.

ⓘ Information

Baden Tourismus (☑ 226 00-600; www.baden.at; Brusattiplatz 3; ⏲ 9am-6pm Mon-Sat, to 4pm Sun May-Sep, to 5pm Mon-Fri Oct-Apr)

ℹ️ Getting There & Around

Bus 360 departs every 30 to 60 minutes (€6, 40 minutes) from the Oper in Vienna. In Baden bus 362 runs between the Thermalstrandbad and Bahnhof via the centre.

Regional and S-Bahn trains connect Baden with Wien-Meidling (€5.80, 20 minutes, three times hourly) and with Wiener Neustadt (€5.80, 20 minutes).

A *Lokalbahn* tram (€6.30, one hour, every 15 minutes, 40 minutes) connects the Oper in Vienna with Josefsplatz in Baden.

Süd-Alpin

This southern corner of Lower Austria, known as the Süd-Alpin (Southern Alps), has some of the province's most spectacular landscapes. Here the hills rise to meet the Alps, peaking at Schneeberg (2076m), a mountain popular among the Viennese for its skiing and hiking possibilities. Nearby Semmering has long been a favourite of the capital's burghers, due mainly to its crisp alpine air. One of the greatest highlights of the area though is the journey there; the winding railway over the Semmering Pass has been designated a Unesco World Heritage site.

Wiener Neustadt

📞 02622 / POP 41,700

Wiener Neustadt used to be known simply as Neustadt (New Town) or Nova Civitas and was built by the Babenbergs in 1194 with the help of King Richard the Lionheart's ransom payment (so if you're English, those town walls, by rights, belong to you!). It became a Habsburg residence in the 15th century during the reign of Friedrich III. His famous AEIOU (*Alles Erdreich Ist Österreich Untertan;* Everything in the world is subservient to Austria) engraving can be found throughout the city. The town was severely damaged in WWII (only 18 homes were left unscathed), so what you see today is mainly a postwar rebuild.

⊙ Sights

Dom CATHEDRAL
(Domplatz; ⊙dawn-dusk) This cathedral runs an architectural gauntlet from the Romanesque (it dates from the late 13th century) to the Gothic and beyond to the baroque. The simplicity of the facade and clear lines are striking from the outside, but inside it will drive those who love the symmetry of the Romanesque style to despair as the nave is noticeably out of kilter with the sanctuary. Fifteenth-century wooden apostles peer down from pillars and there's a baroque high altar and pulpit. To visit the **Turmmuseum** (⊙10.30am-2.30pm Wed-Sun May-Oct), a free-standing tower that provides grand views over the city's rooftops, you need to ask inside the Stadtmuseum. Someone will take you up there, but only in good weather.

Hauptplatz SQUARE
The town's main piazza is closed off on one side by the **Rathaus**, which is something of a hybrid of styles. It began life as a Gothic building, was given some Renaissance flourishes from the late 16th century, and then when imitations came into vogue from the early 19th century a neo-Gothic spire was tacked onto it. In the centre of the square is the **Mariensäule** (Column of Mary) from 1678, flanked by a group of woe-begotten saints.

Neukloster CHURCH
(Ungargasse; ⊙dawn-dusk) Architecturally, this 14th-century church is fairly straight up and down Gothic, with a vaulted ceiling and high windows, but the interior was later refurbished with baroque decorative elements, such as the altar. The clash of styles leaves a little to be desired, and the most attractive feature is the tranquil cloisters, reached by an unmarked door on the right (facing the altar) and sporting a Renaissance-era well. The church is famous as the venue for the very first performance of Mozart's *Requiem* in 1793.

CYCLING THE KAMPTAL

The Waldviertel road trip (p128) can be easily done by bicycle on a slightly different route if you use the **Kamptalradweg** (Kamp Valley Bicycle Path; 107km one way from Krems to Zwettl) and other bike paths in the network. The route runs slightly northwest of the B35 from Krems, but from **Gobelsburg** you can pick up another trail to Hadersdorf, Diendorf and Schloss Grafenegg. It also leaves the Kamp for a while north of Rosenburg, but joins it again from the **Ottensteiner Stausee**. If you do the route, pick up the free *Freizeitkarte Kamptal* from Krems' tourist office (p120) showing routes.

Stadtmuseum
MUSEUM

(☑373-951; www.stadtmuseum.wiener-neustadt.at; Petergasse 2a; adult/child €4/1.50; ⊙10am-4pm Wed-Sun, to 8pm Thu) Partly housed in the former St Peter's monastery, the city museum has artefacts from the Dom and other displays on town history. Its prize item is the 15th-century Corvinus Chalice that, according to legend, was a present from the Hungarian king Matthias Corvinus.

Militärakademie
CASTLE

(Military Academy; Burgplatz 1) **FREE** Dating from the 13th century, this former castle was turned into a military academy in the mid-18th century (founded by Empress Maria Theresia) and was even commanded by the young Rommel in his pre-'desert fox' days.

The academy had to be completely rebuilt after WWII, and its real highlight is **St-Georgs-Kathedrale** (⊙10am-5pm), with a fine late-Gothic interior. Maximilian I, who was born in the castle, is buried under the altar. The eastern wall of the church is packed with heraldic coats of arms dating from 1453 and was the only part of the building to survive WWII unscathed. The relief depicts a genealogy of Austrian rulers. Only 19 of the heraldic arms are real – the rest were invented by Peter von Pusica, the artisan who created it. Entry to the church is on the south side (register with the guard).

Wasserturm
WATER TOWER

(Burgplatz) Just south of the Militärakademie, rising between the convergence of two busy roads, is the town's water tower from 1910. Its shape intentionally apes the gilded goblet donated to the townsfolk by King Matthias Corvinus of Hungary after he took the town in 1487. It's still in operation today, so for reasons of hygiene you can't enter.

🛏 Sleeping

Jugendhotel Europahaus
HOSTEL $

(☑296 95; www.hostel.or.at; Promenade 1; dm/s/d €16/19.50/39; ⊙reception 7-10am & 5-8pm; P) This HI hostel occupying a prime piece of real estate in the *Stadtpark*, near the *Wasserturm*, is often full so call or book ahead.

Hotel Corvinus
HOTEL $$

(☑24 134; www.hotel-corvinus.at; Bahngasse 29-33; s/d €79/122; P🐾) The cubelike exterior may not appeal to all, but this four-star hotel is very comfortable inside. It caters to business and seminar guests as well as tourists and offers 68 bright rooms sweetened with extras such as a wellness area, a bar and a leafy terrace.

Hotel Zentral
HOTEL $$

(☑23 169; www.hotelzentral.at; Hauptplatz 27; s €45-65, d €80-96; @🐾) Located slap-bang on the Hauptplatz, these family-run digs offer a variety of rooms, some with views of the main square. Room sizes and levels of modernity differ throughout, some have little half-baths, all have desks but most parade bathrooms from the 1990s. Not all rooms are nonsmoking. Rates include breakfast.

🍴 Eating

Zum Weissen Rössl
BISTRO PUB $

(Hauptplatz 3; mains €5-11; ⊙7am-8pm Mon-Sat) This cosily curtained eatery, tucked away beneath the arcading of the Rathaus, serves affordable Austrian classics, including a choice of a small or large goulash. There's outdoor seating on Hauptplatz.

Hartig's
AUSTRIAN $$

(Domplatz 2; mains €9-14; ⊙11.30am-midnight) In the shadow of the Dom, this *Gasthof* (restaurant) serves a range of Austrian classics (but not a true Wiener Schnitzel from veal, unfortunately) in a *Beisl* (bsitro pub) atmosphere. The beer garden out the back is one of the most pleasant in town.

Cafe Bernhart
CAFE $

(Hauptplatz 20; mains €7; ⊙8am-6pm Mon-Fri, to 5pm Sat) Standard, unglamourous central cafe with a breakfast and light-lunch menu, where locals linger longer over a caffeine fix and the day's news.

ℹ Information

Tourist office (☑373; www.wiener-neustadt.gv.at; Hauptplatz 3; ⊙8am-5pm Mon-Fri, to noon Sat) Stocks a free English-language booklet, *Cultural Promenade*, describing the central sights and giving their locations on a map.

ℹ Getting There & Away

There are several trains each hour that connect Wiener Neustadt with Wien-Meidling (€10, 30 to 40 minutes).

Postbus services depart from the northern end of Wiener Neustadt train station.

Semmering

📞 02664 / POP 600

With its clean air and grandiose peaks rising out of deeply folded valleys, Semmering is a popular alpine resort for the Viennese, especially among a slightly older crowd who come to this spa town in summer for peaceful walks or to ride the dramatic railway; a younger set hits the ski pistes. There's no real centre to the resort: it's mostly ranged along Hochstrasse, which forms an arc behind the train station.

🏃 Activities

Hiking

Towering over Semmering to the south is the **Hirschenkogel** ('Zauberberg'; 1340m), where a modern cable car whisks walkers (one way/return €10/14) or skiers to the top. The tourist office and Infostelle have maps and brochures on walks.

Two fairly easy trails follow the scenic route of the Semmeringbahn, starting behind the train station. One follows the line for 17km to Mürzzuschlag in Styria, where frequent trains chug you back to Semmering, and a second leads to Breitenstein and Klamm (Lower Austria), 9.5km and 15km respectively from the start. At Klamm the trail divides and one route leads to Payerbach (21km from the start) and another to Gloggnitz (23km from the start).

Skiing

The tourist office can provide information on ski schools. A winter skiing day pass for the Hirschenkogel cable car costs €31.50. Regional skiing day passes are also available for €34.50.

Cycling

If the hills don't kill you, they'll make you stronger. The tourist office rents bicycles (per 24 hours €10).

🛏 Sleeping & Eating

Most sleeping options are situated on Hochstrasse. Many have their own restaurants, which means there's only a short hobble between table and bed.

Panorama Hotel Wagner　　HOTEL **$$**
(📞25 12; www.panoramahotel-wagner.at; Hochstrasse 267; s/d from €74/118; 🅿@🛜) Body and mind are catered for in this ecofriendly hotel: rooms have wood furniture, natural cotton bedding and grand views of the val-

ley. You can chill out with sauna, spa and massage facilities and the highly rated restaurant uses organic ingredients as much as possible. The hotel also has a shop selling organic produce at alpine prices.

Hotel Panhans　　HOTEL **$$**
(📞818 10; www.panhans.at; Hochstrasse 32; s/d from €90/130; 🛜🏊) The four-star Hotel Panhans has a swimming pool and wellness area (that can be used by nonguests), as well as rooms and apartments with a choice of forest or mountain views. The Wintergarten restaurant is regarded as Semmering's best place to dine out.

Hotel-Restaurant Belvedere　　HOTEL **$$**
(📞22 70; www.belvedere-semmering.at; Hochstrasse 60; s/d from €43/92; 🅿🏊🛜) The family-run Belvedere has alpine decor, rooms with balconies, and features such as a small swimming pool, sauna and large garden and patio area. Doubles with connecting doors are suitable for families.

ℹ Information

Infostelle Bahnhof (www.semmeringbahn.at; 🕙9-11.30am & 2-5pm May-Oct) Run by railway enthusiasts stocks material on the Semmeringbahn and the town itself.
Tourismusbüro Semmering (📞200 25; www.semmering.at; Semmering 248; 🕙9am-5pm)

SEMMERING PASS BY TRAIN

For its time, it was an incredible feat of engineering and it took more than 20,000 workers' years to complete. Even today, it never fails to impress with its switchbacks, 15 tunnels and 16 viaducts. This is the **Semmeringbahn** (Semmering Railway; www.semmeringbahn.at), a 42km stretch of track that begins at Gloggnitz and rises 455m to its highest point of 896m at Semmering Bahnhof.

Completed in 1854 by Karl Ritter von Ghega, the Semmering line was Europe's first alpine railway; due to its engineering genius, it gained Unesco World Heritage status in 1998. It passes through some impressive scenery of precipitous cliffs and forested hills en route; the most scenic section is the 30-minute stretch between Semmering and Payerbach.

From Vienna, most express services heading to Graz stop at Mürzzuschlag, from where you take a regional train to Semmering (€21.50, 1¾ hours).

❶ Getting There & Around

If you're driving, consider taking the small back road northwest of Semmering to Höllental via Breitenstein; the road winds its way down the mountain, passing under the railway line a number of times and taking in the spectacular scenery you see on the train trip.

Semmering has train connections with Breitenstein (€2.20, eight minutes), Klamm, (€3.70, 15 minutes), Payerbach (€5.70, 30 minutes) and Gloggnitz (change in Payerbach; €5.80, 40 minutes). At least five direct EuroCity (EC)/InterCity(IC) trains between Graz (€21.80, one hour 20 minutes) and Vienna (€21.50, 1¼ hours) stop at Semmering.

Schneeberg, Raxalpe & Höllental

To the north of Semmering are two of Lower Austria's highest peaks, Schneeberg (2076m) and the Raxalpe (2007m). The area is easily reached by train from Vienna, making it popular for hiking.

The trailhead for hiking or taking the cogwheel railway is **Puchberg am Schneeberg**, where the **tourist office** (☑02636-2256; www.puchberg.at; Sticklergasse 3; ⊙9am-noon & 1-5pm Mon-Thu, 9am-noon & 3-5pm Fri) can tell you about hiking conditions on Schneeberg. The **Schneebergbahn** (☑02636-3661-20; www.schneebergbahn.at; Bahnhofplatz 1, Puchberg am Schneeberg; Salamander 1 way/return €22/35; ⊙late Apr-late Oct) leaves from Puchberg am Schneeberg and takes about an hour on the Salamander and around 1¼ hours on the steam train; check the website for the train timetable.

Several huts are situated on the mountain for sustenance, accommodation or shelter. **Hengsthütte** (www.hengsthuette.at; Hochschneeberg 1; ⊙ Tue-Sun Apr-Oct, Sat & Sun Nov-Mar) and **Baumgartenhütte** (Hochschneeberg 5; ⊙ daily when train runs) are situated along the railway line; **Berghaus Hochschneeberg** (☑02636-2257; www.berghaushochschneeberg.at; Hochschneeberg 6) is at the mountain railway station and **Damböckhaus** (☑02636-2259; www.damboeckhaus.at; Hochschneeberg 8; ⊙May-Oct) is on the plateau.

In Puchberg itself, **Gasthof Pension Schmirl** (☑02636-2277; www.schmirl.at; Muthenhofer Strasse 8; s/d €30/60; ℗ ♠) has comfortable rooms on the edge of town near the railway. Some have balconies; in others you can psyche yourself for the stiff climb ahead with window views of Schneeberg.

On the southern side of Schneeberg is the scenic Höllental (Hell's Valley), a deep, narrow gorge created by the Schwarza River. Rising to the south of Höllental is the Raxalpe, another place for walkers; from Hirschwang, a small village in Höllental, the **Raxseilbahn** (☑02666-524 97; www.raxseilbahn.at; return €20.40) cable car ascends to 1547m and hiking trails. The Raxseilbahn is the site of Austria's first cable car, built in 1926.

In Höllental, the **Hotel Marienhof** (☑02666-529 95; www.marienhof.at; Hauptstrasse 71-73, Reichenau; s/d €91/140; ℗ ✖ ♠), a grand old dame with a restaurant (mains €11 to €14), is not far from the Raxseilbahn. Cycle hire is available.

❶ Getting There & Away

A change in Wiener Neustadt is required to reach Puchberg am Schneeberg from Wien Meidling (€15.10, one hour 20 minutes, hourly). Hirschwang (€18, two hours) is only a little harder to get to from Vienna; a train must first be taken to Payerbach, from where hourly buses run up the Höllental valley.

BURGENLAND

Burgenland is the youngest of Austria's provinces, arising after the collapse of the Austrian empire at the end of WWI. It's named for the 'burg' suffix of the four western Hungarian district names at that time – Pressburg (Bratislava), Wieselburg (Moson), Ödenburg (Soporn) and Eisenburg (Vasvär).

History

In the 10th century the area fell into the hands of Hungary, but German-speaking peasants gradually settled land between the Hungarian villages. The arrival of marauding Turks in the 16th century quashed both the Hungarians and the Austrian-Germans, and devastated the local population. Landlords, without anyone to tend their farms, invited substantial numbers of Croats to settle, laying the foundations for the area's Hungarian and Croatian influences today – around 10% of the population is Croatian, and Croatian (along with Hungarian) is a recognised local language; a few small towns in middle Burgenland bear Croat signs.

With the demise of the Habsburg empire after WWI, Austria lost control of Hungary, but it eventually managed to retain the German-speaking western region of Hungary under the Treaty of St Germain.

THE WINES OF BURGENLAND

The wine produced throughout this province is some of the best in Austria, due in no small part to the 300 days of sunshine per year, rich soil and excellent drainage. Although classic white varieties have a higher profile, the area's reds are more unusual, and the finest of the local wines is arguably the red Blaufränkisch; its 18th-century pedigree here predates its arrival in the Danube region and Germany.

Sweet dessert wines are currently enjoying a renaissance in Austria. *Eiswein* (wine made from grapes picked late and shrivelled by frost) and selected late-picking sweet or dessert wines are being complemented by *Schilfwein*, made by placing the grapes on *Schilf* (reed) matting so they shrivel in the heat. The guru of *Schilfwein* is Gerhard Nekowitsch from **Weingut Gerhard Nekowitsch** (☎ 02175-2039; www.nekowitsch.at; Urbanusgasse 2, Illmitz).

Middle Burgenland, especially around the villages of Horitschon and Deutschkreutz, has a long tradition of Blaufränkisch, which is also at home in southern Burgenland (although this area is better known for Uhudler, a wine with a distinctly fruity taste).

One of the easiest ways to experience wine in the Neusiedler See region is to hire a bicycle in Neusiedl am See and pedal south through the vineyards towards the national park. Along the way you'll pass vineyards and places where you can taste the local wine.

The new province of Burgenland was born, but Hungary was loath to lose Ödenburg (Sopron) to Austria, and a plebiscite held in December 1921 (under controversial circumstances) resulted in the people of Ödenburg opting to stay in Hungary. Burgenland lost its natural capital, and Eisenstadt became the new *Hauptstadt* (capital).

ⓘ Getting There & Around

Lower and middle Burgenland are mostly served by buses, but Sunday services are patchy or nonexistent. The A2 autobahn, heading south from Vienna towards Graz and Carinthia, runs parallel to the western border of Burgenland. Its many exits provide quick, easy access to much of the province. The A4 leads to Neusiedl am See. Eisenstadt and the northern extension of Neusiedler See are easily reached by train from Vienna and Lower Austria.

Eisenstadt

☎ 02682 / POP 13,350

The small capital of Burgenland is best known for its most famous former resident, 18th-century musician and composer, Joseph Haydn. Although it doesn't have a large number of attractions for visitors, it does have a wonderful palace, a couple of good museums and a rather bizarre church. Its nightlife hums rather than buzzes, but taking in its sights can easily be done on a day trip from Vienna or as an excursion from pretty, lakeside Rust.

◉ Sights

★ **Schloss Esterházy** PALACE
(www.schloss-esterhazy.at; Esterházyplatz 1; adult/child palace tour €9/7, Haydn Explosive €7/5; ☺ tours hourly 10am-6pm mid-Mar–mid-Nov, 9am-5pm Fri-Sun mid-Nov–Dec) Schloss Esterházy, a giant, Schönbrunn-yellow castle-palace that dominates Esterházyplatz, is Eisenstadt's most important attraction. Dating from the 14th century, the Schloss (castle) received one makeover in baroque and a later one in the neoclassical style. Many of the 256 rooms are occupied by the provincial government, but 25 can be viewed on tours.

The regular tour covers about seven rooms, giving you an insight into the history of the palace and the lives of the people who inhabited it. The highlight is the frescoed **Haydn Hall**, where during Haydn's employment by the Esterházys from 1761 to 1790 the composer conducted an orchestra on a near-nightly basis.

The **Haydn Explosive exhibition** across the palace courtyard offers an interesting conflux of history and the new: Haydn's music accompanies you as you walk past exhibitions on the life and work of the great composer, a nifty holograph depicts a string quartet, period furniture is projected onto the ceiling and a minuscule hole in the floor has an odd projection of a bare-breasted woman shouting abuse while burning in hell. To get the most out of the palace and Haydn, do the tour, then the Haydn exhibition.

Shortly after Joseph Haydn died in 1809, his skull was stolen from his grave in

Eisenstadt

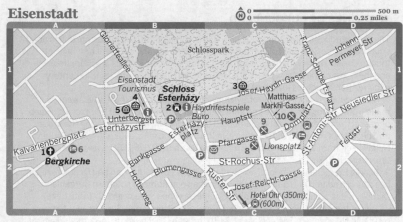

Eisenstadt

⊙ Top Sights

⊙ Sights

🛌 Sleeping

✕ Eating

Vienna. The headless cadaver was returned to Eisenstadt in 1920, but it wasn't until 1954 that the skull rejoined it in the Bergkirche.

★ **Bergkirche**　　　CHURCH
(www.haydnkirche.at; Haydnplatz 1; admission €3; ⊙9am-5pm Apr-Oct) This unusual church contains the white-marble tomb with Joseph Haydn's reunited parts. It began life as a small chapel and in 1701 was transformed into a bizarre representation of Calvary, the mountain outside Jerusalem upon which Christ is thought to have been crucified. Manage all the dungeonlike rooms and you'll be feeling the Stations of the Cross in your feet; get to the top of the 'mountain', though, and awaiting you is not a gaggle of stone throwing sinners but a fantastic view over town.

Haydn-Haus　　　MUSEUM
(www.haydnhaus.at; Josef-Haydn-Gasse 21; adult/child €4/3.50; ⊙9am-5pm Mon-Sat, from 10am Sun Jun-Sep, closed Mon Apr-May & Oct–mid-Nov) Situated in a house dating from the early 18th century, this museum dedicated to Haydn was where the great composer lived from 1766 to 1778. Although the museum won't knock your socks off unless you are an avid fan of Haydn, the collection offers an insight into his private life and has reconstructed rooms with furniture from the era to round off the Haydn experience. Original portraits cover the walls, and there are some rare exhibits such as a fortepiano that was made in Eisenstadt and a letter from Haydn's lover to the son that he is generally believed to have sired.

Landesmuseum　　　MUSEUM
(www.landesmuseum-burgenland.at; Museumgasse 1-5; adult/child €5/4; ⊙10am-5pm Tue-Sun) The Landesmuseum plunges you deep into the local history of the region, and includes a collection of Roman mosaics, ancient artefacts, winemaking equipment and some interesting propaganda posters from the 1920s. There's also a room devoted to Franz Liszt, replete with a warty death mask of the Hungarian composer.

Österreichisches Jüdisches Museum　　　MUSEUM
(Jewish Museum of Austria; www.ojm.at; Unterbergstrasse 6; adult/child €4/3; ⊙10am-5pm Tue-Sun May-Oct) Situated in the former Judengasse (the street where Eisenstadt's Jewish population mostly lived in the Middle Ages), this museum has a permanent exhibition illustrating the rituals and life-

style of Eisenstadt's Jews. Descriptions are in German and Hebrew. Part of the museum is the historic private synagogue of Samson Wertheimer, who was born in Worms in Germany in 1658 and rose to the position of rabbi in Hungary. He financed the synagogue, and it was one of the few to survive the pogroms of 1938.

✴ Festivals & Events

Internationale Haydntage   MUSIC
(www.haydnfestival.at; ⊘ Sep) A two-week series of concerts attracting excellent local acts and top international performers. It features everything from chamber pieces to full-scale orchestral performances. Most events take place in the Haydn Hall or the Bergkirche; for more information contact the **Haydnfestspiele Büro** (☑ 61 866; www.haydnfestival. at; Schloss Esterházy).

🛌 Sleeping

Staff at the tourist office have a complete list of accommodation. While the offerings are fine, splurging is better done by the Neusiedler See rather than in Burgenland's capital.

Hotel-Pension Vicedom   PENSION $$
(☑642 22; www.vicedom.at; Vicedom 5; s/d from €55/95; 🛜) This bright and breezy three-star guesthouse has quite basic but contemporary rooms and is located in a 21st-century building with an epicentral location. Reception is only open between 7am and 9pm, though receptionists can be summoned at any time. Very good breakfast and free wi-fi included.

Hotel Ohr   HOTEL $$
(☑624 60; www.hotelohr.at; Rusterstrasse 51; s €58-122, d €79-152; P 🛜) The Ohr is a family-run hotel with nicely styled modern rooms and within walking distance of the centre. There's quite a large decor difference between *standard* and *komfort* rooms with the higher class more of this millennium than the last. Its rustic-styled restaurant is one of the best in town.

Haus der Begegnung   PENSION $$
(☑632 90; www.hdb-eisenstadt.at; Kalvarienbergplatz 11; s/d €49/83; P) This church-affiliated guesthouse is spotless, very quiet and well run. The 31 rooms are simple but comfortable and it has its own grassed cafe area. It's open to everyone, but obviously not the place to stay if you're planning an all-night rave.

✖ Eating

Haydnbräu   AUSTRIAN $
(www.haydnbraeu.at; Pfarrgasse 22; mains €9-16; ⊘9am-11pm; 🖼) Duck into this microbrewery and restaurant for some of the best-value eating in town: culinary classics like schnitzel and goulash are complemented by seasonal dishes. The lunch menu is an affordable €6.50 and the snack menu has small portions suitable for kids.

Mangoo   TEX-MEX $$
(www.mangoo-bar.at; Domplatz 4; burgers €7, other mains €8-21; ⊘10am-4am Tue-Sat) This lively crossover eatery and lounge serves everything from hamburgers to the full range of Tex-Mex, like burritos, chicken wings, fajitas and good old-fashioned steak. There's a small outdoor area out the back and on Friday and Saturday a DJ works the crowd.

Kredenz   CAFE $$
(www.kredenz.at; Pfarrgasse 33; mains €8-15; ⊘10am-10pm Mon-Thu, to midnight Fri & Sat) This small cafe and bistro-style eatery serves a small range of dishes but it does them superbly – steak, chicken breast in a teriyaki sauce, or a lunch menu (€7.40) that might be carrot and ginger soup with chicken breast and herb-scented risotto.

ℹ Information

Burgenland Tourismus (www.burgenland.info)
Eisenstadt Tourismus (☑673 90; www.eisenstadt.at; Glorietteallee 1; ⊘9am-5pm Apr-Sep, 9am-5pm Mon-Thu, to 3pm Fri Oct)
Main post office (Ignaz-P-Semmelweis-Gasse 7)

ℹ DISCOUNT CARD

If you are staying overnight in Eisenstadt or in towns on the Neusiedler See, make sure you get the **Neusiedler See Card** (www.neusiedler-see.at), which gives you free transport on buses and trains around the lake and on town buses, as well as free or discount admission to many sights.

Take the registration form given to you by your hotel to an issuing office (tourist offices are the easiest) and you'll be given the card free for the duration of your stay. Available between late March and late October only.

❶ Getting There & Away

Hourly direct buses leave from Vienna's Hauptbahnhof (€7.50, one hour 20 minutes). Trains also leave hourly from the Hauptbahnhof (€17, one hour 10 minutes).

Burg Forchtenstein

Straddling a dolomite spur some 20km southwest of Eisenstadt, **Burg Forchtenstein** (www.esterhazy.at; Melinda Esterházy-Platz 1; guided tour of castle & arsenal adult/child €9/7; ⊙10am-6pm mid-Mar–Oct) is one of Burgenland's most imposing castles. This stronghold was built in the 14th century and enlarged by the Esterházys (who still own it today) in 1635. Apart from a grand view from its ramparts, the castle's highlights include an impressive collection of armour and weapons, portraits of regal Esterházys in the **Ahnengalerie** (Ancestral Gallery; adult/child €9/7) and spoils from the Turkish wars (the castle curators will proudly tell you Forchtenstein was the only castle in the area not to fall to the Turks). Its **Schatzkammer** (Treasury; adult/child €9/7) contains a rich collection of jewellery and porcelain. Combination tickets (adult/child €13/6.50) for two of the attractions are also available.

❶ Getting There & Away

On weekdays three buses run direct from Eisenstadt (€6, 45 minutes) and one from Wiener Neustadt (€5, 40 minutes) to Forchtenstein. Frequent indirect buses do the Eisenstadt route, and there's a train and bus (change to bus in Wiesen-Siegless) from Wiener Neustadt.

Neusiedler See

Neusiedler See, Europe's second-largest steppe lake, is the lowest point in Austria. But what it lacks in height, it makes up for in other areas. Ringed by a wetland area of reed beds, it's an ideal breeding ground for nearly 300 bird species – its Seewinkel area is a favourite for birdwatching. The lake's average depth is 1.5m, which means the water warms quickly in summer. Add to this the prevailing warm winds from the northwest and you have a water enthusiast's dream come true. Thousands of tourists flock to the lake for windsurfing and sailing during the summer months. The best swimming beaches are on the eastern side of the lake, as the western shore is thick with reed beds.

The area is also perfect for cycling: a flat cycle track winds all the way round the reed beds, the ferries scuttling across the lake carry bikes, and most hotels and *Pensionen* cater well to cyclists. It's possible to do a full circuit of the lake but the southern section clips Hungarian territory.

To top it all off there are acres of vineyards, making some of Austria's best wines. Rust, on the western shore of the lake, is a perfect place to sample wine in a *Heuriger*.

❶ Information

Neusiedler See Tourismus (☑02167-8600; www.neusiedlersee.com; Obere Hauptstrasse 24, Neusiedl am See; ⊙8am-5pm Mon-Fri) The main information centre for the entire lake region.

❶ Getting Around

From late spring to early autumn ferries connect Illmitz with Mörbisch, Rust, and Fertőrákos in Hungary; Rust with Podersdorf, Breitenbrunn and Fertőrákos; and Breitenbrunn with Podersdorf. See www.neusiedlersee.com for current schedules and prices.

Bus connections are frequent.

Rust

☑02685 / POP 1900

Rust, 14km east of Eisenstadt, is one of the most agreeable towns that cluster around the Neusiedler See. Its reed seashore and hidden boatsheds give it a sleepy, swampy feel on a steamy day, and in the summer months storks glide lazily overhead, make out with each other and clack their beaks from rooftop roosts. Dozens of storks make their homes on chimneys in town, although it's wine, not storks, that has made Rust prosperous. In 1524 the emperor granted local vintners the right to display the letter 'R' (a distinctive insignia as a mark of origin from Rust) on their wine barrels and today the corks still bear this insignia. It's best to sample this history in one of the town's many *Heurigen*.

⊙ Sights & Activities

Rust's affluent past has left a legacy of attractive burgher houses on and around the main squares. Storks, which descend on the town from the end of March to rear their young, take full advantage of these houses (and their kindly owners, who have erected metal platforms on chimneys to entice the storks). The clacking of expectant parents can be heard till late August.

Katholische Kirche
CHURCH

(Haydengasse; ⊙10.30-noon & 2.30-5pm, closed morning Sun) This church's tower is a good vantage point for observing storks. It's at the southern end of Rathausplatz.

Fischerkirche
CHURCH

(Rathausplatz 16; ⊙dawn-dusk Apr-Oct) At the opposite end of Rathausplatz from the Katholische Kirche, this is the oldest church in Rust, built between the 12th and 16th centuries.

Seebad Rust
SWIMMING

(www.seebadrust.at; Ruster Bucht 2; adult/child €4/2; ⊙9am-7pm, May–mid-Sep) Access to the lake and bathing facilities is 1km down the reed-fringed Seepromenade. The swimming is very reedy but refreshing.

🛏 Sleeping

Storchencamp
CAMPGROUND $

(⊡595; office@gmeiner.co.at; Ruster Bucht; camp sites per adult/tent/car €5.80/4.50/4.50; ⊙Apr-Oct; P🐕♿) With a large children's playground, cheap bike rental, close proximity to the lake and free access to the bathing area, this 200-pitch camping ground is great for holidaying families.

Ruster Jugendgästehaus & Pension
HOTEL $

(⊡591; www.seebadrust.at; Ruster Bucht 2; dm €29-34, s/d €44/76; ⊙Jan-Dec; 🛜♿) This HI hostel is right on the harbour, forms part of the bathing complex and has modern, clean rooms.

Hotel Sifkovits
HOTEL $$

(⊡276; www.sifkovits.at; Am Seekanal 8; r €90-130, P🛜♿) Close to the centre of town, Sifkovits is a fine, family-run hotel with 34 large rooms, a lift and extras like its downstairs lounge with a bowl of fruit and a refrigerator stocked with free mineral water. It also has a good restaurant and a soothing garden. Cots and extra beds for kids are available.

★ Mooslechners Bürgerhaus
HOTEL $$$

(⊡6162; www.hotelbuergerhaus-rust.at; Hauptstrasse 1; ste €249-289; P🛜♿) Popular for honeymoon nights and weddings, this exquisite hotel has spiral staircases inside a 1537 building. Rooms are in Biedermeier style, some with vaulted ceilings and drapes around the bed. Mooslechners Bürgerhaus

caters superbly for children, with cots on hand, and the option of an extra bed at a discount. The restaurant downstairs (closed Monday) is top class and has a magnificent garden setting.

🍴 Eating & Drinking

When in Rust, do as the locals do and head for one of the many *Heurigen*. They're easy to spot – just look for the *Buschen* (small wreath) hanging in front of doorways. Some operate under restaurant licences and are therefore open throughout the summer. For some of the finest formal eating in town, head to Mooslechners Bürgerhaus.

Peter Schandl
AUSTRIAN $

(www.schandlwein.com; Hauptstrasse 20; mains €6-12; ⊙4pm-midnight Mon & Wed-Fri, from 11am Sat & Sun mid-Mar–mid-Nov) You can enjoy game goulash and other warm dishes at this place with a restaurant feel, located just off Rathausplatz.

★ Weingut Gabriel
WINE TAVERN $$

(www.weingut-gabriel.at; Hauptstrasse 25; cold platters €12; ⊙from 4pm Thu & Fri, from 2pm Sat & Sun Apr-Oct; ♿) Don't miss this rustic wine spot

---

HIRING BIKES

Burgenland is a cyclist's dream. Much of the landscape is flat or has gently rolling hills and is criss-crossed with well-marked cycle paths.

Local tourist offices can supply cycle maps. From Neusiedl am See the 135-km Neusiedler See bike trail leads south, crossing into Hungary (bring your passport) for 38km before the path re-emerges in Austria just south of Mörbisch am See on the western side of the lake.

Nextbike (⊡02742-229 901; www.nextbike.at; per hour/24hr €1/8) Has over 16 stations around the Neusiedler See and in Eisenstadt where you can hire and drop off a rented bicycle. The website explains the steps and how to register (which you need to do in advance on the website).

Fahrräder Bucsis (⊡02167-207 90; www.fahrraeder-bucsis.at; train station, Neusiedl am See; per day €15; ⊙8.30am-7pm Mar–mid-Oct) The bike path begins at its door.

on the main drag. Not only is the pay-by-weight buffet brimming with delicious sausage and cold cuts, the wine is a treat, and in season the idyllic cobblestone courtyard is a wonderful vantage point to observe the local storks.

ℹ Information

Tourist office (☑502; www.rust.at; Conradplatz 1, Rathaus; ☉9am-noon & 1-4pm Mon-Fri, 9am-6pm Sat, to noon Sun) Has a list of wine-growers offering tastings, plus hotels and private rooms in the town.

ℹ Getting There & Away

Hourly buses connect Eisenstadt and Rust (€3.80, 25 minutes). For Neusiedl am See (€3.80, 40 minutes, every one to two hours), change to the train at Schützen am Gebirge train station. Ferries cross the lake to Podersdorf, Breitenbrunn and Fertörákos.

Mörbisch am See

☑02685 / POP 2300

Mörbisch am See is a sleepy community 6km south of Rust and only a couple of kilometres shy of the Hungarian border. Soaking up the relaxed atmosphere and taking in quaint whitewashed houses with hanging corn and flower-strewn balconies is the order of the day here.

The town's tranquil mood changes dramatically during summer evenings with the **Seefestspiele** (www.seefestspiele-moerbisch. at; ☉mid-July–Aug), a summer operetta festival that attracts some 200,000 people each year. Its biggest competitor is the **Opern**

Festspiele (www.ofs.at; ☉early Jul-late Aug), an opera festival held in an old Roman quarry near St Margareten, around 7km northwest of Mörbisch.

The local **tourist office** (☑8430; www.moerbisch.com; Hauptstrasse 23; ☉9am-5pm Mon-Fri, to noon Sat & Sun) can advise on accommodation, the festivals and lakeside facilities, and give you a list of *Heurigen*.

Frequent buses go to Mörbisch via Rust from Eisenstadt (€3.80, 40 minutes). A foot-and cycle-only border crossing into Hungary, 2km south of Mörbisch, is handy for those circumnavigating the lake. There are no border controls, but you do need to be able to show your passport on demand. Alternatively, jump on the ferry across the lake to stay within Austria.

Purbach am See

☑02683 / POP 2700

Purbach am See, 17km north of Rust, is another pretty town along the lake. Its small, compact centre is filled with squat houses and it is still protected by bastions and three gates – reminders of the Turkish wars. While there isn't a lot to see in the town – nor has it direct access to Neusiedler See – it's nice to soak up the slow pace of life and wander from one wine cellar to the next along historic Kellergasse and Kellerplatz, both outside the town's walls.

The **tourist office** (☑5920; www.purbach. at; Am Kellerplatz 1; ☉9am-7pm) has information on accommodation and wine.

🛏 Sleeping

**Camping Purbach &
Jugendherberge** CAMPGROUND $
(☑51 70; office@gmeiner.co.at; camp sites per adult/child/tent/car €5/3.50/2.90/3, dm €20; ☉Apr-Oct) If you need a place to stay, look no further than this camping ground on the edge of the reed beds.

Gasthof zum Türkentor GUESTHOUSE $
(☑3400; www.foltin.at; Hauptgasse 2; s/d €60/120; 🅿🛜) A guesthouse situated right alongside the old city wall in the historic part of town.

**★Weingut & Weingasthof
Kloster am Spitz** HOTEL $$
(☑5519; www.klosteramspitz.at; Waldsiedlung 2; s €75, d €120-140; 🅿) On the northwestern fringe of town among vineyards (follow Fellnergasse) is a small former monastery with

---

ℹ STAYING IN SOPRON

If you're on a tight budget, staying just over the border in Hungary could save you a bailout of euros. Accommodation in Sopron, just 14km from Mörbisch, can work out vastly cheaper than on the Austrian side of the border, especially when reserving through popular booking websites. However, if you have a hire car and plan to sleep in Hungary, make sure your hire company permits clients to drive vehicles across the border. It is possible to reach Austrian lake communities from Sopron using public transport by changing from Vienna- and Wiener Neustadt–bound trains onto local buses.

a modern hotel. Wines from the vineyard are produced organically and served in its very highly rated (and highly priced) restaurant (open for lunch and dinner Thursday to Sunday and lunch Wednesday March to December).

❶ Getting There & Away

Purbach has direct train connections with Neusiedl am See (€3.70, 12 minutes, hourly), Eisenstadt (€3.80, 15 minutes, hourly) and Vienna Hauptbahnhof (€13.50, one hour, hourly), and direct bus connections with Eisenstadt (€3.80, 20 minutes, at least one every two hours). From Rust, get off in Schützen am Gebirge (centre) and walk 300m to the train station to change to a regional train.

Neusiedl am See

📞 02167 / POP 7300

Neusiedl am See is the region's largest town, the most accessible from Vienna, and a good springboard into the lake area.

If you do stay in town, **Rathausstüberl** (📞 2883; www.rathausstueberl.at; Kirchengasse 2; s €63-75, d €86-118; P) has bright rooms. **Gasthof zur Traube** (www.zur-traube.at; Hauptplatz 9; mains €5.50-14; ⏰ 11am-10pm) offers traditional Austrian edibles for reasonable prices as well as a few vegetarian options.

The city's **tourist office** (📞 2229; www.neusiedlamsee.at; Untere Hauptstrasse 7; ⏰ 8am-6pm Mon-Fri, 8am-noon & 2-6pm Sat, 9am-noon Sun, closed from noon Fri-Sun Nov-Apr) has a map of the town and the lake, as well as information on other lakeside towns.

❶ Getting There & Away

Daily buses leave hourly down the eastern side of the lake, passing through Podersdorf (€3.80, 16 minutes) and Illmitz (€5.70, 30 minutes).

Hourly trains connect Vienna Hauptbahnhof with Neusiedl am See (€11, 45 minutes). Hourly trains to Eisenstadt (€5.80, 30 minutes) pass through Purbach (€3.70, 15 minutes). For Rust, change to the bus in Schützen.

Podersdorf am See

📞 02177 / POP 2100

Podersdorf am See, on the eastern shore, is the only town which can truly claim to be *Am See* (on the lake). This fact combined with a reed-free location are the possible reasons it's become the most popular holiday destination in the Neusiedler See region (and Burgenland).

REED EXPLORATIONS

Although Purbach isn't located directly on the lake shore, it's inside a nature reserve and has reed banks that invite exploration on a bicycle ride or an easy walk. Kirchengasse/Gartengasse one block north of the tourist office leads down to the reeds, and from there a 2.5km path follows a canal out to the lake. An alternative ride or walk is to follow the Kirschblutenradweg (B12) north along the reeds to Breitenbrunn (about 4.5km), turn right onto the Schilflehrpfad (Reed Educational Path) and follow that out to the lake (about 3km), where there's lake swimming. Hire bikes from the camping ground or ask at the tourist office. **Canoe Excursions** (📞 0664 382 85 40; www.natur-neusiedlersee.com; 2hr adult/child €22/15; 👶) takes you out into the reeds and is also suitable for kids. Book at least one day ahead.

🏃 Activities

Water Sports

Podersdorf offers bathing on Neusiedler See, with a long grassy **beach** (adult/child €4/2; ⏰ 7.30am-5pm Apr-Oct) for swimming, boating and windsurfing. Windsurfing costs an extra €3.50, even with your own board, and paddle/electric boat hire is €7/12 per day. Wind and water enthusiasts can head for the Südstrand, where **Mission to Surf** (📞 0680-234 65 29; www.surf-schule.at) has equipment for hire and offers kite-surfing courses. **Surf & Segelschule Nordstrand** (📞 0664-277 61 40; www.nordstrand.at; Seeufergasse 17) rents sailing boats and holds weekday sailing courses.

Bicycle Touring

If you haven't already picked up a bicycle – the perfect way to see the Seewinkel wetlands, which start about 5km south of town – five places around town rent bikes for between €9 and €15 per day.

🛏 Sleeping

Book ahead for July and August. Seestrasse, the street leading from the tourist office to the lake, has many small places to stay.

Steiner   B&B $
(📞 2790; www.steinergg.at; Seestrasse 33; s/d €35.50/71; P 👶) This central *Gästehaus*

SPA & SWIMMING IN FRAUENKIRCHEN

In Frauenkirchen, 8km southeast from Podersdorf, you can take the cure at modern **St Martins Therme & Lodge** (⟐02172-20 500; www.stmartins. at; Im Seewinkel 1, Frauenkirchen; d per person €155-195; P🅿●🛜), a **spa resort** (day tickets adult/child €22.50/9.40; ☉9am-10pm) fed by hot springs. The area around the spa has been landscaped, and it's possible for day or overnight guests of the spa and hotel to swim outdoors in the lake fed by mineral springs.

Book ahead at the hotel for free pickup from Frauenkirchen train station if arriving by rail or bus, but St Martins can also be easily reached by bike on a detour from the main bike path (there's a Nextbike (p145) station at the spa and others at the train station and the basilica in Frauenkirchen).

(guesthouse) has welcoming staff, a tranquil, homey atmosphere and spartanly clean rooms with updated bathrooms and balconies.

Strandcamping CAMPGROUND $
(⟐2279; Strandplatz 19; camp site per adult/child/tent/car €7.20/5/5/5; ☉late Mar-Oct) Right by the beach, this popular camping ground is one of the largest around and has plenty of shade from the sweltering heat.

★**Hotel-Restaurant Pannonia** HOTEL $$
(⟐2245; www.pannonia-hotel.at; Seezeile 20; s/d from €59/€94; P🛜🗲♿) A little way back from the waterfront, this smartly renovated hotel has a New World feel, 21st-century furnishings and a large grassy area where children can go bananas. The owners run a second hotel across the road with family rooms. The restaurant has a wine list the size of a short novel and seasonal dishes such as venison carpaccio served on wild-garlic pesto with tomatoes.

Seewirt HOTEL $$
(⟐2415; www.seewirtkarner.at; Strandplatz 1; s €80-93, d €111-182; P🛜) Having bagged a prime spot right next to the ferry terminal and beach, the four-star Seewirt is understandably popular among those who want to be close to the splashy action. Rooms are

crisp and full of sea-refracted light and the restaurant serves no-nonsense Austrian fare.

✗ Eating & Drinking

★**Zur Dankbarkeit** AUSTRIAN $$
(⟐22 23; www.dankbarkeit.at; Hauptstrasse 39, Podersdorf; mains €9-19; ☉Fri-Tue Apr-Nov, Fri-Sun Jan-Mar, closed Dec) This lovely old restaurant serves some of the best regional cooking around. The inner garden, with its trees and country ambience, is the ideal spot to knock back some local wine.

Weinklub 21 WINE BAR
(www.weinclub21.at; Seestrasse 37; tastings about €10; ☉9am-noon & 4-9pm May-Sep) This excellent *Vinothek* represents 21 wine producers in the town and region; it holds regular tastings and events.

ℹ Information

Tourist office (⟐2227; www.podersdorfamsee.at; Hauptstrasse 2; ☉8am-4.30pm Mon-Fri, 9am-4.30pm Sat, 9am-noon Sun)

ℹ Getting There & Away

Buses leave hourly or two-hourly connecting Neusiedl and Podersdorf (€3.80, 16 minutes). Ferries connect Podersdorf with Rust and Breitenbrunn on the western shore.

Seewinkel

⟐02175
Seewinkel is the heart of the **Neusiedler See-Seewinkel National Park**, and a grassland and wetland of immense importance to birds and other wildlife. The vineyards, reed beds, shimmering waters and constant birdsong make this an enchanting region for an excursion. This is an excellent area for birdwatching and explorations on foot or by bicycle.

The protected areas cannot be directly accessed by visitors, so to really get into the birdwatching you need a pair of binoculars. There are viewing stands along the way.

The park has its own information centre on the northern fringes of Illmitz, the **Nationalparkhaus** (www.nationalpark-neusiedler-see-seewinkel.at; ☉8am-5pm Mon-Fri, 10am-5pm Sat & Sun, closed Sat & Sun Nov-Mar). It has a small display on the ecology and staff can tell you the best places to spot local wildlife.

The town of **Illmitz**, 4km from the lake, is surrounded by the national park and makes for a good base. Staff at its **tourist office**

(✍2383; www.illmitz.co.at; Obere Hauptstrasse 2-4; ☉8am-noon & 1-5pm Mon-Fri, 9am-noon & 1-5pm Sat, 9am-noon Sun, closed Sat & Sun Nov-Jun) can provide information on the region. **Arkadenweingut-Gästehaus** (✍3345; www.arkadenweingut-heiss.at; Obere Hauptstrasse 20; s/d €36/64; P) is a lovely arcaded homestead in the centre of Illmitz.

Illmitz is connected with Möbisch, Rust, and Fertörákos in Hungary by ferry and Neusiedl am See by hourly buses (€5.70, 30 minutes).

Middle & Southern Burgenland

Heading south, the flat expanse of the Neusiedler See is soon forgotten as you enter an undulating landscape replete with lush hills, forested glens and castles that rise up in the distance. It's a region often overlooked by visitors and a place where life is still very much connected to the land; the influence of long-resident Hungarian and Croatian settlers can be felt here.

Lockenhaus & Around

Lockenhaus, in the centre of Burgenland, is famous for its **castle** (✍02616-23 94; www.ritterburg.at; adult/child €8/4; ☉9am-5pm Mar-Oct), or more accurately, for its former resident Elizabeth Báthory. Better known as the 'Blood Countess', she has gone down in history for her reign of terror early in the 17th century, when she reputedly tortured and murdered over 600 mainly peasant women for her own sadistic pleasure. The castle has long been cleansed of such gruesome horrors but still contains an impressive torture chamber, complete with an iron maiden.

If you want to sleep inside a castle, the **Burghotel Lockenhaus** (✍02616-23 94; www.ritterburg.at; s/d €95/130; P) has antique-furnished rooms and a sauna.

Some 13km east of Lockenhaus is the tiny village of **Klostermarienberg**, home to a now-defunct monastery housing what must be the only dog museum in Europe, the **Europäisches Hundemuseum** (www.kulturimkloster.at; Klostermarienberg; admission €5; ☉2-5pm Sun May-Aug). The odd collection of dog paraphernalia includes paintings, statues and intriguing photos of dogs dressed for war during WWI and WWII, complete with gas masks. Take a few minutes to visit the monastery's crypt, a chamber containing ar-

chaeological finds dating from the 13th and 14th centuries.

Bernstein, 15km west of Lockenhaus, is dominated by the impressive **Burg Bernstein** (Bernstein Castle; ✍03354-63 82; www.burgbernstein.at; Schlossweg 1; s €110-170, d €166-196; ☉late Apr–mid-Oct; P). Thirteen of the castle's rooms, all tastefully decorated with period furniture, are now used as a hotel where guests can stay in opulent surroundings. The castle foundations date from 1199, creating the historic setting for a delightful retreat from the stress of modern-day living. In the town centre is a small **Felsenmuseum** (✍03354-6620; www.felsenmuseum.at; Hauptplatz 5; admission €6; ☉9am-6pm daily Mar-Oct, to 5pm Nov & Dec, closed Jan & Feb), which focuses on the gemstone serpentine and local mining (this was first mined in the town in the mid-19th century).

If your body needs some TLC, stop in at the spa town of **Bad Tatzmannsdorf**, 15km south of Bernstein. Aside from taking the waters at the **Burgenland Therme** (✍03353-89 90; www.burgenlandtherme.at; Am Thermenplatz 1; day card adult/child €21.50/14; ☉9am-10pm Mon-Thu & Sun, to 12.30am Fri, to 11pm Sat), you can visit the **Südburgenländisches Freilichtmuseum** (www.freilichtmuseum-badtatzmannsdorf.at; Josef Hölzel-Allee; admission €1; ☉9am-6pm), a small but rewarding open-air museum filled with thatched buildings from 19th-century Burgenland. The local **tourist office** (✍03353-70 15; www.bad.tatzmannsdorf.at; Joseph-Haydn-Platz 3; ☉8am-5.30pm Mon-Fri, 9.30am-2.30pm Sat, 9.30-11.30am Sun, closed Sun Nov-Mar) helps with accommodation.

❶ Getting There & Away

You're better off with your own transport in this region as bus connections can be thin. Three direct weekday buses connect Lockenhaus and Eisenstadt (€14, 1½ hours). On weekdays hourly and on Saturday two-hourly direct buses go north from Oberwart (where there's a train station) to Bad Tatzmannsdorf (€2.50, five minutes); from Oberwart to Bernstein (€5, 30 minutes, every one to three hours) or Lockenhaus (€6.80, one hour, twice each weekday) is also manageable.

Güssing & Around

If you haven't developed castle fatigue by this stage, head 40km south of Bad Tatzmannsdorf to Güssing, a peaceful town on the banks of the Strembach River. Here the arresting **Burg Güssing** (✍03322-43400;

www.burgguessing.info; Batthyanystrasse 10; admission €6; ⊙10am-5pm Tue-Sun Easter-Oct) rises dramatically over the river and town. The castle, which is a mix of ruins and renovations, contains plenty of weapons from the Turks and Hungarians, striking portraits from the 16th century and a tower with 360-degree views of the surrounding countryside. A modern 100m **funicular railway** (Schrägaufzug; tickets €1; ⊙10am-5pm Tue-Sun Easter Mon-Oct) helps those with weary legs reach the castle.

A visit to the **Auswanderer Museum** (Stremtalstrasse 2; adult/child €2/1; ⊙2-6pm Sat & Sun May-Oct), to the north of the castle, is also worthwhile. It relays the story of the mass exodus of Burgenlanders (including Fred Astaire's father) to America before and after WWI – most emigrated due to lack of work or poor living conditions.

If you missed the open-air museum in Bad Tatzmannsdorf, head 5km west of Güssing to the **Freilichtmuseum** (www.freilicht-museum-gerersdorf.at; Gerersdorf bei Güssing 66; admission €5; ⊙9am-5pm Mon-Fri, 10am-6pm Apr–mid-Nov) at **Gerersdorf**. An hour or two could easily slip by while you explore the 30-odd buildings and their traditional furniture and fittings, which capture the rural culture of Burgenland in the 18th and 19th centuries.

The **tourist office** (☑03322-440 03; www.suedburgenland.info; Hauptplatz 7; ⊙9am-noon Mon-Fri) in Güssing can help with private rooms, otherwise try **Landgasthof Kedl** (☑03322-42 40 30; www.tiscover.at/gasthof.kedl; Urbersdorf 33; s/d €32/64; Ⓟ), 3km north of Güssing in Urbersdorf. The castle's restaurant, **Burg Güssing** (☑03322-42 579; www.burgrestaurant.net; mains €10-15, 6-course menus €25; ⊙10am-10pm Tue-Sun Mar-Dec), has a filling six-course Knight's menu and a terrace with extensive views over the countryside.

❶ Getting There & Away

Every one to two hours daily direct buses connect Güssing (€7.50, 45 to 70 minutes) with Oberwart. On weekdays and Saturday several direct buses connect Güssing and Geresdorf (€2, 10 minutes).

Upper Austria

Best Places to Eat

➡ Herberstein (p159)

➡ Verdi Restaurant & Einkehr (p158)

➡ No Solo Vino (p157)

➡ Knapp am Eck (p165)

➡ Löwenkeller (p167)

Best Places to Stay

➡ Spitz Hotel (p157)

➡ Hotel Christkindlwirt (p164)

➡ Baumhotel (p164)

➡ Boutique Hotel Hauser (p164)

➡ Hotel Forstinger (p164)

Why Go?

Upper Austria may not have the in-your-face splendour of the Tyrolean Alps or Vienna's imperial palaces. But, as locals delight in telling you, it has a taste of all that is great about Austria. For starters, there's the mighty Danube and a rich musical heritage, old-world coffee houses and castle-topped medieval towns, and resplendent Augustinian abbeys and spas. And the best bit, they whisper, is that nobody really knows it.

It's true. Beyond the high-tech museums and avant-garde galleries of Linz lies a land in miniature waiting to be un-wrapped. Each layer reveals new surprises: from rustic farmhouses serving home-grown *Most* (cider) to the lime-stone pinnacles of the Kalkalpen where the elusive lynx roams. Whether you're among the mist-enshrouded hills rippling towards the Czech Republic or wheat fields fading into a watercolour distance at dusk, you'll find these land-scapes have a quiet, lingering beauty all of their own.

When to Go

➡ Summer is a fine time to cycle along the Danube and through the countryside. Come in September for cutting-edge technology festivals and free riverside concerts in Linz. Rooms are at a premium from June to September, though, so book ahead.

➡ October to February sees room rates dip, as well as the crowds. Autumn is perfect for crisp walks through the forests, while winter brings glittering Christmas markets galore, and cross-country skiers swish through the Nationalpark Kalkalpen.

➡ The spring shoulder season from March to May is a great time to see the orchards in blossom and to celebrate Schubert in Steyr.

Upper Austria Highlights

1 Playing with pixels and conversing with intelligent robots at Ars Electronica Center in **Linz** (p153).

2 Falling for the storybook lanes and fast-flowing rivers of **Steyr** (p163).

3 Walking and sleeping high above the treetops at the Baumkronenweg in **Kopfing** (p170).

4 Hiking through the rugged limestone wilderness of **Nationalpark Kalkalpen** (p166), Austria's second-biggest national park.

5 Drifting away in a Caribbean lagoon, daiquiri in hand, at **Therme Geinberg** (p171).

6 Being amazed by the grace of the Augustiner Chorherrenstift in **St Florian** (p162).

7 Journeying to the darkest depths of Austria's past at **KZ Mauthausen** (p163) concentration camp.

ℹ Getting There & Around

AIR

Austrian Airlines, Lufthansa, Ryanair and Air Berlin are the main airlines servicing Blue Danube Airport Linz (p160). There are flights to Vienna, as well as Frankfurt, Düsseldorf and Edinburgh. Ryanair has flights to London Stansted every Tuesday, Thursday and Saturday.

CAR & MOTORCYCLE

The A1 autobahn runs east–west to Vienna and Salzburg; the A8 heads north to Passau and the rest of Germany; and the A9 runs south into Styria.

PUBLIC TRANSPORT

Upper Austria's bus and train services are covered by the **Oberösterreichischer Verkehrsverbund** (www.ooevv.at). Prices depend on the number of zones you travel (one zone costs €1.80). As well as single tickets, daily, weekly, monthly and yearly passes are available. Express trains between Vienna and Salzburg pass through Linz and much of southern Upper Austria, and there are also express trains heading south from Linz to St Michael in Styria, from where connections to Klagenfurt and Graz are possible.

LINZ

☑ 0732 / POP 193,500

'In Linz beginnt's' (it begins in Linz) goes the Austrian saying, and it's spot on. This is a city on the move. Daring public art installations, a burgeoning cultural scene, a cybercentre and a cutting-edge gallery that look freshly minted for a sci-fi movie all signal tomorrow's Austria, and reveal that Linz has its finger on the pulse of the country's technology industry.

It took a long time coming, but since Linz seized the reins as European Capital of Culture in 2009, the world has been waking up to the charms of Austria's third city. Sitting astride the Danube, Linz rewards visitors who look beyond its less-than-lovable industrial outskirts.

History

Linz was a fortified Celtic village when the Romans took over and named it Lentia. By the 8th century, when the town came under Bavaria's rule, its name had changed to Linze, and by the 13th century it was an important trading town for raw materials out of Styria. In 1489 Linz became the imperial capital under Friedrich III until his death in 1493.

Like much of Upper Austria, Linz was at the forefront of the Protestant movement in the 16th and 17th centuries. With the Counter-Reformation, however, Catholicism made a spectacular comeback. The city's resurgence in the 19th century was largely due to the development of the railway, when Linz became an important junction.

Adolf Hitler may have been born in Braunau am Inn, but Linz was his favourite city (he spent his schooldays here), and his largely unrealised plans for Linz were grand. His Nazi movement built massive iron- and steelworks, which still employ many locals. After WWII Linz was at the border between the Soviet- and US-administered zones. Since 1955, Linz has flourished to become an important industrial city, port and provincial capital.

◉ Sights & Activities

★ Ars Electronica Center   MUSEUM

(www.aec.at; Ars-Electronica-Strasse 1; adult/child €8/6; ◷ 9am-5pm Tue-Fri, to 9pm Thu, 10am-6pm Sat & Sun) The technology, science and digital media of the future are in the spotlight at Linz' biggest crowd-puller, the Ars Electronica Center. Opened in 2009, the new Treusch-designed centre resembles a futuristic ship by the Danube after dark, when its LED glass skin kaleidoscopically changes colour.

The open-plan interior focuses on themed labs. Head down to **Funky Pixels** to create light drawings and **RoboLab** to interact with cutting-edge robots. Other hands-on highlights include the **BioLab**, where you can clone plants and analyse DNA; the **FabLab**, where you can animate digital objects; and the **GeoCity**, where you can take a virtual round-the-world trip.

★ Lentos   GALLERY

(www.lentos.at; Ernst-Koref-Promenade 1; adult/child €8/4.50, guided tours €2-3; ◷ 10am-6pm Tue-Sun, to 9pm Thu) Ars Electronica's rival icon across the Danube is the rectangular glass-and-steel Lentos, also strikingly illuminated by night. The gallery guards one of Austria's finest modern-art collections, including works by Warhol, Schiele, Klimt, Kokoschka and Lovis Corinth, which sometimes feature in the large-scale exhibitions.

There are one-hour guided tours in German at 7pm on Thursdays and 4pm on Sundays, and 30-minute tours in English at 4pm on the first Saturday of the month. Or download the Lentos app at http://app.lentos.at.

Linz

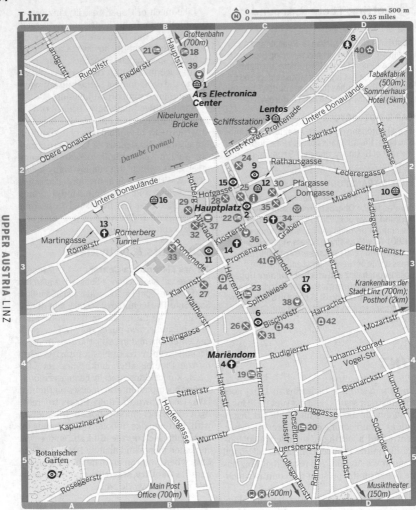

500 m
0.25 miles

Grottenbahn (700m)

Landgutstr
Rudolfstr
Fiedlerstr
Hauptstr

21
18
39

1

Ars Electronica Center

Nibelungen Brücke

8
40

Tabakfabrik (500m); Sommerhaus Hotel (5km)

Lentos
3
Schiffsstation

Ernst-Koref-Promenade
Untere Donaulände
Fabrikstr
Kaisergasse

Obere Donaustr

Danube (Donau)

Untere Donaulände

24
9
Rathausgasse
Lederergasse

Hofberg
15
25
28
12
30
Pfargasse
Domgasse
Museumstr
10

16
29
Hauptplatz
2
35
Altstadt
22
5
34
Graben
Fadingerstr

13
Martingasse
Römerberg Tunnel
Römerstr

32
Klosterstr
14
36
Bethlehemstr

33
Promenade
11
41
Landstr
Danietzstr

Klammstr
27
44
Herrenstr
23
Spittelwiese
17
Krankenhaus der Stadt Linz (700m); Posthof (2km)

38
Harrachstr
42
Mozartstr

Steingasse
26
6
Bischofstr
43
31

Wattherstr

Mariendom
4
19
Herrenstr
Rudigierstr
Johann-Konrad-Vogel-Str
Bismarckstr
Humboldtstr

Stifterstr
Hafnerstr

Kapuzinerstr
Hopfengasse
Wurmstr
Langgasse
Gesellenhausstr
20
Auerspergstr
Südtiroler-Str

Botanischer Garten
7
Rosseggerstr

Main Post Office (700m)
(500m)
Volksgartenstr
Rainerstr
Landstr
Musiktheater (150m)

★ **Mariendom**   CATHEDRAL

(Herrenstrasse 26; ⏱7.30am-7pm Mon-Sat, 8am-
7.15pm Sun) Also known as the Neuer Dom,
this neo-Gothic giant of a cathedral lifts
your gaze to its riot of pinnacles, flying but-
tresses and filigree traceried windows. Designed in the mid-19th century by Vinzenz
Statz of Cologne Dom fame, the cathedral
sports a tower whose height was restricted
to 134m, so as not to outshine Stephansdom in Vienna. The interior is lit by a veritable curtain of stained glass, including
the **Linzer Fenster**, depicting scenes from
Linz' history.

★ **Hauptplatz**   SQUARE

Street performers entertain the crowds, trams
rumble past and locals relax in pavement
cafes on the city's centrepiece square, framed
by ornate baroque and pastel-coloured Renaissance houses. The square's **Dreifaltigkeitssäule** (Trinity Column) – a 20m pillar of
Salzburg marble carved in 1723 to commemorate the town's deliverance from war, fire and
plague – glints when it catches the sunlight.

Landesgalerie   GALLERY

(www.landesgalerie.at; Museumstrasse 14; adult/
child €6.50/4.50; ⏱9am-6pm Tue-Fri, to 9pm Thu,

Linz

10am-5pm Sat & Sun) Housed in a sumptuous late-19th-century building, the Landesgalerie focuses on 20th- and 21st-century paintings, photography and installations. The rotating exhibitions often zoom in on works by Upper Austrian artists, such as Alfred Kubin's expressionist fantasies and Valie Export's shocking Viennese Actionist-inspired pieces. The open-air **sculpture park** contrasts modern sculpture with the gallery's neoclassical architecture.

Pöstlingberg   LOOKOUT
Linz spreads out beneath you atop Pöstlingberg (537m), which affords bird's-eye views over the city and the snaking Danube. It's a precipitous 30-minute ride aboard the narrow-gauge **Pöstlingbergbahn** (Hauptplatz; adult/child return €5.60/2.80; ☉6am-10.30pm Mon-Sat, 7.30am-10.30pm Sun) from the Hauptplatz. This gondola features in the Guinness Book of Records as the world's steepest mountain railway – quite some feat for such a low-lying city!

At the summit is the turn-of-the-20th-century **Grottenbahn** (Am Pöstlingberg 16; adult/child €5/3; ☉10am-5pm, to 6pm Jul & Aug; 🚼), where families – and anyone who loves a bit of cult kitsch – can board the dragon train to trundle past gnomes, glittering stalactites and scenes from Grimms' fairy tales.

Schlossmuseum   MUSEUM
(www.schlossmuseum.at; Schlossberg 1; adult/child €6.50/4.50; ☉9am-6pm Tue-Fri, to 9pm Thu, 10am-5pm Sat & Sun) Romans, Habsburg emperors, fire – Linz' hilltop **castle** has seen the lot. Enjoy the panoramic city views before delving into the museum's trove of treasures, gathered from abbeys and palaces over the centuries. The collection skips through art, archaeology, historical weapons and instruments, technology and folklore. The Gothic ecclesiastical paintings are a real highlight.

Alter Dom   CATHEDRAL
(Domgasse 3; ☉7am-7pm) The twin towers of this late-17th-century cathedral dominate Linz' skyline. With its stucco-work, its

pink-marble altar and its gilt pillars, the interior is remarkably ornate. Famous local lad Anton Bruckner served as organist here from 1856 to 1868.

Donaupark
PARK

Next to Lentos on the southern bank of the Danube is the Donaupark, the city's green escape vault. Modern sculptures rise above the bushes in the well-tended gardens, which are a magnet for walkers, joggers, skaters, picnickers and city workers seeking fresh air in summer.

Botanischer Garten
GARDEN

(Roseggerstrasse 20-22; adult/child €3/2; ☉8am-dusk) These peaceful botanical gardens, south of the centre, nurture 10,000 species, from native alpine plants to orchids, rhododendrons, tropical palms and one of Europe's largest cacti collections.

Zahnmuseum
MUSEUM

(Tooth Museum; www.zahnmuseum-linz.at; Hauptplatz 1; ☉9am-1pm & 2-6pm Mon-Fri) FREE If you're terrified of the whine of the dentist's drill, this is one museum guaranteed to set your teeth on edge. On display are items spanning 300 years of dentistry, from rudimentary 18th-century appliances and chairs through to cavity preparations (gripping stuff) and X-ray devices. Open wide...

Bischofshof
HISTORICAL BUILDING

(Bischofstrasse) This ornate baroque bishop's residence was built by Michael Pruckmayer following designs by Jakob Prandtauer, who also made his mark on the abbeys in St Florian and Melk.

Minoritenkirche
CHURCH

(Church of the Minor Friars; Klosterstrasse 7; ☉8am-4pm) Founded in 1236 and redesigned in rococo style with delicate pink stucco, this church contains altar paintings by Bartolomeo Altomonte.

Landhaus
HISTORICAL BUILDING

(Promenade) This striking Renaissance building with a trio of interlinking courtyards is now the seat of Upper Austrian parliament and government. The bronze **Planet Fountain** dates from 1582.

Martinskirche
CHURCH

(Römerstrasse; ☉7.30am-6pm) One of Austria's oldest churches, first mentioned in 799. Notice the Roman inscriptions and oven through the window.

Ursulinenkirche
CHURCH

(Landstrasse 31; ☉7.30am-6pm) This baroque, twin-domed church was a former nunnery and features altar paintings by the prolific Martin Altomonte.

☞ Tours

If you'd prefer to explore the city with a group, Tourist Information Linz (p160) organises 1½-hour **walking tours** (adult/child €9/free; ☉11am) in German, which run regardless of the weather or the number of people.

✦✦ Festivals & Events

Linz Fest
MUSIC

(www.linzfest.at; ☉May) This huge shindig on the third weekend in May brings free rock, jazz and folk concerts to the city.

Pflasterspektakel
STREET CARNIVAL

(www.pflasterspektakel.at; ☉late Jul) Musicians, jugglers, actors, poets, fire-breathers and acrobats from across Europe descend on Linz for this three-day street festival.

Voestalpine Klangwolke
MUSIC

(www.klangwolke.at; ☉Sep) Modern, classical, children's musicals – it's all in the musical mix at this free concert series held in the Donaupark.

Ars Electronica Festival
CULTURE

(www.aec.at; ☉early Sep) This boundary-crossing event showcases cyber-art, computer music, and other marriages of technology and art.

Brucknerfest
MUSIC

(www.brucknerhaus.at; ☉mid-Sep–early Oct) Linz pays homage to native son Anton Bruckner with classical music.

🛏 Sleeping

Nondescript chain hotels abound in Linz, but you'll also find charming *Pensionen* and design-focused digs in the centre. Tourist Information Linz offers a free accommodation booking service, but only face-to-face and not over the phone.

Sommerhaus Hotel
HOTEL €

(✆24 57 376; www.sommerhaus-hotel.at; Julius-Raab-Strasse 10; s/d €52/80; P🛜🏊) This recently revamped uni hotel sits between the city and open fields. Rooms are no-frills yet comfy, breakfast is filling and there's a big indoor pool for swimming proper laps. Take tram 1 or 2 to Schumpeterstrasse and walk five minutes.

★ **Spitz Hotel** DESIGN HOTEL €€

(☑73 37 33; www.spitzhotel.at; Fiedlerstrasse 6; s €89-168, d €109-188; P✳@🖥) Much-lauded Austrian architect Isa Stein has left her avant-garde imprint on the Spitz. The lobby's molded furnishings and UFO-style lighting set the tone. Each of the hotel's rooms spotlights an aspect of Linz' burgeoning arts scene, and features bespoke pieces by local creatives. Minimalism rules here, with clean lines, open-plan bathrooms and hardwood floors, plus homely perks like DVD players and coffee-making facilities.

Hotel am Domplatz DESIGN HOTEL €€

(☑77 30 00; www.hotelamdomplatz.at; Stifterstrasse 4; s €130-150, d €160-210; ✳@🖥) Sidling up to the neo-Gothic Neuer Dom, this glass-and-concrete cube is a welcome newcomer to Linz' design scene. Streamlined interiors in pristine whites and blonde wood reveal a Nordic-style aesthetic. The rooftop spa is the place to wind down with a view.

Harry's Home APARTMENT €€

(☑75 75 00; www.harrys-home.com; Donaufeldstrasse 3; s €68-131, d €82-146; P@🖥) Slick, pared-down decor, a genuinely warm welcome and light, spacious studios and apartments with kitchenettes make this a great base for exploring Linz under your own steam. Breakfast costs an extra €6 (continental) or €12 (buffet). Harry's is located around 5km north of town; take tram 1 to Linke Brückenstrasse, then bus 33 to Further Weg, a two-minute walk from the apartments.

Zum Schwarzen Bären HISTORIC HOTEL €€

(☑77 24 77; www.linz-hotel.at; Herrenstrasse 9-11; s €80-94, d €116-138, ste €180; P✳@🖥) The birthplace of acclaimed tenor Richard Tauber, this 15th-century hotel is run by the friendly Nell family. Overlooking a courtyard, the rooms have recently been madeover in monochrome hues and parquet; some even sport waterbeds. The woodpanelled restaurant dishes up Austrian classics.

Wolfinger HISTORIC HOTEL €€

(☑77 32 91; www.hotelwolfinger.at; Hauptplatz 19; s €78-92, d €98-126, tr €118-136, q €138-156; P@🖥) This 500-year-old hotel located on the main square has an air of old-world grandeur about it. Archways, stucco and period furniture lend rooms character; those at the back are quieter and some have balconies.

ℹ CITY SAVER

The **Linz Card** (1-day adult/child €15/10, 3-day adult/child €25/20) gives unlimited use of public transport; entry to major museums including the Ars Electronica Center, Schlossmuseum, Lentos and the Landesgalerie; plus discounts on other sights, city tours and river cruises. The three-day card also includes a round-trip on the Pöstlingbergbahn. Buy the Linz Card at the tourist office, airport, museums and some hotels.

Hotel Kolping HOTEL €€

(☑66 16 90; www.hotel-kolping.at; Gesellenhausstrasse 5; s €69-87, d €87-114; P✳🖥) Hidden down a backstreet in central Linz, Kolping has bright, spotless rooms and attentive service. Breakfast is among the best in town with cooked options, homemade cakes and fresh fruit.

Hotel & Loft Landgraf HOTEL €€

(☑70 07 12; http://hotellandgraf.com; Hauptstrasse 12; s/d €89/109, ste €130-160; P🖥) Occupying an art nouveau apartment block, Landgraf is just steps from Ars Electronica and the Danube. Rooms are modern and massive, though furnishings are spartan and bathrooms on the poky side of small. Modern art punctuates the uberchic public spaces.

✕ Eating

Linz takes its innovative spirit to the kitchen and its flair for design to the dining room. Besides Austrian fare, you'll find fusion cuisine, and both locavore and world flavours on many menus. Old-style cafes are the place to try the classic *Linzer Torte*. Made to a 17th-century recipe with almonds, spices and tangy redcurrant jam, the tart is the greatest rival to Vienna's own *Sacher Torte*.

★ **No Solo Vino** DELI, ITALIAN €

(☑79 77 88; www.nonsolovino.at; Bischofstrasse 15; light meals & mains €5-20; ⊙9am-6pm Mon-Fri, to 1pm Sat) Sweet and simple, No Solo Vino believes in careful sourcing; its *formaggi* (cheeses), *salumi* (cold meats), antipasti and pastas are as good as any you'll find in Italy. It knocks superfresh ingredients into lunch dishes such as beef carpaccio with rocket and homemade ravioli. Sit in the courtyard when the weather's fine.

UPPER AUSTRIA LINZ

Spirali
CAFE €

(Graben 32b; mains €5.90-8.90; ☺11am-7pm Mon-Sat; ✍) Staff keep the good vibes and groovy music coming at this ethnic-flavoured cafe. The accent is on regional produce, with great-value lunch specials from pasta to curries. Give the homemade brownies and iced teas a whirl.

Gragger
BAKERY €

(www.gragger.at; Hofgasse 3; snacks €3-6; ☺7.30am-6pm Mon-Fri, 8am-5pm Sat; ✍) ⌕ Breakfast, wholesome soups, salads and delicious organic breads are served at wooden tables in this vaulted cafe.

Promenadenhof
AUSTRIAN €

(✎77 76 61; www.promenadenhof.at; Promenade 39; mains €8-16; ☺10am-1am Mon-Sat; 👶) Promenadenhof enjoys a loyal following for spot-on Austrian grub such as *Tafelspitz* (prime boiled beef) and Styrian-style chicken salad, served in vaulted *Stuben* (parlours) and a beer garden with a kids playground.

k.u.k. Hofbäckerei
CAFE €

(Pfarrgasse 17; coffee & cake €3-6; ☺6.30am-6.30pm Mon-Fri, 7am-12.30pm Sat) The Empire lives on at this gloriously stuck-in-time cafe. Here Fritz Rath bakes the best *Linzer Torte* in town – rich, spicy and with lattice pastry that crumbles just so.

Cafe Jindrak
CAFE €

(www.linzertorte.at; Herrenstrasse 22; lunch menus €5.30-7.10; ☺8am-6pm Mon-Sat, 8.30am-6pm Sun; 👶) Join the cake-loving locals at this celebrated cafe. You'd need a huge fork (and appetite) to tackle the *Linzer Torte* that set a Guinness World Record in 1999, measuring 4m high and weighing 650kg. Bake your own (perhaps not quite as big) at one of the regular cookery workshops.

Bauernmarkt
MARKET €

(Farmers Market; Hauptplatz; ☺9am-2pm Tue & Fri) Twice-weekly market for picnic fixings and fresh local produce.

★ Verdi Restaurant & Einkehr
AUSTRIAN €€

(✎73 30 05; www.verdi.at; Pachmayrstrasse 137; mains €10-28; ☺5pm-midnight Tue-Sat) Linz spreads out picturesquely before you from this gastro duo, a short taxi ride from town. At ultra-chic Verdi, Erich Lukas prepares seasonal dishes with panache and precision, such as quail breast with herby risotto and plump free-range chicken with truffle gnocchi. Wood-beamed Einkehr, in the same building, is an altogether cosier affair and serves Austrian comfort food. They're 5km north of the city centre.

p'aa
INTERNATIONAL €€

(www.paa.cx; Altstadt 28; mains €8.50-12.50; ☺11am-2.30pm & 5.30pm-midnight Mon-Sat; ✍) Choose between the softly lit vaulted interior, decked out with eye-catching photo portraits, and the pavement terrace at worldly, boho-cool p'aa. The vibe is incredibly relaxed and the food places a strong emphasis on vegetarian and organic dishes. Sample the homemade olive focaccia before digging into nicely spiced dishes such as mulligatawny soup and stir-fries.

Cook
INTERNATIONAL €€

(✎78 13 05; www.cook.co.at; Klammstrasse 1; mains €9.50-15; ☺11.30am-2.30pm Mon, 11.30am-2.30pm & 6-10.30pm Tue-Fri) Tossing Scandinavian and Asian flavours into the same pan may seem like folly, but Cook somehow manages to pull it off. A clean-lined, crisp interior forms the backdrop for dishes such as gravlax and *svensk fiksoppa* (fish soup) with a generous pinch of chilli.

Cubus
FUSION €€

(✎94 41 49; www.cubus.at; Ars-Electronica-Strasse 1; mains €11-24; ☺9am-1am Mon-Sat, to 6pm Sun; 📶) On the 3rd floor of the Ars Electronica Center, this glass cube has stellar views over the Danube to the south bank and glows purple after dark. The menu is season-inspired and strictly fusion, along the lines of poached salmon with caper risotto, coffee foam and orange-fennel salad. The two-course lunch is a snip at €7.50.

Alte Welt
AUSTRIAN €€

(✎77 00 53; www.altewelt.at; Hauptplatz 4; mains €9-16; ☺11.30am-2.30pm & 6-11pm Mon-Sat) Set around an arcaded inner courtyard, Alte Welt serves hearty fare, such as roast pork and beef ragout, and a good-value two-course lunch (€7.50). By night the cellar hosts jam sessions, live jazz and plays that attract students and arty types.

Wagnerei
ITALIAN €€

(✎91 89 89; Pfarrgasse 18; mains €16.50-26.50; ☺5pm-midnight Tue & Wed, 11am-3pm & 5pm-midnight Thu-Sun) Chunky wood tables and vaults create a backdrop for clean Italian flavours such as porcini risotto and venison carpaccio at this central foodie haunt. The handwritten menu changes daily.

★ **Herberstein** FUSION €€€
(☑ 78 61 61; www.herberstein-linz.at; Altstadt 10; mains €20-30; ☺4pm-4am Mon-Sat) Chic Herberstein comprises an oriental-style lounge, ivy-draped garden, well-stocked wine cellar and glamorous restaurant. Brick vaults and clever backlighting set the scene for Sascha Wurdinger's crossover dishes, such as caramelised sturgeon with goulash jus and meltingly tender braised beef cheeks with yogurt, aubergines and raisins – all beautifully cooked and presented.

🍷 Drinking & Nightlife

Linz' student population keeps the scene young and upbeat. Your best bet for a bar crawl is the area west of the Hauptplatz, nicknamed the 'Bermuda Triangle'; Altstadt and Hofberg are peppered with pubs, cafes and wine bars.

Domviertel WINE BAR
(www.domviertel.at; Herrenstrasse 36; ☺9am-midnight Mon-Sat, to 5pm Sun; 📶) It's all about the view at this glass-fronted wine bar on the square facing Mariendom. Drink in the view of the cathedral's neo-Gothic pinnacles and spires over a glass of Grüner Veltiner or Zweigelt on the terrace.

Strom BAR
(Kirchengasse 4; ☺2pm-1am Tue-Thu, to 4am Fri & Sat) DJs spin hip-hop, electro and funk at this upbeat bar, where partygoers spill out onto Kirchengasse in summer. Upstairs is rough 'n' ready Stadtwerk, which hosts clubbing events, gigs and party nights.

Cubus Terrace COCKTAIL BAR
(Ars-Electronica-Strasse 1; ☺5pm-midnight; 📶) There's no finer spot to see Linz light up than this glass-walled cafe on the top floor of the Ars Electronica Center. Pick out the landmarks over a sunset cocktail.

Stiegelbräu zum Klosterhof MICROBREWERY
(Landstrasse 30; ☺9am-midnight) Pass on the mediocre food and go straight for the freshly tapped Stiegl beer at the cavernous Klosterhof. The chestnut-tree-shaded beer garden has space for 1500 thirsty punters.

Ignis WINE BAR
(www.ignis-vinotheken.at; Klosterstrasse 3; ☺10am-midnight Mon-Sat) Just off the Hauptplatz, this industro-chic, monochrome bar is a cool spot to converse over Austrian, French and Italian wines, Mühlviertel speciality beers and antipasti.

Madame Wu TEAHOUSE
(www.madamewu.net; Altstadt 13; ☺10am-9pm Mon-Wed, to midnight Thu-Sat, 1-8pm Sun) Full of cosy nooks, this oriental-style tearoom has a terrific tea selection. Afternoon tea (€15) is served daily at 3pm and includes dainty cucumber and salmon sandwiches, and scones with clotted cream and homemade strawberry jam.

☆ Entertainment

★ **Musiktheater** THEATRE
(☑ 761 10; www.landestheater-linz.at; Am Volksgarten 1) Linz is as proud as punch of its new Musiktheater, a strikingly geometric opera house designed by London-based architect Terry Pawson, which opened in April 2013. This is now the city's main stage for operas, operettas, ballets, musicals and children's productions.

Tabakfabrik CULTURAL CENTRE
(www.tabakfabrik-linz.at; Peter-Behrens-Platz 11) Another shining example of Linz' cultural

---

LINZ' HALL OF FAME

Romantic composer **Anton Bruckner** was the organist at the Alter Dom from 1856 to 1868. Today his symphonies still resound at cathedral concerts from July to September and at the annual Brucknerfest. His music is also the focus of the **Linz-Genesis** (Hauptplatz 1; ☺9am-1pm & 2-6pm Mon-Fri) FREE museum in the 17th-century old town hall.

Not to be eclipsed in Linz' hall of fame is great astronomer, mathematician and astrologer **Johannes Kepler**, who lived at Rathausgasse 5, where he completed the groundbreaking Rudolphine Tables. The house now harbours the **Kepler Salon** (www.kepler-salon.at; Rathausgasse 5) FREE, which hosts science-themed events. The genius is also commemorated by the Planet Fountain at the Landhaus, and by the university named after him, where he taught from 1612 to 1626.

A bust of **Mozart** graces the entrance to the grand Renaissance townhouse on the corner of Theatergasse and Altstadt, where he stayed as a guest of the Count of Thun in 1783 and is said to have bashed out the *Linzer Symphony* (No 36) in just four days.

renaissance is this cultural centre, lodged in a former tobacco factory. Check the website program for details of upcoming events from exhibitions to readings, film screenings, concerts and party nights.

Brucknerhaus   LIVE MUSIC
(☑76 12-0; www.brucknerhaus.linz.at; Untere Donaulände 7) Linz' premier music venue stages top-drawer classical and jazz concerts. There is a dedicated program for kids of different ages ('mini' and 'midi' music).

Posthof   MUSIC, THEATRE
(☑77 05 48-0; www.posthof.at; Posthofstrasse 43) Dockside Posthof covers everything from blues, funk and rock gigs to cutting-edge theatre and dance. Festivals are occasionally held here. Take bus 27 or 270 to Hafen/ Posthofstrasse.

🔒 Shopping

The main thoroughfare is Landstrasse, home to high-street stores and malls. Antique and craft shops, galleries, boutiques and jewellers line Bischofstrasse and Herrengasse.

Göttin des Glücks   FASHION
(www.goettindesgluecks.at; Herrenstrasse 2; ⊗10am-6pm Mon-Fri, to 2pm Sat) 🍃 Wear it with a conscience is the maxim at fair-trade and sustainable-fashion-focused Göttin des Glücks, which has a delightfully casual array of supple cotton jerseys, shirts, skirts and shorts. It has sister boutiques in Vienna and Innsbruck.

Glas Galerie   GLASS
(Bischofstrasse 11; ⊗11am-5pm Tue-Fri, 10am-1pm Sat) A gallery specialising in imaginative, contemporary glassware, from decorative objects to candy-coloured jewellery.

Arkade   MALL
(Landstrasse 12; ⊗9.30am-6pm Mon-Fri, to 5pm Sat) This elegant mall shelters names such as Augarten Porzellan, Redl Glass and Marc O'Polo under one glass roof.

Confiserie Isabella   CONFECTIONERY
(Landstrasse 33; ⊗8.30pm-7.30pm Mon-Sat) A nostalgic sweet shop for pralines, bonbons, jellies, marshmallows and other delights.

Imkerhof   FOOD
(Altstadt 15; ⊗9am-6pm Mon-Fri, to noon Sat) Honey you can eat, drink and bathe in (including chestnut and acacia varieties) fills the shelves here.

ℹ Information

There are a number of banks with ATMs in the Innenstadt.

Hotspot Linz (www.hotspotlinz.at) Free wi-fi at 120 hotspots in the city, including Ars Electronica Center and Lentos.

Krankenhaus der Stadt Linz (☑78 06-0; Krankenhausstrasse 9) The main hospital, 1km east of the centre.

Linz Termine (www.linztermine.at) Listings of cultural events and exhibitions throughout the year.

Lonely Planet (www.lonelyplanet.com/austria/the-danube-valley/linz) Planning advice, author recommendations, traveller reviews and insider tips.

Main Post office (Bahnhofplatz 11-13; ⊗8am-6pm Mon-Fri, 9am-noon Sat) Near the Hauptbahnhof; has an ATM.

Post office (Domgasse 1; ⊗8am-6pm Mon-Fri, 9am-noon Sat) Handy to the centre.

Tourist Information Linz (☑7070 2009; www.linz.at; Hauptplatz 1; ⊗9am-7pm Mon-Sat, 10am-7pm Sun May-Sep, 9am-5pm Mon-Sat, 10am-5pm Sun Oct-Apr) Brochures, accommodation listings, free room-reservation service and a separate Upper Austria information desk can be found here.

Unfallkrankenhaus Linz (☑69 20-0; Garnisonstrasse 7) Emergency hospital.

ℹ Getting There & Away

The **Schiffsstation** (Untere Donaulände 1) is on the south bank next to the Lentos Kunstmuseum. From late April to early October, **Wurm + Köck** (☑78 36 07; www.donauschiffahrt.de; Untere Donaulände 1) sends boats westwards to Passau (one way/return €26/29, six hours, 2.20pm Tuesday to Sunday) and east to Vienna (€58, 11½ hours, 9am Saturday).

Regional buses depart from stands at the main bus station adjacent to the Hauptbahnhof.

Linz is on the main rail route between Vienna (€34, 1½ hours) and Salzburg (€24, 1¼ hours), and express trains run twice hourly in both directions. Several trains depart daily for Prague (€47, 5½ hours).

ℹ Getting Around

TO & FROM THE AIRPORT

Blue Danube Airport Linz (☑7221 600-0; www.linz-airport.at; Flughafenstrasse 1, Hörsching) is 13km southwest of town. A direct shuttle-bus service connects the Hauptbahnhof (€2.70, 20 minutes) with the airport hourly from 6am to 7pm Monday to Saturday. Alternatively, there are hourly train connections between Linz and Hörsching (9 minutes, €2.20), a three-minute ride from the airport by free shuttle bus.

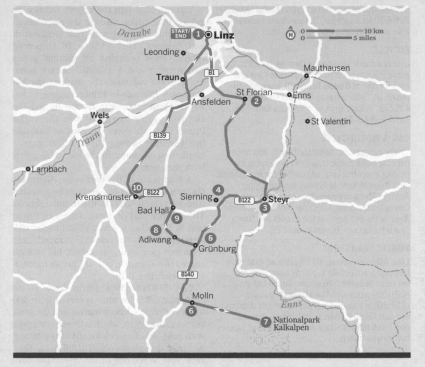

🏃 Driving Tour
Upper Austria Highlights

START LINZ
END LINZ
LENGTH 160KM; ONE DAY

This off-the-beaten-track drive meanders through Upper Austria's bucolic landscapes to resplendent abbeys, rustic villages, spa towns and limestone mountains. It's particularly beautiful on an autumn day, when the apple trees are heavy with fruit and the forests are a vibrant palette of russet and gold.

Heading south of ❶ **Linz**, the city's industrial fringes soon give way to low-rise hills and meadows. Take the B1 to ❷ **St Florian** and explore its majestic Augustinian abbey, a masterpiece of baroque art and the final resting place of Romantic composer Anton Bruckner. Continue south on minor roads through patchwork fields studded with *Vierkanthof,* huge square farmhouses with inner courtyards. The rolling countryside brings you to riverside ❸ **Steyr**, the picture-book town that inspired Schubert's *Trout Quintet* and a relaxed place for lunch. Follow the emerald-tinted Steyr River west

along the B122 to ❹ **Sierning**, dominated by its Renaissance Schloss Sierning. From here, the B140 shadows the river south to the pretty church-topped town of ❺ **Grünburg**, nestled in wooded hills. It's just a 15-minute drive south to ❻ **Molln**, the northern gateway to the spectacular limestone peaks, waterfalls and wilderness of ❼ **Nationalpark Kalkalpen**. Get information on local walks at Molln's national park visitor centre. Refreshed by the mountain air, head north, passing Grünburg and swinging west along a country road to tiny ❽ **Adlwang**. Here Gangl farmhouse is a good stop for home-grown apple juice and *Most* (cider). Five minutes north sits the spa town of ❾ **Bad Hall**, fabled for the healing powers of its iodine-laced waters, in which you can bathe at Mediterrana Therme and inhale (for free) in the sculpture-dotted park. A short drive west along the B122 leads to ❿ **Kremsmünster**, whose opulent Benedictine abbey harbours an incredible library and observatory. Drive back to Linz via the scenic church-dotted villages lining the B139.

Use the free phone at the station to dial ☑ 0800 206 600 for a pick-up. The service is very reliable and runs daily from 5am to 10pm.

BICYCLE

Linz is a major stop on the Danube Trail and has some 200km of bicycle routes. Bikes are available for hire at **Donau Touristik** (www.donaureisen.at; Lederergasse 4-12; per day/week €15/79; ⊙ 8am-6pm Mon-Fri, plus 8am-6pm Sat & Sun Apr-Sep).

CAR & MOTORCYCLE

One-way systems, congested roads and pricey parking make public transport preferable to driving in central Linz, although a car is a definite plus if you're keen to explore more of Upper Austria. There are some free car parks along Obere Donaulände. Major car-hire firms include **Avis** (www.avis.com) at the airport and **Hertz** (www.hertz.com; Bürgerstrasse 19).

PUBLIC TRANSPORT

Linz AG (www.linzag.at) Linz has an extensive bus and tram network, but by early evening services become infrequent. Single tickets (€2), day passes (€4) and weekly passes (€12.20) are available from pavement dispensers and *Tabak* (tobacconist) shops. Drivers don't sell tickets – buy and validate your tickets before you board.

AROUND LINZ

St Florian

☑ 07224 / POP 5990

Unassuming St Florian, a market town 18km southeast of Linz, hides one of Austria's finest Augustinian abbeys. Supposedly buried under the abbey, St Florian was a Roman officer who converted to Christianity and was subsequently tortured and drowned in the Enns River in the year 304 for his pains. In many Austrian churches, the patron saint of fire-fighters and of Upper Austria is depicted as a Roman warrior dousing flames with a bucket of water.

◉ Sights

Augustiner Chorherrenstift   ABBEY
(www.stift-st-florian.at; Stiftstrasse 1; tours adult/child €7.50/5; ⊙11am, 1pm & 3pm May-Sep) Rising like a vision above St Florian, this abbey dates at least to 819 and has been occupied by the Canons Regular, living under Augustinian rule, since 1071. Today its imposing yellow-and-white facade is overwhelmingly baroque.

You can only visit the abbey's interior by guided tour, which takes in the resplendent apartments adorned with rich stuccowork and frescoes. They include 16 emperors' rooms (once occupied by visiting popes and royalty) and a galleried library housing 150,000 volumes. The opulent **Marble Hall** pays homage to Prince Eugene of Savoy, a Frenchman who frequently led the Habsburg army to victory over the Turks. Prince Eugene's Room contains an amusing bed featuring carved Turks, which gives a whole new meaning to the idea of sleeping with the enemy!

A high point of the tour is the **Altdorfer Gallery**, displaying 14 paintings by Albrecht Altdorfer (1480–1538) of the Danube School. The sombre and dramatic scenes of Christ and St Sebastian reveal a skilful use of chiaroscuro. Altdorfer cleverly tapped into contemporary issues to depict his biblical scenes (for example, one of Christ's tormentors is clearly a Turk).

The **Stiftsbasilika** (⊙7am-8pm) is an exuberant affair: its altar is carved from 700 tonnes of pink Salzburg marble and the huge 18th-century organ, which is literally dripping with gold, was Europe's largest at the time it was built. To hear the organ in full swing, time your visit to see one of the 20-minute **concerts** (€4, incl guided abbey tour €9.80; ⊙2.30pm Mon, Wed-Fri & Sun mid-May–mid-Oct).

Alongside Anton Bruckner's simple tomb in the **crypt** are the remains of some 6000 people believed to be Roman, which were unearthed in the 13th century. Stacked in neat rows behind a wrought-iron gate, their bones and skulls create a spine-tingling work of art.

OÖ Feuerwehrmuseum   MUSEUM
(Fire Brigade Museum; www.feuerwehrmuseumstflorian.at; Stiftstrasse 2; adult/child €3/2; ⊙10am-noon & 2-5pm Tue-Sun May-Oct) Opposite the Stiftskirche, this is a child's dream of a museum and an ode to St Florian, patron saint of fire-fighters. The collection comprises historic fire engines, hoses and other paraphernalia.

🛏 Sleeping & Eating

The tourist office hands out a useful accommodation booklet that lists hotels and private rooms in and around St Florian.

Gästehaus Stift St Florian   GUESTHOUSE €
(☑89 02 13; Stiftstrasse 1; s/d €48/76) It's oh-so-quiet at this guesthouse within the abbey's walls, overlooking the cloisters and

manicured gardens. Antique furniture, solid wood floors and candles add character to the fittingly spartan rooms, which are flooded with natural light.

Landgasthof zur Kanne   GUESTHOUSE €€
(⟋ 42 88; www.gasthof-koppler.at; Marktplatz 7; s/d €54/88; P) This yellow-fronted 14th-century guesthouse on the main square scores points for its clean, snug rooms and its restaurant that serves fresh produce from the Koppler family's farm.

Zum Goldenen Löwe   AUSTRIAN €€
(⟋ 89 30; Speiserberg 9; mains €7-13; ◷ 11.30am-10pm Thu-Mon, to 2pm Tue) The sound of the chef pounding humungous schnitzels welcomes you to this wood-panelled restaurant opposite the abbey gates. The sunny terrace out the back overlooks rolling countryside. Lunch specials go for €5.70.

❶ Information

The small **tourist office** (⟋ 56 90; Marktplatz 2; ◷ 9am-1pm Mon-Fri) is in the centre of town on Marktplatz, just below the abbey, where you'll also find a few guesthouses and the post office.

❶ Getting There & Away

St Florian (officially Markt St Florian) is not accessible by train. Buses depart frequently from the main bus station at Linz' Hauptbahnhof (€2.80, 23 minutes); there is a reduced service on Sunday.

Mauthausen
⟋ 07238 / POP 4970

Today Mauthausen is an attractive small town on the north bank of the Danube, east of Linz, but its historic status as a quarrying centre prompted the Nazis to site the **KZ Mauthausen** concentration camp here. Prisoners were forced into slave labour in the granite quarry and many died on the so-called *Todesstiege* (stairway of death) leading from the quarry to the camp. Some 100,000 prisoners died or were executed in the camp between 1938 and 1945.

The camp, which has undergone extensive renovation recently, has been turned into the emotive **Mauthausen Memorial** (www.mauthausen-memorial.at; Erinnerungsstrasse 1; adult/child/family €2/1/4.80; ◷ 9am-5.30pm) museum that tells its history, and that of other camps such as those at Ebensee and Melk. Visitors can walk through the remaining living quarters (each designed for 200, but housing up to 500) and see the disturb-

ing gas chambers. The former Sick Quarters now shelters most of the camp's harrowing material – charts, artefacts and many photos of both prisoners and their SS guards. It is a stark and incredibly moving reminder of human cruelty.

❶ Getting There & Away

From Linz, the quickest way to Mauthausen is by train (€7.60, 25 minutes, hourly). Mauthausen Memorial (follow the KZ Mauthausen signs) is around 3km northwest of the centre; it's a 40-minute walk or a short taxi ride.

THE TRAUNVIERTEL

The pleasantly green and rolling Traunviertel is a great place to abandon the map for a few days. This stretch of Upper Austria is less about sightseeing and more about easing into country life – whether hiking in the hills, sampling homemade *Most* in the apple orchards or bedding down in a rambling *Vierkanthof* farmhouse.

Steyr
⟋ 07252 / POP 38,200

Franz Schubert called Steyr 'inconceivably lovely' and was inspired to pen the sprightly *Trout Quintet* here. And lovely it is: on the confluence of the swiftly flowing Enns and Steyr Rivers, the postcard-like old town of cobbled lanes and candy-hued baroque houses is one of Upper Austria's most attractive. Every April, the town pays homage to the composer at the Schubert Festival.

SANTA'S LETTERBOX

If you happen to arrive in Steyr over Christmas, head for the suburb of Christkindl, to the west of the old centre. During the festive season, a special **post office** (www.christkindl.at; Christkindl; ⊙ 9am-5pm 29 Nov–6 Jan) is set up in the Christkindlkirche to handle the almost two million letters posted around the world.

◉ Sights

Great for an aimless amble, Steyr's well-preserved old town centres on the Stadtplatz and its clutch of graceful Gothic, Renaissance and baroque houses.

Museum Arbeitswelt   MUSEUM
(www.museum-steyr.at; Wehrgrabengasse 7; adult/child/family €5/3.50/9; ⊙ 9am-5pm Tue-Sun Mar-Jul & Sep-Dec) Housed in a converted factory by the river, this excellent museum delves into Steyr's industrial past with exhibits on working-class history, forced labour during WWII and the rise of the Socialist party.

Stadtmuseum   MUSEUM
(Grünmarkt 26; ⊙ 10am-4pm Tue-Sun) **FREE** Set in an early-17th-century granary with an eye-catching sgraffito mural facade, this museum spells out Steyr's culture and folklore in artefacts. The baroque and Biedermeier nativity figurines are the highlight of the permanent collection.

Schlosspark   PARK
(Blumauergasse) Footpaths through this quiet park lead to baroque **Schloss Lamberg**, sitting pretty between the confluence of the Enns and Steyr Rivers. A steep passageway next to the Bummerlhaus, with overhanging arches, squeezes through the old city walls and climbs up to cobbled Berggasse and the park.

Bummerlhaus   HISTORIC BUILDING
(Stadtplatz 32) This Gothic gabled house and former pub takes its name from the figurine of a golden lion, which punters, presumably after one too many, nicknamed *Bummerl* (small, fat dog).

Franz Schubert's House   HISTORIC BUILDING
(Stadtplatz 16) Look out for this fine house on the square, where Schubert apparently found inspiration to pen the *Trout Quintet*.

Stadtpfarrkirche   CHURCH
(Brucknerplatz 4; ⊙ dawn-dusk) The spire of this Gothic church is one of Steyr's most visible landmarks. The church shares features with Stephansdom in Vienna and the same architect, Hans Puchsbaum.

Michaelerkirche   CHURCH
(Michaelerplatz 1; ⊙ dawn-dusk) Just north of the Steyr River, this twin-towered baroque church is embellished with a fresco of St Michael and the fallen angels.

⫟ Tours

The tourist office arranges several themed tours, including three-hour old town **walking tours** (tickets €6; ⊙ 2pm Sat Apr-Oct), in German. Alternatively, you can explore at your own speed with a multilingual MP3 tour for €4.

🛏 Sleeping

The tourist office can help arrange private rooms, which are a good deal if you're willing and able to venture out of the centre.

Gasthof Bauer   PENSION €
(☏ 544 41; www.bauer-gasthof.at; Josefgasse 7; s/d €40/68; P 🖙) Run by the same family since 1880, this homely *Pension* sits on a little island in the Steyr River. The rooms are simple but comfy, and there's a leafy garden and a restaurant serving fresh, local fare (lunch menus €7). It's a 1km walk northwest of Stadtplatz.

Motel Maria   GUESTHOUSE €
(☏ 710 62; www.motel-maria.at; Reindlgutstrasse 25; s/d €37/66; P 🖙) Set in a lovingly converted *Vierkanthof* farmhouse, 2km west of town (bus 2B stops nearby), this peaceful guesthouse offers bright, country-style rooms dressed in wood furnishings.

Campingplatz Forelle   CAMPGROUND €
(☏ 780 08; www.forellesteyr.com; Kematmüllerstrasse 1a; camp sites per adult/child/tent €5.50/2.40/3; 🖙) Open from April to October, this tree-shaded campground on the banks of the Enns River has a playground, activities such as canoeing and tennis, plus facilities for cyclists (take bus 1 from the centre).

★ Hotel Christkindlwirt   HOTEL €€
(☏ 521 84; www.christkindlwirt.at; Christkindlweg 6; s €72-82, d €114-132; @🖙) Slip behind the pilgrimage church in Christkindl to this boutique newcomer. Many of the contemporary, warm-coloured rooms have balco-

nies with river views. Candles create a restful feel in the grotto-like spa, which has a sauna, steam room and treatments such as shiatsu massage.

Stadthotel Styria
HISTORIC HOTEL €€

(📞515 51; www.stadthotel.at; Stadtplatz 40; s/d/tr €90/138/180; 🅿🛜🐕) Welcome to Steyr's most historic hotel. This 400-year-old townhouse has loads of original features, from period furnishings and beams to a frescoed breakfast room overlooking the rooftops. There's a sauna and hammam for guests' use.

✗ Eating

Stadtplatz has lots to offer self-caterers; it hosts an open-air market on Thursday and Saturday mornings, and has snack stands as well as a **Billa Corso** (Stadtplatz 30) supermarket.

Cafe di Fiume
CAFE €

(Michaelerplatz 11; lunch menu €5; ⊙9am-6pm Tue-Sat, from 1pm Sun; 🥗) Mismatching chairs, chipper staff and a terrace with views of the Enns create a laid-back atmosphere at this cafe. Try the excellent vegetarian dishes, organic coffee and freshly squeezed juices.

★ Knapp am Eck
EUROPEAN €€

(📞762 69; www.knappameck.at; Wehrgrabengasse 15; mains €11-19; ⊙11am-2pm & 6pm-midnight Tue-Sat) A cobbled lane shadows the Steyr River to this boho-flavoured bistro. Dishes such as tender lamb with polenta and sage-stuffed pork are inspired by local, seasonal produce. By night, candles and lanterns illuminate the ivy-covered walls, trailing roses and chestnut trees in the garden.

Orangerie im Schlosspark
EUROPEAN €€

(📞740 74; www.orangerie-steyr.at; Blumauergasse 1; 2-course lunch €7.50-9.50, mains €9-17; ⊙11am-midnight) This beautifully converted 18th-century orangery opens onto a leafy terrace facing the Schlosspark. The chef cooks fresh, seasonal dishes ranging from chanterelle tagliatelle to hearty beef broth with homemade dumplings.

Gasthof Mader
AUSTRIAN €€

(📞533 58; Stadtplatz 36; mains €8-24; ⊙8am-1am Mon-Sat) With its Gothic vaults, frescoed Schubertstüberl (parlour) and arcaded inner courtyard, Mader is historic dining at its best. Specialities such as crisp roast pork with dumplings or trout served with parsley potatoes figure on the thoroughly Austrian menu.

Bräuhof
AUSTRIAN €€

(📞420 00; www.braeuhof.at; Stadtplatz 35; mains €10-23.50; ⊙10am-11pm) Dine by lantern light under 300-year-old vaults or on the pavement terrace at the atmospheric Bräuhof. Meaty numbers like pork medallions wrapped in ham and served with a mushroom cream sauce are matched with full-bodied Austrian wines.

❶ Information

The **tourist office** (📞532 29-0; www.steyr.info; Stadtplatz 27; ⊙8.30am-6pm Mon-Fri, 9am-noon Sat) is on the main square in the Rathaus.

The **main post office** (Bahnhofstrasse 15; ⊙9am-5pm Mon-Fri) is close to the Hauptbahnhof; the other **post office** (Grünmarkt 1; ⊙8am-noon & 2-6pm Mon-Fri) is more handy to the Stadtplatz.

❶ Getting There & Away

Regional buses depart from the Hauptbahnhof; city buses leave from outside the Hauptbahnhof to the north.

Steyr is on the B115, the road branching from the A1 and running south to Leoben. There's free car parking at the Hauptbahnhof.

Some trains from Linz (€10, 50 minutes, hourly) require a change at St Valentin; there are fewer services on Sundays. Trains continue south into Styria. Most trains for Wels (€13.60, 1¼ hours, hourly) also require a change in St Valentin.

Bad Hall

📞07258 / POP 4790

A sleepy spa town 18km west of Steyr, Bad Hall's big draw is the new **Mediterrana Therme** (www.eurothermen.at; Kurhausstrasse 10; adult/child day ticket €15.50/12.50; ⊙9am-midnight; 🐕). The iodine-rich waters that gush from its thermal springs are hailed for their therapeutic properties. Outside there are massage jets and mountain views, while inside an iodine steam room, a columned Roman bath and whirlpools pummel you into a blissfully relaxed state. A splash pool keeps tots amused.

After drifting (or possibly dropping) off in the spa, a walk in the sculpture-dotted **Kurpark** (⊙dawn-dusk) opposite is invigorating. Kids love to bash away at the *Klangskulpturen,* larger-than-life musical instruments that include a glockenspiel and wind harp. To inhale the iodized salt for free, head for the central pavilion, where 1000L of the stuff filters through twig walls every hour.

Several family-run farmhouses and guesthouses offer rooms for around €15 to €20 per person. Pick up a list at the **tourist office** (📷72 00-0; www.badhall.at; Kurpromenade 1; ⊙8am-5.30pm Mon-Fri, 9am-noon & 1.30-5.30pm Sat, 1.30-5.30pm Sun).

From Steyr, there are frequent buses to Bad Hall (€4.60, 38 minutes).

Nationalpark Kalkalpen

This little-known, almost untouched wilderness of rugged limestone mountains, high moors and mixed forest is home to the elusive golden eagle and lynx. Bordering Styria, this is Austria's second-largest national park after Hohe Tauern. Its valleys and gorges cut through classic alpine landscapes, dominated by **Hoher Nock** (1963m). It's particularly popular with hikers, cyclists and rock climbers in summer and cross-country skiers in winter. Kompass map 70 (1:50,000) covers the park and its trails in detail. For more information on activities, visit the ultramodern **Nationalpark Zentrum Molln** (📷07584-36 51; www.kalkalpen.at; Nationalpark Allee 1; ⊙9am-4pm Mon-Fri, to 2.30pm Sat & Sun May-Oct, 8am-noon & 1-4pm Mon, Tue & Thu, 8am-1pm Wed & Fri Nov-Apr) 🐾 near the northern entrance to the park. Staff can arrange guided tours in English and help with accommodation, including in the 15 mountain huts within the park. Regular direct buses run from Steyr to Molln (€5.60, 53 minutes).

Kremsmünster

📷 07583 / POP 6460

Looming large above the fertile Krems Valley, Kremsmünster's majestic **Benedictine abbey** (www.stift-kremsmuenster.at; adult/child/family €7/3/14; ⊙tours 10am, 11am, 2pm, 3pm & 4pm May-Oct, 11am, 2pm & 3.30pm Nov-Apr) dates from 777, but was given a baroque facelift in the 18th century. Elaborate stuccowork and frescoes shape the long, low **Bibliothek** (library), where shelves creak under 160,000 volumes, and the **Kaisersaal** (Emperor's Hall). The most prized piece in the **Schatzkammer** (treasury) is the gold Tassilo Chalice, which the Duke of Bavaria donated to the monks in about 780. You can visit all three on a one-hour guided tour.

The other star attraction is the 50m-high **Sternwarte** (Observatory Tower; adult/child €8/3; ⊙tours 10am & 2pm May-Oct), dedicated

to numerous schools of natural history. Spanning seven floors, the mind-boggling collection steps from fossilised starfish to the skeleton of an ice-age cave bear. It's a giddy climb up a spiral staircase to the top floor, which displays the Keppler sextant and affords a bird's-eye perspective of Kremsmünster and the gently rolling countryside.

What can be seen without greasing the palms of the abbey with silver is the **Stiftskirche** (⊙dawn-dusk), a baroque church extravagantly adorned with lacy stucco, Flemish tapestries and frescoes. The 17th-century cloisters contain the **Fischbehälter** (Fish Basin; ⊙10am-4pm) containing five fish ponds, each centred on a mythological statue. The trickling of water is calming and you can feed the carp for €1.

❶ Getting There & Away

Kremsmünster is on the rail line between Linz and Graz (from Linz €7.60, 40 minutes, hourly). Buses to/from Wels (€3.90, 30 minutes) and Steyr (€6.40, 50 minutes) run regularly.

Wels

📷 07242 / POP 58,700

Roman-rooted Wels is the largest town in the Traunviertel. While there are few real sights, this is a handy base for exploring rural Upper Austria. The centre is a pleasure to stroll through, with a clutch of Renaissance and baroque townhouses hiding inner courtyards and walled gardens. In summer the town springs to life with markets, open-air concerts and film festivals.

◉ Sights

Stadtplatz   HISTORIC SITE

Wels' main square is framed by slender townhouses, many of which conceal arcaded inner courtyards. Particularly attractive is the ivy-clad courtyard at No 18, nurturing palms, rhododendrons and Japanese umbrella trees. At the front, glance up to spy the 2000-year-old **Römermedallion** (Roman medallion) relief.

Nearby at No 24, the Renaissance **Haus der Salome Alt** sports a *trompe l'œil* facade and takes its name from one-time occupant Salome Alt, mistress of Salzburg's most famous prince-archbishop, Wolf Dietrich von Raitenau. Opposite is the refreshingly simple **Stadtpfarrkirche** (Stadtplatz 31; ⊙dawn-dusk), noteworthy for its Gothic stained glass.

The stout **Ledererturm** (Tanner's Tower), built in 1326, overshadows the western end of Stadtplatz and is the last remnant of the town's fortifications.

Burg Wels   CASTLE

(Burggasse 13; adult/child €4.50/2; ⊙10am-5pm Tue-Fri, 2-5pm Sat, 10am-4pm Sun) Gathered around a quiet, flower-dotted garden, this castle is where Emperor Maximilian I drew his last breath in 1519. The folksy museum contains everything from cannon balls to Biedermeier costumes. Must-sees include the horse-drawn cider press and the circular room that's a shrine to baking, with walls smothered in animal-shaped pastries and gigantic pretzels.

🛏 Sleeping & Eating

The tourist office can help you find somewhere to stay. In summer, the Stadtplatz and its tributaries offer alfresco dining with a lively vibe.

★Boutique Hotel Hauser   BOUTIQUE HOTEL €€

(⌨454 09; www.hotelhauser.com; Bäckergasse 7; s €91-121, d €121-151; ❄☎🏊) With its polished service, its clean-lined, contemporary rooms and a rooftop pool, sauna and terrace, this boutique hotel outshines most of Wels' midrangers. Organic and regional produce, homemade cakes and jams spice up the breakfast buffet, and guests can refresh with free tea and fruit throughout the day.

Hotel Ploberger   HOTEL €€

(⌨629 41; www.hotel-ploberger.at; Kaiser-Josef-Platz 21; s €80-120, €107-145; ℗❄☎) In the heart of town, this Best Western has fresh, contemporary rooms in monochrome hues, some with comforts such as coffeemakers and DVD players. The sauna and open fire keep things cosy in winter.

★Löwenkeller   INTERNATIONAL €€

(⌨797 85; www.loewenkeller.at; Hafergasse 1; mains €14-24; ⊙dinner Mon-Sat) With its exposed stone, starchy white linen and polished service, Löwenkeller is the most sophisticated restaurant in town. Dishes such as porcini-herb pasta and grilled tuna with wasabi purée are presented with flair, and paired with Austrian wines from the cellar.

Gasthaus zur Linde   AUSTRIAN €€

(⌨460 23; www.gasthaus-zur-linde.at; Ringstrasse 45; mains €9-18; ⊙Tue-Sat; 🐾) Sizzling and stirring for the past 200 years, this family-run place radiates old-fashioned warmth. It dishes up Austrian classics alongside seasonal treats such as asparagus in spring and game in autumn.

Olivi   ITALIAN €€

(⌨911 900; Hafergasse 3; mains €6.50-16; ⊙Mon-Sat) This buzzy pizzeria rustles up tasty antipasti, wood-fired pizza and fresh pasta. The €7.50 lunch buffet is cracking value.

ℹ Information

Information, maps and audioguides (€4) of the city are available from **Wels Info** (⌨677 22-22; www.stadtmarketing-wels.at; Stadtplatz 44; ⊙9am-6pm Mon-Fri, 10am-12.30pm & 1-4pm Sat), situated right on the main square, Stadtplatz.

UPPER AUSTRIA'S SMALL PLEASURES

Village-hopping through Upper Austria's countryside reveals some little-known treasures. In the Traunviertel, take a detour to the orchards in **Adlwang** near Bad Hall, where apples go into making juice, *Most* (cider) and schnapps. Leopold Höllhuber sells award-winning potent stuff at **Gangl** (⌨07258-40 18; Mandorferstrasse 28; apt/d €33/38; ⚑), a *Vierkanthof* farmhouse where you can also spend a very comfortable night.

Wending through the fields of the Mühlviertel, pause in **Hirschbach** to follow a steep 13km trail up to a high-altitude herb garden, which grows 150 different types of herbs, some famed for their healing properties. Organic peppermint and melissa are among hundreds of varieties for sale at **Bergkräuter-Genossenschaft** (www.bergkraeuter.at; Thierberg 32; ⊙8am-5pm Mon-Fri).

Further west, while exploring the misty hills and moor lakes of the Böhmerwald (Bohemian Forest), you can stop off in sweet-toothed **Bad Leonfelden** for homemade gingerbread. **Kastner** (www.kastner-austria.at; Lebzelterstrasse 243; ⊙8.30am-6pm Mon-Fri, 9am-5pm Sat, 1-5pm Sun) has guarded a secret recipe since 1599; sample freshly baked fruit, nut, honey and chocolate varieties at the factory shop.

ⓘ Getting There & Away

Trains and buses arrive at the Hauptbahnhof, 1.25km north of Stadtplatz. The town is on the InterCity (IC) and EuroCity (EC) express rail route between Linz (€5.80, 12 to 22 minutes, several hourly) and Salzburg (€21.50, one hour, hourly). There's also an hourly service to Passau (€17, 1¼ hours, hourly) on the German border.

THE MÜHLVIERTEL

The Mühlviertel is a remote, beautiful region of mist-enshrouded hills, thick woodlands and valleys speckled with chalk-white farmhouses. The scenery (as well as the beer and goulash!) is redolent of the not-so-distant Czech Republic. This offbeat corner of Upper Austria is known for its Gothic architecture, warm-hearted locals, and total peace and quiet.

Freistadt

☏ 07942 / POP 7470

Just 10km from the Czech border as the bird flies, Freistadt has some of the best-preserved medieval fortifications in Austria, and the beer isn't bad either; indeed locals are so passionate about *Freistädter* brews that they avoid places where it isn't on tap. Beer aside, pleasure can be had by strolling through the town's narrow streets to gate towers and the gardens that have taken root in the original moat.

◉ Sights

Pick up the *City Walk* brochure from the tourist office, which pinpoints key attractions.

Stadtmauern   HISTORIC SITE

Topping the must-see list are the sturdy 14th-century city walls, complete with gate towers such as the medieval **Linzertor** and skeletal **Böhmertor**, which reflect Freistadt's past need for strong defences as an important staging point on the salt route to Bohemia. The moat encircling the town is now given over to gardens and allotments.

Hauptplatz   HISTORIC SITE

Freistadt's focal point is the elongated Hauptplatz, jammed between the old city walls. The square has some ornate buildings and a Gothic **Stadtpfarrkirche** (Parish Church; ☺ dawn-dusk) capped with a baroque tower. Some of the houses along Waaggasse, just west of the Hauptplatz, are embellished with sgraffito mural designs.

Schlossmuseum   MUSEUM

(www.museum-freistadt.at; Schlosshof 2; adult/child €3/1; ☺ 9am-noon & 2-5pm Mon-Fri, 2-5pm Sat & Sun) The city's 14th-century castle, with a square tower topped by a tapering red-tiled roof, harbours this museum, exhibiting 600 works of engraved painted glass. Climb the 50m Bergfried tower for far-reaching views over Freistadt.

🛏 Sleeping & Eating

The following recommendations (apart from Camping Freistadt) are in the old town. Self-caterers can buy supplies at **Billa** (Eisengasse 14; ☺ 7.15am-7pm Mon-Fri, to 6pm Sat).

BUYING INTO YOUR FAVOURITE BEER

Freistadt is a *Braucommune*, a town where the citizens actually own their brewery – when you buy a house, you automatically buy a share of your favourite tipple. Ownership is limited to the 149 households within the town walls, but if you have the spare change and *really* like your beer, properties sell for around €350,000. Realistically, the brewery cannot be taken over, as the business would have to buy the whole town in order to take control.

The arrangement started way back in 1777 when the brewery opened. In the ensuing centuries the lucky owners would receive their share of the profits in liquid form, which would be distributed in *Eimer Bier* containers holding 56L. Each owner might get up to 130 containers! Nowadays, for better or worse, owners get a cash payment of equivalent value (which, on Friday and Saturday nights, often goes straight back to the brewery). Brewery tours will run from April 2014 at 10.30am Monday to Saturday.

Practically every bar in town serves the local brew, so it's not hard to see why the brewery remains a profitable business. If you'd like to learn more about Freistadt beer and stock up, nip into the **brewery shop** (www.freistaedter-bier.at; Brauhausstrasse 2; ☺ 8am-6pm Mon-Fri, 9am-6pm Sat & Sun).

Pension Pirklbauer
PENSION €

(☎724 40; www.pension-pirklbauer.at; Höllgasse 2-4; s/d €26/44) Nudging up against medieval Linzertor is this charming *Pension*. Christine makes her guests feel at home, whether on the rooftop terrace or in the country-cottage-style rooms with pinewood, floral fabrics and squeaky-clean bathrooms.

Hotel Goldener Adler
HISTORIC HOTEL €€

(☎721 12; www.hotels-freistadt.at; Salzgasse 1; s/d/ tr €53/84/108; [P][🛜]) Polished stone slabs, wrought-iron banisters and vaulted passages crammed with antique wagons and spinning wheels hint at this hotel's 700-year history. Unwind in the sauna and whirlpool, or tuck into the famous beer-marinated Bohemian pork shoulder in the beer garden (mains €8 to €13).

Freistadt Brauhaus
BREWERY €

(☎727 72; www.freistaedter-bier.at; Brauhausstrasse 2; 2-course lunch €6.90, mains €8-14; ⊙9am-midnight) To sample Freistadt's hoppy brews, head to the town's brewery restaurant, which has a sprawling vaulted interior and beer garden. Meaty Austrian faves such as roast pork drizzled with dark beer sauce, served with lashings of kraut, mop up the beer. A keg is tapped at 6pm daily. There's a playground for the kids.

ⓘ Information

The **Mühlviertler Kernland Tourist Office** (☎757 00; www.oberoesterreich.at/kernland; Waaggasse 6; ⊙8.30am-12.30pm & 1-5pm Mon-Fri) provides information on the town and its surrounds.

ⓘ Getting There & Away

Freistadt is on a direct rail route from Linz (€11.80, one hour, every two hours). This line then wriggles its way north to Prague; Czech rail fares are lower than those in Austria, so you can save money by waiting and buying (in Czech currency) your onward tickets once you've crossed the border.

The B310, which connects to the A7 motorway to Linz, runs adjacent to the walled centre and then continues its way northwards towards Prague.

Kefermarkt

☎07947 / POP 2060

It's silent enough to hear a pin drop in the tiny village of Kefermarkt, home to the **Pfarrkirche St Wolfgang** (Oberer Markt 1; ⊙7am-8pm). The pilgrimage church's main claim to fame is its Gothic *Flügelaltar*

(winged altar). A masterpiece of craftsmanship, the limewood altarpiece towers 13.5m, with latticework fronds rising towards the ceiling. At the centre are three expressive figures, carved with great skill: St Peter, St Wolfgang and St Christopher (left to right as you face them). The wings of the altar bear religious scenes in low relief.

Perched on a hill overlooking the forest and Schloss Weinberg's red turrets is microbrewery-cum-guesthouse **Schlossbrauerei Weinberg** (☎71 11; www.schlossbrauerei.at; Weinberg 2; d €50-58; [P]), 10 minutes' walk from Kefermarkt. Homebrews are paired with hearty flavours including beer-drenched goulash, beer-battered schnitzel and fresh trout in the vaulted restaurant (mains €7 to €12), which opens onto a tree-shaded terrace. The quiet rooms have small windows with views of the castle.

Frequent trains travel between Kefermarkt and Freistadt (€2.20, 10 minutes). The church is about 1km north of the train station.

THE INNVIERTEL

Ping-ponged between Bavaria and Austria over the centuries, the Innviertel is a fertile farming region sliced in two by the Inn River, whose banks are a drawcard for cyclists in summer. As well as beautiful baroque and Gothic architecture in Schärding and Braunau, the region has a few other surprises worth sticking around for: from overnighting in a tree house to splashing around in a Caribbean lagoon.

UPPER AUSTRIA KEFERMARKT

Braunau am Inn

☑ 07722 / POP 16,400

A stone's throw from Germany, Braunau am Inn is a favourite pit stop for cyclists pedalling the Inn Radweg trail to or from Innsbruck. This border town has achieved unwanted attention as the birthplace of Hitler, though it would prefer to be described as *die gotische Stadt* (the Gothic city).

◉ Sights

Stadtplatz HISTORIC SITE
This long main square is lined with elegant pastel-hued townhouses; its southern end narrows to the **Torturm**, a 16th-century gate tower. To the west of Stadtplatz rises the spire of the late-Gothic **Stadtpfarrkirche St Stephan** (Kirchenplatz; ⊙dawn-dusk). At almost 100m, it's one of the tallest in Austria.

Hitler's Geburtshaus LANDMARK
(Hitler's Birthplace) Not far from the Torturm is the house where Hitler was born in 1889; he only spent two years of his life here before moving with his family to Linz. The inscription outside simply reads *Für Frieden, Freiheit und Demokratie, nie wieder Faschismus, Millionen Tote mahnen* (For peace, freedom and democracy, never again fascism, millions of dead admonish).

HIGH ABOVE THE TREETOPS

Never has the phrase 'bird's-eye view' been more appropriate than at the **Baumkronenweg** (www.baumkronenweg.at; Knechtelsdorf 1, Kopfing; adult/child €8.50/5; ⊙10am-6pm Mar–early Nov). At this canopy boardwalk in Kopfing, 21km east of Schärding, you can take a head-spinning walk above the treetops. The 2.5km trail is billed as one of the longest in the world and it's certainly a stunner – snaking high above misty spruce trees and comprising lookout towers, hanging bridges and platforms that afford exhilarating perspectives of the forest. For a peaceful room with a (very green) view, check into the 10m-high **Baumhotel** (☑07763-22 89; per adult/child €62/51), six pine-built tree houses elevated on stilts.

The future of this ill-fated building is still up in the air. In 2012 the Russian MP Franz Klinzewitsch wanted to buy the house and raze it to the ground, which would chime with the sentiments of many locals. Unsurprisingly, its dark past is off-putting for potential buyers, and the word is that it could become an immigrant integration centre, which would be a remarkable volte-face.

🛏 Sleeping & Eating

Hotel am Theaterpark HOTEL €
(☑634 71; www.hotelamtheaterpark-neussl.at; Linzerstrasse 21; s/d/tr €46/68/82; 🅿🤖📶) One of the best deals in town, this hotel has bright, well-kept rooms, bike storage and a little fitness room. You can wind down over a glass of wine in the Gothic cellar or in the tree-shaded garden.

Hotel Mayrbräu HOTEL €€
(☑633 87; www.mayrbraeu.at; Linzer Strasse 13; s €49-55, d €78-90; 🅿) This four-star hotel's large, warm rooms are a decent pick. A vaulted gallery full of contemporary art and a vine-clad inner courtyard lend character to the place.

Brauhaus Bogner MICROBREWERY €
(☑223 58; www.hausbrauerei-bogner.at; Haselbach 26; mains €7-10; ⊙10am-1am) Supposedly Austria's smallest brewery, Bogner is a rustic pub-restaurant with solid Austrian fare, several home-brewed beers to guzzle and, often, live music.

ℹ Information

The **tourist office** (☑626 44; www.tourismusbraunau.at; Stadtplatz 2; ⊙8.30am-6pm Mon-Fri, 10am-3pm Sat) is at the northern end of the Stadtplatz.

ℹ Getting There & Away

By train, at least one change is normally required from either Linz (€22.80, 2¼ hours, hourly) or Salzburg (€13.50, 1½ hours, hourly). From Wels, there are several daily direct trains (€19, 1½ hours).

Schärding

☑ 07712 / POP 4880

Schärding is an easy-going town on the Inn River, with peaceful riverfront walks and a baroque centre studded with merchants' houses in myriad pastel shades, such as the identically gabled ones that line up along the **Silberzeile** (Silver Row).

Standing head and shoulders above most places in town is antique-meets-modern **Hotel Forstinger** (📞 23 02-0; www.hotelforstinger. at; Unterer Stadtplatz 3; s/d/apt €78/128/174; 🅿 ❄ 🛜 🐾), whose tastefully appointed rooms combine a contemporary aesthetic with period features. A fine pick for a bite to eat is slick bistro **Seven** (📞 361 35; www. seven.or.at; Silberzeile 7; light meals & mains €7-18; 🕙 10am-midnight Wed-Mon), with a people-watching terrace on the Silberzeile.

The **tourist office** (📞 43 00-0; www. schaerding.at; Innbruckstrasse 29; 🕙 9am-6pm Mon-Fri, 11am-3pm Sat & Sun, closed weekends Oct-Mar), near the bridge spanning the river into Germany, can assist with booking accommodation.

If you have your own transport, the approach to Schärding from Linz, via Engelhartszell along the Danube, is beautiful and certainly off the beaten track. A more leisurely alternative is a **boat trip** (www. innschifffahrt.at; Kaiserweg 1; adult/child €12/6; 🕙 Tue-Sun Apr-Oct) between Passau (Ingling) and Schärding. Trains connect Linz with Schärding (€19.10, 1¼ hours) roughly every hour.

Geinberg

📞 07723 / POP 1400

A Caribbean-style lagoon fringed by palm trees is maybe not *quite* what you expect in the heart of the rural Innviertel, but that's precisely what you'll find at **Therme Geinberg** (www.therme-geinberg.at; Thermenplatz 1; 4hr ticket adult/child/family €17.50/13/45.50; 🕙 9am-10pm Sat-Thu, to 11pm Fri; 🐾), one of Austria's top spas. St Lucia it isn't, but it is easy to quite forget where you are when sipping a daiquiri on the beach, being massaged with coconut oil on a cabana bed and bathing in thermal, salt- and freshwater pools. The Vitalzentrum offers a huge array of pampering treatments, from goat's milk baths to stimulating Tui-Na massages to get the energy flowing. The massive complex also comprises a fitness centre, sauna area and a Mediterranean restaurant.

Geinberg is between Braunau am Inn and Schärding. Trains operate roughly every hour between Braunau am Inn and Geinberg on weekdays, less frequently at weekends (€3.80, 20 minutes). There are roughly hourly trains daily between Schärding and Geinberg (€11.80, one hour).

UPPER AUSTRIA GEINBERG

Styria

Includes ➡

Best Places to Eat

➡ Aiola Upstairs (p180)

➡ Der Steirer (p180)

➡ Thomawirt (p180)

➡ Tom am Kochen (p186)

➡ Prato im Palais (p181)

Best Places to Stay

➡ Hotel Daniel (p178)

➡ Hotel Erzherzog Johann (p179)

➡ Burg Hotel (p187)

➡ Jugend- und Familiengästehaus Schloss Röthelstein (p193)

Why Go?

Austria's second-largest province is a picturesque combination of culture, architecture, rolling hills, vine-covered slopes and mountains. Graz, Austria's second-largest city, is Styria's attractive and relaxed capital. Head south from Graz and you're in wine country, dubbed the 'Styrian Tuscany'. This is also the land of *Kürbiskernöl* – the strong, dark pumpkin-seed oil ubiquitous in Styrian cooking.

The eastern stretch of Styria is dotted with rejuvenating thermal spas and centuries-old castles. If you're a fan of the former, Bad Blumau is a mandatory stop, not only to take the waters but also to appreciate its unusual architecture, designed by Friedensreich Hundertwasser. If you prefer castles, Schloss Riegersburg is one of Austria's best.

In the north and west, Styria's landscape changes to cold, fast-flowing alpine rivers, towering mountains and carved valleys. Highlights are Admont's abey, charming Murau and Erzberg's open-cast mine. Note that the northwestern reaches of Styria stretch into Salzkammergut.

When to Go

➡ Unless you are here for the skiing, the best time to visit is during the main season from April to October.

➡ The wine roads of southern Styria peak in September, when there are festivals; in October, when the vineyards turn golden brown; and around St Martin's Day (11 November), when the young wine is released.

➡ From November many of the sights and cultural events – such as Graz's best sight, Schloss Eggenberg – close or end for the season.

➡ Skiers usually hit Schladming from mid-December (or year-round on the Dachstein Glacier).

Styria Highlights

1 Visiting Schloss Eggenberg, the beautiful Renaissance palace and museum in **Graz** (p174).

2 Exploring the restaurants and bars of **Graz** (p174), Styria's capital.

3 Discovering the spectacular abbey in **Admont** (p193) and exploring its fascinating museums.

4 Tripping underground, or overground, at the open-cast mine in **Eisenerz** (p191).

5 Hiking the trails around **Schladming** (p195).

6 Cruising the **wine roads** (p185) of southern Styria.

ℹ Getting There & Away

BUS

Postbus departures to Mariazell, which isn't on the train line, are integrated with train arrivals at Bruck an der Mur. To Eisenerz, integrated bus services leave from Leoben. For Admont and the Gesäuse, the towns of Liezen and Hieflau form the main bus-transfer points.

CAR

The A2, from Vienna to Villach in Carinthia, runs through southern Styria, passing just below Graz, while the A9 runs an almost north–south course through the middle of Styria, making it straightforward to travel from Linz and Salzburg to Graz. The A9 also connects Graz with Slovenia, 40km to the south.

TRAIN

Styria's train lines are relatively sparse; the main line between Carinthia and Vienna passes well north of Graz through the region's main railhead, Bruck an der Mur. For Linz and Salzburg, a change is usually required at St Michael, 25km southwest of Bruck.

ℹ Getting Around

Regional and city transport (☎ 050 678 910; www.verbundlinie.at) is based on a system of zones and time tickets. Tickets can be bought from machines for one to 22 zones; the price rises from a single trip in one zone (€2.10, valid for one hour), to 24-hour passes for one (€4.70) or multiple zones (eg €8 for four zones to Bärnbach). Weekly and monthly passes are also available.

In Graz, **Mobilzentral** (☎ 050 678 910; www. mobilzentral.at; Jakoministrasse 1; ⊙ 8am-6pm Mon-Fri, 9am-1pm Sat) is a useful store of information on Styrian regional buses. It also sells international train tickets. The website www.busbahnbim.at has timetable and price information.

GRAZ

☎ 0316 / POP 265,300

Austria's second-largest city is probably Austria's most relaxed. After Vienna, it is also Austria's liveliest for after-hours pursuits. It's an attractive place with bristling green parkland, red rooftops and a small, fast-flowing river gushing through its centre. Architecturally, Graz has Renaissance courtyards and provincial baroque palaces complemented by innovative modern designs. Styria's capital also has a very beautiful bluff connected to the centre by steps, a funicular and a glass lift. Last but not least, a large student population (some 50,000 in four universities) helps propel the nightlife and vibrant arts scene, creating a pleasant, active and liveable city.

◉ Sights

◉ Hauptplatz & Around

Neue Galerie Graz   GALLERY
(www.museum-joanneum.at; Joanneumsviertel; adult/child €8/3; ⊙ 10am-5pm Tue-Sun; 🚊 1, 3, 4, 5, 6, 7 Hauptplatz) The Neue Galerie is the most exciting of the three museums inside the Joanneumsviertel museum complex, which also includes the **Naturkundemuseum** (Museum of Natural History; www. museum-joanneum.at; adult/child €8/3; ⊙ 10am-5pm Tue-Sun; ♿). Level 0 houses the separate **Bruseum**, with changing exhibitions dedicated to the Vienna Actionist Günther Brus.

The stunning collection of paintings from the 19th and early 20th centuries on level 0

is the highlight of this museum ensemble. Though not enormous, the collection showcases richly textured and colourful works by painters such as Ernst Christian Moser, Ferdinand Georg Waldmüller and Johann Nepomuk Passini. Egon Schiele is also represented here.

The upstairs collection on post-1945 art is small and eclectic. Another space on level 1 is also used for temporary exhibitions. Guided tours in English are held at 3.30pm on Sundays (one hour, €2.50).

Landeszeughaus   MUSEUM
(Styrian Armoury; www.museum-joanneum.at; Herrengasse 16; adult/child €8/3; ⊙ 10am-5pm Mon & Wed-Sun; 🚊 1, 3, 4, 5, 6, 7 Hauptplatz) You won't need to have a passion for armour and weapons to enjoy what's on show at the Landeszeughaus. More than 30,000 pieces of glistening weaponry and ways to protect yourself against it are housed here, in an exhibition that is one of Graz's most interesting and the largest of its kind in Austria.

Burg   CASTLE, PARK
(Hofgasse; 🚌 30 Schauspielhaus, 🚊 1, 3, 4, 5, 6, 7 Hauptplatz) **FREE** Graz's 15th-century Burg today houses government offices. At the far end of the courtyard, on the left under the arch, is an ingenious **double staircase** (1499) – the steps diverge and converge as they spiral. Adjoining it is the **Stadtpark**, the city's largest green space.

Domkirche   CHURCH
(www.domgraz.at; Burggasse 3; ⊙ dawn-dusk; 🚊 1, 3, 4, 5, 6, 7 Hauptplatz) The Domkirche dates from the 15th century, and became a cathedral in 1786. The interior combines Gothic and baroque elements, with reticulated vaulting on the ceiling; its highlights are Conrad Laib's panel painting *Crucifixion in the Throng* (1457) and the faded *Gottesplagenbild* fresco on the cathedral's exterior, which dates from 1485.

The fresco depicts life in the early 1480s, when Graz was besieged by its triple tragedy of Turks, the plague and locusts.

Mausoleum of Ferdinand II   MAUSOLEUM
(Burggasse 2; adult/child €4/2; ⊙ 10.30am-12.30pm & 1.30-4pm; 🚊 1, 3, 4, 5, 6, 7 Hauptplatz) The mannerist-baroque Mausoleum of Ferdinand II was designed by Italian architect Giovanni Pietro de Pomis and begun in 1614; after Pomis' death the mausoleum was completed by Pietro Valnegro, while Johann

Bernhard Fischer von Erlach chipped in with the exuberant stuccowork and frescoes inside. Ferdinand (1578–1637), his wife and his son are interred in the crypt.

Another highlight is a red-marble sarcophagus of Ferdinand's parents, Karl II (1540–90) and Maria of Bavaria (1551–1608). Only Maria occupies the sarcophagus – Karl II lies in the Benedictine Abbey in Seckau.

Museum im Palais
MUSEUM

(www.museum-joanneum.at; Sackstrasse 16; adult/child €8/3; ⊙10am-5pm Wed-Sun; 🚊1, 3, 4, 5, 6 ,7 Hauptplatz) The revamped Museum im Palais is housed inside the Baroque Palais Herberstein, which has an elegant staircase dating from 1757 and rooms that more than do justice to the exhibits on the theme of 'status symbols'. This takes in a permanent exhibition of treasures, including a carriage used by Friedrich III, dating from the mid-15th century, and special exhibitions.

Stadtpfarrkirche
CHURCH

(Herrengasse 23; ⊙dawn-dusk; 🚊1, 3, 4, 5, 6, 7 Hauptplatz) Rising up on Herrengasse between the main square and Jakominiplatz, the town parish church has an attractive baroque exterior. Inside, the post WWII stained-glass window by Salzburg artist Albert Birkle has a controversial anomaly: the fourth panel from the bottom on the right (left of the high altar) clearly shows Hitler and Mussolini looking on as Christ is scourged.

Museum der Wahrnehmung
MUSEUM

(Museum of Perception; www.muwa.at; Friedrichgasse 41; adult/child €3.50/2; ⊙1-6pm Wed-Mon; 🚊34, 34E Museum der Wahrnehmung) Exploring sensory illusions, the Museum of Perception features a small changing exhibition of art that has a close or distant relationship to perception, as well as gadgets that help you explore illusion for yourself. The **samadhi** (meditative) bath is a therapeutic bath that deprives the body of all sensory input (book at least a week ahead; €45.60).

Ask for the English information sheet.

Volkskundemuseum
MUSEUM

(www.museum-joanneum.at; Paulustorgasse 11-13a; adult/child €6/2; ⊙4-8pm Wed-Fri, 2-6pm Sat & Sun, closed Dec-Feb; 🚊30 Paulustor, 🚊1, 3, 4, 5, 6, 7 Hauptplatz) The Folk Life Museum is devoted to folk art and lifestyle. Highlights include 2000 years of traditional clothing in an exhibition that has the interesting take of

bringing together ways of life with clothing and belief.

Grazmuseum
MUSEUM

(www.grazmuseum.at; Sackstrasse 18; adult/child €5/free; ⊙10am-5pm Wed-Mon; 🚊1, 3, 4, 5, 6, 7 Hauptplatz) This small museum has a permanent collection with objects from city history and is complemented by changing exhibitions.

⊙ Mur River & Around

★ Kunsthaus Graz
GALLERY

(www.kunsthausgraz.at; Lendkai 1; adult/child €8/3; ⊙10am-5pm Tue-Sun; 🚊1, 3, 6, 7 Südtiroler Platz) Designed by British architects Peter Cook and Colin Fournier, this world-class contemporary art space is a bold creation that looks something like a space-age sea slug. Exhibitions change every three to four months, and tours (in English 2pm Sunday, and in German 3.30pm weekends) cover not only the exhibitions but also the building. Useful multilingual audioguides cost €2.50.

Murinsel
BRIDGE

(🚊4, 5 Schlossplatz/Murinsel, 🚊1, 3, 6, 7 Südtiroler Platz) Murinsel is a constructed island-cum-bridge of metal and plastic in the middle of the Mur. This modern floating landmark contains a cafe, a kids playground and a small stage.

⊙ Schlossberg

★ Schlossberg
VIEWPOINT

(🚊4, 5 Schlossplatz/Murinsel (for lift)) **FREE** Rising to 473m, Schlossberg is the site of the original fortress where Graz was founded. Its wooded slopes can be reached by a number of bucolic and strenuous paths, but also by **glass lift** (1hr ticket adult/child €2/1) or **Schlossbergbahn** (Castle Hill Railway; 1hr ticket adult/child €2/1) funicular for the cost of a regular city transport ticket. The vicinity is a wif-fi hotspot.

Uhrturm
TOWER

(Clock Tower; 🚊4, 5 Schlossplatz/Murinsel (for lift)) **FREE** Perched on the southern edge of Schlossberg is the city's emblem, the Uhrturm. In what must have been a good deal for Europe's modernising midget, the townsfolk paid Napoleon a ransom of 2987 florins and 11 farthings to spare the clock tower during the 1809 invasion.

Graz

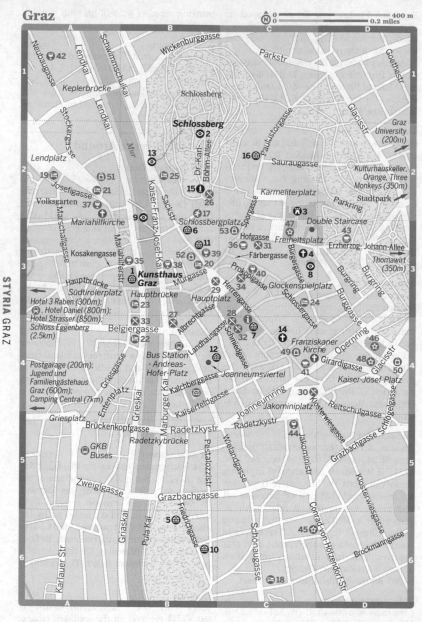

STYRIA GRAZ

◎ **Eggenberg**

Schloss Eggenberg PALACE
(Eggenberger Allee 90; adult/child €8/3; ⏱ tours
10am-4pm Tue-Sun from Palm Sun–Oct; ⓐ1
Schloss Eggenberg) Situated on the western
fringes of the city, Graz' elegant palace was
created for the Eggenberg dynasty in 1625
by Giovanni Pietro de Pomis (1565–1633) at
the request of Johann Ulrich (1568–1634).
Admission is via a highly worthwhile guided
tour, during which you learn about the idi-

Graz

STYRIA GRAZ

osyncrasies of each room, the stories told by the frescoes, and about the Eggenberg family itself.

Johann Ulrich rose from ordinariness to become governor of Inner Austria in 1625, at a time when Inner Austria was a powerful province that included Styria, Carinthia, and parts of Slovenia and northern Italy. His baroque palace was built on a Gothic predecessor (which explains an interesting Gothic chapel in one section of the palace, viewed from a glass cube) and has numerous features of the Italian Renaissance, such as the magnificent courtyard arcades. The guided tour is in English or German and takes you through the 24 *Prunkräume* (staterooms), which, like everything else in the palace and gardens, are based around astronomy, the zodiac, and classical or religious mythology.

The tour ends at Planet Hall, which is a riot of white stuccowork and baroque frescoes.

Alte Galerie & Museums   MUSEUM
(✆58 32 64-9770; Eggenberger Allee 90, Schloss Eggenberg; adult/child €8/3; ☉10am-5pm Wed-Sun Apr-Oct, to 4pm Wed-Sun Nov-Dec, closed Jan-Mar; ☒1 Schloss Eggenberg) Graz' Schloss Eggenberg and park grounds are home to an ensemble of excellent museums, including the **Alte Galerie** (Old Gallery), with its outstanding collection of paintings from the Middle Ages to the baroque. Also very worthwhile are the **Archaeological Museum**, housing relics from pre-history to classical times, and the **Coin Collection**.

Just a few of the highlights in the Alte Galerie are works by Lucas Cranach the Elder, Martin Johann Schmidt and Pieter

Brueghel the Younger. In a clever touch, each room has been individually coloured to highlight and complement the dominant tones of the paintings displayed in them.

While the Coin Collection is more of eclectic interest (magnifying glasses on the case help to see the coins close up), the Archaeological Museum houses the exceptional Strettweg Chariot and a bronze mask, both dating from the 7th century BC, as well as a collection of Roman finds in the province.

Schloss Eggenberg Parkland   GARDEN
(www.museum-joanneum.at; Eggenberger Allee 90, Schloss Eggenberg; adult/child €1/free; ⏰8am-7pm Apr-Oct, to 5pm Nov-Mar; 🚋1 Schloss Eggenberg) Lending Graz' Schloss Eggenberg broad splashes of green, these palace gardens are a relaxing place for whiling away the time amid squawking peacocks and deer that roam among Roman stone reliefs. The **Planetengarten** (Planet Garden; ⏰8am-7pm Apr-Oct, to 5pm Nov-Mar) is based on the same Renaissance theme of planets you find inside the palace itself.

🧭 Tours

Graz Tourismus (p183) offers a walking tour (€9.50/5 per adult/child) in German and English at 2.30pm daily from May to October, and at 2.30pm Saturdays from November to April (except December). Also ask about its theme tours, or weekend day trips outside Graz, or pick up its nifty multimedia (and multilingual) guide to sights, using a handheld computer (€7.50/8.50 for two/four hours).

🎊 Festivals & Events

Graz has a very lively jazz scene. For information of ongoing events, see the **Grazjazz** (www.grazjazz.at) website.

Styriarte   CLASSICAL MUSIC
(www.styriarte.com; ⏰Jun & Jul) Classical festival featuring almost continuous concerts. Pick up information from **Styriarte Kartenbüro** (☑82 50 00; www.styriarte.com; Sackstrasse 17; tickets €18-200; ⏰10am-6pm Mon-Fri). Some concerts are held in Renaissance courtyards and are free.

Stadtfest   MUSIC
(⏰early Jul) Renaissance courtyards are transformed into raucous stages for rock and classical music for the weekend.

Steirischer Herbst   ARTS
(www.steirischerbst.at; ⏰Oct) Includes performances of music, theatre and film, plus exhibitions and art installations. Contact **Steirischer Herbst Informationsbüro** (☑81 60 70; www.steirischerbst.at; Sackstrasse 17; tickets €8-70) for more.

🛏 Sleeping

The tourist office books hotels without charge. Visit the **Ibis** (www.ibishotel.com) and **Mercure** (www.mercure.com) websites for central chain hotels.

⭐**Hotel Daniel**   HOTEL €
(☑71 10 80; www.hoteldaniel.com; Europaplatz 1; r €59-79, breakfast per person €11; 🅿❄@📶; 🚋1, 3, 6, 7 Hauptbahnhof) Perched at the top of Annenstrasse and looking for all the world like a block of 1950s beachside holiday apartments, the Daniel is an exclusive design hotel tastefully furnished in minimalist designs. You can rent a Vespa (€25 per day) as well as e-bikes (electric bikes) and a Piaggio APE Calessino (both €15). In the rooms the bathroom – but, thankfully, not toilet – wall is transparent.

⭐**Hotel Weitzer**   HOTEL €
(☑7030; www.weitzer.com; Grieskai 12; r €69-149, breakfast per person €14; 🅿@📶; 🚋1, 3, 6, 7 Südtiroler Platz) Favoured by tour groups as well as individual travellers on limited budgets, this hotel offers good-value rooms in three comfort categories. Most have been renovated. There are a couple of eateries in the building, as well as sauna and fitness facilities.

Camping Central   CAMPGROUND €
(☑0676-378 51 02; office@campingcentral.at; Martinhofstrasse 3; camp site per 2 adults with car & tent €24, children free; ⏰Apr-Oct; 🅿📶♿👶; 🚋32 Badstrassgang) Excellent camping ground with pool and playground 6km from the centre. Take the bus from Jakominiplatz.

Jugend- und Familiengästehaus Graz   HOSTEL €
(☑70 83 210; www.jufa.eu/jufa-graz-city; Idlhofgasse 74; dm €22.10, s €51, d €82.50; 🅿❄@📶; 🚋31, 32, 33 Lissagasse) This clean and comfortable HI hostel is located about 800m south of the main train station and can be easily reached by bus from Jakominiplatz. Prices can be cheaper according to the demand.

Hotel Strasser   HOTEL €
(☑71 39 77; www.hotelstrasser.at; Eggenberger Gürtel 11; s/d/tr €49/69/93; 🅿@📶; 🚋1, 3, 6, 7 Hauptbahnhof) Hotel Strasser aims above its modest budget class with Tuscan gold and

ochre touches, mirrors, artwork and cast-iron balustrades. Rooms are comfortable, if less elaborately decorated, but ask for one away from the busy street.

★ Hotel Erzherzog Johann   HOTEL €€

(☏81 16 16; www.erzherzog-johann.com; Sackstrasse 3-5; s €134, d €189, ste €249; P🕈; 🚊1, 3, 6, 7 Hauptplatz) Splurge in one of the ostentatious theme rooms such as the Wanda-Sacher-Masoch-Suite, with projections of classical statues in the bathroom, or the Moroccan room. Weekend deals and lower demand periods are especially good value here.

Gasthof-Pension zur Steirer-Stub'n   GUESTHOUSE €€

(☏71 68 55; www.pension-graz.at; Lendplatz 8; s/d €49/92, apt €130-190; P🕈; 🚊58, 58E, 63 Lendplatz, 🚊1, 3, 6, 7 Südtiroler Platz) This homely inn combines the best of a traditional atmosphere with a bright and breezy feel, complemented by features such as tiled floors in the corridors, a potted plant in each room, and patios outside many of the good-sized rooms overlooking Lendplatz.

Hotel Feichtinger Graz   HOTEL €€

(☏72 41 00; www.hotel-feichtinger.at; Lendplatz 1a; s €57, d €106-139, tr €141; P🕈; 🚊1, 3, 6, 7 Südtiroler Platz) This modern seminar and business hotel offers some of the best-value beds in town. Rooms are spacious, and the furnishings are modern and have a light touch, which extends to the very large breakfast room.

Hotel 3 Raben   HOTEL €€

(☏71 26 86; www.dreiraben.at; Annenstrasse 43; s/d/f €69/104/126; P🕈; 🚊1, 3, 6, 7 Esperantoplatz/Arbeiterkammer) This hotel is conveniently located near the main train station and is popular with international visitors. Rooms are well-sized and comfortable, and can be cheaper during low-demand periods. Check the website.

Hotel Wiesler   HOTEL €€

(☏70 66-0; www.hotelwiesler.com; Grieskai 4; r €79-169, ste €339, breakfast €15; P@; 🚊1, 3, 6, 7 Südtiroler Platz) This art nouveau gem has an offbeat edge, a range of comfort categories, and a fully fledged grand suite for up to four people. The foyer and the hotel's abundance of bars and restaurants bear the hallmarks of the new-style Wiesler; the rooms are fairly old-style. Visit the breakfast room to check out Leopold Forstner's (1878–1936) art nouveau mosaic depicting Venus stepping out of an oyster.

Hotel zum Dom   HOTEL €€

(☏82 48 00; www.domhotel.co.at; Bürgergasse 14; s €84, d €129-179, ste €199; P🕈; 🚊30 Palais Trauttmansdorff/Urania, 🚊1, 3, 4, 5, 6, 7 Hauptplatz) Hotel zum Dom is a charming, graceful hotel with tasteful and individually furnished rooms. These come either with steam/power showers or whirlpools, and one suite even has a terrace whirlpool. Ceramic art throughout the hotel is crafted by a local artist. Prices vary by demand.

Schlossberg Hotel   HOTEL €€

(☏80 70-0; www.schlossberg-hotel.at; Kaiser-Franz-Josef-Kai 30; s €100-140, d €135-190, ste €240-280; P@🕈; 🚊4, 5 Schlossbergbahn) Central but away from the city tumult, four-star Schlossberg is blessed with a prime location at the foot of its namesake. Rooms are well-sized and decorated in the style of a country inn. The rooftop terrace with views is perfect for an evening glass of wine.

Augarten Hotel   HOTEL €€

(☏20 800; www.augartenhotel.at; Schönaugasse 53; s €89-169, d €114-194, penthouse ste s €204-280, d €229-305, breakfast €15; P🕈; 🚊4, 5 Finanzamt) Augarten is decorated with the owner's private art collection, which includes a great oil of the German crooning

ⓘ GRAZ' MUSEUMS

Most of Graz' museums are under the umbrella of the Universalmuseum Joanneum, and with almost 20 locations throughout the city, the ensemble is very much the gardener of Graz' rich cultural landscape. Three museums are located inside the Joanneumviertel museum complex, an interesting and eye-catching building that is partially below ground. Admission with a **24-hour ticket** (adult/child/family €11/4/22) allows you to visit the entire museum ensemble over two days (but within 24 hours). The major ones are Schloss Eggenberg (p176) and its museums, Kunsthaus Graz (p175), Landeszeughaus (p174), Museum im Palais (p175), and Naturkundemuseum (p174) and the Neue Galerie Graz (p174) both in the Joanneumsviertel.

An alternative is the **48-hour ticket** (adult/child/family €17/7/34), available from any of the museums. Family tickets, valid for two adults and children under 14, also offer significant discounts.

superstar Heino. All rooms are bright and modern; the end rooms have windows on two walls, and corridors run along the exterior of the building.

✕ Eating

Café Erde VEGETARIAN €
(http://cafeerde.com; Andreas-Hofer-Platz 3; soup & daily dish €7.90, snacks & mains €2.50-6.90; ⊙11am-10pm Mon-Sat; 🛜 🖊) 🍴 Order the daily special accompanied by soup in this upbeat vegan eatery with wooden tables and a friendly atmosphere. From 6pm weekdays and 11.30am Saturdays you can also indulge in one of the good-value dishes from the blackboard, all of which can be washed down with juices or wine.

Mangolds VEGETARIAN €
(www.mangolds.at; Griesgasse 11; meals €5-12; ⊙11am-7pm Mon-Fri, to 4pm Sat; 🖊 🖱; 🚋1, 3, 6, 7 Südtiroler Platz) 🍴 Tasty vegetarian patties, rice dishes and more than 40 different salads are served at this pay-by-weight vegetarian cafeteria.

★ Der Steirer BISTRO PUB €€
(🖉703 654; www.dersteirer.at; Belgiergasse 1; tapas €2, lunch menu €7.90, mains €10-19.50; ⊙11am-midnight; 🖊; 🚋1, 3, 6, 7 Südtiroler Platz) This Styrian neo-*Beisl* (bistro pub) and wine bar has a small but fantastic selection of local dishes (wash them down with a large choice of wines), including a great goulash, and Austro-tapas if you just feel like nibbling. Entrance is from the corner of Belgiergasse and Griesgasse.

FARMERS MARKETS & FOOD STANDS

➡ There are plenty of cheap eateries near Graz University (trams 1 and 7), particularly on Halbärthgasse, Zinzendorfgasse and Harrachgasse.

➡ The freshest fruit and vegetables are at the farmers markets on **Kaiser-Josef-Platz** (⊙6am-noon, Mon-Sat; 🚋1, 7 Kaiser-Josef-Platz) and **Lendplatz** (⊙6am-1pm, Mon-Sat; 🚋1, 3, 6, 7 Südtiroler Platz).

➡ For fast-food stands, head for **Hauptplatz** (🚋1, 3, 4, 5, 6, 7 Hauptplatz) and **Jakominiplatz** (🚋1, 3, 4, 5, 6, 7, 13 Jakominiplatz).

★ Aiola Upstairs INTERNATIONAL €€
(www.aiola.at; Schlossberg 2; pasta €12.50-15.50, mains €19.50-27.50; ⊙9am-midnight Mon-Sat; 🛜; 🚋4, 5 Schlossbergplatz/Murinsel (for lift)) Ask any local where to find the best outdoor dining experience in Graz, and they'll probably say Aiola. Whether it's king prawns with pasta or corn-fed chicken, this wonderful restaurant on Schlossberg has great views, delicious international flavours, a superb wine list, spot-on cocktails and very chilled music.

★ Thomawirt BISTRO PUB €€
(www.thomawirt.at; Leonhardstrasse 40-42; lunch menu €7.90, mains €9.50-15.90; ⊙11am-2am; 🖊; 🚋7 Merangasse) This neo-*Beisl* in the uni quarter serves a lunch special weekdays from 11am, and other excellent lunch and dinner dishes ranging from Styrian classics to steaks and vegetarian mains until 1am. Chill out with occasional music in the bar; the place is divided up into cafe, restaurant and lounge-bar areas.

★ El Gaucho STEAK €€
(🖉83 00 83; www.elgaucho.at/graz; Landhausgasse 1; steak €16-45, side dishes €3; ⊙5pm-midnight Mon-Fri, 11.30am-midnight Sat & Sun; 🚋1, 3, 4, 5, 6, 7 Hauptplatz) Set inside the evocative Renaissance Landhaus building, El Gaucho would seem an unlikely place to feast on Argentine and local steaks. The scene is lit in relaxing crimson and decorated with hanging glass bubbles, lending an easy-going feel, which you can enjoy at the bar till late (2am).

Steaks are grilled to perfection, and the excellent schnapps and liqueur trolley is well worth calling for, whether following a bottom-shelf 'lady steak' (150g) or to digest a top-shelf (600g) rib-eye.

Yamamoto JAPANESE €€
(www.yamamoto-sushibar.at; Prokopigasse 4; udon €7.70-10.20, mains €12-18; ⊙Tue-Sat; 🚋1, 3, 4, 5, 6, 7 Hauptplatz) Yamamoto is refreshingly authentic; it's Japanese owned and run. It gets its sushi delivered throughout the week, so it's always fresh and, like the noodle dishes, delicious.

Hofkeller ITALIAN €€
(www.hofkeller.at; Hofgasse 8; mains €11-23; ⊙Tue-Sat; 🚋1, 3, 4, 5, 6, 7 Hauptplatz) This authentic wine bar and restaurant is the perfect place for sipping from a large selection of Italian wines. Choose a pasta or main dish from the blackboard; expect anything from octopus salad to lamb from a small, changing menu. There's outdoor seating in summer.

Landhauskeller
AUSTRIAN €€

(📱83 02 76; Schmiedgasse 9; mains €10.50-28.50; ⏰11.30am-midnight Mon-Sat; 🚃1, 3 ,4, 5, 6, 7 Hauptplatz) What started as a spit-and-sawdust pub in the 16th century has evolved into an atmospheric, high-quality restaurant serving specialities such as its four different sorts of *Tafelspitz* (prime broiled beef). Flowers, coats of arms and medieval-style murals pack a historical punch and, in the summer, outside tables look onto the stunning Landhaus courtyard.

★ Prato im Palais
AUSTRIAN €€€

(📱23 20 98; www.prato.at; Sackstrasse 16; mains €20-29, 5-/6-course menu €64/74; ⏰11am-midnight Mon-Sat; 🚃1, 3, 4, 5, 6, 7 Hauptplatz) Located inside Palais Herberstein, Prato combines a contemporary atmosphere with elegant dining. The front section allows smoking and has a chilled-out bar area with steel-rim lighting and a lounge feel, while the restaurant serves some of Graz' finest food, either indoors or in a lovely garden setting.

Prato's dishes are inspired by 19th-century chef Katharina Prato, whose book *Die Süddeutsche Küche* (The Southern German Kitchen) is an early gourmet classic.

🍷 Drinking & Nightlife

The cafe and bar scene in Graz is propelled by a healthy student crowd. Some cafes serve food and also transform into bars as the night wears on. Most bars are concentrated in three areas: around the university; on Mehlplatz and Prokopigasse (dubbed the 'Bermuda Triangle'); and a third area near the Kunsthaus.

★ Operncafé
CAFE

(www.ternmel.corn/opernnew; Opernring 22; coffee & cake €7; ⏰7.30am-9pm; 🕿; 🚃1, 3, 4, 5, 6, 7, 13 Jakominiplatz) Operncafé is a traditional cafe with good coffee, homemade pastries, lots of press and pleasant, suited waiters who have found a calling in life.

★ La Enoteca
WINE BAR

(www.laenoteca.at; Sackstrasse 14; ⏰5-11pm Mon, 11.30am-11pm Tue-Fri, 10am-11pm Sat; 🚃1, 3, 4, 5, 6, 7 Hauptplatz) This small wine bar has an informal, relaxed atmosphere and courtyard seating, making it an ideal place to enjoy a Schilcher Sekt (sparkling Schilcher rosé) with mixed antipast. It also does pasta and a few light dishes (from €7 to €13.50).

Flan O'Brien
PUB

(www.flannobrien.at; Paradeisgasse 1; ⏰11am-2am Mon-Thu, to 3am Fri & Sat, 3pm-midnight Sun; 🚃1, 3, 4, 5, 6, 7 Hauptplatz) Flan O'Brien is the largest and liveliest Irish pub in town. It has a courtyard, live music and also serves inexpensive standards such as burgers, Irish stew and very decent fish and chips.

Insel Café
CAFE

(Murinsel; ⏰10am-midnight Mon-Fri, from 9.30am Sat & Sun; 👶; 🚃4, 5 Schlossplatz/Murinsel) This cafe offers a unique experience – you can sip on your drink as the Mur splashes below your feet. Watch the kids climbing on the rope play area while you sip a cocktail or have a snack.

Edegger-Tax
CAFE

(Hofgasse 8; ⏰7am-7pm Mon-Fri, to 3pm Sat; 🚃1, 3, 4, 5, 6, 7 Hauptplatz) This modern cafe is perfectly complemented by its 1569 bakery (open from 7am to 6pm Monday to Friday, to noon Saturday) next door. As well as yummy goodies baked on the premises, it has a stunning wood-carved facade and delicious coffee.

Orange
BAR, CLUB

(www.cbo.at; Elisabethstrasse 30; ⏰8am-3am; 🚃7 Lichtenfelsgasse) A young, fashionable student crowd gets down in this modern lounge, which has a patio perfect for warm summer evenings. DJs spin sounds regularly here. There's a small admission of around €3 from Wednesday to Saturday after 11pm. Minimum age is 19 years. Next door is the student hang-out Kulturhauskeller.

Kulturhauskeller
BAR, CLUB

(www.kulturhauskeller.at; Elisabethstrasse 30; ⊙9pm-5am Tue-Sat; 🚋7 Lichtenfelsgasse) The raunchy Kulturhauskeller is a popular student hang-out with a great cellar-pub feel and a Wednesday karaoke night.

Cafe Centraal
BISTRO PUB, CAFE

(www.centraal.at; Mariahilferstrasse 10; breakfast €3.90-7.90, salad & snacks €3.60-5.90; ⊙8am-2am; 🔊; 🚋1, 3, 6, 7 Südtiroler Platz) This traditional bar and *Beisl* with a dark-wood interior and outside seating has an alternative feel and cheap eats.

Stockwerk Jazz
JAZZ

(http://stockwerkjazz.mur.at; Jakominiplatz 18; concerts €12-18; ⊙4pm-1am Mon-Sat, to midnight Sun; 🚋1, 3, 4, 5, 6, 7, 13 Jakominiplatz) In addition to being Graz' premier jazz-bar-cum-pub for home-grown artists and international acts, this is also a great place to have a drink. It has rustic wooden features and a summer rooftop terrace.

★ Exil
BAR

(Josefigasse 1; ⊙7.30pm-late Tue-Sat; 🚋1, 3, 6, 7 Südtiroler Platz) Exil is a laid-back but smoky alternative bar with outdoor seating and a couple of turntables for Friday and Saturday nights. On busy nights the crowd spills onto the street.

Three Monkeys
BAR

(www.three-monkeys.at; Elisabethstrasse 31; ⊙9pm-6am Mon-Thu, to 7am Fri & Sat; 🚋7 Lichtenfelsgasse) A young crowd flocks to the raunchy Three Monkeys, which is generally known far and wide as a pick-up joint.

Promenade
CAFE

(www.cafepromenade.at; Erzherzog-Johann-Allee 1; snacks & lunch menu €6.90-12; ⊙8am-11pm; 🚋30 Schauspielhaus) Popular with all walks of life, the delightful Promenade is a Graz institution – styled along the lines of a Vienna coffee house on a tree-lined avenue in the Stadtpark.

Dom im Berg
CLUB

(www.domimberg.at; Schlossbergplatz; 🚋4, 5 Schlossplatz/Murinsel) The tunnels under Schlossberg were once used as air-raid shelters. Today, some of them have been refashioned into a large arts-clubbing venue. The sound system and light show are the best in Graz. See the website for opening times and prices.

M1
COCKTAIL BAR

(www.m1-bar.at; Färberplatz 1, 3rd fl; ⊙from 4pm Mon-Fri, from 9am Sat; 🚋1, 3, 4, 5, 6, 7 Hauptplatz) M1 is a modern three-storey cafe-bar replete with rooftop terrace that attracts a mixed crowd. Its spiral staircase can cause a few problems after one or two of the 200 or so cocktails on offer.

Postgarage
CLUB

(www.postgarage.at; Dreihackengasse 42; ⊙from 10pm Fri & Sat; 🚋32, 33, 40 Griesplatz, 🚋1, 3, 6, 7 Südtiroler Platz) Electronic, retro theme nights and everything in between for 20-somethings and upwards, depending on the event. See the website for events and prices.

p.p.c.
CLUB

(www.popculture.at; Neubaugasse 6; admission €7-8; ⊙from 10pm Wed-Sat; 🚋4, 5 Kepplerbrücke) Top-name DJs spin their thing on electronic club nights, in one of Graz' most popular dance places.

Nachtexpress
BAR

(Färberplatz 1; ⊙from 9pm Wed-Sat; 🚋1, 3, 4, 5, 6, 7 Hauptplatz) Situated downstairs in the same building as the bar M1, this cellar joint is the favoured hang-out of Graz' metal connoisseurs, with a video screen showing live headbanger concerts.

☆ Entertainment

To find out what's on and where in the city, pick up a copy of *Megaphon* (€2.50, in German), a monthly magazine that combines entertainment listings with political and social commentary. It's sold on most street corners. For cinema listings, see the website www.uncut.at/graz (in German). The main venue showing films in their original versions is KIZ RoyalKino (Conrad-von-Hötzendorf-Strasse 10; 🚋4, 5 Finanzamt).

Graz is an important cultural centre, hosting musical events throughout the year. Theaterservice Graz (☎8008 1102; www.theater-graz.com; Kaiser-Josef-Platz 10; ⊙9am-6pm Mon-Fri, to 1pm Sat, closed mid-Jul–mid-Aug; 🚋1, 7 Kaiser-Josef-Platz) is the ticket office for the Opernhaus and Schauspielhaus.

Opernhaus OPERA
(www.theater-graz.com/oper; Kaiser-Josef-Platz 10;
⊙ closed early Jul–late Aug; ☐1, 7 Kaiser-Josef-
Platz) The main venue for opera. See the website for upcoming performances and prices.

Schauspielhaus THEATRE
(www.schauspielhaus-graz.com; Hofgasse 11;
⊙ closed early Jul–late Aug; ☐30 Schauspielhaus,
☐1, 3, 4, 5, 6, 7 Hauptplatz) Graz' main venue
for theatre. See the website for dates and
prices.

Shopping

Aside from its divine pumpkin-seed oil, Styria is known for painted pottery and printed
linen.

Good places to pick up quality handi-
crafts are **Steirisches Heimatwerk** (☐82
71 06; www.heimatwerk.steiermark.at; Sporgasse
23; ☐1, 3, 4, 5, 6, 7 Hauptplatz) or **Kastner &
Öhler** (Sackstrasse 7-11; ⊙9.30am-7pm Mon-
Fri, to 6pm Sat), a department store north of
Hauptplatz. The main bookshop in town
is **Buchhandlung Moser** (Am Eisernen Tor 1;
⊙9am-6.30pm Mon-Fri, to 6pm Sat; ☐1, 3, 4, 5, 6,
7, 13 Jakominiplatz).

ℹ Information

INTERNET RESOURCES

Graz (www.graz.at) Provides a snapshot of
most aspects of the city.

InfoGraz (www.info-graz.at) Practical information on life in Graz.

Lonely Planet (www.lonelyplanet.com/austria/
the-south/graz) Planning advice, author recommendations, traveller reviews and insider tips.

Welcome to Graz (www.graztourismus.at) The
city's excellent tourist-information portal.

LEFT LUGGAGE

Lockers (from €2 to €4 for 24 hours) are available inside the train station.

POST

Hauptbahnhof Post office (Hauptbahnhof;
⊙7am-8pm Mon-Fri, 8am-6pm Sat, 1-8pm Sun;
☐1, 3, 6, 7 Hauptbahnhof) Located inside the
main train station.

Main Post office (Neutorgasse 46; ⊙8am-
7pm Mon-Fri, 9am-noon Sat; ☐1, 3, 4, 5, 6, 7,
13 Jakominiplatz)

TOURIST INFORMATION

Graz Tourismus (☐80 75; www.graztouris-
mus.at; Herrengasse 16; ⊙10am-6pm; ☎; ☐1,
3, 4, 5, 6, 7 Hauptplatz) Graz' main tourist office, with loads of free information on the city,
and helpful and knowledgeable staff.

ℹ Getting There & Away

AIR

Graz Airport (GRZ; ☐29 020; www.flughafen-
graz.at) is 10km south of the town centre, just
beyond the A2 and connected by train and bus
with the Hauptbahnhof. Direct connections
with Graz include to/from Berlin with **Air Berlin**
(www.airberlin.com), Frankfurt am Main with
Lufthansa (☐0810 1025 8080; www.lufthansa.
com), Zürich with **InterSky** (www.flyintersky.
com), Rome with **Alitalia** (www.alitalia.com),
and with many other German cities on **Austrian
Airlines** (☐291 669; www.austrian.com); Glasgow and Exeter in the UK with **Niki** (www.flyniki.
com); and inland flights to Vienna with Austrian
Airlines and Niki. Facilities at the airport include
an **information desk** (☐29 02-172; ⊙5am-
10pm), free internet terminals and wi-fi inside
the security zone, and a bank with ATM in arrivals on the ground floor.

BUS

Postbus (☐050 678 910, 05 17 17; www.
postbus.at) services depart from outside the
Hauptbahnhof and from Andreas-Hofer-Platz to
all parts of Styria. Frequent direct **GKB buses**
(☐59 87-0; www.gkb.at) run to Bärnbach (€7.80,
50 minutes) daily, and indirect buses to Piber
(€7.80, 80 minutes) several times each day from
Monday to Friday. All leave from Griesplatz. Six
direct Österreiche Bundesbahn (Austrian Federal
Railways; ÖBB) buses daily (€25.30, two hours)
leave for Klagenfurt from the Hauptbahnhof.

CAR & MOTORCYCLE

Car rental companies include **Avis** (☐81 29
20; www.avis.com; Reinighausstrasse 66),
Hertz (☐82 50 07; www.hertz.com; Andreas-
Hofer-Platz 1), which also has an office at the
airport, and **MegaDrive** (☐050 105 4130; www.
megadrive.at; Kärntnerstrasse 164).

Note that much of Graz is a *Kurzparkzone*
(short-term parking zone); tickets are available
from parking machines (€0.60 per 30 minutes,
maximum three hours).

TRAIN

Trains to Vienna depart hourly (€37, 2½ hours),
and five daily go to Salzburg (€48, four hours).
All trains running north or west go via Bruck an
der Mur (€12, 45 minutes, every 20 minutes),
a main railway junction with more frequent
services. Trains to Klagenfurt (€39, 2¾ hours to 3½
hours, seven daily) require a change in Leoben,
or in Bruck an der Mur and again in Friesach
(check with the conductor).

International direct train connections from
Graz include Zagreb (€38, four hours), Ljubljana
(€41, 3½ hours), Szentgotthárd (€14, 1½ hours)
and Budapest (€70, 5½ hours).

❶ Getting Around

TO/FROM THE AIRPORT
Trains depart the Hauptbahnhof (€2.20) from 4.25am to 12.08am Monday to early Saturday morning, from 5.57am Saturday and Sunday to 12.08am the next morning. Trains leave the airport from 4.47am to 10.47pm Monday to Friday, from 5.17am to 10.47pm Saturday and from 5.17am to 9.47pm Sunday, at least hourly. The trip between the train station and airport takes 18 minutes. An infrequent bus also runs to the airport from the Hauptbahnhof; it takes 20 minutes and can be convenient between trains. Expect to pay about €20 for a taxi.

BICYCLE
Rental is available from **Bicycle** (☑ 68 86 45; www.bicycle.at; Körösistrasse 5; per 24hr €10, weekend (Fri-Mon) €16; ☺ 7am-1pm & 2-6pm Mon-Fri). Mobilzentral (www.mobilzentral.at) has city rental bicycles for €10 per day or €40 per week and **Radstation am Hauptbahnhof** (http://grazbike.at; Europaplatz 4; from €10 per day, €40 per week; ☺ 8am-11.45am & 12.45-5pm) has bike hire outside the main train station.

PUBLIC TRANSPORT
Graz has one zone (zone 101). Single tickets (€2.10) for buses and trams are valid for one hour, but you're usually better off buying a 24-hour pass (€4.70). Ten one-zone tickets cost €19.20, and weekly/monthly passes cost €12.70/42.60. Hourly and 24-hour tickets can be purchased from the driver; other passes can be purchased from *Tabak* (tobacconist) shops, pavement ticket machines or the tourist office.

TAXI
Call ☑ 2801, ☑ 878 or ☑ 889.

TRAM
Trams 1, 3, 6 and 7 connect Jakominiplatz with the Hauptbahnhof every five to 20 minutes from around 4.45am to early evening Monday to Saturday. After that, trams 1 and 7 do the run alone until services end just before midnight.

AROUND GRAZ

There are a number of sights within easy distance of Graz that make for a pleasant excursion into the countryside.

Stübing

Located some 15km northeast of Graz and consisting of about 100 Austrian farmstead buildings, the **Österreichisches Freilichtmuseum** (Austrian Open-Air Museum; www.freilichtmuseum.at; adult/child/family €9/5/26; ☺ 9am-5pm Tue-Sun Apr-Oct) in Stübing is ideal for a family outing. The museum is about a 20-minute walk from the Stübing train station; turn left out of the train station and pass over the tracks, then under them before reaching the entrance. Hourly trains make the journey from Graz (€4, 15 minutes). Pick up a copy of the English-language guidebook (€2.90) at the entrance.

On the last Sunday in September the **Erlebnistag**, a special fair with crafts, music and dancing, takes place here.

Bundesgestüt Piber

Piber is home to world-famous Lipizzaner stallion stud farm **Bundesgestüt Piber** (Piber Stud Farm; www.piber.com; Piber 1; tours adult/child €12/7.50; ☺ tours 10am, 11am & hourly 1-4pm Apr-Oct, 11am & 2pm Nov-Mar; ☑). Originally the farm was based in Lipica (Slovenia) but was moved here when Slovenia was annexed after WWI. About 40 to 50 foals are born at the farm every year, but of these only about five stallions have the right stuff to be sent for training to the Spanische Hofreitschule (Spanish Riding School) in Vienna. In summer, you have the choice of a do-it-yourself tour using a sheet map of the stud, using the free multi-lingual audioguide (deposit €10) or taking a fully fledged tour. For information, head to the **Tourismusverband Lipizzanerheimat** (☑ 03144-72 777-0; www.lipizzanerheimat.com; An der Quelle 3, Köflach; ☺ 9am-noon & 2-5pm Mon-Fri, 9am-noon Sat May-Oct, 9am-1pm Mon-Fri Nov-Apr) in Köflach, 3km south of Piber. The foyer has brochures and an information PC and is open from 6am to 10pm.

To get to Piber from Graz, the most convenient option is to catch the **GKB** (ww.gkb.at) morning bus 700 at 8am from Graz' Griesplatz, arriving in Piber at 9.15am (you have to change to connecting bus 705 at Voitsberg Hauptplatz). The last bus leaves Piber at 4.57pm. This only works weekdays. Frequent trains also go to Köflach (€9.90, one hour), from where it's a 3.5km walk from Hauptplatz along Piberstrasse (follow the signs). A **taxi** (☑ 03144-26 26; fares €6.50) from the Köflach train station to Piber is an option. Bundesgestüt Piber is also close to Bärnbach (€7 by taxi).

Bärnbach

☎ 03142 / POP 5250

Otherwise unremarkable, Bärnbach is famous for its **St Barbara Kirche** (Piberstrasse; ☉ dawn-dusk) FREE, a church redesigned by Friedensreich Hundertwasser. Completed in 1988, it is a visual treat of bright colours and glistening copper dome. Leave a donation and pick up the explanation card in English, which reveals the symbolism behind the architectural features.

Tourist information is available from the glass-making centre and from **Bärnbach Information** (☎ 615 50; www.baernbach.at; Hauptplatz 1; ☉ 8-11.30am Tue, Wed & Fri, 8-11.30am & 2-4.30pm Mon & Thu), which is located inside the town hall.

ⓘ Getting There & Away

Hourly trains run from Graz (€7.90, 50 minutes). The train station is 2.5km south of the church. Follow Bahnhofweg and Neue Landstrasse (turn right) to Piberstrasse. A **taxi** (☎ 0664-340 2247) to the centre of town costs about €6.

SOUTHERN STYRIA

Southern Styria is known as *Steirische Toskana* (Styrian Tuscany), and for good reason. Not only is this wine country, but the landscape is reminiscent of Chianti; gentle rolling hills cultivated with vineyards or patchwork farmland, and capped by clusters of trees. It's also famous for *Kürbiskernöl*, the rich pumpkin-seed oil generously used in Styrian cooking.

Region Süd und West Steiermark (☎ 03462-43152; www.sws.st; Hauptplatz 36, Deutschlandsberg) handles telephone, email and postal enquiries for western and southern Styria.

Styrian Wine Roads

The *Weinstrassen* (wine roads) of southern Styria comprise an idyllic bundle of winding roads criss-crossing a picturesque landscape that is reminiscent of Tuscany. The region is at its best about two weeks after the grape harvest (usually September), when *Sturm* (young wine) is sold. The **Weinlesefest** (Wine Harvest Festival; ☎ 03454-70 70 10; www.rebenland.at) takes

place in Leutschach on the last weekend in September, with lots of wine and song.

The main towns in the region are Ehrenhausen, Gamlitz and Berghausen in the north, and the town of Leutschach in the west, less than 20km away but best reached via a serpentine route partly along the Slovenian border. Settlements and vineyards rather than fully fledged villages dot the region, some of these offering picturesque and romantic places to stay overnight. Less-rural accommodation is available in Ehrenhausen (p187), whereas Berghausen is quieter and more remote. On weekends in September and October, accommodation is usually booked out. During the week and at other times it's usually fine if you're flexible.

If you're without your own wheels, take a train from Graz to Leibnitz. A bus runs five to eight times daily from Monday to Saturday via Grossklein from Leibnitz to Leutschach (€8, 40 minutes), where there's bike hire, easy access to hiking trails, and numerous wine and panorama roads. Car hire is in Graz.

To explore further, from Leutschach a road veers left at the top of the main street at Rebenlandhof restaurant. This leads to Eichberg-Trautenburg, a pretty region with *Buschenschänke* (wine taverns) and narrow sealed roads. A walking trail (560) goes through forest, across meadows and partly alongside the road. Regions along and south of the Alte Weinstrasse (Old Wine Road) are more remote, with lesser-used wine and panorama roads but fewer vineyards.

STYRIA BÄRNBACH

THE WINE ROADS OF SOUTHERN STYRIA

This 50km circuit takes you from Ehrenhausen to Leutschach and back to Gamlitz, along the wine roads of southern Styria, traversing some of the most attractive areas. Along the way you will find lookouts where you can leave the main road and enjoy broad panoramas.

From the Hauptstrasse (B69) in **Ehrenhausen** veer left on the southern edge of town at the **Südsteirische Weinstrasse** (L613) signpost. Almost immediately you see vineyards and *Buschenschänke* (wine taverns) where you can taste wines. After **Berghausen** and **Grassnitzberg** the road reaches the Slovenian border (the left of the road is Slovenia, the right Austria) and veers west, where about 2km from Berghausen settlement you reach **Gästehaus & Atelier Sonnenberg** (☑ 0664-971 2961; www.msonnenberg.at; Wielitsch 34, Berghausen; holiday houses per person €45, minimum 3 nights), situated across the road from Slovenia. Here the Hannover-born artist Manfred Sonnenberg has holiday flats sleeping two to six, and offers sculpting and painting courses over three days for around €350 with accommodation. Just before an outlying part of Ratsch an der Weinstrasse, a road leads right for about 500m to the **Bärengehege Berghausen** (Berghausen-Ratsch an der Weinstrasse; ⊙ 8am-6pm), a refuge for bears no longer able to live in the wild. This was established in 1980 for maltreated circus bears and today has enclosures where injured or 'problem' bears are housed.

Continuing along the L613, you reach **Rebenhof** (☑ 03453-25 750; www.rebenhof.at; Ottenberg 38, Ratsch an der Weinstrasse; light dishes €6-12; ⊙ Easter-Dec). This *Buschenschank* has wine, *Flammkuchen* (flambée) and mostly light Styrian dishes to go with the vintages. At the junction settlement of Eckberg, a road leads north 5km to Gamlitz. If doing the complete circuit, turn left at the junction (away from Gamlitz), and continue along the L613 to Schlossberg and **Leutschach**, where you will need to reserve ahead for a table at the gourmet restaurant **Tom am Kochen** (☑ 03454-700 99; www.tomamkochen.at; Arnsfelder Strasse 2, Leutschach; 'Genussreise' meal €85; ⊙ dinner Tue-Sat; ℗), run by Tom Riedere. He also conducts cooking courses. Other eating and drinking options are on the pretty main street of Leutschach, including **Tscheppes Lang-Gasthof** (☑ 03454-246; www.langgasthof-tscheppe.at; Hauptplatz 6; s/d/f €65/98/114, mains €8.50-18.80; ℗), a four-star hotel with a sauna and a herbal bath filled with hops (this is also a big hop-growing district). As well as traditional Austrian seasonal favourites like roast goose on the Wednesday before November 11 (around St Martin's Day), the restaurant offers seasonal cuisine such as game in September and October, and dishes using regional herbs, wines or locally grown hops. Leutschach's **tourist office** (☑ 03454-70 70 10; www.rebenland.at; Hauptplatz 2, Leutschach; ⊙ 9am-noon Mon, Tue & Thu, 9am-1pm & 2-6pm Fri, 9am-noon Sat) has a free **Freizeitkarte** with hiking trails and *Buschenschänke* (with opening times) marked. Brochures and maps are on racks outside, even when the office is closed.

From Leutschach, backtrack to Schlossberg and follow the **Alte Weinstrasse** east to **Langegg**. This wine road has mostly fallen into disuse, and partly follows the course of a small river before it swings north at Langegg to join the Südsteirische Weinstrasse at Gasthof Mahorko. Turn right and follow the signs to Gamlitz.

Deutschlandsberg

☑ 03462 / POP 8130

In the heart of the Schilcher wine region, Deutschlandsberg is a bustling little town dominated by a well-restored castle, some 25 minutes' walk uphill from the town centre. Inside the castle is a **museum** (www.burgmuseum.at; Burgplatz 2; adult/child €9/4; ⊙ 10am-6pm Tue-Sun Apr-Oct) with exhibits on ancient history, the Celts, historical weapons and antique jewellery. The extensive collection, whose highlights include a delicate gold necklace from the 5th century BC, takes about 1½ hours to see. As with any good castle, there's a torture chamber in the underground vaults.

The **tourist office** (☑ 75 20; www.schilcherland-deutschlandsberg.at; Hauptplatz 34; ⊙ 9am-1pm & 2-5pm Mon-Fri, 9am-noon Sat Mar-Oct,

9am-1pm Mon-Fri Nov-Feb) is a good source of information on the town and environs.

For sleeping arrangements, look no further than the **Burg Hotel** (⊿56 56-0; www. burghotel-dl.at; Burgplatz 1; s €65-90, d €120-135, ste €160-250; P🛜), located in the castle. Its crowning glory is the tower suite, which comes with complimentary champagne and a fruit basket; rooms are large and quiet and have views of the woods.

If Burg is out of your budget, the **Jugend- und Familiengästehaus Deutschlandsberg** (⊿05 7083-260; www. jufa.eu/jufa-deutschlandsberg-sport-resort; Burgstrasse 5; s/d €53/85; P@🛜) is a good option. It's set in a vineyard at the foot of the castle. Wi-fi is in the foyer only.

At least hourly trains (€10, one hour) connect Graz and Deutschlandsberg.

Grossklein

Southern Styria was once a stomping ground of the Celts, and this legacy has gradually been unearthed by archaeologists. Some of their finds are housed in the four exhibition rooms of the **Hallstattzeitliches Museum** (Hallstatt Period Museum; www.archaeo-grossklein. com; adult/child/family €4/2/9; ⊙10am-noon & 2-5pm Wed-Sun Apr-Oct; 🚻) in the small town of Grossklein, 26km southeast of Deutschlandsberg. Most of the exhibits are from the nearby grave mounds and include coins, pottery and tools, and a copy of a bronze mask dating from 600 BC (the original is housed in Graz' Schloss Eggenberg. A 9km archaeology trail heading northwest from town towards Kleinklein takes in approximately 700 Celtic grave mounds.

Five to 10 buses (€4, 25 minutes) connect Leibnitz and Grossklein from Monday to Saturday. Weekdays, a train-bus connection (€9.35, 1¼ hours) from Graz via Leibnitz works well.

Ehrenhausen

⊿03453 / POP 1050

The picturesque town of Ehrenhausen, near the A9 connecting Graz with the Slovenian border, makes a fine base for exploring the vineyards of southern Styria.

The town is little more than one street of pastel-coloured houses dominated by the baroque **Pfarrkirche** (Hauptplatz; ⊙dawn-dusk). Before setting off for the wine country, follow the path (three minutes' walk) on the

right of the Rathaus up to the **mausoleum** (⊙groups only) of Ruprecht von Eggenberg (1546–1611), hero of the Battle of Sisak against the Turks. This attractive white-and-yellow building is guarded by two impressive Roman-like bruisers.

If travelling the wine roads, consider the newly opened **Wine & Spa Resort Loisium Südsteiermark** (⊿288 00; www.loisium-suedsteiermark.at; Am Schlossberg 1a, Ehrenhausen; s €133-143, d €178-198, ste €228, day spa (nonguests) €35), which brings together wine and bodily TLC in a contemporary hotel and spa facility.

Hourly trains (€10, 45 minutes) run from Graz to Ehrenhausen. The train station is about four minutes' walk east of Hauptplatz.

Riegersburg

⊿03153 / POP 2400

Located 50km southeast of Graz at Riegersburg and perched on a 200m-high rocky outcrop, **Schloss Riegersburg** (www.veste-riegersburg.at; adult/child/family €12/7/30; ⊙10am-5pm Apr & Oct, 9am-5pm May-Sep) is a hugely impressive 13th-century castle built against invading Hungarians and Turks; today it houses a **Hexenmuseum** on witchcraft, a **Burgmuseum** featuring the history of the Liechtenstein family, who acquired it in 1822, and an impressive collection of weapons. A **war memorial** is a reminder of fierce fighting in 1945, when Germans occupying the castle were attacked by Russian troops.

A cable car on the north side whisks you up in 90 seconds (one way €2.50).

For more information on the Schloss or activities, contact the **tourist office** (⊿86 70; www.riegersburg.com; Riegersburg 26; ⊙8.30am-3pm Mon & Wed-Sat May-Oct, 8am noon Mon & Wed-Fri Nov-Apr)

If you have your own transport, consider stopping in at **Schloss Kapfenstein** (⊿03157-300 30-0; www.schloss-kapfenstein. at; Kapfenstein 1; s €100-127, d €140-194, 4-course menu €32 per person; P@), a hotel-restaurant 17km south of Riegersburg. Weekdays are less expensive; on weekends, only Friday-to-Sunday packages are possible. The restaurant serves delightful Styrian cuisine in its outer courtyard overlooking the valley.

Frequent trains run from Graz to nearby Feldbach, and from there six weekday buses head for Riegersburg (€2, 20 minutes). The last bus back is at around 6pm (check before setting out).

NORTHERN STYRIA

Heading north from Graz the landscape of Styria begins to change; gentle hills and flat pastures are replaced by jagged mountains, virgin forests, deep valleys and cold, clear mountain streams. This is also the region's industrial heartland, home to the Steirische Eisenstrasse (Styrian Iron Road), where for centuries iron mining was the backbone of the economy. Two of its cultural highlights are the pilgrimage church of Mariazell and the abbey of Admont.

Mariazell

☎ 03882 / POP 1500

Mariazell, situated on the lower reaches of the eastern Alps, is one of Austria's icons. It offers opportunities for hiking, mountain biking and skiing, but what makes Mariazell so well known is its status as Austria's most important pilgrimage site. Its basilica, founded in 1157, holds a sacred statue of the Virgin, and busloads of Austrians flock to the site on weekends and on 15 August (Assumption) and 8 September (Mary's name day). The mountain above town, **Bürgeralpe** (1270m), has a couple of restaurants and a small museum.

◎ Sights

★**Basilika** CHURCH
(Kardinal Eugen Tisserant Platz 1; ⊗7am-8pm) Originally Romanesque, Mariazell's basilica underwent a Gothic conversion in the 14th century, followed by a massive baroque facelift in the 17th century. The result is a strange clash of styles, with the original Gothic steeple bursting like a wayward skeletal limb from between two baroque onion domes. Inside, Gothic ribbing combines with baroque frescoes and lavish stuccowork, while in the upper galleries there's a quite interesting **Schatzkammer** (Treasury; adult/child €4/1; ⊗10am-3pm Tue-Sat, 11am-3pm Sun May-Oct).

Unusually, the church is centred on a small but exquisite chapel, known as the **Gnadenkapelle** (Chapel of Grace). This gold and silver edifice houses the Romanesque statue of the Madonna, whose healing powers reputedly helped King Louis of Hungary defeat the Turks in 1377. Except for two days each year, she's dressed up rather doll-like in her *Liebfrauenkleid* (dress of Our Lady). Both Johann Bernhard Fischer von Erlach

and his son Josef Emmanuel had a hand in the baroque interior features; the crucifixion group sculpture (1715) on the high altar is by Lorenzo Mattielli. The Schatzkammer contains votive offerings spanning six centuries, mainly naive-style paintings.

Erlebniswelt Holzknechtland MUSEUM
(entry & cable car adult/child €17.20/9.90; ⊗9am-5pm Apr-Oct) A small museum on Bürgeralpe is devoted to wood and all its wonderful uses.

🏃 Activities

The region has lots of small, winding roads and forest/mountain-bike trails for two-wheeled exploration. Pick up the *Mariazeller Land* brochure, which has a good pull-out map, from the tourist office. A handful of treking and mountain bikes are rented out by **Hotel Schwarzer Adler** (☎2863; www.hotelschwarzeradler.at; Hauptplatz 1; per day €12-16).

Bürgeralpe HIKING, SKIING
This mountain is a great starting or finishing point for hiking in the summer months, and also has skiing in winter. The **cable car** (www.mariazell-buergeralpe.at; adult/child return €14/9) operates year-round. It has an artificial lake used as a setting for special events. During winter, adult ski passes cost around €31 (daily) and €162 (weekly).

Erlaufsee WATER SPORTS, WALKING
This small lake a few kilometres to the northwest of town reaches about 22°C in summer and, apart from swimming, it offers good opportunities for windsurfing and scuba diving; contact addresses for water sports are listed in the booklet *Mariazellerland von A-Z*, available at the tourist office.

An easy four-hour **Rundwanderweg** (circuit trail) runs past the lake and south through forest back into Mariazell; alternatively, you can take the steam **Museumstramway** (one way/return €5/8), which runs at weekends and holidays in July and August. It leaves from the Museumstramway Bahnhof.

🛏 Sleeping & Eating

The only problem times for finding a room in Mariazell are around the pilgrim days. Aside from hotels and pensions, there is a smattering of private rooms.

Jugend- und Familiengästedorf HOSTEL €
(☎05 7083 390; www.jufa.eu/jufa-erlaufsee-sport-resort; Erlaufseestrasse 49; s/d €54.30/88.60;

P @ 🛜 🏊 🚹) Located halfway between Mariazell and Erlaufsee, this hostel has a sauna, solarium and fitness room.

Campingplatz Erlaufsee　　CAMPGROUND €
(☑ 49 37; www.st-sebastian.at; camp sites per adult/child/tent/car €4.20/2/3.20/2.90; ⊙ May–mid-Sep; P) A small camping ground in St Sebastian on the Erlaufsee, flanked by pine trees. Bus 197 runs regularly to St Sebastian from the bus station.

Goldene Krone　　HOTEL €
(☑ 25 83; www.mariazell.at/krone; Grazer Strasse 1; s €44, d €76; @ 🛜 🚹) Goldene Krone's big and bright rooms have a homely feel, which is complemented by a Finnish sauna and billiard room (also with table football). The ground floor has an excellent restaurant (mains €8 to €13), featuring traditional Austrian cuisine and street-side seating.

★ Hotel Drei Hasen　　HOTEL €€
(☑ 24 10; www.dreihasen.at; Wiener Strasse 11; s €80, d €130, ste €180; ⊙ closed mid-Mar–mid-Apr & Nov; P 🛜) This comfortable hotel has some of the most pleasant and comfortable rooms in town, with the added bonus of a sauna, relaxation room and sundeck. The first-class restaurant (mains €9 to €24) specialises in seasonal game dishes.

Brauhaus Mariazell　　BREWERY €€
(☑ 25 23-0; www.bierundbett.at; Wiener Strasse 5; mains €12.90-17.70; ⊙ 10am-11pm Wed-Sat, 2-11pm Sun; 🛜) This lovely, rustic microbrewery has some of the best Styrian cuisine in these parts and brews its own light and dark beer. There's a garden out back and accommodation upstairs (rooms from €70 per person; suites €119 per person).

Questers　　DELI €€
(www.questers.at; Grazer Strasse 4; mains €8.90-15.60; ⊙ 10am-5pm Mon-Thu, to 6pm Fri & Sat, to 4pm Sun) This gourmet shop serves sit-down meals and snacks but also has lots of tasty fish dishes and delicacies for a picnic, including mouth-watering *Krainer* sausage made from game.

ℹ Information

Tourist office (☑ 23 66; www.mariazell-info.at; Hauptplatz 13; ⊙ 9am-5.30pm Mon-Fri, to 4pm Sat, to 12.30pm Sun, closed Sat & Sun Nov-Apr) Has a town map and brochure with walking trails marked; doesn't book rooms but has accommodation listings.

Mariazell

◎ Top Sights

✚ Activities, Courses & Tours

◉ Sleeping

✖ Eating

ℹ Getting There & Away

A narrow-gauge train departs from St Pölten, 84km to the north, every two to three hours. It's a slow trip (€16, 2½ hours), but the scenery is good for the last hour approaching Mariazell.

Bus is the only option for further travel from Mariazell into Styria; four direct buses run daily to/from Bruck an der Mur (€11.60, 1½ hours), with train connections to/from Graz (€24, 2¼ hours). There is also one early-morning and one afternoon direct bus each way daily between Vienna (Südtiroler Platz) and Mariazell (€20, three hours).

ⓘ TRANSPORT CONNECTIONS IN NORTHERN STYRIA

Travelling in northern Styria requires bus travel between some towns. Plan your arrivals and getaways using www.verbundlinie.at, www.postbus.at or www.oebb.at. Some useful direct connections:

➡ Leoben–Eisenerz: €7.80, one hour, six to 10 daily.

➡ Eisenerz–Hieflau: €4, 25 minutes, three to four daily; another four on weekdays during school term.

➡ Hieflau–Admont: €4, 30 minutes, three to 10 daily.

➡ Admont–Liezen–Schladming: €12.40, 80 minutes to 1¾ hours, five to 18 daily. Change to train in Liezen.

➡ Admont–Gesäuse: €4, 12 minutes, five to 10 daily.

➡ Schladming–Graz: €36.40, 2½ hours, daily every two hours. Trains run via Stainach-Irdning (the main transfer point for trains north to the Hallstätter See and elsewhere in the Salzkammergut) and Liezen (the transfer point for buses to Admont and the Gesäuse).

Bruck an der Mur

✍ 03862 / POP 12,500

Bruck, at the confluence of the Mur and Mürz rivers, is the Mur Valley's first real town and an important railway junction for Styria. Attractions are limited but if you're on a stopover, check out the attractive **Koloman-Wallisch-Platz**, the historic town square with a food and flower market each Wednesday and Saturday; and the castle ruins of **Schloss Landskron**, which can be easily reached from the centre on winding paths. On the way, drop by the 15th-century Gothic **Pfarrkirche** (Kirchplatz; ☉ dawn-dusk). The **tourist office** (✍ 890-121; www.tourismus-bruckmur.at; Koloman-Wallisch-Platz 1; ☉ 9am-5pm Mon-Thu, to 1pm Fri) is on the main square.

ⓘ Getting There & Away

Along with Leoben, Bruck is the region's main rail hub; all fast trains to Graz (€12, 45 minutes, hourly) pass through here. Other direct trains go hourly to Klagenfurt (€30.50, two hours) and hourly to Vienna (€27.80, 1¾ hours). By road, the main autobahn intersect southeast of town. If you're planning to cycle in the region, the tourist office has useful maps. Postbus services arrive and depart next to the train station.

Leoben

✍ 03842 / POP 24,600

Unprepossessing Leoben reveals a few surprises once you dig down into its modest urban soul. A revamped museum quarter is one very good reason to prolong a flying visit here between trains. The town is also a centre for metallurgical industries and home to Gösser beer, and achieved ultimate fame with the peace treaty signed here in 1797 by Napoleon and Emperor Franz II.

◉ Sights & Activities

Tourismusverband Leoben can help arrange tours into an early-Romanesque crypt of the **Stiftkirche** (foundation church) or visits to the local **Gösser Brewery**, both about 4km south of the centre in the suburb of Göss.

Hauptplatz   SQUARE
Dating from the 13th century, this long, rectangular square has an attractive **Pestsäule** (Plague Column; 1717). Many of the elegant facades lining the square were created in the 17th century, including the baroque **Hacklhaus** (Hauptplatz 9) from 1660. Leoben's connection with the iron industry is seen in the curious town motif displayed on the **Altes Rathaus** (Hauptplatz 1) facade, which shows an ostrich eating horseshoes.

At the northern end you find a fountain from 1794 with an angel holding the town's heraldic shield, and at the opposite end is a fountain dedicated to miners (1799).

Pfarrkirche St Xaver   CHURCH
(Kirchplatz 1; ☉ 8am-7pm) The simple exterior of this early baroque church, built in 1665 as a Jesuit church, belies a complex interior of white walls and black-and-gold baroque altars.

Kunsthalle
MUSEUM

(www.kunsthalle-leoben.at; Kirchgasse 6; ⊙9am-6pm) This museum complex stages some of Austria's best temporary exhibitions to be found outside the capital. Its permanent Schienen der Vergangenheit (Tracks of the Past) in the **MuseumsCenter Leoben** (www.museumscenter-leoben.at; Kirchgasse 6; adult/child/family €5/3.50/11; ⊙10am-5pm Tue-Sat, longer hours during Kunsthalle exhibitions) tells the history of Leoben and the town's industries. Check the website for information on prices and temporary exhibitions, which are staged for seven to eight months every second year. Combined tickets are available.

Asia Spa
SPA

(☑245 00; www.asiaspa.at; In der Au 3; 4hr spa adult/child €7/3, 4hr sauna adult €18) Leoben's spa centre offers massages and treatments. Note that children under 16 may not enter the sauna.

🛏 Sleeping & Eating

Pension Jahrbacher
PENSION €

(☑436 00; www.jahrbacher.at; Kirchgasse 14; s/d €39/69; 🖧) This small, centrally located *Pension* has comfortable rooms and is associated with **Cafe am Schwammerlturm** (☑436 00; www.jahrbacher.at; Homanngasse 11; ⊙11am-6pm Tue-Sun), a tiny cafe with wonderful outdoor seating on top of the circular city tower. From here you have breathtaking views over the town and countryside. Book ahead for the *Pension*, and if no one answers the door, drop by the antique shop next door or the cafe.

Hotel Kindler
HOTEL €€

(☑432 020; www.kindler.at; Straussgasse 7-11; s €51-57, d €92; 🖧) This clean, renovated hotel in the centre offers excellent value and is comfortable; its only drawback is that wooden-tiled floors cause sound to travel between rooms.

Falkensteiner Hotel
HOTEL €€

(☑40 50; www.leoben.falkensteiner.com; In der Au 1-3; s €100-200, d €120-250; 🅿@🖧🏊💪) This seminar and business hotel is part of the Asia Spa complex and offers quality, stylish rooms with high-speed cable or wi-fi (€9 per day; free in reception area). Tones are warm and attractive, and one wall of the shower cubicle is glass and fronts the double bed (but has a curtain for the discreet). A night here includes use of the Asia Spa.

★ Stadt Meierei
AUSTRIAN, INTERNATIONAL €€

(☑446 03; www.stadt-meierei.at; Homanngasse 1; lunch menu €8.90, mains €16.50-25.90; ⊙lunch & dinner Tue-Sat) Run by chef Martin Neuretter and *chef de rang* and sommelier Isabella Pichler, this restaurant offers quality cuisine from a menu featuring lamb, beef, poultry and fish specialities.

ℹ Information

Tourismusverband Leoben (☑481 48; Peter Tunner-Strasse 2; ⊙9am-5pm Mon-Fri) Main information centre for Leoben; stocks a *Bei uns zu Gast* booklet with useful listings. Its Leoben map also includes a great environs map with hiking trails.

Stadt Information Leoben (☑440 18; www. leoben.at; Hauptplatz 12; ⊙8am-5pm Mon-Fri, 9am-noon Sat) Community and tourist-information centre with brochures.

ℹ Getting There & Away

Leoben is 16km west of Bruck an der Mur (€3.80, 15 minutes, hourly) and is on the main rail route from there to Klagenfurt or Linz. The town centre is 10 minutes' walk from Leoben Hauptbahnhof: cross the Mur and bear right.

Eisenerz

☑03848 / POP 4800

Eisenerz, nestled at the foot of the extraordinary Erzberg (Iron Mountain), is one of the important stops along the **Steirische Eisenstrasse** (Styrian Iron Road). This unusual peak has been completely denuded by open-cast stope mining and resembles a step pyramid. The outcome is eerie and surprisingly beautiful, with its orange and purple shades contrasting with the lush greenery and grey crags of surrounding mountains.

◉ Sights & Activities

Erzberg
INDUSTRIAL MUSEUM

(☑32 00; www.abenteuer-erzberg.at; Erzberg 1; tours adult/child €15/7.50, combined tours €26/12.50, Hauly explosion tour €21/15.50; ⊙tours 10am-3pm May-Oct, advance booking required; 💪) Eisenerz' main attraction is its Erzberg ironworks, which can be seen up close on underground *Schaubergwerk* tours of the mine, abandoned in 1986, or alternatively on overground tours in a 'Hauly' truck along roads cut into the mountain. Both tours are usually in German, with English-language notes available. Each Thursday at 9am you can also ride up in a Hauly and watch the rock being exploded. The departure point is a 10-minute walk from the centre, following the course of the river.

Dress warmly for the 90-minute *Schaubergwerk* tours. There are fine views along the way of the 60-minute *Hauly Abenteuerfahrt* tours.

Wehrkirche St Oswald
CHURCH

(Kirchenstiege 4; ⊙9am-7pm Apr-Oct) More a fortress than a Gothic church, this soaring bastion gained its heavy walls in 1532 as protection against the Turks.

Hiking Trails
HIKING

Eisenerz is surrounded by lots of hiking trails. The tourist office has a free town map with trails marked, including to the idyllic **Leopoldsteiner See**, only 3km north on the road towards Admont. This small lake has a wall of granite rising to 1649m as a backdrop; you can hire boats in summer – it's a very chilly swim, though.

🛏 Sleeping & Eating

There are several good *Pensionen* and hotels in the old town, but not so many good eating options.

Jugend- und Familiengästehaus
HOSTEL €

(☑05 7083 340; www.jufa.eu/jufa-eisenerzer-ramsau-almerlebnisdorf; Ramsau 1; s/d €34.20/68.40; P@⊜🚻) This lovely HI hostel is 5km south of Eisenerz. It's at an altitude of 1000m, and has a sauna and indoor and outdoor climbing walls, as well as hiking trails going off into the mountains. There's a restaurant on-site. You will need a car to get here (a taxi costs about €13).

Gästehaus Tegelhofer
GUESTHOUSE €

(☑20 86; www.gaestehaus-tegelhofer.at; Lindmoserstrasse 8; s/d €37/64; P⊜🚻) This modern guesthouse offers great value, with spacious and clean rooms, and a free sauna and fitness room. There's also an inexpensive family apartment for two to six people.

Gästehaus Weninger
GUESTHOUSE €

(☑22 580; www.gaestehaus-weninger.at; Krumpentalerstrasse 8; s/d €39/66; P⊜) A very decent guesthouse with a fitness room and sauna, Weninger aims at those staying for a few days, but does take guests for one night at very short notice. Some bathrooms are cramped, but rooms are a good size.

Gasthof zu Post
AUSTRIAN €

(Lindmoserstrasse 10; mains €8-12; ⊙lunch & dinner Tue-Sat, lunch Sun; P) The traditional Gasthof zu Post prides itself on local classics such as *Beuschel* (lung and heart) or inexpensive goulash and venison ragout.

Barbarastub'n
CAFE €

(Bergmannplatz 2; ⊙8.30am-7pm Mon-Sat, 2-6pm Sun) Drop by here for delicious apple strudel or simply relax on the comfy chairs out back over a tea or coffee. Sometimes it has brochures and maps of town, which are useful when the tourist office is closed.

ℹ Information

Tourist office (☑37 00; www.eisenerz-heute. at; Dr Theodor Körner Platz 1; ⊙9am-noon & 3-5pm Mon-Fri) Helpful and in the centre of town. Good maps for hiking.

ℹ Getting There & Away

Direct buses run hourly from Leoben to Eisenerz (€7.80, one hour), less frequently on Sundays. Several daily connect Eisenerz and Hieflau (€4, 25 minutes), where you can pick up buses and the occasional train to Selzthal and Liezen.

Trains no longer operate to Eisenerz, and at the time of research landslides had halted the special Vordernberg–Eisenerz **Nostalgie** (Nostalgic Train; ☑03849-832; www.erzberg-bahn.at) train. See the website for the latest on whether the service has resumed.

For a taxi, call ☑4636.

Nationalpark Gesäuse

Established in 2003, Gesäuse is Austria's newest national park, set in a pristine region of jagged mountain ridges, rock towers, deep valleys, alpine pastures and dense spruce forests. It is washed by the Enns River, which is a favourite of rafting connoisseurs, and a number of companies offer rafting trips during the summer months. Hiking and mountain climbing, and to a lesser extent mountain biking, also feature among the park's outdoor activities; of the six peaks over 2000m within the park, **Hocktor** (2369m) is the highest and is popular among hikers.

The staffed **national park pavilion** (☑03611-21 101-20; Gstatterboden 25; ⊙10am-6pm May-Oct) is a useful source of information, and the tourist office in Admont also has information on accommodation and activities in the park.

Buses connect with Admont (€4, 22 minutes, four to seven daily), via Bachbrücke/Weidendom (€4, 12 minutes).

Admont

☎ 03613 / POP 2540

Admont, nestled in a broad section of the Enns Valley, is a low-key town that revs up during the day when groups arrive in buses to see its spectacular abbey. Each night it sinks back into pleasant oblivion. The town makes a good base for kicking off deeper into the region.

◉ Sights

Benedictine Abbey ABBEY
(www.stiftadmont.at; Admont 1; adult/child/family €9.50/5.30/22; ☉10am-5pm late Mar-early Nov, to 2pm early Nov-late Dec, by arrangement late Dec-late Mar) Admont's Benedictine Abbey is arguably Austria's most elegant and exciting baroque abbey. It brings together museums, religion, and modern art and architecture into an award-winning cultural ensemble.

The centrepiece of the abbey is its **Stiftsbibliothek**, the largest abbey library in the world. Survivor of a fire in 1865 that severely damaged the rest of the abbey, it displays about 70,000 volumes of the abbey's 200,000-strong collection, and is decorated with heavenly ceiling frescoes by Bartolomeo Altomonte (1694–1783) and statues (in wood, but painted to look like bronze) by Josef Stammel (1695–1765).

The abbey is also home to the **Kunsthistorisches Museum** (Art History Museum), featuring rare pieces such as its tiny portable altar from 1375, made from amethyst quartz and edged with gilt-silver plates; some Gerhard Mercator globes from 1541 and 1551; and monstrances from the 15th and 16th centuries. Each year innovative temporary exhibitions complement the permanent ones.

Another museum, the **Museum für Gegenwartkunst** (Museum for Contemporary Art), contains works by about 100 mainly Austrian artists, and has pieces you can explore with your hands. The **Naturhistorisches Museum** (Natural History Museum) began in 1674 with a small collection and today includes rooms devoted to flying insects (one of the largest collections in the world), butterflies, stuffed animals, wax fruits (bizarrely) and reptiles. From the glass stairway and **Herb Garden** there are views to the National Park Gesäuse.

⌂ Sleeping

★ **Jugend- und Familiengästehaus Schloss Röthelstein** HOSTEL €€
(☎05 7083-320; roethelstein@jufa.at; Aigen 32; s/d/tr/q €54/88/132/176; ℗⌖) This is where the monks from the abbey used to stay in summer. It's located in a baroque castle from the 17th century, about 5km southwest

STYRIA ADMONT

LOCAL KNOWLEDGE

THE GESÄUSE REGION

Andreas Hollinger, a ranger from Nationalpark Gesäuse outside Admont, explains what makes the Gesäuse special.

Character of the Gesäuse

The Gesäuse is the last of the regions in the eastern Alps where the mountains rise up so powerfully. It's a rocky, mountainous landscape with enormous differences in altitude in a small area. If you stand at Johnsbachsteg, near the Weidendom national park complex, you can see the Enns River in the valley, the surrounding forest, and the peak region, an altitude difference of 1800m all at a glance.

Trails

From Weidendom there are various theme trails leading out into the valley that are suitable for children and two trails, the Lettmair Au trail and the Leierweg, for those travellers in wheelchairs. I think the trail that best gives you the Gesäuse feeling with altitude differences leads to the **Haindlkarhütte** (☎0664-114 00 46; www.haindlkar-huette.at; Johnsbach; ☉Sep–mid-Oct) at 1121m. It's 1½ hours each way and accessed from the Haindlkarhütte bus stop between Gstatterboden and the turn-off to Johnsbach. It's an easy trail, and from there you've got access to extreme climbing tours.

WORTH A TRIP

JOHNSBACH

Situated 17km southeast of Admont, the tiny settlement of Johnsbach is the focal point for hiking, climbing and water sports in the region. It is wedged on a bucolic stream, with rugged mountains rising up on virtually all sides.

This is one of Austria's earliest mountain-climbing centres, and testimony to this is the whimsical **Bergsteiger-Friedhof** (Mountain Climber Cemetery; www.johnsbach.at; ☺dawn-dusk) `FREE`, where buried alongside local citizens are mountain climbers who have come to grief in the Gesäuse over the centuries. With its pretty white-washed church, this is a beautiful and strangely touching place.

Both easy and difficult trails lead off into the mountains from Johnsbach or the turn-off from the B146 main road. The tourist office and national park information offices can help. A couple of rafting companies also have bases here, including **AOS Adventures** (☑03612-25 343; www.rafting.at; 3-4hr Enns rafting tours €50; ☺8.30am-5pm Mon-Fri, tours 9am & 2pm, Gesäuse camp closed mid-Oct–Apr).

There are several good guesthouses offering food and a bed in the settlement. **Gasthof zum Donner** (☑03611-218; www.donnerwirt.at; Johnsbach 5; s €30-35, d €60-70, mains €9-13.50) sits alongside the church and rafting base camp, while **Gasthof Kölblwirt** (☑03611-216; www.koelblwirt.at; Johnsbach 65; s €39, d €66-72) is about 800m further up the road and has it all: a *Pension*, a restaurant specialising in Styrian beef, yodelling courses and Nordic ski hire, through to suggestions for hikes and winter tours.

With your own wheels, take the B146 east and the signposted turn-off to Johnsbach. By bus, call about two hours ahead for the **Rufbus** (Taxi bus; ☑03613-2406, 03613-4170), which runs out four to five times daily from Admont Bahnhof (€4). Regular buses also run from Admont to the turn-off at Bachbrücke/Weidendom (€4, 12 minutes), from where it's a 5km walk.

of the centre off Aignerstrasse. The renovated palace is flanked by carefully manicured lawns, has an elegant glass-roofed, arcaded inner courtyard, and tastefully decorated rooms with wooden floors and subtle tones. Some of its 40 rooms are located in towers.

Hotel Gastof Traube HOTEL €€
(☑24 400; www.hotel-die-traube.at; Hauptstrasse 3; s €58-68, d €96-116; P🐾) One of the best places to stay in the centre of town, with modern rooms that are a notch above the others on Hauptstrasse.

Hotel Spirodom Admont HOTEL €€
(☑36 600; www.spirodom.at; Eichenweg 616; s/d €100/166; P@🐾🏊) Admont's new four-star hotel is located about 600m north of the abbey and lures guests with a pool, wellness facilities and views to either the abbey or parkland.

❶ Information

The **tourist office** (☑21 1 60; www.gesaeuse.at; Hauptstrasse 35; ☺8am-6pm Mon-Fri, 10am-4pm Sat mid-May–mid-Oct, 9am-5pm Mon-Fri mid-Oct–mid-May) is opposite the Rathaus and near the abbey church. It doubles as a national-park office.

❶ Gettting There & Away

Admont is 15km to the east of Selzthal, but served by only very limited train services. Buses departing from Hieflau (€4, 30 minutes, three to nine daily) and Liezen (€4, 30 minutes, seven to 15 daily) are the two main approaches to Admont. Buses connect Admont with the national park office in Gstatterboden (€4, 22 minutes, four to seven daily), via Bachbrücke/Weidendom (€4, 12 minutes). **Gasthaus Kamper** (☑3688; www.gh-kamper.at; Hauptstrasse 19; per hr €1.50, per day €7; 🚲) hires out trekking and mountain bikes as well as a couple of children's bikes.

WEST STYRIA

Like northern Styria, west Styria is a mountainous region divided by jagged ranges and alpine streams. Murau is a picturesque town well placed for hikes and cycle trips into the surrounding forests. If you're heading this way from Graz, consider a detour to **Seckau** or **Oberzeiring**. The former is famous for its **Benedictine Abbey** (www.abtei-seckau.at; Seckau 1; tours adult/child €5/3.50; ☺8am-8pm year-round, tours 11am & 2pm May–late Oct), a stunning Romanesque basilica and the mausoleum of Karl II, while the latter is known for its old **silver mine** (www.silbergruben.at; adult/child/family €9/5/18; ☺ tours 10.30am, 1.30pm & 3pm daily May-Oct, 3pm Wed Nov-Apr), now resurrected as an exhibition mine and small health resort for sufferers of respiratory diseases.

Schladming

📶 03687 / POP 4370

Situated deep in the Ennstal (Enns Valley) in western Styria at the foot of the glacial Dachsteingebirge (Dachstein mountains), Schladming is a winter ski resort that in summer also offers glacier skiing and snowboarding, easy access to hiking trails, white-water rafting on the Enns River and excellent mountain biking. On Hoher Dachstein (2995m), don't miss the opportunity to walk through a glacier crevice in the Eispalast or to admire views over the Ennstal from the Skywalk high-altitude panorama platform.

⊙ Sights

Dachstein Eispalast   GLACIER

(www.dachsteingletscher.at; Ramsau am Dachstein; adult/child €10/5.50, gondola return adult/child €33/18; ☺ 8.30am-4.30pm, gondola every 20min 7.50am-5.10pm) Situated in a crevice of the Dachstein Glacier at the sheer cliff face of the mountains, the **Eispalast** (Ice Palace) creates the strange effect of walking through an enormous, hollow ice cube. A **gondola**, one of the world's most spectacular, whisks you up and terminates with a vertical thrust at the spectacular **Skywalk** viewing platform. About 10 buses daily (€8.10, 45 minutes) leave Lendplatz or Rathausplatz in Schladming for the base station near Ramsau.

🏃 Activities

The area around Schladming has more than 900km of mountain-bike trails, divided among 20 routes shown on the excellent, free mountain-bike map from the tourist office. Hiking trails begin almost from the centre of town – the tourist office's town map has trails marked.

Schladming Ski Fields   SKIING, SNOWBOARDING

(day pass adult/child €45/23, alpine ski set per day €30) The winter ski period from December to March is the peak season in Schladming, when the area's 223km of downhill ski pistes and more than 100 ski lifts rev into action.

Skiing and snowboarding on the Dachstein Glacier can be done year-round (but not all lifts are open in summer).

Most of the cross-country skiing is done across the valley in Ramsau (about €16 for ski hire). A medium-quality snowboard for the pistes costs €20 and snow-hiking shoes €15. Prices on the glacier are similar.

Riesachfälle Waterfalls   HIKING

You can begin this popular walk from Talbachgasse in Schladming. Follow the stream for about 40 minutes along a shared mountain-bike and walking trail to Untertal. From there it's about another 3½ hours to the waterfalls. An alternative is to take the bus to the popular valley restaurant **Gasthof zu Riesachfall** (📶 61678; www.gasthaus-riesachfall.at; Untertalstrasse 66, Untertal; ☺ lunch & dinner late Apr–late Oct) and walk the forest trail (1½ hours; good shoes and head for heights required) or the gravel forestry road (two hours) to the falls and beyond to the Riesachsee (Lake Riesach).

[pi:tu] Bikecenter   BICYCLE RENTAL

(📶 0680-320 78 62; www.bikeparkplanai.at; Coburgstrasse 52; per day €30-80) This mountain-bike rental place is located at the Planai Stadium.

Trittscher   BICYCLE, SKI RENTAL

(📶 226 47-11; www.trittscher.at; Salzburgerstrasse 24) In summer Trittscher rents mountain bikes for €15 per day and e-bikes for €29 per day; in winter it hires out ski equipment for €15 to €29 depending on the type, ski shoes for €8.40 per day and snowboards for €19.

🛏 Sleeping

Book ahead during the ski season to be sure of a room. The tourist office can help place you.

STYRIA SCHLADMING

ⓘ SOMMERCARD

Bus and cable-car rides can soon eat into a budget in Schladming. From late May to late October a Sommercard is issued by many places to stay; it gives discounts and all-important free transport on the buses (but not for the Eispalast or Postbus services) and cable cars. You can't buy it, but when booking your accommodation ask whether one is issued.

★ Post Hotel
HOTEL €€

(☎ 225 71; www.posthotel-schladming.at; Hauptplatz 10; r €90-130, apt €95-135, ste €220-300; P @ 🛜 🐾) The four-star Post Hotel has spacious, modern rooms decorated in tasteful tones. Some of its doubles have connecting doors for families, and its family apartment is in fact a fully fledged suite with a separate living room. It also has a sauna and issues the Sommercard.

Jugendgästehaus Schladming
HOSTEL €€

(☎ 05 7083-330; www.jufa.at/schladming; Coburgstrasse 253; s/d €55/80; 🛜) Situated in the pedestrian zone close to the Planai base station, this excellent hostel has maisonette rooms with upstairs and downstairs beds, doubles with beds you can shift together, as well as standard rooms. It issues the Sommercard.

Hotel Landgraf
HOTEL €€

(☎ 223 95; www.landgraf.cc; Hauptplatz 37; s/d/tr/q €55/110/150/180; P 🐾) Hotel Landgraf is a comfortable abode situated right in the centre of Schladming. As well as offering good-value standard rooms, it has some spacious apartments suitable for families (it doesn't issue the Sommercard).

✖ Eating & Drinking

Bio Chi
HEALTH FOOD €

(www.biochi.at; Martin Luther Strasse 32; breakfasts €4.50-9.10, buffet salads €3.90-5.60, mains €6.20-8.20; ⊙ 8am-6pm Mon-Fri, to 2pm Sat; 🖉) 🌿 This health-food shop whips up healthy salads and vegetarian mains using organic ingredients, which you can wash down with freshly squeezed juices.

HUNDERTWASSER SPA

East Styria is well known throughout Austria for its thermal activity, and in particular for the spa centres that have sprung up around its thermal springs. Fans of the architectural style of Friedensreich Hundertwasser won't want to miss the unusual spa **Rogner-Bad Blumau** (☎ 03383-51 00; www.blumau.com; adult/child weekdays €41/23, weekends €50/28; ⊙ 9am-11pm), near the town of Bad Blumau, 50km east of Graz. The spa has all the characteristics of his art, including uneven floors, grass on the roof, colourful ceramics and golden spires. Overnight accommodation includes entry to the spa.

Johann
AUSTRIAN €€

(www.posthotel-schladming.at; Hauptplatz 10; mains €12.90-24.90; ⊙ lunch & dinner) Affiliated with the Post Hotel, Johann has cosy shades of striped green and is the best restaurant act in town, with an excellent selection of wines to go with its Styrian and Austrian dishes.

Maria's Mexican
TEX-MEX €€

(Steirergasse 3; light mains & salads €9.10-18.50, mains €9.80-19.40; ⊙ dinner, closed Mon & Tue Apr-Oct; 🛜) This Tex-Mex joint in the centre has a good range of salads served with meat accompaniments, as well as burgers, steaks, spare ribs and chicken wings. When the snow's on the slopes, it kicks on till late.

Hohenhaus Tenne
BAR

(www.tenne.com/schladming; Coburgstrasse 512; ⊙ 11am-4am, closed Apr-Oct) Finding après-ski in Schladming in the ski season is as easy as falling down an icy hill. The Hohenhaus Tenne is the hottest place to tumble.

① Information

Tourismusverband Schladming-Rohrmoos (☎ 22 777 22; www.schladming.at; Rohrmoosstrasse 234; ⊙ 9am-6pm Mon-Sat, closed Sat Apr & Nov) Stocks mountain-bike-trail and hiking maps, has lots of tips on the region and will organise accommodation if you call ahead. A useful accommodation board and free telephone are situated outside.

① Getting There & Around

Every two hours, trains pass through on their way to Graz (€36, 2½ hours) and at least five times daily to Salzburg (€19, 1½ hours). The Dachsteinstrasse toll road to the gondola costs €6/2.80 per adult/child.

In summer five buses daily leave from Rathausplatz and Lendplatz to Riesachfall Wilde Wasser (€5.90, 35 minutes), the access point to the Riesachfälle waterfalls and the lake.

For a taxi, call ☎ 222 63 or ☎ 222 22.

Murau

☎ 03532 / POP 2120

Murau, in the western reaches of the Murtal (Mur Valley) on the banks of the river, is an attractive town filled with pastel-coloured houses. It's also surrounded by forested hills and alpine meadows. Its close proximity to Stolzalpe to the north and the Metnitzer mountains to the south makes it an excellent base for hiking and cycling during the summer months.

⊙ Sights & Activities

Schloss Murau — CASTLE
(Schlossberg 1; tours adult/child €6/3; ☺ tours 2pm Wed & Fri Jun–late Sep) Built in 1250 by the Liechtenstein family, which once ruled the region, Schloss Murau assumed its present Renaissance form in the 17th century. Tours take you through seven rooms, including the chapel and the **Rittersaal** (Knight's Room), where concerts are often held. The altar in the chapel dates from 1655 and was created by masters from the town of Judenberg.

Stadtpfarrkirche St Matthäus — CHURCH
(Schlossberg 8; ☺ dawn-dusk) Situated just below the castle, this restored church has Gothic and baroque elements that work surprisingly well together, especially in the combination of the Gothic crucifixion group (1500) and the baroque high altar (1655). The beautiful frescoes date from the 14th to the 16th centuries.

Brewery Museum — MUSEUM
(Raffaltplatz 19-23; adult/child €6/free; ☺ 2-6pm Fri May, Jun & Oct, 2-6pm Wed & Fri Jul-Sep) 🅿 Murau is also famous for its Brauerei Murau, which has a museum on the processes of making beer. Entry includes a glass of the local brew or a soft drink.

🛏 Sleeping & Eating

Jugend- und Familiengästehaus — HOSTEL €
(☎ 05 7083-280; www.jufa.at/en/accomodations/jufa-murau.html; St Leonhard Platz 4; s/d €42.50/65; 🅿🔌) This HI hostel is situated in four buildings near the train station, and has a sauna and a peaceful inner courtyard. Call ahead in September or October, when it closes for at least one month.

★ Hotel Ferner's Rosenhof — HOTEL €€
(☎ 23 18; www.hotel-ferner.at; Rosseggerstr 9; s from €70, d €130-170; 🅿@🔌👪) With lovely rooms, a sauna and herbal steam bath, and an attractive restaurant terrace (mains €11 to €27), Hotel Ferner's Rosenhof has style and cosiness. The more expensive rooms have balconies and are larger, and some have connecting doors for families.

Hotel Gasthof Lercher — HOTEL, PENSION €€
(☎ 24 31; www.meisterstrasse.at/hotel.lercher; Schwarzenbergstrasse 10; s €39-78, d €68-156; 🅿@🔌) Hotel Lercher is two places in one – a three-star Gasthof with inexpensive rooms and – still excellent value – a four-star hotel. Many of the rooms have views to the Stolz-

CYCLING & HIKING AROUND MURAU

Almost a dozen cycling tracks and mountain-bike trails can be accessed from Murau. The granddaddy of them all is the 450km-long Murradweg, which follows the course of the Mur River. Trails are numbered and routes marked on the Murau tourist office's useful *Rad & Mountainbike* booklet, also in English.

Hiking trails also branch out from here, some from the train station and others from the Bundesstrasse around Billa supermarket. A strenuous five-hour return hike to the Stolzalpen peak (1817m) begins at Billa. The tourist office has a useful *Wandern* booklet on hikes.

Intersport Pintar (☎ 23 97; www.sportpintar.at; Bundesstrasse 7a; per day bike €12, e-bike €22), about 500m past the Billa supermarket, rents trekking and e-bikes.

alpe, and even the cheapest are comfortably furnished. There's a sauna and steam bath. The restaurant serves delicious seasonal Styrian and Austrian classics (mains €12 to €18).

Pizzeria Restaurant Platzhirsch — ITALIAN, AUSTRIAN €
(☎ 33 39; Schillerplatz 10; pizza €6.90-9.50, pasta €7.90-9.90, mains 10.90-17.90; ☺ 11am-11pm) Serves good eat-in and takeaway pizza, pasta and Austrian classics.

ℹ Information

Tourist office (☎ 27 20-0; www.murau-kreischberg.at; Liechtensteinstrasse 3-5; ☺ 9am-6pm Mon-Fri, till noon Sat) Has loads of brochures on the town and its surrounds, including hiking trails and bicycle tracks.

ℹ Getting There & Away

If you're coming from Salzburgerland, the most pleasant mode of transport is the **Murtalbahn** (www.stlb.at; return €17), a steam train that chugs its way between Tamsweg and Murau once every Tuesday and Thursday from mid-June to mid-September on a narrow-gauge line.

Every two hours direct ÖBB trains connect Murau with Tamsweg (€7.80, one hour). Trains to Leoben (€13.60, 1½ hours, every two hours) require a change in Unzmarkt, also the junction for trains from Murau to Klagenfurt (€17.20, 2¼ hours, every two hours).

STYRIA MURAU

The Salzkammergut

Best Places to Eat

➡ Restaurant zum Salzbaron (p204)

➡ Restaurant-Pizzeria Simmer (p205)

➡ Landhotel Grünberg am See (p211)

Best Places to Stay

➡ Seehotel Grüner Baum (p203)

➡ Heritage.Hotel Hallstatt (p203)

➡ Schlosshotel Freisitz Roith (p211)

➡ Im Weissen Rössl (p212)

➡ Gjaid Alm (p205)

Why Go?

The Salzkammergut is a spectacular region of alpine and subalpine lakes, picturesque valleys, rolling hills and rugged, steep mountain ranges rising to almost 3000m. Much of the region is remote wilderness and, even in those heavily visited parts such as the Wolfgangsee and Mondsee, you'll always find isolated areas where peaceful, glassy waters provide limitless opportunities for boating, swimming, fishing or just sitting on the shore and chucking stones into the water. The popular Hallstätter See, flanked by soaring mountains that offer great hiking, is arguably the most spectacular of the lakes. Salt is the 'white gold' of the Salzkammergut, and the mines that made it famous now provide an interesting journey back in time to the settlers of the Iron Age Hallstatt culture, and to the Celts and Romans.

When to Go

➡ Head to the mountain lakes from July to early September for lake swimming. Lakes can be chilly or cold outside these months; the Wolfgangsee and Mondsee are warmest.

➡ The shoulder season (spring and autumn) has changeable weather, and in midsummer short, sudden rain showers are not unusual.

➡ There's good skiing on the Dachstein mountains once the snow settles, from December to March. With the right experience, equipment and maps you can ski to the Schladming side of the range on a cross-country trail.

The Salzkammergut Highlights

1 Reeling from views at the 5Fingers platform in the **Dachstein mountains** (p205).

2 Hiking around the **Hallstätter See** (p202) from Obertraun to Hallstatt and cooling off in the crystal waters between trails.

3 Exploring the Wolfgangsee and the pilgrimage church filled with priceless works of art in **St Wolfgang** (p211).

4 Strolling through the Kaiservilla, Franz Josef's summer residence in **Bad Ischl** (p200).

5 Plunging into the chilling depths to masterfully illuminated towers of ice in the **Dachstein caves** (p204).

6 Finding the toilet in K-Hof – a museum with a sanitary objects section in **Gmunden** (p208), for whenever nature calls.

7 Winter skiing on the 11km downhill piste from Krippenstein in the **Dachstein mountains** (p205).

ⓘ Getting There & Away

To reach the Salzkammergut from Salzburg by car or motorcycle, take the A1 to reach the north of the region, or Hwy 158 to Bad Ischl. Travelling north–south, the main road is Hwy 145 (the Salzkammergut Bundesstrasse), which follows the train line for most of its length. By rail, the main routes into the province are from Salzburg or Linz, with a change at Attnang-Puchheim onto the regional north–south railway line. From Styria, change at Stainach-Irdning.

ⓘ Getting Around

BOAT

Ply the waters between towns on the Attersee, Traunsee, Mondsee, Hallstätter See and Wolfgangsee.

BUS

Regular bus services connect all towns and villages in the area; services on weekends run less frequently or not at all. Hourly buses depart Salzburg for various towns in the region, including Bad Ischl, Mondsee and St Wolfgang; for services from Styria, see www.busbahnbim.at.

TRAIN

The Salzkammergut is crossed by regional trains on a north–south route, passing through Attnang-Puchheim on the Salzburg–Linz line and Stainach-Irdning on the Bischofshofen–Graz line. Hourly trains take 2½ hours to complete the journey. Small stations are not staffed; at an *unbesetzter Bahnhof* (unattended train station), use a platform ticket machine or pay on the train. Attersee is also accessible by rail.

BAD ISCHL

🕿 06132 / POP 13,900

This spa town's reputation snowballed after the Habsburg Princess Sophie took a treatment here to cure her infertility in 1828. Within two years she had given birth to Emperor Franz Josef I; two other sons followed and were nicknamed the Salzprinzen (Salt Princes). Rather in the manner of a salmon returning to its place of birth, Franz Josef made an annual pilgrimage to Bad Ischl, making it his summer home for the next 60 years and hauling much of the European aristocracy in his wake. The fateful letter he signed declaring war on Serbia and sparking off WWI bore a Bad Ischl postmark.

Today's Bad Ischl is a handsome town that makes a handy base for visiting the region's five main lakes.

◉ Sights & Activities

Kaiservilla PALACE
(www.kaiservilla.com; Jainzen 38; adult/child €13/7.50, grounds only €4.50/3.50; ⊗ 9.30am-4.45pm daily, Wed only Jan-Mar, closed Nov) Franz Josef's summer residence, the Kaiservilla is an Italianate building that was bought by his mother, Princess Sophie, as an engagement present for her son and Princess Elisabeth of Bavaria. Elisabeth, who loathed the villa and her husband in equal measure, spent little time here, but the emperor came to love it and it became his permanent summer residence for more than 60 years. His mistress, Katharina Schratt, lived nearby in a house chosen for her by the empress. Tours of the villa give interesting insights into the life of the family here and the objects on display include a death mask of Empress Elisabeth made after she was killed by a knife-wielding madman at the age of 60. Franz Josef was a passionate hunter, and the stuffed corpse of the 2000th chamois he shot is also on display.

Stadtmuseum MUSEUM
(www.stadtmuseum.at; Esplanade 10; adult/child €5.10/2.50; ⊗ 10am-5pm Thu-Sun, 2-7pm Wed Apr-Oct & Dec, 10am-5pm Fri-Sun Jan-Mar, closed Nov) The City Museum showcases the history of Bad Ischl and stages changing exhibitions inside the building where Franz Josef and Elisabeth were engaged (the day after they met at a ball).

Salzkammergut Therme SPA
(www.eurothermen.at; Voglhuberstrasse 10; 4hr ticket adult/child €15.50/11.50; ⊗ 9am-midnight) If you'd like to follow in Princess Sophie's footsteps, check out treatments at this historic spa.

★ Festivals & Events

The home of operetta composer Franz Lehár, Bad Ischl hosts the **Lehár Festival** (www.leharfestival.at; ⊗ Jul & Aug), which stages works by Lehár and other composers.

🛏 Sleeping

Jugendgästehaus HOSTEL €
(🕿 265 77; www.jugendherbergsverband.at/herbergen/badischl; Am Rechensteg 5; dm €20-24.50, s/d €34.50/54; ⊗ reception closed from 1pm Mon-Fri; @) The characterless but clean HI guesthouse is in the town centre behind Kreuzplatz.

Hotel Stadt Salzburg
HOTEL €

(☏235 640; www.stadtsalzburg.at; Salzburger Strasse 25; s/d €53/90; ☎) Rooms are a little on the worn side, but staff are efficient and the hotel has two advantages – budget price, and the bus to St Gilgen and Salzburg stops at the door.

Hotel Garni Sonnhof
HOTEL €€

(☏230 78; www.sonnhof.at; Bahnhofstrasse 4; s €65-95, d €90-150; P☎) Nestled in a leafy glade of maple trees next to the station, this lovely hotel has cosy, traditional decor; a beautiful garden (complete with a pond); a sunny conservatory; and large bedrooms with interesting old furniture, rag rugs and wooden floors. Use of the sauna and steam bath is included.

Landhotel Hubertushof
HOTEL €€

(☏24 445; www.hubertushof.co.at; Götzstrasse 1; s €64-76, d €120-148, tr €162-207; P@☎⚹⛷) This neo-rustic hotel has well-styled rooms that manage to lend a traditional edge without the heavy stuffiness. The tranquil swimming pool has an outdoor section, and there's a sauna and an infrared cabin located on-site – all geared to the wellness visitor.

Goldenes Schiff
HOTEL €€

(☏242 41; www.goldenes-schiff.at; Adalbert-Stifter-Kai 3; s €87-117, d €136-184, apt €184-198, junior ste €184-198; P@☎) Most double rooms in this four-star hotel have bathtubs, and the best rooms (junior suites) have large windows and overlook the river. Some rooms can be very plain, though. There's also a wellness centre that has a solarium and sauna, and a good restaurant that serves classic Austrian cuisine (from €13 to €29; closed Tuesday).

✖ Eating & Drinking

Restaurant Esplanade
CAFE €

(Pfarrgasse 7; pastries €3.50-5; ⊘8.30am-6pm) Little has changed here since its opening in 1882. Its elegant interior with antique furnishings makes it the perfect place to relax over a delicious pastry and coffee.

Heurigen-Stöckl
WINE TAVERN €

(www.heli-pizza.at; in the Kurpark; ⊘from 4pm Wed-Sun) Set among trees with a yard for outside eating and drinking, this *Heuriger* (wine tavern) crosses the culinary line to serve pizza as well as light meals with wine.

Restaurant Esplanade
AUSTRIAN €€

(Hasner Allee 2; mains €11.50-19.90; ⊘10am-10pm) This offshoot of Café Zauner, the famous pastry shop at Pfarrgasse 7, serves quite decent Austrian staples, some using organic local meats, in a pleasant location beside the river.

★ K.u.K. Hofbeisl
BISTRO PUB, BAR €€

(www.kukhofbeisl.com; Wirerstrasse 4; mains €10.50-20; ⊘Beisl lunch & dinner, bar 8am-4am Mon-Sat, from 9am Sun) This rambling place has a *Beisl* (bistro pub) in one building connected with a bar in the other – the bar is the liveliest late-night party place in town. DJs do their thing most Friday and Saturday nights, and the cocktail list would do a Russian novelist proud – about 150 cocktails in all.

Café Sissy
AUSTRIAN €€

(www.cafe-sissy.at; Pfarrgasse 2; mains €7.90-27.80; ⊘8am-midnight) Sissy was the nickname of the Kaiserin Elisabeth, unhappy wife of Emperor Franz Josef, and her pictures hang on the walls of this popular riverside bar-cafe. You can breakfast here, lunch or dine on a Wiener Schnitzel and other simple fare, or simply nighthawk at the front-room bar till the midnight hour.

❶ Information

Salzkammergut Touristik (☏24 000; www.salzkammergut.co.at; Götzstrasse 12; ⊘9am-7pm daily Apr-Sep, closed Sun Oct-Mar) A helpful private regional agency that rents trekking and mountain bikes as well as Movelo electric bikes (e-bikes; from €13 to €20 per 24 hours). Internet available (€1 per 15 minutes).

Tourist office (☏277 57; www.badischl.at; Auböckplatz 5; ⊘9am-6pm Mon-Sat, 10am-6pm Sun) Runs a telephone service until 10pm for rooms and information.

> ### SALZKAMMERGUT REGION
>
> The Salzkammergut, a cultural region that centres on Bad Ischl and the Hallstätter See, falls within three provinces: Upper Austria, which takes the lion's share; Styria, comprising the small area around Bad Aussee; and Salzburg province. For general information, check out www.salzkammergut.at. The nontransferable **Salzkammergut Erlebnis Card**, available from tourist offices and hotels, costs €4.90 and offers significant discounts for 21 days between 1 May and 31 October.

THE SALZKAMMERGUT BAD ISCHL

❶ Getting There & Away

BUS

Postbus services depart from outside the train station, with hourly buses to Salzburg (€9.90, 1½ hours) via St Gilgen (€5.10, 40 minutes). Buses to St Wolfgang (€3.90, 36 minutes) go via Strobl.

CAR

Most major roads in the Salzkammergut go to or near Bad Ischl. Hwy 158 from Salzburg and the north–south Hwy 145 intersect just north of the town centre.

TRAIN

Hourly trains to Hallstatt (€3.80, 25 minutes) go via Steeg/Hallstätter See and continue on to Obertraun (€5.70, 30 minutes). There are also hourly trains to Gmunden (€7.80, 40 minutes), as well as to Salzburg (€22.70, two hours) with a change at Attnang-Puchheim.

SOUTHERN SALZKAMMERGUT

The Dachstein mountain range provides a stunning 3000m backdrop to the lakes in the south. Transport routes go round rather than over these jagged peaks.

Hallstätter See

The Hallstätter See, set among sharply rising mountains at an altitude of 508m in the southern Salzkammergut, is one of the prettiest and most accessible lakes in the region. It offers some of the best hiking and swimming in summer, good skiing in winter, and a fascinating insight into the cultural history of the region any time of year. Just 5km around the lake lies Obertraun, the closest resort to the Dachstein ice caves. The whole Hallstatt-Dachstein region became a Unesco World Heritage site in 1997.

Hallstatt

📞 06134 / POP 790

With pastel-coloured houses that cast shimmering reflections onto the glassy waters of the lake and with towering mountains on all sides, Hallstatt's beauty alone would be enough to guarantee it fame. Boats chug tranquilly across the lake from the train station to the village, situated precariously on a narrow stretch of land between mountain and shore. So small is the patch of land

occupied by the village that its annual Corpus Christi procession takes place largely in small boats on the lake.

Salt in the hills above the town have made it a centre of salt mining. The Hallstatt Period (800 to 400 BC) refers to the early Iron Age in Europe, named after the village and the Iron Age settlers and Celts who worked the salt mines here.

Today the sheer volume of visitors can get annoying at times, and makes finding a hotel room difficult in midsummer. Consider staying in Obertraun, which retains its sleepy feel.

The centre of Hallstatt is at Hallstatt Markt, and Hallstatt Lahn is on the edge of town near the funicular to the Salzbergwerk. The train station is across the lake from Hallstatt; to get into town you have to take the ferry.

◎ Sights & Activities

Salzbergwerk   SALT MINE
(funicular return plus tour adult/child/family €26/13/54, tour only €19/9.50/40; ☺9.30am-4.30pm, closed late Oct–late Apr) The fascinating Salzbergwerk is situated high above Hallstatt on Salzberg (Salt Mountain) and is the lake's major cultural attraction. The German–English tour details how salt is formed and the history of mining, and takes visitors down into the depths on miners' slides – the largest is 60m, during which you have your photo taken (€5 to purchase).

The Hallstätter Hochtal (Hallstatt High Valley) near the mine was also an Iron Age burial ground. An audioguide (€2; bring photo ID) available from the base station of the funicular takes you through the numbered stations and explains the site and rituals of burial.

The **funicular** (one way adult/child €7/3.50) is the easiest way up to the mountain station, from where the mine is 15 minutes' walk; a switchback trail takes about 40 minutes to walk. Another option is to take the steps behind the Beinhaus and follow the trail until it joins the picturesque Soleleitungsweg; go left and follow the very steep trail past the waterfall and up steps. It's a tough climb, and not really for children.

Beinhaus   CHURCH
(Bone House; Kirchenweg 40; admission €1.50; ☺10am-6pm, closed Nov-Apr) This small charnel house contains rows of neatly stacked skulls, painted with decorative designs and the names of their former owners. Bones

have been exhumed from the overcrowded graveyard since 1600, and the last skull in the collection was added in 1995. It stands in the grounds of the 15th-century Catholic *Pfarrkirche* (parish church), which has some attractive Gothic frescoes and three winged altars inside.

Weltkulturerbe Museum MUSEUM
(☎8206; www.museum-hallstatt.at; Seestrasse 56; adult/child/family €7.50/4/18; ⏲10am-6pm daily Apr-Oct, closed Mon & Tue Nov-Mar) This multimedia museum covers the region's history of Iron Age/Celtic occupation and salt mining. All explanations are in German and English. Celtic and Roman excavations can be seen downstairs in **Dachsteinsport Janu** (Seestrasse 50; ⏲8am-6pm) FREE, a shop opposite the tourist office, or near the Salzbergwerk, where there is an exhibition grave.

Hallstätter See LAKE
(boat hire per hr from €11) You can hire boats and kayaks to get out on the lake, or scuba dive with the **Tauchclub Dachstein** (☎676 99 89, 644 99 89; www.zauner-online.at; 2-3hr course from €35).

Sleeping

Rooms fill quickly in summer, so book ahead. The tourist office can help you if you arrive without a booking. Many places provide free parking for guests within the town limits.

Campingplatz Klausner-Höll CAMPGROUND €
(☎8322; www.camping.hallstatt.net; Lahnstrasse 7; camp sites per adult/child/tent/car €8/4.50/5/4; ⏲mid-Apr–mid-Oct; P ᯤ) Located on a grassy meadow in Hallstatt Lahn, conveniently close to the centre and almost right on the lake, this camping ground has a small kiosk, a common room for camping guests and an on-site laundry.

Gasthaus Mühle HOSTEL €
(☎8318; www.hallstatturlaub.at; Kirchenweg 36; dm €23; ⏲closed Tue & Nov) This youth hostel is part of the restaurant of the same name. It's handily situated on the way up to the church, and the dorms are quite decent.

★ **Heritage.Hotel Hallstatt** HOTEL €€
(☎200 36-0; www.heritagehotel.at; Landungsplatz 102; s €139, d €195-325, ste €395; ᯤ) Rooms in this luxury hotel are spread across three buildings, with prime position in the main building at the landing stage on the lake. Most rooms offer stunning views and all have modern decor. Wi-fi in the main building.

★ **Seehotel Grüner Baum** HOTEL €€
(☎8263; www.gruenerbaum.cc; Marktplatz 104; s €95, d €135-165, d or ste with lake view €195-230; P ᯤ) Rooms in the four-star Grüner Baum are tastefully furnished without going overboard on decor to impress; three suites have enormous patios to the lake, and doubles have smaller balconies large enough for seating, making this the ideal place for romantic lakeside sojourns.

Gasthof Zauner GUESTHOUSE €€
(☎8246; www.zauner.hallstatt.net; Marktplatz 51; s/d €60/120; ⏲closed 3 weeks Nov; P) This quaint, ivy-covered guesthouse has very tasteful, pine-embellished rooms, some with balconies and lake views. The restaurant (mains from €10.60 to €23.40) is excellent, not just for fish.

Bräugasthof am Hallstätter See GUESTHOUSE €€
(☎8221; www.brauhaus-lobisser.com; Seestrasse 120; s/d/tr €65/105/155) A central, friendly guesthouse with comfortable rooms decked out in light wood.

TRANSPORT ON & AROUND HALLSTÄTTER SEE

As well as excursions, **Hemetsberger** (☎06134-8228; Am Hof 126; 80min excursions €9.50; ⏲mid-Jul–mid-Sep) does a scheduled run between Obertraun and Hallstatt Markt (€5.50, 25 minutes, four or five times daily from June to September) and the all-important year-round service between Hallstatt Markt and Hallstatt train station (€2.40, 10 minutes, 15 times daily). This connects (separate tickets) with trains in both directions. If you're going to Bad Aussee, your last boat leaves Hallstatt Markt at 5.15pm. Going to Bad Ischl, 6.15pm is your last boat–train connection.

Between Obertraun and Hallstatt town, a taxi (p206) costs about €12. Reserve ahead.

Bus 543 connects Hallstatt (Lahn) town with Obertraun Dachsteinseilbahn (cable car station; €2.20, nine to 16 minutes) at least eight times daily. Not all buses run to the centre of Obertraun – get off at Obertraun Traunbrücke in that case.

✗ Eating

Balthazar im Rudolfsturm CAFE €
(Rudolfsturm; mains €10.80-14.20; ⊘9am-6pm, closed Nov-Apr) Balthazar is situated 855m above Hallstatt and has the most spectacular terrace in the region. The views over the lake are fantastic; the kitchen is currently a little flat in terms of quality, but that can quickly change.

★Restaurant zum Salzbaron EUROPEAN €€
(Marktplatz 104; mains €15.90-22.90; ⊘lunch & dinner; 🤝🐕) One of the best gourmet acts in town, the Salzbaron is perched alongside the lake inside the Seehotel Grüner Baum and serves a seasonal pan-European menu; local trout features strongly in summer.

ℹ Information

For internet access, try the **Umbrella Bar** (Seestrasse 145; per 15min €1; ⊘ 9.30am-10pm May–mid-Oct). To reach the **tourist office** (📞82 08; www.dachstein-salzkammergut.at; Seestrasse 169; ⊘ 9am-6pm Mon-Fri, 9am-1pm & 1.30-4pm Sat & Sun, closed Sat & Sun Sep-Jun) turn left from the ferry. It stocks a free leisure map of lakeside towns that shows hiking and cycling trails.

ℹ Getting There & Around

BOAT

Ferry excursions do the Hallstatt Lahn via Hallstatt Markt, Obersee, Untersee and Steeg circuit (€10, 90 minutes, three daily) from mid-July to August.

BUS

At least nine daily buses connect Hallstatt (Lahn) town with the cable car at Obertraun-Dachsteinseilbahn (€2.20, from nine to 16 minutes).

CAR

Access into the village is restricted: electronic gates are activated during the day. Staying overnight in the centre gives you a parking rate of €9 per 24 hours in the P1 parking zone (follow the signs, press 'Hotel Ticket' when entering and contact the attendant); you also get use of the special shuttle bus. See www.hallstatt.net/parking-in-hallstatt/cars for more. The rate otherwise is €12 per 24 hours.

TRAIN

Trains connect Hallstatt and Bad Ischl (€3.80, 25 minutes, hourly), and Hallstatt every two hours with Bad Aussee (€3.80, 15 minutes). Hallstatt train station is across the lake from the village, and boat services coincide with train arrivals (€2.40, 10 minutes, last ferry to Hallstatt Markt 6.50pm).

Obertraun

📞06131 / POP 720

More low-key than Hallstatt, this broad settlement offers great access to the Dachstein caves. It's also a good starting point for hikes around the lake, or more strenuous treks up to the caves themselves and beyond through alpine meadows. Signs from the train station point the way to the cable-car station and ice caves. The trail (No 16) to the caves is a stiff 2½-hour hike from the valley station.

⊙ Sights & Activities

Dachstein Caves CAVES
(Dachsteinhöhlen; www.dachstein-salzkammergut.com; adult/child 2 caves €21.50/12, cable-car return & 1 cave €28/15.50, cable-car return & 2 caves €34/19.50; ⊘9am-4pm May-Oct) Climb to the Dachstein caves and you'll find yourself in a strange world of ice and subterranean hollows extending 80km in some places. The two caves, the **Dachstein Eishöhle** (tour adult/child €13.50/8; ⊘core tour 9.20am-4pm May-Oct) and the **Mammuthöhle** (Mammoth Cave; tour adult/child €13.50/8; ⊘core tour 10.30am-2.30pm mid-May–Oct), take about 15 minutes to reach by foot in different directions from the Schönbergalm cable-car station at 1350m. Tours of each cave last an hour.

The ice in the **Dachstein Eishöhle** is no more than 500 years old, and forms an 'ice mountain' up to 8m high – twice as high now as it was when the caves were first explored in 1910. The formations here are illuminated with coloured light and the shapes they take are eerie and surreal. This cave can only be seen on a guided tour; if you let the tour guide know, they will do the tour with English as well as German commentary.

The **Mammuthöhle** is among the 30 or so deepest and longest caves in the world and is free of ice. Tours offer insight into the formation of the cave, which also has installations and artworks based on light and shadow to heighten the experience.

Cable Car CABLE CAR
(all sections return adult/child €27/15, 1 section return adult/child €12.50/7.50; ⊘closed late Oct–Nov & Easter-Apr) A highlight in itself, the cable car departs about every 15 minutes from the valley station and has several stages, becoming more low-key and remote

the further you go. After the middle station (for the caves), **Schönbergalm** (return adult/child €16.20/9; ☻ from May), it continues to the highest point (2109m) of **Krippenstein** (return adult/child €23/14; ☻ from mid-May), which has the eerie **5Fingers viewing platform** dangling over the precipice. On a clear day the views from this platform down across the lake are little short of magnificent, and a glass floor allows you to peer directly down beyond your feet into a gaping void. Each 'finger' has a different form, one of these reminiscent of a diving board.

The final stretch is to **Gjaid Alm** (return adult/child €27/15; ☻ from mid-Jun), taking you away from the crowds to an area where walking trails wind across the rocky meadows or lead higher into the mountains. Some of these trails begin at the simple Gjaid Alm guesthouse and working organic farm situated 10 minutes by foot from the cable-car station.

🛏 Sleeping & Eating

Campingplatz Hinterer   CAMPGROUND €
(☑ 265; www.camping-am-see.at; Winkl 77; camp sites per adult/child/tent/car €10.50/7/8/3; ☻ May-Sep; P 🛜) This informal, grassy campground is by the lake south of the river.

Hotel Haus am See   HOTEL €€
(☑ 26 777; www.hotel-hausamsee.at; Obertraun 169; s/d €46/90; P 🛜) Situated conveniently alongside the boat station and swimming area, this no-frills hotel has lots of clean rooms with balconies and views over the lake. Only some rooms have wi-fi.

★**Restaurant-Pizzeria Simmer**   AUSTRIAN, ITALIAN €
(Seestrasse 178; mains €9.90-14, pizza €7.20-8.50; ☻ 10am-midnight Wed-Sun) Easily the most atmospheric of all the budget restaurants in the region, this Italo-Austrian place has cosy indoor seating and outdoor tables alongside a gurgling brook; the pizza is great, and there's ten-pin bowling out the back.

GETTING THE MOST OUT OF THE DACHSTEIN CAVES & MOUNTAINS

Planning the Day

To view one or both caves and the 5Fingers viewing platform (about 15 minutes by foot from the Krippenstein station), allow a whole day, setting off from the valley cable-car station around 10am. Take the cable car up to the first stop (Schönbergalm) by noon or earlier, and register at the information desk for the cave tours. Do the Mammuthöhle first, and allow 30 to 45 minutes to reach the Dachstein Eishöhle from there afterwards. If you only have time to see one cave, we recommend the Dachstein Eishöhle.

Over two days you can view one or both of the caves and the 5Fingers viewing platform, and also take the final section of the cable car to Gjaid Alm station, drop by the Gjaid Alm meadow hut, and explore the area on walks or hike back down to the valley.

Discounts

There are various combined tickets and deals, including a ticket for all sections of the cable car and the caves in summer (return adult/child €40/23). Check them out at the valley station.

Winter Skiing

In winter Krippenstein is a ski and snowboard free-riding area (day pass costs €32). The cable car begins service in December, depending on completion of maintenance and snow conditions; it usually ends around Easter. Advanced cross-country ski hiking is also possible on the mountain. For downhill skiers, the best piste is an 11km downhill run beginning at Krippenstein and going via Gjaid Alm station to the valley station. Hold onto your hat!

Staying & Eating on the Peaks

★**Gjaid Alm** (☑ 06131-596; www.gjaid.at; s/d incl half-board €46/92; ☻ closed May & Nov; 🛜) is set in a rocky hollow replete with grazing cattle and horses, an easy 10-minute walk from the cable-car station. Rooms are bright, heated and very comfortable. They're furnished in light woods and offer views through the windows to the meadow. Remove your shoes before climbing the stairs. All dishes in the restaurant (daily mains €10) are prepared with organic ingredients. Regular meditation, climbing and qigong courses are held here.

ℹ Information

The very helpful **tourist office** (☑ 351; www. dachstein-salzkammergut.at; ☻ 8am–noon & 1-5pm Mon-Fri, 9am–noon Sat, closed Sat Sep-Jun) has a free map detailing lakes and hiking trails It's on the way to the Dachstein cable car from the train station. There's an ATM next door.

ℹ Getting There & Away

At least nine daily buses connect Hallstatt (Lahn) town with the cable car at Obertraun-Dachsteinseilbahn (€2.20, nine to 16 minutes). A ferry runs from Hallstatt Markt via Hallstatt Lahn to Obertraun (€5.50, 25 minutes, five daily). Obertraun-Dachsteinhöhlen is the train station for Obertraun settlement. There are trains to Bad Ischl (€5.70, 30 minutes, 12 daily) via Hallstatt (€2.20, three minutes).

A **taxi** (☑ 06131-542) to the cable-car valley station or between Hallstatt and Obertraun costs about €12. Mountain and trekking bikes can be hired from **Seecafe Obertraun** (☑ 0650-6177 165; Strandbad Obertraun; per day €15; ☻ closed Oct-Apr) and from **Sportshop Feuerer** (☑ 0664-342 0885; Seestrasse 59; per day bikes €15, e-bikes €20).

Gosausee

☑ 06136 / ELEV 923M

This small lake is flanked by the impressively precipitous peaks of the Gosaukamm range (2459m). The view is good from the shoreline, and it takes a little over an hour to walk around the entire lake. The **Gosaukammbahn** (return adult/child €13/8.10; ☻ mid-May–late Oct) cable car goes up to 1475m, where there are spectacular views and walking trails. One- to two-hourly Postbus services run to the lake from Bad Ischl (€6.10, one hour) via Steeg.

Before reaching the lake you pass through the village of **Gosau**, which has its own **tourist office** (☑ 8295; www.dachstein-salz-kammergut.at; house 547, Gosau; ☻ 8am–noon & 2-6pm Mon-Fri, 9am–noon Sat, closed Sat Sep-Jun) with an accommodation board outside. Gosau is at the junction of the only road to the lake and can be reached by Hwy 166 from Hallstätter See.

Bad Aussee

☑ 03622 / POP 4880

Quiet, staid Bad Aussee is the largest Styrian town in the southern Salzkammergut. It is close to two lakes, and convenient by rail and a walking trail to a third, the Hallstätter See. Stay in Bad Ischl, though, if you prefer a little nightlife.

The train station is located 1.5km south of the town centre. After getting off the train, dash to the bus stop out front for the connecting bus.

◉ Sights

Altaussee Salzbergwerk MUSEUM
(www.salzwelten.at; adult/child/family €16/8/34; ☻ tours hourly 9am-4pm Jun–mid-Sep, 9am, 11am, 1pm & 3pm mid-Sep–late Oct, 7pm Wed year-round; ♿) Situated near the Altaussee about 6km north of Bad Aussee, this working salt mine was the secret hiding place for art treasures stolen by the Nazis during WWII. All tours are bilingual in German and English. Bus 955 runs a few times each day to the nearby stop 'Altaussee Scheiben' from the post office (€2, 10 minutes). Bike is a better option as the bus is infrequent.

Tours include the treasure chambers, an underground lake, and a chapel dedicated to St Barbara, the patron saint of miners, that's made of blocks of salt.

Kammerhof Museum MUSEUM
(www.badaussee.at/kammerhofmuseum; Chlumeckyplatz 1; adult/child/family €4/2/6; ☻ 10am–noon & 3-6pm May-Oct) Kammerhof Museum, housed in a beautiful 17th-century building, covers local history and salt production. It also has some portraits of Anna Plöchl, the local postmaster's daughter who scandalously married a Habsburg prince. All explanations are in German but there's an English sheet available.

Panoramastrasse SCENIC AREA
(toll per car €15) A scenic road climbs most of the way up **Loser** (1838m), the main peak overlooking the Altausseer See. Snow chains are required in winter.

🏃 Activities

Bike trails lead off from Bad Aussee to all the major lakes, including the Hallstätter See, and where there aren't trails the roads are generally suitable for riding. **Zweirad Friedl** (☑ 52 918; www.badaussee.net/zweirad. friedl; Meranplatz 38; mountain bikes per day €12) hires out mountain bikes, and **Sport Käfmüller** (☑ 54 911; www.sport-kaefmueller. at; Ischler Strasse 121; per day mountain bikes €15, e-bikes €18) does the same, as well as offering e-bikes.

Grundlsee
WATER SPORTS

Five kilometres northeast of Bad Aussee, Grundlsee has a good lookout at its western end as well as water sports (including a sailing school) and walking trails. Extending from the eastern tip of the lake are two smaller lakes, **Toplitzsee** and **Kammersee**. Between May and October, three-hour **boat tours** (☑ 86 13; www.3-seentour.at; adult/child €23/12) take you through all three. Bus 956 departs almost hourly from the post office to Grundlsee Seeklause weekdays, every two hours weekends (€2, 10 minutes).

Koppentalweg
HIKING, CYCLING

The Koppentalweg is a picturesque 10km hiking and cycling trail that runs west through the lush Traun River valley; it connects via the Koppenbrüllerhöhlen (caves) with the Ostuferwanderweg running along the Hallstätter See. The trail begins at the train station.

🛏 Sleeping

Outside the tourist office there's a 24-hour information touch screen and a free phone to contact hotels. You can also find an accommodation brochure there.

HI Jugendgästehaus
HOSTEL €

(☑ 0570 83 520; www.jufa.eu/jufa-bad-aussee; Jugendherbergsstrasse 148; s/d €55/87; P @ 🛜 🐾) This hostel has a wellness area with sauna and fitness facilities, as well as a playground for kids and a terrace for soaking up the mountain sunshine. HI Jugendgästehaus is located 15 minutes' walk from the post office by road, or by quicker (unlit) footpaths.

Pension Stocker
PENSION €

(☑ 524 84; www.zimmer-ausseerland.at/stocker; Altausseer Strasse 245; s/d €35/66; P 🛜) Located 500m northwest of Kurhausplatz, this is a very pretty *Pension* with wooden balconies, flower-filled window boxes and a large garden.

Josefinum
HOSTEL €

(☑ 521 24; www.tiscover.at/josefinum; Gartengasse 13; s/d €39/78; P 🛜) Peaceful retreat in the centre, run by nuns. Telephone ahead for evening arrival.

★ Erzherzog Johann
HOTEL €€

(☑ 525 07; www.erzherzogjohann.at; Kurhausplatz 62; r per person €99-143; P @ 🛜 🏊 🐾) Bad Aussee's four-star hotel has rooms with comforts, but the facilities are what really catapult you into seventh heaven: a wonderfully large sauna and wellness area, a 10m private swimming pool, and excellent bikes free for guests (or e-bikes for €20 per day). The hotel also caters to kids with a program of special activities.

Gasthof Blaue Traube
GUESTHOUSE €€

(☑ 523 63-0; www.blauetraube.at; Kirchengasse 165; s/d €58/100) Historic guesthouse in the centre with modern and well-sized but somewhat bland rooms. There's wi-fi in the hall.

🍴 Eating & Drinking

Bad Aussee is no great shakes when it comes to eating and drinking – save your splurging for elsewhere.

Konditerei Lewandofsky-Temmel
CAFE €

(Kurhausplatz 144; apple strudel €2.70; ⊙ 8am-10pm Mon-Sat, from 9am Sun) Drop in for coffee and a slice of delicious apple strudel with crispy pastry, best enjoyed on the terrace alongside the Kurpark.

Restaurant Erzherzog Johann
AUSTRIAN €€

(www.erzherzogjohann.at; Kurhausplatz 62; mains €14-24, lunch buffet €15; ⊙ lunch & dinner daily, lunch buffet Mon-Fri) The restaurant at the Hotel Erzherzog Johann has a very strong wine list, some good dishes and service with character.

Vinothek Annamax
WINE BAR

(www.annamax.at; Meranplatz 36; ⊙ 10am-7pm Mon-Thu, to 10pm Fri, to 1pm Sat) Small wine bar with a great selection of wine and a mixed antipasto (about €8 to €10).

ℹ Information

Tourist office (☑ 523 23; www.ausseerland. at; Ischlerstrasse 94; ⊙ 9am-6pm Mon-Fri, to noon Sat) Excellent tourist office with helpful staff, located in the post-office building. Pick up the town map, which has hiking trails marked for the region.

ℹ Getting There & Around

Bad Aussee is on the rail route between Bad Ischl (€7.60, 35 minutes) and Stainach-Irdning (€5.80, 35 minutes), and trains run hourly in both directions. Buses arrive and depart from the tourist office/post office. A **taxi** (☑ 521 75, 540 08) from the train station to the centre costs about €6.

NORTHERN SALZKAMMERGUT

The two most popular of the northern lakes are Traunsee – with the three resorts of Gmunden, Traunkirchen and Ebensee on its shores – and Wolfgangsee, home to the villages of St Wolfgang and St Gilgen (the latter provides access to Schafberg mountain).

Traunsee

Traunsee is the deepest lake in Austria, going down to a cool 192m. The eastern flank is dominated by rocky crags, the tallest of which is the imposing **Traunstein** (1691m).

Gmunden

☑ 07612 / POP 13,080

With its yacht marina, lakeside square and promenades, Gmunden exudes a breezy, Riviera feel. It was formerly known for its ceramics and as a centre for the salt trade.

⊙ Sights & Activities

★**K-Hof**   MUSEUM

(www.k-hof.at; Kammerhofgasse 8; adult/child €6/2; ⊙10am-5pm Tue-Sun, closed Tue Sep-May) The K-Hof museum complex is a double act with one of Austria's most unusual and refreshing museums, the **Museum for Sanitary Objects**. The museum complex gives a fascinating insight into the history of the region. The exhibition covers ceramics manufacture (for which Gmunden was famous in its early years), salt, fossils, and the life of the 15th-century astronomer Johannes von Gmunden, whose theories influenced Copernicus.

The museum integrates into the building the Gothic St Jakob's, Gmunden's first church. The sanitary objects collection is monumental and includes a toilet regularly mounted by the royal *Po* (bottom) of Kaiser Franz Josef in his hunting lodge near Ebensee.

★**Seeschloss Ort**   CASTLE

(www.schlossorth.com; Orth 1) **FREE** Flanking the lake on the eastern side, a pretty nature reserve known as **Toscana Park** forms a backdrop to Seeschloss Ort. This lakeside castle is believed to have been built on the ruins of a Roman fortress. It dates from 909 or earlier (rebuilt in the 17th century after

a fire) and has a picturesque courtyard, a late-Gothic external staircase and sgraffito from 1578.

★**Pfarrkirche**   CHURCH

(Kirchplatz) North of the Rathausplatz lies the 12th-century Pfarrkirche, a Gothic church later remodelled in baroque style and with an altar (dating from 1678) by the sculptor Thomas Schwanthaler (1634–1707).

Schloss Weyer   PALACE

(Freygasse 27; admission €9.50; ⊙10am-noon & 2-5.30pm Tue-Fri, 10am-1pm Sat Jun-Sep) Palace containing a good collection of Meissen porcelain, silver and jewellery.

Grünberg Lookout   SCENIC AREA

(cable car return adult/child €15/7) A cable car whisks visitors 984m up to the local mountain, Grünberg. This was revamped in 2013 and will reopen for summer 2014. Trails also lead up here on an easy walk from the base station.

Kajak & Kanu Salzkammergut   CANOEING

(☑ 62 496; www.kajak-kanu.at; Traunsteinstrasse 13; kayaks & canoes per day €40-50, SUP boards €30; ⊙2-6pm Wed & Thu, 9am-1pm & 3-6.30pm Fri, 9.30am-1.30pm Sat, closed Oct-Apr) Kayaks, Canadian canoes and SUP (stand-up paddle) boards can be hired here for paddling along the isolated eastern shore. Call ahead from October to April to arrange hire.

Mountainbiker.at   BICYCLE RENTAL

(www.mountainbiker.at; Bahnhofstrasse 47; bikes per day €20; ⊙9am-6pm Mon-Fri, to 1pm Sat) Rents out mountain bikes, e-mountain bikes and is a Movelo e-bike station.

🛏 Sleeping & Eating

Private rooms are the best deal for budget travellers – ask the excellent tourist office to help you find one.

★**Keramikhotel Goldener Brunnen**   BOUTIQUE HOTEL €€

(☑ 644 310; www.goldenerbrunnen.at; Traungasse 10; s €75, d €140-160; ℗🐾) This excellent boutique hotel in the centre has very tastefully appointed rooms with modern fittings. Ceramic art adds a decorative touch and its restaurant (mains €7 to €14) is a plus, with Austrian dishes such as Styrian chicken and some international favourites.

Hotel Magerl   HOTEL €€

(☑ 636 75; www.pension-magerl.at; s €54-62, d €88-104; ℗@🐾) This rambling *Pension* is

Gmunden

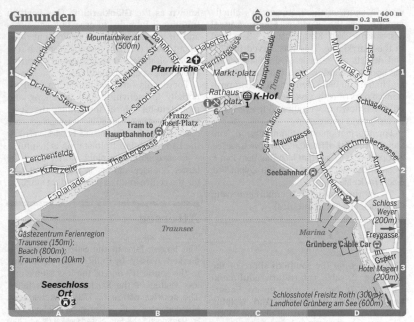

spread over three buildings near the cable-car station. From the outside the main building looks very drab, but rooms are clean and modern. The other buildings are newer.

Café Brandl CAFE, BAR €
(Rathausplatz 1; light dishes €2-5; ☺ from 8am) This smart cafe-bar has bright-yellow walls, black leather sofas and cubist artworks spiking its interior. It serves breakfast, cakes and light meals during the day, and turns into a drinking venue (with snacks) at night.

ⓘ Information

Gästezentrum der Ferienregion Traunsee
(☏ 07612-64 305; www.traunsee.at; Toscanapark 1; ☺ 8am-6pm Mon-Fri, 9am-5pm Sat & Sun) Regional tourist office for the lake, with accommodation booking service and Movelo e-bike station.

Tourist office (☏ 657 520; www.traunsee.at/gmunden; Rathausplatz 1; ☺ 9am-5pm Mon-Fri) Information and maps of town and the lake. Helps with accommodation bookings.

ⓘ Getting There & Around

The Gmunden Hauptbahnhof on the Salzkammergut Attnang-Puchheim to Stainach-Irdning line is the main train station for the town. The Bad Ischl–Gmunden train fare (€7.80, 45 min-

Gmunden

◎ Top Sights
1 K-Hof C1
2 Pfarrkirche B1
3 Seeschloss Ort A3

☺ Activities, Courses & Tours
4 Kajak & Kanu Salzkammergut D2

⊜ Sleeping
5 Keramikhotel Goldener
   Brunnen C1

⊗ Eating
6 Café Brandl C1

utes, every 1 to 1½ hours) includes the connecting tram to Gmunden's centre. The Seebahnhof, near the marina, services the slow, private train line from Vorchdorf-Eggenburg.

The main train station is 2km northwest of the town centre: tram G (€1.90) runs to Franz-Josef-Platz after every train arrival. Bus tickets for city services cost €1.90.

Traunkirchen

☏ 07617 / POP 1640
The attractive hamlet of Traunkirchen sits on a spit of land about halfway along the

western shore of the Traunsee. It's chiefly famous for the wooden **Fischerkanzel** (Fisherman's Pulpit; Klosterplatz 1; ⊘8am-5pm) in the Pfarrkirche. This was carved in 1753 and depicts the miracle of the fishes, with the apostles standing in a tub-shaped boat and hauling in fish-laden nets. The composition, colours (mostly silver and gold) and detail (even down to wriggling, bug-eyed fish) create a vivid impression.

For information on accommodation, contact the **tourist office** (☑22 34; www.traunsee. at; Ortsplatz 1; ⊘9am-1pm Mon-Thu, 9am-1pm & 3-5pm Fri Jun-Sep, 9am-noon Tue-Thu, 2-4pm Wed, 3-5pm Fri Oct-May).

Trains run hourly to Traunkirchen from Gmunden (€2.20, 10 minutes).

Ebensee

☑06133 / POP 7830
Ebensee lies on the southern shore of the Traunsee. A cable car (return adult/child €19.50/€9.70, hourly) runs up to **Feuerkogel** (1592m), where you find walking trails leading across a flattish plateau. Within an hour's walk, **Alberfeldkogel** (1708m) is a nature reserve popular for hiking and for cross-country skiing in winter, and has an excellent view over the two Langbath lakes. Feuerkogel also provides access to winter **skiing** (day pass €33) with easy to medium slopes.

In early January every year, the men of Ebensee don giant illuminated headdresses made of tissue paper in a bizarre ritual known as the **Glöcklerlauf**. This heathen tradition is intended to drive out evil spirits and to win the favour of benevolent ones. About 300 *Glöckler* parade through the streets on the evening of 5 January wearing enormous wedge-shaped hats.

For details on accommodation, and especially for activities such as hiking and mountain-bike hire and trails, the local **tourist office** (☑8016; www.ebensee.com; Hauptstrasse 34; ⊘9am-noon & 1-5pm Mon-Fri) by the Landungsplatz train station is helpful.

Ebensee-Landungsplatz, rather than the larger Ebensee station, is the train station for the centre and the boat landing stage.

Attersee

☑07666 / POP 1500
The largest lake in the Salzkammergut is flanked mostly by hills, with mountains in the south. It's one of the less scenic and less visited of the Salzkammergut's lakes. The **tourist office** (☑7719; www.attersee.at; Nussdorferstrasse 15; ⊘9am-noon & 2-5pm Mon-Fri, 9am-noon Sat & Sun, closed weekends Sep-Jun) in the resort of Attersee can help with accommodation and has a telephone service from May to September from 9am to 8pm.

Attersee-Schifffahrt (www.atterseeschifffahrt.at) does mostly alternating boat circuits of the north (adult/child €10/5, 1¼ hours) and south (€16/8, 2¼ hours) regions of the lake several times most days from Easter to early October. Full circuits combining both

---

ⓘ TRANSPORT AROUND THE TRAUNSEE

Train
The Traunsee resorts are strung along the western shore and are connected by rail. Trains run between Gmunden and Traunkirchen (€2.20, 10 minutes, hourly) and Ebensee (€3.80, 20 minutes, hourly), continuing to Bad Ischl (€7.80, 40 minutes).

Boat
Traunsee Schiffahrt (www.traunseeschiffahrt.at; Rathausplatz, Gmunden) vessels tour the shoreline between mid-May and early October. There are connections from Gmunden's Rathausplatz to Landhotel Grünberg am See (adult/child €3/2.50, seven minutes, three daily), Traunkirchen (adult/child €8/6, 45 minutes, four daily) and Ebensee (adult/child €10/7.50, 70 minutes, four daily). Some boats do round-trips of the lake (adult/child €19/13, 125 minutes, four daily).

Electric Shuttle Bus
A **Bummelzug** (adult/child €5/3; ⊘every 30min 10am-5.30pm, from 2pm Tue May-Sep) runs to Seeschloss Ort on the western shore and **Panorama Shuttle** (adult/child one way €3.50/2; ⊘8.50am-6.40pm early May–early Oct) runs seven trips daily to the end of the road on the eastern shore.

The Traunsee has two interesting hotels on its eastern shore, both unique in different ways.

★**Landhotel Grünberg am See** (☑777 00; www.gruenberg.at; Traunsteinstrasse 109; s €60-80, d €100-120, restaurant mains €10-17.50; [P] [@] [🛜]) is a homely guesthouse and restaurant situated 2km from Rathausplatz in Gmunden. It has a loyal following as an informal getaway, especially in summer. Rooms are modern, and the more expensive ones have lake views. Ingrid Pernkopf, part-owner, writes cooking books and gives cooking courses on Upper Austrian and Austrian specialities, so expect fish and local favourites, some using organic ingredients. There's outdoor seating with lake views, as well as waterskiing from the private jetty for the actively inclined. A section of the walking trail leading to the pretty Laudachsee (three hours) begins behind the building.

Nearby, **Schlosshotel Freisitz Roith** (☑649 05; www.freisitzroith.at; Traunsteinstrasse 87; s €95-135, d €200-230, ste €270-310, restaurant mains €17 to €22; [P] [@] [🛜]) is a great wellness hotel set on a rise slightly back from the road, in grounds replete with a fountain and fruit trees. There are rapturous views from the rooms (less-expensive rooms don't have lake views), and from the atrium and terrace restaurant.

Taxi (☑679 09) is the easiest way to reach the hotels, but the Panorama Shuttle and Traunsee Schiffahrt run out here in summer months.

segments can be done on weekends from Easter to September, and daily in July and August (adult/child €20/10, 3¾ hours).

The two lakeside towns of Attersee and Schörfling are each connected to the rail network by a line branching from the main Linz–Salzburg route (only regional trains make stops): for Kammer-Schörfling change at Vöcklabruck, and for Attersee change at Vöcklamarkt.

Wolfgangsee

Named after a local saint, this lake has two very popular resorts, St Wolfgang and St Gilgen, of which St Wolfgang is the most appealing. The third town on the lake, Strobl (population 2750), is a less remarkable but pleasant place at the start of a scenic toll road (per car and per person €3) to Postalm (1400m).

A **ferry** (www.wolfgangseeschifffahrt.at; ⊙late Mar–Oct) service operates from Strobl to St Gilgen (€9.50, 75 minutes), stopping at points en route. Services are most frequent from late June to early September. Children pay half-price.

The Wolfgangsee is dominated by the 1783m Schafberg mountain on its northern shore. At the summit you'll find a hotel, restaurant and phenomenal views over mountains and lakes (especially Mondsee, Attersee and, of course, Wolfgangsee). If you don't fancy the three- to four-hour walk from St Wolfgang (early tourists were carried

up in sedan chairs), ride the **Schafbergbahn** (adult/child one way €21.40/10.70, return €31/15.50; ⊙May-Oct), which takes 35 minutes one way. Departures are approximately hourly between 9.15am and 3pm (last trip down 5.15pm), but the trip is so popular that you probably won't be able to simply jump on the next train. Queue early, purchase a ticket for a specific train, and then go for a wander along the lake or around St Wolfgang until your time comes to depart.

St Wolfgang

☑06138 / POP 2850

St Wolfgang is a charming town situated on the steep banks of the Wolfgangsee. Although its streets can get clogged with visitors during the day, things usually settle down by early evening, which is the best time for a tranquil stroll along the forested lakeshore past the gently creaking wooden boathouses.

The village's main fame arose as a place of pilgrimage, and today's visitors still come to see the 14th-century pilgrimage church, packed with art treasures. Note that Markt in the centre of town is a wi-fi hotspot.

⊙ Sights & Activities

Wallfahrtskirche   CHURCH
(Pilgrimage Church; Markt; donation €1; ⊙9am-6pm) St Wolfgang's impressive Wallfahrtskirche is a spectacular gallery of religious art, with glittering altars (from Gothic to baroque), an extravagant pulpit, a fine organ,

LOW-KEY STROBL

While high-profile Wolfgangsee towns such as St Wolfgang and St Gilgen justifiably attract large numbers of visitors, the lesser-known and more low-key Strobl at the eastern end of the lake is well worth a visit.

From the shoreline in Strobl you can walk northeast along the lake for about five to 10 minutes towards Bürglstein, the high bluff rising above the lake. Just over the bridge, an easy-going trail (also a bike trail, though you'll need to dismount at a few sections) leads to St Wolfgang (6km, 1½ hours) along the shore. This follows a path and boardwalks around the bluff (the nicest stretch) to the settlement of Schwarzenbach (which is also a ferry stop). From Schwarzenbach the road runs near the trail, so it's not as secluded or tranquil. Locals who are reasonably strong swimmers sometimes enter the water near the bridge and even swim part or all of the way to Schwarzenbach. Joggers, cyclists and hikers can also do the easy trail around Bürglstein (9km, 1½ hours) or join other trails going away from the Wolfgangsee.

You can hire bikes from **Sport Girbl** (☑0664-221 79 85; Bahnstrasse 300; 7-gear bicycles per day €10, mountain e-bikes €28, e-bikes €20; ⊙8am-noon & 2.30-6pm).

Strobler Hof (☑06137-7308; www.stroblerhof.at; Ischler Strasse 16; per person €78-98 incl 1 meal; ⊙lunch & dinner; ℗@🖤), an upmarket hotel with an inexpensive Tex-Mex restaurant upstairs (mains €7.50 to €17.50) and a formal Austrian restaurant (mains €10.50 to €22) set in the grounds, is a great place to stay or eat in Strobl. Reserve ahead for an outside table in summer; some ingredients are organic.

and countless statues and paintings. The most impressive piece is the winged high altar, created by celebrated religious artist Michael Pacher between 1471 and 1481 – it's a perfect example of the German Gothic style, enhanced with the technical achievements of Renaissance Italy.

Wolfgangsee   SWIMMING
A number of hotels have jetties for swimming, and a tourist-office booklet details the many water sports on offer. A nice thing to do is to walk or cycle to Strobl, 6km away (around 1½ hours on foot), ending the excursion with a swim.

🛏 Sleeping

St Wolfgang has some good private rooms in village homes or in farmhouses in the surrounding hills. Lists are available from the tourist office, which will phone places on your behalf.

Haus am See   PENSION €
(☑22 24; Michael Pacher Strasse 98; s/d without bathroom €30/50; ⊙closed Oct–mid-May; ℗) This is a remarkable *Pension* with features ripe for a Wolfgangsee mystery novel: it's run by a retired professor and his wife, and evokes earlier decades. The owners also rent out four rooms in their boatshed down on the water (for the same price). Guests get free use of a boat and bike. It's conveniently opposite the Au bus stop.

Hotel Peter   HOTEL €€
(☑23 04; www.hotelpeter.at; Au 140; s/d €89/150, ste €178; ℗@🖤) The generous-sized rooms at this four-star hotel have balconies looking onto the lake, large bathrooms and tasteful decor. The restaurant (most mains €13 to €17) has a terrace overlooking the lake, and serves pasta and a good fish platter filled with poached, fried and baked local fish. The restaurant has wi-fi.

★ Im Weissen Rössl   LUXURY HOTEL €€€
(☑23 06; www.weissesroessl.at; Markt 74; s €158-184, d €228-388; ℗@🖤🏊) St Wolfgang's most famous hotel was the setting for Ralph Benatzky's operetta *The White Horse*. Rooms are individually styled and somewhat idiosyncratic, but the more expensive ones have a balcony and view over the lake. There's a large wellness area, and two pools – one pool literally floats on the lake (heated to 30°C), and another is indoors. It also has several good junior suites.

🍴 Eating

Kraftstoff-Bar   MEXICAN €
(www.kraftstoffbar.at; Markt 128; mains €10-20; ⊙from 11am Wed-Mon May-Sep, from 5pm Mon-Sat Oct-Apr) Decked out like a petrol station, this chilled-out restaurant-bar is an unusual place to curl your fingers around a drink, accompanied by wings and potato wedges, pasta, salads or grills. Check out the charming balcony.

Im Weissen Rössl AUSTRIAN €€
(Markt 74) There are two restaurants and a lovely wine cellar in this highly respected hotel. The Seerestaurant (kitchen open all day, most mains €12.50 to €19) tempts with regional and international dishes, while the Romantik has à la carte dining (dinner only, mains €25 to €31) and an exceptional six-course menu for €60.50.

❶ Information

Tourist office (☑ 80 03; www.wolfgangsee. at; Au 140; ⊙9am-7pm Mon-Fri, to 6pm Sat, 10am-5pm Sun) Helpful staff, at the eastern tunnel entrance; a wi-fi hotspot. A smaller branch (Michael-Pacher-Haus; Pilgerstrasse; ⊙9am-noon & 2-5pm Jun-Sep) is located near the northwest end of the road tunnel.

❶ Getting There & Around

The only road to St Wolfgang approaches from Strobl in the east. Boats run to St Gilgen roughly half-hourly May to early September (adult/child €7.10, 45 minutes), tailing off to every couple of hours in shoulder seasons (May, September and October). Paddle-wheel and vintage boats complement these (€1 surcharge). A Postbus service runs between St Wolfgang and St Gilgen (€4.20, 50 minutes) with a connecting transfer in Strobl. For buses to Salzburg (€9.10, 1¾ hours) you need to connect in St Gilgen or Strobl (€2.20, 12 minutes).

Wolfgangsee ferries stop at the village centre (Markt stop) and at the Schafberg railway. **Pro Travel** (☑ 25 25; www.protravel.at; Markt 152; mountain bike per day €17-27, e-bikes €20; ⊙9am-6.30pm) rents bikes.

St Gilgen

☑ 06227 / POP 3780

The ease of access to St Gilgen, 29km from Salzburg, makes this town very popular for day trippers, but it has also grown in recent years because of its very scenic setting. Along with quieter Strobl, it's a good base for lake water sports, and is not quite as crowded as St Wolfgang.

◉ Sights

Mozarthaus MUSEUM
(www.mozarthaus.info; Ischler Strasse 15; adult/child €4/2.50; ⊙10am-noon & 3-6pm Tue-Sun May-Sep) There are five houses worldwide dedicated to Mozart, but this one takes the interesting approach of focusing mostly on the family – especially his sister 'Nannerl', an accomplished composer and musician

in her own right. Multilingual films tell the story, and there's a small exhibition.

Muzikinstumente-Museum der Völker MUSEUM
(Folk Music Instrument Museum; Aberseestrasse 11; adult/child €4/2.50; ⊙9-11am & 3-7pm Tue-Sun) This cosy little museum is home to 1500 musical instruments from all over the world, all of them collected by one family of music teachers. The son of the family, Askold zum Eck, can play them all and will happily demonstrate for hours. Visitors are allowed to play one or two.

Heimatkundliches Museum MUSEUM
(Pichlerplatz 6; adult/child €4/2.50; ⊙10am-noon & 3-6pm Tue-Sun Jul-Sep) The town museum has an eclectic collection ranging from embroidery (originally manufactured in the building) to animal specimens (about 4700) and religious objects.

⚡ Activities

Water sports such as windsurfing, waterskiing and sailing are popular activities in St Gilgen. There's a town swimming pool and a small beach (free) with a grassy area beyond the yacht marina.

The mountain rising over the resort is 1520m **Zwölferhorn** (www.12erhorn.at; return cable car adult/child €22/14.50), from where there are good views and trails (two to 2½ hours) leading back to St Gilgen. Skiers ascend in winter.

🛏 Sleeping & Eating

Pension Falkensteiner PENSION €
(☑ 2395; www.pension-falkensteiner.at; Salzburgerstrasse 13; s/d €54/99; 🅿@) Some of the rooms have balconies and all are large in this no-frills but spotless *Pension* that has helpful management.

Jugendgästehaus Schafbergblick HOSTEL €
(☑2365; jgh.stgilgen@oejhv.or.at; Mondseer Strasse 7; dm/s/d €24.50/34.50/52; ⊙reception

THE SALZKAMMERGUT WOLFGANGSEE

KIDS PLAYGROUND

St Gilgen has one of the lake's best kids playgrounds, situated at the shore near the ferry landing. As well as swings, there's a nifty flying fox and slides, and things to climb or hang around on. It's partly shaded.

8am-1pm & 5-7pm Mon-Fri, 5-7pm Sat & Sun; P@⊚) This hostel gets lots of school groups; it has a good location near the town beach.

Gasthof Zur Post
GUESTHOUSE €€

(☑2157; www.gasthofzurpost.at; Mozartplatz 8; s €115, d €178, f €222; P @ ⊚ ⊕) Expect heavy wooden beds, interesting colour schemes and wooden floors in this hotel. The 'Post-Geschichten' rooms at this old inn are beautifully designed in a cosily rustic style with shades of minimalism. The restaurant (mains €15 to €20) serves national and regional specialities in a low-ceilinged, whitewashed dining room or outside on the elegant terrace.

★ M-Place
ITALIAN €€

(www.marvins-gastro.com; Ischler Strasse 18; steaks €13.90-23,90, pasta €9.20-14.40, pizza €7.20-11.20; ⊘5-10pm Mon-Fri, 11am-10.30pm Sat & Sun) This relaxed Italian restaurant by the lake has eat-in (inside or in the garden) and takeaway food. The bar-disco downstairs, the Zwolfer Alm Bar (⊘9pm Thu-Sun) hosts lots of events.

Fischer-Wirt Restaurant
SEAFOOD €€

(www.fischer-wirt.at; Ischlerstrasse 21; ⊘lunch & dinner) Situated on the water's edge, this popular seafood restaurant was preparing for a revamp in late 2013. When it reopens in spring 2014 it will have accommodation to complement its restaurant – both should be worth watching out for.

Restaurant Timbale
AUSTRIAN €€€

(☑7587; www.timbale.at; Salzburger Strasse 2; mains €23-32, 3-course lunch menu €23, 5-course dinner menu €75; ⊘lunch & dinner, closed Thu & lunch Fri) Reserve ahead for a table in one of the finest restaurants on the Wolfgangsee. The atmosphere is informal and it specialises in seasonal regional dishes and Mondsee fish.

ℹ Information

The **tourist office** (☑06227-23 48; www.wolfgangsee.at; Mondsee Bundesstrasse 1a; ⊘9am-7pm Mon-Fri, to 6pm Sat, 10am-5pm Sun) can help with finding accommodation. Brochures are also available inside the Rathaus on Mozartplatz.

ℹ Getting There & Away

St Gilgen is 50 minutes from Salzburg by Postbus (€8.10), with hourly departures until early evening; buses continue on to Strobl and Bad Ischl (€5.10, 40 minutes). The bus station is near the base station of the cable car. Hwy 154 provides a scenic route north to Mondsee. Boats run to St Wolfgang roughly hourly May to early September, tailing off in shoulder seasons (adult/child €7.10, 45 minutes).

Mondsee

☑06232 / POP 3300

The town of Mondsee extends along the northern tip of this crescent-shaped lake, noted for its warm water. Coupled with its closeness to Salzburg (30km away), this makes it a highly developed, popular lake for weekending Salzburgers.

⊙ Sights & Activities

Parish Church
CHURCH

(www.pfarre-mondsee.com; Kirchengasse 1; ⊘8am-7pm) If you're allergic to the film *The Sound of Music*, there's just one piece of advice: skip town. Even the lemon-yellow baroque facade (added in 1740, incidentally) of the

WORTH A TRIP

SCHWARZENSEE

Situated 9km from Strobl at an altitude of 715m, Schwarzensee makes for a perfect day outing with conventional or e-bikes, which can be rented in Strobl from Sport Girbl (p212). This picturesque and isolated swimming lake has a couple of small restaurants, including **Alm-Stadl Schwarzensee** (☑0664-266 4498; Schwarzensee; mains €8.50-13.90; ⊘10am-10pm, closed Nov-Apr), which serves delicious smoked lake trout. (The restaurant is also a battery exchange station for Movelo e-bikes.)

Those on a conventional or electric mountain bike can press further along the forestry track to the idyllic restaurant **Eisenauer Almhütte** (☑06227-2405, mobile 0664-2105 333; Eisenauer Alm; ⊘May-Sep, closed Mon) where a plate of smoked trout and a beer costs €12. If walking, it's a three-hour walk from Schwarzensee, partly on a spectacular trail running along a gorge. Bring a good hiking map and don't attempt the hike in poor weather. If cycling, take the road right at the parking area kiosk at Schwarzensee,

15th-century parish church achieved notoriety by featuring in those highly emotional von Trapp wedding scenes in the film.

Museum Mondseeland und Pfahlbaumuseum
MUSEUM

(Wrede Platz; adult/child €3/1.50; ⊙10am-6pm Tue-Sun May–late Oct) Next door to the parish church, this museum has displays on Stone Age finds and the monastic culture of the region (Mondsee is a very old monastery site).

Segelschule Mondsee
WATER SPORTS

(☑3548-200; www.segelschule-mondsee.at; Robert Baum Promenade 3; 1-week course €238 plus exam fee €20, kayak per day €40) Large outfit offering sailing and windsurfing courses as well as hire.

🛏 Sleeping & Eating

Jugendgästehaus
HOSTEL €

(☑2418; www.jugendherbergsverband.at/herbergen/mondsee; Krankenhausstrasse 9; dm/s/d €20/34.50/52; P) This HI hostel is a few minutes' walk from the centre of town.

★Seegasthof-Hotel Lackner
HOTEL €€

(☑2359; www.seehotel-lackner.at; Mondseestrasse 1; r €180-250, junior ste €290-320; P) Situated 15 minutes by foot from the centre (turn right heading towards the lake from the tourist office) on the shore of the Mondsee, the four-star Lackner offers rooms with balconies and lake views. A private beach is set among the reeds and the excellent terrace restaurant (mains €17 to €28, six-course menu €75, closed Tuesdays) serves venison

and lamb dishes as well as fish, complemented by a *Vinothek* (wine bar).

Hotel Krone
HOTEL €€

(☑2236; www.hotelkrone.org; Rainerstrasse 1; s €70, d €108-144; P🖨📶♿) The more expensive rooms in this attractive, comfortable, centrally located three-star hotel are larger and have balconies. Some doubles have a connecting door that families will find useful, and there's a restaurant (mains €10.50 to €14.50, open for lunch and dinner Wednesday to Monday).

Iris Porsche Hotel & Restaurant
HOTEL €€€

(☑2237; www.irisporsche.at; Marktplatz 1; s €130-200, d €180-290; P✳📶) Rooms in this modern, upmarket tourist and business hotel with lovely wooden floors are priced according to size and are cheaper during the low season. There's a lift, wellness area, bathtubs and steam showers, and a writing desk in all rooms. The restaurant (lunch mains €10 to €16, dinner mains €18 to €28) serves well-prepared fish and Austrian dishes.

ℹ Information

The **tourist office** (☑22 70; www.mondsee.at; Dr Franz Müller Strasse 3; ⊙8am-7pm Mon-Fri, 9am-7pm Sat & Sun, closed Sat & Sun Oct-May) can help with accommodation.

ℹ Getting There & Away

Hourly Postbus services connect Mondsee with Salzburg (€9.10, 45 minutes), and five direct buses run weekdays to St Gilgen (€3.10, 20 minutes). Expect to pay €25 for a ride to St Gilgen by **taxi** (☑0664-22000 22).

Salzburg & Salzburgerland

Best Places to Eat

➡ Magazin (p234)

➡ Gasthof Schloss Aigen (p232)

➡ Obauer (p244)

➡ Mayer's (p254)

➡ Lutter & Wegner (p258)

Best Places to Stay

➡ Haus Ballwein (p228)

➡ Hotel & Villa Auersperg (p228)

➡ Bio-Hotel Hammerhof (p245)

➡ Pension Hubertus (p251)

➡ Hoteldorf Grüner Baum (p258)

Why Go?

One of Austria's smallest provinces, Salzburgerland is proof that size really doesn't matter. Well, not when you have Mozart, Maria von Trapp and the 600-year legacy of the prince-archbishops behind you. This is the land that grabbed the world spotlight and shouted 'Visit Austria!' with Julie Andrews skipping joyously down the mountainsides. This is indeed the land of crisp apple strudel, dancing marionettes and high-on-a-hilltop castles. This is the Austria of your wildest childhood dreams.

Salzburg is every bit as grand as you imagine it: a baroque masterpiece, a classical-music legend and Austria's spiritual heartland. But it is just the prelude to the region's sensational natural beauty. Just outside the city, the landscape is etched with deep ravines, glinting ice caves, karst plateaux and mountains of myth – in short, the kind of alpine gorgeousness that no well-orchestrated symphony or yodelling nun could ever quite capture.

When to Go

➡ Prices peak in family-friendly alpine resorts during winter, from December to early April. Salzburg twinkles at its Christmas markets. In January orchestras strike up at Mozartwoche, while hot-air balloons glide above Filzmoos' summits.

➡ Summer sees room prices soar in Salzburg and nosedive in alpine resorts from June to September. Book months ahead for the colossal feast of opera, classical music and drama that is the Salzburg Festival from late July to August. Head for high-altitude hiking in the limestone Tennengebirge and Dachstein ranges, and the glacier-capped Hohe Tauern National Park, or lakeside chilling in Zell am See.

➡ Shoulder-season months April, May, October and November bring few crowds and low room rates. Salzburg hosts Easter classical-music festivals.

Salzburg & Salzburgerland Highlights

1 Surveying the baroque cityscape of **Salzburg** (p218) from the heights of Festung Hohensalzburg.

2 Going subzero in the frozen depths of Eisriesenwelt in **Werfen** (p243).

3 Getting drenched by the fountains at **Schloss Hellbrunn** (p240).

4 Singing 'Do-Re-Mi' in the gardens of Schloss Mirabell in **Salzburg** (p218).

5 Donning a boiler suit for a ride at the Salzwelten salt mine in **Bad Dürrnberg** (p241).

6 Buckling up for an alpine roller-coaster ride on **Grossglockner Road** (p246).

7 Bathing in the healing, radon-laced waters of **Bad Gastein** (p256).

8 Hearing the thunder of Europe's highest waterfall, Krimmler Wasserfälle, in **Krimml** (p255).

9 Being awed by alpine views on the high-altitude **Pinzgauer Spaziergang** (p253).

History

Salzburg had a tight grip on the region as far back as 15 BC, when the Roman town Iuvavum stood on the site of the present-day city. This Roman stronghold came under constant attack from warlike Celtic tribes and was ultimately destroyed or abandoned due to disease.

St Rupert established the first Christian kingdom and founded St Peter's church and monastery around 700. As centuries passed, the successive archbishops of Salzburg gradually increased their power and eventually were given the grandiose titles of princes of the Holy Roman Empire.

Wolf Dietrich von Raitenau, Salzburg's most influential prince-archbishop from 1587 to 1612, spearheaded the total baroque makeover of the city, commissioning many of its most beautiful churches, palaces and gardens. He fell from power after losing a fierce dispute over the salt trade with the powerful rulers of Bavaria, and died a prisoner.

Another of the city's archbishops, Paris Lodron (1619–53), managed to keep the principality out of the Europe-wide Thirty Years' War. Salzburg also remained neutral during the War of the Austrian Succession a century later, but bit by bit the province's power waned and Salzburg came under the thumb of France and Bavaria during the Napoleonic Wars. In 1816 Salzburg became part of the Austrian empire and was on the gradual road to economic recovery.

The early 20th century saw population growth and the founding of the prestigious Salzburg Festival in 1920. Austria was annexed to Nazi Germany in 1938 and during WWII some 40% of the city's buildings were destroyed by Allied bombings. These were restored to their former glory, and in 1997 Salzburg's historic Altstadt (old town) became a Unesco World Heritage site.

🅸 Getting There & Around

AIR

Both scheduled and no-frills flights from Europe and the USA serve Salzburg airport (p239), a 20-minute bus ride from the city.

BUS

Salzburg's efficient bus network, run by Salzburger Verkehrsverbund (p239), makes it easy to reach the province's smaller villages.

CAR & MOTORCYCLE

By road, the main routes into the region are the A8/E52 from Munich and the A1/E60 from Linz. To enter the province from Carinthia and the south, you can use the A10 from Spittal an der Drau or the Autoschleuse Tauernbahn south of Bad Gastein.

TRAIN

Salzburg is well connected to the rest of Austria by public transport, with excellent rail connections to Hohe Tauern National Park and neighbouring Salzkammergut. Salzburg's Hauptbahnhof has good services to Germany, Italy and the Czech Republic.

SALZBURG

🅹 0662 / POP 149,800

Salzburg is storybook Austria. Standing beside the fast-flowing Salzach River, your gaze is raised inch by inch to the Altstadt's mosaic of graceful domes and spires, the formidable clifftop fortress and the mountains beyond. It's a view that never palls. It's a backdrop that once did the lordly prince-archbishops and home-grown genius Mozart proud.

As tempting as it is to spend every minute in the Unesco-listed Altstadt, drifting from one baroque church and monumental square to the next in a daze of grandeur, Salzburg rewards those who venture further. Give Getreidegasse's throngs the slip, meander side streets where classical music wafts from open windows, linger decadently over coffee and cake, and let Salzburg slowly, slowly work its magic.

Beyond Salzburg's two biggest money-spinners – Mozart and *The Sound of Music* – hides a city with a burgeoning arts scene, wonderful food, manicured parks and concert halls that uphold musical tradition 365 days a year. Everywhere you go, the scenery, the skyline, the music and the history send your spirits soaring higher than Julie Andrews' octave-leaping vocals.

🅾 Sights

Salzburg's trophy sights huddle in the pedestrianised Altstadt, which straddles both banks of the Salzach River but centres largely on the left bank. Here the tangled lanes are made for a serendipitous wander, leading to hidden courtyards and medieval squares framed by burgher houses and baroque fountains.

Many places close slightly earlier in winter and open longer – usually an hour or two – during the Salzburg Festival.

★**Festung Hohensalzburg**　　　FORT
(www.salzburg-burgen.at; Mönchsberg 34; adult/
child/family €7.80/4.40/17.70, incl Festungsbahn
funicular €11/6.30/25.50; ◷9am-7pm) Salzburg's most visible icon is this mighty
900-year-old clifftop fortress, one of the
biggest and best preserved in Europe. It's
easy to spend half a day up here, roaming the ramparts for far-reaching views
over the city's spires, the Salzach River
and the mountains. The fortress is a steep
15-minute jaunt from the centre or a speedy
ride in the glass **Festungsbahn funicular**
(Festungsgasse 4).

The fortress began life as a humble bailey,
built in 1077 by Gebhard von Helffenstein
at a time when the Holy Roman Empire
was at loggerheads with the papacy. The
present structure, however, owes its grandeur to spendthrift Leonard von Keutschach, prince-archbishop of Salzburg from
1495 to 1519 and the city's last feudal ruler.
Highlights of a visit include the **Golden
Hall**, where lavish banquets were once held,
with a gold-studded ceiling imitating a starry night sky. Your ticket also gets you into
the **Marionette Museum**, where skeleton-
in-a-box Archbishop Wolf Dietrich steals
the (puppet) show, as well as the **Fortress
Museum**, which showcases a 1612 model

of Salzburg, medieval instruments, armour
and some pretty gruesome torture devices.

The Golden Hall is the backdrop for
year-round **Festungskonzerte** (Fortress
Concerts), which often focus on Mozart's
works. See www.mozartfestival.at for times
and prices.

★**Salzburg Museum**　　　MUSEUM
(www.salzburgmuseum.at; Mozartplatz 1; adult/
child €7/3; ◷9am-5pm Tue-Sun, to 8pm Thu)
Housed in the baroque Neue Residenz palace, this flagship museum takes you on a
fascinating romp through Salzburg's past.
A visit starts beneath the courtyard in the
strikingly illuminated **Kunsthalle**, presenting rotating exhibitions of art, such as one
spotlighting Hohe Tauern landscape paintings. On the 1st floor, **Ars Sacra** zooms in on
medieval art treasures, from altarpieces and
embroidery to monstrances, chalices, Latin
manuscripts and a Romanesque crucifix.

Upstairs, prince-archbishops glower down
from the walls at **Mythos Salzburg**, which
celebrates the city as a source of artistic and
poetic inspiration. Showstoppers include
Carl Spitzweg's renowned *Sonntagsspa-
ziergang* (Sunday Stroll; 1841) painting, the
portrait-lined prince-archbishop's room and
the Ständesaal (Sovereign Chamber), an
opulent vision of polychrome stucco curling

SALZBURG IN...

Two Days

Get up early to see **Mozarts Geburtshaus** (p224) and boutique-dotted **Getreidegasse**
before the crowds arrive. Take in the baroque grandeur of **Residenzplatz** (p224) and
the stately prince-archbishop's palace, **Residenz** (p223). Coffee and cake in the decadent surrounds of **Café Tomaselli** (p235) fuels an afternoon absorbing history at the
hands-on **Salzburg Museum** or monastic heritage at **Stiftskirche St Peter** (p225).
Toast your first day with homebrews and banter in the beer garden at **Augustiner
Bräustübl** (p236).

Begin day two with postcard views from the ramparts of 900-year-old **Festung
Hohensalzburg**, or absorbing cutting-edge art at **Museum der Moderne** (p223).
Have lunch at **M32** (p234) or bag goodies at the **Grünmarkt** (p232) for a picnic in the
sculpture-strewn gardens of **Schloss Mirabell** (p225). Chamber music in the palace's
sublime **Marble Hall** or enchanting puppetry at **Salzburger Marionettentheater**
(p236) rounds out the day nicely.

Four Days

With another couple of days to explore, you can join a Mozart or *Sound of Music* **tour**.
Hire a bike to pedal along the Salzach's villa-studded banks to summer palace **Schloss
Hellbrunn** (p240) and its trick fountains. Dine in old-world Austrian style at **Alter Fuchs**
(p234) before testing the **right-bank nightlife**.

The fun-packed salt mines of **Hallein** (p241) and the Goliath of ice caves, **Eisriesenwelt** (p243) in Werfen, both make terrific day trips for day four. Or grab your walking boots
or skis to head up to Salzburg's twin peaks: **Untersberg** (p242) and **Gaisberg** (p242).

Salzburg

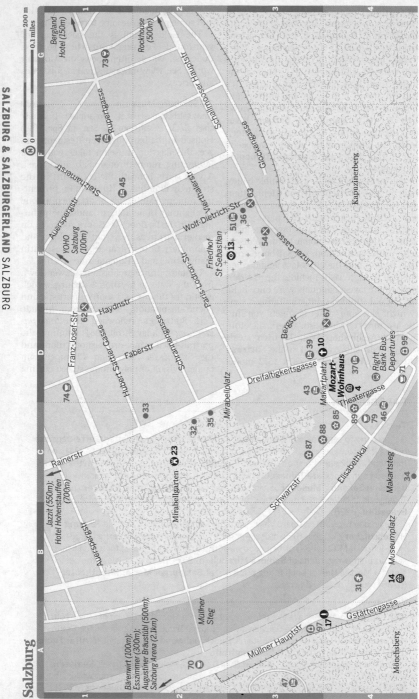

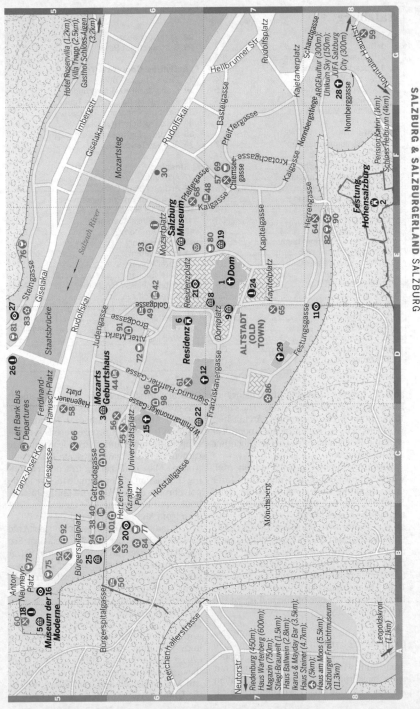

Salzburg

around frescoes depicting the History of Rome according to Titus Livius. The early-16th-century Millefiori tapestry, Archbishop Wolf Dietrich's gold-embroidered pontifical shoe and Flemish tapestries are among other attention-grabbers.

Salzburg's famous 35-bell **glockenspiel**, which chimes daily at 7am, 11am and 6pm, is on the western flank of the Neue Residenz. You can ascend the tower on a behind-the-scenes **tour**. Tickets are sold at the **Panorama Museum** (Residenzplatz 9; adult/concession €3/2.50; ◷9am-5pm) next door to the Salzburg Museum. The Panorama Museum is Johann Michael Sattler's 360-degree painting of Salzburg as it was in 1829. The museum plays host to rotating exhibitions, such as one on the real life of the von Trapp family.

★ **Dom** CATHEDRAL
(Domplatz; ◷8am-7pm Mon-Sat, 1-7pm Sun) Gracefully crowned by a bulbous copper dome and twin spires, the Dom stands out as a masterpiece of baroque art. Italian architect Santino Solari redesigned the ca-

thedral during the Thirty Years' War and it was consecrated in 1628. Its origins, though, date to an earlier cathedral founded by Bishop Virgil in 767. Bronze portals symbolising faith, hope and charity lead into the cathedral. In the nave, intricate stucco and Arsenio Mascagni's ceiling frescoes recounting the Passion of Christ guide the eye to the polychrome dome. For more on the history, hook onto one of the free guided tours at 2pm from Monday to Friday.

The adjacent **Dommuseum** (adult/child €5/1.50; ◷10am-5pm Mon-Sat, 11am-6pm Sun May-Oct) is a treasure trove of sacred art. A visit whisks you past a cabinet of Renaissance curiosities crammed with crystals, coral and oddities such as armadillos and pufferfish, through rooms showcasing gem-encrusted monstrances, stained glass and altarpieces, and into the Long Gallery, which is graced with 17th- and 18th-century paintings, including Paul Troger's chiaroscuro *Christ on the Mount of Olives* (c 1750). From the organ gallery, you get close-ups of the organ Mozart played and a bird's-eye view of the Dom's nave.

⭐ Residenz   PALACE

(www.residenzgalerie.at; Residenzplatz 1; combined ticket state rooms & gallery adult/child €9/3; ⏱10am-5pm) Nowhere is the pomp and circumstance of Salzburg more tangible than at the regal Residenz. A man of grand designs, Wolf Dietrich von Raitenau, prince-archbishop of Salzburg from 1587 to 1612, gave the go-ahead to build this baroque palace on the site of an 11th-century bishop's residence. The prince-archbishops held court here until Salzburg became part of the Habsburg empire in the 19th century.

An audioguide tour takes in the exuberant **state rooms**, a hotchpotch of baroque and neoclassical styles, which are lavishly adorned with tapestries, stucco and frescoes by Johann Michael Rottmayr.

Admission also covers the **Residenz Galerie**. Here the focus is on Flemish and Dutch masters, with must-sees such as Rubens' *Allegory on Emperor Charles V* and Rembrandt's chiaroscuro *Old Woman Praying*. Thomas Ender's alpine landscapes and Heinrich Bürkel's Salzburg scenes are among the 19th-century standouts.

⭐ Museum der Moderne   GALLERY

(www.museumdermoderne.at; Mönchsberg 32; adult/child €8/6; ⏱10am-6pm Tue-Sun, to 8pm Wed) Straddling Mönchsberg's cliffs, this contemporary glass-and-marble oblong of a gallery stands in stark contrast to the fortress. The gallery shows first-rate temporary exhibitions of 20th- and 21st-century art. The works of Alberto Giacometti, Dieter Roth, Emil Nolde and John Cage have previously featured. There's a **free guided tour** of the gallery at 6.30pm every Wednesday. The **Mönchsberg Lift** (Gstättengasse 13; one way/return €2.10/3.40, incl gallery €9.70/6.80; ⏱8am-7pm Thu-Tue, to 9pm Wed) whizzes up to the gallery year-round.

Mönchsberg commands broad outlooks across Salzburg's spire-dotted cityscape and its woodland walking trails are great for tiptoeing away from the crowds for an hour or two. While you're up here, take in the far-reaching views over Salzburg over coffee or lunch at M32 (p234).

DIY SOUND OF MUSIC TOUR

Do a Julie and sing as you stroll on a self-guided tour of *The Sound of Music* film locations. OK, let's start at the very beginning:

➡ **The Hills are Alive** Cut! Make that *proper* mountains. The opening scenes were filmed around the jewel-coloured Salzkammergut lakes. Maria makes her twirling entrance on alpine pastures just across the border in Bavaria.

➡ **A Problem Like Maria** Nuns waltzing on their way to mass at Benedictine Stift Nonnberg is fiction, but it's fact that the real Maria von Trapp intended to become a nun here before romance struck.

➡ **Have Confidence** Residenzplatz is where Maria belts out 'I Have Confidence' and playfully splashes the spouting horses of the Residenzbrunnen fountain.

➡ **So Long, Farewell** The grand rococo palace of Schloss Leopoldskron, a 15-minute walk from Festung Hohensalzburg, is where the lake scene was filmed. Its Venetian Room was the blueprint for the von Trapp's lavish ballroom, where the children bid their farewells.

➡ **Do-Re-Mi** Oh the Pegasus fountain, the steps with fortress views, the gnomes...the Mirabellgarten at Schloss Mirabell might inspire a rendition of 'Do-Re-Mi', especially if there's a drop of golden sun.

➡ **Sixteen Going on Seventeen** The loved-up pavilion of the century hides out in Hellbrunn Park (p240), where you can act out those 'Oh Liesl', 'Oh Rolf' fantasies.

➡ **Edelweiss and Adieu** The Felsenreitschule (Summer Riding School) is the dramatic backdrop for the Salzburg Festival in the movie, where the von Trapp Family Singers win the audience over with 'Edelweiss' and give the Nazis the slip with 'So Long, Farewell'.

➡ **Climb Every Mountain** To, erm, Switzerland. Or content yourself with alpine views from Untersberg (p242), which appears briefly at the end of the movie when the family flees the country.

★ **Mozarts Geburtshaus**   MUSEUM
(Mozart's Birthplace; www.mozarteum.at; Getreidegasse 9; adult/child/family €10/3.50/21; ☺9am-5.30pm) Wolfgang Amadeus Mozart, Salzburg's most famous son, was born in this bright-yellow townhouse in 1756 and spent the first 17 years of his life here. Today's museum harbours a collection of instruments, documents and portraits. Highlights include the mini-violin he played as a toddler, plus a lock of his hair and buttons from his jacket. In one room, Mozart is shown as a holy babe beneath a neon blue halo – we'll leave you to draw your own analogies...

★ **Mozart-Wohnhaus**   MUSEUM
(Mozart's Residence; www.mozarteum.at; Makartplatz 8; adult/child €10/3.50, incl Mozarts Geburtshaus €17/5; ☺9am-5.30pm) Tired of the cramped living conditions on Getreidegasse, the Mozart family moved to this more spacious abode in 1773, where a prolific Mozart composed works such as the *Shepherd King* (K208) and *Idomeneo* (K366).

Emanuel Schikaneder, a close friend of Mozart and the librettist of *The Magic Flute,* was a regular guest here. An audioguide accompanies your visit, serenading you with opera excerpts. Alongside family portraits and documents, you'll find Mozart's original fortepiano.

Under the same roof and included in your ticket is the **Mozart-Ton- und Filmsammlung**, a film and music archive of interest to the ultra-enthusiast, with some 25,000 audiovisual recordings.

Residenzplatz   SQUARE
With its horse-drawn carriages, palace and street entertainers, this stately baroque square is the Salzburg of a thousand postcards. Its centrepiece is the **Residenzbrunnen**, an enormous marble fountain ringed by four water-spouting horses and topped by a conch-shell-bearing Triton. The plaza is the late-16th-century vision of Prince-Archbishop Wolf Dietrich von Raitenau who, inspired by Rome, enlisted Italian architect Vincenzo Scamozzi.

Stiftskirche St Peter
CHURCH

(St Peter's Abbey Church; St Peter Bezirk 1-2; catacombs adult/child €1.50/1; ☉ church 8.30am-noon & 2.30-6.30pm, cemetery 6.30am-7pm, catacombs 10.30am-5pm Tue-Sun) A Frankish missionary named Rupert founded this abbey church and monastery around 700, making it the oldest in the German-speaking world. Though a vaulted Romanesque portal remains, today's church is overwhelmingly baroque, with rococo stucco, statues – including one of archangel Michael shoving a crucifix through the throat of a goaty demon – and striking altar paintings by Martin Johann Schmidt.

Take a stroll around the **cemetery**, where the graves are mini works of art with their intricate stonework and filigree wrought-iron crosses. Composer Michael Haydn (1737–1806), opera singer Richard Mayr (1877–1935) and renowned Salzburg confectioner Paul Fürst (1856–1941) lie buried here; the last is watched over by skull-bearing cherubs.

The cemetery is home to the **catacombs**, cavelike chapels and crypts hewn out of the Mönchsberg cliff face.

Schloss Mirabell
PALACE

(Mirabellplatz 4; ☉ palace 8am-4pm Mon, Wed & Thu, 1-4pm Tue & Fri, gardens dawn-dusk) FREE
What a way to woo your mistress: Prince-Archbishop Wolf Dietrich had this splendid palace built for his mistress Salome Alt in 1606. It must have done the trick because she went on to bear the archbishop some 15 children; sources disagree on the exact number – poor Wolf was presumably too distracted by spiritual matters to keep count himself. Johann Lukas von Hildebrandt, of Schloss Belvedere fame, remodelled the palace in baroque style in 1721. The lavish baroque interior, replete with stucco, marble and frescoes, is free to visit. The **Marmorsaal** (Marble Hall) provides a sublime backdrop for evening chamber concerts.

The flowery parterres, rose gardens and leafy arbours are less overrun first thing in the morning and early evening. The lithe *Tänzerin* (dancer) sculpture is a great spot to photograph the gardens with the fortress as a backdrop. *The Sound of Music* fans will of course recognise the **Pegasus statue**, the steps and the gnomes of the **Zwerglgarten** (Dwarf Garden), where the von Trapps practised 'Do-Re-Mi'.

Rupertinum
GALLERY

(www.museumdermoderne.at; Wiener-Philharmoniker-Gasse 9; adult/child/family €6/4/8; ☉ 10am-6pm Tue-Sun, to 8pm Wed) In the heart of the Altstadt, the Rupertinum is the sister gallery of the Museum der Moderne (p223) and is devoted to rotating exhibitions of modern art. There is a strong emphasis on graphic works and photography.

Friedhof St Sebastian
CEMETERY

(Linzer Gasse 41; ☉ 9am-6.30pm) Tucked behind the baroque **Sebastianskirche** (St Sebastian's Church), this peaceful cemetery and its cloisters were designed by Andrea Berteleto in Italianate style in 1600. Mozart family members and well-known 16th-century physician Paracelsus are buried here, but out-pomping them all is Prince Archbishop Wolf Dietrich von Raitenau's mosaic-tiled mausoleum, an elaborate memorial to himself.

Stift Nonnberg
CHURCH

(Nonnberg Convent; Nonnberggasse 2; ☉ 7am-dusk) A short climb up the Nonnbergstiege staircase from Kaigasse or along Festungsgasse brings you to this Benedictine convent, founded 1300 years ago and made famous as *the* nunnery in *The Sound of Music*. You can visit the beautiful rib-vaulted church, but the rest of the convent is off limits.

Steingasse
HISTORIC SITE

On the right bank of the Salzach River, this narrow, cobbled lane was, incredibly, the main trade route to Italy in medieval times.

ℹ DISCOUNT CARDS

If you're planning on doing lots of sight-seeing, save by buying the **Salzburg Card** (1-/2-/3-day card €26/35/41). The card gets you entry to all of the major sights and attractions, a free river cruise, unlimited use of public transport (including cable cars) plus numerous discounts on tours and events. The card is half-price for children and €3 cheaper in the low season.

If you're venturing outside of Salzburg consider purchasing the **Salzburgerland Card** (www.salzburgerlandcard.com, adult/child 6-day card €59/29.50), which provides discounts on 190 attractions in the province. These are available online and at tourist offices in the province.

Look out for the 13th-century **Steintor** gate and the house of **Joseph Mohr**, who wrote the lyrics to the all-time classic carol 'Silent Night'. The street is at its most photogenic in the late morning when sunlight illuminates its pastel-coloured townhouses.

Kollegienkirche   CHURCH
(Universitätsplatz; ⊙8am-6pm) Johann Bernhard Fischer von Erlach's grandest baroque design is this late-17th-century university church, with a striking bowed facade. The high altar's columns symbolise the Seven Pillars of Wisdom.

Pferdeschwemme   FOUNTAIN
(Horse Trough; Herbert-von-Karajan-Platz) Designed by Fischer von Erlach in 1693, this fountain is a horse-lover's delight, with rearing equine pin-ups surrounding Michael Bernhard Mandl's statue of a horse tamer.

Franziskanerkirche   CHURCH
(Franziskanergasse 5; ⊙6.30am-7.30pm) A real architectural hotchpotch, Salzburg's Franciscan church has a Romanesque nave, a Gothic choir with rib vaulting, and a baroque marble altar (one of Fischer von Erlach's creations).

Dreifältigkeitskirche   CHURCH
(Church of the Holy Trinity; Dreifaltigkeitsgasse 14; ⊙6.30am-6.30pm) Baroque master Johann Bernhard Fischer von Erlach designed this graceful right-bank church, famous for Johann Michael Rottmayr's dome fresco of the Holy Trinity.

Domgrabungsmuseum   MUSEUM
(Residenzplatz; adult/child €2.50/1; ⊙9am-5pm Jul & Aug, on request Sep-Jun) Map out the city's past with a romp of the rocks at this subterranean archaeology museum beside the Dom. Particularly of interest are fragments of Roman mosaics, a milestone hewn from Untersberg marble, and the brickwork of the former Romanesque cathedral.

🏃 Activities

Salzburg's rival mountains are 540m Mönchsberg and 640m Kapuzinerberg – Julie Andrews and locals who are used to bigger things call them 'hills'. Both are thickly wooded and criss-crossed by **walking trails**, with photogenic views of the Altstadt's right bank and left bank respectively.

There's also an extensive network of **cycling routes** to explore: from a gentle 20-minute trundle along the Salzach River to Hellbrunn, to the highly scenic 450km Mozart Radweg through Salzburgerland and Bavaria.

☞ Tours

Both the *Fiaker* (horse-drawn carriages) and the colourful rickshaws that pull up in front of the Residenz will take you on a guided tour of the Altstadt; prices depend on your itinerary.

One-hour guided tours (in German and English; €9) of the historic centre depart daily at 12.15pm and 2pm from Mozartplatz. If you would rather go it alone, the tourist office has four-hour **iTour** audioguides (€9), which take in big-hitters such as the Residenz, Mirabellgarten and Mozartplatz.

WALK OF MODERN ART

Eager to slip out of its baroque shoes and show the world that it can do cutting edge, too, Salzburg commissioned a clutch of public artworks between 2002 and 2011. Internationally renowned artists were drafted in to create contemporary sculptures that provide striking contrast to the city's historic backdrop, many of which can be seen on a wander through the Altstadt.

On Mönchsberg you will find Mario Merz' 21 neon-lit **Numbers in the Woods** and James Turrell's elliptical **Sky Space**, the latter creating a play of light and shadow at dawn and dusk. Back in town, you will almost certainly stroll past Stephan Balkenhol's **Sphaera** on Kapitelplatz, a huge golden globe topped by a startlingly realistic-looking man. Tucked away on Ursulinenplatz is Markus Lüpertz' **Mozart – Eine Hommage**, an abstract, one-armed bronze sculpture of the genius, sporting his trademark pigtail and the torso of a woman. Another tribute to Mozart stands across the river in the shape of Marina Abramovic's **Spirit of Mozart**, a cluster of chairs surrounding a 15m-high chair, which, as the name suggests, is said to embody the spirit of the composer.

For more, visit the Salzburg Foundation (www.salzburgfoundation.at), the driving force behind this display of open-air art installations and sculpture.

Fräulein Maria's Bicycle Tours   BIKE TOUR
(www.mariasbicycletours.com; Mirabellplatz 4;
adult/child €26/18; ⊙9.30am May-Sep, plus
4.30pm Jun-Aug) Belt out *The Sound of Music*
faves as you pedal on one of these jolly 3½-
hour bike tours, taking in film locations including the Mirabellgarten, Stift Nonnberg,
Schloss Leopoldskron and Hellbrunn. No
advance booking is necessary; just turn up
at the meeting point on Mirabellplatz.

Segway Tours   TOUR
(www.segway-salzburg.at; Wolf-Dietrich-Strasse 3;
City/Sound of Music tour €33/65; ⊙tours 9am,
noon, 3pm & 5pm Mar-Oct) These guided Segway tours take in the big sights by zippy
battery-powered scooter. Trundle through
the city on a one-hour ride or tick off *The
Sound of Music* locations on a 2½-hour tour.

Salzburg Schiffsfahrt   BOAT TOUR
(www.salzburghighlights.at; Makartsteg; adult/
child €15/7; ⊙Apr-Oct) A boat ride along the
Salzach is a leisurely way to pick out Salzburg's sights. Hour-long cruises depart from
Makartsteg bridge, with some of them chug-
ging on to Schloss Hellbrunn (adult/child
€18/10, not including entry to the palace).

Stiegl-Brauwelt   BREWERY TOUR
(www.brauwelt.at; Bräuhausstrasse 9; adult/child
€9/4; ⊙10am-5pm) Brewing and bottling
since 1492, Stiegl is Austria's largest private
brewery. A tour takes in the different stages
of the brewing process and (woohoo!) the
world's tallest beer tower. A free Stiegl beer
and pretzel are thrown in for the price of a
ticket. The brewery is 1.5km southwest of the
Altstadt; take bus 1 or 8 to Bräuhausstrasse.

Bob's Special Tours   COACH TOURS
(📱84 95 11; www.bobstours.com; Rudolfskai 38;
⊙office 8.30am-5pm Mon-Fri, 1-2pm Sat & Sun)
Minibus tours to *The Sound of Music* locations (€45), the Bavarian Alps (€45) and
Grossglockner (€90). Prices include a free
hotel pick-up for morning tours starting at
9am. Reservations essential.

Salzburg Panorama Tours   COACH TOURS
(📱87 40 29; www.panoramatours.com; Mirabellplatz; ⊙office 8am-6pm) Boasts the 'original
Sound of Music Tour' (€40) as well as a huge
range of others, including Altstadt walking
tours (€15), Mozart tours (€25) and Bavarian
Alps and Salzkammergut excursions (€40).

Salzburg Sightseeing Tours   BUS TOUR
(📱88 16 16; www.salzburg-sightseeingtours.at;
Mirabellplatz 2; ⊙office 8am-6pm) Sells a 24-

THE ROOT OF THE PROBLEM

While exploring Festung Hohensalzburg (p219), keep your eyes peeled for
turnips – there are 58 in total. Rumour
has it that Prince-Archbishop Leonard
von Keutschach was a spendthrift, so
his miserly uncle flung a turnip at his
head to (literally) knock some sense
into him. Ironically, the turnip became
a symbol for Leonard's new-found wisdom and features prominently on the
family coat of arms.

hour ticket (adult/child €16/8) for a multilingual hop-on hop-off bus tour of the city's
key sights and *The Sound of Music* locations.

🎭 Festivals & Events

Mozartwoche   MUSIC FESTIVAL
(Mozart Week; www.mozarteum.at; ⊙late Jan)
World-renowned orchestras, conductors
and soloists celebrate Mozart's birthday
with a feast of his music.

Osterfestspiele   MUSIC FESTIVAL
(Easter Festival; www.osterfestspiele-salzburg.at;
⊙Apr) This springtime shindig brings orchestral highlights, under Christian Thiele-
mann's sprightly baton, to the Festspielhaus.

SommerSzene   CULTURAL FESTIVAL
(www.sommerszene.net; ⊙Jul)   Boundary-
crossing performing arts are the focus of this
event.

Salzburg Festival   MUSIC FESTIVAL
(Salzburger Festspiele; www.salzburgerfestspiele.
at; ⊙late Jul–Aug) You'll need to book tickets
months ahead for this venerable summer
festival, running since 1920. See p230.

Jazz & the City   JAZZ FESTIVAL
(www.salzburgjazz.com; ⊙mid-Oct) Salzburg
gets its groove on at some 100 free concerts
in the Altstadt.

Christkindlmarkt   CHRISTMAS MARKET
(www.christkindlmarkt.co.at; ⊙Dec) Salzburg is
at its storybook best during Advent, when
Christmas markets bring festive sparkle to
Domplatz and Residenzplatz.

🛏 Sleeping

Salzburg's accommodation is pricey by Austrian standards, but you can get a good deal
if you're willing to go the extra mile or two.
Ask the tourist office for a list of private

rooms and *Pensionen*; some of the best are along Moosstrasse, just south of the centre. Medieval guesthouses that ooze history, avant-garde design hotels with river views, and chilled-out hostels all huddle in the Altstadt, where booking ahead is advisable.

Bear in mind that high-season prices are jacked up another 10% to 20% during the Salzburg Festival. If Salzburg is booked solid, consider staying in Hallein or just across the border in Bavaria.

★ Haus Ballwein GUESTHOUSE €
(☑82 40 29; www.haus-ballwein.at; Moosstrasse 69a; s €35-45, d €58-68, apt €100-115; P 🛜 ♿) Country or city? Why not both at this farmhouse guesthouse. With its bright, pine-filled rooms, mountain views, free bike hire and garden patrolled by duck duo Rosalee and Clementine, this place is big on charm. The largest, quietest rooms face the back and have balconies and kitchenettes. Breakfast is a wholesome spread of fresh rolls, eggs, fruit, muesli and cold cuts. It's a 10-minute trundle from the Altstadt; take bus 21 to Gsengerweg.

Haus Steiner GUESTHOUSE €
(☑83 00 31; www.haussteiner.com; Moosstrasse 156; s/d €35/58; P 🛜 ⛷ ♿) Kind-natured Rosemarie runs a tight ship at this sunny yellow chalet-style guesthouse, ablaze with flowers in summer. The pick of the petite rooms, furnished in natural wood, come with fridges, balconies and mood-lifting mountain views; family-sized apartments have kitchenettes. Breakfast is copious and the Altstadt is a 15-minute ride away on bus 21; get off at Hammerauerstrasse.

Haus am Moos GUESTHOUSE €
(☑82 49 21; www.ammoos.at; Moosstrasse 186a; s/d/apt €32/60/70; P 🛜 ♿) A slice of rural calm just a 15-minute ride from town on bus 21, this alpine-style chalet is a find. Many of the rooms have balconies with gorgeous mountain views and some come with canopy beds. A breakfast of muesli, cold cuts, eggs and fresh breads gears you up for the day, and there's an outdoor pool for an afternoon dip.

YOHO Salzburg HOSTEL €
(☑87 96 49; www.yoho.at; Paracelsusstrasse 9; dm €15-23, d €45-75; @ 🛜) This fun-loving hostel has got it sussed. Free wi-fi, secure lockers, comfy bunks, plenty of cheap beer and good-value schnitzels – what more could a backpacker ask for? Except, perhaps, a merry sing-along with *The Sound of Music*

screened daily (yes, *every* day). The friendly crew can arrange tours, adventure sports such as rafting and canyoning, and bike hire.

JUFA Salzburg City HOSTEL €
(☑05-7083 613; www.jufa.eu; Josef-Preis-Allee 18; dm €21, s €59-69, d €75-119; P 🛜 ♿) True, its plain, modern facade won't bowl you over, but this budget pick has got plenty going for it: superclean dorms, bike rental, generous breakfasts, *The Sound of Music* shown daily at 8pm and a sun-trap of a cafe terrace with views of Festung Hohensalzburg. It's a five-minute stroll southeast of the Altstadt.

Stadtalm HOSTEL €
(☑841 729; www.diestadtalm.com; Mönchsberg 19c; dm €19) This turreted hostel plopped on top of Mönchsberg takes in the entire Salzburg panorama, from the city's spires and fortress to Kapuzinerberg. There's a good-value restaurant on-site.

★ Hotel & Villa Auersperg BOUTIQUE HOTEL €€
(☑88 94 40; www.auersperg.at; Auerspergstrasse 61; s €129-155, d €165-205, ste €235-310; P @ 🛜 ♿) 🖉 This charismatic villa and hotel duo fuse late-19th-century flair with contemporary design. Guests can relax by the lily pond in the vine-strewn garden or in the rooftop wellness area with its sauna, tea bar and mountain views. Free bike hire is a bonus. Local organic produce features at breakfast.

Arte Vida GUESTHOUSE €€
(☑87 31 85; www.artevida.at; Dreifaltigkeitsgasse 9; s €55-140, d €80-152; 🛜) Arte Vida has the boho-chic feel of a Marrakech riad, with its lantern-lit salon, communal kitchen and serene garden. Asia and Africa have provided the inspiration for the rich colours and fabrics that dress the individually designed rooms, all with DVD players and iPod docks. Reinhold gives invaluable tips on Salzburg, and arranges yoga sessions and outdoor activities.

Hotel Am Dom BOUTIQUE HOTEL €€
(☑84 27 65; www.hotelamdom.at; Goldgasse 17; s €90-160, d €130-280; ❄ 🛜) Antique meets boutique at this Altstadt hotel, where the original vaults and beams of the 800-year-old building contrast with razor-sharp design features. Artworks inspired by the musical legends of the Salzburg Festival grace the rooms, which sport caramel-champagne colour schemes, funky lighting, velvet throws and ultraglam bathrooms.

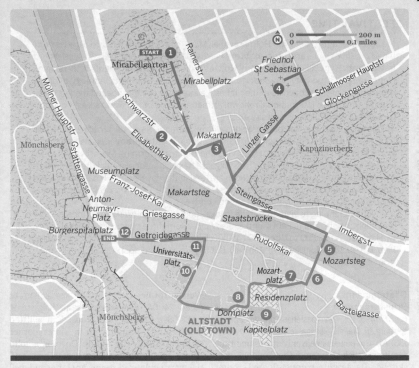

City Walk
In Mozart's Footsteps

START SCHLOSS MIRABELL
FINISH FÜRST
LENGTH 3KM; 1½ HRS

Mozart was the ultimate musical prodigy: he identified a pig's squeal as G-sharp when he was two years old, began to compose when he was five and first performed for Empress Maria Theresia at the age of six. Follow in his footsteps on this classic walking tour.

Begin at baroque ❶ **Schloss Mirabell** (p225), where the resplendent Marmorsaal is often the backdrop for chamber concerts of Mozart's music. Stroll south through the fountain-dotted gardens, passing the strikingly angular ❷ **Mozarteum** (p237), a foundation honouring Mozart's life and works, and the host of the renowned Mozartwoche festival. Around the corner on Makartplatz is the 17th-century ❸ **Mozart-Wohnhaus** (p224), where you can see how the Mozart family lived and listen to rare recordings of Mozart's symphonies. Amble north along Linzer Gasse to ❹ **Friedhof St Sebastian** (p225), the arcaded

cemetery where Wolfgang's father Leopold and wife Constanze lie buried. Now retrace your steps towards the Salzach River, turning left onto medieval Steingasse and crossing the art nouveau ❺ **Mozartsteg** (Mozart Bridge). Look out for the ❻ **memorial plaque** at No 8, the house where Mozart's beloved Constanze died, as you approach ❼ **Mozartplatz**. On this elegant square, Mozart is literally and metaphorically put on a pedestal. Across the way is the ❽ **Residenz** (p223) palace where Mozart gave his first court concert at the ripe old age of six. Beside it rests the baroque ❾ **Dom** (p222), where Mozart's parents were married in 1747 and little Mozart was baptised in 1756. Mozart later composed sacred music here and was cathedral organist. Follow Franziskanergasse to reach the ❿ **Kollegienkirche** (p226) on Universitätsplatz, where Mozart's *D Minor Mass*, K65, premiered in 1769. On Getreidegasse, stop to contemplate the birthplace of a genius at ⑪ **Mozarts Geburtshaus** (p224) and buy some famous chocolate Mozartkugeln (Mozart balls) at ⑫ **Fürst** (p238).

FESTIVAL TIME

In 1920, dream trio Hugo von Hofmannsthal, Max Reinhardt and Richard Strauss combined creative forces and the **Salzburg Festival** (Salzburger Festspiele; www.salzburger-festspiele.at; ⊙ late Jul–Aug) was born. Now, as then, one of the highlights is the staging of Hofmannsthal's morality play *Jedermann* (Everyman) on Domplatz. A trilogy of opera, drama and classical concerts of the highest calibre have since propelled the five-week summer festival to international renown, attracting some of the world's best conductors, directors, orchestras and singers.

Come festival time, Salzburg crackles with excitement, as a quarter of a million visitors descend on the city for some 200 productions. Theatre premieres, avant-garde works and the summer-resident Vienna Philharmonic performing Mozart works are all in the mix. The Festival District on Hofstallgasse has a spectacular backdrop, framed by Mönchsberg's cliffs. Most performances are held in the cavernous **Grosses Festspielhaus**, which accommodates 2179 theatregoers, the **Haus für Mozart** in the former royal stables, and the baroque **Felsenreitschule**.

If you're planning to visit during the festival, don't leave *anything* to chance – book your flights, hotel and tickets months in advance. Sometimes last-minute tickets are available at the **ticket office** (☑ 80 45-500; info@salzburgfestival.at; Herbert-von-Karajan-Platz 11; ⊙ 9.30am-1pm & 2-5pm Mon-Sat), but they're like gold dust. Ticket prices range from €5 to €370.

Gästehaus im Priesterseminar
GUESTHOUSE €€

(☑ 877 495 10; www.gaestehaus-priesterseminar-salzburg.at; Dreifaltigkeitsgasse 14; s €60, d €106-136) Ah, the peace is heavenly at this one-time seminary, tucked behind the Dreifältigkeitskirche. Its bright, parquet-floored rooms were recently given a total makeover, but the place still brims with old-world charm with its marbles staircase, antique furnishings and fountain-dotted courtyard. It's still something of a secret, so whisper about it quietly...

Hotel Rosenvilla
GUESTHOUSE €€

(☑ 62 17 65; www.rosenvilla.com; Höfelgasse 4; s €68-97, d €113-143, ste €146-233; P ⊛ ☎ ⛟) This guesthouse goes the extra mile with its sharp-styled contemporary rooms, faultless service and incredible breakfasts with spreads, breads, cereals, eggs and fruit to jump-start your day. Take bus 7 to Finanzamt or walk 15 minutes along the tree-lined riverfront into the centre.

Wolf Dietrich
HISTORIC HOTEL €€

(☑ 87 12 75; www.salzburg-hotel.at; Wolf-Dietrich-Strasse 7; s €90-130, d €155-225, ste €195-280; P ⊛ ☎ ⛟) For old-fashioned elegance you can't beat this central hotel, where rooms are dressed in polished wood furnishings and floral fabrics. There's even a suite based on Mozart's *The Magic Flute*, which has a star-studded ceiling and freestanding bath. By contrast, the spa and indoor pool are ultramodern. Organic produce is served at breakfast.

Weisse Taube
HISTORIC HOTEL €€

(☑ 84 24 04; www.weissetaube.at; Kaigasse 9; s €88-98, d €139-152; ☎) Housed in a listed 14th-century building in a quiet corner of the Altstadt, the 'White Dove' is a solid choice. Staff go out of their way to help, and the warm-coloured rooms are large and well kept (some have fortress views). Breakfast is a generous spread.

Pension Katrin
PENSION €€

(☑ 83 08 60; www.pensionkatrin.at; Nonntaler Hauptstrasse 49b; s €56-69, d €93-115, tr €129-158, q €146-176; P ☎ ⛟) With its flowery garden, bright and cheerful rooms and homemade goodies at breakfast, this *Pension* is one of the homiest in Salzburg. The affable Terler family keeps everything spick and span. Be prepared to lug your bags as there's no lift. The *Pension* is 1km south of the Altstadt; take bus 5 to Wäschergasse.

Haus Wartenberg
GUESTHOUSE €€

(☑ 84 84 00; www.hauswartenberg.com; Riedenburgerstrasse 2; d €128; P @ ☎) This welcoming family-run *Pension* is just a 15-minute stroll southwest of the Altstadt. It's set in vine-strewn gardens and housed in a gorgeous 17th-century chalet full of creaky floors and family heirlooms. The chunky pinewood and florals in the country-style rooms are in keeping with the character of the place. To get there, take bus 1, 4 or 5 to Moosstrasse.

Hotel Elefant
HISTORIC HOTEL €€

(☑84 33 97; www.elefant.at; Sigmund-Haffner-Gasse 4; s €86-109, d €102-192, tr €142-245; ✳☎♨) Occupying a 700-year-old building and run by the good-natured Mayr family, this central Best Western hotel has loads of charm. Bright colours add a modern touch to the spacious, elegantly furnished rooms. A generous breakfast is available.

Bergland Hotel
BOUTIQUE HOTEL €€

(☑87 23 18; www.berglandhotel.at; Rupertgasse 15; s €60-80, d €70-150, tr €120-180; P♨☎) Don't be fooled by the nondescript exterior. Belonging to the Kuhn family since 1912, the Bergland is ever so homely inside, with art (courtesy of the owner) on the walls, touches such as traditional Austrian hats and painted furnishings in the rooms, and a handsome piano room.

Hotel Mozart
HISTORIC HOTEL €€

(☑87 22 74; www.hotel-mozart.at; Franz-Josef-Strasse 27; s €95-105, d €140-155, tr €160-175; P☎♨) An antique-filled lobby gives way to spotless rooms with comfy beds and sizeable bathrooms at the Mozart. You'll have to fork out an extra €12 for breakfast, but it's a good spread with fresh fruit, boiled eggs, cold cuts and pastries.

Hotel Hohenstauffen
HOTEL €€

(☑87 21 93; www.hotel-hohenstauffen.at; Elisabethstrasse 19; s/d €97/145; P☎) Granted, it's not in the nicest part of town (erotica shops and all), but don't be put off. This genuinely friendly, family-run place has comfy old-style rooms and is geared up for cyclists, as the bicycle bell at reception confirms.

Hotel Wolf
HISTORIC HOTEL €€

(☑84 34 53-0; www.hotelwolf.com; Kaigasse 7; s €80-120, d €110-214; ☎) Tucked in a quiet corner of the Altstadt, Hotel Wolf occupies a lovingly converted 15th-century building. Uneven stone staircases and antique furnishings are a nod to its past, while the light, parquet-floored rooms range from modern to rustic.

Hotel Zur Goldenen Ente
HISTORIC HOTEL €€

(☑84 56 22; www.ente.at; Goldgasse 10; s/d/apt €125/180/350; ✳@☎) Bang in the heart of the Altstadt, this 700-year-old townhouse has oodles of charm – some rooms have four-poster beds, while Emperor Franz Josef guards over others. The sunny terrace overlooks the rooftops of the old town.

★Hotel Schloss Mönchstein
LUXURY HOTEL €€€

(☑84 85 55-0; www.monchstein.at; Mönchsberg Park 26; d €345-590, ste €595-2100; P✳@☎) On a fairy-tale perch atop Mönchsberg and set in hectares of wooded grounds, this 16th-century castle is honeymoon (and second mortgage) material. Persian rugs, oil paintings and Calcutta marble finish the rooms to beautiful effect. A massage in the spa, a candlelit tower dinner for two with Salzburg views, a helicopter ride – just say the word.

Hotel Sacher
LUXURY HOTEL €€€

(☑88 97 70; www.sacher.com; Schwarzstrasse 5-7; s €226-336, d €241-651, ste €502-3898; P✳☎♨) Tom Hanks, the Dalai Lama and Julie Andrews have all stayed at this 19th-century pile on the banks of the Salzach. Scattered with oil paintings and antiques, the rooms have gleaming marble bathrooms, and fortress or river views. Compensate for indulging on chocolate *Sacher Torte* in the health club.

Arthotel Blaue Gans
BOUTIQUE HOTEL €€€

(☑84 24 91; www.hotel-blaue-gans-salzburg.at; Getreidegasse 41-43; s €129-205, d €149-329; ✳☎) Contemporary design blends harmoniously

---

NO TOURIST TRAPP

Did you know that there were 10, not seven von Trapp children, the eldest of whom was Rupert (so long, Liesl)? Or that the captain was a gentle, family-loving man and Maria no soft touch? Or, that in 1938 the von Trapp family left quietly for the US instead of climbing every mountain to Switzerland? For the truth behind the Hollywood legend, stay the night at **Villa Trapp** (☑63 08 60; www.villa-trapp.com; Traunstrasse 34; d €109-500), tucked away in Salzburg's biggest private park in the Aigen district, 3km east of the Altstadt.

Marianne and Christopher have transformed the original von Trapp family home into a beautiful guesthouse (for guests only, we might add). The 19th-century villa is elegant, if not as palatial as in the movie, with tasteful wood-floored rooms and a balustrade for sweeping down á la Baroness Schräder. Family snapshots and heirlooms, including the baron's model ships and a photo of guest Pink Floyd guitarist David Gilmour strumming 'Edelweiss', grace the dining room. From the main station, take a train or bus 160 to Aigen.

with the original vaulting and beams of this 660-year-old hotel. Rooms are pure and simple, with clean lines and lots of white and streamlined furnishings. The restaurant is well worth a visit.

Goldener Hirsch
LUXURY HOTEL €€€

(☑80 84-0; www.goldenerhirschsalzburg.com; Getreidegasse 37; s €190-455, d €220-560; P❄@🛜) A skylight illuminates the arcaded inner courtyard of this 600-year-old Altstadt pile, where famous past guests include Queen Elizabeth and Pavarotti. Countess Harriet Walderdorff tastefully scattered the opulent rooms with objets d'art and hand-printed fabrics. Downstairs are two restaurants: beamed S'Herzl and vaulted Restaurant Goldener Hirsch (mains €20 to €38).

Hotel Bristol
LUXURY HOTEL €€€

(☑87 35 57; www.bristol-salzburg.at; Makartplatz 4; s/d/ste €240/355/630; P❄🛜) The Bristol transports you back to a more decadent era. Chandelier-lit salons, champagne at breakfast, exquisitely crafted furniture, service as polished as the marble – this is pure class. Even Emperor Franz Josef and Sigmund Freud felt at home here.

🍴 Eating

Salzburg's eclectic dining scene skips from the traditional to the supertrendy to the downright touristy. This is a city where schnitzel is served with a slice of history in vaulted taverns; where you can dine in Michelin-starred finery or be serenaded by a warbling Maria wannabe. Save euros by taking advantage of the lunchtime *Tagesmenü* (fixed menu) served at most places.

Knödlerei
AUSTRIAN €

(☑0660-540 56 64; www.knoedlerei.at; Nonntaler Hauptstrasse 9; lunch €5.50, mains €8.50-13; ⊙11.30am-9pm Mon, to 11.30pm Tue-Fri, 5.30-11.30pm Sat) The humble *Semmelknödel* (bread dumpling) is elevated to a whole new level here. Chunky benches, funky wooden stag heads and lanterns create a retro-cool, boho-flavoured backdrop for *Knödel* like you've never tasted before, from wasabi-potato varieties with sweet chilli sauce to Thai curry with coriander dumplings. The creative salads are excellent, too.

Spicy Spices
INDIAN €

(☑87 07 12; Wolf-Dietrich-Strasse 1; mains €7; ⊙11.30am-9.30pm Mon-Fri, noon-9.30pm Sat & Sun; ☑) 'Healthy heart, lovely soul' is the mantra of this all-organic, all-vegetarian haunt. Service is slow but friendly. It's worth the wait for the satisfyingly wholesome *thali* (appetisers), dhal and curries mopped up with *paratha* (flatbread) and washed down with mango lassis or *chai* (spiced tea).

Mensa Toskana
CAFE €

(Sigmund-Haffner-Gasse 11; lunch €4.50-5.40; ⊙11.30am-2pm Mon-Fri) University cafe in the Altstadt, with courtyard seating and pocket-money-priced lunches.

★ Gasthof Schloss Aigen
AUSTRIAN €€

(☑62 12 84; www.schloss-aigen.at; Schwarzenbergpromenade 37; mains €14-34.50, menus €39-54; ⊙6-10pm Wed, noon-2pm & 6-10pm Thu-Sun) A country manor with an elegantly rustic interior and a chestnut-shaded courtyard presents Austrian dining at its finest. The Forstner family's house speciality is '*Wiener*

DON'T MISS

TOP SNACK SPOTS

Want to grab a bite on the hoof or pick up some picnic fixings? Here's where to head.

Grünmarkt (Green Market; Universitätsplatz; ⊙7am-7pm Mon-Fri, 6am-3pm Sat) A one-stop picnic shop on one of Salzburg's grandest squares, for regional cheese, ham, fruit, bread and gigantic pretzels.

Stiftsbäckerei St Peter (Kapitelplatz 8; ⊙8am-5.30pm Mon & Tue, 7am-5.30pm Thu & Fri, 7am-1pm Sat) Next to the monastery where the watermill turns, this 700-year-old bakery bakes Salzburg's best sourdough loaves (€3.10 per kilogram) from a wood-fired oven.

Kaslöchl (Hagenauerplatz 2; ⊙9am-6pm Mon-Fri, 8am-1pm Sat; 🛜) A mouse-sized Austrian cheese shop, crammed with creamy alpine varieties, holey Emmental and fresh cheese with herbs.

IceZeit (Chiemseegasse 1; scoop €1.30; ⊙11am-8pm) Grab a cone at Salzburg's best ice-cream parlour, and choose flavours from poppy seed to passionfruit.

SALZBURG FOR CHILDREN

With dancing marionettes, chocolate galore and a *big* fairy-tale-like fortress, Salzburg is kid nirvana. If the crowds prove unbearable with tots in tow, take them to the city's adventure **playgrounds** (there are 80 to pick from); the one on **Franz-Josef-Kai** is a central choice. In summer, children love to race down the slides at Austria's largest outdoor pool, **Leopoldskron** (Leopoldskronstrasse 50; adult/child €4.40/2.40; ☺9am-7pm May-Aug), just 1km south of the centre (take bus 21 or 22 to Nussdorferstrasse).

Salzburg's sights are usually half-price for children and most are free for under-six-year-olds. Many galleries, museums and theatres also have dedicated programs for kids and families. These include the Museum der Moderne (p223), which has 90-minute Sunday art workshops for children (€4), which begin at 2.45pm, and the matinée performances at the enchanting Salzburger Marionettentheater (p236). The Salzburg Museum (p219) has lots of hands-on displays, from harp-playing to old-fashioned writing with quills. Pick up 'Wolf' Dietrich's cartoon guide at the entrance.

Kids will love the **Haus der Natur** (www.hausdernatur.at; Museumsplatz 5; adult/child/family €7.50/5/18.50; ☺9am-5pm), where they can bone up on dinosaurs and alpine crystals in the natural-history rooms, gawp at snakes and crocs in the reptile enclosure, and glimpse piranhas and coral reefs in the aquarium. Blink-and-you'll-miss-them baby clownfish splash around in the 'Kinderstube'. Shark and octopus feeding time is 10.15am on Mondays and Thursdays. On the upper levels is a **science museum** where budding scientists can race rowboats, take a biological tour of the human body and – literally – feel Mozart's music by stepping into a giant violin case.

On the arcaded Bürgerspitalplatz, the **Spielzeugmuseum** (Toy Museum; www. salzburgmuseum.at; Bürgerspitalgasse 2; adult/child/family €4/1.50/8; ☺9am-5pm Tue-Sun) takes a nostalgic look at toys, with its collection of doll's houses and Steiff teddies. Wednesday-afternoon Punch and Judy shows start at 3pm and cost €4. There's also dress-up fun, marble games and a Bosch workshop. Parents can hang out in the 'adult parking areas' and at the free tea bar while the little ones let off excess energy.

Outside Salzburg, near Untersberg, the open-air **Freilichtmuseum** (www.freilichtmuseum.com; Hasenweg; adult/child/family €10/5/20; ☺9am-6pm Tue-Sun Apr-Oct) harbours 100 archetypal Austrian farmhouses and has tractors to clamber over, goats to feed and a huge adventure playground. Kids can come face to face with lions, flamingos and alpine ibex at **Salzburg Zoo** (www.salzburg-zoo.at; Anifer Landesstrasse 1; adult/child/family €10/4/23; ☺9am-7pm, to 4.30pm in winter) near Schloss Hellbrunn.

Melange', different cuts of meltingly tender Pinzgauer beef, served with apple horseradish, chive sauce and roast potatoes, best matched with robust Austrian wines. Bus 7 stops at Bahnhof Aigen, a 10-minute stroll away.

Bärenwirt AUSTRIAN €€
(☑42 24 04; www.baerenwirt-salzburg.at; Müllner Hauptstrasse 8; mains €9.50-20; ☺11am-11pm) Sizzling and stirring since 1663, Bärenwirt is Austrian through and through. Go for hearty *Bierbraten* (beer roast) with dumplings, locally caught trout or organic wild boar bratwurst. A tiled oven warms the woody, hunting-lodge-style interior in winter, while the river-facing terrace is a summer crowd-puller. The restaurant is 500m north of Museumplatz.

St Paul's Stub'n INTERNATIONAL €€
(☑43 33 203; Herrengasse 16; ☺5-11pm Mon-Sat) Up cobbled Herrengasse lies this gloriously old world tavern, with a dark-wood interior crammed with antique curios, which attracts a regular crowd of locals. In summer, guests spill out into the beer garden to dig into authentically prepared classics such as roast pork in wheat-beer sauce.

Hagenauerstuben AUSTRIAN €€
(☑84 26 57; www.hagenauerstuben.at; Universitätsplatz 14; 2-course lunch €6.90, mains €8-17; ☺9am-midnight Mon-Sat, noon-8pm Sun) You'd be forgiven for thinking a restaurant tucked behind Mozarts Geburtshaus would have 'tourist trap' written all over it. Not so. The baroque-contemporary Hagenauerstuben combines a stylishly converted vaulted interior with a terrace overlooking

the Kollegienkirche. Pull up a chair for good old-fashioned Austrian home cooking – pork medallions with herb mash, spinach *Knödel* and the like.

Zwettler's
AUSTRIAN €€

(☑ 84 41 99; www.zwettlers.com; Kaigasse 3; mains €9-18; ☺ 11am-2am Tue-Sun) This gastro-pub has a lively buzz on its pavement terrace. Local grub such as schnitzel with parsley potatoes and goulash goes well with a cold, foamy Kaiser Karl wheat beer.

Triangel
AUSTRIAN €€

(☑ 84 22 29; Wiener-Philharmoniker-Gasse 7; lunch €4.90, mains €9-30; ☺ noon-midnight Mon-Sat) The menu is market-fresh at this arty bistro, where the picture-clad walls pay tribute to Salzburg Festival luminaries. It does gourmet salads such as saddle of veal with rocket and parmesan, a mean Hungarian goulash with organic beef, and delicious homemade ice cream.

Zum Fidelen Affen
AUSTRIAN €€

(☑ 87 73 61; www.fideleraffe.at; Priesterhausgasse 8; mains €10.50-19.50; ☺ 5pm-midnight Mon-Sat) The Jovial Monkey lives up to its name with a sociable vibe. Presuming you've booked ahead, you'll dine heartily under vaults or on the terrace on well-prepared Austrian classics including goulash, *Schlutzkrapfen* (Tyrolean ravioli) and sweet curd dumplings.

M32
FUSION €€

(☑ 84 10 00; www.m32.at; Mönchsberg 32; 2-course lunch €14, 5-course dinner €68-70, mains €14-23; ☺ 9am-1am Tue-Sun; ☑ ☒) Bold colours and a veritable forest of stag antlers reveal architect Matteo Thun's imprint at Museum der Moderne's ultrasleek restaurant. The food matches the seasons with specialities such as tortellini of organic local beef with tomato ragout, and tangy green-apple sorbet with cassis. The glass-walled restaurant and terrace take in the full sweep of Salzburg's mountain-backed skyline.

Afro Café
AFRICAN €€

(☑ 84 48 88; www.afrocoffee.com; Bürgerspitalplatz 5; lunch €7.20, mains €10-15; ☺ 9am-midnight Mon-Sat; ☎) Hot-pink walls, butterfly chairs, artworks made from beach junk and *big* hair...this afro-chic cafe is totally groovy. Staff keep the good vibes and food coming – think springbok in a sesame-coriander crust on lentils, and lemongrass-zucchini cake.

Alter Fuchs
AUSTRIAN €€

(☑ 88 20 22; Linzer Gasse 47-49; mains €10-17; ☺ noon-midnight Mon-Sat; ☑ ☒) This sly old fox prides itself on witty service and old-fashioned Austrian fare – both rarities in the Altstadt. Go for a schnitzel fried to golden perfection or pumpkin-seed-coated cordon bleu. Bandana-clad foxes guard the bar in the vaulted interior, and there's a courtyard for good-weather dining. In the cosy *Stube* (parlour) out back, scribbling on the walls (chalk only, please) is positively encouraged.

Sarastro
INTERNATIONAL €€

(☑ 84 35 32; www.sarastro.co.at; Wiener-Philharmoniker-Gasse 9; mains €10-21.50; ☺ 10am-10pm; ☑ ☒) Colourful stained glass illuminates this vaulted place at the Rupertinum, which opens to a vine-draped courtyard. The food is Austro-Italian: seafood goulash; summery, herb-dressed salads; parmesan-sprinkled spinach *Knödel* and the like. The two-course lunch is a snip at €7.90.

Pescheria Backi
SEAFOOD €€

(Franz-Josef-Strasse 16b; mains €9-15; ☺ 9am-10pm Mon-Sat) A clapboard shed of a fishmonger-bistro dishing up fish, fresh and simple, to a hungry crowd of regulars.

Wilder Mann
AUSTRIAN €€

(☑ 84 17 87; Getreidegasse 20; mains €9-17; ☺ 11am-9pm Mon-Sat) *Dirndl*-clad waitresses bring goulash with dumplings, boot-sized schnitzels and other light and airy fare to the table at this old-world Austrian tavern in the Altstadt.

★ Magazin
MODERN EUROPEAN €€€

(☑ 84 15 84; www.magazin.co.at; Augustinergasse 13a; mains €25-31, tasting menus €57-79; ☺ 10am-midnight Mon-Sat) Chef Richard Brunnauer's culinary flair and careful sourcing have gastronomes whispering 'Michelin star'. Gathered around a courtyard below Mönchsberg's sheer rock wall, Magazin shelters a deli, wine store, cookery school and restaurant. Menus fizzing with seasonal flavours – scallops with vine-ripened peaches, celery and buttermilk; venison medallions in porcini sauce – are matched with wines from the 850-bottle cellar and served alfresco or in the industrochic, cavelike interior. Hands-on cookery classes (€130 to €150) must be prebooked. Buses 4 and 21 stop at Augustinergasse.

Esszimmer
FRENCH €€€

(☑ 87 08 99; www.esszimmer.com; Müllner Hauptstrasse 33; 3-course lunch €38, tasting menus

€64-105; ☉noon-2pm & 6.30-9.30pm Tue-Sat) Andreas Kaiblinger puts an innovative spin on market-driven French cuisine at Michelin-starred Esszimmer. Eye-catching art, playful backlighting and a glass floor revealing the Almkanal stream keep diners captivated, as do gastro showstoppers such as Artic char with calf's head and asparagus. Buses 7, 21 and 28 to Landeskrankenhaus stop close by.

Riedenburg   MODERN EUROPEAN €€€
(☑83 08 15; www.riedenburg.at; Neutorstrasse 31; mains €18.50-30; ☉noon-2pm & 6-10pm Tue-Sat) Martin Pichler works the stove at this Michelin-starred restaurant with a romantic garden pavilion. His imaginative, seasonally inflected flavours, such as quail breast on asparagus with Bloody Mary and strawberry *Knödel*, are expertly matched with top wines. The €14 two-course lunch is a bargain. Riedenburg is a 10-minute walk southwest of the Altstadt along Neutorstrasse; take bus 1, 4 or 5 to Moosstrasse.

Ikarus   MODERN EUROPEAN €€€
(☑21 97 77; www.hangar-7.com; tasting menus €150-180; ☉noon-2pm & 7-10pm) At the space-age Hangar-7 complex at the airport, this glamorous restaurant is the epitome of culinary globetrotting. Each month, Roland Trettl invites a world-famous chef to cook for a serious foodie crowd.

Blaue Gans Restaurant   AUSTRIAN €€€
(☑84 24 91-50; www.blauegans.at; Getreidegasse 43; mains €17-25, tasting menus €41-54; ☉noon-midnight Mon-Sat) In the 650-year-old vaults of Arthotel Blaue Gans, this restaurant is a refined setting for regional cuisine, such as roast saddle of Hohe Tauern venison and poussin with nettle ravioli and chanterelles, which are married with full-bodied wines. The olive-tree-dotted terrace is popular in summer.

Alt Salzburg   AUSTRIAN €€€
(☑84 14 76; Bürgerspitalgasse 2; mains €19.50-30, tasting menus €43-58; ☉11.30am-2pm & 6-10pm Mon-Sat) Tucked into a courtyard at the base of Mönchsberg, this supremely cosy restaurant has attentive service, hearty regional specialities such as venison and veal knuckle, and fine Austrian wines.

☍ Drinking

A stein-swinging beer hall, a sundowner on the Salzach, an intimate wine bar for appreciating the subtle nuances of Grüner Veltiner wines – all possible ideas for a good night out in Salzburg. Nobody's pretending this is rave city, but the days of lights out by

---

CAFE CULTURE

Who says only the Viennese have great coffee houses? You can make yourself pretty *gemütlich* (comfy) over coffee and people-watching in Salzburg's grand cafes. Expect to pay around €4 for a slice of cake and €8 for a daily special (more in fancy places). Here are five favourites:

Café Tomaselli (www.tomaselli.at; Alter Markt 9; ☉7am-9pm Mon-Sat, 8am-9pm Sun) Going strong since 1705, this marble and wood-panelled cafe is a former Mozart haunt. It's famous for having Salzburg's flakiest strudels, best *Einspänner* (coffee with whipped cream) and grumpiest waiters.

Sacher (www.sacher.com; Schwarzstrasse 5-7; ☉7.30am-midnight) Nowhere is the chocolate richer, the apricot jam tangier and the cream lighter than at the home of the legendary *Sacher Torte*. The cafe is pure old-world grandeur, with its picture-lined walls and ruby-red banquettes. Sit on the terrace by the Salzach for fortress views.

Fingerlos (Franz-Josef-Strasse 9; ☉7.30am-7.30pm Tue-Sun) Salzburgers rave about the dainty petits fours, flaky pastries and creamy tortes served at this high-ceilinged cafe. Join a well-dressed crowd for breakfast or a lazy afternoon of coffee and newspapers.

Café Bazar (www.cafe-bazar.at; Schwarzstrasse 3; ☉7.30am-11pm Mon-Sat, 9am-6pm Sun) It's all chandeliers and polished wood here. Locals enjoy the same river views today over breakfast, cake and intelligent conversation as Marlene Dietrich did in 1936.

Niemetz (Herbert-von-Karajan-Platz 11; ☉10am-6pm Mon-Sat) Tucked behind the Pferdeschwemme fountain, this gloriously old-world cafe and cake shop has a small courtyard where you can dig into nut-poppy-seed tart and strudel that crumbles just so.

11pm are long gone. You'll find the biggest concentration of bars along both banks of the Salzach and some of the most upbeat around Gstättengasse. Rudolfskai can be on the rough side of rowdy at weekends.

★ Augustiner Bräustübl   BREWERY

(www.augustinerbier.at; Augustinergasse 4-6; ⊙3-11pm Mon-Fri, 2.30-11pm Sat & Sun) Who says monks can't enjoy themselves? This cheery monastery-run brewery has been serving potent homebrews in traditional ceramic *Stein* mugs since 1621. Fill yours from the pump in the foyer, visit the snack stands and take a pew in the vaulted hall or beneath the chestnut trees in the 1000-seat beer garden.

Republic   BAR

(www.republic-cafe.at; Anton-Neumayr-Platz 2; ⊙8am-1am Sun-Thu, to 4am Fri & Sat) One of Salzburg's most happening haunts, this backlit lounge-bar opens onto a popular terrace on the square. By night, DJs spin to a 20-something, cocktail-sipping crowd in the club. Check the website for free events from blues, rock and indie-pop breakfasts to salsa nights.

StieglKeller   BEER HALL

(Festungsgasse 10; ⊙11am-midnight Mon-Sat, 10am-midnight Sun) For a 365-day taste of Oktoberfest, try this cavernous Munich-style beer hall, which shares the same architect as Munich's Hofbräuhaus. It has an enormous garden above the city's rooftops and a menu of meaty mains (€11 to €18) such as fat pork knuckles and schnitzel. Beer is cheapest from the self-service taps outside.

Die Weisse   PUB

(www.dieweisse.at; Rupertgasse 10; ⊙pub 10.30am-midnight Mon-Sat, Sudwerk bar 5pm-4am Mon-Sat) The cavernous brewpub of the Salzburger Weissbierbrauerei, this is the place to guzzle cloudy wheat beers in the wood-floored pub and in the shady beer garden out back. DJs work the decks in Sudwerk bar, especially at the monthly Almrausch when locals party in skimpy *Dirndls* and strapping Lederhosen.

Unikum Sky   CAFE

(Unipark Nonntal; ⊙10am-7pm Mon-Fri, 8am-7pm Sat) For knockout fortress views and a full-on Salzburg panorama, head up to this sun-kissed terrace atop the new Unipark Nonntal campus, 300m south of Schanzlgasse in the Altstadt. It's a relaxed spot to chill over drinks and inexpensive snacks.

220 Grad   CAFE

(Chiemseegasse 5; ⊙9am-7pm Tue-Sat) Famous for freshly roasted coffee, this retro-chic cafe serves probably the best espresso in town and whips up superb breakfasts.

Mayday Bar   COCKTAIL BAR

(www.hangar-7.com; ⊙noon-midnight Sun-Thu, to 1am Fri & Sat) Peer down at Flying Bulls' aircraft through the glass walls at this crystalline bar, part of the airport's futuristic Hangar-7 complex. Strikingly illuminated by night, it's a unique place for a fresh-fruit cocktail or 'smart food' appetisers served in Bodum glasses.

Steinterrasse   COCKTAIL BAR

(Giselakai 3; ⊙3pm-midnight Sun-Thu, to 1am Fri & Sat) Hotel Stein's 7th-floor terrace attracts Salzburg's Moët-sipping socialites and anyone who loves a good view. It isn't cheap, but it is the best spot to see the Altstadt light up against the theatrical backdrop of the fortress.

Köchelverzeichnis   WINE BAR

(Steingasse 27; ⊙5-11pm Tue-Fri) This is a real neighbourhood bar with jazzy music, antipasti and a great selection of wines. Taste citrusy Grüner Veltliner and Riesling from the family's vineyards in the Wachau.

Café am Kai   CAFE

(Müllner Hauptstrasse 4; ⊙9am-9pm daily) On the banks of the Salzach River, this is a pleasantly low-key cafe, in which to kick back over coffee and cake, ice cream or a cold beer.

Salzburger Heimatwerk   CAFE

(Residenzplatz 9; ⊙9am-6pm Mon-Fri, to 5pm Sat) As well as knocking fine fabrics into *Dirndls* and selling Austrian schnapps, preserves and honeys, Salzburger Heimatwerk has an uncrowded cafe terrace that offers prime views across Residenzplatz.

Humboldt Stub'n   BAR

(www.humboldtstubn.at; Gstättengasse 4-6; ⊙11am-3am; 🛜) Following a recent makeover, this rustic-cool bar opposite Republic is once again a prime gathering spot, with a pavement terrace for sipping a cold, foamy one.

☆ Entertainment

★ Salzburger Marionettentheater   THEATRE

(☑87 24 06; www.marionetten.at; Schwarzstrasse 24; 🚼) The red curtain goes up on a miniature stage at this marionette theatre, a lavish stucco, cherub and chandelier-lit affair, which celebrated its centenary in 2013. The repertoire star is *The Sound of Music,* with a life-sized Mother Superior and a marionette-packed finale. Other enchanting productions include Mozart's *The Magic Flute,* Tchaikovsky's *The Nutcracker* and Strauss' *Die Fledermaus.* All have multilingual surtitles. Tickets cost between €18 and €35.

Landestheater
THEATRE

(☑ 87 15 12; www.salzburger-landestheater.at; Schwarzstrasse 22; 🖶) Opera, operetta, ballet and musicals dominate the stage at this elegant 18th-century playhouse. There's a strong emphasis on Mozart's music, with the Mozarteum Salzburg Orchestra often in the pit. There are dedicated performances for kids, and the *Sound of Music* musical is a winner with all ages.

Schlosskonzerte
CLASSICAL MUSIC

(www.salzburger-schlosskonzerte.at; ⊙ concerts 8pm) A fantasy of coloured marble, stucco and frescoes, Schloss Mirabell's baroque Marmorsaal (Marble Hall) is the exquisite setting for chamber-music concerts. Internationally renowned soloists and ensembles perform works by Mozart and other well-known composers such as Haydn and Chopin. Tickets costing between €31 and €37 are available online or at the **box office** (☑ 84 85 86; Theatergasse 2; ⊙ 9am-2pm Mon-Fri).

Mozarteum
CLASSICAL MUSIC

(☑ 889 40; www.mozarteum.at; Schwarzstrasse 26) Opened in 1880 and revered for its supreme acoustics, it highlights the life and works of Mozart through chamber music (from October to June), concerts and opera. The annual highlight is Mozart Week in January.

ARGEkultur
CONCERT VENUE

(www.argekultur.at; Ulrike-Gschwandtner-Strasse 5) This alternative cultural venue was born out of protests against the Salzburg Festival in the 1980s. Today it's a bar and performing-arts hybrid. Traversing the entire arts spectrum, the line-up features concerts, cabaret, DJ nights, dance, poetry slams and world music. It's at the Unipark Nonntal campus, a five-minute walk east of the Altstadt.

Rockhouse
LIVE MUSIC

(www.rockhouse.at; Schallmooser Hauptstrasse 46) Salzburg's hottest live-music venue, Rockhouse presents first-rate rock, pop, jazz, folk,

SALZBURG & SALZBURGERLAND SALZBURG

LOCAL KNOWLEDGE

AN INSIDER'S TAKE ON SALZBURG

Salzburg guide, Christiana Schneeweiss, runs us through the best of the city.

Best Time to Visit

May when everything is in bloom and the mountains are still dusted with snow. September is lovely, too, with mild days and fewer crowds than in summer.

Salzburg Festival

Even if you don't have tickets, you can still join in the fun! Opera and concert highlights are shown on a big screen against the spectacular backdrop of the fortress illuminated at the free Siemens Festival Nights on Kapitelplatz. If the weather is fine, little beats a performance of Jedermann on Domplatz – it is the very essence of the festival (p230). Last-minute tickets are often available.

Great Escapes

Kapuzinerberg and Mönchsberg for shady strolls and magnificent panoramas of the Altstadt. For quiet contemplation, head to Friedhof St Sebastian (p225) or Stift Nonnberg (p225), where the chapel choir contains wonderful 10th-century Byzantine frescoes, which are among Austria's oldest.

Top Day Trips

Gaisberg and Untersberg for hiking in alpine surrounds; the Bavarian lakes, such as Königssee just across the border; and Waldbad Anif for a swim in beautiful forested surrounds.

Sightseeing Tips

Avoid the groups by visiting the big sights after 4pm. To feel the true spirit of the Dom (p222), attend Sunday morning mass. Don't overlook lesser-known sights: the Dommuseum (p222), for instance, is fascinating and rarely crowded.

RETURN OF THE TRACHT

Ever thought about purchasing a tight-fitting *Dirndl* or a pair of strapping Lederhosen? No? Well, Salzburg might just change your mind with its *Trachten* (traditional costume) stores that can add alpine oomph to your wardrobe. If you have visions of old maids in gingham and men in feathered hats, you might be surprised. Walk the streets where 20-somethings flaunt the latest styles or hit the dance floor at Die Weisse's Almrausch club night and you'll see that hemlines have risen and necklines have plunged over the years; that young Salzburger are reinventing the style by teaming Lederhosen with T-shirts and trainers, or pairing slinky off-the-shoulder numbers with ballet pumps. Their message? *Trachten* can be cool, even sexy.

Embracing the trend is **Ploom** (www.ploom.at; Ursulinenplatz 5; ⊙ 11am-6pm Thu & Fri, to 5pm Sat), where designer Tanja Pflaum has playfully and successfully reinvented the *Dirndl;* her boutique is a wonderland of floaty femininity: a sky-blue bodice here, a frothy cotton blouse, a wisp of a turquoise *Schürze* (pinafore) or silk evening gown there.

For a more classic look, there's **Lanz Trachten** (www.lanztrachten.at; Schwarzstrasse 4; ⊙ 9am-6pm Mon-Fri, to 5pm Sat) and upscale **Stassny** (www.stassny.at; Getreidegasse 30; ⊙ 9.30am-6pm Mon-Fri, to 5pm Sat), which combine *Tracht*-making know-how with high-quality fabrics and age-old patterns (stag prints, polka dots, gingham etc). For a fusion of modern and traditional *Trachten* in myriad colours, try midrange **Forstenlechner** (www.salzburg-trachtenmode.at; Mozartplatz 4; ⊙ 9.30am-6pm Mon-Fri, to 5pm Sat) and **Wenger** (www.wenger.at; Getreidegasse 29; ⊙ 10am-6pm Mon-Fri, to 5pm Sat); the latter stocks figure-hugging Lederhosen for ladies and *Dirndln* from below-the-knee Heidi to thigh-flashing diva creations trimmed with ribbons and lace.

metal and reggae concerts – see the website for details. There's also a tunnel-shaped bar that has DJs (usually free) and bands. Rockhouse is 1km northeast of the Altstadt; take bus 4 to Canavalstrasse.

Jazzit
JAZZ CLUB

(☑ 88 32 64; www.jazzit.at; Elisabethstrasse 11) Hosts regular concerts from tango to electro alongside workshops and club nights. Don't miss the free Tuesday-night jam sessions in Jazzit:Bar. It's 350m southwest of the Hauptbahnhof along Elisabethstrasse.

Salzburg Arena
CONCERT VENUE

(☑ 24 04-0; www.salzburgarena.at; Am Messezentrum 1) Under a domed wooden roof, this is Salzburg's premier stage for sporting events, musicals and big-name concerts (Santana and Bob Dylan have played here). The arena is 3km north of town; take bus 1 to Messe.

Das Kino
CINEMA

(www.daskino.at; Giselakai 11) Shows independent and art-house films from Austria and across the globe in their original language. The cinema hosts the mountain-focused Bergfilmfestival in November.

Sound of Salzburg Show
SHOW

(☑ 82 66 17; www.soundofsalzburgshow.com; Festungsgasse 10; tickets with/without dinner €48/33; ⊙ dinner 7.30pm, show 8.30pm May-Oct) This all-singing show at StieglKeller is a triple bill of Mozart, *The Sound of Music* and operetta faves performed in traditional costume. Kitsch but fun.

Mozart Dinner
CONCERT SHOW

(☑ 82 86 95; www.mozartdinnerconcert.com; Sankt-Peter-Bezirk 1; adult/child €54/33; ⊙ 8pm) You'll love or hate this themed dinner, with Mozart music, costumed performers and (mediocre) 18th-century-style food. It's held in Stiftskeller St Peter's lavish baroque hall.

🔒 Shopping

Whether you're after a bottle of Mozart eau de toilette or a pair of yodelling Lederhosen, Getreidegasse is your street. Traditional wrought-iron signs hang above the shops, which sell everything from designer fashion to hats. Goldgasse, where goldsmiths once plied their trade, has accessories, antiques and porcelain. A popular street for a shop and stroll is Linzer Gasse.

★ Fürst
CONFECTIONERY

(www.original-mozartkugel.com; Getreidegasse 47; ⊙ 10am-6.30pm Mon-Sat, 11am-5pm Sun) Pistachio, nougat and dark-chocolate dreams, the *Mozartkugeln* (Mozart balls) here are still handmade to Paul Fürst's original 1890 recipe. Other specialities include cube-shaped *Bach Würfel* – coffee, nut and marzipan truffles dedicated to yet another great composer.

Musikhaus Katholnigg   MUSIC
(Sigmund-Haffner-Gasse 16; ⊙9am-6pm Mon-Fri, 9.30am-5pm Sat) Housed in a 16th-century townhouse, Musikhaus Katholnigg has been a music shop since 1847. This is the place to pick up high-quality recordings of the Salzburg Festival. There's a huge selection of classical, jazz, chanson and folk CDs and DVDs.

Zotter   CHOCOLATE
(Herbert-von-Karajan-Platz 4; ⊙10am-6pm Mon-Fri, 9.30am-6pm Sat) Made in Austria, Zotter's organic chocolate – including unusual varieties like Styrian pumpkin, ginger-carrot and mountain cheese-walnut – is divine. Dip a spoon into the choc fountain and try samples from the conveyor belt.

Alte Hofapotheke   PHARMACY
(Alter Markt 6; ⊙8am-6pm Mon-Fri, to noon Sat) For a whiff of nostalgia and a packet of sage throat pastilles, nip into this wonderfully old-fashioned, wood-panelled pharmacy, Salzburg's oldest, founded in 1591.

Salzburg Salz   GIFTS
(Wiener-Philharmoniker-Gasse 6; ⊙10am-6pm Mon-Fri, to 5pm Sat) Pure salt from Salzburgerland and the Himalaya, herbal salts and rock-salt tea lights are among the high-sodium wonders here.

Drechslerei Lackner   GIFTS
(Badergasse 2; ⊙9.30am-6.30pm Mon-Fri, to 5pm Sat) The hand-carved nutcrackers, nativity figurines and filigree Christmas stars are the real deal at this traditional craft shop.

Spirituosen Sporer   WINE
(Getreidegasse 39; ⊙9.30am-7pm Mon-Fri, 8.30am-5pm Sat) In Getreidegasse's narrowest house, family-run Sporer has been intoxicating local folk with Austrian wines, herbal liqueurs and famous *Vogelbeer* (rowan berry) schnapps since 1903.

ℹ Information

EMERGENCY
Hospital (⊉44 82; Müllner Hauptstrasse 48) Just north of Mönchsberg.
Police Headquarters (⊉63 83; Alpenstrasse 90) Police headquarters.

INTERNET ACCESS
There are several cheap internet cafes near the train station. A central choice is **City Net Café** (Gstättengasse 11; per hr €2; ⊙10am-10pm), which also offers discount calls. Many hotels, bars and cafes offer free wi-fi

MONEY
Bankomaten (ATMs) are ubiquitous. Exchange booths are 24/7 at the airport. There are also plenty of exchange offices downtown, but beware of potentially high commission rates.

POST
Main post office (Residenzplatz 9; ⊙8am-6pm Mon-Fri, 9am-noon Sat)
Station post office (Südtiroler Platz 1; ⊙8am-8.30pm Mon-Fri, to 2pm Sat, 1-6pm Sun)

TOURIST INFORMATION
The main **tourist office** (⊉889 87-330; www.salzburg.info; Mozartplatz 5; ⊙9am-7pm daily Jun-Aug, to 6pm Mon-Sat Sep-May) has stacks of information about the city and its immediate surrounds. There's a **ticket booking agency** (www.salzburgticket.com) in the same building. For information on the rest of the province, visit **Salzburgerland Tourismus** (⊉6688-0; www.salzburgerland.com; ⊙8am-5.30pm Mon-Thu, 8am-5pm Fri), 6.5km north of Salzburg.

ℹ Getting There & Away

AIR
Salzburg airport (⊉858 00; www.salzburg-airport.com; Innsbrucker Bundesstrasse 95), a 20-minute bus ride from the centre, has regular scheduled flights to destinations all over Austria and Europe.

Low-cost flights from the UK are provided by **Ryanair** (www.ryanair.com) and **EasyJet** (www.easyjet.com). Other airlines include **British Airways** (www.britishairways.com) and **Jet2** (www.jet2.com).

BUS
Salzburger Verkehrsverbund (SVV; www.svv-info.at) makes it easy to reach the province's smaller villages. Buses depart from just outside the Hauptbahnhof on Südtiroler Platz, where timetables are displayed.

Bus information and tickets are available from the information points on the main concourse. For more information on buses in and around Salzburg and an online timetable, see www.svv-info.at and www.postbus.at.

Hourly buses leave for the Salzkammergut:
Bad Ischl €10.10, 1½ hours
Mondsee €6.30, 53 minutes
St Gilgen €6.30, 49 minutes
St Wolfgang €9.20, 1¾ hours

CAR & MOTORCYCLE

Three motorways converge on Salzburg to form a loop around the city: the A1/E60 from Linz, Vienna and the east; the A8/E52 from Munich and the west; and the A10/E55 from Villach and the south. The quickest way to Tyrol is to take the road to Bad Reichenhall in Germany and continue to Lofer (B178) and St Johann in Tirol.

TRAIN

Salzburg has excellent rail connections with the rest of Austria, though the Hauptbahnhof is undergoing extensive renovation until 2014.

Trains leave frequently for Vienna (€49.90, 2½ to three hours) and Linz (€23.70, 1¼ hours). There is a two-hourly express service to Klagenfurt (€38.70, three hours).

The quickest way to Innsbruck is by the 'corridor' train through Germany; trains depart at least every two hours (€37.80, two hours) and stop at Kufstein. Direct trains run at least hourly to Munich (€35, 1½ to two hours); some of these continue to Karlsruhe via Stuttgart.

There are also several trains daily to Berlin (€139, eight hours), Budapest (€80.60, 5¾ hours), Prague (€67.60, 6½ hours) and Venice (€34 to €91, six to nine hours).

ⓘ Getting Around

TO/FROM THE AIRPORT

Salzburg airport is around 5.5km west of the centre along Innsbrucker Bundesstrasse. Buses 2, 8 and 27 (€2.40) depart from outside the terminal roughly every 10 to 15 minutes and make several central stops near the Altstadt; buses 2 and 27 terminate at the Hauptbahnhof. Services operate roughly from 5.30am to 11pm. A taxi between the airport and the centre costs €15 to €20.

BICYCLE

Salzburg is one of Austria's most bike-friendly cities. It has an extensive network of scenic cycling trails heading off in all directions, including along the banks of the Salzach River. See www.movelo.com (in German) for a list of places renting out electric bikes (e-bikes).

A Velo (Mozartplatz; 1hr/half-/full day €4.50/10/16, e-bike €6/16/22; ◷9am-6pm mid-Apr–Oct) Bicycle rentals, just across the way from the tourist office.

Top Bike (www.topbike.at; Staatsbrücke; per day €15; ◷10am-5pm) Bicycle rental joint with half-price rental for kids. The Salzburg Card yields a 20% discount.

BUS

Bus drivers sell single (€2.40), 24-hour (€5.30) and weekly tickets (€14). Single tickets bought in advance from machines are slightly cheaper. If you're planning on making several trips, *Tabak* (tobacconist) shops sell tickets even cheaper still (€1.60 each), in units of five. Under-six-year-olds travel free, while all other children pay half-price.

Bus routes are shown at bus stops and on some city maps; buses 1 and 4 start from the Hauptbahnhof and skirt the pedestrian-only Altstadt.

BUS TAXI

'Bus taxis' operate from 11.30pm to 1.30am (3am on weekends) on fixed routes, dropping off and picking up along the way, for a cost of €4.50. Ferdinand-Hanusch-Platz is the departure point for suburban routes on the left bank, and Theatergasse for routes on the right bank.

CAR & MOTORCYCLE

Parking places are limited and much of the Altstadt is only accessible on foot, so it's easier to leave your car at one of three park-and-ride points to the west, north and south of the city. The largest car park in the centre is the Altstadt Garage under Mönchsberg (€18 per day); some restaurants in the centre will stamp your ticket for a reduction. Rates are lower on streets with automatic ticket machines (blue zones); a three-hour maximum applies (€3.90, or €0.60 for 28 minutes) from 9am to 7pm on weekdays. For car hire, try **Avis** (www.avis.com; Ferdinand-Porsche-Strasse 7), **Europcar** (www.europcar. com; Gniglerstrasse 12) or **Hertz** (www.hertz. com; Ferdinand-Porsche-Strasse 7).

FIAKER

A *Fiaker* (horse-drawn carriage) for up to four people costs €40 for 25 minutes. The drivers line up on Residenzplatz. Not all speak English, so don't expect a guided tour.

AROUND SALZBURG

Hellbrunn

A prince-archbishop with a wicked sense of humour, Markus Sittikus built **Schloss Hellbrunn** (www.hellbrunn.at; Fürstenweg 37;

adult/child/family €10.50/5/25; ☉9am-5.30pm, to 9pm Jul & Aug; ♿) in the early 17th century as a summer palace and an escape from his functions at the Residenz. The Italianate villa became a beloved retreat for rulers of state who flocked here to eat, drink and make merry. It was a Garden of Eden to all who beheld its exotic fauna, citrus trees and *Wasserspiele* (trick fountains) – designed to sober up the clergy without dampening their spirits. Domenico Gisberti, poet to the court of Munich, once gushed: 'I see the epitome of Venice in these waters, Rome reduced to a brief outline.'

While the whimsical palace interior – especially the oriental-style Chinese Room and frescoed Festsaal – is worth a peek, the eccentric **Wasserspiele** are the big draw in summer. Be prepared to get soaked in the mock Roman theatre, the shell-clad Neptune Grotto and the twittering Bird Grotto. No statue here is quite as it seems, including the emblematic Germaul mask with its tongue poking out (Sittikus' answer to his critics). The tour rounds out at the 18th-century water-powered Mechanical Theatre, where 200 limewood figurines depict life in a baroque city. Tours run every 30 minutes.

Studded with ponds, sculptures and leafy avenues, the palace **gardens** are free and open until dusk year-round. Here you'll find the pavilion of 'Sixteen Going on Seventeen' fame from *The Sound of Music*.

Hellbrunn is 4.5km south of Salzburg, a scenic 20-minute bike ride (mostly along the Salzach River) or a 12-minute ride on bus 25 (€2.40, every 20 minutes) from Mozartsteg/Rudolfskai in the Altstadt.

Hallein & Around

☑ 06245 / POP 21,600 / ELEV 460M

Too few people visit Hallein in their dash north to Bavaria or south to Salzburg, but those who do are pleasantly surprised. Beyond its industrial outskirts lies a pristine late-medieval town, where narrow lanes are punctuated by courtyards, art galleries and boho cafes. Hotels are cheaper and less sought-after here than in Salzburg, a 25-minute train ride away – a point worth considering during the Salzburg Festival. Hallein's major family attraction, the Salzwelten salt mine, is actually located in Bad Dürrnberg, 6km southwest of town.

◉ Sights & Activities

★ **Salzwelten** MINE
(www.salzwelten.at; Ramsaustrasse 3, Bad Dürrnberg; adult/child/family €19/9.50/48.50; ☉9am-5pm; ♿) The sale of salt filled Salzburg's coffers during its princely heyday. At Austria's biggest show mine, you can slip into a boiler suit to descend to the bowels of the earth. The tour aboard a rickety train passes through a maze of claustrophobic passageways, over the border to Germany and down a 27m slide – don't brake, lift your legs and ask the guide to wax for extra speed! After crossing a salt lake on a wooden raft, a 42m slide brings you to the lowest point (210m underground) and back to good old Austria. Guided tours depart every half-hour. Bus 41 makes the 11-minute journey from Hallein train station to the salt mine hourly on weekdays, less often at weekends.

Keltenmuseum MUSEUM
(Celtic Museum; www.keltenmuseum.at; Pflegerplatz 5; adult/child €6/2.50; ☉9am-5pm; ♿) Overlooking the Salzach, the glass-fronted Keltenmuseum runs chronologically through the region's heritage in a series of beautiful vaulted rooms. It begins with Celtic artefacts, including Asterix-style helmets, an impressively reconstructed chariot, and a selection of bronze brooches, pendants and buckles. The 1st floor traces the history of salt extraction in Hallein, featuring high points such as a miniature slide and the mummified Mannes im Salz (Man in Salt) unearthed in 1577. There is a pamphlet with English explanations.

> ### SILENT NIGHT
>
> Hallein's festive claim to fame is as the one-time home of Franz Xaver Gruber (1787–1863) who, together with Joseph Mohr, composed the carol 'Stille Nacht' (Silent Night). Mohr penned the poem in 1816 and Gruber, a schoolteacher at the time, came up with the melody on his guitar. The fabled guitar takes pride of place in Gruber's former residence, now the **Stille Nacht Museum** (www.stillenachthallein.at; Gruberplatz 1; adult/child €2/0.70; ☉3-5pm 2nd Fri of month), next to Hallein's parish church. The museum tells the story of the carol through documents and personal belongings.

SALZBURG'S TWIN PEAKS

Rising above Salzburg and straddling the German border, the rugged 1853m peak of **Untersberg** affords a spectacular panorama of the city and the Tyrolean, Salzburg and Bavarian alpine ranges. The mountain is a magnet to local skiers in winter, and hikers, climbers and paragliders in summer. A cable car to the top (up/down/return €13/11.50/21) runs every half-hour; closed from late October to mid-December. Take bus 25 from Salzburg's Hauptbahnhof to St Leonhard and the valley station.

A road snakes up to 1287m **Gaisberg**, where stellar views of the Salzburg Valley, Salzkammergut lakes, the limestone Tennengebirge range and neighbouring Bavaria await. The best way to appreciate all this is on the 5km around-the-mountain circuit trail. Salzburgers also head up here for outdoor pursuits from mountain biking to cross-country skiing. Bus 151 (€4.30, 40 minutes, hourly) runs from Mirabellplatz to Gaisberg in summer. From November to March the bus only goes as far as Zistelalpe, 1.5km short of the summit.

Keltenblitz TOBOGGANING
(Bad Dürrnberg; adult/child €9/6.20; ☺10am-6pm, closed mid-Oct–Apr; ⚐) In summer, families pick up speed on this toboggan run close to Salzwelten. A chairlift takes passengers up to the top of Zinken mountain, where they board little wheeled bobsleds to race 2.2km down hairpin bends. The ride is over in a flash and affords fleeting views of the Salzach Valley.

⭐ Festivals & Events

First-rate musicians and artists draw crowds to the two-week **Halleiner Festwochen** in June. The festival is one of the headliners on the summer events program in Salzburger-land, with everything from classical concerts to live jazz, theatre, comedy acts, readings and exhibitions. For more details, see www.forum-hallein.at.

🛏 Sleeping & Eating

Hallein can be a day trip from Salzburg, but there are lots of value-for-money places to stay if you'd rather base yourself here. The tourist office helps book private rooms.

Pension Sommerauer GUESTHOUSE €
(☎800 30; www.pension-hallein.at; Tschusistrasse 71; s/d/tr/q €43/69/92/117; P⛄⚐) Housed in a 300-year-old farmhouse, the rustic rooms at this guesthouse are a bargain. There's a heated pool and conservatory as well as kiddie stuff including a playroom, sandpit and swings.

Pension Hochdürrnberg GUESTHOUSE €
(☎751 83; Rumpelgasse 14, Bad Dürrnberg; d/tr €60/70; P⚐) Surrounded by meadows, this farmhouse in Bad Dürrnberg has countrified rooms with warm pine furnishings and

downy bedding. The animal residents (rabbits, sheep and cows) keep children amused.

Hotel Auwirt HOTEL €€
(☎804 17; www.auwirt.com; Salzburgerstrasse 42; camp sites per adult/child/tent €6/4.40/4, s €58-78, d €88-108, tr €120-140, q €140-160; P⛄🛜⚐) Auwirt's light-filled rooms are a tad dated but comfy (ask for one with a balcony). The hotel is a good family base with its tree-shaded garden and playground. You can also pitch a tent here.

Koi ASIAN €
(Schanzplatz 2; lunch €7.90; ☺8am-2am Mon-Sat; ⚐) A Buddha welcomes you to this industrial-style cafe. The menu tempts with fresh-from-the-wok noodles and crunchy beansprout salads, which you can wash down with organic juices. There's a cool breeze to be had on the raised terrace by the stream.

Stadtkrug Hallein AUSTRIAN €€
(☎830 85; Bayrhamerplatz 10; 2-course lunch €7.50, mains €9.50-15; ☺11am-2pm & 5pm-midnight Mon-Fri, 5pm-midnight Sun; ⚐) Tables fill quickly at midday at this bustling wood-beamed *Gasthaus*. If it's warm, pull up a chair beside the trickling fountain on the square for an enormous schnitzel or plate of goulash.

Bistro Barock ITALIAN €€
(☎705 86; Gollinger-Tor-Gasse 1; 2-course lunch €7.30-8.60, mains €7-16; ☺10am-midnight Mon-Sat; ⚐) Hidden down an old-town backstreet, the cobbled terrace at this art-strewn bistro is a draw for lunching locals. The menu emphasises bright, herby Italian flavours such as homemade pasta with lemon, prawns and rocket. The pizza is pretty good, too.

Pur CAFE €€

(Schiemerstrasse 2; breakfast & light meals €5-15; ⊙8am-8pm; 🛜📷) 🍴 Opposite the Kelten-museum, this relaxed cafe has a terrace by the Salzach and is done up in zesty colours and fruit-themed artworks. The organic breakfasts are great, as are the wraps, baguettes, ice creams and the coffee (roasted in Hallein).

ℹ️ Information

The **tourist office** (📞853 94; www.hallein.com; Mauttorpromenade 6; ⊙9am-5pm Mon-Fri) is on the narrow Pernerinsel island adjoining the Stadt-brücke. Here you can borrow an iPhone for the day (€9.50) for a self-guided spin of the sights.

ℹ️ Getting There & Away

Hallein is close to the German border, 18km south of Salzburg via the B150 and A10/E55 direction Graz/Villach. It's a 25-minute train journey from Salzburg, with departures roughly every 30 minutes (€3.80).

Werfen

📞06468 / POP 3020 / ELEV 525M

The world's largest accessible ice caves, the soaring limestone turrets of the Tennenge-birge range, and a medieval fortress are but the tip of the superlative iceberg in Wer-fen. Such salacious natural beauty hasn't escaped Hollywood producers – Werfen stars in WWII action film *Where Eagles Dare* (1968) and makes a cameo appearance in the picnic scene of *The Sound of Music*.

Both the fortress and the ice caves can be squeezed into a day trip from Salzburg; start early, visit the caves first and be at the fortress for the last falconry show.

👁 Sights & Activities

⭐**Eisriesenwelt** CAVE

(www.eisriesenwelt.at; adult/child €9/4.50, incl cable car €20/10; ⊙9am-3.45pm May-Oct, to 4.45pm Jul & Aug) Billed as the world's largest accessible ice caves, Eisriesenwelt is a glittering ice empire spanning 30,000 sq metres and 42km of narrow passages burrowing deep into the heart of the mountains. Even if it's hot outside, entering the caves is like stepping into a deep freeze – bring warm clothing and sturdy footwear year-round. Photography is not permitted inside the caves.

A 75-minute tour through these Narnia-esque chambers of blue ice is a unique experience. As you climb up wooden steps and down pitch-black passages, with carbide lamps aglow, otherworldly ice sculptures shaped like polar bears and elephants, frozen columns and lakes emerge from the shadows. A highlight is the cavernous **Eispalast** (Ice Palace), where the frost crystals twinkle when a magnesium flare is held up to them. A womblike tunnel leads to a flight of 700 steps, which descends back to the entrance. The last guided tour leaves at 3.45pm.

In summer, minibuses (adult/child return €6.10/4.50) operate every 25 minutes between Gries car park in Werfen and the Eisriesenwelt car park, which is a 20-minute walk from the bottom station of the cable car, as well as every two hours from Werfen station from 8.20am to 2.20pm. The last bus down is at 5.34pm. Allow roughly three hours for the return trip (including tour). You can walk the whole route, but it's a challenging four-hour ascent, rising 1100m above the village.

LIECHTENSTEINKLAMM

One of the deepest and longest ravines in the Alps, the **Liechtensteinklamm** (Liechtenstein Gorge; www.liechtensteinklamm.at; adult/child €4/3; ⊙8am-6pm May-Sep, 9am-4pm Oct; ♿) is well worth a detour. The jaw-dropping chasm was carved out during the last ice age and takes its name from Johann II, Prince of Liechtenstein, who dipped into the royal coffers to render the gorge accessible in the 19th century.

Today, a footpath burrows into the gorge, past swirling ultramarine waters, glistening boulders and 300m-high cliffs, and through tunnels gouged into slate cliffs veined with white granite. The ravine is at its loveliest in the late afternoon when the light turns the water opal-blue. The trail culminates at a 50m-high waterfall. Allow at least an hour to explore the ravine.

Trains run frequently between Werfen and St Johann im Pongau (€3.80, 18 minutes), a 4km walk from the gorge, where free parking is available.

Burg Hohenwerfen CASTLE
(adult/child/family €11/6/25, incl lift €14.50/8/33; ☺9am-5pm Apr-Oct; 🅿) Slung high on a wooded clifftop and cowering beneath the majestic peaks of the Tennengebirge range, Burg Hohenwerfen is visible from afar. For 900 years this fortress has kept watch over the Salzach Valley, its current appearance dating to 1570. The big draw is the far-reaching view over Werfen from the 16th-century belfry, though the dungeons (displaying the usual nasties such as the iron maiden and thumb screw) are worth a look. The entry fee also covers a **falconry show** in the grounds (11.15am and either 2.15pm or 3.15pm), where falconers in medieval costume release eagles, owls, falcons and vultures to wheel in front of the ramparts. There is commentary in English and German. The brisk walk up to the fortress from the village takes 20 minutes.

🛏 Sleeping & Eating

Mariannenschlössl PENSION €
(☎420 93 80; Poststrasse 10; d €60) What a view! A five-minute uphill trot from the centre of the village, this family-run guesthouse offers an entrancing vista of the fortress and of the Tennengebirge's magnificent rock turrets and spires from its garden and the sweet, spotlessly kept rooms. A generous breakfast is served in a room adorned with hunting trophies.

Camping Vierthaler CAMPGROUND €
(☎56 57; www.camping-vierthaler.at; Reitsam 8; camp sites per adult/child/tent €5.50/2.50/6, bungalows d/tr/q €27/35/43; ☺mid-Apr–Sep; 🅿) This lovely campground on the bank of the Salzach River has a back-to-nature feel. Facilities include a snack bar and playground. Bungalows with kitchenettes, patios and barbecue areas are also available.

Oedlhaus AUSTRIAN €€
(Eishöhlenstrasse; snacks €3.50-8, mains €8-12.50; ☺9am-3.45pm May-Oct, to 4.45pm Jul & Aug) Next to Eisriesenwelt cable-car top station, this woodsy hut at 1574m fortifies walkers with mountain grub such as *Gröstl* (pan-fried potatoes, pork and onions topped with a fried egg). The terrace has views to rave about: looking across the Salzach Valley to the chiselled limestone peaks of the Hochkönig range.

★Obauer MODERN EUROPEAN €€€
(☎52 12-0; www.obauer.com; Markt 46; 3-course lunch €35, tasting menus €58-110; ☺noon-2pm & 7-9pm Wed-Sun; 🅿) Culinary dream duo Karl and Rudi Obauer run the show at this highly regarded, ingredient-focused restaurant. Sit in the rustic-chic restaurant or the garden, where most of the fruit and herbs are grown. Signatures such as meltingly tender Werfen lamb and flaky trout strudel are matched with the finest of Austrian wines. It also has a dedicated kids menu.

ℹ Information
The **tourist office** (☎53 88; www.werfen.at; Markt 24; ☺9am-12.30pm Mon-Fri, plus 2-4pm Sat Jun-Sep) hands out information and maps, and makes hotel bookings free of charge.

ℹ Getting There & Away
Werfen is 45km south of Salzburg on the A10/E55 motorway. Trains run frequently to Salzburg (€10, 40 minutes).

SOUTHERN SALZBURG PROVINCE
If you're driving to Radstadt or Mauterndorf in the remote Lungau region, look out for the Roman milestones along the Tauern Pass road.

Filzmoos
☎06453 / POP 1470 / ELEV 1055M
Theatrically set amid the jagged limestone spires of the Dachstein massif, rolling pastures and the aptly named Bischofsmütze (Bishop's Mitre) peaks, Filzmoos is quite the alpine idyll. Despite some wonderful hiking and skiing, the resort's out-of-the-way location deters the masses and the village has kept its rural charm and family-friendly atmosphere.

🏃 Activities
Overshadowed by the iconic Bischofsmütze (2454m), the village shares 32km of downhill slopes with neighbouring Neuberg and is criss-crossed with 50km of serene winter **walking trails**.

Queues are practically unheard of on Filzmoos' ski slopes, which mostly suit beginners. The resort's nursery slopes, central ski schools and floodlit toboggan run appeal to families. A day ski pass costs €37.50, and free ski buses shuttle between lifts. On a grander scale, Filzmoos is part of the huge Ski

Amadé (p256) arena, which covers 860km of varied terrain in five regions.

Hiking and rock climbing are Filzmoos' raisons d'être in summer. A network of well-graded, colour-coded trails takes walkers to the glaciated peaks and bizarre limestone formations of the Dachstein range. The two-day **Gosaukamm circuit** via Hofalm provides a fantastic overview of the area, as does the eight-day **Dachstein circuit**. The tourist office has trail maps and information on family hikes, such as the marmot-dotted **Bachalm Trail**, and can arrange guided hikes.

Other popular activities include Nordic walking in the surrounding hills, and mountain biking the challenging 182km **Dachsteinrunde** (Dachstein Tour) through Salzburgerland, Upper Austria and Styria. Pick up a map of the latter at the tourist office.

Mountain bikes, skis, snowshoes, sledges and cross-country equipment are available for hire at **Intersport Flory** (www.flory.at; Filzmoos 103; ⊗8.30am-noon & 2-6pm Mon-Fri, 8.30am-noon Sat).

✯✯ Festivals & Events

Thanks to its central alpine location and stiff winds, Filzmoos has become something of a ballooning mecca. In mid-January the village hosts the spectacular **Hanneshof Hot Air Balloon Week**. The highlight is the magical Night of Balloons, when 40 balloons illuminate the night sky.

🛏 Sleeping & Eating

Filzmoos is scattered with characterful, modestly priced chalets, private rooms and hotels. High-season rates are in winter; expect substantial reductions in summer.

Pension Wieser   PENSION €
(☑83 56; www.wieser-filzmoos.at; Neuberg 123; d €64-70, incl half-board €82-84; ⊞) Handy for the slopes, this sweet, rustic pension sits opposite the Filzmoos-Neuberg chairlift. A fire blazes downstairs in winter and the spotless rooms come with mountain-facing balconies. It's worth shelling out extra for half-board, which includes breakfast, a packed lunch, all-day soft drinks and a delicious three-course dinner. There's table tennis and a games room for kids.

★ Bio-Hotel Hammerhof   HOTEL €€
(☑82 45; www.hammerhof.at; Filzmoos 6; s/d €90/174; ℗@⊞) ✎ Set in a beautifully converted 400-year-old farmhouse, this eco-friendly hotel is a find. Bathed in soft light,

the rooms are decorated with natural wood and country touches; some have balconies and tiled ovens. The restaurant serves home-grown organic produce. Unwind in a herbal bath at the beauty centre or saddle a horse to canter off into the hills (the owner, Matthias, is a riding instructor and arranges tours).

Haus Obermoos   GUESTHOUSE €€
(☑0664-1261 403; www.hausobermoos.com; Neuberg 190; d €129, apt €169-189; ℗📶⊞) Lily and Stephen extend the warmest of welcomes at Haus Obermoos. Their love for this guesthouse shows in bright, immaculate rooms and apartments, tastefully done out in wood, marble and earthy hues. A heated ski room and a spa area are welcome touches. Haus Obermoos is near the ski lifts, a 10-minute walk from the centre.

Fiakerwirt   AUSTRIAN €
(☑82 09; Filzmoos 23; mains €5.50-11; ⊗10am-11pm Tue-Sun; ⊞) This rambling farmhouse and beer garden serves meaty fare such as schnitzel, goulash and pork roast. Kids love the pet goats, ducks and ponies. In winter, horse-drawn sleighs depart from here (from €15 to €17 per person). They pass through the village and snowy forest en route to one of the surrounding *Almen* (alpine meadows).

ℹ Information

The centrally located **tourist office** (☑82 35; www.filzmoos.at; Filzmoos 50; ⊗8.30am-12.30pm & 2-6pm Mon-Fri, 8.30am-12.30pm & 3-6pm Sat, 10am-noon Sun) provides stacks of information on activities in the region and will also help book accommodation.

ℹ Getting There & Away

Filzmoos is a 10km detour from the A10/E55 Tauern-Autobahn motorway. Several train–bus connections operate daily between Salzburg Hauptbahnhof and Filzmoos (€13.40, 1¾ hours); most require a change at Bischofshofen.

Radstadt

☑06452 / POP 4810 / ELEV 856M
Low-key Radstadt has an attractively walled town centre, with round turrets and a *Stadtpfarrkirche* (town parish church) that is a potpourri of Gothic and Romanesque elements. Most people come for the varied skiing and snowboarding. The resort is part of the vast Ski Amadé (p34) arena that is covered by a single ski pass and interconnected by ultramodern lifts and free ski buses.

The same mountains attract active types in summer, too, with more than 1000km of walking trails and opportunities for canyoning, climbing, white-water rafting and mountain biking. For information, contact the **Salzburger Sportwelt Tourist Office** (www.salzburgersportwelt.com).

ℹ Getting There & Away

Radstadt is on the route of a regular bus–train service running between Innsbruck (€34.40 to €50, 3¼ to four hours) and Graz (€38.60, three hours); the former involves at least one change, in Bischofshofen, the latter a change at Stainach-Irdning. Zell am See (€15, 1½ hours) and Bruck an der Mur (€27.70, three hours) are on this route. From Radstadt, the B99 climbs to the dramatic Radstädter Tauern Pass (1739m), then over to Carinthia. Just to the west is the A10/E55, which avoids the high parts by going through a 6km tunnel.

Mauterndorf

☏ 06472 / POP 1720 / ELEV 1122M

Sleepy little Mauterndorf has fairy-tale appeal; its narrow streets are dotted with candy-coloured houses and fountains. While the surrounding high moors and exposed bluffs are set up for walking and skiing, its remote setting in the Lungau region keeps things quiet.

The village centrepiece is medieval **Burg Mauterndorf** (adult/child €8.50/5.50; ⏰ 10am-6pm May-Oct). Dominating a rocky outcrop, this 13th-century castle was built by the prince-archbishops of Salzburg on the site of a Roman fort. The castle now houses a regional museum and provides the backdrop for various cultural events. It is believed that in the Middle Ages the main road passed directly through the castle courtyard and tolls were extracted from road users.

Mauterndorf is on Hwy 99. Bus 780 runs from Radstadt to the Mauterndorf post office (€8.20, 50 minutes, three times daily).

HOHE TAUERN NATIONAL PARK

If you thought Mother Nature pulled out all the stops in the Austrian Alps, think again: Hohe Tauern National Park was her magnum opus. Welcome to Austria's outdoor wonderland and one of Europe's biggest nature reserves (1786 sq km), which straddles Tyrol, Carinthia and Salzburgerland and is overshadowed by the 3798m hump of Grossglockner, the country's highest peak. Try as we might, no amount of hyperbole about towering snow-clad mountains, shimmering glaciers, impossibly turquoise lakes and raging waterfalls can quite do this place justice. Go see it for yourself.

History

The Austrian Alps once formed the boundary between the more-established southern Roman territories and their newer, less stable conquests to the north. The main trade route for pack animals ran along the pass at the end of the Tauern Valley, but few settlements were established due to the Romans' distrust of the treacherous climate (tales of malevolent snowy spirits abounded) and difficult mountainous topography. In 1971 the provinces of Carinthia, Salzburg and Tyrol agreed to the creation of a national park; regions were added in stages between 1981 and 1991 until it became Europe's largest national park. Today Hohe Tauern is widely regarded as one of Europe's biggest conservation success stories, an example of an approach where the needs of the local population are addressed right from the start.

ℹ Getting There & Around

CAR & MOTORCYCLE

To limit traffic through the park, many of the roads have toll sections and some are closed in winter. The main north–south road routes are the year-round Felber-Tauern-Strasse (B108) between Mittersill and Lienz, and the spectacular Grossglockner Road (open May to October). The 5.5km-long Felbertauerntunnel is on the East Tyrol–Salzburgerland border; the toll is €10 for cars and €8 for motorcycles. Buses on the Lienz–Kitzbühel route operate along this road.

TRAIN

The main hubs for train services are Zell am See (for services to Salzburg and points north via St Johann im Pongau) and Lienz (for trains east and west into Tyrol and Carinthia).

Grossglockner Road

A stupendous feat of 1930s engineering, the 48km **Grossglockner Road** (www.grossglockner.at; Hwy 107; car/motorcycle €33/23; ⏰ May-early Nov) swings giddily around 36 switchbacks, passing jewel-coloured lakes, forested slopes and above-the-clouds

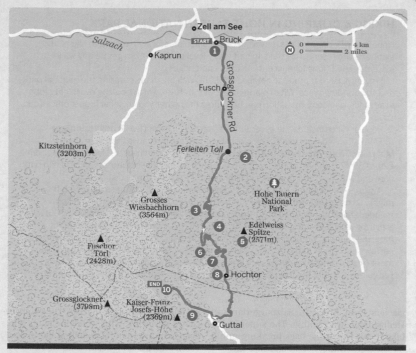

Driving Tour
Grossglockner Road

START BRUCK
FINISH BRUCK
LENGTH 96KM; FOUR TO SIX HOURS

Buckle up for one of Europe's greatest alpine drives. Grossglockner Road consists of 48 head-spinning, glacier-gawping, wow-what-a-mountain kilometres.

Leaving **1 Bruck**, enter the wild, mountainous Fuschertal (Fuscher Valley), passing Fusch and **2 Wildpark Ferleiten** (p251). Once through the toll gate, the road climbs steeply to **3 Hochmais** (1850m), where glaciated peaks including 3564m Grosses Wiesbachhorn crowd the horizon. The road zigzags up to **4 Haus Alpine Naturschau** (2260m), which spotlights local flora and fauna. A little further along, a 2km side road (no coaches allowed) corkscrews up to **5 Edelweiss Spitze** (2571m), the road's highest viewpoint. Climb the tower for staggering 360-degree views of more than 30 peaks of 3000m. Refuel with coffee and strudel on the terrace at the hut.

Get your camera handy for **6 Fuscher Törl** (2428m), with super views on both sides of the ridge, and gemstone of a lake **7 Fuscher Lacke** (2262m) nearby. Here a small exhibition documents the construction of the road, built by 3000 men over five years during the Great Depression.

The road wriggles on through high meadows to **8 Hochtor** (2504m), the top of the pass, after which there's a steady descent to **9 Schöneck**. Branch off west onto the 9km Gletscherstrasse, passing waterfalls and *Achtung Murmeltiere* (Beware of Marmots) signs.

The Grossglockner massif slides into view on the approach to flag-dotted **10 Kaiser-Franz-Josefs-Höhe** (2369m), with memorable views of the bell-shaped Grossglockner (3798m) and the rapidly retreating Pasterze Glacier. The 8km swirl of fissured ice is best appreciated on the short and easy Gamsgrubenweg and Gletscherweg trails. Allow time to see the glacier-themed exhibition at the visitor centre and the crystalline Wilhelm-Swarovski observatory before driving back to Bruck.

HIKING & CLIMBING IN HOHE TAUERN NATIONAL PARK

Hohe Tauern's deep valleys, towering peaks and plateaux are a mecca to hikers and climbers. The reserve has treks to suit every level of ability, from gentle day walks to extreme expeditions to inaccessible peaks and ridges.

Freytag & Berndt produce detailed 1:50,000 walking maps covering the national park and surrounding areas. When planning a major trek, it's worth booking overnight stops in advance, as accommodation can be sparse the higher you go; local tourist offices can advise.

Popular hikes include the ascent of the eternally ice-capped **Grossvenediger** (3674m), flanked by glaciers. The closest you can get by road is the 1512m-high **Matreier Tauernhaus** (☑ 04875-88 11; www.matreier-tauernhaus.at; Matrei in Osttirol; dm €29, s €39-47, d €58-74) at the southern entrance to the Felbertauerntunnel. You can park here and within an hour's walk gain fine views of the mountain.

Anyone with climbing experience and a reasonable level of fitness can climb the mighty **Grossglockner** (3798m) via the 'normal' route, though a guide is recommended. The main trail begins at the **Erzherzog-Johann-Hütte** (☑ 04876-85 00; www.erzherzog-johann-huette.at; dm/r €21/30), a four- to five-hour hike from Heiligenblut. From here, the roughly two-hour route crosses ice and rocks, following a steel cable over a narrow snow ridge, to the cross at the summit. It's essential to have the proper equipment (maps, ropes, crampons etc) and to check weather conditions before setting out. For guides, contact the tourist office in Heiligenblut or visit www.glocknerfuehrer.at.

glaciers from Bruck in Salzburgerland to Heiligenblut in Carinthia. The superfit can bike it: it's worth the back-breaking uphill for the exhilarating downhill, some say.

Between toll gates, all attractions are free. Begin your drive bright and early to beat the crowds, as the road is often bumper-to-bumper by midday, especially in July and August. It's also worth checking the forecast before you hit the road, as the drive is not much fun in snow or a storm. Variations of the route include overnighting in Heiligenblut or continuing on to Lienz.

The route is doable by bus, albeit a time-consuming option. Bus 5002 runs frequently between Lienz and Heiligenblut on weekdays (€8.40, one hour); less frequently at weekends. From late June to late September, four buses run from Monday to Friday, and three at weekends between Heiligenblut and Kaiser-Franz-Josefs-Höhe (€5.70, 30 minutes).

Heiligenblut

☑ 04824 / POP 1070 / ELEV 1301M

One of the single-most striking images on the Grossglockner Road is Heiligenblut, the needle-thin spire of its pilgrimage church framed by the glaciated summit of Grossglockner. The village's iconic scenery and easily accessible mountains lure skiers, hik-

ers and camera-toting tourists. The compact centre is stacked with wooden chalets and, despite an overload of yodelling kitsch souvenirs, retains some traditional charm.

In summer, serious mountaineers head here to bag peaks in the Hohe Tauern National Park. Enquire at the tourist office for details on mountain-bike trails in the park.

⊙ Sights & Activities

Wallfahrtskirche St Vinzenz CHURCH
(Hof 2; ⊙ dawn-dusk) As though cupped in celestial hands and held up to the mighty Alps, this 15th-century pilgrimage church lifts gazes and spirits. Inside is a tabernacle which purportedly contains a tiny phial of Christ's blood; hence the village name (*Heiligenblut* means 'Holy Blood'). Legend has it that the phial was discovered by a saint named Briccius, who was buried in an avalanche on this spot more than a thousand years ago.

Schareck & Gjaidtroghöhe SKIING
(1-day lift pass €40) Skiers can play on 55km of snow-sure slopes in the shadow of Grossglockner in Heiligenblut. This is perfect cruising terrain for beginners and easy-going intermediates, and families often choose the resort for its Snowland Kids Club and gentle slopes. Most of the skiing takes place on Schareck (2604m) and Gjaidtroghöhe (2969m) peaks.

🛏 Sleeping

Heiligenblut has a handful of places to stay and eat, most clustered around the village centre. The tourist office can book private rooms. Rates jump between 20% and 30% in winter.

Jugendherberge HOSTEL €
(☑ 22 59; www.oejhv.or.at; Hof 36; dm/s/d €21/29/50; Ⓟ ◎) Near the church, this chalet-style HI hostel has light, spacious dorms and handy extras including ski storage and a common room. It's right next to the public swimming pool, sauna and climbing wall.

Camping Grossglockner CAMPGROUND €
(☑ 20 48; Hadergasse 11; camp sites per adult/child/car €6.90/3/2.50) Open year-round, this green and pleasant site on the outskirts of the village features a restaurant, and affords prime vistas of Grossglockner.

★ Chalet-Hotel Senger HOTEL €€
(☑ 22 15; www.romantic.at; Hof 23; s €50, d €112-116; Ⓟ 🛜) Colourful prayer flags flutter at this farmhouse, a tribute to the Tibetan monks who once stayed here. All cosy nooks, warm wood and open fireplaces, this is just the spot for a little mountain hibernation and soul-searching. Most of the snug rooms have balconies; room 24 offers Grossglockner views instead.

ℹ Information

Tourist office (☑ 27 00; www.heiligenblut. at; Hof 4; ◎ 8am-6pm Mon-Fri, 9am-noon & 2-6pm Sat & Sun) On the main street, close to the Hotel Post bus stop. Books mountain guides.

ℹ Getting There & Away

As well as buses running to/from Kaiser-Franz-Josefs-Höhe from late June to September, there is a year-round service to/from Lienz.

Zell am See

☑ 06542 / POP 9,990 / ELEV 757M
Zell am See is an instant heart-stealer with its bluer-than-blue lake (Zeller See), pocket-sized centre studded with brightly painted chalets, and the snowcapped peaks of the Hohe Tauern that lift your gaze to postcard heaven. You can dive into the lake and cycle its leafy shores, hike and ski in the mountains and drive high on the Grossglockner Road. Every year, more than one million visitors from all round the world – from families to playboys in souped-up Mustangs – do just that, in search of the Austrian dream.

🏃 Activities

Alpine Walks
Hiking around Zell am See is among the finest in the Alps. Almost everywhere, you're rewarded with staggering views of the Hohe Tauern range – whether you opt for a gentle walk through alpine pastures tinkling with cow bells or a high-altitude day hike. For the 'greatest hits' of regional scenery, consider walking the **Pinzgauer Spaziergang** (p253), accessed by the Schmittenhöhebahn (Schmittenhöhe cable car) and the Schattberg X-press gondolas.

Boat Trips
Laid-back **Rundfahrt Schmittenhöhe boat tours** (adult/child €11/5.50; ◎ 10am-5pm Jun-Sep, 11am-4pm May & Oct) leave from Zell am See Esplanade for a 45-minute spin on the lake. Boats occasionally stop at Seecamp Zell am See (one way/return €3.20/5.40). If you'd prefer to go it alone, a number of places along the promenade hire out pedalos/motorboats for around €13/16 per hour from April to October.

Skiing
Together with neighbouring Kaprun, Zell am See has 138km of downhill skiing in its mountainous backyard. The two must-ski biggies are **Schmittenhöhe** (1965m) and the **Kitzsteinhorn Glacier** (3203m); the latter also offers cross-country skiing, year-round glacier skiing on a variety of pistes, and an all-level snowpark with rails, kickers, tubes, boxes and a 160m superpipe for boarders. The terrain is more tree-lined

---

DON'T MISS

FREE GUIDED HIKES
From mid-June to October, the tourist office arranges free guided walks on Schmittenhöhe and Kitzsteinhorn, including glacier hikes, herb walks and five-hour treks to 2995m Maurerkogel. The staff can also advise you on family-friendly llama treks in the Kaprun area, and have maps and GPS devices to help you plan your route.

Zell am See

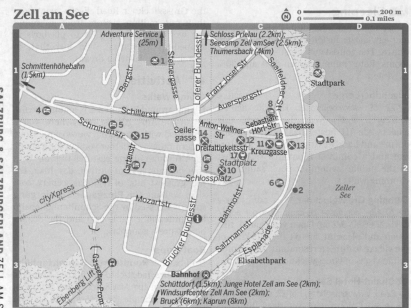

Zell am See

☼ Activities, Courses & Tours

🛏 Sleeping

✗ Eating

🍸 Drinking & Nightlife

and scenic than hair-raising, but there are a couple of steep black pistes for experts. Expect fairly long lift queues in the high winter season.

Ski passes for the Zell am See–Kaprun region cost €46/130/225 for one/three/six days. Ski buses are free for ski-pass holders. The most convenient way to reach the slopes is by taking the **cityXpress** gondola from central Zell am See. About 1.5km west of town, and served by bus 71 from Postplatz in central Zell am See to the cablecar base station, the **Schmittenhöhebahn** takes you even higher – to the summit of Schmittenhöhe.

Zeller See   SWIMMING

The Zeller See may be on the cold side of refreshing, but the views are marvellous. There's also loads of high-speed action on the water in summer, from waterskiing to wakeboarding. If you'd rather not grit your teeth as you swim, try the **Zell am See Lido** (€6.90/3.70; ⊙9am-7pm), or those in Thumersbach and Schüttdorf. They all feature sunbathing lawns, solar-heated pools and children's splash areas. Entry is free with the Zell am See–Kaprun Card.

Adventure Service   ADVENTURE SPORTS

(📞735 25; www.adventureservice.at; Steinergasse 9) A one-stop daredevil shop, this offers a long list of adrenaline-charged activities from tandem paragliding (€110) and whitewater rafting (€45) to canyoning (€59 to

€95), climbing (€50 to €105) and guided half-day mountain-bike tours (€27). Less physically exerting are the 1½ hour Segway tours (€40), taking in the lake and mountain scenery. Bike hire costs €13/23 per half/full day.

Freizeitzentrum SWIMMING
(www.freizeitzentrum.at; Steinergasse 3-5; pool adult/child €12.40/6.70; ⊙10am-10pm; 🚗) Preferable to a dip in the icy Zeller See in winter, this leisure centre shelters a 25m pool, whirlpool and saunas. There's also a bowling alley, ice rink and (in summer) a lido.

Windsurfcenter Zell am See WINDSURFING
(🛈0664-644 36 95; Seespitzstrasse 13; ⊙May-Sep) Stiff mountain breezes create the ideal conditions for windsurfing on Zeller See. This reputable windsurfing centre is 2km south of town. Call for more information on its wide range of courses. You can also rent stand-up paddleboards/windsurfers/funboards for €5/9/16.50 respectively.

✨ Festivals & Events

Zell am See swings into summer with live music, fireworks and sports events at its two **lake festivals**, held in mid-July and early August. The free **Zell Summer Night** festival draws bands, street entertainers and improvised theatre to streets and squares every Wednesday night in July and August.

🛏 Sleeping

Winter prices are roughly 50% higher than summer rates. Note that many places close between seasons – usually from October to November and April to May.

Haus Wilhelmina PENSION €
(🛈726 07; www.haus-wilhelmina.at; Schmittenstrasse 14; r €72-80, apt €71-163; P🛜🚗) Just a joyous skip from the ski lift and centre, this friendly *Pension* has simple but homey rooms with lots of pine, floral prints and balconies. There are also family-sized apartments, and a playground to keep the little ones amused.

Haus Haffner GUESTHOUSE €
(🛈23 96-0; www.haffner.at; Schmittenstrasse 29; s €27-41, d €50-82, apt d €72-114; 🛜🚗) Tucked down a quiet backstreet near the ski lift, this cheery guesthouse has spacious rooms and family apartments with rag rugs, kettles and chunky wood furniture (the owner is a cabinetmaker).

Junge Hotel Zell am See HOSTEL €
(🛈571 85; www.hostel-zell.at; Seespitzstrasse 13; dm/s/d €23.50/34/56; @🛜🛜) Right at the lake and beach, a 15-minute walk south of town, this hostel is a great budget deal. Dorms are well kept, the mountain views dreamy and there's always plenty going on – from volleyball matches to weekly barbecues. Half-board costs an extra €8 per day.

Seecamp Zell am See CAMPGROUND €
(🛈721 15; www.seecamp.at; Thumersbacherstrasse 34; camp sites per adult/child/tent €9.10/5.90/7.10; P🛜🚗) If waking up to views of the snow-capped Kitzsteinhorn mountains appeals, camp out at this tree-shaded site on the lakeshore. Facilities include a shop, restaurant and kids club. Guided mountain-bike and hiking tours are available.

★ Pension Hubertus PENSION €€
(🛈724 27; www.hubertus-pension.at; Gartenstrasse 4; s €56-61, d €98-108; P🚗) 🍴 Beate and Bernd extend a warm welcome at their eco-savvy chalet. Situated opposite the ski lifts, the pension uses 100% renewable energy (solar and wind power), and organic produce and fair-trade coffee are served at breakfast. The bright, airy rooms are decked out country-style, with lots of pine, floral drapes and downy bedding.

Hotel Seehof HOTEL €€
(🛈726 66; www.seehof.at; Salzmannstrasse 3; s/d/apt €55/94/95; P🛜🚗) This lemon-fronted chalet is just steps from the lake. Rooms are cosy, if a tad small, with good beds and pine trappings. Light sleepers may hear the trains; rooms at the back are quieter but sacrifice the fine lake views. The family puts on a generous breakfast spread.

ⓘ CENT SAVER

If you're in town in summer, ask your host for the free **Zell am See–Kaprun Card**. The card gets you free entry to all major sights and activities in the region, including the swimming pools around the lake, **Wildpark Ferleiten** (www.wildpark-ferleiten.at; adult/child €7/3.50; ⊙8am-dusk May-Nov) and the Krimmler Wasserfälle (p255). It also gives you a boat trip on the lake and one free ride per day on the cable cars that ascend to Schmittenhöhe and Kitzsteinhorn.

Steinerwirt
BOUTIQUE HOTEL €€€

(🖉725 02; www.steinerwirt.com; Dreifaltig-keitsgasse 2; s €59-65, d €118-130; @🛜🏠) A 500-year-old chalet turned boutique hotel, Steinerwirt has light-filled rooms tastefully done out in muted tones and untreated pinewood, with flat-screen TVs and DVD players. The rooftop whirlpool, mountain-facing sauna and meditation room invite relaxation. There are incredible views of Kitzsteinhorn Glacier and Schmittenhöhe from the roof terrace.

Schloss Prielau
HISTORIC HOTEL €€€

(🖉729 11-0; www.schloss-prielau.at; Hofmannsthal-strasse 10; s €145, d €180-260; 🅿@🛜) A once-upon-a-dream fairy tale of a hotel, this 16th-century castle set in mature grounds was once the haunt of Bavarian prince-bishops. Wood panelling and antiques add a touch of romance to the rustic-chic rooms, many of which feature lake and mountain views. With its private beach, mini-spa and Michelin-starred restaurant, Mayer's (p254), this is luxury all the way. Schloss Prielau is 2.5km northeast of the centre along the lakefront promenade.

Romantik Hotel Zell am See
HOTEL €€€

(🖉725 20; www.romantik-hotel.at; Sebastian-Hörl-Strasse 11; s €90-115, d €186-228; 🅿@🛜🏊) This dark-wood chalet, ablaze with geraniums in summer, looks back on a 500-year history. Antique wood furnishings in the cosy rooms, a solar-heated pool with mountain views and a small spa with pampering treatments such as chocolate baths create an ambience of discreet luxury.

✖️ Eating

The cafes and restaurants lining the lakefront and the old town serve up everything from Middle Eastern snacks to Michelin-starred finery. Many places close in shoulder seasons.

VESPA VA-VA-VOOM

What could be cooler in summer than hiring a Vespa to cruise along the winding mountain roads surrounding Zell am See for the day? You can pick up a quality scooter at **Vespa Verleih** (🖉0664-201 08 28; www.vespa-verleih.at; per day €50-90).

Ristorante Giuseppe
PIZZERIA €

(🖉723 73; Kirchengasse 1; pizza €7-11, mains €10-22; ⏰10am-11pm) Large and crisp, the pizzas tend to be a better choice than pasta at this upbeat Italian place in the pedestrian-only centre. Choose to eat in either the pavement terrace or the rustic, wood-panelled restaurant. Lunch is good value at €7.20.

Feinkost Lumpi
DELI €

(Seegasse 6; ⏰8.30am-6.30am Mon-Fri, to 5pm Sat) This deli is picnic central. Stop by for dense rye bread, Pinzgauer ham and cheese, and homemade *Knödel*. The farm-fresh ice cream is superb, too.

Steinerwirt
AUSTRIAN €€

(🖉725 02; Dreifaltigkeitsgasse 2; mains €9-17.50; ⏰7am-midnight) Whether you dine in the contemporary bistro or in the old-world ambience of the wood-panelled Salzburger Stube, you get the same great food and service at Steinerwirt. The Austrian menu emphasises locally sourced meat and fresh lake fish, accompanied by wines drawn from the 600-year-old cellar.

Villa Crazy Daisy
INTERNATIONAL €€

(🖉725 26; www.villa-crazydaisy.at; Salzmann-strasse 8; 2-course lunch €7.50, mains €11-25; ⏰10am-late; 🍴) In a rambling villa opposite the Grand Hotel, Daisy hosts full-on après-ski parties in winter and has the most popular terrace in town in summer. Pizza, *gambas piri-piri* (piri-piri prawns) and giant salads are on the menu in the restaurant, where service can be hit or miss. Head upstairs for live music, DJs and a real party vibe.

Deins & Meins
FUSION €€

(🖉472 44; www.deins-meins.at; Schlossplatz 5; mains €10-33; ⏰10am-midnight Mon-Sat; 🛜🍴) Floor-to-ceiling glass, red velvet chairs and rotating exhibitions of modern art define this slinky lounge-restaurant. Local chef and confectioner David Fischböck has put his stamp on the slow-food menu: herby Mediterranean-inspired mains and spot-on steaks are followed by his delectable homemade desserts.

Zum Hirschen
AUSTRIAN €€

(🖉77 40; www.hotel-zum-hirschen.at; Dreifaltig-keitsstrasse 1; lunch special €8.50-9.50, mains €18-26; ⏰11am-11pm) Warm pine panelling, flickering candles and friendly yet discreet service create an intimate feel in this smart restaurant. The chef makes the most of local ingredients, so expect dishes like organic

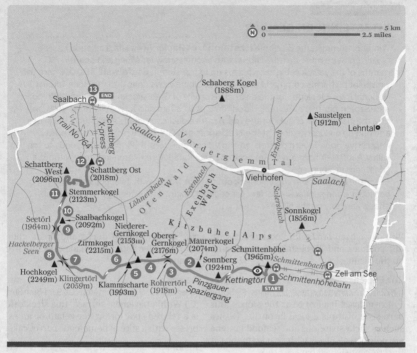

🏃 Walking Trail
Pinzgauer Spaziergang

START ZELL AM SEE
FINISH SAALBACH
LENGTH 19KM; FIVE TO SIX HOURS

This moderately challenging day hike affords magnificent views of the Kitzbühel Alps and Hohe Tauern range. Bring supplies and consider buying Kompass 1:35,000 map No 30 *Zell am See–Kaprun*.

At ❶ **Schmittenhöhebahn** top station, begin a gradual descent from Saalbach/Pinzgauer Spaziergang, enjoying views of Zeller See and the glaciated Hohe Tauern range. The ever-narrowing path continues up an incline and passes through tarn-studded forest, occasionally drawing your gaze to shimmering Grossglockner and the Kitzsteinhorn Glacier to the south.

The landscape soon opens up as you wend through wildflower-streaked meadows and, after roughly an hour, contour the rounded summit of ❷ **Maurerkogel**. Make a short, painless ascent to ❸ **Rohrertörl** saddle, where you can contrast the limestone Kaisergebirge to the north with the icy Hohe Tauern peaks to the south.

Passing two junctions, follow a balcony trail that contours the base of ❹ **Oberer-Gernkogel** and gently mounts ❺ **Niederer-Gernkogel**. You'll soon reach the foot of ❻ **Zirmkogel**, which, with will and expertise, can be climbed in little over an hour.

The rocky trail runs through high meadows and mottled mountains, passing a small hut near a stream. Around four hours from the trailhead, the path ascends a steepish incline to the ❼ **Klingertörl** saddle, where a sign shows the way to Saalbach. Traverse the base of cliffs that sweep down from ❽ **Hochkogel** and make a short descent to the grassy col of ❾ **Seetörl**.

Walk north from here, either climbing over the ❿ **Saalbachkogel** or skirting its western slopes. The same option is repeated for ⓫ **Stemmerkogel**. Descend the ridge and continue towards Schattberg, making a final ascent to the ⓬ **Schattberg X-press** gondola and then down to ⓭ **Saalbach**.

DON'T MISS

KITZSTEINHORN GLACIER

Winter or summer, the 3029m **Kitzsteinhorn Glacier** (www.kitzsteinhorn.at) is one of Zell am See's must-do attractions, with enough snow for skiing and boarding 10 months of the year. A cable car whizzes up to top-station **Gipfelwelt 3000**, where two viewpoint platforms command phenomenal alpine views deep into the Hohe Tauern National Park – look out for the distinctive profile of Grossglockner. From mid-May to mid-September there are free guided tours at 10.30am and 1pm. In summer you can hike the glacier trail, check out the **Ice Arena**'s deckchair-clad snow beach and slides, and buff up on local geology at the **Nationalpark Gallery**, which has some pretty impressive Hohe Tauern crystals on show. For free-riders, a 12km trail descends to the valley. A Kitzsteinhorn day ticket costs €35/17 for adults/children for those without a guest card in summer.

For the chill factor in winter, check out the **Ice Camp** with its spectacularly lit igloo bar, lounge and sundeck – perfect for cocktail sipping and listening to mellow beats after a hard day on the slopes.

Pinzgauer beef *Tafelspitz*, local trout with dill potatoes and Tyrolean mountain lamb on the menu.

Zur Einkehr AUSTRIAN €€
(☑723 63; Schmittenstrasse 12; mains €9.50-19; ⊙4pm-midnight Thu-Tue) Near the slopes, this barn-style bistro is a local favourite. Dishes such as sticky spare ribs and seafood lasagne are polished off nicely with pear schnapps at the crescent-shaped bar.

★ **Mayer's** GASTRONOMIC €€€
(☑72 91 10; www.mayers-restaurant.at; Hofmannsthalstrasse 10; tasting menus €79-185; ⊙6.30pm-midnight Wed-Sun) Andreas Mayer heads the stove at Schloss Prielau's refined restaurant, awarded Austria's restaurant of the year 2011 and holder of two Michelin stars. Freshness is key, with home-grown vegetables and organic produce shining through in French-infused specialities such as *pot au feu* of guinea fowl, and Pinzgauer camembert served with red-wine pears – all totally divine and creatively presented. If you fancy getting behind the stove yourself, see the website for details on cookery courses.

Drinking

Zell am See's nightlife gathers momentum in winter when skiers descend on the town and many restaurants and bars double as après-ski haunts.

Grand Café CAFE
(Esplanade 4; ⊙noon-6pm) You don't have to stay in the belle-époque finery of Grand Hotel Zell am See to appreciate the dreamy lake and mountain views from its tree-shaded

cafe terrace. Watch ducks and boats glide by over coffee with homemade cake and live piano music.

Seegasse CAFE
(Seegasse 10; ⊙8am-8pm Mon-Sat, 9am-8pm Sun; ☎) With a pavement terrace, this sleek cafe is a relaxed spot for proper gelato or an espresso with a slice of homemade carrot cake.

Insider BAR
(Kreuzgasse 1; ⊙4pm-late) Join the cocktail sippers for a daiquiri or Cuba libre at this upbeat, backlit lounge bar, which has occasional live music and DJ nights.

ℹ Information

Tourist office (☑770; www.zellamsee-kaprun.com; Brucker Bundesstrasse 1a; ⊙8am-6pm Mon-Fri, 9am-6pm Sat, 9am-1pm Sun) Staff at this office will help you find rooms; there's also an accommodation board in the foyer with a free 24-hour telephone.

ℹ Getting There & Away

BICYCLE
You can hire bikes to pedal around the lake at any of the sports shops in town.

BUS
Buses leave from outside the Hauptbahnhof and from the **bus station** behind the post office. They run to Kaprun (€3.20, 17 minutes, twice hourly) and Krimml (€10.20, 1½ hours, every two hours).

CAR & MOTORCYCLE
Zell am See is on the B311 running north to Lofer, where it joins the B178, which connects St Johann in Tirol with Salzburg (passing through

Germany). It's also just a few kilometres north of the east–west highway linking St Johann im Pongau with Tyrol (via the Gerlos Alpine Rd).

TRAIN
Hourly trains run from Zell am See to destinations including Salzburg (€21.50, 1½ to two hours), Kitzbühel (€12, 55 minutes) and Innsbruck (€27.70, 2½ hours).

Krimml

📞06564 / POP 840 / ELEV 1076M

A real crash-bang spectacle, the 380m-high, three-tier Krimmler Wasserfälle, Europe's highest waterfall, is the thunderous centrepiece of this tiny village. Those who look beyond the falls find even more to like about Krimml – gorgeous alpine scenery, fine mountain walks and farmstays that are great for tiptoeing back to nature for a few days.

⊙ Sights & Activities

The tourist office has details on activities for kids, from pony riding to climbing.

★Krimmler Wasserfälle WATERFALL
(Krimml Falls; www.wasserfaelle-krimml.at; adult/child €2.50/0.50; ⊗ticket office 8am-6pm mid-Apr–late Oct) Enshrouded in mist, arched by a rainbow, frozen solid – this waterfall always looks extraordinary, no matter the time of year. The **Wasserfallweg** (Waterfall Trail), which starts at the ticket office and weaves gently uphill through mixed forest, has numerous viewpoints with photogenic close-ups of the falls.

It's about a two-hour round-trip walk, or double that if you want to continue along the glacial Achental valley, which shadows a burbling brook to Hölzlahneralm. Up here, you'll have fantastic views of boulder-strewn pastures and 3000m-high peaks – you can even stay the night if you're too tired to head back down to Krimml.

Wasserwunderwelt THEME PARK
(adult/child €7.50/3.70, incl waterfall €8.50/4.20; ⊗9.30am-5pm May-Oct) A water-related theme park with loads of hands-on activities for kids, from physics experiments to art installations and outdoor games, where the aim is to get completely soaked.

Zillertal Arena SKIING
(www.zillertalarena.at; 1-/3-/6-day ski pass €46.50/129/224) Krimml is part of the Zillertal Arena, which covers 166km of pistes that are mostly geared towards intermediates. Krimml also appeals to families and non-skiers in winter, with low-key activities such as tobogganing, snowshoeing and horse-drawn sleigh rides.

Tauernradweg CYCLING
(www.tauernradweg.com) Well-marked cycling and hiking trails fan out from Krimml into the surrounding Alps. The Tauernradweg is a 310km bike route through the mind-blowing scenery of the Hohe Tauern National Park to Salzburg and then to Passau. The route covers some high-altitude stretches and demands a good level of fitness. The Krimmler Wasserfälle Wasserfallweg walking trail begins near the Tauernradweg's starting point.

🛏 Sleeping

Krimml makes an easy day trip from Zell am See or Mayrhofen in Tyrol, but it's a shame not to stay the night as the village has *Pensionen* and farmstays with bags of character. Winter prices go up by roughly a third from standard rates.

Burgeck Panorama Hotel GUESTHOUSE **€**
(📞72 49; www.burgeck.com; Oberkrimml 79; s/d/apt €54/84/85; 🅿🛜👶) Scenically perched above the village and next to forest, this guesthouse is run by the kindly Bachmaier family and has terrific waterfall views. The recently renovated rooms are modern, while others are done out in rustic alpine style. Kids are well catered for with a playground and, in winter, an illuminated toboggan track right on the doorstep.

ROAM RANGER

If you want to get out and stride in the Hohe Tauern National Park, consider signing up for one of the back-to-nature **guided tours** led by a team of well-informed rangers. From Monday to Friday from July to September, Hohe Tauern offers 30 hikes, several of which are free with a guest card. The broad spectrum covers everything from herb discovery trails to high-altitude hikes, around-the-glacier tours, gorge climbing and wildlife spotting. For the complete program and price list, visit www.nationalpark.at.

MOVING ON?

For tips, recommendations and reviews, head to shop.lonelyplanet.com to purchase a downloadable PDF of the Germany chapter from Lonely Planet's *Western Europe* guide.

Hölzlahneralm
HOSTEL €

(☑0664-402 68 78; www.hoelzlahner.at; dm €20, without breakfast €14; ⊙May-Oct) This wood-shingled farmhouse is a superb budget choice. You'll need to do the legwork – it's a two-hour hike from Krimml via the Krimmler Wasserfälle – but that makes the *Kaspressknödel* (dumpling in gooey Pinzgauer cheese) all the more welcome. The ecofriendly chalet generates its own electricity, uses natural spring water and has comfy bunks for weary walkers upstairs.

Hotel Klockerhaus
HOTEL €€

(☑72 08; www.klockerhaus.com; Oberkrimml 10; d incl half-board €106-116; P🅿🛜♨♿) Plenty of pine keeps things cosy in the rooms that have waterfall views and in the lounge with an open fire. There's a small spa with a sauna, saline steam bath and treatments such as Tibetan massage, as well as an untreated outdoor pool.

ℹ Information

The **tourist office** (☑72 39; www.krimml.at; Oberkrimml 37; ⊙8am-6pm Mon-Fri, 8.30-11.30am Sat) is in the village centre next to the church. The post office is next door.

ℹ Getting There & Away

Buses run year-round from Krimml to Zell am See (€10.20, 1½ hours, every two hours).

The village is about 500m north of the Krimmler Wasserfälle, on a side turning from the B165. There are parking spaces near the path to the falls, which branches to the right just before the toll booths for the Gerlos Alpine Road to Mayrhofen.

Bad Gastein

☑06434 / POP 4360 / ELEV 1000M

Spiritually somewhere between Brighton and St Moritz, Bad Gastein runs hot and cold, with therapeutic spas year-round and first-class skiing in winter. Though the damp is rising in places, the resort has kept some of the grandeur of its 19th-century heyday, when Empress Elisabeth came to bathe and pen poetry here. And the backdrop is timeless: belle-époque villas cling to forest-cloaked cliffs that rise above thunderous falls and springs still hailed for their miraculous healing properties.

⊙ Sights

★**Gasteiner Wasserfall**
WATERFALL

Bad Gastein's star attraction is this 341m waterfall, which rages over rugged cliff faces and through thick forest to tumble into three turquoise pools. The waterfall's wispy, ethereal beauty captured the imagination of Klimt, Max Liebermann, Schubert and Empress Elisabeth. The stone **Wasserfallbrücke** (waterfall bridge) is the best vantage point and the trailhead for the **Wasserfallweg** (waterfall path) that shadows the magnificent cataract and provides some great photo ops.

Nikolauskirche
CHURCH

(Bismarckstrasse) The late-Gothic Nikolauskirche is a little gem of a church, tiled with wood shingles and built around a central pillar. Its interior is simple yet beautiful with an uneven flagstone floor, baroque altar and rudimentary frescoes that are fading with age. Look out for the statue of the 16th-century physician Paracelsus outside.

Gasteiner Museum
MUSEUM

(www.gasteinermuseum.com; Kaiser-Franz-Josef-Strasse 14, Grand Hotel de l'Europe; adult/child €6/free; ⊙2.30-6.30pm Wed-Sun) Tap into the source of Bad Gastein at this museum, which spells out the town's history and the wonders of its thermal waters, from the bath-loving Romans to the Romantic painters inspired by its waterfall. The collection spans everything from *Krampus* (devil) costumes to vintage tourist posters and 19th-century oil paintings of Bad Gastein. English audioguides are available.

🏃 Activities

From mid-May to mid-September, the tourist office organises daily guided walks that range from half-day hikes to herb trails and dairy visits.

Ski Amadé
SKIING

(1-day ski pass adult/child €46/23.50) The Gasteinertal's slopes and spas are a match made in heaven in winter. The 220km of varied pistes challenge confident beginners and intermediates, with attractive wooded

Bad Gastein

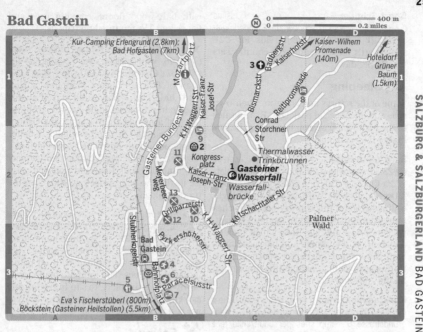

runs and some great carving opportunities. Mountain transport is not brilliant, and reaching the slopes in neighbouring resorts can be time-consuming unless you have your own wheels.

The resort is part of the expansive Ski Amadé arena, which comprises 865km of slopes, with skiing and snowboarding centred on **Stubnerkogel** (2246m) and **Graukogel** (2492m). Cross-country skiing is also big in Bad Gastein, with 90km of prepared *Loipe* (tracks) including a flood-lit trail at **Böckstein** (3km south of Bad Gastein).

Kaiser-Wilhem-Promenade   WALKING TRAIL
There's no need to exert yourself for a view in Bad Gastein. Simply follow this balcony trail along Kaiserhofstrasse for deep views into the forest-cloaked, mountain-rimmed, villa-studded Gastein Valley. It's an easy-going, 45-minute walk, with prime photo ops at the statue of **Kaiser Wilhelm**, who gave Bad Gastein's curative waters the royal seal of approval by coming here 20 times in the late 19th century.

Stubnerkogel & Graukogel   WALKING
Both Stubnerkogel and Graukogel are excellent for summertime walking, with high-altitude trails traversing alpine pastures and craggy peaks, and taking you up to authentic mountain huts. The two-section **Stubnerkogelbahn** cable car is near Bad Gastein's train station and the **Graukogel-bahn** cable car 300m northeast of the centre; both cost €22.50 return.

Sport Schober
SKIING

(☑32 68; www.sport-schober.at; Stubnerkogel-strasse 21; ☺8am-6pm) Rents skis for €21, snowboards for €25 and cross-country sets for €12 per day.

🛏 Sleeping

Some of the resort's hotels feature their own spas and offer special packages. Expect rates in the high winter season to be roughly 30% higher than standard.

Euro Youth Hotel
HOSTEL €

(☑23 30; www.euro-youth-hotel.at; Bahnhofsplatz 8; dm €16-22, s €30-55, d €50-96; ☺closed Apr & Oct-Nov; P@🛜) With its well-kept, high-ceilinged rooms, this century-old manor has more charm than your average hostel. Back-packers praise the facilities, which include a restaurant, TV lounge and barbecue area. Staff can arrange adventure sports such as rafting, canyoning, paragliding, mountain biking and snowshoeing.

Kur-Camping Erlengrund
CAMPGROUND €

(☑302 05; www.kurcamping-gastein.at; Erlen-grundstrasse 6; camp sites per adult/child/tent €7.75/4.60/8.35; P🛜🍴) Close to a natural lake, this campground has shady pitches and, in summer, a heated pool. It's an hour's walk following the waterfall north of Bad Gastein to Kötschachdorf; buses run from the train station.

Hotel Miramonte
DESIGN HOTEL €€

(☑25 77; www.hotelmiramonte.com; Reitlprom-enade 3; s €79-129, d €138-268; P🛜) This hill-top hotel impressed the likes of *Vanity Fair* with its retro-chic design and phenomenal mountain backdrop. A terrace overlooking forested peaks, a thermal spa with pamper-ing Aveda treatments and yoga classes draw a style-conscious crowd. The studio-style rooms are all about pared-down glamour,

---

ⓘ GASTEIN CARD

Pick up the free Gastein Card from your host for some great freebies, includ-ing guided hikes and bike tours, spa concerts and history walks; the tourist office has full details. The card also yields substantial discounts on cable cars, buses, spas and activities. The winter card offers similar reductions plus free use of all buses, the ice-skat-ing rink, toboggan rental and guided ski safaris.

---

with bare-wood floors, cowskin rugs and flat-screen TVs mounted on tripods.

★Hoteldorf Grüner Baum
LUXURY HOTEL €€€

(☑25 16; www.hoteldorf.com; Kötschachtal 25; s €87-137, d €174-300, f €302-402; P🛜🍴🚼) The Shah of Persia, Princess Margaret of Hol-land, Jude Law – they've all stayed at this mountain retreat set in 30-hectare grounds. More of a hamlet than a hotel, the Grüner Baum's cluster of alpine chalets shelter rooms beautifully furnished with antiques. A spa and thermal pools, an outdoor activity program, delicious food and polished serv-ice justify the hefty price tag. Kids love the resident alpacas.

Villa Solitude
HISTORIC HOTEL €€€

(☑51 01; www.villasolitude.com; Kaiser-Franz-Josef-Strasse 16; d €180-260; P🛜) Once home to an Austrian countess, this belle-époque villa shelters six suites crammed with oil paint-ings and antiques. The intimate piano room downstairs is the place to slip into your role as lord or lady of the manor. Lutter & Weg-ner restaurant is next door.

🍴 Eating

Most of Bad Gastein's eating options line up along Kaiser-Franz-Josef-Strasse. Many places close or have shorter opening hours in the shoulder seasons.

Silver Bullet Bar
INTERNATIONAL €

(☑22 53 60; www.silverbulletbar.com; Grill-parzerstrasse 1; mains €7.50-10; ☺3.30pm-2am daily winter, 3-11pm Thu-Tue summer) Wagon wheels, a stuffed buffalo head and cow-print benches give this barn-style restaurant and bar a mock Wild West look. Finger-lickin' snacks like 100% Austrian beefburgers are accompanied by a party vibe and regular live music. In summer families gravitate here for the sunny terrace and activities such as a climbing wall, minigolf and boules.

Revolution
SNACK BAR €

(Grillparzerstrasse 14; snacks €3-5.50; ☺4pm-midnight Tue-Sat; 🛜) Crimson walls and cush-ion-filled nooks create a warm, relaxed set-ting for drinks or a bite to eat at Revolution. The day's snacks, such as tortilla wraps, are scrawled on a blackboard.

★Lutter & Wegner
AUSTRIAN €€

(☑51 01; Kaiser-Franz-Josef-Strasse 16; mains €14-25, 4-course menu €38; ☺6-9.30pm) Big on atmosphere, this smart restaurant at Villa Solitude has a fairy-tale tower setting,

DON'T MISS

TAKING THE WATERS

Bad Gastein is famous for its radon-laced waters, which trickle down from the mountains, heat up to temperatures of 44°C to 47°C around 2000m underground, then gush forth at 18 different springs in the area. Renowned since Roman times for their healing properties and described by 16th-century physician Paracelsus as 'God's own composita', the therapeutic waters are said to boost potency, alleviate rheumatism and respiratory ailments, stop inflammation, stimulate circulation and (phew!) stabilise the immune system. Strauss and Empress Elisabeth (Sisi) both put the waters' benefits to the test; the empress was so impressed that she penned a poem in 1886 beginning: 'Only sick bones I thought of bringing, where mystically your hot water springs...'

The product of 3000 years of geological forces, the radon is absorbed through the skin and retained in the body for nearly three hours. Vapour tunnels burrowed deep in the rock and emitting radon gases are used for more intensive treatments.

A glass elevator zooms up to **Felsentherme Gastein** (222 30; Bahnhofplatz 5; 3hr/day ticket adult €20.50/24, child €11.50/15; 9am-9pm), where you can splash around in the rejuvenating waters. The spa shelters grottolike pools and an outdoor thermal bath that has pummelling massage jets and stellar mountain views. For those prepared to bare all, there are panoramic saunas and salty steam baths to test out. Treatments such as radon baths (€20), fango mud packs (€18) and electrotherapy (€23.50) are available next door in the **Thermalkurhaus** (www.thermalgastein.com; Bahnhofplatz 7; 8am-noon & 2-5pm Mon-Fri, 8am-noon Sat).

To feel the water's benefits without tapping into your euros, fill your bottle at one of the town's **Thermalwasser Trinkbrunnen** (thermal water drinking fountains), such as those on Kongressplatz and Mozartplatz. Two to six cups per day are recommended for glowing health.

award-winning fusion cuisine and a terrace with knockout views over the Gasteinertal and the falls. Fine wines (choose from 150 bottles) are expertly matched with flavours such as pike perch in wild garlic and rabbit served two ways with kohlrabi.

Jägerhäusl
AUSTRIAN €€

(202 54; www.gastro-gastein.at; Kaiser-Franz-Josef-Strasse 9; mains €7-18.50; 10am-11pm) Besides wood-fired pizza, the menu is packed with Austrian faves such as schnitzel and venison goulash with dumplings at this galleried villa. Pull up a chair on the maple-tree-shaded terrace when the sun's out. There's often live Tyrolean music on summer evenings (see the website for details).

Eva's Fischerstüberl
AUSTRIAN €€

(45 05; www.evas-fischerstueberl.at; Schareck-strasse 17; €12-18; 11.30am-2pm & 5.30-9pm Wed-Mon;) Trout fresh from the stream outside is the big deal at this quaint chalet restaurant, with a terrace for warm-day dining. You might begin with creamy pumpkin soup and move on to, say, grilled trout served with parsley-butter potatoes. There's a dedicated menu for kids. Eva's Fischerstüberl is 1km south of the train station.

Hofkeller
AUSTRIAN €€

(203 70; Grillparzerstrasse 1; mains €19-27; 7-10pm Mon-Sat;) In winter, there's no place like this stone cellar beneath the Salzburger Hof hotel for warming up over fondue, a raclette cheese fest or hot stone specialities. Kids menus are available.

ℹ Information

Post office (Bahnhofplatz 9; 8am-noon & 2-5.30pm Mon-Fri) Next to the train station.

Tourist office (3393 560; www.gastein. com; Kaiser-Franz-Josef-Strasse 27; 8am-6pm Mon-Fri) To get here, go left from the train station exit and walk down the hill. Staff will find you accommodation free of charge. There's information on the national park in the foyer.

ℹ Getting There & Away

CAR & MOTORCYCLE

Driving south, you'll need to use the Autoschleuse Tauernbahn (railway car-shuttle service) through the tunnel that starts at Böckstein (one way/return €17/30). On the A10 Tauern-Autobahn from the north (Salzburg), take the Gasteinertal exit near Bischofshofen, then the B167.

TRAIN

Trains trundle through Bad Gastein's station every two hours, connecting the town to points north and south including Spittal-Millstättersee (€11.80, 40 minutes), Salzburg (€19.20, 1½ hours) and Innsbruck (€37, 3½ hours). When travelling north from Bad Gastein to Bad Hofgastein, sit on the right side of the train for the best views.

Around Bad Gastein

Stepping 3.5km south of Bad Gastein, you reach the unassuming village of **Böckstein**, whose medieval gold mine has been re-invented as a much-celebrated health centre, the **Gasteiner Heilstollen** (Gastein Healing Gallery; ☑ 6434-375 30; www.gasteiner-heilstollen.com; Heilstollenstrasse 19; ⊙ mid-Jan–late Oct). Visitors board a small train at the Gasteiner Heilstollen that chugs 2km into the depths of Radhausberg mountain, where you absorb the healing radon vapours. The trial session costs €29.90, while the full three-week cure will set you back €591 (includes 10 entries to the tunnel).

Seven kilometres north of Bad Gastein is the sibling spa town of **Bad Hofgastein** (858m), home to the architecturally innovative **Alpen Therme** (☑06432-829 30; www.alpentherme.com; Senator-Wilhelm-Wilfling-Platz 1; 4hr ticket adult/child €23.50/14.50; ⊙9am-9pm Sun-Wed, 9am-10pm Thu-Sat) This mammoth spa is split into four different 'worlds', where experiences stretch from relaxing in radon-rich thermal baths to racing down white-knuckle flumes. The sauna village comprises brine grottoes, loft saunas, red-hot Finnish saunas and an ice-cold plunge pool. For some pampering, pop over to the beauty centre for treatments such as goat's-milk wraps and hot-chocolate massages.

Bad Gastein, Bad Hofgastein and Böckstein are linked by both bus and rail. The scenic 7km Gastein Alpine Road (per person €5; price included in the Ski Amadé ski pass) links Böckstein to Sportgastein via tunnels and galleries.

Carinthia

Best Places to Stay

➡ Arcotel Moser Verdino (p265)

➡ Hotel Palais Porcia (p265)

➡ Hotel Mosser (p269)

Best Places to Eat

➡ Restaurant Maria Loretto (p266)

➡ Princs (p266)

➡ Dolce Vita (p266)

Why Go?

Few regions in Europe match the rugged beauty of Carinthia, and you'll find that travelling through it is often a serpentine journey in valleys and natural conduits. Carinthia can also, at times, seem larger than life with its spectacularly high peaks; its gouged valleys and glistening lakes; the flamboyant show of opulence in the capital, Klagenfurt; and the resorts around the more famous of the region's 1270 pristine mountain lakes. The most popular of these lakes, such as the large Wörthersee, have waters warmed to a comfortable swimming temperature by thermal springs.

Carinthia's deep medieval heritage is another attraction – celebrated in picturesque walled villages such as Friesach and Gmünd, and impressive castles such as the hilltop fortress of Hochosterwitz. Many of the towns and villages nestled in Carinthia's rolling hills hold an annual summer festival, with roving performers coming from neighbouring Italy and Slovenia to take part alongside the locals.

When to Go

➡ Midsummer is the time to make the most of Carinthia's lakes and excellent mountain hiking. Because it gets more sunshine than elsewhere in Austria, lake temperatures are warmer.

➡ In winter the province morphs into one of Austria's best ski regions, despite having a shorter ski season than elsewhere due to the warmer temps.

➡ The shoulder-season periods are less interesting here except for valley hiking or cycling. Despite a couple of gems, the museum landscape is fairly limited in Carinthia – the activities seasons are therefore the best time to visit.

Carinthia Highlights

1 Cycling and hiking the forest trails above the **Weissensee** (p280).

2 Visiting the Eboard Museum in **Klagenfurt** (p263) and playing vintage predigital keyboards – 1300 in all, the largest collection in Europe.

3 Swimming the shores of the **Wörthersee** (p268) and enjoying a lakeside meal at Restaurant Maria Loretto.

4 Stopping in **Villach** (p268) for skiing in winter, splashy fun in summer in the lakes, or hiking in the mountains.

5 Transporting yourself to the tranquil ambience of Tibet at the Heinrich Harrer Museum in **Hüttenberg** (p274).

6 Admiring the views from the top of **Burg Hochosterwitz** (p274), a spectacular medieval castle.

7 Winter skiing near **Hermagor** (p272) at the top of the 6km-long Millennium-Express cable car.

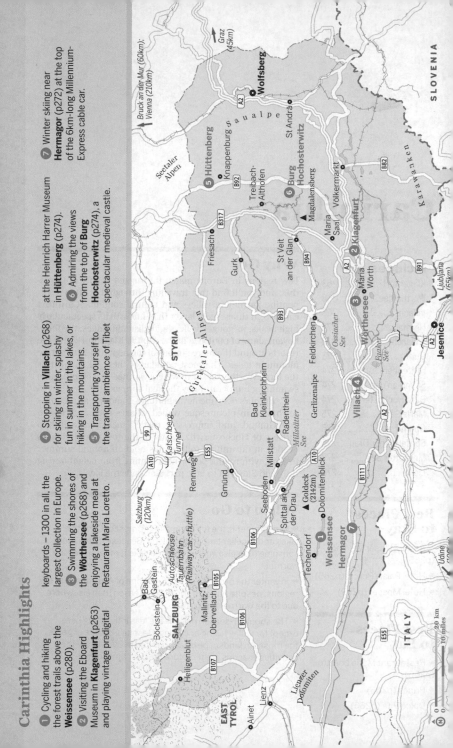

❶ Getting There & Around

Klagenfurt airport has cheap connections with the UK (Ryanair; www.ryanair.com) and Germany (Air Berlin; www.airberlin.com). Klagenfurt and Villach are the main hubs for trains from elsewhere in Europe.

Carinthia is divided into regional zones for public transport, with either single tickets or passes that are valid for one day or longer. Ask what's cheapest when buying a ticket, or contact **Kärntner Linien** (☎ 0463-546 1821; www.kaerntner-linien.at) in Klagenfurt. Many of the lakes are served by boat services in summer.

The **Kärnten Card** (www.kaerntencard.at; 1-/2-week card €36/44) gives free or cheaper access to the province's major sights plus 50% discount on buses and trains. It's sold at hotels and tourist offices from mid-April to late October.

KLAGENFURT

☎ 0463 / POP 94,800

Klagenfurt is not an urban centre that's comparable with Graz or Vienna; it walks a very fine line between being Austria's boondocks capital and a playground for a partying set. It's an enjoyable, sunny city, however, that offers easy access to lakeside villages on and around the beautiful Wörthersee. At the town's western limit is the wide green space of Europapark, home to a couple of children's attractions including the bizarre world-in-miniature of Minimundus.

◉ Sights & Activities

◉ Central Klagenfurt

Landesmuseum Rudolfinum   MUSEUM
(Map p264; www.landesmuseum-ktn.at; Museumgasse 2) Carinthia's flagship museum has lots of exhibitions on natural and cultural history. It was closed for restoration in 2013 and is expected to reopen again by 2016.

★ Eboard Museum   MUSEUM
(☎ 0699-1914 41 80; www.eboardmuseum.com; Florian Gröger Strasse 20; adult/family €10/20; ⊙ 2-7pm Sun-Fri, call ahead Sat) With the largest collection of keyboard instruments in Europe (more than 1300), this quirky museum is literally a 'fingers-on' museum: you are able play most of the organs, including rare items such as a Model A Hammond from 1934 and many more. Live bands perform on Friday nights (except July and August) at 8pm (€10).

❶ WALKS

Pick up the excellent free walking brochure (in English) from the Klagenfurt tourist office. Free guided tours depart from the office at 10am each Friday and Saturday in July and August.

Stadtgalerie   GALLERY
(Map p264; www.stadtgalerie.net; Theatergasse 4; adult/child €5/2.50; ⊙ 10am-6pm Tue-Sun) Some excellent rotating art exhibitions are held at this gallery, which has a main venue on Theaterstrasse and a second nearby in the **Alpen-Adria-Galerie Im Stadthaus** (Map p264; Theaterplatz 3; ⊙ 10am-6pm Tue-Sun).

Dragon Fountain   MONUMENT
(Map p264) Neuer Platz, Klagenfurt's central square, is dominated by the 16th-century Dragon Fountain, the emblem of the city. The blank-eyed, wriggling statue is modelled on the *Lindwurm* (dragon) of legend, which is said to have resided in a swamp here long ago, devouring cattle and virgins.

Landhaus   PARLIAMENT
(Map p264; www.landesmuseum.ktn.gv.at; Landhaushof 1; adult/child €3/2; ⊙ 9am-4pm Tue-Fri, to 2pm Sat, closed Nov-Mar) The Renaissance *Landhaus* (state parliament) building dates from the late 16th century and is still the centre of political power today. The stairs on the right (facing the portico) lead up the **Grosser Wappensaal** (Heraldic Hall), with its magnificent *trompe l'œil* gallery painted by Carinthian artist Josef Ferdinand Fromiller (1693–1760).

Stadthauptpfarrkirche St Egyd   CHURCH
(Map p264; http://st-egid-klagenfurt.at; Pfarrplatz; church free, tower adult/child €1/0.50; ⊙ tower 10am-5.30pm Mon-Fri, to 11.30pm Sat Easter–mid-Sep) Climb the 225 steps of this church's 45m-high tower for a bird's-eye view of town and the surrounding mountains.

Dom   CATHEDRAL
(Map p264; Domplatz 1; ⊙ dawn-dusk) Klagenfurt's cathedral is a monolith with an ornate marble pulpit and a sugary pink-and-white stuccoed ceiling. Its highlight is an altar painting by Paul Troger in one of the chapels.

MMKK   GALLERY
(Museum für Moderne Kunst Kärnten; Map p264; www.mmkk.at; Burggasse 8; adult/child €5/free;

Klagenfurt

CARINTHIA KLAGENFURT

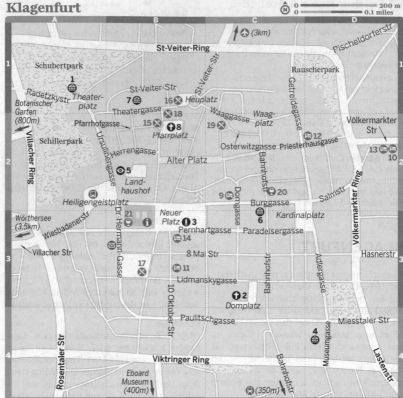

Klagenfurt

◎ Sights
1	Alpen-Adria-Galerie im Stadthaus	A1
2	Dom	C3
3	Dragon Fountain	B3
4	Landesmuseum Rudolfinum	D4
5	Landhaus	B2
6	MMKK	C3
7	Stadtgalerie	B1
8	Stadthauptpfarrkirche St Egyd	B2

◎ Sleeping
9	Arcotel Moser Verdino	C2
10	Cityhotel Ratheiser	D2
11	Hotel Garni Blumenstöckl	B3
12	Hotel Geyer	D2
13	Hotel Liebetegger	D2
14	Hotel Palais Porcia	B3

◎ Eating
15	Bierhaus zum Augustin	B2
16	Dolce Vita	B1
17	Fruit & Vegetable Market	B3
18	Princs	B2
19	Zauberhutt'n	C2

◎ Drinking & Nightlife
20	Kamot	C2
21	The Claddagh	B3

◎ 10am-6pm Tue, Wed & Fri-Sun, to 8pm Thu, closed Mon) This gallery for modern and contemporary art stages three or four excellent temporary exhibitions each year based on its collection of Carinthian and mostly national artists, including the likes of Arnulf Rainer and Hans Staudacher.

Botanischer Garten   GARDEN
(◎ 9am-6pm daily May-Sep, to 4pm Mon-Thu Oct-Apr) **FREE** The small botanical garden is especially popular for its evocative landscape of small cliffs with alpine plants, and for another section with a waterfall and ponds. Adjoining it is the **Kreuzberglkirche**,

perched on a hillock with some pretty mosaics of the Stations of the Cross on the path leading up to it. Take bus 60 or 61 from Heiligengeistplatz to Kreuzbergl.

👁 Europapark

Minimundus   AMUSEMENT PARK
(Map p266; www.minimundus.at; Villacher Strasse 241; adult/child €13/8; ⊙9am-7pm Mar-Oct; 🅖) Down near the Wörthersee, Minimundus has around 140 replicas of some of the world's architectural icons, downsized to a scale of 1:25. By lying on the ground with a camera, you can later impress your friends at parties with great snaps of the Taj Mahal, Eiffel Tower or Arc de Triomphe. Guides in English (€4) are sold.

Happ's Reptilienzoo   ZOO
(Map p266; 🕿234 25; www.reptilienzoo.at; Villacher Strasse 237; adult/child €13/8; ⊙8am-5pm winter, to 6pm summer, closed Nov; 🅖) Crocodiles plus all manner of creepers, crawlers and slitherers are here for kids and adults to admire. Some signs are in English.

★Strandbad   SWIMMING
(Map p266; www.stw.at; Metnitzstrand 2; day card adult/child €4.10/1.70, 1hr before closing €1.50/ free, paddle or electric boat per 30min €3.50-8.50; ⊙8am-8pm Jun-Aug, to 7pm May & Sep, closed late Sep–early May; 🅖) Klagenfurt's wonderful lakeside beach has cabins, restaurants and piers for basking like a seal. *Kästchen* (lockers large enough for day packs) in the *Strandbad* cost €2 plus €20 deposit. There's also good swimming outside the buoys further south, past the Maria Loretto beach. You can indulge in paddle or electric boat escapades alongside the *Strandbad*.

✿✶ Festivals & Events

Klagenfurter Stadtfest   MUSIC, THEATRE
(www.altstadtzauber.at; ⊙Aug) Annual two-day music and theatre festival.

Wörthersee Festspiele   ARTS
(www.klagenfurt-tourismus.at; tickets €40-80; ⊙late Jun–mid-Aug) Every summer, operas, ballets and pop concerts take place on an offshore stage on the Wörthersee.

🛏 Sleeping

Camping Klagenfurt am
Wörthersee   CAMPGROUND €
(Map p266; 🕿287 810; www.camping-woerthersee. at; Metnitzstrand 5; camp site per adult/child/tent

€6.90/6.80/9.90; ⊙May-Sep; 🅿🛜🏊🅖) This attractive, shady camping ground offers free use of the *Strandbad* and has bike rental.

Jugendgästehaus Klagenfurt   HOSTEL €
(Map p266; 🕿23 00 20; www.oejhv.or.at; Neckheimgasse 6; dm/s/d €20.50/28.50/49; 🅿@🛜) The modern HI hostel is near Europapark. To get here from the centre, take bus 81 from the train station or 10 from Heiligengeistplatz and get off at Jugendgästehaus or (depending on the bus route) Neckheimgasse.

Hotel Garni Blumenstöckl   HOTEL €
(Map p264; 🕿577 93; www.blumenstoeckl.at; 10 Oktober Strasse 11; s €47.20, d €76.30) Rooms are arranged around a plant-filled courtyard in this two-star, family-run place in a 400-year-old building. The traditionally furnished rooms aren't terribly grand, but the hotel's location and very friendly owners make up for this.

★Arcotel Moser Verdino   HOTEL €€
(Map p264; 🕿578 78; www.arcotel.at/moserverdino; Domgasse 2; s €80-144, d €91-155, apt €149-192, breakfast €13; @🛜🅖) Prices in this excellent four-star hotel vary by demand, making it always worth a phone call, even if your budget is tight. What you get are high-quality modern rooms with flair, very helpful staff, and a free stay for kids under 16 in many rooms.

★Hotel Palais Porcia   HOTEL €€
(Map p264; 🕿51 15 90-0; www.palais-porcia.at; Neuer Platz 13; s €84-182, d €113-197, ste €197-349; 🅿❄@🛜) This marvellously ornate and old-fashioned hotel has gilt, mirrors and red-velvet couches, with pink marble and gold taps in the bathrooms. It also has a private beach that guests can use near its other hotel in Pörtschach.

Hotel Liebetegger   HOTEL €€
(Map p264; 🕿569 35; www.liebetegger.com; Völkermarkter Strasse 8; s €47.50-77.50, d €75-115, tr €112.50-145; 🅿🛜) Rooms are bland in this clean hotel, but this is offset by its prices, hospitable management and the free use of good bikes. It sometimes gets large tour groups.

Cityhotel Ratheiser   HOTEL €€
(Map p264; 🕿512 994; www.cityhotel-ratheiser.at; Völkermarkter Strasse 10; s €58-65, d €75-85, ste €95-130; 🅿) This quirky hotel has two extraordinary suites (8 and 10) with upstairs and downstairs sections joined by a spiral staircase. This hotel is not bright and modern, but it is central, comfortable and has a free sauna.

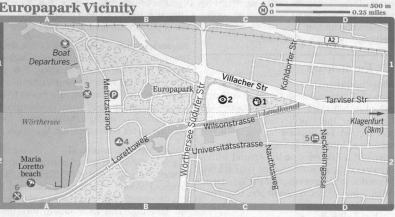

Europapark Vicinity

Hotel Geyer   HOTEL €€
(Map p264; ☑578 86; www.hotelgeyer.com; Priesterhausgasse 5; s €70-88, d €102-135, q €155-170; P🕲) Expect modern and comfortable rooms in this three-star hotel, complemented by a bright and tasteful breakfast room. Bonuses are the sauna and steam bath, and free use of the fitness centre around the corner.

✗ Eating & Drinking

A **fruit and vegetable market** (Map p264) as well as a flower market come to life on Benediktinerplatz on Thursday and Saturday mornings.

★ Restaurant Maria Loretto   AUSTRIAN €€
(Map p266; ☑24 465; Lorettoweg 54; mains €15.80-25.80; ☺lunch & dinner, closed mid-Jan–Feb) Situated on a headland above Wörthersee, this wonderful restaurant is easily reached by foot from the *Strandbad*. It does very good trout and some flavoursome meat dishes, but it's the sheer character of the place that makes it a wonderful choice for food and casual drinks.

★ Princs   INTERNATIONAL €€
(Map p264; ☑0676-470 06 76; www.princs.com; Heuplatz 1; mains €12.80-24.80; ☺7am-midnight Mon-Wed, 7am-2am Thu-Sat) The kitchen of this restaurant and bar serves pasta, pizza and international dishes that are so good that during peak periods you might need to reserve ahead. The bar is also one of Klagenfurt's liveliest and some nights has a DJ spinning sounds from the corner.

Zauberhutt'n   ITALIAN, AUSTRIAN €€
(Map p264; Osterwitzgasse 6; mains €10.70-15.30; ☺lunch & dinner Mon-Fri) The fried squid in a light garlic oil is a delight, and pasta, pizza and classic meat dishes all feature on the menu of this inexpensive, family-run restaurant. It's also the headquarters of the Magic Club of Klagenfurt (with a very unexpected visiting card).

Bierhaus zum Augustin   BISTRO PUB €€
(Map p264; Pfarrhofgasse 2; mains €8.90-22.60; ☺11am-midnight Mon-Sat) *Beisl* (bistro pub) Bierhaus zum Augustin is one of Klagenfurt's liveliest haunts for imbibers, thanks especially to its traditional pub atmosphere. There's a cobbled courtyard at the back for alfresco eating.

★ Dolce Vita   ITALIAN €€€
(Map p264; ☑554 99; Heuplatz 2; lunch menu €11-28, dinner mains €21-28, 5-9 course menu €69-99; ☺Lunch & Dinner Mon-Fri) In a region strongly

influenced by northern Italian cuisine, this restaurant is something of a local flagship. Inexpensive it is not, but it builds a seasonal menu mostly around fresh local produce and game, while in summer also offering a lunchtime Venetian *Sarde in saor* (sardines in a marinade). Expect to pay about €14 for a pasta entrée.

The Claddagh
PUB

(Map p264; www.claddagh.at; Pernhartgasse 4; ☺5pm-2am) This Irish pub is co-managed by a dyed-in-the-wool Irishman and is the scene of some of Klagenfurt's most convivial drinking. It has a great selection of Irish beers and live music many nights.

Kamot
JAZZ BAR

(Map p264; www.kamot.at; Bahnhofstrasse 9; ☺8pm-2am) This jazz joint has a warm pub atmosphere. It hosts some of the top national jazz names on the pub circuit, and it's a nice place for a drink anytime.

ⓘ Information

Café-bar G@tes (Waagplatz 7; internet per 10min €1; ☺9am-1am Mon-Fri, 7pm-1am Sat & Sun; ☎) Wi-fi and internet are free if you buy a drink.

Main post office (Map p264; Dr-Herrmann-Gasse 4; ☺7am-6pm Mon-Fri, 8am-noon Sat)

Tourist office (Map p264; ☎53 722 23; www.info.klagenfurt.at; Neuer Platz 1, Rathaus; ☺8am-6pm Mon-Fri, 10am-5pm Sat, 10am-3pm Sun) Sells Kärnten Cards (p263) and books accommodation.

ⓘ Getting There & Away

AIR

Klagenfurt's **airport** (☎41 500; www.klagenfurt-airport.com; Flughafenstrasse 60-66) is 3km north of town. Ryanair connects Klagenfurt with London Stansted; germanwings flies to Cologne-Bonn in Germany.

BOAT

The **departure point** (Map p266) for boat cruises on the lake is a few hundred metres north of the *Strandbad*.

BUS

Postbus services depart outside the Hauptbahnhof, where there's an **information office** (☎543 40; ☺7.15am-3.15pm Mon-Fri) with a timetable board outside. Direct two-hourly Österreiche Bundesbahn (Austrian Federal Railways; ÖBB) buses connect Klagenfurt with Graz (€25.30, two hours). At least four daily buses run via Villach to Venice (Italy; €25, 4¼ hours).

CAR & MOTORCYCLE

The A2/E66 between Villach and Graz skirts the north of Klagenfurt. **Avis** (☎559 38; www.avis.at; Klagenfurt Airport; ☺7am-10pm) and **Megadrive** (Denzeldrive; ☎050105 4140; www.megadrive.at; Klagenfurt Airport; ☺7.30am-6pm Mon-Fri, to noon Sat) are among the car-rental companies at the airport.

TRAIN

Two-hourly direct IC/EC (InterCity/EuroCity) trains run from Klagenfurt to Vienna (€50, 3¾ hours) and Salzburg (€38.70, three hours). Trains to Graz depart every two to three hours (€38.70, 2¾ hours), with a change at Leoben or Bruck an der Mur. Trains to western Austria, Italy, Slovenia and Germany go via Villach (€7.80, 25 to 40 minutes, two to four per hour).

ⓘ Getting Around

TO/FROM THE AIRPORT

Klagenfurt airport is a 10-minute walk from the train station Klagenfurt Annabichl, which is served by IC and S-Bahn trains (€2.20, five minutes). Better is bus 40 or 42 from Hauptbahnhof to the airport, which runs every 30 minutes to one hour (every two hours Sunday; €2, 30 minutes). A taxi costs about €12 from the centre of town.

BICYCLE

In summer the tourist office cooperates with a bicycle rental company. **Bicycles** (per 24hr €11-19) can also be picked up and dropped off at various points around the lake. The tourist office has a brochure with the points.

BUS

Single bus tickets (which you buy from the driver) cost €1.20 for two or three stops or €2 for one hour. Drivers also sell 24-hour passes

---

ⓘ REACHING EUROPAPARK

The large, green expanse of Europapark and the *Strandbad* (beach) on the shores of the Wörthersee are centres for splashy fun, and especially good for kids. Boating and swimming are usually possible from May to September. To get there, take bus 10 from Heiligengeistplatz via Minimundus to Strandbad. To get to the Wörthersee by bicycle, avoid Villacher Strasse and take the bicycle path running along the northern side of Lendl Canal. You can access it from the small streets running west from the junction of Villacher Ring and Villacher Strasse.

for €4.40. You can also buy tickets at the **STW Verkehrsbetriebe office** (⏹521 542; Heiligengeistplatz 4; ⏲6.30am-2.30pm Mon-Fri) near the city bus station. Validate your advance tickets after boarding.

TAXI

Call ⏹311 11, ⏹23 222 or ⏹499 799. A taxi between the Wörthersee and the city costs about €10.

CENTRAL CARINTHIA

Wörthersee

The Wörthersee stretches from west to east between Velden and Klagenfurt and can be easily explored by bicycle on a 50km circuit. The southern shore is the most picturesque, but the northern shore has the best public-transport access and is the busiest section.

A trip around the lake takes you past the exclusive resort of Pörtschach, the night-life hub of Velden and the small town of Maria Wörth. Five kilometres south of Velden is Rosegg, with its **Tierpark** (Animal Park; ⏹04274-523 57; www.rosegg.at; adult/child €8.50/5.50; ⏲9am-6pm mid-Apr–Oct) and a **Schloss** (⏹04274-30 09; www.rosegg.at; adult/child €7/4.50; ⏲10am-6pm daily May-Sep, closed Mon Oct-Apr), and 8km southwest of Maria Wörth is the **Pyramidenkogel** (⏹04273-2443; www.pyramidenkogel.info; Linden 62, Keutschach am See; adult/child/family €10/5.50/24; ⏲10am-6pm), a hill topped by a new 71m tower made of steel with wooden beams spiralling up its exterior. This vertiginous tower has three viewing platforms, two of which are open and the lowest, the Sky Box, glass encased. Those with strong legs can climb the 400-odd steps; others can take the glass panorama lift. The relatively easy St Anna-Weg trail (90 minutes one way) leads here through forest from Maria Wörth.

Tourist offices in **Pörtschach** (⏹04272-23 54; www.poertschach.at; Hauptstrasse 153; ⏲8am-6pm Mon-Fri, 10am-1pm & 4-6pm Sat & Sun, closed Sat & Sun Oct-Apr), **Velden** (⏹21 03-0; www.velden.at; Villacher Strasse 19; ⏲8am-6pm Mon-Sat, 9am-5pm Sun, closed Sun late Oct–mid-Apr) and **Maria Wörth** (⏹04273-22400; www.maria-woerth.at; Seepromenade 5; ⏲8am-5pm Mon-Fri, 10am-12.30pm & 1-3.30pm Sat & Sun) can help with accommodation, or book through the website, www.woerthersee.com.

Villach

⏹04242 / POP 59,600

Although there are more picturesque cities in the region, and the town itself has little in the way of sights, Villach is a very lively and liveable city. Consider using it as a base for activities and for exploring the region.

◉ Sights

Pick up a copy of the tourist office's free walking booklet in English with descriptions of buildings and sights.

Stadtpfarrkirche St Jakob   CHURCH
(Oberer Kirchenplatz 8; ⏲dawn-dusk) The Stadtpfarrkirche St Jakob dominates the old town and has frescoes, a stuccoed ceiling and a vast rococo altar in gold leaf, arrayed with fresh flowers. The walls are studded with the ornate memorial plaques of the region's noble families. Each summer a pair of falcons nests in the **tower** (adult/child & student €2/1; ⏲10am-6pm Jul & Aug, to 4.30pm May, Jun, Sep & Oct, closed Nov-Apr).

Relief Von Kärnten   MUSEUM
(Peraustrasse; ⏲10am-6pm Mon-Sat, closed Nov-Apr) Relief Von Kärnten is a huge relief model of Carinthia housed in Schillerpark, south of the old town. It covers 182 sq metres and depicts the province at a scale of 1:10,000 (1:5000 vertically, to exaggerate the mountains).

Villacher Fahrzeugmuseum   MUSEUM
(www.oldtimermuseum.at; Ferdinand-Wedenig-Strasse 9; adult/child €7/5; ⏲10am-6pm) Located 3km outside town, the Villach Automobile Museum focuses on icons of everyday motoring such as the Fiat Topolino, BMW Isetta and about 250 others. Take bus 5179 from the train station to Zauchen (Bundestrasse stop).

Museum der Stadt Villach   MUSEUM
(Widmanngasse 38; adult/child €5/free; ⏲10am-4.30pm Mon-Sat) This museum covers local history, archaeology and medieval art but also has occasionally interesting special exhibitions.

✦ Festivals & Events

On the first Saturday in August, the pedestrian centre is taken over by the **Kirchtag** (⏹205 66 00; www.villacherkirchtag.at), a folk-music festival featuring national and local musicians. Many events begin during the preceding week, culminating on the Saturday.

Central Carinthia

🛏 Sleeping

Jugendherberge
HOSTEL €

(☎563 68; www.oejhv.or.at; Dinzlweg 34; dm/s/d €21/28/50; P@♿) Located 1km west of the centre, off Sankt-Martiner-Weg. Sauna facilities and a children's playground are on-site.

★ Hotel Mosser
HOTEL €€

(☎241 15; www.hotelmosser.at; Bahnhofstrasse 9; s €62-98, d €99-198, ste €195-250, apt €145-220; P@♞) Some rooms in this friendly and efficient historic hotel have angled mirrors above the headboards, others have whirlpools for romantic interludes, whereas cheaper singles are functional and unremarkable.

★ Holiday Inn
HOTEL €€

(☎225 220; www.hi-villach.at; Europaplatz 1-2; s €114-139, d €154-179, ste €265-510; P♞) All rooms in this chain hotel have partial stone tiling, are strong on burgundy tones, and have a nifty toilet and shower section with a smart use of doors to create privacy; the best have views to the Drau River. Prices vary according to demand.

Romantik Hotel Post
HOTEL €€

(☎261 01-0; www.hotel-villach.com; Hauptplatz 26; s €85-150, d €100-180, tr €134-199, ste €205-270; P@♞♿) The corridors of this smart hotel offer a foretaste of its charms, which include chandeliers and oriental rugs. The wooden furnishings have a light and breezy feel, and the lift and some of the doubles connected by doors make it ideal for families.

Kramer Hotel-Gasthof
HOTEL €€

(☎249 53; www.hotelgasthofkramer.at; Italiener Strasse 14; s €49-69, d €94-106, tr €130; P@♞♿) You'll find very good value among contemporary furnishings at this hotel just up the road from the Stadtpfarrkirche. Rooms are spacious and priced by size and demand.

🍴 Eating & Drinking

★ Stern
INTERNATIONAL, STEAK €€

(☎247 55; www.stern-villach.com; Kaiser Josef Platz 5; mains €7.90-23.90, steaks €18.30-22.30, lunch menu €4.90-6.90; ⊗7am-midnight Mon-Thu, 7am-2am Fri, 9am-2am Sat; ♞) This lounge-restaurant is a perfect place to hang out over a drink, inside or outdoors on the square. Its speciality is steak, which you get by filling out a menu sheet.

★ Trastavere
ITALIAN €€

(☎21 56 65; www.trastavere.at; Widmanngasse 30; pasta €8.90-12.80, pizza €7.80-11.80, mains €12.80-26; ⊗11am-midnight Mon-Sat) Book ahead for a courtyard table on weekend summer evenings in this trattoria situated in a lovely courtyard. It has a broad range of seafood dishes, excellent pizzas and a selection of Argentinian steaks.

Romantik Restaurant Post
AUSTRIAN €€

(www.stadtrestaurant.at; Hauptplatz 26; mains €14.50-23.50; ⊗lunch & dinner; ♫) The restaurant of the Romantik Hotel Post serves well-prepared regional specialities in a cosy and intimate atmosphere. The midday meat or veg *Menü* (set menu) is good value and there's also a healthy selection of salads.

Villach

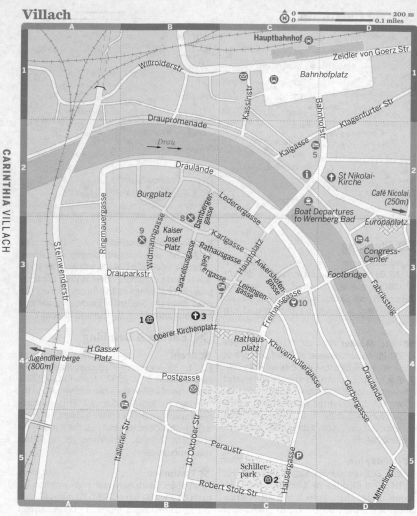

Soho   BAR
(Freihausgasse 13; ⊙9pm-2am Wed-Sat) On a good night, this is one of Villach's best bars, with a DJ and relaxed crowd.

ℹ Information

Café Nicolai (☑22 511; Nikolaigasse 16; per 10min €1.50; ⊙7am-9.30pm Mon-Fri, to noon Sat) has fast internet access, or try **Bouhia Internet Callshop** (☑22 511; Bahnhofplatz; per hr €2; ⊙9am-9pm), a cheaper call shop.

Tourismusinformation Villach-Stadt (☑20 5-2900; www.villach.at; Bahnhofstrasse 3; ⊙9am-7pm Mon-Fri, 10am-4pm Sat) is the city tourist office. It helps with accommodation, has a free city map and excellent free city environs map, as well as a free internet terminal.

ℹ Getting There & Around

BICYCLE

Das Radl (☑0664-226 9540, 269 54; www.das-radl.at; Italiener Strasse 25; per day city bike or mountain bike €11; ⊙8am-6pm Mon-Fri, 9am-noon Sat, bike hire closed Oct-Apr) rents bikes in Villach. It also rents from Bodensdorf and Faak train stations on the Ossiacher and Faaker Sees respectively.

Villach

◎ **Sights**
1 Museum der Stadt Villach B4
2 Relief Von Kärnten...............................C5
3 Stadtpfarrkirche St Jakob B4

⊜ **Sleeping**
4 Holiday Inn..D3
5 Hotel Mosser C2
6 Kramer Hotel-Gasthof.......................B4
7 Romantik Hotel Post C3

⊗ **Eating**
Romantik Restaurant Post .... (see 7)
8 Stern..B3
9 Trastavere..B3

⊜ **Drinking & Nightlife**
10 Soho..C3

BUS

Call ☎ 44410-1510 or ☎ 0810 222 33 39 for Postbus information. The **bus station** is opposite the Hauptbahnhof. At least four InterCity (IC) buses go to Venice daily (€25, 3½ hours).

TRAIN

Villach is situated on three Austrian IC/EC (InterCity/EuroCity) rail routes, which serve Salzburg (€31, 2½ hours, every two hours), Lienz (€20, 1¾ hours, hourly) and Klagenfurt (€7.20, 30 to 40 minutes, two to four per hour).

Direct services run to seemingly everywhere: Munich (€70, 4½ hours, four daily) in Germany; Ljubljana (€23, 1¾ hours, four daily) in Slovenia; Zagreb (€45, four hours, four daily) in Croatia; and Belgrade (€82, 11 hours, one daily) in Serbia.

Faaker See & Ossiacher See

Villach is blessed with two major lakes nearby with low-key summer resorts. Both the Faaker See, 6km east of Villach and close to the Karawanken Range, and the Ossiacher See, 4km to the northeast, provide plenty of camping, boating and swimming opportunities.

Above Annenheim and providing a backdrop to the Ossiacher See is **Gerlitzen** (1909m), a popular ski area. Expect to pay about €40 for a ski pass here.

Browse through the region-wide accommodation brochure obtainable from the Villach tourist office, or contact the **regional tourist office** (☎ 04242-420 00; www.region-villach.at; Töbringer Strasse 1, Villach; ☉ 8am-5pm Mon-Thu, to 4pm Fri), near St Ruprecht, for more on the lakes and skiing.

On the Ossiacher See, **boats** (www.schiffahrt.at/drau) run by Drau Fluss Schifffahrt complete a criss-cross circuit between St Andrä and Steindorf (adult/child €12.80/6.40, 2½ hours, approximately hourly from May to October). Boats run by the same company also navigate the Drau River from Villach Congress-Center to Wernberg Bad (one way adult/child €7.50/3.75, 45 minutes) via St Niklas an der Drau (about 2km northeast of the Faaker See) up to four times a day between early May and mid-October.

Regular train and Postbus services leave weekdays from the Villach bus station and train station, running along the northern shore of Ossiacher See via Annenheim (€2, 12 minutes) and Bodensdorf (€3.40, 20 minutes). Regular trains run to Faak am See (€3.40, 30 minutes), and regular buses run to Drobollach (€2, 20 minutes), both on the Faaker See.

You can also explore the region by bicycle through Das Radl. These can be hired in Villach if you call ahead, and at the Bodensdorf (Ossiacher See) and Faak (Faaker See) train stations; hotels and camping ground in the region hire them out, too.

Burg Landskron

Situated between Villach and the Ossiacher See, the castle ruins of Burg Landskron are home to the impressive **Adler Flugschau** (Falconry Show; ☎ 04242-428 88; www.adlerflugschau.com; Schlossweg, Burgruine Landskron; adult/child €10/5; ☉11am & 2.30pm May-Oct, closed Nov-Apr), a 40-minute spectacle featuring birds of prey.

Five to 11 buses (€2, nine minutes) daily leave from alongside Villach's train station and stop in St Andrä, below the castle.

Dreiländereck

Walkers and mountain bikers will find much to do in the **Dobratsch** (2166m) area, in the Villacher Alpen about 12km west of Villach. Just south of here, hiking trails go from the small town of Arnoldstein to the Dreiländereck – the point where Austria, Italy and Slovenia meet. At 1500m there's an **alpine garden** (www.alpengarten-villach.at; adult/child €2.50/1, free May, Sep & Oct; ☉ 9am-6pm daily Jun-Aug, 9am-3pm Wed & Thu May, Sep & Oct) with flora from the southern Alps.

> ### ℹ SHUTTLE BUSES TO NATURPARK DOBRATSCH
>
> Although the Naturpark Dobratsch is quite isolated, getting to it is easy even without your own vehicle. Postbus runs shuttle buses between Villach and Naturpark Dobratsch from mid-June to mid-September, and from late December to mid-February. Buses leave Villach Wednesday, Saturday and Sunday at 9.15am and return the same day at 4pm (adult/child €4/1, including toll). See www.naturparkdobratsch.info for more.

To reach the garden, follow the Villacher Alpenstrasse from town. This is a toll road (€15 per car), but it's free from about mid-November to mid-April, or free in summer if all occupants have the Kärnten Card (p263). Dobratsch is popular with cross-country skiers.

Buses run to Villacher Alpe Rosstratte in the **Naturpark Dobratsch** (www.naturpark-dobratsch.info), via the Alpenstrasse and the alpine garden. Frequent trains connect Villach and Arnoldstein (€3.60, 25 minutes).

Hermagor

☑ 04282 / POP 7060

Situated about 50km west of Villach, Hermagor is popular as a base for skiing in the nearby Nassfeld ski pistes, where you can zip around 110km of pistes (day pass €42) and explore Nordic skiing trails and snowboarding runs; in summer it morphs into a low-key spot for hikers and mountain bikers. Hermagor is also the starting point for hiking the spectacular **Garnitzenklamm**, a narrow gorge some 2.5km west of town. Ask at the tourist office for advice.

The **Millennium-Express cable car** (adult/child €16/8 return) climbs 6km up to Nassfeld (mountain station: Madritsche), making it Austria's longest. The valley station is in Tröpolach, 8km west of town along the B111 and then B90, or also reached by train.

Situated on a lovely rise about a 10-minute walk north of town along Radnigger Strasse, **Villa Blumegg** (**☑** 20 92; www.villa-blumegg. at; Neupriessenegg 2; s €55, d €84-92, tr €109, apt €168-243; **P ≉**) has been recently renovated and offers comfortable rooms with and with-

out balconies. There are also holiday apartments here accommodating up to seven people.

The **tourist office** (**☑** 2043; www.hermagor.info; Göseringlände 7; ⊗ 8.30am-6pm Mon-Fri, 10am-2pm Sat & Sun) is about 400m west of the train station on the B111. It has well-informed staff with information on skiing, guided and unguided hiking, and mountain biking in the area. Facilities such as banks, supermarkets and a post office are all central or near the tourist office.

ℹ Getting There & Around

Trains run to Hermagor from Villach (€10, 70 minutes) every one to two hours, some continuing to Tröpolach (€2.20, 10 minutes), complemented by bus services from Hermagor to Tröpolach. **Bike Paradies** (**☑** 2010; www.bikeparadies.zeg.de; Obervellach 48; per day trekking bike/e-bike & e-mountain bike €15/29; ⊗ closed Dec-Jan), at the Rudolf service station 1km towards Villach on the B111, has a good range of bikes, including models for children.

EASTERN CARINTHIA

Eastern Carinthia's prettiest medieval towns and most impressive castles lie north of Klagenfurt, on or close to Hwy 83 and the rail route between Klagenfurt and Bruck an der Mur. There are mountain ranges on either side: the Seetaler Alpen and Saualpe to the east, and the Gurktaler Alpen to the west.

Friesach

☑ 04268 / POP 5180

Once a key staging post on the Vienna–Venice trade route, Friesach is Carinthia's oldest town. The hills on either side of town bristle with ruined fortifications, and the centre is surrounded by a moat (it's the only town in Austria that still has one) and a set of imposing, grey-stone walls. Once a year Friesach's gates are locked, everyone in town dresses up in medieval costumes and Friesach re-enacts its history.

◉ Sights

Medieval Fortifications & Churches   CHURCH, FORTRESS

FREE Friesach has four medieval fortress ruins ranged along the hills rising above Hauptplatz to the west, all offering excellent views. The northernmost is **Burg Geyersberg**; the furthest south are the **Virgilienberg** ruins. The middle two (**Rotturm** and **Petersberg**) are the most easily visited from the centre. There are lovely views from **Peterskirche** (⊙ 11am-5pm Tue-Sun May-Sep), accessible by paths ascending from the front of the Gothic **Stadtpfarrkirche** (⊙ dawn-dusk), with Romanesque elements dating from 927.

All fortresses are connected by the Burgwanderweg that winds through the bucolic landscape with views over town.

☆ Festivals & Events

Spectaculum   MEDIEVAL
(⊙ Jul) On the last Saturday in July, electric lights are extinguished and the town is closed off and lit by torches and flares as jesters, princesses and armoured knights stroll around juggling, fire-eating and staging jousting tournaments and duels. Friesach reverts to the currency that made it famous, with medieval meals from street stalls being paid for with Friesach pennies. Contact the tourist office for event information.

Petersberg Fortress   THEATRE
(tickets €15-25) The site for open-air theatre in summer, where performances range across anything from Shakespeare to Brecht. Obtain details and tickets from the tourist office.

🛏 Sleeping & Eating

Several hotels and eating options are on Hauptplatz and around.

Metnitztalerhof   HOTEL €€
(✆ 25 10-0; www.metnitztalerhof.at; Hauptplatz 11; s €57, d €96-108; P@☎) This pastel-pink edifice at the far end of the town square is the only four-star hotel in Friesach; rooms are modern and comfortable and have small balconies. There's a sauna, Jacuzzi and steam room on-site, plus a **restaurant** (mains €16-23.50; ⊙ lunch & dinner, restaurant closed Thu) that serves Austrian and Carinthian dishes.

Cafe Konditorei Craigher   CAFE
(www.craigher.at; Hauptplatz 3; ⊙ 7am-8pm Mon-Fri, 8am-7pm Sat & Sun) Connoisseurs of chocolate will love dipping into this place – all chocolate is made on the premises.

ℹ Information

Tourist office (✆ 43 00; www.friesach.at; Fürstenhofplatz 1; ⊙ 8am-4pm Mon-Fri, 10am-3pm Sat & Sun, closed weekends Oct-May) Located a couple of minutes by foot north of Hauptplatz.

ℹ Getting There & Away

Friesach has direct connections with Vienna's Meidling (€42.50, 3¼ hours, three daily), Villach (€15.30, 1½ hours, hourly), Bruck an der Mur (€23.10, 1¾ hours, four daily), St Veit (€7.20, 30 minutes, hourly) and Klagenfurt (€10.60, 60 minutes, hourly).

Gurk
✆ 04266 / POP 1280

This small town (Krka in Slovenian), some 18km west of the Friesach–Klagenfurt road, is famous for its former **Dom** (✆ 8236; Domplatz 11; combined tours adult/child €6.20/5.70; ⊙ 9am-7pm, Sunday service 10-10.45am, combined 70-minute tours Dom, crypt & Bischofskapelle 10.30am, 1.30pm & 3pm), which was built between 1140 and 1200 and still operates as a church. With its harmonious pillared crypt, this is Austria's foremost church from the Romanesque epoch. Inside you will also find Gothic reticulated vaulting, and most of the church fittings are either baroque or rococo. The early-baroque high altar has a startling 72 statues and 82 angel heads.

The frescoes in the **Bischofskapelle** (Episcopal Chapel; adult/child €3.70/2.90; ⊙ guided tours 11.20pm, 2.20pm & 3.50pm), dating from around 1200, are all the more beautiful for the use of raw colours.

Visit on a weekday if using public transport – an 8.04am train from Klagenfurt to Treibach-Althofen connects with a bus (€11.90, 1¾ hours). Returning, the last bus from Gurk leaves at 6.06pm. With your own transport, take Hwy 93.

ℹ MOUNTAIN BIKING

Mountain bikers should pick up a copy of *The Best Bicycle & Bike Tours* from the tourist office in Hermagor. This gives an overview of trails, including an 11.7km downhill trail from the top of the Millennium-Express cable car to the Gmanberg station. Bikes are carried free of charge but can also be hired at the valley station.

Hüttenberg

☎ 04263 / POP 1800

Step off the bus in the tiny mining village of Hüttenberg and you might be forgiven for thinking you've stumbled into Tibet, for here you see fluttering prayer flags rising up the cliff. Hüttenberg is the birthplace of Heinrich Harrer, who famously spent seven years in Tibet and was immortalised by Brad Pitt in film.

Outside the **Heinrich Harrer Museum** (www.harrermuseum.at; Bahnhofstrasse 12; adult/child €13.50/8; ⊙ 10am-5pm May-Oct) you can sip on a bowl of butter tea and listen to the rush of water through wooden prayer wheels, before going inside the beautiful stone-and-wood building to see the huge collection of objects and photographs Harrer brought back from his world travels. The steep admission price to the Heinrich Harrer Museum includes the inconveniently located **Puppenmuseum** (Doll Museum) and the **Mineralienschaubergwerk** (Mineral Mining Museum), 3km away in Knappenberg.

ⓘ Getting There & Away

One direct bus runs to Hüttenberg weekdays from St Veit an der Glan (€9, one hour), and a train and bus connecting service operates from St Veit an der Glan via Treibach-Althofen (€17.50, 75 minutes). From Klagenfurt frequent buses run with a change either in Görtschitztal Vierlinden or in Mösel Ort (€11.40, one to 1½ hours). Buses continue on to Knappenberg.

St Veit an der Glan

☎ 04212 / POP 12,600

St Veit was historically important as the seat of the dukes of Carinthia from 1170 until 1518. These days it's a mildly interesting, mid-sized town with a lovely baroque square.

The highlight on the town square is the Gothic **Rathaus** from the 15th century, with its magnificent courtyard featuring sgraffito (a mural or decoration in which the top layer is scratched off to reveal the original underneath). St Veit's other main attraction is the **Kunsthotel Fuchspalast** (☎ 4660-601; www.hotel-fuchspalast.at; Prof-Ernst-Fuchs-Platz 1; r per person €49; P @ 🛜). This surrealist structure was designed by mystical artist Ernst Fuchs, and has blue and red glass tiles in fantastical

and astrological designs – a theme that you find throughout St Veit's best place to sleep.

For good food and a great atmosphere, **La Torre** (☎ 39 250; www.latorre.at; Grabenstrasse 39; mains €15.50-28, 6-course menu €69; ⊙ Tue-Sat) is an Italian restaurant set in one of the towers of the 14th-century town wall. As well as the smart, romantic interior, there's a beautiful walled garden and terrace, and an Italian owner who exudes bonhomie.

The reception of Kunsthotel Fuchspalast doubles as the **tourist office** (☎ 4660-0; www.stveit.com; Hauptplatz 23; ⊙ 10am-4pm).

ⓘ Getting There & Away

St Veit is 33km south of Friesach and 20km north of Klagenfurt. Two-hourly express trains run to Villach (€12, 37 minutes), stopping at Klagenfurt (€3.80, 12 minutes). There are no left-luggage lockers at the station.

Burg Hochosterwitz

This fairy-tale fortress (it claims to be the inspiration for the castle in *Sleeping Beauty*) drapes itself around the slopes of a hill, with 14 gate towers on the path up to the final bastion. These were built between 1570 and 1586 by its former owner, Georg Khevenhüller, to ward off invading Turks. A *Burgführer* information booklet (in English; €4) outlines the different challenges presented to attackers by each gate – some have spikes embedded in them, which could be dropped straight through unwary invaders passing underneath. The **castle** (www.burg-hochosterwitz.com; adult/child incl tour €12/8; ⊙ 9am-6pm Palm Sunday–Oct; 🚻) has a museum featuring the suit of armour of one Burghauptmann Schenk, who measured 225cm at the tender age of 16.

ⓘ Getting There & Away

Regional trains on the St Veit–Friesach route stop at Launsdorf Hochosterwitz station, a 3km walk from the car park and the first gate, where a lift (€6) ascends to the castle.

Maria Saal

☎ 04223 / POP 3830

Maria Saal, a small town perched on a fortified hill 10km north of Klagenfurt, is easily visited on an excursion from Klagenfurt or St Veit. Its **Pilgrimage Church** (Domplatz 1; ⊙ dawn-dusk) was built in the early 15th century from volcanic stone, some of it filched from a nearby Roman ruin. The exterior south wall is embedded with relief panels and ancient gravestones.

The **tourist office** (⌨22 14-25; www.maria-saal.at; Am Platzl 7; ☺7.30am-12.30pm & 1-4pm Mon-Fri) is just off Hauptplatz.

There are no left-luggage facilities in the small train station. Regional trains run from St Veit (€3.70, eight minutes, every one to two hours) and Klagenfurt (€2.20, nine minutes, every one to two hours).

WESTERN CARINTHIA

The main attractions of western Carinthia are Millstatt with its serene and pretty lake for swimming and boating, and its abbey and famous music festival; Spittal an der Drau, with its stately Renaissance palace and pretty, floral park; and the remote and beautiful Weissensee.

Both Millstatt and Spittal an der Drau are close to the primary road route north from Villach, the A10/E55 that leads to Salzburg. It has a special vehicle toll section (€10 on top of the normal autobahn toll) covering the two long tunnel sections north of Renn-weg – the Tauerntunnel and Katschbergtun-nel. Traffic jams are common.

Gmünd

⌨ 04732 / POP 2590

Gmünd is an attractive 11th-century village with a delightful walled centre and a 13th-century hilltop castle, **Alte Burg**. From 1480, Hungarians conducted a seven-year siege of the city, breaking through and partially destroying the castle. Today it's the setting for plays and musical events.

Gmünd's most unusual attraction is the **Pankratium** (www.pankratium.at; Hintere Gasse 60; 1hr tour adult/child €8.50/4.90; ☺10am-5pm May-Oct), an extraordinary space bringing together water, light and sound (ie vibration) in hands-on pieces designed for the senses. You can bring sound gadgets and all manner of instruments to life on a tour that culminates in bubble-blowing in the yard.

While in town, visit the excellent, privately owned **Porsche Museum Helmut Pfeifhofer** (www.auto-museum.at; Riesertratte 4a; adult/child €7/3.50; ☺9am-6pm mid-May–mid-Oct, 10am-4pm mid-Oct–mid-May), a Porsche factory that operated in Gmünd from 1944 to 1950. The first car to bear that famous

name (a 356) was handmade here. There's a 15-minute film (in German and English) on Ferdinand Porsche's life and work.

Gmünd has a range of inexpensive accommodation options, including hotels offering child-minding that are geared towards families with young children. Staff at the tourist office can outline options. **Gasthof Kohlmayr** (⌨2149; www.gasthof-kohlmayr.at; Hauptplatz 7; s/d/q €42/70/96; 🅿) has an eclectic mix of historic and modern rooms in a 400-year-old building right in the heart of Gmünd. It also has a restaurant (mains €8.90 to €17.90) serving tasty local fare.

The **tourist office** (⌨22 1514; www.familien-tal.com; Hauptplatz 20; ☺8am-5pm Mon-Fri, 9am-3pm Sat, closed Sat Sep-Jun) has an excellent sheet map of town in English, German and Italian, with sights and galleries numbered and briefly explained.

❶ Getting There & Away

Gmünd is not on a rail route; one to two hourly buses connect it with Spittal an der Drau (€4.40, 30 minutes) from Monday to Friday.

Spittal an der Drau

⌨ 04762 / POP 15,770

Spittal is an important economic and administrative centre in upper Carinthia. Its name comes from a 12th-century hospital and refuge that once succoured travellers on this site. Today it's a town with an impressive Italianate palace at its centre and a small attractive park with splashing fountains and bright flower beds.

◎ Sights

Schloss Porcia & Museum für Volkskultur PALACE, MUSEUM
(Local Heritage Museum; www.museum-spittal.com; adult/child €8/4; ☺9am-6pm daily mid-Apr–mid-Oct, 1-4pm Mon-Thu mid-Oct–mid-Apr; ♿) Boasting an eye-catching Renaissance edifice, Schloss Porcia was built between 1533 and 1597 by the fabulously named Graf von Salamanca-Ortenburg. Inside, Italianate arcades run around a central courtyard used for summer theatre performances. The top floors contain the enormous Local Heritage Museum, which has lots of displays about Carinthia and 3-D projections, such as a virtual navigation through the Hohe Tauern National Park.

Goldeck   MOUNTAIN

(cable car one way/return €12.50/18, Goldeckstrasse toll road cars & motorbikes €13, lift pass adult/child €36/18) In summertime, this peak (2142m) can be reached by cable car, or by the Goldeckstrasse toll road (free with the Kärnten Card; p263). The road stops 260m short of the summit. In winter, Goldeck is popular for skiing. The cable car doesn't operate from mid-April to mid-June or from mid-September to mid-December.

🛏 Sleeping

Staff at the tourist office help with accommodation free of charge.

Draufluss Camping   CAMPGROUND €

(☑24 66; www.drauwirt.com; Schwaig 10; camp site per adult/child/tent/car €6/3/4/4, s/d incl breakfast €30/60; ☉ Jun-Sep) Spittal's camping ground is about 3.5km from the town centre on the southern bank of the Drau River. The *Gasthof* has six simple rooms.

★ Hotel Erlebnis Post   HOTEL €€

(☑22 17 0; www.erlebnis-post.at; Hauptplatz 13; s €66-77, d €111-122, tr €166, ste €188; ᴾ🛜) Rooms in this unusual hotel might be described as 'room-vertisements', as they're sponsored by local companies (usually with the name inside). One non-sponsored room has beds from the local juvenile prison and an original cell door. Bonuses are the ski-storage room and transfers to the pistes.

Hotel Ertl   HOTEL €€

(☑204 80; www.hotel-ertl.at; Bahnhofstrasse 26; s/d/tr/q €69/118/135/152; ᴾ@🛜🏊) Smack-bang across the road from the railway station, this comfortable hotel has the ochre

---

ⓘ THE AUTOSCHLEUSE TAUERNBAHN

If you're driving to Bad Gastein from Spittal an der Drau, you'll need to use the **Autoschleuse Tauernbahn** (Railway Car Shuttle Service; www. gasteinertal.com/autoschleuse) through the tunnel from Mallnitz to Böckstein. The fare for cars is €17 one way or €30 return (valid for two months). For motorcycles, the price is €16/28. For information, call ☑05 717. Departures are every 60 minutes, with the last train departing at 11.20pm heading south, and 10.50pm going north. The journey takes 11 minutes.

---

colours of its Tex-Mex restaurant downstairs trickling into the interior design. The pool is about 25m and outdoors.

🍴 Eating & Drinking

The main nightlife area is on Brückenstrasse and Bogengasse. It's a thin and eclectic line of low-life bars and regular pubs.

★ Restaurant Zellot   AUSTRIAN €€

(Hauptplatz 12; mains €10.50-18.50; ☉ lunch & dinner Mon-Sat) This is possibly the most important address in town: it's a funky and rather eccentric restaurant that does a good steak as well as Austrian staples. On top of this, it has the Glashaus bar and bistro (open from 9am to 1am Monday to Saturday), and the Garage, a space for live acts and DJs that is decked out like a garage – its features become even more intriguing after your second drink. Garage is open from 9.30pm to 4am Friday and Saturday.

Mettnitzer   AUSTRIAN €€

(☑358 99; Neuerplatz 17; mains €16.90-26.90; ☉Wed-Sun) Mettnitzer is a class act that serves a small range of classic, local and seasonal dishes in a formal atmosphere.

ⓘ Information

Post office (Egarterplatz 2; ☉8am-6pm Mon-Fri, 9am-noon Sat)

Tourist office (☑56 50 220; www.spittaldrau.at; Burgplatz 1; ☉9am-6pm Mon-Fri year round, plus 9am-noon Sat Jul & Aug) On one side of Schloss Porcia, with maps and lots of useful information.

ⓘ Getting There & Around

BICYCLE

More (☑2555-0; www.more-der-spezialist. at; Bahnhofstrasse 11) rents city and mountain bikes per day/week for €12/60 (top mountain bikes cost €20 per day) and electric bicycles (€19 per day, range 60km, 120km with auxiliary battery).

Pick up the tourist office's free city/regional map, which has paths marked.

BUS

One- to two-hourly Postbuses leave from outside the train station, Spittal-Drau Zentrum and Neuer Platz to Gmünd (€4.40, 30 minutes) from Monday to Saturday, but none on Sunday. Call ☑0180 222 333 for schedule information. Postbus services to Millstatt depart from outside Spittal train station (€3.40, 20 minutes, two hourly), with some continuing to Bad Kleinkirchheim (from Spittal €7, one hour).

TAXI

Call ☑ 5580 or ☑ 3802. Expect to pay €24 to get to Millstatt.

TRAIN

Spittal-Millstättersee is an important rail junction: two-hourly IC/EC services run north to Bad Gastein (€11.80, 40 minutes); at least hourly regional services run west to Lienz (€12.20, one hour) and to Villach (€7.20, 35 minutes), 37km to the southeast. The railway line north via Mallnitz-Obervellach clings spectacularly to the valley walls.

Millstätter See

Stretching out 12km but just 1.5km wide, the Millstätter See is second in size in Carinthia after the Wörthersee. It was gouged out during the ice age about 30,000 years ago, and today is studded with a handful of small towns. Millstatt on the north shore and Seeboden at the western end are the most important. The warm waters of the lake (about 22°C to 26°C in summer) lend themselves to sailing, kayaking and open-water swimming.

The central information office, **Infocenter Millstätter See** (☑ 04766-3700-0; www.millstaettersee.at; Thomas-Morgenstern-Platz 1; ☺ 9am-6pm Mon-Fri, 10am-5pm Sat, 10am-2pm Sun), is situated in a modern building in Seeboden, doubling as a call centre with English- and Italian-speaking staff. The bus to Millstatt stops here (ask the driver).

Millstatt

☑ 04766 / POP 3390

The genteel lakeside village of Millstatt lies 10km east of Spittal an der Drau on the northern shore. It got its name from Emperor Domition, an early Christian convert who tossed *mille statuae* (1000 heathen statues) into the lake. A gaunt and crazed-looking sculpture of the emperor stands in the lake, portrayed in the act of consigning a Venus to a watery grave.

⊙ Sights & Activities

East of Millstatt lies **Bad Kleinkirchheim**, a spa resort and large winter skiing centre with 26 lifts and cable cars. The **tourist office** (☑ 04240-82 12; www.badkleinkirchheim.at; Dorfstrasse 30) there has good skiing info.

Stift Millstatt   ABBEY
(tours in German adult/child €5/2.50; ☺ tours 10.30am Wed Jun–mid-Sep) Apart from Lake Millstatt itself, the town's main attraction is

> **ⓘ ACCESS TO JETTIES & THE LAKE**
>
> The public bathing foreshore in Millstatt is a bustling place in midsummer. If you're after tranquillity, hire a boat or kayak and head for the leafy shore opposite. For swimming, private jetties belonging to the hotels are the nicest options. Many places have private jetties or offer lake access.

its Romanesque Benedictine abbey, founded in 1070. This pretty complex consists of a moderately interesting **Stiftsmuseum** (Abbey Museum; ☑ 0660-506 80 66; Stiftsgasse 1; admission adult/child €3/2.50, tours €6; ☺ 10am-4pm May, Jun, Sep & Oct, to 6pm Jul & Aug, tours 2pm Mon & Thu), the attractive 11th century abbey **church**, a **graveyard**, and **abbey buildings** south of the church with lovely yards and arcades. If you walk downhill along Stiftsgasse from the church, you see on the left a **1000-year-old lime tree**. The abbey grounds and magnificent arcades and cloisters are free to visit.

Surf- und Segelschule Millstatt   WATER SPORTS
(☑ 0676-751 19 39; www.surf-segelschulemillstatt. at; Seestrasse, alongside Villa Verdin; hire per hr windsurfing board & rig €17-23, kayak €10, sailing boats €10, e-boats €12-14) This reliable outfit rents equipment, and holds individual and group windsurfing, sailing and kayak courses.

Wassersport Strobl   WATER SPORTS
(☑ 22 63; Seemühlgasse 56a; per hr e-boats €7-14) Wassersport Strobl has two landing stages where you can rent boats and Canadian canoes.

🎊 Festivals & Events

Musikwochen Millstatt (Millstatt Music Weeks; ☑ 2023-35; www.musikwochen.com; tickets €16-39; ☺ May-Sep) brings performances of classical and jazz music every year from May to September; most performances take place in the abbey church.

🛏 Sleeping

Früstuckspension Strobl   PENSION €
(☑ 3142; pension-hansstrobl@aon.at; Kaiser-Franz-Josef-Strasse 59; s/d €38/76) This budget hotel is back from the lake but has views across it from most of the rooms. It's in a

400-year-old Gothic building that once belonged to the monastery. Almost all rooms have balconies.

★**Villa Verdin** HOTEL €€
(⏰374 74; www.villaverdin.at; Seestrasse 69; s €60-65, d €110-160; 🅿@🛜) This converted 19th-century villa-hotel mixes contemporary design with antiques and interesting junk to create a comfortable, informal yet stylish atmosphere. It's gay-friendly and has a retro beach cafe. Wi-fi is in public areas.

★**Hotel See-Villa** HOTEL €€
(⏰21 02; www.see-villa-tacoli.com; Seestrasse 68; s €73-92, d €140-196, ste per person €89-106; 🅿@🛜) This very comfortable turn-of-the-20th-century hotel has genuine historic charm. It is located right on the shore (perfect for sleeping with windows open), with a huge terrace restaurant, a private sauna and a swimming jetty. Its restaurant (mains €14.50 to €20) is open daily for lunch and dinner.

Die Forelle HOTEL €€€
(⏰2050-0; www.hotel-forelle.at; Fischergasse 65; s €113-140, d €225-311, 2-6 person apt per person €65; 🅿@🛜🏊) Some guests like its lakeside bar, others gravitate towards this large lakeside hotel for its wellness facilities, including whirlpool and baths. Rooms are well-sized, and the more expensive doubles have a balcony to the lake. Its midpriced restaurant opens for lunch and dinner, and offers a reduced menu between meal times; half-board is available (€25 extra).

✖ Eating & Drinking

★**Fisch-Häusl Stark** FISH
(Kaiser-Franz-Josef-Strasse 134; mains €17-22, smoked trout about €8; ⏰from 11am, closed Oct-May) This small place serves delicious fish from the Millstätter See and the Weissensee,

including smoked trout the owners will pack for a picnic. Grab a bread roll from the bakery across the street.

★**Kap 4613** BAR
(www.kap4613.at; Kaiser-Franz-Josef-Strasse 330; ⏰from noon, closed Mon & Tue Nov-Feb) Combining an atrium with a deck area, and a beach bar extending over the water for summer sipping, this lakeside bar is easily Millstatt's best drinking venue. It opens from 10am in many months.

ⓘ Information

Tourist office – Millstatt (⏰20 23; www.millstaettersee.com; Marktplatz 8; ⏰8am-6pm Mon-Fri, 10am-noon Sat & Sun) Located inside Millstatt's Rathaus; has useful information on the town.

ⓘ Getting There & Around

Postbus services to Millstatt depart from outside Spittal train station (€3.40, 20 minutes, two hourly), with some continuing to Bad Kleinkirchheim (from Spittal €7, one hour). **Mountainbike Station Thomas Graf** (⏰0650-356 3181; www.mountainbike-station.at; Kaiser-Franz-Josef-Strasse 59; ⏰9am-6pm Mon-Fri, to 3pm Sat & Sun May–mid-Oct) rents mountain bikes for €21 and electric bikes for €24 per 24 hours.

Lienz

⏰04852 / POP 11,820 / ELEV 673M
The Dolomites rise like an amphitheatre around Lienz, which straddles the Isel and Drau Rivers and lies just 40km north of Italy. Those same arresting river and mountain views welcomed the Romans, who settled here some 2000 years ago and whose legacy is explored at medieval castle Schloss Bruck and archaeological site Aguntum. Looking up to the blushing Dolomites at sunset, it's easy to see why they were so taken with this region, which is an exclave of Tyrol.

◉ Sights

Schloss Bruck CASTLE
(www.museum-schlossbruck.at; Schlossberg 1; adult/child €7.50/2.50; ⏰10am-6pm daily Jul & Aug, 10am-6pm Tue-Sun May, Jun, Sep & Oct) Lienz' famous **medieval fortress** has a museum chronicling the region's history, as well as Roman artefacts, Gothic winged altars and local costumes. The **castle tower** is used for changing exhibitions; a highlight for art enthusiasts is the **Egger-Lienz-**

Lienz

Galerie devoted to the emotive works of Albin Egger-Lienz (see the boxed text, p282.)

Stadtpfarrkirche St Andrä CHURCH
(Pfarrgasse 4; ☺ dawn-dusk) The town's main church has an attractive Gothic rib-vaulted ceiling, startling baroque altar, 14th-century frescoes and a pair of unusual tombstones sculpted in red Salzburg marble. Alongside is the solemn **Kriegergedächtniskapelle** (War Memorial Chapel) sheltering Albin Egger-Lienz's controversial frescoes, one depicting an emaciated Jesus after the resurrection, which in 1925 scandalised the Vatican; religious activity was banned in the chapel for about the next 60 years. To visit, pick up the keys hanging on the door at Pfarrgasse 13 (across the little bridge behind the Kirchenwirt restaurant).

Aguntum MUSEUM, RUINS
(www.aguntum.info; Stribach 97; archaeological park adult/child €6/4, museum €7.50/2.50, combined admission adult/child €10.50/8.50; ☺ 9.30am-6pm, closed Nov-Apr) Excavations are still under way at the Aguntum archaeological site in nearby Dölsach to piece together the jigsaw puzzle of this 2000-year-old *municipium*, which flourished as a centre of trade and commerce under Emperor Claudius. Take a stroll around the excavations, then

visit the glass-walled museum to explore Lienz' Roman roots, with interactive stuff for the kids (a virtual tour through Aguntum and dress-up costumes) and an exhibition featuring fun elements such as traditional Roman recipes. Bus 4406 runs out here from Monday to Saturday.

WORTH A TRIP

WEISSENSEE

Wedged within a glacial cleft in the Gailtal Alps with mountain ridges flanking its northern and southern shores, the Weissensee is Austria's highest swimmable glacial lake, the least developed of Carinthia's large lakes, and a spectacular and peaceful nature reserve. It stretches as a turquoise and deep-blue slither for almost 12km and in most parts is about 1km wide. Because it's at an altitude of 930m, the water is cooler than the Wörthersee, but in July and August you can expect temperatures of above 20° in most parts.

Consider staying in **Naggl**, a small settlement on the southern shore about 3.5km from Techendorf, as it has a quiet shoreline, low-key accommodation options, and good access to hiking and mountain-biking trails.

With its large network of forestry tracks, the Weissensee has some great hiking trails to *Almhütten* (meadow huts) on easy return day walks. **Trail 27** can be picked up from the boat landing at Paterzipf (near Naggl) on a walk to the **Hermagorer Bodenalm** (☑ 0650-400 2488; Bodenalm; per person half-board €32, mains €8; ☉ closed Oct-Apr) farmstay and beyond to Dolomitenblick at the eastern end of the lake. There you can catch a boat back to Techendorf.

From the top of the chairlift, **Bergbahn Weissensee** (Techendorf; one way adult/child €8.60/5.30; ☉ 9am-5pm, closed Mon May, Jun & Sep, closed early Mar–mid-May & early Oct–Nov), a walk to the farmstay, **Kohlröslhütte** (☑ 0664-8850 1860; www.kohlroesl.at; above Techendorf in Gailtal Alps; per person full board €31, snacks €4-11; ☉ mid-May–mid-Oct; 🐕) takes you from **Naggler Alm** (www.naggleralmut.at; Naggler Alm; mains €8.90-14.50; ☉ 9am-5pm Tue-Sun, closed Nov-Apr) restaurant across lush alpine meadows to the other side of the ridge. Here you have fantastic views into the Gitschtal (Gitsch Valley) and over to dramatic peaks. Both of these walks are also suitable for mountain bikes.

The **tourist office** (☑ 04173 2220-0; www.weissensee.com; Techendorf-Süd; ☉ 8.30am-12.30pm & 1.30-5pm Mon-Fri, 9am-noon & 4-6pm Sat, 10am-noon & 4-6pm Sun, closed Sat & Sun mid-Sep–mid-Jun) can help with addresses for diving, sailing, canoing and kayaking, as well as with accommodation on the lake.

The nearest train station is Greifenburg-Weissensee, 11km from the lake on the Villach–Spittal an der Drau–Lienz line. From there **Mobil Büro Hermagor** (☑ reservations 0800 500 1905; www.mobilbuero.com; one way €7; ☉ mid-May–late Sep & mid-Dec–Feb) runs a bus service to/from your place of stay on the Weissensee. It's for overnight guests only. Book by telephone or online by 4pm the day before. Day guests can buy a day pass (€7) but only to Hotel Kreuzwirt, 4km from Techendorf. You can pick up the free but often infrequent Naturpark bus from there.

To reach the lake by car, take Bundestrasse 87 from Greifenburg or Hermagor. From Spittal an der Drau, a road (L32) runs to the eastern end of the lake but ends there.

Boat services run by **Weissensee Schifffahrt** (www.schifffahrt-mueller.at; 1-7 stops €2.50-7, round trip €10.50; ☉ mid-May–early Oct) run to all stops between Techendorf and Dolomitenblick three to 11 times daily, peaking in July and August.

🏃 Activities

Lienz has 64km of groomed cross-country trails. It also hosts the Dolomitenlauf cross-country skiing race, which is held in mid-January.

The fast-flowing rivers, narrow gorges and forests of the Dolomites around Lienz are the perfect place for adrenalin-pumping sports, including rafting and canyoning. Expect to pay between €29 and €80 for rafting tours, for canyoning between €69 and €160. **Osttirol Adventures** (☑ 04853-200 30, mobile 0664-356 0450; www.ota.at; Ainet 108b), in the small town of Ainet 8km west of Lienz, is the largest outfit. Thomas Zimmermann of **La Ola** (☑ 611 99; www.laola.at; Mühlgasse 15) organises the whole gamut – from canyoning, kayaking and climbing in summer to ski touring, snowshoeing and ice climbing in winter. Call for times and prices.

Galitzenklamm WALKING TRAIL

(adult/child €4.50/3.50; ⊙10am-5pm Jun-Sep)
This vertiginous walkway clings to the sheer
cliffs of a gorge that rises above the swirling
waters of the Drau River. To get there, take
bus 4421 to Leisach, 3km from Lienz.

Zettersfeld SKIING

(www.topskipass.at; 1-day ski pass €41, multiday
passes for all East Tyrol lifts from €83) Beginners
and intermediates should find enough of a
challenge on Lienz' 40km of pistes, which
afford seductive views of the rugged Dolomites. Most of the action takes place around
Zettersfeld, located slightly west of Lienz.
A cable car and six lifts whizz skiers up to
slopes reaching between 1660m and 2278m.
Free buses link the Lienz train station to the
cable-car valley stations.

Hochstein SKIING

(www.topskipass.at; 1-day ski pass €41, multiday
passes for all East Tyrol lifts from €83) Slightly
west of Lienz, Hochstein (2057m) is a ski
area popular for its groomed pistes and
2.5km floodlit toboggan run; free buses link
the train station to the cable-car valley stations in summer and winter high seasons.

Dolomites Trails WALKING

The tourist office sells walking (€4) and *via
ferrate* (€1) maps, and can advise on the
high-altitude trails that thread through the
steely peaks of the Dolomites. See p283 for
cable cars and summer prices.

Dolomiten Lamatrekking HIKING

(☑68 087; www.dolomitenlama.at) Dolomiten
Lamatrekking is a dab hand at getting those
stubborn llamas to walk the right way. The
llamas obligingly lug the packs on anything
from two-hour to four-day uphill hikes.

Drau Radweg CYCLING

(www.drauradweg.com) A network of well-
signposted mountain-bike trails radiates
from Lienz, taking in the striking landscape
of the Dolomites. The scenic 366km Drau
Radweg passes through Lienz en route to
Maribor in Slovenia. Ask the tourist office
for the free map *Rad und Mountainbike
Karte Osttirol,* which details cycling routes.
Probike Lienz (☑735 36; www.probike-lienz.at;
Amlacherstrasse 1a; per day mountain bike €18, city
bike €15, e-bike €25; ⊙9am-noon & 2-6pm Mon-
Fri, 9am-noon Sat) is the most central place to
hire your own set of wheels.

★ Festivals & Events

Lienz hosts the testosterone-fuelled **Dolomiten Mann** (www.dolomitenmann.com) in September, a sponsored iron-man competition
billed as the world's toughest team challenge.
Headlining the program is the cross-country
relay race, where teams of runners, paragliders, kayakers and mountain bikers battle it
out for the title. Lively open-air concerts and
parties complement the line-up.

In late July, a free street festival draws
top circus and theatre acts from around
the world. Summer also welcomes a series
of events celebrating Tyrolean culture, plus
free concerts on Hauptplatz and in other
squares (8pm on Wednesdays and Sundays
from June to September).

⌨ Sleeping

Camping Falken CAMPGROUND €

(☑0664-410 79 73; www.camping-falken.com;
Eichholz 7; camp sites per adult/child/tent €6/5/5;
⊙mid-Dec–mid-Oct; P😊) Wake up to Dolomite views at this leafy campground, a
20-minute walk south of the centre. There's
a minimarket, restaurant and playground
on-site, and guests get free access to swimming pools in Lienz.

Goldener Stern PENSION €

(☑621 92; www.goldener-stern-lienz.at; Schweizer-
gasse 40; s/d €45/84; P) Framed by neat

CLIFF-HANGER: THE DOLOMITENHÜTTE ALPINE HUT

Clinging to a 1600m clifftop like an
eagle's nest and watched over by jagged
peaks, the **Dolomitenhütte** (☑0664-
225 37 82; www.dolomitenhuette.at; Amlach
39; mains €9.80-23.50) is extraordinary.
With the Dolomites and larch woods
as its mesmerising backdrop, this cosy
alpine hut is like something out of a fairy
tale. In summer, walkers and cyclists
make the 12km jaunt south of Lienz
for the enticing views from the terrace
and the home cooking, which includes
the likes of *Kaspressknödel* (fried
cheese dumpling) and *Schlipfkrapfen*
(Tyrolean-style ravioli). Snowy winter
days up here are equally enchanting –
bring your sled and you'll be able to
race back down to Lienz on a scenic
toboggan track.

gardens, this 600-year-old *Pension* has spacious, old-fashioned rooms. Breakfast is served in the tiny courtyard in summer.

Hotel Haidenhof
HOTEL €€

(☑624 40; www.haidenhof.at; Grafendorferstrasse 12; s €77-86, d €146-166; P ⑤) Fringed by pear and plum orchards, Haidenhof is where rustic farmhouse meets 21st-century chic. Rooms have plenty of natural light and honey pine and there's a sauna and roof terrace with vistas of the Dolomites. In the South Tyrolean–style restaurant (mains €9.20 to €14.50), nearly everything that lands on your plate is home-grown.

Goldener Fisch
HOTEL €€

(☑621 32; www.goldener-fisch.at; Kärntnerstrasse 9; s/d €53/92; P⑤⑨) The chestnut-tree-shaded beer garden is a big draw at this family-friendly hotel. The rooms are light and modern (if not fancy) and you can wind down in the sauna and herbal steam baths.

Romantik Hotel Traube
HOTEL €€

(☑644 44; www.hoteltraube.at; Hauptplatz 14; s €67, d €138-190; P@⑤⑨) Right on the main square, Traube races you back to the Biedermeier era with its high ceilings and antique-meets-boutique rooms. The 10m pool and the wellness area afford lovely views over Lienz to the Dolomites.

ALBIN EGGER-LIENZ

Lienz' most famous son is artist Albin Egger-Lienz (1868–1926), who grew up here and then studied at the Fine Arts Academy in Munich before becoming a member of the Vienna Secession in 1909. After a brief spell teaching art in Weimer, Egger-Lienz spent much of WWI capturing wartime horrors and the pervading spirit of hopelessness on canvas. Ghostlike corpses on battlefields and soldiers walking hand in hand with skeletons are among the deeply moving motifs that won the artist international acclaim (and criticism). The Tyrolean struggle for liberation (1809), the hardship and anguish of rural life and destiny are other recurring themes in his sombre, fatalistic works. The new seven-stop **Albin Egger-Lienz Trail**, from the Hauptplatz to Schloss Bruck, takes you in the footsteps of the artist in his hometown; stop by the tourist office for more details.

Moarhof
HOTEL €€

(☑675 67; www.hotel-moarhof.at; Moarfeldweg 18; incl half-board s €79-87, d €166-170; P ⑤) Set in serene gardens, 10 minutes' stroll from the centre, this chalet-style hotel has big, modern rooms with mountain views. In the restaurant you'll dine heartily on farm-fresh produce. The stone-clad spa is the hotel's showpiece, with assorted saunas, whirlpools and relaxation rooms.

Grand Hotel Lienz
HOTEL €€€

(☑640 70; www.grandhotel-lienz.com; Fanny-Wibmer-Peditstrasse 2; ste €170-420; P⑤⑨⑨) This hotel designed in fin-de-siècle style is a classy new addition to Lienz. Every imaginable luxury comes with the price tag: impeccable service, a first-rate spa and pool, fine dining on a terrace overlooking the Isel River and Dolomites – you name it. The bright suites with canopy beds are rather grand, too.

✖ Eating & Drinking

Da Leonardo
PIZZA €

(www.daleonardo.at; Tiroler Strasse 30; pizza €5.50-8.40; ⊙11am-11pm) Not many chefs can claim to be a world champion of pizza making, but Leonardo Granata can – he's picked up the title of World Champion, and many other awards, using dough he allows to stand for 24 to 48 hours.

Kirchenwirt
AUSTRIAN €€

(☑625 00; www.kirchenwirt-lienz.at; Pfarrgasse 7; mains €12.90-26.90; ⊙9am-11.30pm Sun-Thu, to 1.30am Fri & Sat) Up on a hill opposite Stadtpfarrkirche St Andrä, this is Lienz' most atmospheric restaurant. Dine on a selection of local dishes under the vaults or on the streamside terrace. The lunch special costs under €10.

La Taverna
AUSTRIAN €€

(☑647 85; Hauptplatz 14; mains €8.50-16; ⊙Tue-Sun) A staircase twists down to this excellent wood-panelled tavern in the bowels of Romantik Hotel Traube.

Gösser Bräu im Alten Rathaus
INTERNATIONAL €€

(☑721 74; Johannesplatz 10; mains €9.50-22; ⊙9am-1am Mon-Fri, to 2am Sat, 9.30am-midnight Sun) Gather around a horseshoe-shaped bar at this vaulted brewpub; it's draught Gösser Brau beers go well with traditional favourites. The vine-clad terrace is popular in summer.

Almrausch
COCKTAIL BAR

(Hauptplatz 14; ⏱ from 8pm Thu-Sat) This groovy underground lounge harbours an aquarium that even Nemo would surely sacrifice the sea for. Plastic fish continue the aquatic theme.

ℹ Information

Osttirol Werbung (☏ 050-212 212; www.ost-tirol.com) For information about the wider East Tyrol area. The office sends brochures, but isn't set up for visits.

Stadtbücherei (Egger-Linz-Platz 2; per 20min €1.20; ⏱ 10am-noon & 3-6pm Mon-Wed & Fri, 10am-6pm Thu, 10am-noon Sat) Free internet with a Gästekarte, available from your hotel.

Tourist office (☏ 050-212 400; www.lienzer-dolomiten.info; Europaplatz 1; ⏱ 8am-6pm Mon-Fri, 9am-noon & 4-6pm Sat) Staff will help you find accommodation (even private rooms) free of charge.

ℹ Getting There & Away

Regional transport in Tyrol comes under the wing of the **Verkehrsverbund Tirol** (VVT; www.vvt.at).

BUS

Buses pull up in front of the train station, where you'll find the **Postbus information office** (☏ 930 00 187; Hauptbahnhof; ⏱ 8am-12.30pm & 1-2.30pm Mon-Fri). There are bus connections to regional ski resorts and northwards to the Hohe Tauern National Park. Buses to Kitzbühel (€15, 1¾ hours) are quicker and more direct than the train, but less frequent.

CAR & MOTORCYCLE

To head south, you must first divert west or east along Hwy 100, as the Dolomites are an

---

ℹ CABLE CARS & SUMMER PRICES

Cable cars to **Zettersfeld** and **Hochstein** go into hibernation from November to 8 December, and pause again after Easter. The Hochstein cable car starts running to the first station, Hochstein 1 (return adult/child €10.50/7.50), from Thursday to Sunday from May to mid-June, after which all summer cable cars are back in full swing daily. Hochstein 2 is winter only. The return cost to Zettersfeld per adult/child is €11.50/6 (or €19/9.50 including the chairlift to 2214m). If you're planning on making several trips, it's worth investing in the Osttirol Card (p278).

---

impregnable barrier. The main north–south road routes are the year-round Felber-Tauern-Strasse (B108) between Mittersill and Lienz, the spectacular Grossglockner Road (open May to October) and the 5.5km-long Felbertauerntunnel (cars and motorcycles €10).

Hauptplatz has lots of parking in its Kurzparkzone, or park for free in front of Stadtpfarrkirche St Andrä.

TRAIN

Most trains to the rest of Austria, including Salzburg (€37, 3½ hours, hourly), go east via Spittal-Millstättersee, where you usually have to change. The quickest and easiest route to Innsbruck (€34, 4½ hours) is to go west via Sillian and Italy, with a change in San Candido/Innichen and again in Fortezza/Franzensfeste.

Tyrol & Vorarlberg

Best Places to Eat

➡ Die Wilderin (p294)

➡ Wirtshaus Zum Griena (p305)

➡ Museum Restaurant (p321)

➡ Restaurant Zur Tenne (p309)

Best Places to Stay

➡ Villa Licht (p308)

➡ Hotel Weisses Kreuz (p292)

➡ Enzianhof (p302)

➡ Hotel Helga (p313)

Why Go?

There's no place like Tyrol for the 'wow, I'm in Austria' feeling. Nowhere else in the country is the downhill skiing as exhilarating, the après-ski as pumping, the wooden chalets as chocolate box, the food as hearty. Whether you're schussing down the legendary slopes of Kitzbühel, cycling the Zillertal or hiking in the Alps with a big, blue sky overhead – the scenery here makes you glad to be alive. Welcome to a place where snowboarders brag about awesome descents under the low beams of a medieval tavern; where *Dirndls* (women's traditional dress) and Lederhosen have street cred; and where *Volksmusik* (folk music) features on club playlists.

The Arlberg Alps give way to rolling dairy country in pleasingly low-key Vorarlberg. Spilling east to the glittering expanse of Bodensee (Lake Constance), this eastern pocket of the country swings happily between ecofriendly architecture on the cutting edge of design and deeply traditional hamlets with more cows than people.

When to Go

➡ In winter (December to early April), skiers flock to the Tyrolean Alps for snow and après-ski fun and prices soar, making advance booking essential. At Christmas, markets bring festive sparkle to towns and cities.

➡ In summer (June to September), room rates are lower in alpine resorts and this is prime time for high-altitude and hut-to-hut hikes, lake swimming and adventure sports like rafting, paragliding and mountain biking. Zillertal rocks to summer folk music; the Bregenz Festival in mid-July lures opera fans to Bodensee.

➡ Crowds are few and room rates low in the shoulder seasons of April/May and October/November, though many places close in alpine resorts. Seasonal colour is at its best, with wildflowers in spring and foliage in autumn.

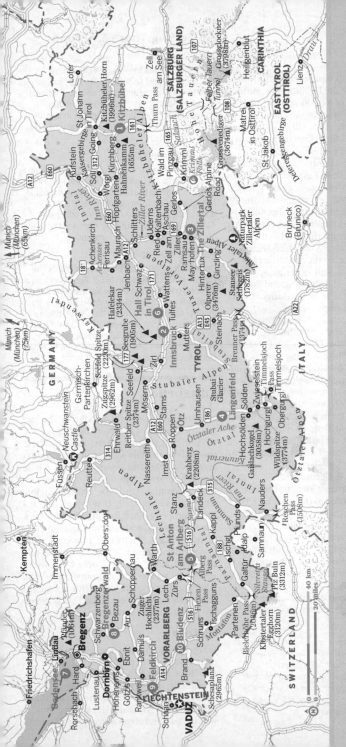

Tyrol & Vorarlberg Highlights

1. Saving your best schuss (and snowsuit) for the slopes of **Kitzbühel** (p306).

2. Seeing the midday sun burnish Innsbruck's iconic **Goldenes Dachl** (p289).

3. Cycling pulse-racing descents in the **Zillertal** (p299).

4. Bathing in out-of-this-world whirlpools at **Aqua Dome** (p314) in Längenfeld.

5. Partying in your snow boots in the après-ski bars of **St Anton am Arlberg** (p320).

6. Slipping back 500 years in the pristine medieval old town of **Hall in Tirol** (p297).

7. Splashing and cycling over borders on **Bodensee** (p328). Europe's third-largest lake.

8. Eating cheese, cheese and more glorious cheese in **Bregenzerwald** (p331).

9. Tiptoeing back to medieval times at the castles and towers in **Feldkirch** (p334).

10. Going to purple-cow heaven gorging on Milka chocolate in **Bludenz** (p336).

TYROL

History

Despite its difficult alpine terrain, Tyrol has been settled since the Neolithic age, verified by the discovery of a 5400-year-old body of a man preserved in ice in the Ötztal Alps in 1991. The Brenner Pass (1374m), crossing into Italy, allowed the region to develop as a north–south trade route.

Tyrol fell to the Habsburgs in 1363, but it wasn't until the rule of Emperor Maximilian I (1490–1519) that the province truly forged ahead. He boosted the region's status by transforming Innsbruck into the administrative capital and a cultural centre. In 1511 the emperor drew up the Landibell legislation, allowing Tyroleans to defend their own borders, thus creating the *Schützen* (marksmen militia) which still exists today. When the last Tyrolean Habsburg, Archduke Sigmund Franz, died in 1665, the duchy of Tyrol was directly ruled from Vienna.

In 1703 the Bavarians attempted to capture Tyrol in the War of the Spanish Succession. In alliance with the French, they reached the Brenner Pass before being beaten back by the *Schützen*. In 1805 Tyrol passed into Bavarian hands under Napoleon, a rule that was short-lived and troublesome. In 1809 South Tyrolean innkeeper Andreas Hofer led a successful fight for independence, winning a famous victory at Bergisel. The Habsburg monarchy did not support his heroic stance and Tyrol was returned to Bavaria later that year.

The Treaty of St Germain (1919) dealt a further blow to Tyrolean identity; prosperous South Tyrol was ceded to Italy and East Tyrol was isolated from the rest of the province.

A staunch ally of Mussolini, Hitler did not claim back South Tyrol when his troops invaded Austria in 1938. In the aftermath of WWII, Tyrol was divided into zones occupied by Allied forces until the country proclaimed its neutrality in 1955. Since then Tyrol has enjoyed peace and prosperity, and tourism, particularly the ski industry, has flourished.

MOVING ON?

For tips, recommendations and reviews, head to shop.lonelyplanet.com to purchase a downloadable PDF of the Italy chapter from Lonely Planet's Western Europe guide.

ℹ Getting There & Around

AIR

Lying 4km west of Innsbruck's city centre, Innsbruck Airport (p393), caters to a handful of national (Vienna and Graz) and international (London, Amsterdam, Frankfurt, Hamburg, Palma and Antalya) flights, handled mostly by Austrian Airlines, British Airways, easyJet, Niki and Lufthansa.

CAR & MOTORCYCLE

The main road and rail route in and out of Tyrol follows the Inntal (Inn River), with the east–west A12/E60 cutting the province into almost equal halves, entering from Germany near Kufstein and exiting west of St Anton in Vorarlberg. The A13 connects Tyrol with Italy, crossing the Brenner Pass directly south of Innsbruck.

PUBLIC TRANSPORT

Regional transport, covering buses, trams and Österreiche Bundesbahn (ÖBB; Austrian Federal Railway) trains, is run by the **Verkehrsverbund Tirol** (www.vvt.at). Ticket prices depend on the number of zones you travel through; a single ticket costs €1.90, a day pass €3.80. Additionally, Tyrol is divided into 12 overlapping transport zones. A regional pass covering all 12 zones costs €38.60/135.10 per week/month.

Innsbruck

🖉 0512 / POP 121,329 / ELEV 574M

Tyrol's capital is a sight to behold. The jagged rock spires of the Nordkette range are so close that within minutes it's possible to travel from the city's heart to over 2000m above sea level and alpine pastures where cowbells chime. Summer and winter activities abound, and it's understandable why some visitors only take a peek at Innsbruck proper before heading for the hills. But to do so is a shame, for Innsbruck is in many ways Austria in microcosm: its late-medieval Altstadt (old town) is picture-book stuff, presided over by a grand Habsburg palace and baroque cathedral, while its Olympic ski jump with big mountain views make a spectacular leap between the urban and the outdoors.

History

Innsbruck dates from 1180, when the little market settlement on the north bank of the Inn River spread to the south bank via an eponymous new bridge – Ynsprugg.

In 1420 Innsbruck became the ducal seat of the Tyrolean Habsburgs, but it was under the reign of Emperor Maximil-

Innsbruck

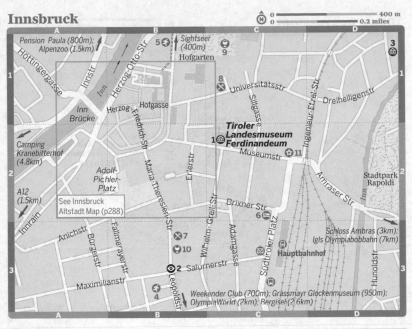

N 0 ————— 400 m
   0 ————— 0.2 miles

Innsbruck

⊙ Top Sights
1 Tiroler Landesmuseum
   Ferdinandeum.....................................C2

⊙ Sights
2 Triumphpforte..B3
3 Zeughaus...D1

⊕ Activities, Courses & Tours
4 Die Börse...B3
  Inntour...(see 4)
5 Nordkettenbahnen...................................B1

⊜ Sleeping
6 Grand Hotel Europa.................................C2

⊗ Eating
7 Chez Nico...B3
8 Himal..C1

⊜ Drinking & Nightlife
9 Hofgarten Café...C1
10 Theresienbräu...B3

⊛ Entertainment
11 Cinematograph..C2

ian I (1490–1519) that the city reached its pinnacle in power and prestige; many of the emperor's monuments, including the shimmering Goldenes Dachl, are still visible today. Maximilian was not the only Habsburg to influence the city's skyline: Archduke Ferdinand II reconstructed the Schloss Ambras, and Empress Maria Theresia the Hofburg.

Two world wars aside, Innsbruck has enjoyed a fairly peaceful existence over the centuries. More recently, the city held the Winter Olympics in 1964 and 1976, and the Winter Youth Olympic Games in 2012.

⊙ Sights

Many of the sights in Innsbruck close an hour or two earlier in winter (generally from November to early May).

★ **Hofkirche**
CHURCH
(Map p288; www.tiroler-landesmuseum.at; Universitätstrasse 2; combined ticket with Volkskunst Museum adult/child/family €10/6/20; ⊙ 9am-5pm Mon-Sat, 12.30-5pm Sun) Innsbruck's pride and joy is the Gothic Hofkirche, one of Europe's finest royal court churches. It was commissioned in 1553 by Ferdinand I, who enlisted top artists of the age such as Albrecht Dürer, Alexander Colin and Peter Vischer the Elder.

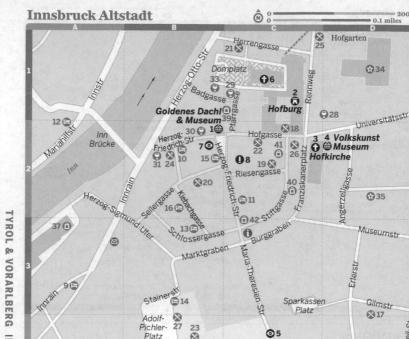

Innsbruck Altstadt

Top billing goes to the empty **sarcophagus of Emperor Maximilian I** (1459–1519), a masterpiece of German Renaissance sculpture, elaborately carved from black marble.

The tomb is embellished with Alexander Colins' white marble reliefs based on Dürer's *Ehrenpforte* (Triumphal Arch) woodcuts, depicting victorious scenes from Maximilian's life such as the Siege of Kufstein (1504). The twin rows of 28 giant bronze figures that guard the sarcophagus include Dürer's legendary King Arthur, who was apparently Emperor Maximilian's biggest idol. You're now forbidden to touch the statues, but numerous inquisitive hands have already polished parts of the dull bronze, including Kaiser Rudolf's codpiece!

Andreas Hofer (1767–1810), the Tyrolean patriot who led the rebellion against Napoleon's forces, is entombed in the church. In the **Silberkapelle**, a dazzling silver Madonna keeps watch over the marble tomb of Archduke Ferdinand II and his first wife, Philippine Welser.

★**Volkskunst Museum** MUSEUM
(Folk Art Museum; Map p288; www.tiroler-landes-museum.at; Universitätstrasse 2; combined ticket with Hofkirche adult/child/family €10/6/20; ⊙9am-5pm) Next door to the Hofkirche, Volkskunst Museum presents a fascinating romp through Tyrolean folk art from hand-carved sleighs and Christmas cribs to carnival masks and cow bells. On the 1st floor is a beautifully restored Gothic *Stube* (parlour) complete with low ceiling, wood panelling and an antique tiled oven.

Schloss Ambras CASTLE
(www.schlossambras-innsbruck.at; Schlossstrasse 20; adult/child/family €10/free/18; ⊙10am-5pm; ⓓ) Picturesquely perched on a hill, this Renaissance pile was acquired in 1564 by Archduke Ferdinand II, then ruler of Tyrol, who transformed it from a fortress into a

Innsbruck Altstadt

palace. He was the mastermind behind the **Spanische Saal** (Spanish Hall), a 43m-long banquet hall with a wooden inlaid ceiling and Tyrolean nobles gazing from the walls. Also note the grisaille (grey relief) around the courtyard and the sunken bath-tub where his beloved Philippine used to bathe.

Ferdinand instigated the magnificent Ambras Collection, encompassing three elements. Highlights of the **Rüstkammer** (Armour Collection) include the archduke's wedding armour – specially shaped to fit his bulging midriff ! – and the 2.6m suit created for giant Bartlmä Bon. The **Kunst und Wunderkammer** (Art and Curiosity Cabinet) is crammed with fantastical objects, including a petrified shark, gravity-defying stilt shoes and the Fangstuhl – a chair designed to trap drunken guests at Ferdinand's raucous parties.

The **Portraitgalerie** features room upon room of Habsburg portraits, with paintings by Titian, Velázquez and van Dyck. Maria Anna of Spain (No 126, Room 22) wins the prize for the most ludicrous hairstyle. When Habsburg portraits begin to pall, you can stroll or picnic in the extensive **castle** gardens (⊙6am-8pm) **FREE**, home to strutting peacocks. Schloss Ambras is 4.5km southeast of the centre. The Sightseer bus (p292) runs every half hour between the castle and central stops like the Hauptbahnhof (central train station) and Hofburg.

★**Goldenes Dachl & Museum**   MUSEUM
(Golden Roof; Map p288; Herzog-Friedrich-Strasse 15; adult/child €4/2; ⊙10am-5pm, closed Mon Oct-Apr) Innsbruck's golden wonder is this Gothic oriel, built for Emperor Maximilian I and glittering with 2657 fire-gilt copper tiles. An audio guide whizzes you through the history in the museum; look for the grotesque tournament helmets designed to resemble the Turks of the rival Ottoman Empire.

★**Hofburg**   PALACE
(Imperial Palace; Map p288; www.hofburg-innsbruck.at; Rennweg 1; adult/child €8/free; ⊙9am-5pm) Demanding attention with its imposing facade and cupolas, the Hofburg was built as a castle for Archduke Sigmund the Rich in the 15th century, expanded by Emperor Maximilian I in the the 16th century and

THE BELLS OF INNSBRUCK

En route to Bergisel, consider stopping at the **Grassmayr Glockenmuseum** (www.grassmayr.at; Leopoldstrasse 53; adult/child €7/4.50; ☺9am-5pm Mon-Fri, plus 9am-5pm Sat May-Sep) to discover the Grassmayr family's 400 years of bell-making tradition. Besides exhibits including some formidable Romanesque and Gothic bells, you can watch the casting process and have a go at ringing the bells to achieve different notes.

given a total baroque makeover by Empress Maria Theresia in the 18th century.

The centrepiece of the lavish rococo state apartments is the 31m-long **Riesensaal** (Giant's Hall), adorned with frescoes and paintings of Maria Theresia and her 16 children (including Marie Antoinette), who look strangely identical – maybe the artist was intent on avoiding royal wrath arising from sibling rivalry in the beauty stakes.

★**Tiroler Landesmuseum Ferdinandeum** GALLERY
(Map p287; www.tiroler-landesmuseum.at; Museumstrasse 15; adult/child/family €10/6/20; ☺9am-5pm Tue-Sun) This treasure trove of Tyrolean history and art moves from Bronze Age artefacts to the original reliefs used to design the Goldenes Dachl. Alongside brooding Dutch masterpieces of the Rembrandt ilk, the gallery displays an astounding collection of Austrian art including Gothic altarpieces, a handful of Klimt and Kokoschka paintings, and some shocking Viennese Actionist works (for a description of Actionism, see p370).

More specific to Tyrol are the late-baroque works by fresco master Paul Troger, Alfons Walde's Kitzbühel winterscapes and Albin Egger-Lienz' sombre depictions of rural life in postwar Tyrol.

ℹ ONE TICKET: TIROLER LANDESMUSEEN

One ticket (adult/child €10/6) gets you entry to all of the Tiroler Landesmuseen museums, including the Ferdinandeum, Hofkirche, Volkskunstmuseum and Zeughaus. For more details, visit www.tiroler-landesmuseen.at.

Dom St Jakob CATHEDRAL
(St James' Cathedral; Map p288; Domplatz; ☺10.15am-7.30pm Mon-Sat, 12.30-7.15pm Sun) **FREE** Innsbruck's 18th-century cathedral is a feast of over-the-top baroque. The Asam brothers from Munich completed much of the sumptuous art and stucco work, though the Madonna above the high altar is by the German painter Lukas Cranach the Elder.

Bergisel SKI JUMP
(www.bergisel.info; adult/child €9/4; ☺9am-6pm) Rising above Innsbruck like a celestial staircase, this glass-and-steel ski jump was designed by much-lauded Iraqi architect Zaha Hadid. From May to July, fans pile in to see athletes train, while preparations step up a gear in January for the World Cup Four Hills Tournament.

It's 455 steps or a two-minute funicular ride to the 50m-high **viewing platform**. Here, the panorama of the Nordkette range, Inntal and Innsbruck is breathtaking, though the cemetery at the bottom has undoubtedly made a few ski-jumping pros quiver in their boots.

Bus 4143 and line TS run from the Hauptbahnhof to Bergisel.

Alpenzoo ZOO
(www.alpenzoo.at; Weiherburggasse 37; adult/child €9/4.50; ☺9am-6pm) Billing itself as a conservation-oriented zoo, this is where you can get close to alpine wildlife like golden eagles, chamois and ibex. To get there, walk up the hill from Rennweg or take bus W from the Marktplatz.

Zeughaus MUSEUM
(Map p287; Zeughausgasse 1; adult/child/family €10/6/20; ☺9am-5pm Tue-Sun) Emperor Maximilian's former arsenal, the Zeughaus runs chronologically through Tyrol's cultural history. It kicks off with geological and mineral history, including the silver that made Hall and Schwaz medieval powerhouses, but mostly concentrates on Tyrol's greatest hero, Andreas Hofer.

Stadtturm TOWER
(Map p288; Herzog-Friedrich-Strasse 21; adult/child €3/1.50; ☺10am-8pm) Climb this tower's 148 steps for 360-degree views of the city's rooftops, spires and surrounding mountains.

Hölblinghaus LANDMARK
(Map p288; Herzog-Friedrich-Strasse) A late-Gothic-turned-rococo townhouse that is the architectural equivalent of a wedding cake,

with its stuccolike piped icing, pastel colours and naturalistic ornament.

Annasäule
LANDMARK

(St Anne's Column; Map p288; Maria-Theresien-Strasse) Topped by a statue of the Virgin Mary, this column was erected in 1703 to mark the repulsing of a Bavarian attack.

Triumphpforte
LANDMARK

(Map p287; Salurnerstrasse) This triumphal arch was built in 1765 to commemorate the marriage of the then emperor-to-be Leopold II.

🏃 Activities

Anyone who loves the great outdoors will be just itching to head up into the Alps in Innsbruck. Aside from skiing and walking, rafting, mountain biking, paragliding and bobsledding tempt the daring.

Summer Activities

Nordkettenbahnen
FUNICULAR

(Map p287; www.nordkette.com; 1 way/return to Hungerburg €4.30/7.10, Seegrube €15.40/25.70, Hafelekar €17.10/25.80; ⊙ Hungerburg 7am-7.15pm Mon-Fri, 8am-7.15pm Sat & Sun, Seegrube 8.30am-5.30pm daily, Hafelekar 9am-5pm daily) Zaha Hadid's space-age funicular runs every 15 minutes, whizzing you from the Congress Centre to the slopes in no time. Walking trails head off in all directions from **Hungerburg** and **Seegrube**. For more of a challenge, there is a downhill track for mountain bikers and two *Klettersteige* (via ferrate; fixed-rope routes for climbers). Patrolled by inquisitive alpine sheep, the 2334m summit of **Hafelekar** affords tremendous views over Innsbruck to the snowcapped giants of the Austrian Alps, including 3798m **Grossglockner**.

Innsbrucker Klettersteig
VIA FERRATA

(adult/child incl cable car €26/14.30; ⊙ Jun-Sep) Hafelekar cable car top station (2256m) is the starting point for Innsbruck's head-spinning, seven-hour via ferrata. The trail is not for the faint-hearted – it traverses seven peaks and affords tremendous views of the Stubaier, Zillertaler and Ötztaler Alps. You can rent equipment at the sports shop at Seegrube.

Nordkette Singletrail
MOUNTAIN BIKING

(http://nordkette-singletrail.at; ⊙ late May-early Nov) A magnet to hard-core downhill mountain bikers, this *very* steep, technically demanding track begins 200m below Seegrube. It's free to transport your bike

on the cable car but make sure it is clean. There is a special half-/one-day ticket costing €21/28 in case you want to ride it more than once.

Die Börse
ADVENTURE SPORTS

(Map p287; www.dieboerse.at; Leopoldstrasse 4; ⊙ 9am-6.30pm Mon-Fri, to 5pm Sat & Sun) Rents skis and snowboards (€19 to €35 per day) and city, electro, mountain, free-ride and downhill bikes (€19 to €35).

Inntour
ADVENTURE SPORTS

(Map p287; www.inntour.com; Leopoldstrasse 4; ⊙ 9am-6.30pm Mon-Fri, to 5pm Sat & Sun) Based at Die Börse, Inntour arranges all manner of thrillseeking pursuits, including canyoning (€80), tandem paragliding (€105), white-water rafting (€48) and bungee jumping from the 192m Europabrücke (€175).

Winter Activities

Innsbruck is the gateway to a formidable ski arena, the **Olympia SkiWorld Innsbruck**, covering nine surrounding resorts and 300km of slopes to test all abilities. The most central place to pound powder is the **Nordpark** (⊙ cable cars every 15min 8am-7pm). At the top, boarders can pick up speed on the quarter-pipe, kickers and boxes at **Nitro Skylinepark** (www.skylinepark.at), while daring skiers ride the Hafelekar-Rinne, one of Europe's steepest runs with a 70% gradient. The **OlympiaWorld Ski Pass** (3-/6-day pass €117/197) covers all areas; ski buses are free to anyone with an Innsbruck Card (p293).

Nonskiers can find their snowy fun on cross-country trails, toboggan runs, ice rinks and winter walking trails.

WORTH A TRIP

OLYMPIC BOBSLED

For a minute in the life of an Olympic bobsleigh racer, you can't beat the **Olympiabobbahn** (☑ 377 160; www.olympiaworld.at; Heiligwasserwiese, Igls; summer/winter €28/30; ⊙ Dec-Mar & Jul-Aug), built for the 1976 Winter Olympics. Zipping around 10 curves and picking up speeds of up to 100km/h, the bob run is 800m of pure hair-raising action. You can join a professional bobsled driver in winter or summer; call ahead for the exact times. To reach it, take bus J from the Landesmuseum to Igls Olympiaexpress.

☞ Tours

Innsbruck Information (p296) organises guided city walks, which meander through the historical centre. One-hour tours leave at 2pm daily (plus 11am in July and August) and cost €8. If you would rather go it alone, pick up an iTour guide (€7.50), which takes you on a two-hour, 23-stage walk through town.

To capture more than the Altstadt in a tour, jump on a bright-red Sightseer bus (www.sightseer.at; adult/child day pass €6.50/4.70), running between Messe/Zeughaus and Schloss Ambras. Buses depart from Congress/Hofburg on Rennweg every 40 minutes roughly between 10am and 5.30pm. Innsbruck Information sells tickets.

✷ Festivals & Events

Tanzsommer   PERFORMING ARTS
(www.tanzsommer.at; ⊙ mid-Jun–mid-Jul) From classical ballet to gravity-defying acrobatics, dance takes the stage by storm at this festival.

Festwochen der Alten Musik   MUSIC
(Festival of Early Music; www.altemusik.at; ⊙ Aug) This festival brings baroque concerts to venues such as Schloss Ambras, the Landestheater, Goldenes Dachl and Hofburg.

Christkindlmarkt   CHRISTMAS MARKET
(www.christkindlmarkt.cc; ⊙ mid-Nov–6 Jan; ⋒) Innsbruck twinkles festively at Christmas markets in the Altstadt, Marktplatz and Maria-Theresien-Strasse from mid-November to Epiphany. Kids love the fairytale-themed Kiebachgasse and Köhleplatzl.

Vierschanzentournee   SKIING
(Four Hills Tournament; http://vierschanzentournee.com; ⊙ Dec-Jan) Innsbruck sees in the New Year by hosting one of four World Cup ski-jumping events at Bergisel.

DON'T MISS

FREE GUIDED HIKES

From late May to October, Innsbruck Information arranges daily guided hikes from sunrise walks to lantern-lit strolls and half-day mountain jaunts, which are, incredibly, free to anyone with an Innsbruck guest card. Pop into the tourist office to register and browse the program.

🛏 Sleeping

Innsbruck and the villages of Igls and Mutters offer private rooms that cost between €20 and €40; Innsbruck Information (p296) can make bookings.

★ Nepomuks   HOSTEL €
(Map p288; ☎ 584 118; www.nepomuks.at; Kiebachgasse 16; dm/d €24/58; ⋒) Could this be backpacker heaven? Nepomuks sure comes close, with its Altstadt location, well-stocked kitchen and high-ceilinged dorms with homely touches like CD players. The delicious breakfast in attached Café Munding, with homemade pastries, jam and fresh-roasted coffee, gets your day off to a grand start.

Pension Paula   GUESTHOUSE €
(☎ 292 262; www.pensionpaula.at; Weiherburggasse 15; s €35-44, d €58-68, tr €89, q €100; 🅿) This *Pension* (guesthouse) occupies an alpine chalet and has superclean, homely rooms (most with balcony). It's up the hill towards the zoo and has great vistas across the city.

Camping Kranebitterhof   CAMPGROUND €
(☎ 279 558; www.campingplatz-innsbruck.at; Kranebitterallee 216; camp site incl tent/caravan, car & 2 people €25-30; ⋒⋒) This modern camping ground west of town has alpine views and a rural feel. There's an on-site pizzeria and playground. Bus line O stops nearby or take the scenic cycle route along the River Inn into town, 5.5km away.

★ Hotel Weisses Kreuz   HISTORIC HOTEL €€
(Map p288; ☎ 594 79; www.weisseskreuz.at; Herzog-Friedrich-Strasse 31; s €40-76, d €77-132; 🅿⊙⋒⋒) Beneath the arcades, this atmospheric Altstadt hotel has played host to guests for 500 years, including a 13-year-old Mozart. With its wood-panelled parlours, antiques and twisting staircase, the hotel oozes history with every creaking beam. Rooms are supremely comfortable, staff charming and breakfast is a lavish spread.

Goldener Adler   HISTORIC HOTEL €€
(Map p288; ☎ 571 111; www.goldeneradler.com; Herzog-Friedrich-Strasse 6; s €115, d €140-260; 🅿❄⋒⋒) Since opening in 1390, the grand Goldener Adler has welcomed kings, queens and Salzburg's two biggest exports: Mozart and Mrs Von Trapp. Rooms are elegant with gold drapes and squeaky-clean marble bathrooms.

Weinhaus Happ GUESTHOUSE €€

(Map p288; ☑582 980; www.weinhaus-happ.at; Herzog-Friedrich-Strasse 14; s/d €75/110) Happ exudes old-world atmosphere. The rooms haven't been decorated in donkeys' years, but its plus points are many: prime views of the Goldenes Dachl, a cavernous wine cellar and a rustic restaurant (mains €11 to €21).

Basic Hotel HOTEL €€

(Map p288; ☑586 385; www.basic-hotel.at; Innrain 16; s €68-100, d €95-130; ⓢ) For central, simple digs bang in the heart of town, Basic Hotel takes some beating. It goes for a stream-lined, ultramodern look in its bright, open-plan rooms and bistro, and has 24-hour self check-in. Breakfast is served in Stefan's bakery.

Mondschein HOTEL €€

(Map p288; ☑227 84; www.mondschein.at; Mariahilfstrasse 6; s €87-110, d €125-188, f €230-318; Ⓟ✳@ⓢ⌨) The moon beams down as you enter this riverside hotel, harboured in a 15th-century fisherman's house. Rooms painted in blues and sunny yellows give way to Swarovski-crystal-studded bathrooms glittering like a night sky.

Weisses Rössl GUESTHOUSE €€

(Map p288; ☑583 057; www.roessl.at; Kiebach-gasse 8; s €70-110, d €100-160; @ⓢ⌨) An antique rocking horse greets you at this 600-year-old guesthouse. The vaulted entrance leads up to spacious rooms recently revamped with blonde wood, fresh hues and crisp white linen. The owner is a keen hunter, so it's no surprise that the restaurant (mains €9 to €18) has a meaty menu.

Penz Hotel HOTEL €€€

(Map p288; ☑575 657; www.the-penz.com; Adolf-Pichler-Platz 3; s €145-265, d €185-295; Ⓟ✳ⓢ⌨) Behind a sheer wall of glass, the Penz is a contemporary design hotel next to the Rathaus Galerien. The minimalist rooms in muted hues are spruced up with flat-screen TVs and shiny chrome fittings. At breakfast, a whole table is piled high with exotic fruits.

Grand Hotel Europa LUXURY HOTEL €€€

(Map p287; ☑59 31; www.grandhoteleuropa.at; Südtiroler Platz 2; s €145-185, d €204-264, ste €324-424; Ⓟ✳@ⓢ) This luxurious pile opposite the station has been given a facelift. Pared-down chic now defines the rooms, though old-world grandeur lingers in the opulent Baroque Hall and wood-panelled restaurant.

ⓘ CITY SAVERS

The money-saving **Innsbruck Card** allows one visit to Innsbruck's main sights and attractions, a return journey with any cable car or funicular, five hours' bike rental and unlimited use of public transport including the Sightseer and Kristallwelten shuttle bus. The card also yields numerous discounts on tours and activities. It's available at the tourist office and costs €31/39/45 for 24/48/72 hours (half-price for children).

Stay overnight in Innsbruck and you'll receive a **guest card**, giving discounts on transport and activities, entry to a number of pools and lidos, and allowing you to join the tourist office's free guided hikes in summer.

Mick Jagger and Queen Elizabeth II are famous past guests.

✕ Eating

A mix of Austrian and international restaurants, bistros and pavement cafes cluster in the pedestrianised Altstadt.

Cafe Munding CAFE €

(Map p288; www.munding.at; Kiebachgasse 16; cake €2-4; ⏱8am-8pm) Modern art hangs on the walls of this 200-year-old cafe. Besides whipping up delicious cakes – try the moist chocolate raspberry *Haustorte* or the chocolate-marzipan *Mozarttorte* – the family roast their own coffee and make preserves with fruit freshly picked from local farms.

Mamma Mia PIZZERIA €

(Map p288; ☑562 902; Kiebachgasse 2; mains €7-9; ⏱10.30am-midnight) This no-frills Italian bistro has a great buzz, alongside huge pizzas, fresh salads and healthy pasta dishes. The sunny terrace is a favourite spot in summer.

Kröll SNACKS €

(Map p288; Hofgasse 6; snacks €3-4.50; ⏱6am-9pm) Forget plain apple, this hole-in-the-wall cafe's strudels include rhubarb, poppy, feta and plum. The fresh juices pack a vitamin punch.

Cafe Katzung CAFE €

(Map p288; www.cafe-katzung.at; Herzog-Friedrich-Strasse 16; snacks €5-8; ⏱8am-midnight Mon-Sat, from 9am Sun) Katzung attracts a faithful local following for its laid-back vibe, Goldenes

Dachl–facing terrace and homemade cakes and ice cream. Menu favourites include all-day breakfasts, toasted sandwiches and wholesome soups.

★ Die Wilderin
AUSTRIAN €€

(Map p288; ☑ 562 728; www.diewilderin.at; Seilergasse 5; ⊙ 5pm-2am Tue-Sat, 4pm-midnight Sun) 🌾 Take a gastronomic walk on the wild side at this artily understated, fashionably relaxed restaurant. The menu sings of the seasons, be it asparagus, game or strawberries. The chef believes adamantly in local sourcing and knows his suppliers by name, so what you can expect are farm-fresh and foraged ingredients of prime quality, all expertly cooked and seasoned. Live music jazzes up Tuesday nights, but be sure to book ahead.

Pavillon
FUSION €€

(Map p288; ☑ 257 000; www.der-pavillon.at; Rennweg 4; mains €26.50-33; ⊙ cafe 9am-midnight, restaurant 6pm-midnight Tue-Sat) A rising star on Innsbruck's gastro scene, this glass-cube restaurant-cafe is all clean-lined, backlit minimalism, with a terrace on Landestheaterplatz. Manning the stove is 27-year-old

---

THE PERFECT PICNIC

With the Alps and River Inn as its backdrop, Innsbruck has some incredibly scenic spots for a picnic. Here's where you'll find goodies:

s'Speckladele (Map p288; Stiftgasse 4; ⊙ 9am-1pm & 2-6pm Mon-Fri, 9am-3pm Sat) Two at a time please... This Lilliputian shop has been doing a brisk trade in quality regional sausages, hams and speck made from 'happy pigs' for the past 60 years. Mini Teufel sausages with a chilli kick are the must-try.

s'Culinarium (Map p288; Pfarrgasse 1; ⊙ 10am-6pm Mon-Sat) The charming Herby Signor will help you pick an excellent bottle of Austrian wine at his shop-cum-bar. s'Culinarium also stocks other Tyrolean specialities from honey to schnapps.

Markthalle (Map p288; www.markthalle-innsbruck.at; Innrain; ⊙ 7am-6.30pm Mon-Fri, to 1pm Sat) Fresh-baked bread, Tyrolean cheese, organic fruit, smoked ham and salami – it's all under one roof at this riverside covered market.

---

chef Manuel Hanser. Served with imagination, his Med-inflected specialities strongly invoke the seasons, from elderflower soup with marinated Artic char, cow parsley and vanilla asparagus to venison served with a poached peach.

Chez Nico
VEGETARIAN €€

(Map p287; ☑ 0650-451 06 24; www.chez-nico.at; Maria-Theresien-Strasse 49; 2-course lunch €13.50, 6-course menu €55; ⊙ noon-2pm Tue-Fri, 6.30-10pm Mon-Sat; 🌱) Take a creative Parisian chef with an artistic eye and a passion for herbs, *et voilà*, you get Chez Nico. At this intimate bistro, Nicolas Curtil (Nico) treats a handful of lucky, lucky diners to an all-vegetarian, season-inspired menu, with beautifully presented dishes along the lines of smoked aubergine wonton and chanterelle-apricot goulash. You won't miss the meat, we swear.

Dengg
INTERNATIONAL €€

(Map p288; ☑ 582 347; www.dengg.co.at; Riesengasse 11; mains €13-23; ⊙ 8.30am-11pm) A cool curiosity shop of a bistro, with a minimalist, snow white interior that contrasts strikingly with the old-fashioned kitchen appliances plastered to its walls, Dengg feels like a secret despite its Altstadt location. The chef rustles up regional-meets-Med taste sensations like pike perch with red port sauce and fennel puree, and summer tiramisu with espresso sorbet.

Fischerhäusl
AUSTRIAN €€

(Map p288; ☑ 583 535; www.fischerhaeusl.com; Herrengasse 8; 2-course lunch €7.80, mains €9-23; ⊙ 10am-1am Mon-Sat) The lemon-fronted Fischerhausl has stood in this hidden spot between Domplatz and the Hofburg since 1758. On the menu is Tyrolean grub such as *Kaspressknödelsuppe*, cheesy dumplings swimming in broth, and *Gröstl*, a potato, bacon and onion fry-up. The terrace fills quickly on warm days.

Himal
ASIAN €€

(Map p287; ☑ 588 588; Universitätsstrasse 13; mains €9.50-14.50; ⊙ 11.30am-2.30pm & 6-10.30pm Mon-Sat, 6-10.30pm Sun; 🌱) Friendly and intimate, Himal delivers vibrant, robust Nepalese flavours. Spot-on curries are mopped up with naan and washed down with mango lassis. Vegetarians are well catered for.

Thai-Li-Ba
THAI €€

(Map p288; ☑ 567 888; Rathaus Galerien; mains €12-18; ⊙ 9am-midnight Mon-Sat; 🍴) Get your noodle fix at this open-plan Thai place centred on an open kitchen. The wok, rice and curry dishes are well spiced and brilliantly fresh.

Cafe Sacher
CAFE €€

(Map p288; www.sacher.com; Rennweg 1; mains €9-17; ⊙8.30am-midnight) Sidling up to the Hofburg, this grand chandelier-lit cafe is the place to linger over chocolate *Sacher Torte*, salads or lunch. There are free classical concerts in the courtyard in summer.

Cafe Central
CAFE €€

(Map p288; www.central.co.at; Gilmstrasse 5; mains €8-16; ⊙7am-10pm; ✍) Little has changed since this old-world, Viennese-style cafe opened in 1889. Come to lunch on schnitzel or goulash or to browse the daily papers over a slice of torte. There's live piano music on Sunday evenings in winter.

Stiftskeller
AUSTRIAN €€

(Map p288; Hofgasse 6; mains €8-15; ⊙10am-midnight) A vaulted restaurant with a large beer garden for Augustiner Bräu beers and hearty fare like pork roast with beer sauce, dumplings and sauerkraut.

Lichtblick
INTERNATIONAL €€€

(Map p288; ☑566 550; www.restaurant-lichtblick. at; Maria-Theresien-Strasse 18, Rathaus Galerien; lunch €9.90-13, set menus €40-50; ⊙10am-1am Mon-Sat) On the 7th floor of the Rathaus Galerien, this chic glass-walled restaurant has sweeping views over Innsbruck to the Alps beyond. Backlighting and minimalist design create a sleek backdrop for Mediterranean-inspired cuisine such as crayfish gazpacho and herby polenta with chanterelles, rocket and parmesan.

⏺ Drinking & Nightlife

Innsbruck's student population keeps the bar and clubbing scene upbeat. Besides a glut of bars in the Altstadt, a string of bars huddles under the railway arches on Ingenieur-Etzel-Strasse, otherwise known as the Viaduktbögen.

Moustache
BAR

(Map p288; www.cafe-moustache.at; Herzog-Otto-Strasse 8; ⊙11am-2am Tue-Sun; ☎) You too can try your hand at playing Spot-the-Moustache (Einstein, Charlie Chaplin and others), the preferred pastime at this retro bolthole. It has a terrace overlooking pretty Domplatz, as well as Club Aftershave in the basement.

Hofgarten Café
BAR

(Map p287; Rennweg 6a; ⊙10am-2am Tue-Thu & Sun, to 4pm Fri & Sat) DJ sessions and a tree-shaded beer garden are crowd-pullers at this trendy cafe-cum-bar set in the greenery of Hofgarten. Sip cocktails beneath the stars or gaze up at the star-studded ceiling in the pavilion.

360°
BAR

(Map p288; Rathaus Galerien; ⊙10am-1am Mon-Sat) Clean lines, cream leather and lounge music create a relaxed mood in this sphere-shaped bar beside Lichtblick. Grab a cushion and drink in 360-degree views of the city and Alps from the balcony skirting the bar.

Theresienbräu
PUB

(Map p287; Maria-Theresien-Strasse 53; ⊙11am-1am Mon-Wed, to 2am Thu-Sat, noon-9pm Sun) Copper vats gleam and rock plays at this lively microbrewery, which opens onto a garden seating 120 beer guzzlers and pretzel munchers. The ceiling is studded with 10,000 dried roses.

Das Stadtcafe
BAR

(Map p288; www.das-stadtcafe.at; Universitätsstrasse 1; ⊙6pm-4am Tue-Sat, to midnight Sun) Das Stadtcafe sports a glam interior and a people-watching terrace facing the Hofburg. It can feel a bit *schickimiki* (self-consciously cool) at times, but there's a great events line-up: from Wednesday's Caribbean nights to funky house at Friday's City Club.

Elferhaus
PUB

(Map p288; Herzog-Friedrich-Strasse 11; ⊙10am-2am) Eleven is the magic number at Elferhaus, where you can nurse a beer beside Gothic gargoyles at the bar or take a church-like pew to hear live rock bands play. The haunt attracts a 20-something crowd that spills out onto Herzog-Friedrich-Strasse.

Krahvogel
PUB

(Map p288; Anichstrasse 12; ⊙10am-2am Mon-Sat, 5pm-1am Sun) A big black crow guards the bar at this industrial-style pub. It doesn't make much noise, but the punters do after one drink too many. There are regular live bands and big-screen sports.

In Vinum
WINE BAR

(Map p288; www.invinum.com; Innrain 1; ⊙11am-midnight Mon-Sat, 4-9pm Sun) This snug Altstadt wine bar is a relaxed choice to sample Austria's finest wines, which start at €2.80 a glass; see the website for details of the regular tastings. If you get peckish, you can snack on local cheese and ham.

Dom Cafe-Bar
BAR

(Map p288; www.domcafe.at; Pfarrgasse 3; ⊙11am-2am) Chandeliers, vaulted ceilings and an HMV gramophone set the scene in this convivial Gothic-style bar.

Weekender Club
CLUB

(www.weekenderclub.net; Tschamlerstrasse 3; ⊙9pm-4am Mon, 10pm-4am Fri & Sat) Happening warehouse club, with top DJs and gigs. It's a 10-minute walk south of Maria-Theresien-Strasse along Leopoldstrasse.

☆ Entertainment

For more entertainment options, pick up a copy of *Innsider*, found in cafes across town, or visit www.innsider.at. Schloss Ambras hosts a series of classical concerts in summer.

Tiroler Landestheater
THEATRE

(Map p288; ☑520 744; www.landestheater.at; Rennweg 2; ⊙ticket office 8.30am-7pm Mon-Sat) Innsbruck's imposing neoclassical theatre stages year-round performances of opera, dance, drama and comedy. Tickets cost between €3 and €59.

Treibhaus
CULTURAL CENTRE

(Map p288; www.treibhaus.at; Angerzellgasse 8; ⊙10am-1am) This cultural complex draws a boho crowd with its big terrace, regular DJs and live music. In August it hosts an open-air cinema.

OlympiaWorld
CONCERT VENUE

(www.olympiaworld.at; Olympiastrasse 10) This cutting-edge venue hosts big-name concerts, musicals and sports events from football to ice-hockey matches. Take bus J from the Landestheater to Landessportcenter.

Cinematograph
CINEMA

(Map p287; www.cinematograph.at; Museumstrasse 31) Independent films are screened in their original language here.

🛍 Shopping

When in the Altstadt, try Seilergasse for jewellery and accessories by local creators, Herzog-Friedrich-Strasse for everything from chocolates to crystals, and Maria-Theresien-Strasse for high-street brands.

Spezialitäten aus der Stiftsgasse
FOOD

(Map p288; Stiftsgasse 2; ⊙9.30am-6.30pm Mon-Fri, to 4pm Sat) An Aladdin's cave of home-made goodies, this vine-clad shop stocks all-Austrian honeys, oils, preserves, wines and spirits from gentian liqueur to hay schnapps.

Tiroler Heimatwerk
CRAFT

(Map p288; Meraner Strasse 2; ⊙9am-6pm Mon-Fri, to noon Sat) Great for traditional gifts, this place sells everything from *Dirndls* to hand-carved nativity figurines, stained glass and Tyrolean puppets.

Swarovski Crystal Gallery
GIFTS

(Map p288; Herzog-Friedrich-Strasse 39; ⊙8am-7.30pm) Swarovski's flagship store in Innsbruck is this gallery-style boutique, crammed with sparkling crystal trinkets, ornaments and jewellery.

Rathaus Galerien
MALL

(Map p288; www.rathausgalerien.at; Maria-Theresien-Strasse 18; ⊙9am-7pm Mon-Fri, to 6pm Sat; 🖥) High-street shops, boutiques and cafes line this glass-roofed mall.

Kaufhaus Tyrol
MALL

(Map p288; http://kaufhaus-tyrol.at; Maria-Theresien-Strasse 31; ⊙9am-7pm Mon-Wed, to 8pm Thu & Fri, to 6pm Sat; 🖥) Shopping mall with big-name stores and eateries.

🛈 Information

The Hauptbahnhof and Innsbruck Information have exchange facilities and *Bankomaten* (ATMs) are ubiquitous in the Altstadt.

Bubble Point (Innstrasse 11; ⊙7.30am-10.30pm Mon-Fri, to 10pm Sat & Sun) Self-service laundries with internet access for €2 per hour.

Innsbruck Information (Map p288; ☑535 60; www.innsbruck.info; Burggraben 3; ⊙9am-6pm) Main tourist office with truckloads of info on the city and surrounds, including skiing and walking. Sells ski passes, public-transport tickets and city maps (€1); will book accommodation (€3 commission); has an attached ticketing service (open 9am to 6pm Monday to Friday, and 9am to 12.30pm Saturday); and has internet access (€1 for 10 minutes).

Landeskrankenhaus (☑50 40; Anichstrasse 35) The *Universitätklinik* (University Clinic) at the city's main hospital has emergency services.

Main post office (Map p288; Innrain 15; ⊙7am-8pm Mon-Fri, 9am-3pm Sat, 10am-6pm Sun)

Post office (Map p287; Südtiroler Platz 10; ⊙8am-6pm Mon-Fri, 9am-noon Sat) This second post office is handy to the Hauptbahnhof.

STA Travel (Wilhelm-Greil-Strasse 14; ⊘9am-6pm Mon-Fri, 10am-2pm Sat) Student-focused travel agency.

❶ Getting There & Away

BUS
The **bus station** (Map p287) is at the southern end of the Hauptbahnhof; its ticket office is located within the station.

CAR & MOTORCYCLE
The A12 and the parallel Hwy 171 are the main roads heading west and east. The B177, to the west of Innsbruck, continues north to Germany and Munich. The A13 is a toll road (€8.50) running south through the Brenner Pass to Italy and crossing the 192m Europabrücke, spanning the Sill River. Toll-free Hwy 182 follows the same route, passing under the bridge.

TRAIN
Fast trains depart daily every two hours for Bregenz (€34.40, 2¾ hours) and Salzburg (€41.30, two hours). From Innsbruck to the Arlberg, the best views are on the right-hand side of the train. Two-hourly express trains serve Munich (€40.60, two hours) and Verona (€37, 3½ hours). Direct services to Kitzbühel also run every two hours (€19.20, 1¾ hours). There are roughly hourly connections to Lienz (€33.80, three to five hours); some pass through Italy while others take the long way round via Salzburgerland.

❶ Getting Around

TO/FROM THE AIRPORT
The airport is 4km west of the centre and served by bus F. Buses depart every 15 or 20 minutes from Maria-Theresien-Strasse (€2); taxis charge about €10 for the same trip.

CAR & MOTORCYCLE
Most of central Innsbruck has restricted parking, indicated by a blue line. You can park within these areas for a maximum of 1½ or three hours during set times (approximately shop hours). Parking garages (such as the one under the Altstadt) will set you back about €2.50/17 per hour/day.
Avis (www.avis.com; ⊘7.30am-6pm Mon-Sat, 9am-6.30pm Sun) At the airport.
Hertz (www.hertz.com; Südtiroler Platz 1; ⊘7.30am-6pm Mon-Fri, 8am-1pm Sat)

PUBLIC TRANSPORT
Single tickets on buses and trams cost €2 from the driver, €1.80 if purchased in advance. If you plan to use the city's public transport frequently you're better off buying a 24-hour ticket (€4.40). Weekly and monthly tickets are also available (€13.90 and €45.20, respectively). Tickets bought in advance, which are available from ticket machines, *Tabak* (tobacconist) shops and Innsbruck Information, must be stamped in the machines at the start of the journey.

Hall in Tirol

📞 05223 / POP 12,895 / ELEV 574M

Nestled beneath the Alps, just 9km east of Innsbruck, Hall is a beautiful medieval town that grew fat on the riches of salt in the 13th century. The winding lanes, punctuated by pastel-coloured townhouses and lantern-lit after dark, are made for aimless ambling. If you're in town for the **Weinherbst** festival on the first weekend in September, watch as the water in the Wilden Mannes fountain miraculously turns to wine.

⊙ Sights

All streets in Hall lead to the medieval Obererstadt (Upper Town), which centres on the main square, Oberer Stadtplatz.

Burg Hasegg   CASTLE
(Burg Hasegg 6; adult/child €8/6; ⊘10am-5pm Tue-Sun; ⓘ) Stepping south of the medieval centre is the Burg Hasegg, where a spiral staircase coils up to the 5th floor for far-reaching views over Hall. The castle had a 300-year career as a mint for silver *Thalers* (coins, the root of the modern word 'dollar'), and this history is unravelled in the **Münze Hall**, displaying water-driven and hammer-striking techniques. Audio guides are included in the price and kids can mint their own coin.

Pfarrkirche St Nikolaus   CHURCH
(St Nicholas Parish Church; ⊘dawn-dusk) This graceful 13th-century church is best known for its **Waldaufkapelle**, home to Florian Waldauf's grisly collection of 45 skulls and 12 bones, picked from the remains of minor saints. Each rests on embroidered cushions, capped with veils and elaborate headdresses, reminiscent of spiked haloes; the whole effect is both repulsive and enthralling.

Bergbau Museum   MUSEUM
(Fürstengasse; adult/child €3.50/2; ⊘tours 11.30am Mon, Thu & Sat) This reconstructed salt mine, complete with galleries, tools and shafts, can only be visited by 40-minute guided tour.

Rathaus
TOWN HALL

(Oberer Stadtplatz) Bordering the main square is Hall's 15th-century town hall, with its distinctive courtyard, complete with crenellated edges and mosaic crests.

🛏 Sleeping & Eating

Gasthof Badl
GUESTHOUSE €

(📞 567 84; www.badl.at; Innbrücke 4; s €48-65, d €78-102; 🅿 🛜 🚲) A short dash across the Inn River, this gem of a guesthouse has immaculate rooms (most with river view) and a tavern that knocks up a great strudel. Children will love the playground and docile St Bernard, Max. Rent a bike here to pedal along the banks to Innsbruck.

Parkhotel
HOTEL €€

(📞 537 69; www.parkhotel-hall.com; Thunfeldgasse 1; s €105-115, d €172-198; 🅿 @ 🛜) It's a surprise to find such an avant-garde design statement as this cylindrical hotel in tiny Hall. The mountains seem close enough to touch in the curvy glass-walled rooms, done out in minimalist style and earthy hues.

Goldener Löwe
AUSTRIAN €€

(📞 415 50; www.goldenerloewe-hall.at; Obere Stadtplatz; mains €8-20; ⊙ 11am-2.30pm & 5.30pm-midnight Tue-Sat) The ambience is wonderfully cosy in this historic tavern on the main square. Join locals for Austrian comfort food like *Tafelspitz* (boiled beef with horseradish) and sweet dumplings, paired with local wines.

Rathaus Cafe
CAFE €€

(Oberer Stadtplatz 2; snacks €3-6.50; ⊙ 8am-1am Mon-Thu, to 2am Fri & Sat, 9am-midnight Sun) Part of Hall's vaulted town hall has been transformed into this modern cafe. There's a terrace for people-watching over breakfast, a baguette or drink.

ℹ Information

Staff at the **tourist office** (📞 455 44; www.regionhall.at; Wallpachgasse 5; ⊙ 8.30am-6pm Mon-Fri, 9am-1pm Sat) can help you sort out accommodation. They also organise **guided tours** (adult/child €6/3.50; ⊙ 10am Mon-Sat Apr-Sep).

ℹ Getting There & Away

The B171 goes almost through the town centre, unlike the A12/E45, which is over the Inn River to the south. The train station is about 1km southwest of the centre; it is on the main Innsbruck–Wörgl train line. Trains run frequently to/from Innsbruck (€2.20, eight minutes).

Wattens

The quaint village of Wattens has one claim to fame: it's the glittering heart of the Swarovski crystal empire. Call them kitsch or classy, but there is no doubting the pulling power of these crystals at the fantastical **Swarovski Kristallwelten** (Swarovski Crystal Worlds; http://kristallwelten.swarovski.com; Kristallweltenstrasse 1; adult/child €11/free; ⊙ 9am-6.30pm), one of Austria's most visited attractions. A giant's head spewing water into a pond greets you in the park. Inside you'll find Alexander McQueen's crystal winterscape, a kaleidoscopic crystal dome and even zebras drifting past on ruby slippers in a twinkling theatre. A play on light and dark, the Conran-designed shop is where, budget depending, you can buy a bejewelled pen for a few euros or spend thousands on a crystal-encrusted elephant. Decisions, decisions...

Trains run roughly half-hourly from Innsbruck to Fritzens-Wattens (€3.80, 16 minutes), 3km north of Swarovski Kristallwelten and on the opposite side of the river.

Schwaz

📞 05242 / POP 13,058 / ELEV 545M

What is today a sleepy little town with pastel-washed houses and winding streets was once, believe it or not, Austria's second-largest city after Vienna. Schwaz wielded clout in the Middle Ages when its eyes shone brightly with silver, past glory that you can relive by going underground to the show silver mine.

◉ Sights

★ Silberbergwerk Schwaz
MINE

(Silver Mine; www.silberbergwerk.at; Alte Landstrasse 3a; adult/child/family €16/8/38; ⊙ 9am-5pm) You almost feel like breaking out into a rendition of 'Heigh-Ho' at Silberbergwerk Schwaz, as you board a mini train and venture deep into the bowels of the silver mine for a 90-minute trundle through Schwaz' illustrious past. The mine is about 1.5km east of the centre.

Altstadt
HISTORIC SITE

Schwaz' other big draw is its well-preserved Altstadt. Taking pride of place on pedestrianised Franz-Josef-Strasse, the Gothic **Pfarrkirche** (Parish Church; ⊙ dawn-dusk) immediately catches your eye with its step-gabled roof bearing 14,000 copper tiles. The web-vaulted interior purportedly harbours the largest symphonic organ in Tyrol, which is put to use at 8.15pm every Monday.

Not far south is the Gothic-meets-baroque **Franziskanerkirche** (Gilmstrasse; ⊙ dawn-dusk); Gothic windows and unfinished frescoes line its inner courtyard.

Museum der Völker MUSEUM
(www.hausdervoelker.com; St Martin; adult/child €7/5; ⊙10am-6pm) Local photographer Gert Chesi set up this museum, showcasing a rich collection of African and Asian ritual art. Rotating exhibitions home in on elements of the collection, such as spiritual Tanzania or African textile art.

🛏 Sleeping & Eating

Gasthof Einhorn Schaller GUESTHOUSE €
(☑740 47; www.gasthof-schaller.at; Innsbruckerstrasse 31; s €46-51, d €74-84, tr €92.50-105, q €111-126; P🅿❸⊕) This supercentral, family-friendly *Gasthof* (inn) combines modern rooms, done out in light pinewood and splashes of bright colour, with a traditional restaurant dishing up regional fare (mains €9 to €18), such as *Tiroler Käsespätzle*, eggy noodles topped with cheese and onions.

Villa Masianco INTERNATIONAL €€
(☑629 27; Münchner Strasse 20; lunch €5.50-6.50, pizzas €6-10, mains €8-22; ⊙10am-midnight Mon-Fri, 11am-midnight Sat, 11am-11pm Sun; ⊕) A restaurant with pizza, pasta, steaks, Tex-Mex, Thai curry and Austrian classics on the same menu might cause foodies to raise a sceptical eyebrow. Yet this ambitious culinary globetrotter manages to consistently deliver quality, which has won it a faithful local following. The vibe is relaxed in the contemporary brasserie, with terrace seating in summer and a children's play area.

ℹ Information

Tourist office (☑632 40; www.silberregionkarwendel.at; Münchnerstrasse 11; ⊙9am-5.30pm Mon-Fri, to noon Sat) The helpful tourist office provides information on sights and accommodation in Schwaz.

ℹ Getting There & Away

Schwaz is 30km east of Innsbruck and 10km west of the Zillertal on the A12 Inntal-Autobahn. There are frequent trains between Innsbruck and Schwaz (€5.80, 19 minutes).

The Zillertal

Sandwiched between the Tuxer Voralpen and the Kitzbüheler Alpen, the Zillertal (Ziller Valley) is storybook Tyrol. A steam train chugs through the broad valley, passing fertile farmland and wooded mountains, and affording snatched glimpses of snowy peaks and the fast-flowing Ziller River.

🏃 Activities

Adrenalin-based activities include rafting, rock climbing, paragliding and cycling. The Ziller and its tributaries are also good for fishing, but permits are only valid for certain stretches.

Winter Activities

While Mayrhofen is the prime spot for serious skiing, there is plenty of downhill and cross-country skiing elsewhere. The **Zillertaler Superskipass** (4 days/4 out of 6 days €161/178) covers all 487km of slopes in the valley, including the snow-sure pistes at the Hintertuxer Glacier. Ski buses connect the resorts.

Summer Activities

In summer the alpine valley morphs into excellent walking territory, with high-altitude trekking in the Tuxer Voralpen and myriad trails fanning out from the resorts of Ried, Kaltenbach, Aschau, Zell am Ziller and Ramsau. Mountain huts at elevations of around 1800m beckon weary hikers; visit www.alpenverein.at for details of huts in the valley. A detailed walking map covering the

LOCAL KNOWLEDGE

GET INTO THE ALPINE GROOVE

As well as skis or walking boots, the Zillertal is one place you'll be glad you packed that figure-hugging *Dirndl* (women's traditional dress) or extra pair of Lederhosen. This valley is the Austrian Alps' land of song and thigh-slapping tradition, where down-to-earth locals tune into *Alpenrock* (alpine rock), every *Gasthaus* (inn or restaurant) worth its weight swings to accordion-loaded *Volksmusik* (folk music) in summer, and names like the Zillertaler Haderlumpen (literally the 'Zillertal good-for-nothings') are sacrosanct. Go, enjoy!

entire region is the Kompass *Zillertaler Alpen-Tuxer Alpen* (scale 1:50,000).

If you're planning on spending a week or more in the valley between late May and mid-October, the value-for-money **Zillertal Activecard** (6/9/12 days €55/76/95.50) covers public transport, one journey per day on any of the Zillertal cable cars and entry to swimming pools.

✦ Festivals & Events

Zillertal Bike Challenge   SPORT
(www.zillertal-bikechallenge.com; ☺early Jul) Hard-core mountain bikers with nerves of steel descend on the Zillertal for this three-day bike race.

Almabtriebe   HERITAGE
(☺late Sep-early Oct) The Zillertaler celebrate the coming home of the cows, which are adorned with elaborate floral headdresses and bells. The event is a valley-wide party with feasting, *Volksmusik* and schnapps before another harsh winter shovelling cow dung.

🛏 Sleeping & Eating

Four campgrounds are situated in the valley and there is the chalet-style **Finsingerhof Hostel** (☎05288-620 10; www.finsingerhof. at; Finsingerhofweg 1; dm €20; P🐕🛜) at Uderns, 17km south of Jenbach. Local tourist offices will usually help you find *Pensionen*, private rooms, holiday apartments and farmhouses for free. Wherever you stay, enquire about the resort's *Gästekarte* (guest card).

Note that many hotels, restaurants and bars close in shoulder seasons: early April to late June and early November to mid-December.

ℹ Information

Practically every resort has its own tourist office, but the main **tourist office** (☎05288-871 87; www.zillertal.at; ☺8.30am-noon & 1-5.30pm Mon-Fri, 8.30am-noon Sat) covering the whole valley is in Schlitters, 6km from Jenbach. It stocks plenty of information on outdoor activities, along with the *Zillertaler Gästezeitung* (partially in English) magazine.

ℹ Getting There & Away

The Zillertal is serviced by a private train line, the **Zillertalbahn** (www.zillertalbahn.at), which travels the 32km from Jenbach to Mayrhofen. Those with a thirst for nostalgia can take a *Dampfzug* (steam train) along the valley. It runs at 10.30am from Jenbach to Mayrhofen and at 2.04pm and 4.34pm from Mayrhofen to Jenbach. A one-way/return ticket for the 1¾-hour journey costs €12.80/18.60. If you just want to get from A to B, it's better to take the ordinary train (€7.10, 52 minutes), which runs twice hourly.

Zell am Ziller
📞 05282 / POP 1743 / ELEV 575M

Scenically located at the foot of knife-edge Reichenspitze (3303m), Zell am Ziller is a former goldmining centre. There's now less sparkle and more swoosh about this rural and deeply traditional little village, with its fine skiing and thrilling 7.5km floodlit to-boggan run. In summer active types come to hike in the mountains or pedal up the Gerlos Alpine Road to Krimml in the Hohe Tauern National Park.

◉ Sights & Activities

Pfarrkirche   CHURCH
(Parish Church; ☺dawn-dusk) The spire of this pink-and-white parish church dominates the village centre and is surrounded by a sea of filigree crosses. You can peek inside the church, but you do so at your own risk – a sign on the door issues a warning that it is *not* a museum!

Abenteuer Goldbergbau   MINE
(www.goldschaubergwerk.com; Hainzenberg 73; adult/child €11/5.50; ☺9am-5pm) Abenteuer Goldbergbau is a two-hour tour of a gold mine, 2km east of Zell on the Gerlos road. The entry price covers a cheese tasting in the show dairy and a visit to the animal enclosure with deer, emus and llamas.

Freizeitpark Zell   SWIMMING
(www.freizeitparkzell.at; Schwimmbadweg 7; ice rink adult/child €4/2.50, swimming pool €6/3.50; ☺9am-7pm; 🔸) There's ice skating, tennis, football, bowling and a fun pool with plenty to amuse the kids at this riverside sports centre.

Arena Coaster   ROLLER COASTER
(adult/child €4.50/2.70; ☺9.30am-6pm; 🔸) Feel your stomach do backflips with a whizzy, loop-the-loop ride on Zell's 1.5km roller-coaster bob. Kids love it.

Aktivzentrum Zillertal   ADVENTURE SPORTS
(☎0664-505 95 94; www.aktivzentrum-zillertal. at; Freizeitpark Zell; 🔸) Craving a little adventure? This specialist takes you paragliding (€55 to €130), rafting on the Ziller (€35), canyoning (€35 to €59), via ferrata climbing

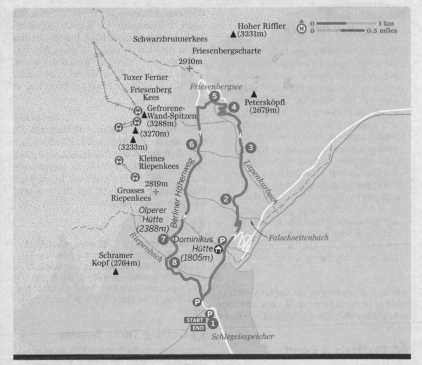

Walking Trail
Zillertal Circuit

START SCHLEGEISSPEICHER
END SCHLEGEISSPEICHER
LENGTH 11KM; FIVE TO SIX HOURS

This high-level circuit provides tremendous views to the turquoise Schlegeisspeicher and snowcapped Zillertal Alps. Though the trek involves 850m of incline, the path is well graded and mostly gentle; however, use care in bad weather. Kompass 1:50,000 map No 37 *Zillertaler Alpen-Tuxer Alpen* covers the walk in detail. Begin at the **①Schlegeisspeicher**, ringed by rugged 3000m-high peaks. From the northeast end of the car park follow signs towards the Dominikus Hütte, bearing right towards Friesenberghaus alpine hut. The path emerges at the treeline near the alpine pasture of **②Friesenbergalm** after about 45 minutes. It flattens to cross tarn-dotted pastures. Sidle around a shoulder and enter a valley overshadowed by Hoher Riffler.

Boulder-strewn meadows give way to scree patches and the **③Lapenkarbach** stream. The trail winds uphill via long bends, then tight switchbacks, to the **④Friesenberghaus** at the head of the valley around 1½ hours from Friesenbergalm. This is a scenic spot for a break.

Retrace your steps for 50m, following the signs right towards the Olperer Hütte and the Berliner Höhenweg. The trail descends slightly, crossing the outlet stream of **⑤Friesenbergsee**, then makes a short, steep ascent up the rocky slope on the other side. Turn left when you reach a junction and contour the mountainside ahead. The next 1½ hours follow an easygoing balcony trail, part of the multiday **⑥Berliner Höhenweg** route. It leads under the glacier-capped peaks of the Gefrorene-Wand-Spitzen.

About two hours from Friesenberghaus, cross a stream to reach **⑦Olperer Hütte**, a great place for a drink. Then it's a steady descent to the reservoir, winding gently over grassy hummocks before zigzagging down beside the **⑧Riepenbach** stream to the road (1½ hours from the Olperer Hütte). Turn left and head 1km to the parking area.

DON'T MISS

YODEL-WAY-HEE-HO!

If you've ever felt the urge to burst out into song Julie Andrews–style as you skip through meadows ablaze with wildflowers, you'll love the **Jodel Wanderweg** (Yodel Hiking Trail; ☑ 06565-82 43; visit www.jodelweg.at) in Königsleiten, on the Gerlos Alpine Road between Zell am Ziller and Krimml. You can either go it alone and practise your high notes at huts with giant cowbells, alpine horns and listen-repeat audio clippings, or join one of the guided sing 'n' stroll hikes with trail founder Christian Eder. The three-hour ambles begin at 10.30am every Wednesday from late June to mid-September and cost €7.60/3.80 per adult/child. Reserve by 5pm the previous day by calling ahead.

(€45 to €80) and – one for the kids – llama trekking (€20) in summer. Winter activities include snowshoe hikes (€35) and ice climbing (€70).

✦✦ Festivals & Events

Gauderfest   BEER

(www.gauderfest.at; ☉ early May) Overstrenuous activities are not recommended after a bellyful of superstrong Gauderbier (reputedly over 10% alcohol), brewed specially for this shindig. As well as eating, dancing and excessive drinking, there's a historical parade and alpine wrestling.

🛏 Sleeping & Eating

In winter expect room rates to be roughly a third higher than standard rates. There are several mediocre restaurants in the village centre.

★ Enzianhof   FARMSTAY €

(☑ 22 37; www.enzianhof.eu; Gerlosberg 23; s €32-52, d €52-94; P🛜🐾) High on a hilltop, this rustic farmhouse is perfectly located for hiking and skiing, and has warm, spacious rooms. The farmer makes his own gentian schnapps and smokes his own ham, and you can fill up on Zillertaler specialities like *Pressknödelsuppe* (Tyrolean dumpling soup) in the wood-beamed restaurant. Half board costs an extra €11 per person.

Gästehaus Brindlinger   PENSION €

(☑ 26 71; Gaudergasse 4; s & d €50-60; P @) Tucked down a quiet lane, this chalet has bright rooms with plenty of pine, rag rugs and balconies affording mountain views. Guests can wind down in the small sauna and Mrs Brindlinger lends out bikes free of charge.

Camping Hofer   CAMPGROUND €

(☑ 22 48; www.campingdorf.at; Gerlosstrasse 33; camp sites per adult/child/tent €7.10/4.80/8.20, d €40-66; P @ 🛜 🐾) This tree-shaded site's first-rate facilities include a playground, barbecue area and heated pool. If you don't fancy roughing it, check out the well-kept rooms in the guesthouse.

ⓘ Information

The **tourist office** (☑ 22 81; www.zell.at; Dorfplatz 3a; ☉ 8.30am-12.30pm & 2-6pm Mon-Fri, 8.30am-12.30pm Sat) near the train tracks is a mine of information on walking, skiing and adventure activities in the area. At the other end of Dorfplatz is the post office, with bus stops at the rear.

ⓘ Getting There & Away

Normal trains to Mayrhofen (€2.70, 10 minutes) and Jenbach (€6.10, 40 minutes) are cheaper than the steam train. Twice hourly trains to and from Innsbruck (€11.50, 1½ hours) require a change at Jenbach.

Zell am Ziller is the start of the Gerlos Alpine Road.

Gerlos Alpine Road

Open year-round, the highly scenic **Gerlos Alpine Road** (www.gerlosstrasse.at; toll per car/motorcycle €8/5) links the Zillertal in Tyrol to Krimml in Salzburgerland, winding 12km through high moor and spruce forest, and reaching a maximum elevation of 1630m.

The lookout above the turquoise *Stausee* (reservoir) is a great picnic stop, with a tremendous vista of the Alps. On the approach to Krimml near Schönmoosalm, there are bird's-eye views of the Krimml Falls.

Buses make the trip between Krimml and Zell am Ziller (one way including toll €8.70, 1½ hours) in Tyrol from 1 July to 30 September. By car, you can avoid using the toll road by following the (easy-to-miss) signs to Wald im Pinzgau, 6km north of Krimml.

Mayrhofen

📞 05285 / POP 3821 / ELEV 630M

Mayrhofen is ever so traditional in summer, with its alpine dairies, trails twisting high into the mountains and stein-swinging *Volksmusik* pouring out of every *Gasthof*. But it dances to a different tune in winter. The skiing at Ahorn and Penken is some of the country's finest, a double whammy of cruising and kamikaze in the shadow of the glaciated Zillertal range, and the après-ski is the hottest this side of the Tyrolean Alps.

🏃 Activities

Winter Activities

Snow-sure Mayrhofen has varied skiing on 159km of slopes, mostly geared towards confident intermediates, as well as some great off-piste opportunities. The skiing ranges from scenic tree-lined runs for cruisers to knee-trembling black runs, including the infamous Harakiri, to challenge experts. The **ski pass** (one-day pass €47) is valid for all cable cars, snowboard parks and lifts in Mayrhofen.

Hintertuxer Gletscher .... SKIING
(Hintertux Glacier; www.hintertuxergletscher.at; day ski pass summer/winter €39.50/47) Mayrhofen provides easy access to year-round skiing on the Hintertuxer Gletscher; the cable car is an attraction in itself, gliding above sheer cliff faces and jagged peaks to the tip of the ice blue glacier. The sundeck at 3250m affords phenomenal views of the Tuxer Alps and, on clear days, Grossglockner, the Dolomites and Zugspitze. From Christmas until early May, a free bus shuttles skiers from Mayrhofen to the glacier (included in the ski pass).

Vans Penken Park .... SNOW SPORTS
(www.vans-penken-park.com) Snowboarders are in their freestyle element in six areas with 11 kickers, 34 boxes and rails and a half-pipe at the Vans Penken Park in the Penken area, ranked one of Europe's best terrain parks.

Summer Activities

Walking is the big deal in Mayrhofen in summer, particularly in the glorious alpine country of the Naturpark Zillertaler Alpen (p305). The tourist office website, www.mayrhofen.at, has excellent information on walks, maps and GPS downloads. From the village itself, two **cable cars** (one way/return €11.30/17.80) give walkers a head start to Ahorn (1965m) and Penken (1800m). If you know your karabiner from your crampons, Mayrhofen also has some prime rock climbing and via ferrate on its doorstep.

The **Run & Walk Park** challenges Nordic walkers and joggers. Spanning a total of 130km, the 18 different routes, colour coded according to difficulty – blue is easy, red moderate, black difficult – include the Harakiri, only slightly easier to run than it is to ski! The tourist office has a route map.

Penken .... MOUNTAIN BIKING
(day pass €25) Downhill mountain bikers are in heaven on Penken. The tourist office can point you in the direction of bike rental, routes and hotels, as can its website, www.mayrhofen.at, which has a virtual bike map.

Sennerei Zillertal .... SHOW DAIRY
(www.sennerei-zillertal.at; Hollenzen 116; admission with/without tasting €11.90/5.80; ◷10am-3pm) For a fly-on-the-wall tour of a working dairy, head to the Sennerei Zillertal, where a 30-minute tour guides you through the cheese-making processes, from culturing in copper vats to mould ripening. The final products are huge wheels of Tilsiter, Bergkäse and Graukäse, a grey cheese that is virtually fat free. A tasting lets you try seven different cheeses. In summer this is accompanied by live Tyrolean music at 3pm every Friday.

Action Club Zillertal .... ADVENTURE SPORTS
(📞629 77; www.actionclub-zillertal.com; Hauptstrasse 458; ◷10am-noon & 4-6pm) Action Club Zillertal is the place to go for adventure sports from rafting the raging waters of the Ziller River (€29) to canyoning (€29 to €79),

---

THE HARAKIRI

With a 78% gradient, the Harakiri is Austria's steepest piste. This is half diving, half carving; a heart-stopping, hell-for-leather descent that leaves even accomplished skiers quaking in their ski boots. Only superfit, experienced skiers with perfect (think Bond) body control should consider tackling this monster of a run. Test out slope 17 first to see if you're able, and check piste conditions before heading out as ice renders the slope treacherous. For bragging rights in the après-ski bars, you can pick up 'survivor' souvenirs in the shop at the base of the Ahornbahn.

tubing (€35), climbing (€35 to €60), abseiling (€35) and tandem paragliding (€80 to €160).

Stocky Air
PARAGLIDING

(☑0664-340 79 76; www.stockyair.com; Hauptstrasse 456; ☺9am-noon & 3-6pm) This paragliding specialist will help you spread your wings in the surrounding Zillertaler Alps, with tandem flights costing between €75 and €145.

Salewa Mountain Shop
ROCK CLIMBING

(☑632 58; www.zillertal-alpin.at; Hauptstrasse 412; ☺8.30am-6pm Mon-Fri, 8am-4.30pm Sat) Runs climbing, via ferrata, glacier and ice-climbing tours and rents out climbing equipment (€12).

🛏 Sleeping

The tourist office can help you trawl through the mountain of sleeping options in the village; rates are roughly 30% higher in winter. Bear in mind that many hotels and restaurants close between seasons.

Stoanerhof
GUESTHOUSE €

(☑627 98; www.stoanerhof.at; Dorf Haus 764; s €49, d €58-70; P🖸🌐) Serenely located in meadows yet just a joyous hop from the Ahorn and Penken lifts, Stoanerhof is a bargain. Expect a genuinely warm welcome, cosy rooms done out in pine and big mountain views from the garden with kids' play area. It's worth forking out an extra €10 for breakfast and €12 for dinner. Ski and bike storage is available.

★ Hotel Garni Glockenstuhl
HOTEL €€

(☑631 28; www.glockenstuhl.com; Einfahrt Mitte 431; s €49-52, d €90-95, tr €140-150, q €170-180; P🖸🌐) Good old-fashioned Austrian hospitality, dreamy alpine views, free bike rental and a relaxing spa make this chalet stand head and shoulders above most in town. If you can drag yourself out of the comfiest of beds, you'll find a delicious breakfast with fresh eggs on the table.

Hotel Kramerwirt
HOTEL €€

(☑67 00; www.kramerwirt.at; Am Marienbrunnen 346; s incl half board €57-133, d €90-176; P🖸🌐) Ablaze with geraniums in summer, this rambling 500-year-old chalet has corridors full of family heirlooms, spacious rooms and an outside whirlpool. Get your tongue in a twist at the restaurant (mains €8 to €21) asking for the tasty *Zillertaler Bauernschmaus* (farmers' platter with meat, dumplings and sauerkraut).

Hotel Rose
HOTEL €€

(☑622 29; www.hotel-rose.at; Brandbergstrasse 353; s €51.50-57.50, d €91-103; P🖸) In the capable hands of the fourth-generation Kröll family, this place has spacious rooms with chunky pine furnishings and balconies. There's a little sauna and whirlpool for après-ski relaxing. The garden pumps to live *Volksmusik* daily in summer.

🍴 Eating

Metzgerei Kröll
BUTCHER €

(Scheulingstrasse 382; snacks €3-8; ☺7.30am-12.30pm & 2.30-6pm Mon-Fri, 7am-noon Sat) This family-run butchery is famed for its unique *Schlegeis-Speck* ham, cured in a hut at 1800m for three months to achieve its aroma. There are a handful of tables where you can sample this speciality and the delicious homemade sausages.

Cafe-Konditorei Kostner
CAFE €

(Hauptstrasse 414; snacks & mains €4,.50-10.50; ☺6.30am-6pm) 🌿 Great organic wholemeal bread and homemade cakes, alongside salads and heart-warming dishes like goulash.

CYCLING THE ZILLERTAL

The Zillertal is cycling nirvana, particularly for serious mountain bikers, many of whom limber up here before taking part in the gruelling three-day Zillertal Bike Challenge (p300) in July. The wide, sunny valley and surrounding 3000m peaks are laced with 800km of well-marked routes that reach from easygoing two-hour jaunts along the valley floor to panoramic mountain passes, such as the notoriously tough 56km trail from Fügen to Kellerjoch, a test of stamina and condition.

You can access many of the high-altitude and downhill routes using the cable cars in the valley, and local trains will transport your bike for free. Bikes are available for hire at major stations throughout the Zillertal, including Zell am Ziller and Mayrhofen, for €8/12 per half-/full day. For free maps, detailed route descriptions and downloadable GPS bike tours, visit www.zillertal.at or www.best-of-zillertal.at.

Mamma Mia PIZZERIA €
(🖉 67 68; Einfahrt Mitte 432; mains €7-9; ⊙ 11am-midnight) Skip more complicated dishes and go for wood-fired pizza at Mamma Mia, a kitsch-cosy slice of Italy with its terracotta floor and murals of Florence.

★**Wirtshaus Zum Griena** AUSTRIAN €€
(🖉 62 778; www.wirtshaus-griena.at; Dorfhaus 768; mains €8-16; ⊙ 11am-2pm & 5-10pm Tue-Sun; 🖢) Set in high pastures, this woodsy 400-year-old chalet is the kind of place where you pray for a snow blizzard, so you can huddle around the fire and tuck into *Schlutzkropf'n* (fresh pasta filled with cheese).

Schneekarhütte AUSTRIAN €€
(🖉 649 40; www.schneekarhütte.com; mains €12.50-43.90; ⊙ 8am-5pm Dec-Apr) Upping the ante in slopeside dining, this sophisticated hut has terrific views and an enticing open fire. Regional organic produce goes into dishes from *tarte flambée* to meltingly tender steaks. Reach it by taking the Horbergbahn cable car in Schwendau.

🍷 **Drinking & Entertainment**

Mayrhofen's après-ski scene rocks; most bars go with the snow and open from mid-December to early April.

Mo's BAR
(Hauptstrasse 417; ⊙ noon-1am) An American-themed bar with an upbeat vibe, great cocktails, finger food and burgers, and regular live music.

White Lounge BAR
(www.white-lounge.at; Ahorn; ⊙ 10am-4.30pm) Kick your skis off and chill over cocktails at this 2000m ice bar, with a big sunny terrace for catching rays. Things heat up with DJs and night sledding at Tuesday's igloo party (begins 8pm).

Ice Bar BAR
(Hauptstrasse 470, Hotel Strass; ⊙ 3-10pm) A loud, lairy, anything-goes après-ski haunt brimming with boot-stomping revellers and, occasionally, go-go polar bears (we kid you not!). Arena nightclub is under the same roof.

Scotland Yard PUB
(www.scotlandyard.at; Scheulingstrasse 372; ⊙ 7pm-late) Scotland Yard is a British pub with all the trimmings: Guinness, darts and a red phone box where expats can pour their hearts out to folk back home after a pint or three.

DON'T MISS

SNOWBOMBING

The self-proclaimed greatest show on snow, **Snowbombing** (www.snowbombing.com) in early April is Mayrhofen's biggest shindig. Some of the world's top boarders compete on the slopes, but most people are just here for the party – six solid days of drinking and dancing to a cracking line-up of bands and DJs, plus fun from igloo raves to fancy-dress street parties in the mix.

Brück'n Stadl LIVE MUSIC
(Ahornstrasse 850, Gasthof Brücke; ⊙ 5pm-2am Jun-Sep, 3pm-2am Dec-Apr) For year-round *Spass* (fun), you can't beat this lively barn and marquee combi. Lederhosen clad folk stars get beer glasses swingin' in summer, while plentiful schnapps and DJ Mütze fuel the après-ski party in winter.

ℹ **Information**

The ultramodern **tourist office** (🖉 67 60; www.mayrhofen.at; Dursterstrasse 225; ⊙ 9am-6pm Mon-Fri, 2-6pm Sat, 9am-1pm Sun) stocks loads of information and maps on the resort. Look for the comprehensive *Info von A-Z*; it's free and written in English. There is a handy topographic model of the surrounding Alps, a 24-hour accommodation board and free wi-fi.

ℹ **Getting There & Away**

By the normal train that runs twice hourly, it's €7.10 each way to Jenbach (52 minutes). For the Zillertal Circuit, buses run between Mayrhofen and the Schlegeisspeicher reservoir (one way €6.10, one hour, seven daily).

Ginzling
🖉 05286 / POP 400 / ELEV 999M

For a taste of what the Austrian Alps looked like before the dawn of tourism, head to Ginzling, an adorable little village 8km south of Mayrhofen.

The main draw for hikers is the **Naturpark Zillertaler Alpen** (www.naturpark-zillertal.at), a 379-sq-km nature park and pristine alpine wilderness of deep valleys and glaciated peaks. The **Naturparkhaus Zillertaler Alpen** (🖉 521 81; www.ginzling.at; ⊙ 8am-noon & 1-5pm May-Oct) is the park's information centre and runs 200 excellent themed **guided hikes**, most costing between €5 and €7, from May to October. The extensive program includes everything from llama trekking to sunrise photo excursions, herb walks and alpine hikes. Be sure to reserve your place by 5pm on the day before your planned hike.

The most charming place to stay is **Gasthof Alt-Ginzling** (☑202 96; www.ferien-wohnungen-ginzling.at; 240 Ginzling; s/d €47/82, apt €90-120, mains €7-16; ℗), once a wayside inn for smugglers travelling to Italy. The 18th-century farmhouse oozes history from every creaking beam and the low-ceilinged, pine-panelled rooms are supremely cosy. The restaurant serves local rainbow trout.

In winter free ski buses run frequently to Mayrhofen; otherwise there is an hourly service (€2.70, 12 minutes). A road (toll €12) snakes on from Ginzling up the valley to the **Schlegeisspeicher** reservoir, the trailhead for the stunning Zillertal Circuit (p301).

Achensee

Around 6km north of Jenbach, the fjord-like Achensee is Tyrol's largest lake and one of its loveliest, flanked by thickly wooded mountains. The **Achenseebahn** (www.achen-seebahn.at; 1 way/return €22.50/29.50), a private cogwheel steam train, trundles to the lake from Jenbach between May and October, connecting with two-hour **boat tours** (www.tirol-schiffahrt.at; adult/child €17.50/8.75) of the lake. Sweeping views over the lake and the surrounding peaks can be had from Erfurter (1831m), which is easily reached by the **Rofanseilbahn** (www.rofanseilbahn.at; adult/child return €18.50/11; ☉8.30am-5pm) cable car from Maurach.

Kitzbühel

☑05356 / POP 8450 / ELEV 762M

Ask an Austrian to rattle off the top ski resorts in the country, and Kitzbühel will invariably make the grade. Ever since Franz Reisch slipped on skis and whizzed down the slopes of Kitzbüheler Horn way back in 1893, so christening the first alpine ski run in Austria, Kitzbühel has carved out its reputation as one of Europe's foremost ski resorts. Legends have been made and born on these pistes, not least three-time Olympic medallist Toni Sailer.

Kitzbühel began life in the 16th century as a silver and copper mining town, and today continues to preserve a charming medieval centre despite its other persona as a fashionable and prosperous winter re-

sort. It's renowned for the white-knuckled Hahnenkamm-Rennen downhill ski race in January and the excellence of its slopes.

⊙ Sights

It's a joy simply to stroll the cobbled lanes of Kitzbühel's late-medieval town, stopping to people-watch at one of the many pavement cafes.

★**Museum Kitzbühel**　　　　　MUSEUM
(www.museum-kitzbuehel.at; Hinterstadt 32; adult/child €6/free; ☉10am-5pm) This museum traces Kitzbühel's heritage from its Bronze Age mining beginnings to the present day. The big emphasis is on winter sports, and the permanent collection pays tribute to home-grown legends like ski racing champ Toni Sailer and winter landscape painter Alfons Walde.

★**Alpine Flower Garden**　　　　GARDEN
(cable car return adult/child €19.20/10.60; ☉8.30am-5pm May-Sep) Arnica, edelweiss and purple bellflowers are among the 400 alpine blooms flourishing at this quiet garden atop Kitzbüheler Horn. It's a four-hour (14km) hike one way, or a speedy cable-car ride. A road also twists up to the mountain (toll per car/motorcycle €6/3, plus €3 per person).

Pfarrkirche St Andreas　　　　CHURCH
(Pfarrau) Slightly above the town is this Gothic-meets-baroque parish church, identified by its steep, wood-shingled roof.

Liebfrauenkirche　　　　　　CHURCH
(Pfarrau; ☉dawn-dusk) Next to Pfarrkirche St Andreas, this rococo church has a chunky 48m belfry and an elaborately frescoed interior.

🏃 Activities

Winter Sports

Downhill skiers flock here for the 170km of groomed slopes that are mostly intermediate and focused on **Hahnenkamm-Pengelstein**, while off-piste enthusiasts find plenty of backcountry powder to play with at high elevations. **Kitzbüheler Horn** is much loved by beginners for its gentle cruising on sunny slopes. Confident intermediates up for a challenge can tackle the incredibly scenic 35km **Ski Safari**, linking the Hahnenkamm to Resterhöhe/Pass Thurn. The alpine tour is marked by elephant signs and is a good introduction to the entire ski area.

Kitzbühel

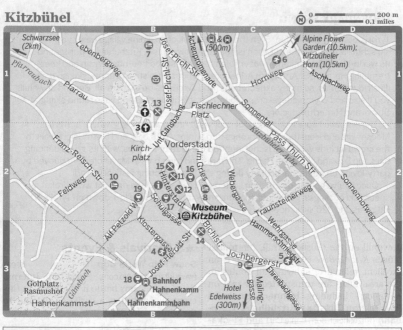

Kitzbühel

The mind-bogglingly sheer, breathtakingly fast **Streif** downhill course lures hard-core skiers to Kitzbühel – even experts feel their hearts do somersaults on the Mausefalle, a notoriously steep section with an 85% gradient. **Snowpark Hanglalm** is rider heaven with its rails, kickers and obstacles.

The tourist office website, www.kitzbuehel.com, has up-to-date lift and slope reports, as well as the low-down on non-ski-focused activities like winter hiking, ice skating and sledding.

Summer Sports

Kitzbühel makes a terrific base for walking in summer, with scores of well-marked trails, including the 15km **Kaiser Trail** with superlative views of the jagged Kaisergebirge massif. The website www.kitzbuehel.com has plenty of inspiration, or pick up the handy *Kitz Mountain Guiding* booklet at the tourist office for themed walking suggestions and mini maps.

As the trailhead for the epic 1000km, 32-stage **Bike Trail Tirol**, Kitzbühel is mountain-biking central. Whether you want to pedal gently through the valley or rattle

LEGENDARY SKIING

Tyrol is powdery perfection. Even the tiniest speck of an alpine village has its own ski school and lift, so the question is not *if* but *how* you ski. Kitzbühel for purists and its world-class Hahnenkamm, Mayrhofen for its fantastic free-ride terrain and knee-trembling Harakiri, St Anton am Arlberg for glorious off-piste and après-ski...so many illustrious names, so many expectations. And Tyrol lives up to them all. Beyond downhill, you'll also find Olympic-level cross-country tracks in Seefeld and year-round skiing at Stubai and Hintertux glaciers.

The unrivalled après-ski king is, of course, St Anton am Arlberg, where barns like Mooserwirt and Heustadl whip throngs into a frenzy with beer and live music. Rivals to the crown include wild child Ischgl, dubbed the Ibiza of the Alps, with its go-go dancing bars, top DJs and clubs like Pacha. The pubs and igloo bars in Mayrhofen are buoyed by party-loving boarders, particularly during the Snowbombing festival in April.

Once you've got the destination sorted, you can start planning. Visit www.tirol.at for special ski packages, guide information, snow reports and the low-down on Tyrol's 70 ski areas and 220 ski schools.

downhill on the Gaisberg Trail, the tourist office's *KitzAlpBike* cycling map (€3) is an excellent reference, showing all routes in the area. Bikes are transported for free on cable cars including **Hahnenkammbahn** (Hahnenkamm Cable Car), **Kitzbüheler Hornbahn** (Kitzbüheler Horn Cable Car) and **Fleckalmbahn**. These cable cars cost €16/19.20 one way/return for adults in summer, with substantial reductions for children and youths. All are covered by ski passes in winter

Along with these activities, Kitzbühel gets pulses racing in summer with scenic flights, skydiving, ballooning, golf, water sports and even bungee jumping.

Element 3   ADVENTURE SPORTS
(☑ 723 01; www.element3.at; Klostergasse 8; ⊗ 9am-1pm & 2.30-6pm) A ski school in winter, in summer this is a one-stop shop for adventure sports, including rafting (€65), canyoning (€60 to €70) and paragliding (€110). Mountain and electric bikes (e-bikes) are available for hire at €25 and €35 per day.

Schwarzsee   SWIMMING
(adult/child €4.20/1.70) For a cool summer swim, venture 3km northwest of the centre to Kitzbühel's natural swimming hole, the tree-flanked Schwarzsee. This lakeside lido has open-air pools and pedalo rental.

Intersport   BICYCLE RENTAL
(www.kitzsport.at; Jochbergerstrasse 7; ⊗ 9am-12.30pm & 2-6.15pm Mon-Fri, 9am-1pm Sat) Rents e-bikes (€20 per day) that take the uphill slog out of cycling.

★ Festivals & Events

Snow Polo World Cup   SPORT
(www.kitzbuehelpolo.com; ⊗ mid-Jan) International polo teams battle it out on ice at this event, which brings a spritz of glamour to the winter calendar.

Hahnenkamm-Rennen   SPORT
(www.hahnenkamm.com; ⊗ late Jan) Perhaps the most enthralling of all Fédération International de Ski (FIS; International Ski Federation) Alpine World Cup stages, this is the mother of all downhill races.

bet-at-home Cup   SPORT
(www.bet-at-home-cup.com; ⊗ early Aug) Tennis stars compete in the bet-at-home Cup for the much-coveted Kitzbühel Trophy.

⌴ Sleeping

Budget digs are not Kitzbühel's forte, but the tourist office has a list of good-value private rooms and guesthouses. Rates leap up by 50% in the high winter season.

Snowbunny's Hostel   HOSTEL €
(☑ 067-6794 0233; www.snowbunnys.co.uk; Bichlstrasse 30; dm €25-40, d €120; @ 🛜) Friendly, laid-back hostel, a bunny-hop from the slopes. Dorms are fine, if a tad dark; breakfast is DIY-style in the kitchen. There's a TV lounge, ski storage room, cats to stroke and a shop for backpacker staples (Vegemite, Jägermeister etc).

★ Villa Licht   HOTEL €€
(☑ 622 93; www.villa-licht.at; Franz-Reisch-Strasse 8; d €150-180, apt €170-360; 🅿 @ 🛜 🖂 ♿) Pretty gardens, warm-hued rooms with pine

trappings, balconies with mountain views, peace – this charming Tyrolean chalet has the lot, and owner Renate goes out of her way to please. Kids love the outdoor pool in summer.

Hotel Edelweiss HOTEL €€

(☑752 52; www.edelweiss-kitzbuehel.at; Marfeldgasse 2; d incl half board €140; P🐕) Near the Hahnenkammbahn, Edelweiss oozes Tyrolean charm with its green surrounds, alpine views, sauna and cosy interiors. Your kindly hosts Klaus and Veronika let you pack up a lunch from the breakfast buffet and serve delicious five-course dinners.

Pension Kometer PENSION €€

(☑622 89; www.pension-kometer.com; Gerbergasse 7; s/d €65/110; P🐕) Make yourself at home in the bright, sparklingly clean rooms at this family-run guesthouse. There's a relaxed lounge with games and DVDs. Breakfast is a treat with fresh breads, fruit and eggs.

Hotel Erika HISTORIC HOTEL €€€

(☑648 85; www.erika-kitz.at; Josef-Pirchl-Strasse 21; d incl half board €174-220; P🐕🏊🍴) This turreted art nouveau villa has luxurious high-ceilinged rooms and polished service. The rose-strewn garden centres on a vine-clad pagoda and pond that are illuminated by night. Unwind with treatments from thalassotherapy to hay baths in the spa.

✗ Eating

Metzgerei Huber SNACKS €

(Bichlstrasse 14; snacks €4-8; ⊙8am-6pm Mon-Fri, to 12.30pm Sat) A great local butcher's for a meaty snack like *Schweinebauch* (pork belly) and quality sausages.

★ Restaurant Zur Tenne AUSTRIAN €€

(☑644 44-606; www.hotelzurtenne.com; Vorderstadt 8-10; lunch €9.90, mains €15.50-40; ⊙11.30am-1.30pm & 6.30-9.30pm) Choose between the rustic, beamed interior where an open fire crackles and the more summery conservatory at Hotel Tenne's highly regarded restaurant. Service is polished and the menu puts a sophisticated twist on seasonal Tyrolean dishes such as catfish with wild garlic pasta and artichokes.

Lois Stern FUSION €€

(☑748 82; www.loisstern.com; Josef-Pirchl-Strasse 3; mains €25-33; ⊙6pm-midnight Tue-Sat) Lois works his wok in the show kitchen of this bistro, which has understatedly chic de-

cor of wood floors and caramel-hued banquettes. Clean, bright flavours such as tempura of wild gambas and Thai-style ceviche with chilli-lime salsa shine on the Asian-Mediterranean crossover menu.

Centro ITALIAN €€

(☑658 62; www.centro-kitzbuehel.at; Vorderstadt 12; 2-course lunch €7.80, pizzas €6-14.50, mains €13-24.50; ⊙9am-midnight; 🍴) On a sunny evening, it seems as though the whole of Kitzbühel congregates on the street-facing terrace of Centro to chat and people-watch over Italian salads, wood-oven pizzas, pasta and grilled fish. The slick vaulted interior entices in winter. It's popular, so book ahead.

Huberbräu Stüberl AUSTRIAN €€

(☑656 77; Vorderstadt 18; mains €8.50-18; ⊙8am-midnight Mon-Sat, from 9am Sun) An old-world Tyrolean haunt with vaults and pine benches, this tavern favours substantial portions of Austrian classics, such as schnitzel, goulash and dumplings, cooked to perfection.

🍷 Drinking & Nightlife

Kitzbühel rocks with fun-seeking skiers during the winter season; join them if you can muster up the energy after a day on the slopes.

Hahnenkamm Pavillon BAR

(www.pavillon-kitz.at; Hahnenkammstrasse 2; ⊙2-10.30pm winter) This slopeside pick opposite Hahnenkammbahn is a rollicking après-ski haunt in winter, with DJs, singing, schnapps-drinking and skiers jiggling to Austrian beats in their ski boots.

ⓘ KITZBÜHEL AREA SKI PASSES

One-/three-/six-day passes in the high winter season cost €45/127/225, and €40.50/114.50/202.50 at all other times. Passes cover lifts, cable cars and ski buses as far south as Thurn Pass. If you plan to cover a lot of terrain, the **Kitzbüheler Alpen AllStarCard** (www.allstarcard.at; 1-/3-/6-day pass €49/137/241) is your best bet; it spans the whole region, including Kitzbühel, Wilder Kaiser-Brixental, Saalbach-Hinterglemm and Zell am See-Kaprun (some 1088km of pistes).

> **ⓘ OUTDOOR SAVERS**
>
> Stay in Kitzbühel and you'll automatically receive a guest card, which allows you to hook onto half-day guided hikes arranged by the tourist office for free. Engelbert and Madeleine are the hiking guides that run the tours at 8.45am (summer) and 9.45am (winter) from Monday to Friday.
>
> You can save in summer by investing in the **Kitzbüheler Alpen Summer Card** (3-day pass with/without bus €47/39.50), which covers 29 lifts and cable cars.

Londoner   PUB
(www.londoner.at; Franz-Reisch-Strasse 4; ☺3pm-late) This raucous British den has great beer, crazy events and plenty of slapstick fun.

Bergsinn   BAR
(www.bergsinn.at; Vorderstadt 21; ☺9am-1am Mon-Sat, from 11am Sun; 🛜) This slinky, backlit lounge bar has a cocktail happy hour (8pm to 9pm), DJ nights and free wi-fi.

Club Take Five   CLUB
(www.club-takefive.com; Hinterstadt 22; ☺10pm-late) Chic and pricey club with a trio of bars, a VIP area and DJs spinning house, soul and funk.

ⓘ Information

Post office (Josef-Pirchl-Strasse 11; ☺8am-6pm Mon-Fri, 9am-noon Sat) The post office is midway between the train station and tourist office.

Tourist office (📞666 60; www.kitzbuehel.com; Hinterstadt 18; ☺8.30am-6pm Mon-Fri, 9am-6pm Sat, 10am-noon & 4-6pm Sun) Kitzbühel's central tourist office has loads of info in English and a 24-hour accommodation board.

ⓘ Getting There & Away

Kitzbühel is on the B170, 30km east of Wörgl and the A12/E45 motorway.

The main train station is 1km north of central Vorderstadt. Trains run frequently from Kitzbühel to Innsbruck (€19.20, 1¼ hours) and Salzburg (€28, 2½ hours). To travel to Kufstein by train (€10, one hour), you'll need to change at Wörgl.

Kufstein
📱 05372 / POP 17,550 / ELEV 499M

In the 1970s, Karl Ganzer sang the praises of Kufstein in his hit yodelling melody 'Perle Tirols' (The Pearl of Tyrol) and rightly so. Resting at the foot of the mighty limestone Kaisergebirge and crowned by a fortress, Kufstein's backdrop is picture-book stuff. Control of the town was hotly contested by Tyrol and Bavaria through the ages until it finally became Austrian property in 1814.

◉ Sights

★ Festung Kufstein   FORT
(www.festung.kufstein.at; Oberer Stadtplatz 6; adult/child €11/6.50; ☺9am-6pm) For an insight into Kufstein's turbulent past, head up to cliff-top Festung Kufstein. The castle dates from 1205 (when Kufstein was part of Bavaria) and was a pivotal point of defence for both Bavaria and Tyrol during the struggles. The round **Kaiserturm** (Emperor's Tower) was added in 1522.

The lift to the top affords sweeping views over Kufstein and the surrounding peaks. Inside is the small but imaginatively presented **Heimatmuseum** (Heritage Museum), showcasing everything from Bronze Age urns to folk costumes and – drum roll please – Andreas Hofer's shoe. Below the Kaiserturm is the **Heldenorgel** (Heroes Organ) with 4307 pipes, 46 organ stops and a 100m gap between the keyboard and the tip of the pipes; the delay in the sounding of the notes makes playing it a tricky business. Catch recitals at noon and, in July and August, 6pm.

When the fortress is closed in the evening you can walk up the path in under 15 minutes and roam the ramparts and grounds free of charge.

Römerhofgasse   HISTORIC STREET
A classic saunter leads along gingerbready Römerhofgasse, a reconstructed medieval lane that looks fresh-minted for a Disney film set with its overhanging arches, lanterns and frescoed facades. Even the crowds and souvenir kitsch – marmot ointment, *Dirndls*, strapping Lederhosen, you name it – detract little from its appeal.

🏃 Activities

Kaisergebirge   HIKING, SKIING
The Kaisergebirge range is a sheer wall of limestone to the east of Kufstein, rising to 2300m and stretching as far as St Johann in

Tirol. It attracts walkers, mountaineers and skiers alike. The Kaisergebirge is actually two ranges, split by the east–west Kaisertal valley. The northern range is the **Zahmer Kaiser** (Tame Emperor) and the southern is the **Wilder Kaiser** (Wild Emperor) – no medals for guessing which has the smoother slopes! Pick up a free *Wanderkarte* (walking map) from the tourist office.

Hechtsee & Stimmersee
SWIMMING

(adult/child €4/1.60) The tree-fringed lakes around Kufstein are best explored on foot or by bike; the closest are in the wooded area west of the Inn River, where there's a network of walking trails. Hechtsee, 3km to the northwest, and Stimmersee, 2.5km to the southwest, both have swimming areas open from late May to September. A free city bus goes to Hechtsee in summer during fine weather (ask at the tourist office).

🛏 Sleeping

Camping Maier
CAMPGROUND €

(☑583 52; www.camping-maier.com; Egerbach 54, Schwoich; camp sites per adult/child/tent €4/2.70/6; ❄🛏) Bordering woodland, this friendly campground 5km south of Kufstein has tree-shaded pitches, plus a playground and an outdoor pool.

★ Auracher Löchl
HISTORIC HOTEL €€

(☑621 38; www.auracher-loechl.at; Römerhofgasse 2-5; s €63, d €120-132; @🛜🛏) Squeezed between Römerhofgasse and the Inn River, this hotel marries medieval charm with 21st-century comfort; river or fortress views cost a little extra. Cross the footbridge to the low-beamed restaurant (mains €10 to €20), one-time haunt of Andreas Hofer, where creaking floors and grinning badgers create a rustic feel. Austrian classics like *Schwein-shaxe* (basically half a pig) are served in gut-busting portions.

Hotel Kufsteinerhof
HOTEL €€

(☑714 12; www.kufsteinerhof.at; Franz-Josef-Platz 1; s €51, d €102-122; 🛜) With its recently spruced-up rooms in clean, contemporary style and substantial breakfasts, the Kufsteinerhof is one of the best central picks in Kufstein. It's just a three-minute walk from the fortress.

🍴 Eating

Inn-Café Hell
CAFÉ €

(Unterer Stadtplatz 3; snacks €3-7, lunch €8.50; ❄8.30am-8pm) Sit on the riverside terrace

for a good-value, two-course lunch or a scrummy homemade strudel with ice cream.

Batzenhäusl
TYROLEAN €€

(☑624 33; Römerhofgasse 1; mains €10-15; ❄9am-11pm Tue-Sat) Murals of merry wine-guzzlers welcome you to Tyrol's oldest wine tavern. Burrowing into cliffs below the fortress, this 530-year-old haunt is packed with curios like 16th-century cannonballs. The food is thoroughly Austrian: *Tafelspitz, Gröstl* and the fluffiest *Salzburger Nockerl* (Austrian soufflé) ever. Reserve ahead.

Purlepaus
FUSION €€

(☑636 33; www.purlepaus.at; Unterer Stadtplatz 18; lunch €5.90-7.20, mains €8.50-16; ❄11am-10pm) This is a perennially popular choice with a stylish vaulted interior and a big chestnut-tree-shaded terrace. The wordly menu skips from pasta and tarte flambé to Thai curries and Tyrolean grub.

ℹ Information

At the **tourist office** (☑622 07; www.kufstein.com; ❄8am-6pm Mon-Fri, 9am-1pm Sat), staff will hunt down accommodation without charging commission. If you stay overnight, ask for the *Gästekarte*, which has different benefits in summer and winter.

ℹ Getting There & Away

The frequent trains to Kitzbühel (€10, one hour) require a change at Wörgl. The easiest road route is also via Wörgl. Kufstein is on the main Innsbruck–Salzburg train route. Direct trains to Salzburg (€33.40, 1¼ hours) run at least every two hours; those to Innsbruck (€15, 50 minutes) are half-hourly. Buses leave from outside the train station.

Söll

☑05333 / POP 3500 / ELEV 703M

Söll is a well-known ski resort 10km south of Kufstein. Once a favourite of boozy, boisterous visitors in the 1980s, the resort has successfully reinvented itself and is now a family-oriented place with myriad outdoor activities.

The highest skiing area overlooking the resort is Hohe Salve at 1828m, though Söll has also combined with neighbouring resorts Itter, Brixen, Scheffau, Hopfgarten and Going to form the mammoth Skiwelt (www.skiwelt.at) area, comprising 279km of mostly red and blue pistes. Passes are €44 a day in the high season. Cross-country skiing is also popular, with trails running as far as St Johann in Tirol.

In summer walkers are drawn to **Hohe Salve** (www.hohe-salve.com; cable car 1 way/return €11.50/16; 🚠) and the **Hexenwasser**, a fun-loaded family walking trail with water obstacles, sundials, playgrounds, a working mill and bakery and an apiary. Throughout the summer you can see (and sample) bread, schnapps and cheese made the traditional way.

The **tourist office** (☑050-509 201; www.wilderkaiser.info; Dorf 84; ⊗8am-noon & 1-6pm Mon-Fri, 3-6pm Sat, 9am-noon Sun), in the centre of the village, provides information on activities and will help you find accommodation.

❶ Getting There & Away

Söll is on the B178 between Wörgl and St Johann in Tirol. It's not on a train line, but there are plenty of buses from Kufstein (€4.20, 25 minutes).

Stubai Glacier

It's a bizarre feeling to slip out of sandals and into skis in midsummer, but that's precisely what draws people to the Stubai Glacier. Just 40km south of Innsbruck, the glacier is a year-round skiing magnet with more than 110km of wide, snow-sure pistes that are great for cruising and intermediate skiing. Summer skiing is limited to between 2900m and 3300m. Walkers are attracted to the network of trails lower down in the valley; a good hiking map for the area is Kompass' *Stubaier Alpen* (scale 1:50,000). The Stubaital branches off from the Brenner Pass route (A13/E45) a little south of the Europabrücke and runs southwest.

Stubaitalbahn (STB) buses from Innsbruck journey to the foot of the glacier (€8.80, 1½ hours) twice hourly.

If you're based in Innsbruck and want to go skiing for the day on the glacier, consider the package tour offered by Innsbruck Information (p296). For €99, you get an overnight stay, ski or snowboard rental and a ski pass.

Seefeld

☑ 05212 / POP 3241 / ELEV 1180M

Seefeld sits high on a south-facing plateau, ringed by the rugged limestone peaks of the Wetterstein and Karwendel Alps. While most Tyrolean resorts are crazy about downhill, Seefeld's first love is *Langlauf* (cross-country skiing), and fans of the sport flock here to skate and glide along 279km of prepared trails in winter.

Seefeld was the proud cohost of the Winter Olympic Games in 1964, 1976 and, more recently, the Winter Youth Olympics in 2012.

◉ Sights & Activities

Pfarrkirche St Oswald   CHURCH
(Dorfplatz; ⊗8am-7pm) Seefeld's trophy sight is this late-Gothic parish church, the supposed location of a miracle. The story goes that Oswald Milser gobbled a wafer reserved for the clergy at Easter communion here in 1384. After almost being swallowed up by the floor, the greedy layman repented, but the wafer was streaked with blood – not from foolish Oswald but from Christ, naturally. You can view the **Blutskapelle** (Chapel of the Holy Blood), which held the original wafer, by climbing the stairway.

Strandbad Strandperle   SWIMMING, WALKING
(Innsbrucker Strasse 500; adult/child €4.90/3; ⊗9am-9pm late May-Sep) After following the 45-minute lakeside **walking trail** that wriggles around bottle green, pine-fringed Wildsee, a short stroll from the centre in the Reither Moor conservation area, you can stop off for a refreshing dip at the Strandbad lido.

For longer, more challenging walks, cable cars ascend nearby Seefeld Spitze (2220m) and Reither Spitze (2374m); consult the tourist office for more information or join one of its regular **guided walks**.

Cross-Country Skiing   SKIING
Seefeld's raison d'être is cross-country skiing. Well-groomed *Loipen* (trails) criss-cross the sunny plateau to Mösern, 5km away, where there are fine views of the Inn River and the peaks beyond. A day pass costs €3.

The 48km of downhill skiing here is best suited to beginners and intermediates. Your pass to the slopes is the multiday **Happy Ski Card** (3-day pass adult/child €107/64.50), covering all lifts in Seefeld. The two main areas are Gschwandtkopf (1500m) and Rosshütte (1800m); the latter connects to higher lifts and slopes on the Karwendel range.

🛌 Sleeping & Eating

Rates jump by around a third during the high winter season. Ask at you accommodation for a guest card for discounts on activities. Many places close in the shoulder seasons.

★ **Hotel Helga** FAMILY HOTEL **€**
(☑ 23 26; www.hotel-helga.at; Haspingerstrasse
156; s incl half board €52-71, d €100-142; ◉) Helga
and Franz bend over backwards to please at
this homely chalet, with sweet and simple
rooms dressed in traditional Tyrolean style,
with lots of wood and florals. Stay here for
the mountain views, the terrific four-course
dinners, the familiar atmosphere and the
silence needed for a sound night's sleep. A
sauna takes the chill out of winter.

Central HOTEL **€€**
(☑ 26 88; www.central-seefeld.at; Münchnerstrasse
41; s €69-79, d €98-118, apt €108-148, half board
€14; P🖥📶🛗) 🍴 Friendly service, an attractive spa and a kids' play areas make the Central a good choice. The well-lit rooms with
balconies are contemporary Tyrolean in
style, with light birch wood and earthy hues.
The food makes the most of local products
and there are organic options at breakfast.

Waldgasthaus Triendlsäge AUSTRIAN **€€**
(☑ 25 80; www.triendlsaege.at; Triendlsäge 259;
mains €10-22; ☺11.30am-10pm Thu-Tue) A romantic slice of Tyrolean rusticity, this woody
restaurant, named after its sawmill, hides in
the forest, a 20-minute walk north of town.
Or reach it on cross-country skis or by horse-
drawn carriage in winter. Sit by the open
fire or on the terrace for regional dishes that
play up seasonal, farm-fresh ingredients,
from trout to game and wild mushrooms.

Strandperle INTERNATIONAL **€€**
(☑ 24 36; www.strandperle.at; Innsbrückerstrasse
500; mains €9-18; ☺10am-10pm) Overlooking
the calm waters of Wildsee, Strandperle is
a funky glass-and-granite place. The menu
delivers Med-inspired flavours like pepper-
crusted tuna with lemon rice and saffron
risotto. The decked terrace has the finest
views of the Alps anywhere in Seefeld.

ℹ Information

The central **tourist office** (☑ 05-088 050; www.
seefeld.com; Klosterstrasse 43; ☺8.30am-
6.30pm Mon-Sat, 10am-12.30pm & 3-5pm Sun)
has stacks of info on accommodation and outdoor activities.

ℹ Getting There & Away

Seefeld is 25km northwest of Innsbruck, just
off the Germany-bound B177. The track starts
climbing soon after departing Innsbruck, providing spectacular views across the whole valley.
There are hourly buses to Mittenwald (€4.20, 25

minutes) and Garmisch-Partenkirchen (€11.80,
45 minutes) in Germany. Trains run to/from
Innsbruck (€5.80, 36 minutes) at least hourly.

Stams

☑ 05263 / POP 1340 / ELEV 672M
One of Tyrol's true architectural highlights
is the ochre-and-white **Zisterzienstift**
(www.stiftstams.at; Stiftshof 1; tours adult/child
€4.70/2.50; ☺ guided tours hourly 9-11am & 1-4pm
Jun-Sep, 2pm Wed Oct-May) in Stams. The abbey was founded in 1273 by Elisabeth of Bavaria, the mother of Konradin, the last of the
Hohenstaufens. Set in pristine grounds, the
monumental facade is identified by its twin
silver cupolas, which were added as a final
flourish when the abbey was revamped in
baroque style in the 17th century. The exuberant church interior is dominated by the
high altar: the intertwining branches of this
version of the 'tree of life' support 84 saintly
figures surrounding an image of the Virgin.
Near the entrance is the **Rose Grille**, an exquisite iron screen made in 1716. Crane your
neck to admire the ceiling which swirls with
rich stuccowork, gilding and elaborate frescoes by Georg Wolker.

Marmalade, juice, honey and schnapps
made on the premises can be bought from
the **Kloster shop** (☺9am-noon & 1-5pm Mon-
Sat, 1-5pm Sun).

Stams is on the train route between Innsbruck and Landeck (both €7.80, 38 minutes).
Both the A12 and B171 pass near the abbey.

The Ötztal

POP 12,000
Over millenniums, the Ötztal (Ötz Valley)
has been shaped into rugged splendour. No
matter whether you've come to ski its snowcapped mountains, raft its white waters or
hike to its summits, this valley is all about
big wilderness. Guarding the Italian border and dominated by Tyrol's highest peak,
Wildspitze (3774m), this is one of three river
valleys running north from the Ötztaler Alpen to drain into the Inn River.

⊙ Sights & Activities

Ötzi Dorf MUSEUM
(www.oetzi-dorf.at; Umhausen; adult/child
€6.80/3.30; ☺9.30am-5.30pm May-Oct; 🛗)
This small open-air museum brings to life
the Neolithic world of Ötzi the ice man. A
visit takes in traditional thatched huts, herb

TYROL & VORARLBERG STAMS

gardens, craft displays and enclosures where wild boar and oxen roam. Multilingual audio guides are available.

Stuibenfall
WATERFALL

From Ötzi Dorf, it's a beautiful 20-minute forest walk to Tyrol's longest waterfall, the wispy Stuibenfall, cascading 159m over slate cliffs and moss-covered boulders. You can continue for another 40 minutes up to the top viewing platform and hanging bridge. A thrilling new 450m *Klettersteig* takes you right over the waterfall; bring your own karabiner and helmet.

★ Aqua Dome
SPA

(☑ 05243-6400 6001; www.aqua-dome.at; Oberlängenfeld 140, Längenfeld; 3hr card adult/child Mon-Fri €18.50/9.50, Sat & Sun €21.50/12.50, sauna world €11; ⊙ 9am-11pm, sauna world 10am-11pm) Framed by the Ötztaler Alps, this crystalline spa looks otherworldly after dark when its trio of flying-saucer-shaped pools are strikingly illuminated. And there's certainly something surreal about gazing up to the peaks and stars while floating in a brine bath, drifting around a lazy river or being pummelled by water jets.

The 'textile-free' **sauna world** is an adult-only wonderland, with a hay-barn sauna, steam dome and canyon sauna with the occasional thunderstorm. To cool off, there's an ice grotto and a rain temple where you can choose between mist, tropical rain and a raging waterfall – it's quite a Niagara, so stand back. For full-on pampering, there are treatments from energising Ötztal stone massage to fango (volcanic mud) wraps.

Area 47
ADVENTURE SPORTS

(☑ 05266-876 76; www.area47.at; Ötztaler Achstrasse 1, Ötztal Bahnhof; water park adult/child/family €18/10/48; ⊙ 10am-7pm May-Sep; ⚑) Billing itself as the ultimate outdoor play-ground, this huge sports and adventure park is the Ötztal's flagship attraction, dramatically set at the foot of the Alps and on the edge of a foaming river. The place heaves with families and flirty teenagers in summer.

Besides a water park with a natural lake and some pretty hairy diving boards and waterslides, there is a thrilling flying fox (€23), climbing walls (€8) and an adventure centre offering canyoning (€78) and rafting (€49 to €105). Events from party nights to concerts are held in summer and there's a tepee village for overnight stays (€22 per person). A free shuttle bus runs here from Ötztal Bahnhof.

Sölden
SKIING

(www.soelden.com; 6-day pass €246) Sölden is a snow-sure ski resort with a high-speed lift network and fun-loving après-ski scene. The resort's 144km of slopes particularly appeal to confident intermediates and are complemented by glacier skiing at Rettenbach and Tiefenbach. For many, the highlight is the panoramic 50km **Big 3 Rally**, a four-hour downhill marathon which begins at Giggijoch gondola and takes in three 3000m peaks.

Obergurgl & Hochgurgl
SKIING

(www.obergurgl.com; day ski pass €47; ⚑) Around 14km south of Sölden is family-friendly Obergurgl (1930m), Austria's highest parish, with skiing largely aimed at beginners and intermediates. Obergurgl is actually at the head of the valley, but the road doubles back on itself and rises to Hochgurgl (2150m), where the pistes are steeper and the views equally impressive.

Rocky Nature
ROCK CLIMBING

(☑ 0650-266 52 92; www.rockynature.at; Winklen 188b, Längenfeld) Climbing-pro Markus Morandell helps you come to grips with the Ötztal's high-altitude wonderland. See the website for courses and prices, including the introductory two-hour *Schnupperklettern* (€30).

🛏 Sleeping

Nearly every village in the valley has a supermarket and camping ground. Room rates are 30% to 50% higher in winter.

★ Hotel Rita
SPA HOTEL €€

(☑ 05253-53 07; www.hotel-rita.com; Oberlängenfeld 44a, Längenfeld; s €84-90, d €148-166, ste €174-202; P 🕿 🖼 ⚑) The Lengler family ex-

---

> ### ℹ ÖTZTAL CARD
>
> You can save in summer by investing in the **Ötztal Card** (www.premiumcard. oetztal.com; 3/7/10 days €49/69/87), which is half-price for children. From mid-June to September, the pass covers public transport and cable cars in the valley, attractions like Ötzi Dorf, activities from outdoor swimming pools to bike rental, plus one free entry to Aqua Dome and Area 47.

tend a heartfelt welcome at this pretty chalet hotel, a five-minute walk from Aqua Dome. Set in gardens with mountain views, Hotel Rita has spacious, contemporary rooms and a terrific spa area with an indoor pool, whirlpool, herb-scented saunas and *hammam*. It's all about the details here: from lovingly prepared six-course dinners to free guided hikes and bicycle, map and walking-pole rental.

Nature Resort Ötztal   RESORT €€
(☑05252-603 50; www.nature-resort.at; Piburgerstrasse 6, Ötz; s incl half board €90-100, d €150-210; P@🐕🏠) 🍴 This riverside retreat has eco-chic chalet rooms, warmly decorated in sustainable pine. It's a solid family choice, with free activities like guided mountain hikes and bike tours, plus deals on rafting and canyoning. That's if you can tear your self away from the saunas and open fire in the spa.

Hotel Garni Granat   HOTEL €€
(☑05254-20 62; www.hotel-granat.at; Gemeindestrasse 2, Sölden; s €33-43, d/tr €66/99; P@🐕🏠) This friendly *Pension* in Sölden is near the ski lifts in winter and runs free guided hikes in summer. Many of the bright, traditional rooms have whirlpool bath-tubs. A playground and sandpit occupy kids, and guests have free use of the pool, sauna and tennis court at the nearby leisure centre.

ℹ Information

The valley's main **tourist office** (☑057200-200; www.oetztal.com; Gemeindestrasse 4, Sölden; ⊙8am-6pm Mon-Sat, 9am-noon & 3-6pm Sun) is in Sölden, though there are others in villages like Ötz and Längenfeld. All can arrange accommodation and have brochures on activities in the area.

ℹ Getting There & Away

From Ötztal Bahnhof, buses head south roughly hourly to destinations including Ötz (€2.70, 13 minutes), Umhausen (€4.20, 30 minutes) and Sölden (€8, one hour).

With your own wheels you should be able to get at least as far as Hochgurgl all year, but the road beyond into Italy via the high-alpine 2509m **Timmelsjoch Pass** (car/motorbike €14/12; ⊙7am-8pm) is often blocked by snow in winter.

Trains arrive at Ötztal Bahnhof at the head of the valley and run frequently to Innsbruck (€10, 34 minutes), Imst-Pitztal (€2.20, eight minutes) and Landeck (€5.80, 25 minutes).

Imst
☑05412 / POP 9523

Beautifully situated in the wide Gurgltal (Gurgl Valley) and spreading towards a range of thickly wooded mountains, Imst is famous for its many springs. While the town itself won't keep you long, its surrounding meadows, rugged peaks and gorges might. Imst makes a fine base for hiking and skiing in the nearby Ötztal.

⊙ Sights & Activities

The tourist office sells the good-value **Gletscherpark Card** (3/7 days €43/63), which covers all public transport, cable cars and most attractions in the region.

Haus der Fasnacht   MUSEUM
(www.fasnacht.at; Streleweg 6; adult/child €4/1; ⊙4-7pm Fri) Every four years, Imst plays host to a Shrovetide festival, the Unesco-listed **Schemenlaufen** (ghost dance); the next takes place on 31 January 2016. The highlight is the vibrant parade of characters, from hunchback *Hexen* (witches) to *Spritzer* that squirt water at spectators. This museum homes in on this centuries-old tradition and exhibits many of the hand-carved ghost masks.

Starkenberger Biermythos   BREWERY
(☑662 01; www.starkenberger.at; Griesegg 1, Tarrenz; adult/child €7/6; ⊙10am-5pm) Housed in a medieval castle, this 200-year-old brewery sits 3km north of Imst in Tarrenz. A visit dashes through the brewing process and includes a beer tasting. If you can't get enough of the stuff, you can even bathe in it by calling ahead – it does wonders for the complexion, apparently.

🛏 Sleeping

Romedihof   HOSTEL €
(☑222 12 10; www.romedihof.at; Brennbichl 41; dm €20-23, d/tr €50/72; @🐕) Lodged in 16th-century farmhouse, Romedihof is a terrific base for hiking, cycling and skiing. The interiors have been carefully restored, with beams, fireplaces and stucco adding historic edge. Room rates include bread delivered fresh from a local baker for preparing your own breakfast in the shared kitchen. Take the train to Imst-Pitztal then walk 10 minutes; see the website for a detailed map.

Hotel Hirschen
HOTEL €€

(☑69 01; www.hirschen-imst.com; Thomas-Walch-Strasse 3; s/d €68/130; P@☎️≋) This central guesthouse has comfy rooms, an indoor pool and modern spa area (check out the water beds in the relaxation room). A plate of venison ragout is never far away in the wood-panelled restaurant (mains €10 to €18), where stag heads stud the walls.

ℹ️ Information

The **tourist office** (☑69 10-0; www.imst.at; Johannesplatz 4; ☉8am-6pm Mon, 9am-6pm Tue-Fri, 10am-noon Sat; ☎️) is highly informed on accommodation and activities in Imst and its surrounds; there's also free wi-fi.

ℹ️ Getting There & Around

The town is slightly to the north of the main east–west roads (the A12 and B171), and is served by frequent buses and trains (from Innsbruck €11.90, 50 minutes).

Grown men may feel slightly silly boarding the Imster Bummelbär (€1.50, three daily) tourist train, but it's handy for reaching nearby sights like Starkenberger Biermythos.

The tourist office has a list of outfits with bike and e-bike rental.

ROSENGARTENSCHLUCHT CIRCUIT

An easygoing family hike is the 5km (approximately three-hour) loop through the dramatic 200m-high Rosengartenschlucht (Rose Garden Ravine), where boarded walkways make for a gentle ascent and afford sterling views of a waterfall. At the top, the walk continues through forest and along a trail overlooking the Lechtaler Alps. Look out for the Blaue Grotte, a cave pool that is a startling shade of blue. In Hoch-Imst, you can board the exhilarating **Alpine Coaster** (adult/child €6.60/4.30; ☉10am-5pm), touted as the world's longest alpine roller coaster, before a gradual descent back to Imst. From May to October, you can hook onto the tourist office's free guided hike at 2pm on Monday (reserve your place by 10am).

The trail starts and ends at the Johanneskirche (St John's Church) opposite the tourist office, which stocks maps of the walk.

Ehrwald

☑05673 / POP 2581

Ehrwald's crowning glory is the glaciated 2962m **Zugspitze** (www.zugspitze.at; cable car 1 way/return €25.50/37.50), Germany's highest peak, straddling the Austro-German border. From the crest there's a magnificent panorama of the main Tyrolean mountain ranges, as well as the Bavarian Alps and Mt Säntis in Switzerland. North of Zugspitze is Garmisch-Partenkirchen, Germany's most popular ski resort.

Ehrwald is linked with other resorts in Tyrol and Germany (including Garmisch-Partenkirchen) under the **Top Snow Card** (2-day pass adult/child €79/43.50), covering 207km of pistes. For information on accommodation and activities, contact the **tourist office** (☑20 000 201; www.ehrwald.com; Kirchplatz 1; ☉8.30am-6pm Mon-Fri, 9am-5pm Sat, 9am-noon Sun) in the heart of the town. Staff will help find rooms free of charge.

Trains from Innsbruck (€15.60, 1¾ hours) to Ehrwald pass through Germany; you must change at Garmisch-Partenkirchen. Austrian train tickets are valid for the whole trip.

Landeck

☑05442 / POP 7742

Landeck is an ordinary town with an extraordinary backdrop: framed by an amphitheatre of forested peaks, presided over by a medieval castle and bordered by the fast-flowing Inn and Sanna Rivers. The town makes a good-value base for outdoor activities and exploring the nearby Inntal and Patznauntal valleys.

◎ Sights & Activities

Landeck attracts the odd skier to its 22km of mostly intermediate slopes (a day ski pass costs €32), but is better known for its hiking trails. The magnificent **Adlerweg** (Eagle Trail) stops off in Landeck on its 280km journey through Tyrol. Many footpaths can be accessed by taking the **Venet** (adult/child 1 way €13.50/8, return €15.50/9.50) cable car up to Krahberg (2208m).

If you're staying overnight in summer, pick up the **TirolWestCard** (www.tirolwest.at) for free access to the major sights, outdoor pools and the bus network. In summer the tourist office arranges guided walks from herb strolls to mountain hikes (free with the

TirolWestCard), and can advise on activities from llama trekking to via ferrate.

Schloss Landeck
CASTLE

(www.schlosslandeck.at; Schlossweg 2; adult/child €7.50/4; ⊙10am-5pm Sun-Fri; 🎫) Standing sentinel above Landeck, this 13th-century hilltop castle is visible from afar. The 1st-floor **museum** showcases everything from Celtic figurines to hand-carved *Krampus* masks, as well as a wonderful mechanised nativity scene during aAdvent. Climb the dizzying staircase to the tower for sweeping views over Landeck and the Lechtaler Alps.

Zammer Lochputz
GORGE

(www.zammer-lochputz.at; Zams; adult/child €4/3; ⊙9.30am-5.30pm May-Sep, 10am-5pm Oct) A roller-coaster of water thrashes the limestone cliffs at Zammer Lochputz gorge just outside of Landeck. Leading up through pine forest, a trail passes viewpoints and some interesting rock formations – look out for the head of a bull and a nymph.

Sport Camp Tirol
ADVENTURE SPORTS

(📞626 11; www.sportcamptirol.at; Mühlkanal 1) This is a one-stop action shop for activities like paragliding, canyoning, white-water rafting and hydrospeeding. You can also rent mountain bikes here (half-/full day €18/22) to head off on one of the tourist office's free GPS tours or tackle the downhill Inn Trail.

🛏 Sleeping & Eating

Gasthof Greif
GUESTHOUSE €

(📞622 68; www.gasthof-greif.at; Marktplatz 6; s €38-42, d €60-68; 🅿) Greif sits on a quiet square above the main street just down from the castle. Its 1970s-style rooms are large and tidy, and its restaurant (mains €9 to €16) serves solid Tyrolean cuisine.

Tramserhof
HOTEL €€

(📞622 46; www.tramserhof.at; Tramserweg 51; s/d/tr/q incl half board €60/120/180/240; 🅿🛜♨🎫) 🏊 Nestled among trees, this is a calm retreat 20 minutes' walk from the centre. The rooms are country-style with loads of natural light and warm pine. The spa shelters a whirlpool and sauna. Tuck into organic produce at breakfast.

Hotel Mozart
HOTEL €€

(📞642 22; www.mozarthotels.at; Adamhofgasse 7; s/d/f incl half board €77/128/201; 🅿🎫) It's amazing how far Amadeus travels in Austria. This particular Mozart pleases with big sunny rooms opening onto balconies. The

---

> **PASS THE SCHNAPPS**
>
> If all that fresh air and activity have worked up a thirst, pop over to **Stanz** (www.brennereidorf.at), 3km away. Set on a sunny plateau dotted with apple and plum orchards, the village has 150 houses and a mind-boggling 53 schnapps distilleries. There are a number of rustic huts where you can kick back and taste the local firewater before rolling back down to the valley.

flowery gardens and indoor pool with a little spa area invite relaxation.

Cafe Haag
CAFE €

(Maisengasse 19; snacks €3.50-6; ⊙7.30am-7pm Mon-Fri, 8am-12.30pm Sat) Locally picked plums are the key ingredient in this cafe's divine chocolates, and the cakes are just the sugar kick needed for an uphill trudge to the castle.

Schrofenstein
AUSTRIAN €€

(📞623 95; Malserstrasse 31; mains €14-27; ⊙11am-11pm; 🎫) Schrofenstein's restaurant dishes up Austrian classics such as Tyrolean cream of garlic soup and *Tafelspitz* in wood-panelled surrounds and on the chestnut-tree-shaded terrace.

ℹ Information

The friendly staff at the **tourist office** (📞656 00; www.tirolwest.at; Malserstrasse 10; ⊙8.30am-noon & 2-6pm Mon-Fri; 📞) can help book accommodation and have a list of local *Pensionen*.

ℹ Getting There & Away

Trains run roughly hourly to Innsbruck (€15.10, 50 minutes) and at least every two hours to Bregenz (€23.30, 1¾ hours). Buses depart from outside the train station and/or from the bus station in the centre. The train station is 1.5km to the east; to get into town walk left on leaving the station and stay on the same side of the river.

The A12 into Vorarlberg passes by Landeck, burrowing into a tunnel as it approaches town. The B171 passes through the centre of town.

The Inntal

POP 11,250

Shadowing the turquoise Inn River, the Inntal (Inn Valley) has few major sights but the scenery is beautiful, particularly around **Pfunds** with its jagged peaks and thickly forested slopes. Many homes here are similar in design to those found in the Engadine in Graubünden, Switzerland, further up the Inntal.

South of Pfunds, you have a choice of routes. If you continue along the Inn you'll end up in Switzerland (infrequent buses). Alternatively, if you bear south to Nauders you'll soon reach South Tyrol (Italy) by way of the Reschen Pass (open year-round). Eleven buses daily run from Landeck to Nauders (€8.80, one hour), where it's possible to head on with public transport to Merano in Italy, but at least three changes are required.

The Paznauntal

POP 5950

Grazing the Swiss border and running west of the Inntal, the Paznauntal (Paznaun Valley) is a dramatic landscape overshadowed by the pearly white peaks of the Silvretta range. The villages are sleepy in summer, a lull that is broken in winter when skiers descend on party-hearty resorts like Ischgl.

The valley is undoubtedly one of Austria's best ski areas, despite (or because of) its relative isolation. The **Silvretta Ski Pass** (2-day pass adult/child €95/53.50) covers Ischgl, Galtür, Kappl and Samnaun, a duty-free area in Switzerland. Its summer equivalent is the **Silvretta Card** (3-day pass adult/child €41/24.50), comprising cable cars, lifts, public transport over the Bielerhöhe Pass into Vorarlberg, and numerous swimming pools in Ischgl and Galtür.

Around 10km from Ischgl is the uncrowded resort of **Galtür**. This unspoilt village suffered in February 1999 when an avalanche all but swept it away. A museum documenting the event has been built on the spot, the **Alpinarium Galtür** (www.alpinarium.at; Hauptstrasse 29c, Galtür; adult/child €8/4; ☉ 10am-6pm Tue-Sun). Inside you'll find many poignant reminders of the devastation in the shape of photos, newspaper reports and some incredible video footage.

❶ Getting There & Away

Only a secondary road (B188) runs along the valley, crossing into Vorarlberg at the Bielerhöhe Pass (toll cars/motorcycles €14/11), where the views are sensational. This pass, closed in winter, rejoins the main highway near Bludenz. Regular buses travel as far as Galtür (€8, one hour) from Landeck.

Ischgl

☑ 05444 / POP 1596 / ELEV 1377M

Ischgl becomes a quintessential powdersville in winter, with snow-sure slopes and a boisterous après-ski scene. The resort is a bizarre combination of rural meets raunchy; a place where lap-dancing bars, folk music and techno happily coexist. That said, summer here can be *tote Hose* (totally dead) and you may prefer to base yourself in one of the more authentic neighbouring villages.

⭤ Activities

Silvretta Arena   SKIING
(www.silvretta.at; full-region 6-day pass €257) Ischgl is the centrepiece of the vast Silvretta Arena, offering fabulous skiing on 238km of groomed slopes, ultramodern lifts (heated seats and all) and few queues. Suited to all except absolute beginners, the resort has great intermediate runs around Idalp, tough black descents at Greitspitz and Paznauer Taya, and plenty of off-piste powder to challenge experts. Skiing to Samnaun in Switzerland for lunch adds the novelty factor. Boarders can play on the half-pipe, jumps, rails and boarder-cross at two snowparks.

Toboggan Track   SNOW SPORTS
(adult/child €12.50/7) The 7km toboggan track offers a bumpy downhill dash through the snow from Idalp to Ischgl, which is particularly scenic when floodlit on Monday and Thursday nights. Toboggans can be hired at the mountain station for €8/4.50 per adult/child.

Silvretta Mountain
Bike Arena   MOUNTAIN BIKING
Few Austrian resorts can match Ischgl for mountain biking. The mammoth Silvretta Mountain Bike Arena features 1000km of bikeable territory, ranging from downhill tracks to circular trails. Pick up a free map of the area at the tourist office.

For bike rental, try **Intersport Bründl** (www.bruendl.at; Dorfstrasse 64; per day €24-49) or **Silvretta Bike Academy** (www.silvretta-bikeacademy.at; Paznaunweg 15), which also offers GPS rental (€25) and arranges technique training and free-ride day tours costing €40 to €50.

Klettersteige   WALKING
Walking is the other big draw in summer, ranging from gentle lakeside rambles to ambitious scrambling on the *Klettersteige* at 2872m Greitspitz and 2929m Flimspitze.

✨ Festivals & Events

Top of the Mountain CONCERT
(☺late Nov & late Apr) This winter-season opening and closing concert has welcomed a host of stars, including pop divas Kylie Minogue and Alicia Keys in recent years.

Ironbike SPORTS EVENT
(☺Aug) Superfit mountain bikers compete in this 79km obstacle course of a race, involving steep climbs and exhilarating descents.

🛏 Sleeping & Eating

Rates double in the high winter season and nearly everywhere closes between seasons. Cafes, pizzerias and snack bars cluster on Dorfstrasse.

Hotel Alpenstern HOTEL €
(☑512 01; www.alpenstern.at; Versahlweg 5; s/d €36/60; P@�) Nice surprise: one of Ischgl's sweetest hotels is also among its cheapest. The friendly Walser family keep the modern alpine-style rooms spotless and serve generous breakfasts. In winter the spa is great for postski downtime.

AlpVita Piz Tasna HOTEL €€
(☑52 77; www.piztasna.at; Stöckwaldweg 5; s €59, d €106-116, half board €14; P@�) Picturesquely set on a slope, Piz Tasna gets rave reviews for its heartfelt welcome, big and comfy rooms and superb food (half board is worth the extra). The spa has an indoor pool, saunas, herbal steam rooms and a relaxation zone with hay and water beds.

Kitzloch INTERNATIONAL €€
(☑5618; http://kitzloch.at; Galfeisweg 3; ☺après-ski 3-7pm, dinner 8-11pm) Wild après-ski shenanigans with DJ Boris at Kitzloch (fancy dress and all) should work up an appetite for dinner in the rustic, fire-warmed restaurant. Go for the famous sticky spare ribs or a pot of bubbling fondue. Portions are very generous.

Paznaunerstube GASTRONOMIC €€€
(☑600; www.trofana-royal.at; Hotel Troyana Royal, Dorfstrasse 95; menus €55-110) Celebrity chef Martin Sieberer turns every meal into a gastronomic event at this Michelin-starred hotel restaurant. In a refined wood-panelled parlour, regional specialities like milk-fed Galtür lamb are given a creative twist and paired with top wines.

🍸 Drinking & Nightlife

The snow doesn't get hotter than in Ischgl, famous Europe-wide for its pumping après-ski scene. Oompah-playing barns, raunchy go-go bars and chichi clubs shake the resort. Most places go with the snow and open in winter only.

Schatzi Bar BAR
(Fimbabahnweg 4, Hotel Elizabeth; ☺4-8pm) This rollicking après-ski bar is full of *Schatzis* (little treasures) in the form of go-go dancing girls in skimpy *Dirndls* that look like they've shrunk in the wash. Madness.

Niki's Stadl BAR
(www.nikis-stadl.com; Pizbuin Hotel; ☺1pm-3am) German singalongs and swinging steins – it's Oktoberfest every day in this rustic barn.

Kuhstall BAR
(www.kuhstall.at; Ischgl 80; ☺3pm-midnight) *The* place for slopeside socialising to gear up for a big night out in Ischgl.

Trofana Alm BAR
(www.trofana-alm.at; Dorfstrasse 91; ☺3-8pm) A huge wooden barn with live Austrian bands and potent apple schnapps working the crowd into a singing, dancing, drunken frenzy.

Pacha CLUB
(www.pacha.at; Hotel Madlein; ☺10pm-5am) Victoria Beckham (performing), Paris Hilton (posing)...they've all been spotted at this glamorous club brimming with beautiful people.

ℹ Information

The **tourist office** (☑050-990 100; www.ischgl.com; Dorfstrasse 43; ☺8am-6pm Mon-Fri, to 5pm Sat, to 1pm Sun) stocks heaps of literature on hiking, biking and skiing in the area, plus accommodation brochures.

ℹ Getting There & Away

Bus 4240 operates hourly between Ischgl and Landeck (€7.10, 55 minutes).

Arlberg Region

The wild and austerely beautiful Arlberg region, shared by Vorarlberg and Tyrol, comprises several linked resorts and offers some of Austria's finest skiing. Heralded as the cradle of alpine skiing, St Anton am Arlberg is undoubtedly the best known and most popular resort.

St Anton am Arlberg

☑ 05446 / POP 2564 / ELEV 1304M

Once upon a time St Anton was but a sleepy village, defined by the falling and melting of snow and the coming and going of cattle, until one day the locals beheld the virgin powder on their doorstep and discovered their happy-ever-after... In 1901 the resort founded the first ski club in the Alps and downhill skiing was born, so if ever the ski bug is going to bite you it will surely be here. Nestled at the foot of 2811m-high Valluga and strung out along the northern bank of the Rosanna River, St Anton am Arlberg is a cross between a ski bum's Shangri La and Ibiza in fast-forward mode – the terrain fierce, the nightlife hedonistic.

◉ Sights

St Anton Museum   MUSEUM

(Rudi-Matt-Weg 10; adult/child €4/free; ⊙noon-6pm Tue-Sun) Set in attractive gardens with a trout lake, playground and minigolf course, this nostalgic museum traces St Anton's tracks back to the good old days when skis were little more than improvised wooden planks.

🏃 Activities

Arlberg Well.com   SWIMMING

(http://wellness.arlberg-well.com; Hannes-Schneider-Weg 11; adult/child €6.50/3.50, incl sauna €10.50; ⊙9am-9pm) You can gaze up to the Alps from the indoor and outdoor pools or warm up in the sauna complex at this striking glass-and-wood leisure centre. There's also curling (summer) and ice skating (winter), plus a tennis court and fitness centre.

Arlrock   ADVENTURE SPORTS

(www.arlrock.at; Bahnhofstrasse 1; climbing wall adult/child €9/5, boulder wall €6.50/5; ⊙9am-9pm Mon-Fri, 4-9pm Sat & Sun) This all-new leisure centre by the train station has climbing and boulder walls, kids' play areas, a bowling alley and tennis courts. It's also the home base of **H2O Adventure** (☑05472 66 99; www.h2o-adventure.at; Bahnhofstrasse 1, Arlrock; ⊙May–mid-Oct), offering adrenalin-based activities from rafting on the Sanna River to canyoning, ziplining and downhill mountain biking.

Winter Activities

St Anton is the zenith of Austria's alpine skiing, and the spacey Galzigbahn gondola, launched in 2007, has further improved conditions. The terrain is vast, covering 280km of slopes, and the skiing challenging, with fantastic backcountry opportunities and exhilarating descents including the **Kandahar** run on Galzig.

Cable cars ascend to **Valluga** (2811m), from where experts can go off-piste all the way to Lech (with a ski guide only). For fledglings, there are nursery slopes on **Gampen** (1850m) and **Kapall** (2330m). **Rendl** is snowboarding territory with jumps, rails and a half-pipe. A 10-minute stroll east of St Anton is **Nasserein**, where novices can test out the nursery slopes. Further east still are the quieter slopes of **St Jakob**, easily accessed by the Nasserein gondola.

A single **ski pass** (1-/3-/6-day pass €48/134/235) covers the whole Arlberg region and is valid for all 84 ski lifts.

Summer Activities

Walking in the mountains is the most popular summertime activity, and the meadows full of wildflowers and grazing cattle are pure Heidi. A handful of cable cars and lifts (€5 to €23 one way, €6 to €25 return) rise to the major peaks. If you're planning on going hiking, pick up a detailed booklet and map from the tourist office. Also consider purchasing a **Wanderpass** (3-/7-day pass €32/37), providing unlimited access to all lifts, or a **St Anton Card** (3-/7-day pass €47/54), which offers the same benefits plus entrance to the town's indoor and outdoor swimming pools.

The tourist office also produces a small booklet (in German only) with a number of suggested **cycling** trails in the area.

✺ Festivals & Events

The **Arlberg Adler** (www.arlbergadler.eu) triathlon kicks off with *der weisse Rausch* (the white thrill) ski race in April; then the Jakobilauf half-marathon in July, and the Bike Marathon in August. The cows come home in their floral finery at September's **Almabtrieb**, a villagewide excuse for a party.

🛏 Sleeping

The best places fill up in a flash in winter, so book well ahead. For cheaper *Pensionen*, try nearby Nasserein and St Jakob. Some of the smaller places only open in winter, when rates can as much as double.

★ Hotel Garni Ernst Falch   GUESTHOUSE €

(☑28 53; www.hotelfalch.at; Ing-Gomperz-Weg 26; r €60; @ 🕾 🛉) Rainer and his kindly mum are the heart and soul of this wonderful B&B, perched above St Anton, a five-minute stroll from the Nassereinbahn. The homely rooms are bright, immaculately kept and pine-clad, with balconies for soaking up the alpine views. Nothing is too much trouble for the family, so whether you need a pick-up from the station or Nordic poles for a hike, just say the word.

Himmlhof   GUESTHOUSE €€

(☑232 20; www.himmlhof.com; Im Gries 9; d €96-100, ste €116-422; 🅿 @ 🕾) This *himmlisch* (heavenly) Tyrolean chalet has wood-clad rooms brimming with original features (tiled ovens, four-poster beds and the like). An open fire for afternoon tea and a cosy spa with a grottolike plunge pool beckon after a day's skiing.

Altes Thönihaus   GUESTHOUSE €€

(☑28 10; www.altes-thoenihaus.at; Im Gries 1; s €62-66, d €120-128; 🅿 🕾) Dating to 1465, this listed wooden chalet oozes alpine charm from every last beam. Fleecy rugs and pine keep the mood cosy in rooms with mountain-facing balconies. Downstairs there's a superb little spa and restored *Stube* (parlour).

Rundeck   HOTEL €€

(☑31 33; www.hotelrundeck.at; Arlbergstrasse 59; d €84-106; @ 🕾 🛉) Clean lines, earthy tones and nutwood panelling define the streamlined rooms at design-focused Rundeck. There's a sleek spa and a backlit bar with an open fire for relaxing moments, plus a playroom for the kids.

Lux Alpinae   DESIGN HOTEL €€€

(☑301 08; www.luxalpinae.at; Arlbergstrasse 41; d incl half board €296-374; 🅿 🛎) This design hotel wings you into the 21st century with glass-walled rooms that bring the mountains indoors and industrial-chic interiors blending concrete, wood and steel. Personalised service (including a driver to take you to the slopes), a first-rate restaurant and a spa add to its appeal. Lux Alpinae is only open in winter.

✖ Eating

Because of the lopsidedness of St Anton's seasons, many restaurants only open in winter, when reservations are recommended.

Most places double as vibrant bars after dinner, especially along the pedestrian-only Dorfstrasse.

★ Museum Restaurant   AUSTRIAN €€

(☑24   75; www.museum-restaurant.at; Rudi-Matt-Weg 10; mains €23.50-32.50; ⊙6-10pm) Arlberger hay soup with smoked wild boar and lavender served in a bread bowl, and the most succulent Tyrolean beef and trout fished fresh from the pond outside land on your plate at this intimate wood-panelled restaurant, housed in the picture-perfect chalet of the St Anton Museum.

Hazienda   INTERNATIONAL €€

(☑29 68; www.m3hotel.at; Dorfstrasse 56; mains €16-33; ⊙cafe 8am-midnight year-round, restaurant 6pm-1am winter) A prime people-watching terrace fronts this smart restaurant-cafe hybrid. Thai-style Argentine beef fillet, herby homemade pasta with sheep's cheese, proper Italian espresso – everything here strikes a perfect balance.

Fuhrmann Stube   AUSTRIAN €€

(☑29 21; Dorfstrasse 74; mains €10-16; ⊙10am-10pm) When snow blankets the rooftops, this is a cosy hideaway for tucking into *Knödel* (dumplings) or a carnivorous *Tiroler Bauernplatte* (Tyrolean farmers' platter).

Bodega   TAPAS €€

(☑427 88; Dorfstrasse 40; tapas €2.50-10; ⊙3pm-1am) Excellent tapas, vino and live music reel in the crowds to this buzzy Spanish haunt. You can't book, so be prepared to wait for a table.

A DOWNHILL SLED TO DINNER

Fancy a twilight dash through the snow? Every Tuesday and Thursday evening in winter, the 4km-long **Rodelbahn** (adult/child €10.50/5.50, sled rental €8) toboggan run from Gampen to Nasserein is floodlit. Simply grab your sled and away you go! Most ruddy-faced sledders stop to defrost over schnapps and enormous portions of Tyrolean dumplings and pork knuckles in the warm, woody halfway hut, **Rodelalm** (☑0676-886 486 000; www.rodelalm.com; Nassereinerstrasse 106; mains €9.50-14.50; ⊙11am-11pm, closed Wed; 🛉). Reservations are highly advisable.

St Anton am Arlberg

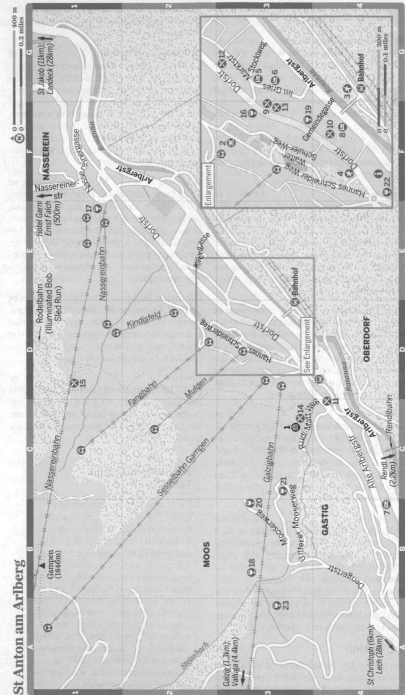

St Anton am Arlberg

Sights
1 St Anton Museum...............................C3

Activities, Courses & Tours
2 Arlberg Well.com F3
3 Arlrock..G4
H2O Adventure..........................(see 3)
4 Intersport Arlberg............................F4

Sleeping
5 Altes Thönihaus G3
6 Himmlhof..G3
7 Lux Alpinae B4
8 Rundeck...F4

Eating
9 Bobo's F3
10 Bodega..F4
11 Floriani..C4
12 Fuhrmann Stube G3
13 Hazienda F3
14 Museum Restaurant.........................C3
15 Rodelalm..D1

Drinking & Nightlife
16 Bar Cuba...F3
17 Fanghouse...E1
18 Heustadl..B3
19 Kandahar...F3
20 Krazy Kanguruh B3
21 Mooserwirt.......................................C3
22 Piccadilly...F4
23 Sennhütte...A3
Taps...(see 20)

Bobo's TEX-MEX €€
(☑ 27 14; www.bobos.at; Dorfstrasse 60; mains €13-19; ☺ 5pm-2am; ☑) Tex-Mex food and potent cocktails make Bobo's a perennial favourite. The party cranks up after fajitas and a fistful of nachos, with everything from karaoke to live bands and DJs.

Floriani PIZZERIA €€
(☑ 23 30; Alte Arlbergstrasse 13; mains €7-10; ☺ 5-11pm) The pizzas – thin, crisp and filling – are the stars of the menu at this sweet and simple place.

🍷 Drinking & Nightlife

St Anton is Austria's unrivalled après-ski king. Dancing on tables, *Schlager* (a broad genre of soft pop or even folk with a sentimental edge) singalongs, Jägermeister after Jägermeister – it's just an average night out in St Anton, where people party as hard as they ski. Pace yourself.

Mooserwirt BAR
(www.mooserwirt.at; Unterer Mooserweg 2; ☺ 3.30-8pm) One word: *craaaazy*. Come tea-time Mooserwirt heaves with skiers guzzling beer (the place sells around 5000L a day), dancing to DJ Gerhard's Eurotrash mix and sweating in their salopettes. The first challenge is to locate your skis, the second to use them to get back to St Anton in one piece.

Krazy Kanguruh BAR
(www.krazykanguruh.com; Mooserweg 19; ☺ 10am-8pm) Owned by St Anton ski legend and two-time slalom world champion Mario Matt, this slopeside hot spot is loud, fun and jam-packed after 5pm. One too many tequilas will indeed send you bouncing (on skis) back to the valley.

Heustadl BAR
(www.heustadl.com; Dengerstrasse 625; ☺ 9.30am-6.30am) Just north of Sennhütte, this shack is always fit to bursting with beery throngs. There's live music from 3pm to 6pm most days. Yes, the bar stools have legs; yes, you are still sane if not sober.

Sennhütte BAR
(Dengerstrasse 503; ☺ 3-6pm; 🚼) A sunny terrace, feisty schnapps, locals jiggling on the tables – what more après-ski could one ask for? In summer there's a wonderful herb garden, treehouse and cow-themed walking trail for kids.

Taps BAR
(Mooserweg 15; ☺ 10am-8pm) Taps is a pumping après-ski place with the cheapest beer on the mountain and DJ Beni keeping the party in full swing. There's a huge sun terrace for chilling and often free homemade schnapps (mind-blowing stuff) doing the rounds.

Fanghouse BAR
(www.fanghouse.com; Nassereinerstrasse 6; ☺ 10am-10pm) At the base of the slopes in Nasserein, this laid-back hang-out has a big, sunny terrace, fun staff (including the crazy Swedish owner, Hasse) and lethal Jägermeister shots served at -17°C. The pub also occasionally hosts events, from live music to quiz nights.

Bar Cuba BAR
(www.barcuba-stanton.com; Dorfstrasse 33; ☺ 4pm-3am) Live music, Wednesday-night fancy-dress parties, chipper bar staff and cocktails named Cuban Cocaine and Love Juice – say no more.

LOCAL KNOWLEDGE

LOCALS' APRÈS-SKI FAVOURITES

Taps (p323) 'The après-ski here has to be seen here to be believed – crazy but not a *Schlager* bash! Great place run by a terrific local family' – *Beni, snowboard instructor*

Fanghouse (p323) 'Fanghouse is always a great place to visit. Hasse the boss loves a *Jägi* and hates to drink alone. A party is always on the cards!' – *Maggie Ritson, waitress*

Piccadilly 'Massive parties kick off at 4pm at the Piccadilly, with live music from the '80s to the current. I've had a blast there.' – *Lush, pizza chef*

Heustadl (p323) 'It's the biggest and best. Top location, good all-day après-ski and a very entertaining band where the waitresses are part of the show...' – *Chris Ritson, powerline contractor*

Mooserwirt (p323) 'If you want to let your hair down, get up and dance on the tables, and sing along to some dodgey music, Mooserwirt is the place. It is expensive but there is no other place like it. You have to come here at least once on your ski holiday.' – *Shane Pearce, Funky Foods*

Piccadilly BAR
(Dorfstrasse 2; ☻4pm-2am) This loud, crowded British pub with daily live music is known as Pickawilly (the mind boggles) to locals.

Kandahar CLUB
(www.kandaharbar.com; Dorfstrasse 50; ☻10pm-4am) Top British and Ibiza DJs play house and keep the dance floor packed till dawn here.

❶ Information

You can check emails for free in most ski shops. The centrally located **tourist office** (☎226 90; www.stantonamarlberg.com; Dorfstrasse 8; ☻8am-6pm Mon-Fri, 9am-noon Sat & Sun) has information on outdoor activities, maps and places to stay. There's an accommodation board and a free telephone outside.

❶ Getting There & Away

St Anton is the easiest access point to the region. Buses depart from stands southwest of the tourist office.

St Anton and St Christoph are close to the eastern entrance of the Arlberg Tunnel (cars and minibuses €8.50), the toll road connecting Vorarlberg and Tyrol. You can avoid the toll by taking the B197, but no vehicles with trailers are allowed on this winding road.

The ultramodern train station is on the route between Bregenz (€19.20, 1½ hours) and Innsbruck (€21.50, 1¼ hours), with fast trains every one or two hours.

❶ Getting Around

Bicycles can be rented (half-/full day €16/23) from **Intersport Arlberg** (www.intersport-arlberg.com; Dorfstrasse 1; ☻9am-1pm & 2-6pm Mon-Fri, 9am-1pm Sat).

Free local buses go to outlying parts of the resort (such as St Jakob). Buses run to Lech and Zürs in Vorarlberg (one way €6.10); they are hourly (till about 6pm) in winter, reducing to four a day in summer.

A minibus taxi can be shared between up to eight people; the trip from St Anton to Lech costs €37/55 in the day/night.

VORARLBERG

History

Vorarlberg has been inhabited since the early Stone Age but it wasn't until the Celts arrived in 400 BC, followed by the Romans in around 15 BC, that lasting settlements were maintained. Brigantium, the forerunner of Bregenz, was a Roman stronghold until around the 5th and 6th centuries, when the raiding Germanic Alemanni tribes increased their influence and effectively took over.

Peace reigned in the province until the early 15th century, when it suffered substantial damage during the Appenzell War with the Swiss Confederation. Relations with its neighbour later improved to such an extent that in 1918 Vorarlberg declared independence from Austria and sought union with Switzerland. The move was blocked by the Allied powers in the postwar reorganisation of Europe; fears that an even smaller Austria would be easily absorbed by a recovering Germany were certainly founded.

Today, Vorarlberg still looks first towards its westerly neighbours, and then to Vienna, 600km to the east.

ℹ Getting There & Around

AIR

Austrian Airlines flies to **St Gallen Altenrhein** (www.airport-stgallen.com) in Switzerland, the nearest airport. **Friedrichshafen airport** (www.fly-away.de), in Germany, is the closest major airport serving domestic and European destinations.

CAR & MOTORCYCLE

The A14/E43 connects the province to Germany in the north and the rest of Austria via the 14km Arlberg tunnel, which runs under the Arlberg mountains. To the west, there are plenty of border crossings into Liechtenstein and Switzerland.

PUBLIC TRANSPORT

Vorarlberg is broken down into Domino (individual zones). A Regio travel pass covering one region costs €6.20/€15.50 for one day/week while a Maximo pass, costing €12.80/26.50, covers the entire province. Single Domino tickets cost €1.30 and a day pass is €2.40; these cover city transport in Bregenz, Dornbirn, Götzis, Feldkirch, Bludenz, Lech and Schruns/Tschagguns. Information and timetables are available from the **Verkehrsverbund Vorarlberg** (www.vmobil.at).

Bregenz

📞 05574 / POP 28,000 / ELEV 427M

What a view! Ah yes, the locals proudly agree, Bregenz does indeed have the loveliest of views: before you the Bodensee, Europe's third-largest lake, spreads out like a liquid mirror; behind you the Pfänder (1064m) climbs to the Alps; to the right you see Germany, to the left the faint outline of Switzerland. Just wow.

Whether contemplating avant-garde art and architecture by the new harbour, sauntering along the promenade on a summer's evening or watching opera under the stars at the much-lauded *Festspiele* (festival), you can't help but think – clichéd though it sounds – that Vorarlberg's pocket-sized capital has got at least a taste of it all.

◉ Sights

★ Kunsthaus GALLERY
(www.kunsthaus-bregenz.at; Karl-Tizian-Platz; adult/child €9/free; ⊙10am-6pm Tue, Wed & Fri-Sun, to 9pm Thu; ♿) Designed by Swiss architect Peter Zumthor, this giant glass and steel cube is said to resemble a lamp, reflecting the changing light of the sky and lake. The stark, open-plan interior is perfect for rotating exhibitions of contemporary art – the work of New York graffitti artist Keith Haring and Mexican sculptor Gabriel Orozco have recently been in the spotlight. Check the website for details on everything from guided tours to kids' workshops.

★ Vorarlberg Museum MUSEUM
(www.vlm.at; Kornmarktplatz 1; adult/child €9/6.50; ⊙10am-6pm Tue, Wed & Fri-Sun, to 9pm Thu) Following a three-year, €34-million makeover, the Vorarlberg Museum reopened in June 2013 to much acclaim. Its striking new home is a white cuboid emblazoned with what appears to be 16,656 flowers (actually PET bottle bases imprinted in concrete). The gallery homes in on Vorarlberg's history, art and architecture in its permanent exhibitions, including one on the Roman archaeological finds of Brigantium. It also stages rotating exhibitions, such as the inaugural one on African lace, highlighting the textile trade between Vorarlberg and Nigeria.

★ Pfänder Cable Car CABLE CAR
(www.pfaenderbahn.at; Steinbruchgasse 4; 1 way adult/child €6.70/3.40, return €11.50/5.80; ⊙8am-7pm) A cable car whizzes to the 1064m peak of the Pfänder, a wooded mountain rearing above Bregenz and affording a breathtaking panorama of the Bodensee and the snow-capped summits of the not-so-distant Alps. At the top, a 30-minute circular trail brings you close to deer, wild boar, ibex and whistling marmots at the year-round **Wildpark** (nature reserve). There's also a **Greifvogelflugschau** (adult/child €5.60/2.80; ⊙11am & 2.30pm May-early Oct), where birds of prey amaze with aerial feats.

Oberstadt HISTORIC QUARTER
Slung high above the lake is the Oberstadt, Bregenz' tiny old town of winding streets, candy-coloured houses and flowery gardens. It's still enclosed by defensive walls and the sturdy **Martinstor** (St Martin's Gate), guarded by a grotesque mummified shark.

MOVING ON?

For tips, recommendations and reviews, head to shop.lonelyplanet.com to purchase a downloadable PDF of the Switzerland chapter from Lonely Planet's Western Europe guide.

Bregenz

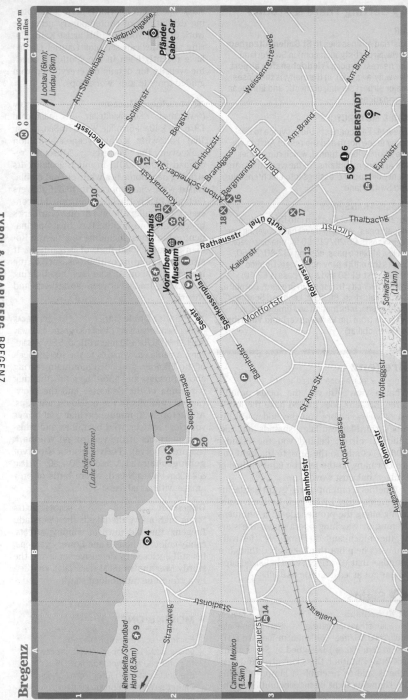

TYROL & VORARLBERG BREGENZ

Map labels:

Lochau (6km); Lindau (8km)

Pfänder Cable Car 2

OBERSTADT 7

6

5 11

Steinbruchgasse

Am Steinenbach

Reichsstr

Schillerstr

Bergstr

Eichholzstr

Weissenreuteweg

Brandgasse

Belruptstr

Am Brand

Eponastr

12

Kornmarktstr

Anton-Schneider-Str

Bergmannstr

16

10

Kunsthaus

1 15

22

18

17

Thalbachg

Vorarlberg Museum 3

Rathausstr

Leutbühel

Kirchstr

8

Kaiserstr

13

Schwärzler (1.1km)

21

Sparkassenplatz

Montfortstr

Römerstr

Seestr

Bahnhofstr

St-Anna-Str

Wolfeggstr

Seepromenade

20

Klostergasse

Römerstr

19

Augasse

Bodensee (Lake Constance)

4

Bahnhofstr

Quellerstr

Rheindelta/Strandbad Hard (8.5km) 9

Strandweg

Stadtonstr

Mehrerauerstr

14

Camping Mexico (1.5km)

200 m
0.1 miles

Martinsturm TOWER
(St Martin's Tower; www.martinsturm.at; Martinsgasse; adult/child €3.50/1; ⊙10am-5pm Tue-Sun Apr-Oct) Not far past Martinstor is this baroque tower, topped by the largest onion dome in Central Europe. It's worth seeing the 14th-century frescoes in the **chapel** before climbing up to the small **military museum** for fine views over Bregenz' rooftops.

Festspielhaus LANDMARK
(www.festspielhausbregenz.at; Platz der Wiener Symphoniker 1) Even if you can't bag tickets for the Bregenzer Festspiele (p329), the Festival Hall is a must-see. All tinted glass, smooth concrete and sharp angles, this is one of Bregenz' most visible icons. Many festival performances are held on the semicircular **Seebühne** stage jutting out onto the lake.

🏃 Activities

Bregenz' shimmering centrepiece is the Bodensee, Europe's third-largest lake, straddling Austria, Switzerland and Germany. In summer the well-marked trail that circumnavigates the lake becomes an autobahn for lycra-clad *Radfahrer* (cyclists); shoulder seasons are considerably more peaceful. For informtion on Visas, see p390.

Other lakeside activities include sailing and diving at Lochau, around 6km north of town, and swimming. The most central place for a quick dip or a barbecue is the **Pipeline**, a stretch of pebbly beach north of Bregenz, so named for the large pipeline running parallel to the lake.

Vorarlberg Lines CRUISE
(www.vorarlberg-lines.at; Seestrasse) This is one of a number of companies taking you out onto the lake from May to mid-October. There are two-hour Bodensee panorama cruises (adult/child €16.90/8.40), one-hour Bregenz trips (€10.20/5.10) and regular boat transfers to lake destinations including Lindau, Mainau, Friedrichshafen and Konstanz.

Strandbad Bregenz OUTDOORS
(Strandweg; adult/child €4.40/2.10; ⊙9am-8pm early May-early Sep; ☝) Packed with bronzed bods, overexcited kids and flirty teens in summer, this central lido has a lakeside beach, several outdoor pools with waterslides, and activities like volleyball and table tennis.

Rheindelta WALKING, CYCLING
(www.rheindelta.com; Hard) Easily explored on foot or by bike, this nature reserve sits 5km south of Bregenz, where the Rhine flows into the Bodensee. The mossy marshes, reeds and mixed woodlands attract more than 300 bird species, including curlews, grey herons and rare black-tailed godwits.

Strandbad Hard SWIMMING
(www.hard-sport-freizeit.at; Hard; adult/child €3.90/2; ⊙9am-8pm early May-early Sep) A lake front contender 5km south of town, this lido has outdoor pools, barbecue areas, minigolf and a secluded Frei Körper Kultur (FKK; nudist) beach for skinny-dippers.

ONE LAKE, TWO WHEELS, THREE COUNTRIES

When the sun's out, there's surely no better way to explore Bodensee than with your bum in a saddle. The well-marked **Bodensee Cycle Path** (www.bodensee-radweg.com) makes a 273km loop of the Bodensee, taking in vineyards, meadows, orchards, wetlands and historic towns. There are plenty of small beaches where you can stop for a refreshing dip in the lake. Visit the website for itineraries and maps.

A day suffices to tick off some highlights in three countries on a 30km stretch of the route. Catch a morning ferry to the story-book old town of **Lindau** in Germany, then roll along the lakeshore back to **Bregenz**. Continue southwest along a woodland path to the broad banks of the **Bregenzerach**, a beautiful meltwater river where locals bathe and fly-fish on hot days. From here it's just a short pedal to the Rheindelta wetlands (p327) and the wide bay of **Rorschach** in Switzerland, where you can stop for Swiss chocolate before catching a train back to Bregenz.

Sleeping

Stop by the tourist office for a list of private rooms (around €30 per person). Prices soar and beds are at a premium during the Bregenzer Festspiele in late July to late August, when it's highly advisable to book ahead. If Bregenz is booked solid, consider hopping over the border to Lindau in Germany, around 8km away.

JUFA Gästehaus Bregenz   HOSTEL €
(☎05708-35 40; www.jufa.eu; Mehrerauerstrasse 5; dm €28; P @) Housed in a former needle factory near the lake, this HI hostel now reels backpackers in with its superclean dorms and excellent facilities including a common room and restaurant.

Camping Mexico   CAMPGROUND €
(☎732 60; www.camping-mexico.at; Hechtweg 4; camp sites per adult/child/tent €7.50/4/6; ⊗ May-Sep; ⊛) 🖉 This eco-labelled camping ground by the lake uses solar energy, recycles waste and serves organic food in its restaurant. The leafy pitches offer plenty of shade. You can rent a canoe/kayak here for €21/27 per day.

Hotel Weisses Kreuz   HOTEL €€
(☎498 80; www.hotelweisseskreuz.at; Römerstrasse 5; s €109-119, d €126-186; P ✳@⊛) Service is attentive at this central pick, with a cocktail bar and a restaurant rolling out seasonal Austrian fare (mains €16 to €34). The smart rooms sport cherry-wood furnishings, flat-screen TVs and organic bedding.

Schwärzler   HOTEL €€
(☎49 90; http://schwaerzler.s-hotels.com; Landstrasse 9; P ✳⊛) This turreted, ivy-clad pick is a far cry from your average business hotel. Rooms are understated and contemporary, done out in earthy hues and blonde wood,

and with the comforts you'd expect for the category – bathrobes, flat-screen TVs, mini-bars. Regional produce from organic farms features on the breakfast buffet, and there's a pool and sauna area for downtime. Buses 4 and 5 from the train station stop in front of the hotel.

Hotel Bodensee   HOTEL €€
(☎423 00; www.hotel-bodensee.at; Kornmarktstrasse 22; s/d €69/122; ⊛⊛) Right in the thick of things, this hotel's best rooms are spacious, tastefully decorated in muted tones and sport flat-screenTVs. Breakfast is a wholesome fresh fruit, muesli and regional produce affair.

★ **Deuring-Schlössle**   HISTORIC HOTEL €€€
(☎478 00; www.deuring-schloessle.at; Ehre-Guta-Platz 4; d €218-252, ste €330-440; P @⊛) Perched above Bregenz in the Oberstadt, this is your archetypal fairy-tale hotel with a turret and ivy-draped walls. Rooms have medieval charm with antiques and low beams, while marble bathrooms, designer furnishings and wi-fi wing you back to the 21st century.

Eating

Restaurants and cafes huddle along the lake front and the streets of the Unterstadt. In summer little beats a picnic on the banks of the Bodensee; stock up on farm-fresh produce at the weekly **Bauernmarkt** (Kaiserstrasse; ⊗8am-noon Fri).

Buongustiao   DELI, ITALIAN €
(☎581 29; www.buongustaio.at; Anton-Schneider-Strasse 10; lunch €9.80; ⊗9am-10pm Tue-Fri, to 4pm Sat; ⊛) For an authentic Italian lunch or picnic goodies, drop by this deli-restaurant. The split-level, open-plan interior is a socia-

ble setting for homemade pasta or a glass of prosecco with antipastos. The €19.90 Saturday brunch, with wood-oven bread, Italian *salumi*, cheese and *dolci* (sweets) is legendary. Buongustiao's events – from cookery workshops to live-music nights – are listed on its website.

Cafesito
CAFE €

(Maurachgasse 6; bagels €2.50-4.50; ⊘ 7.45am-6.30pm Mon-Fri, 9am-2.30pm Sat) 🍴 Tiny Cafesito does the best bagels, brownies and smoothies in town. Bright-hued, art-plastered walls create a boho-cool backdrop for a light lunch or cup of fair-trade coffee.

KUB Nam Viet
CAFE €

(📞 580 70; www.namviet.at; Karl-Tizian-Platz 1; lunch €9.50, mains €10-17; ⊘ 9am-2am; 🚼) In front of the Kunsthaus, this anthracite-clad cafe opens onto a buzzy terrace. It's a popular choice for breakfast, salads, coffee and cake, and Vietnamese dishes like yellow curry and *pho bo* (beef noodle soup).

Neubeck
INTERNATIONAL €€

(📞 436 09; www.neubeck.at; Anton-Schneider-Strasse 5; lunch €11, mains €20-35; ⊘ 11.45am-2pm & 6-10pm Tue-Sat) Crisp white linen and soft lighting keep the mood intimate and refined at this fin de siècle bistro, with a secluded courtyard garden. Chef Nina Sotriffer puts a creative, herby spin on seasonal dishes like Singapore-style noodles with wild *gambas* (shrimp) and stuffed Breton quail with truffle mash.

Wirtshaus am See
AUSTRIAN €€

(📞 422 10; www.wirtshausamsee.at; Seepromenade 2; mains €10.50-29; ⊘ 9am-midnight) Snag a table on the lake-front terrace at this mock half-timbered villa, dishing up local specialities like buttery Bodensee whitefish and venison ragout. It's also a relaxed spot for quaffing a cold one.

Kornmesser
AUSTRIAN €€

(📞 548 54; www.kornmesser.at; Kornmarktstrasse 5; lunch €8.10-8.90, mains €8-27; ⊘ 9.30am-midnight Tue-Sun) Baroque meets Bavaria at this attractively converted 18th-century *Gasthaus* (inn). Wash down *Weisswürste* (herby veal sausages), pork knuckles and other hearty fare with Augustiner Bräu beer in the vaulted interior or chestnut-shaded beer garden.

★ Deuring-Schlössle
GASTRONOMIC €€€

(📞 478 00; www.deuring-schloessle.at; Ehre-Guta-Platz 4; mains €19-34, 3-/4-course menu €74/89; ⊘ 6-10pm Wed-Sat) Whether by the fireside in the wood-panelled salon or in the walled garden, this restaurant is romantic stuff. Chef Heino Huber makes the most of organic, market-fresh produce, with specialities like *Felchen* (Bodensee whitefish) with chive mash and organic chicken on lime risotto. Deuring-Schlössle regularly hosts wine tastings and cookery classes.

🍷 Drinking & Entertainment

Wunderbar
BAR

(Bahnhofstrasse 4; ⊘ 10am-4am Mon-Sat, 2pm-1am Sun; 🛜) Bordello meets neobaroque at the Wunderbar, where candles illuminate blood red walls, cherubs and velvet sofas. Browse the papers, bag a swing on the terrace or sip cocktails as smooth funk plays.

Beach Bar Bregenz
BAR

(Seepromenade; ⊘ 4pm-midnight Mon-Fri, from 2pm Sat, 11am-midnight Sun late Apr-early Sep) Cool cocktails, palm trees, chilled DJ beats – it's the Costa del Bodensee every summer at this lake-front beach bar. Work your relaxed look in a *Strandkorb* (wicker basket chair).

Cuba
BAR

(www.cuba-club.at; Bahnhofstrasse 9; ⊘ 11am-2am Mon-Sat, from 2pm Sun) Glammed up with chandeliers and a sweeping staircase, this gallery-style bar attracts trendy types with Latin tunes and a top line-up of DJs.

Vorarlberger Landestheater
THEATRE

(📞 428 70; www.landestheater.org; Seestrasse 2; ⊘ ticket office 8am-12.30pm Mon-Fri) Also known as the Theater am Kornmarkt, this German-language theatre is Vorarlberg's main stage for opera, drama, comedy and musicals.

OPERA UNDER THE STARS

The **Bregenzer Festspiele** (Bregenz Festival; 📞 407-6; www.bregenzerfestspiele.com; ⊘ mid-Jul–mid-Aug) is the city's premier cultural festival. World-class operas, orchestral works and other highly imaginative productions are staged on the open-air Seebühne, a floating stage on the lake, in the Festspielhaus and at the Vorarlberger Landestheater. Information and tickets (€28 to €132) are up for grabs about nine months before the festival.

ⓘ Information

You'll find plenty of banks and *Bankomat* machines in central Bregenz, including on Sparkassenplatz and Bahnhofstrasse.

Bodensee-Vorarlberg Tourism (🖉434 43; www.bodensee-vorarlberg.com) Free regional accommodation-booking service.

Main post office (Seestrasse 5; ☉8am-6pm Mon-Fri, 9am-noon Sat) Also has a *Bankomat* (ATM) machine.

Tourist office (🖉49 59; www.bregenz.travel; Rathausstrasse 35a; ☉9am-6pm Mon-Fri, to noon Sat) Information on the city and the surrounding area and help with accommodation.

Unfallkrankenhaus (🖉4901; Josef Huter Strasse 12) Provincial hospital with emergency ward.

ⓘ Getting There & Around

BICYCLE

Fahrradverleih Bregenz (Seepromenade; per day city bike €15-18, e-bike €25; ☉9am-7pm Apr-Oct) rents quality bikes and has free Bodensee cycling maps.

BUS

A daily bus service runs to Dornbirn (€2.60, 30 minutes) at least four times an hour.

TRAIN

Four direct trains daily head for Munich (€46.40, three hours) via Lindau (€2.20, 11 minutes), while trains for Konstanz (€19.40, two hours) go via the Swiss shore of the lake and may be frequent, but require up to four changes. There are frequent

departures for Zürich (€34.20, two hours), all of which call in at St Gallen (€14.20, 56 minutes). There are roughly hourly trains to Innsbruck (€34.40, 2½ hours), calling en route at Dornbirn (€3.80, eight minutes), Feldkirch (€7.80, 30 minutes) and Bludenz (€12, 45 minutes).

Dornbirn & Around

ELEV 437M

Ragged, thickly wooded limestone pinnacles are the dramatic backdrop to Dornbirn, Vorarlberg's largest city. While nowhere near as appealing as Bregenz, it's worth a visit for its refreshing lack of tourists and remarkable museums.

Hohenems, 6km south of Dornbirn, sheltered a large Jewish community in the 17th century. Their numbers dwindled in the 1860s, when Jews were eligible to live anywhere under Habsburg rule.

◉ Sights & Activities

★**Inatura**　　　　　　　　　MUSEUM
(www.inatura.at; Jahngasse 9, Dornbirn; adult/child/family €10.50/5.30/23.10; ☉10am-6pm; ⏩) Dornbirn's biggest draw is this hands-on museum. It's a wonderland for kids who can pet (stuffed) foxes and handle (real) spiders, whip up tornadose, conduct light experiments and generally interact with science, nature and technology. There's also a climbing wall and 3D cinema.

Altstadt　　　　　　　　HISTORIC SITE
(Dornbirn) Dornbirn's compact old town centres on the Marktplatz, where your gaze is drawn to the crooked, 17th-century **Rotes Haus**, which owes its intense red hue to an unappetising mix of ox blood and bile. Next door, the neoclassical columns and freestanding Gothic belfry of **Pfarrkirche St Martin** catch your eye.

Rolls-Royce Museum　　　　MUSEUM
(www.rolls-royce-museum.at; adult/child €9/4.50; ☉10am-6pm) Situated at the bottom of Rappenlochschlucht and ensconced in a 19th-century cotton mill, this museum harbours the world's largest collection of Rolls-Royces. Highlights include a reconstruction of Royce's Cooke St factory in Manchester and a hall of fame showcasing vintage Rollers that once belonged to the likes of Queen Elizabeth, Franco and George V. Stay for tea in the ever-so-British rosewood tearoom.

VORARLBERG: AN ARCHITECTURAL TRAILBLAZER

Rural though it may seem, Vorarlberg is among the most progressive places on the planet when it comes to architecture. It all started back in the mid-1980s when a group of forward-thinking architects began calling themselves Baukünstler (building artists). Today, almost everywhere you look – private homes, hotels, office blocks, supermarkets – you'll find cutting-edge buildings of glass, wood and steel. Some, like Inatura in Dornbirn and the Kunsthaus (p325) in Bregenz, make urban design statements; others, like the alpine Silvrettahaus (p339), integrate seamlessly into the natural environment.

Jüdisches Museum Hohenems   MUSEUM

(www.jm-hohenems.at; Schweizer Strasse 5, Hohenems; adult/child €7/4; ⊘10am-5pm Tue-Sun) Housed in the Rosenthal villa, this museum zooms in on Hohenems' long-defunct Jewish community with photos, documents and religious artefacts. The Rosenthals built up a considerable textile business in the town, and part of their wealth – especially gorgeous period furniture – is also on show.

Huddled against a tree-lined hill just outside the town on the road to Götzis is the **Jewish cemetery**; get the key from the museum.

Rappenlochschlucht   WALKING

(Rappenloch Gorge; www.rappenlochschlucht.at) Just 4km south of Dornbirn is the narrow Rappenlochschlucht, gouged out by the thundering Dornbirner Ache. A 10-minute walk leads up to a good viewpoint and a 30-minute trail to the **Staufensee**, a turquoise lake ringed by forest.

ⓘ Getting There & Away

Bus 47 departs from Dornbirn train station and passes by the Rappenlochschlucht (€1.80, 30 minutes, nine daily).Dornbirn has frequent connections to Bregenz (€3.80, eight minutes) and Hohenems (€2.20, eight minutes) on the Bregenz–Innsbruck railway line.

Bregenzerwald

The wooded limestone peaks, cow-nibbled pastures and bucolic villages of the Bregenzerwald unfold to the south of Bregenz. This rural region is great for getting back to nature for a few days, whether cheese tasting in alpine dairies, testing out hay and herbal treatments in spa hotels, or curling up by the fireside in a cosy farmhouse. One lungful of that good clean air and you'll surely want to grab your boots, slip into your skis or get on your bike and head outdoors.

◉ Sights

★ **Angelika Kauffmann Museum**   MUSEUM

(www.angelika-kauffmann.com; Brand 34, Schwarzenberg; adult/child €7/1.50; ⊘10am-5pm Tue-Sun) This ultramodern museum houses a permanent collection in winter and rotating exhibitions in summer of Swiss-Austrian neoclassical painter Angelika Kauffmann's works. The artist had strong connections to the village where her father was born.

A ticket covers entry to the neighbouring **Heimat Museum** (Heritage Museum), a pristine alpine chalet. Displays of traditional painted furniture, extraordinary headwear, hunting paraphernalia and filigree iron crosses focus on rural 19th-century life.

Bergkäserei Schoppernau   SHOW DAIRY

(www.bergkaeserei.at; Unterdorf 248, Schoppernau; ⊘8.30-11.30am Mon-Sat) Discover cheesemaking secrets (including why Emmentaler is holey) at this show dairy, famous for its award-winning tangy *Bergkäse*, matured for up to 12 months.

Käse-Molke Metzler   SHOW DAIRY

(☑05512-30 44; www.molkeprodukte.com; Bruggan 1025, Egg; ⊘8.30am-noon & 2-6pm Mon-Fri, 8.30am-noon Sat) This architecturally innovative dairy churns out fresh *Wälderkäsle*, arranges tours and tastings (€13.50) and runs four-hour cheese-making workshops (€59). See the website for exact dates and times; booking is essential.

Käsekeller Lingenau   SHOW DAIRY

(www.kaesekeller.at; Zeihenbühel 423, Lingenau; ⊘10am-6pm Mon-Fri, 9am-5pm Sat) Step into the foyer of this modern cheese-maturation cellar to glimpse robots attending to wagon-wheel-sized cheeses through a glass wall. A tasting of *Bergkäse* with juice/wine costs €6.90/8.90.

⚡ Activities

The hills buzz with hikers, climbers and cyclists in summer. Local tourist offices also arrange **themed walks**, including some geared towards families. Paragliders can launch themselves off mountains in Andelsbuch, Bezau and Au-Schoppernau; tandem flights cost around €100.

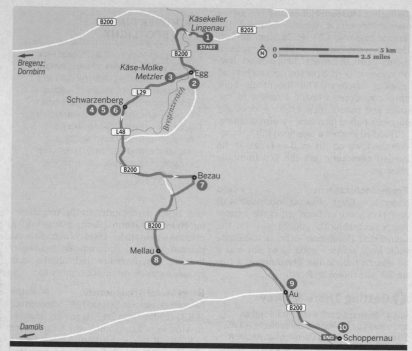

Driving Tour
Bregenzerwald Käsestrasse

START KÄSEKELLER LINGENAU
END SCHOPPERNAU
LENGTH 35KM; FOUR HOURS

The Bregenzerwald's rolling dairy country is best explored on the Käsestrasse (Cheese Rd), which refers to the cheese-producing region rather than a specific route. This tour (40 minutes' driving without stops) takes in the highlights, threading through quaint villages and stopping en route for silo-free buttermilk and cheese at local *Sennereien* (dairy farms). Spring through autumn is the best time to visit. See www.kaesestrasse.at for details.

Take a peek inside the huge cellars of the ultramodern ❶ **Käsekeller Lingenau** (p333) to see how cheese is matured, and taste flavoursome *Bergkäse* with a glass of local wine. Hit the pretty village of ❷ **Egg** and, 2.5km west, ❸ **Käse-Molke Metzler** (p331), an avant-garde dairy and farmhouse duo. Here you can sample creamy *Wälderkäsle*, made from cow's and goat's milk, or call ahead to join a cheese-making workshop.

Veer southwest to the village of ❹ **Schwarzenberg**, where old farmhouses tiled with wood shingles and studded with scarlet geraniums crowd the narrow streets. Contemplate art in the ❺ **Angelika Kauffmann Museum** (p331) before lunching on cheese-rich *Kässpätzle* (egg noodles) in the wood-panelled parlour or garden at ❻ **Gasthof Hirschen**. The narrow country lane now wends its way gently to ❼ **Bezau**, 7km southeast, where the Bregenzerach river flows past forest-cloaked slopes rising to jagged limestone crags. In the village you can buy cheese, honey, herbs and schnapps. Continue southeast towards the Arlberg and mountainous ❽ **Mellau**, where the tourist office organises cheese walks in summer.

Driving southeast brings you to peaceful ❾ **Au**, affording deep views into a U-shaped valley, particularly beautiful on a golden autumn day. Round out your tour with total cheese immersion at the ❿ **Bergkäserei Schoppernau** (p331), where you can try the famous *Bergkäse*.

Downhill Skiing

SKIING

(3-valley 3-/6-day pass adult €113/192, child €57/96) Though lesser known than other Austrian ski regions, the Bregenzerwald has fine downhill skiing on 273km of slopes, well suited to beginners, intermediates and ski tourers. Lift queues are virtually nonexistent and free ski buses shuttle between resorts. Nonskiers can shuffle through snowy forests on cross-country or snowshoe trails, go winter hiking or bump downhill on toboggan runs in Au and Damüls.

🛏 Sleeping

The Bregenzerwald has some incredibly charming places to sleep and eat. Local tourist offices can help you book farmstays and holiday homes. You'll receive the Bregenzerwald Guest Card when you stay more than three nights, giving free access to cable cars, buses and outdoor pools.

⭐ Gasthof Hirschen

HISTORIC HOTEL €€

(☑ 05512-29 44; www.hirschenschwarzenberg. at; Hof 14, Schwarzenberg; s/d incl half board €117/256; P 🛜) This is a 250-year-old dream of a *Gasthof*. The wood-shingle facade is festooned with geraniums, while inside low-ceilinged corridors lead to antique-filled nooks and individually designed rooms. *Dirndl*-clad waitresses serve up spot-on regional fare like saddle of venison in a walnut crust and *Bregenzerwälder Käsknöpfle* (cheese noodles) in the restaurant (mains €14 to €27).

Bio-Pension Beer

PENSION €€

(☑ 05515-23 98; www.bio-pension.at; Gräsalp 357, Schoppernau; d €60-70) 🍃 The light, cheery rooms at this *Pension* are done out in sustainable wood from the Beer family forest. You'll feel right at home at this ecofriendly country retreat, complete with pure spring water, clucking chickens and organic produce at breakfast.

Hotel Gasthof Gams

BOUTIQUE HOTEL €€€

(☑ 05514-22 20; www.hotel-gams.at; Platz 44, Bezau; d €206-246, ste €310-350; P 🛜🐾) A real glamour puss of a hotel, the Gams (chamois) whispers romance from every last gold-kissed, heart-strewn, candlelit corner. An open fire in the dreamlike Da Vinci spa, starry ceilings, a whirlpool with mountain views, a gourmet restaurant (seven-course menu €115) with a walk-in wine tower – this is definite honeymoon material.

A DATE WITH DAISY

Elsa, Klara, Bibi, Dora and their sisters are there for the milking at the **Kräuterbauernhof** (☑ 05515-22 98; www. kuhforyou.at; Argenau 116, Au; d/tr/q €45/56/67). The Erlach-Dorle family will rent you the cow of your choice (€29 per week for a minimum of two months, though you don't have to stay the whole time). The price includes 8kg of cheese which they can post to your home country, regular visits and milking sessions, and a keepsake photo of your long-lashed alpine beauty. Cow or no cow, this 300-year-old farmhouse is a fantastic place to stay, with spacious apartments full of woody charm, a herb garden and plenty of dairy goodness at breakfast.

❶ Information

The **Bregenzerwald tourist office** (☑ 05512-23 65; www.bregenzerwald.at; Impulszentrum 1135, Egg; ⊙9am-5pm Mon-Fri, 8am-1pm Sat) should be your first port of call for details on the region's sights, activities and accommodation. The shelves are well stocked with maps and brochures.

❶ Getting There & Away

Buses run roughly twice hourly to Bezau (€4.90, one hour) from Bregenz, but for most other destinations a change at Egg is required. From Dornbirn, Schwarzenberg (€3.30, 25 minutes), Bezau (€4.10, 50 minutes), Mellau (€4.90, 50 minutes), Au (€7.60, 70 minutes) and Schoppernau (€6.70, 80 minutes) can all be reached a couple of times daily (times vary from season to season). For Damüls (€8.50, 1¾ hours), a change at Au is required.

Feldkirch

☑ 05522 / POP 31,269 / ELEV 458M

On the banks of the turquoise Ill River, Feldkirch sits prettily at the foot of wooded mountains, vineyards and a castle-crowned hill. It's a joy to stroll the well-preserved old town, which wings you back to late-medieval times with its cobbled, arcaded lanes, towers and pastel-coloured townhouses. The town springs to life in summer with pavement cafes and open-air festivals.

Feldkirch

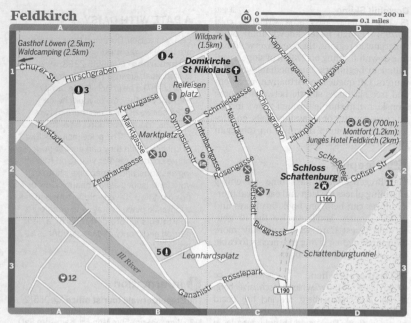

Feldkirch

◎ Sights

Feldkirch has several towers surviving from the old fortifications. These include the 40m-high, late-15th-century **Katzenturm** (Hirschgraben), where Vorarlberg's biggest bell (weighing 7500kg) still tolls. The **Mühletor** (Mühletorplatz), also known as the Sautor, is where the pig market was held in the Middle Ages. The step-gabled **Churertor** (Heiligkreuzbrücke; off Hirschgraben) is the gateway to the bridge that was once used to transport salt across the Ill River to Switzerland.

★ Schloss Schattenburg   CASTLE

(www.schattenburg.at; Burggasse 1; adult/child €6/4.50; ⊙9am-noon & 1.30-5pm Mon-Fri, 10am-5pm Sat & Sun) This 13th-century hilltop castle is story-book stuff with its red turrets and creeping vines. It's a steep climb up to the ramparts, which command far-reaching views over Feldkirch's rooftops. Once the seat of the counts of Montfort, the castle now houses a small **museum** displaying religious art, costumes and weaponry.

★ Domkirche St Nikolaus   CATHEDRAL

(Domplatz; ⊙8am-6pm) Identified by a slender spire, Feldkirch's cathedral has a large, forbidding interior complemented by late-Gothic features and dazzling stained glass. The painting on the side altar is by local lad Wolf Huber (1480–1539), a leading member of the Danube school.

Wildpark   WILDLIFE PARK

(Ardetzenweg 20; ⊙dawn-dusk; ⊞) **FREE** Facing the castle across the town is Ardetzenberg (631m), a heavily forested hill. At its northern end is this wildlife park, with a woodland trail, adventure playground, barbecue areas, and animal-friendly enclosures home to marmots, ibex and wild boar.

🏃 Activities

Dreiländerweg　　　　　CYCLING
(Three Country Trail) The Feldkirch region is criss-crossed with cycling trails, including the 30km Dreiländerweg, taking in beautiful scenery in Austria, Switzerland and Liechtenstein. Pick up the free *Feldkircher Radwegkarte* map from the tourist office.

Gasthof Löwen　　　　BICYCLE RENTAL
(www.hotel-loewen.at; Kohlgasse 1; per day €12) Bike hire is available at this place, 2.8km north of the centre.

🎉 Festivals & Events

Montfortspektakel　　　　FESTIVAL
(☺early Jun) Feldkirch revisits the Middle Ages with troubadours, knights and nonstop feasting.

Gauklerfestival　　　　FESTIVAL
(☺late Jul) Jugglers, fire-eaters and clowns entertain the crowds at this huge street party.

🛏 Sleeping

Junges Hotel Feldkirch　　　HOSTEL €
(☑731 81; www.oejhw.at; Reichsstrasse 111; dm/s/d €14/28/42; P🛜) A 700-year-old infirmary has been converted into this HI hostel, which exudes charm with its creaking beams, vaulted lounge and ivy-clad courtyard. A spiral staircase twists up to light-filled dorms with pine bunks. Buses 59, 60 and 68 stop here.

Waldcamping　　　　CAMPGROUND €
(☑760 01 3190; www.waldcamping.at; Stadionstrasse 9; camp sites per adult/child/car & tent €6.40/3.75/11; ☺Apr-Oct; P🛜🏊) Pine trees shade this quiet camping ground, where facilities include a barbecue area, playground and free entry to the Waldbad leisure pool. Take bus 2 from the train station to the last stop (3.5km).

Hotel Alpenrose　　　BOUTIQUE HOTEL €€
(☑721 75; www.hotel-alpenrose.net; Rosengasse 4-6; s/d €91/160; @🛜) Hidden down a quiet old-town backstreet, this 16th-century merchant's house is a touch of old-fashioned romance, with its dusky pink facade, rose garden and Biedermeier salon. The rooms blend contemporary and classic – polished wood, muted colours and flat-screen TVs.

Montfort　　　　HOTEL €€
(☑721 89; www.montfort-dashotel.at; Galuragasse 7; s/d/tr €95/149/160; P🛜) Run by the friendly Oberhöller family, Montfort is a business hotel with personality. Set in attractive gardens, the hotel has bright, contemporary rooms with flat-screen TVs and monochrome bathrooms. It goes the extra mile at breakfast, with freshly baked croissants, eggs and bacon, salmon and antipastos. Montfort is a 10-minute stroll northeast of the centre.

🍴 Eating

April　　　　CAFE €
(www.aprilcafe.at; Neustadt 39; breakfast €4.10-13.70, lunch €8.10; ☺9am-6pm Thu-Tue) Bright flower pots and upside-down watering cans guide the way to this wholesomely hip and wonderfully laid-back cafe. Bag a spot on one of the sofas or on the pocket-sized terrace for a latte adorned with flowers or butterflies (Ingo is a 'coffee artist'). Lavish breakfasts, open sandwiches and homemade cakes feature on the all-organic menu.

Möbelle　　　　CAFE €
(www.moebelle.at; Schmiedgasse 12; snacks €3.50-7.50; ☺10am-midnight Wed-Thu, to 1am Fri & Sat, 2-11pm Sun & Tue; 🛜) Like the look of that groovy lamp, vase or chair? No problem. This cafe-cum-lounge bar doubles as a contemporary design store and everything's for sale. It's a chilled spot for an espresso, snack or DIY breakfast.

Rauch Cafe　　　　CAFE €€
(www.rauchgastronomie.at; Marktgasse 12-14; 2-course lunch €8.40, mains €12.50-25; ☺9am-1am Wed-Mon, 10am-1am Sun) This vaulted

> ### POOL PARTY
>
> Feldkirch's old public swimming pool in the Reichenfeld district has been born again as the ultrahip **Poolbar** (Reichenfeldgasse 9), the venue of the summertime **Poolbar Festival** (www.poolbar.at; ☺Jul & Aug). If you're in town during the festival be sure to check out the top-notch line-up of mostly free events, skipping from concerts, dance and poetry slams to juggling shows and DJ nights.

cafe-restaurant opens onto a buzzy terrace. If you can stomach chilli first thing, try the 'how to cure the hangover' breakfast (€12.90), egg and bacon topped with cheese, chilli and garlic. The menu is a medley of Austrian staples and more imaginative dishes like stuffed calamari with sweet potato spaghetti. DJs spin house here after dark.

Dogana INTERNATIONAL €€
(☎751 26; www.dogana.com; Neustadt 20; 2-course lunch €8.20, mains €9-27; ⏲8.30am-1am Tue-Thu, to 2am Fri & Sat) This slinky lounge bar-restaurant hybrid has a popular terrace for alfresco dining and imbibing. The menu has Mediterranean overtones, with antipastos, summery salads (try the curried chicken *kikeriki*), pasta, steaks and fish dishes – many pepped up with a pinch of chilli.

Wirtschaft Zum Schützenhaus AUSTRIAN €€
(☎852 90; www.schuetzenhaus.at; Göfiser Strasse 2; mains €11.50-17.50; ⏲10am-midnight Thu-Mon; 👪) *Schiessen und Geniessen* (shoot and enjoy!) is the motto at this half-timbered tavern, where Lederhosen-clad staff bring humungous schnitzels to the table. The tree-shaded beer garden has prime views of the castle and a pet corner with fluffy rodents to keep kids amused.

Information

The helpful **tourist office** (☎734 67; http://feldkirch.at/stadtmarketing; Schlossergasse 8; ⏲9am-5.30pm Mon-Fri, 9am-noon Sat) has stacks of information and free town maps. The post office is opposite the train station.

Getting There & Away

Trains head north to Bregenz (€7.80, 30 minutes) and Dornbirn (€5.80, 20 minutes), and southeast to Bludenz (€5.70, 12 minutes).

Bludenz

☎05552 / POP 13,858 / ELEV 588M

The Alps provide a spectacular backdrop to Bludenz, the only town in Austria – perhaps the world – that can lay claim to having purple cows; the Milka ones churned out from the Suchard factory. Gorging on chocolate aside, Bludenz' arcaded old town takes you back to its heyday as the seat of the Habsburg governors from 1418 to 1806. Bludenz also makes a good base for exploring the surrounding valleys.

Sights & Activities

To explore Bludenz' attractions, join a free **city tour** organised by the tourist office, departing at 10am on Friday from mid-May till October.

There are 15 skiing areas within a 30km radius and ski bus transport to/from Bludenz is sometimes included in the price of ski passes. Walking and cycling are other popular activities; the tourist office has thick booklets on summer and winter outdoor pursuits.

St Laurentiuskirche CHURCH
(Mutterstrasse; ⏲9am-5pm) Climb the covered staircase to this Gothic parish church, dominated by an octagonal onion-domed spire. There are stellar views over the town's rooftops to the Alps beyond from up here.

Stadtmuseum MUSEUM
(Kirchgasse 9; adult/child €2/1.50; ⏲3-5pm Mon-Sat) This museum houses a small display on folk art and prehistoric finds.

Muttersberg WALKING
(www.muttersberg.eu; Hinterplärsch; cable car adult/child 1 way €7.10/4.50, return €11.90/7.40; ⏲cable car 9am-5pm) About 1km north of the town centre, a **cable car** rises up to this 1401m peak, the starting point for numerous hiking, Nordic walking and cycling trails. If you don't want to walk it, catch bus 1 from in front of the train station to the cable-car station.

Kletterhalle ROCK CLIMBING
(Untersteinstrasse 5; adult/child €5/3; ⏲hall 6am-10pm, ticket office 8am-noon & 1-5pm Mon-Fri) Practise clambering up boulders before tackling the real thing in the Alps at this excellent hall, run by the Austrian Alpine Club. The ticket office is on the 1st floor.

Sleeping

Private rooms usually offer the best value, even though a surcharge of around €3.50 per day applies for stays under three days.

Gasthof Hotel Löwen HOTEL €€
(☎322 70; www.loewen-bludenz.at; Mutterstrasse 7a; s/d €69/90; P 📶) A recent makeover has brought this central hotel bang up to date. Rooms now sport parquet floors, crisp white bedding and walk-in showers.

Schlosshotel Dörflinger HISTORIC HOTEL €€
(☎630 16; www.schlosshotel.cc; Schlossplatz 5; s/d €88/130; P @) Clinging to the cliffs above

Bludenz, this smart hotel shelters modern rooms, many with balconies. There's a mountain-facing terrace for warm evenings, free mountain-bike hire for guests and a smart restaurant (mains €10 to €25) dishing up Austrian fare.

Val Blu　　　　　　　　SPA HOTEL €€
(☑631 06; www.valblu.at; Haldenweg 2a; s/d/tr/q €69/120/168/196; [P][📶][🏊]) Glass walls and smooth contours define this ultramodern spa hotel, a 10-minute walk east of the centre along Untersteinstrasse. The functional, minimalist-style rooms feature wi-fi and flat-screen TVs.

✗ Eating

Remise　　　　　　　　　　CAFE €
(www.remise-bludenz.at; Am Raiffeisenplatz; lunch €7.60, snacks €2-10; ⊘11am-midnight; 🅿) This contemporary cafe attracts arty types and serves snacks from polenta pizza to creative salads. The cultural centre next door regularly hosts exhibitions, film screenings and concerts. There's a kids' playground outside.

Altes Rathaus　　　　　　ITALIAN €€
(Rathausgasse 1a; mains €7-22; ⊘10am-11pm Mon-Sat) Opening onto a terrace under the arcades, this minimalist glass-fronted cafe rustles up predominantly Italian food, with a menu heavy on pizza, pasta and grilled fish. It's also a relaxed spot for an espresso or ice cream.

Wirtshaus Kohldampf　　AUSTRIAN €€
(☑653 85; www.fohren-center.at; Werdenbergerstrasse 53; mains €8-16; ⊘11am-midnight Mon-Wed, 10am-4am Thu-Sat, 9am-midnight Sun) A five-minute amble west of the centre lies this cavernous brewpub-cum-beer garden. Meaty grub like schnitzel, pork roast and goulash is washed down with Fohrenburger beer from the brewery opposite.

ℹ Information

The town centre sits on the northern bank of the III River. The **tourist office** (☑636 217 90; www.bludenz.travel; Werdenbergerstrasse 42; ⊘7.30am-noon & 2-5.30pm Mon-Thu, 7.30am-noon Fri) is five minutes' walk from the train station and has free internet access.

ℹ Getting There & Away

The A14 motorway passes just south of the III River and the town centre. Buses run down all five valleys around Bludenz.

Bludenz is on the east–west InterCity express rail route to Innsbruck (€24.70, 1¾, every two hours) and Bregenz (€12, 45 minutes, hourly).

Montafon

POP 16,544

The Montafon's pristine wilderness and potent schnapps had Ernest Hemingway in raptures when he wintered here in 1925 and 1926, skiing in blissful solitude and penning *The Sun Also Rises*. Silhouetted by the glaciated Silvretta range and crowned by the 3312m arrow of Piz Buin, the valley remains one of the most serene and unspoilt in the Austrian Alps.

Partenen marks the start of the serpentine 23km **Silvretta Hochalpenstrasse** (www.silvretta-bielerhoehe.at; car/motorcycle €14/11; ⊘Jun-Oct), which wends its way under peaks rising to well over 2500m before climbing over the 2036m Bielerhöhe Pass via a series of tight switchbacks. At the top of the pass is the **Silvretta Stausee** (2030m), a startlingly aquamarine reservoir, which mirrors the snowcapped peaks of Piz Buin and Klostertaler Egghorn on bright mornings.

🏃 Activities

Mile upon glorious mile of alpine trails, including the Radsattel Circuit, attract hikers in summer. Cable cars and lifts can be accessed with the regional **Montafon-Silvretta-Card** (3-/7-day €41/55).

In winter Montafon is a magnet for families who come to carve its 246km of uncrowded pistes and go cross-country skiing,

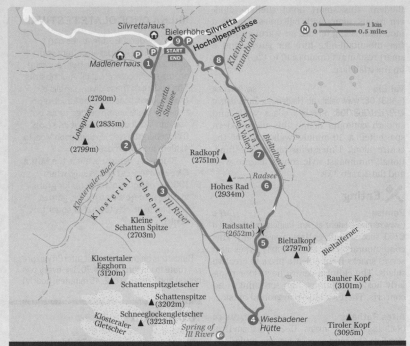

Walking Trail
Radsattel Circuit, Bierlehöhe

START BIELERHÖHE
END BIELERHÖHE
LENGTH 15KM; FIVE TO SIX HOURS

This is one of Vorarlberg's most spectacular hikes, exploring two valleys and taking you high into the realms of 3000m mountains and glaciers. Best tackled in July or August, the route demands a moderate level of fitness. The Alpenvereinskarte 1:25,000 map No 26 *Silvrettagruppe* covers the trail in detail.

From the ❶ **Silvretta Stausee** car park in Bielerhöhe, walk over the dam to join the well-worn path skirting the western shore of the turquoise reservoir. Stick to the shoreline around the southern end of the lake, crossing one bridge over the ❷ **Klostertaler Bach**, then another over the fast-flowing ❸ **Ill River**. At the junction, turn right up the trail signed to the Wiesbadener Hütte.

An amphitheatre of glistening blue, heavily crevassed glaciers appears as you gradually gain height. Continue your steady ascent, stopping for refreshment on the sunny terrace of the ❹ **Wiesbadener Hütte** after two to 2¼ hours. At the back of the hut, veer left towards the Radsattel on a red-and-white-marked trail that becomes increasingly narrow and rough underfoot. The path zigzags steeply up the slope and over a small stream. Keep right and ascend a rise topped by a large cairn. Cross a shallow pool outlet before the final steep climb to the 2652m ❺ **Radsattel**, where a sign marks the Vorarlberg–Tyrol border, one to 1½ hours from the hut.

Drop steeply down the boulder-strewn eastern side of the pass, keeping an eye out for ibex. You will pass several small lakes including the jewel-like ❻ **Radsee** as you take the small path down to the remote meadows of the ❼ **Bieltal** (Biel Valley). Follow the path along the west bank of the babbling ❽ **Bieltalbach** stream and continue west to the Silvretta Stausee, turning right along the reservoir. Back at the main road, turn left and walk 300m to return to ❾ **Bielerhöhe** (1½ to two hours from the Radsattel).

snowshoeing, ski touring and sledding. The **Skipass-Montafon** (3-/7-day pass €120/237) covers public transport and the 61 lifts in the valley.

⊨ Sleeping

Every village in the valley has a tourist office that can help you find a *Pension* (expect to pay €20 to €30 per person).

Madlenerhaus   HUT €
(☑ 05558-42 34; www.madlenerhaus.at; dm €10-12, half board per person €25; ⊙ Feb-May, late Jun-Oct) This DAV (German Alpine Club) hut at 1986m is a good-value place to bed down at Bielerhöhe. The four- to 12-bed dorms are comfy and the restaurant serves satisfying Austrian food.

Posthotel Rössle   HISTORIC HOTEL €€
(☑ 05558-833 30; www.posthotel-roessle.at; Dorfstrasse 4, Gaschurn; d incl half board €130-274; P ☒) Hemingway once stayed in this 200-year-old chalet – whether with his mistress or wife remains a mystery. The friendly Kessler family will show you the guestbook he signed and the bed he slept in. Within easy reach of the Silvretta Nova ski arena, the hotel has well-kept rooms, a superb wood-panelled restaurant, indoor and outdoor pools, and a spa.

Silvrettahaus   HUT €€
(☑ 05558-42 46; www.silvretta-bielerhoehe.at; s/d €59/92, incl half board €72/118; ⊙ Jul–mid-Oct & mid-Dec–Easter) For more creature comforts at 2000m, check into the architecturally innovative Silvrettahaus at Bielerhöhe, which has bright, contemporary rooms and spellbinding mountain views.

❶ Information

Montafon Tourism (☑ 05556-721 660; www.montafon.at; Silvrettastrasse 6, Schruns; ⊙ 8am-6pm Mon-Fri, 9am-noon & 4-6pm Sat, 10am-noon Sun) Has the low-down on accommodation and activities in the valley.

❶ Getting There & Away

Trains run frequently from Bludenz to Schruns (€3.20, 20 minutes), from where up to five buses daily continue onto Partenen (€3.30, 35 minutes) at the base of the Silvretta pass. From mid-July to mid-October, eight buses daily climb from Partenen to the Silvretta Stausee (€3.30, 35 minutes).

Western Arlberg
☑ 05583

Mountains huddle conspiratorially around the snow-sure slopes of the rugged Arlberg region, one of Austria's top ski destinations. The best-known villages are picture-postcard Lech (1450m) and its smaller twin Zürs (1716m), 6km south. Because of their relative isolation, fabulous skiing and five-star hotels, the resorts are a magnet to royalty (Princess Diana used to ski here), celebrities and anyone who pretends to be such from behind Gucci shades.

☂ Activities

Remember Bridget Jones hurtling backwards down the mountain on skis in *The Edge of Reason?* That was filmed on Lech's scenic, forest streaked runs. You can surely do a better job skiing on the Arlberg region's 280km of slopes. These are interlinked by free solar-powered buses and covered by a regional ski pass, which costs €48/235 for one/six days. The terrain is best suited to beginners and intermediates, with off-piste possibilities and the famous 21km Weisse Ring (White Ring) appealing to more advanced skiers.

Themed Walks   WALKING
From July to September, the tourist office organises free themed walks such as sunrise hikes and botanical strolls every Monday and Thursday. You can also go it alone on 250km of signed hiking trails, ranging from high-alpine treks to gentle lake walks, as well as dedicated running and Nordic walking trails.

⊨ Sleeping & Eating

Many of the hotels in Lech and Zürs are five-star, including the superluxurious Hotel Aurelio which made Condé Nast's Hotlist in 2010. Expect prices to be 30% to 50% higher in the winter high season.

★ Hotel Gotthard   HOTEL €€
(☑ 35 60; www.gotthard.at; Omesberg 119, Lech; s €71-79, d €146-164, ste €196-208; P ☒ ☒) It's the little touches that make all the difference at this chalet hotel, such as the oven-warm bread at breakfast (owner Clemens is a baker) and yoga room for Zen moments. Splashes of fuchsia and forest green jazz up the contemporary, pine-wood rooms, most of which have balconies, DVD players and

iPod docks. There's a spa, an indoor pool and a children's playroom.

Theodul
HOTEL €€

(☎ 23 08; www.theodul.at; Omesberg 332; s €75, d €132-174; P 🛜 📶) The Walch family make you feel instantly at ease at this chalet hotel, handily positioned for the slopes. Rooms are decorated in classic alpine style, with white bedding, pine furnishings and mountain views. Slip into your bathrobe for a postski or posthike steam and unwind in the spa. Organic produce and speciality teas kick off the day healthily at breakfast.

Gästehaus Lavendel
PENSION €€

(☎ 26 57; www.lavendel.at; Dorf 447, Lech; d €80-110, apt €160-180; 🛜 📶) The affable Mascher family make you feel at home at this cosy *Pension* next to the ski lifts. Many of the spacious, immaculate rooms and apartments sport balconies and there's a little spa for a posthike or après-ski unwind.

Hûs Nr. 8
AUSTRIAN €€

(☎ 332 20; www.hus8.at; Lech 8; mains €9-20; ⊙ 11am-midnight Tue-Sun, from 4pm Mon) Raclette, fondue and crispy roast chicken are the stars of the menu at this rustic chalet, going strong since 1760. Snuggle up in an all-wood interior in winter or sit on the patio when the sun's out.

Fux
FUSION €€€

(☎ 29 92; www.fux-mi.net; Omesberg 587, Lech; mains €28-50; ☑) Asian art gives a decadent touch to Fux, a steakhouse-restaurant hybrid. The food is top notch, whether you go for succulent charcoal-grilled steaks daubed with herb butter or Asian signatures like yellow-fin tuna with wok vegetables. The award-winning wine list comprises 2700 bottles.

❶ Information

Tourist office (☎ 21 61-0; www.lech-zuers.at; Dorf 2, Lech; ⊙ 8am-6pm Mon-Sat, 8am-noon & 3-5pm Sun) The central tourist office has bags of info on skiing and walking possibilities, and an accommodation board.

❶ Getting There & Around

Buses run between Lech and Zürs (€1.30, seven minutes); both resorts have connections to St Anton am Arlberg. For Bludenz (€5.80, two hours) and beyond, a change in Ratzalpe is required.

One kilometre south of Zürs is the Flexen Pass (1773m), occasionally blocked off by snow in winter, after which the road splits: the western fork leads to Stuben (1407m), the eastern one to St Anton am Arlberg in Tyrol. In summer, Lech can also be approached from the north, via the turning at Warth (1494m).

Understand
Austria

Austria Today

Despite recent financial and currency crises in Europe, most Austrians today remain buoyant about the future. The country has held up well so far and has one of the world's highest standards of living. Continuing political stability and social and economic equality are what people think about most. Fear of the widening gap between the well-off and poor was a strong underlying issue in the most recent national elections, held in late 2013.

Best in Print (Travel)

A Time of Gifts (Patrick Leigh Fermor; 1977) First volume of trilogy about an epic walk from the Hook of Holland via Austria to Constantinople in 1933–34.

Vienna: The Image of a Culture in Decline (Edward Crankshaw; 1938) Travel description and history.

Danube (Claudio Magris; 1986) Mid-1980s Italian travel journal covering the river's length.

Last Waltz in Vienna: The Destruction of a Family 1842–1942 (George Clare; 1982) Autobiographical account of a Jewish family's fate.

Best on Film

The Third Man (1949) Classic film noir set in Vienna.

The Piano Teacher (2001) Masterpiece directed by Michael Haneke about a masochistic piano teacher.

Metropolis (1927) Industry and prescient futuristic grunge by director Fritz Lang.

Amour (2012) Michael Haneke directed and wrote the screenplay of a film about an old couple's tested love.

The Counterfeiters (2007) A Jew whose remarkable skill in counterfeiting puts him in the service of Nazis.

Stable but Fragmenting Politics

Austria's national anthem, 'Land of Mountains and Flowing Rivers', is a song of praise for the spectacular landscape, but what goes for the natural landscape cannot really be said of politics, which is among Europe's least spectacular. This is not necessarily a bad thing: Austria is one of the world's most stable countries. Stability partly comes from the astounding degree of consensus, with the two largest parties, the Sozialdemokratischen Partei Österreichs (SPÖ ; Social Democratic Party of Austria) and Österreichische Volkspartei (ÖVP; Austrian People's Party) having ruled together in grand coalitions 18 times out of 27 governments since 1945.

Changing Coalition Landscape

Austria's characteristic consensus is gradually giving way to fragmentation and greater diversity, with the growth in support for smaller parties breaking the stronghold of the SPÖ and ÖVP on federal office. Die Grünen (Green Party) has gained political momentum and support, while the more established populist Freiheitliche Partei Österreichs (FPÖ; Freedom Party of Austria) – and to a lesser extent its breakaway groups – continues to play an important role, especially in traditionally conservative regions outside the cities.

While the Greens go to the polls on their primary reason for being – environmental issues – the FPÖ and its breakaway groups pursue a populist, right-wing, if somewhat nebulous agenda focusing on reduced immigration, and promotion of regional identity, the family and traditional values. It's also a loud voice in disputes about bilingual (Slovenian and German) signposting in Carinthia. About 20% of Austria's population has an immigrant background.

With the establishment of the populist Team Stronach by the influential businessman Frank Stronach (b 1932), a new player has emerged who is set to challenge the FPÖ grip on populist issues. Key tenets of the Team Stronach platform are euroscepticism, immigration to Austria predominantly on the basis of the country's economic needs, and administrative reforms. On the whole, it leans towards laissez-faire economics. Unlike in neighbouring Germany, die Piraten (the Pirate Party) has been unable to get a foot in the door of federal or regional parliaments.

2013 Elections

Regional elections in many provinces in 2013 produced extended grand coalitions of the large parties, such as in Carinthia, where the SPÖ, ÖVP and Greens formed the so-called Kenya Coalition (based on the party colours of red, black and green, those of Kenya's flag). This government includes minsters from Team Stronach and the FPÖ – a situation unimaginable in many countries.

Following national elections held in late 2013, Austria continued to be governed by a grand coalition of the SPÖ and ÖVP, with Team Stronach and a newly formed Neos liberal party winning seats in parliament.

'Red' Vienna Calling

With a population of more than 1.7 million, Vienna makes up over 20% of Austria's population and is an exception to the rest of the country as it has been ruled by the SPÖ uninterrupted since 1945; the SPÖ has won an outright majority in all but two elections. 'Red' Vienna therefore stands in stark contrast to the rural population, which is generally conservative in spirit, and the consensus-focused federal government. The popularity of the SPÖ in Vienna is based on its achievements in fostering a high quality of urban life and its infrastructure and equal-opportunity policies.

Crisis, What Crisis?

Austria has been riding through the crises in recent years afflicting the banking system and euro with relatively little turbulence. Its banks are highly exposed to Eastern European markets, but otherwise the fallout has been minimal, thanks in part to the extent to which the Austrian economy is integrated into the Europe's economic powerhouse – Germany.

While the average Austrian is having to pay higher rents on properties, and the value of properties especially in resort areas around the lakes has risen sharply of late, the country has largely avoided real-estate bubbles of the kind that have afflicted the US and some European countries. The crises, therefore, are perceived as developments happening elsewhere, for the most part, and as being unlikely to affect people's lives dramatically in the near future.

POPULATION: **8.42 MILLION**

GDP: **€307 BILLION**

INFLATION: **1.9%**

UNEMPLOYMENT: **4.3%**

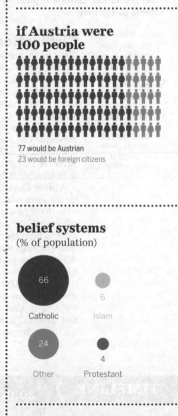

if Austria were 100 people

77 would be Austrian
23 would be foreign citizens

belief systems
(% of population)

66
Catholic

6
Islam

24
Other

4
Protestant

population per sq km

AUSTRIA   USA   GERMANY

≈ 30 people

History

Although Austria's territorial heartland has always been modest in size, its monarchy ruled an empire that spanned continents and was once the last word in politics and high culture. Austria's history is a story of conflated empires and powerful monarchs, war and revolution, cultural explosion, Austro-Fascism, occupation by foreign powers, and stable democracy.

Discover more about the history of Austria from the Babenbergs through to the country's entry into the EU in *The Austrians: A Thousand Year Odyssey* by Gordon Brook-Shepard.

Civilisations & Empires

The alpine regions of Austria were cold, inhospitable places during the Ice Age 30,000 years ago and virtually impenetrable for human and beast. So it's not surprising that while mammoths were lumbering across a frozen landscape, the more accessible plains and Danube Valley in Lower Austria developed into early centres of civilisation. Several archaeological finds can be traced back to this period, including ancient Venus figurines that are today housed inside Vienna's Naturhistorisches Museum. The starlet among the collection is the Venus of Willendorf, discovered in 1908 in the Wachau region of the Danube Valley. The diminutive and plump 11cm figurine is made of limestone and estimated to be around 25,000 years old.

A proto-Celtic civilisation known as the Hallstatt Culture – named after the town of Hallstatt in the Salzkammergut where there was a burial site – took root in the region around 800 BC. These proto-Celts mined salt in the Salzkammergut and maintained trade ties with the Mediterranean. When other Celts settled in the late Iron Age (around 450 BC) from Gaul (France) they chose the valley of the Danube River, but also the salt-rich regions around Salzburg, encountering Illyrians who had wandered there from the Balkan region as well as the Hallstatt proto-Celts. Gradually an Illyric-Celtic kingdom took shape, known as Noricum, that stretched from eastern Tyrol to the Danube and the eastern fringes of the Alps in Carinthia, also extending into parts of Bavaria (Germany) and Slovenia. Today the towns of Hallstatt and Hallein have exhibits and salt works focusing on the Hallstatt Culture and these Celtic civilisations.

TIMELINE	30,000 BC	3300 BC	800–400 BC
	The 30,000-year-old Venus of Galgenberg (aka Dancing Fanny) and the 25,000-year-old buxom beauty the Venus of Willendorf are crafted – both are now in Vienna's Naturhistorisches Museum.	The Neolithic 'Ötzi' dies and is mummified in a glacier in the Ötztal. He's found in 1991; several Austrian and Italian women ask to be impregnated with his frozen sperm.	The Iron Age Hallstatt-Kultur (Hallstatt Culture) develops in southern Salzkammergut, where settlers work salt mines. Around 450 BC Celts arrive in the region and build on this flourishing culture.

ICE MAN

In 1991 German hiker Helmut Simon came across the body of a man preserved within the Similaun Glacier in the Ötztaler Alpen, some 90m within Italy. Police and forensic scientists were summoned to the scene. Carbon dating revealed that the ice man, nick-named 'Ötzi', was nearly 5400 years old, placing him in the late Stone Age and making him the oldest and best-preserved mummy in the world.

Ötzi became big news, more so because his state of preservation was remarkable; even the pores of his skin were visible. In addition, Ötzi had been found with 70 arte-facts, including a copper axe, bow and arrows, charcoal and clothing. Physiologically he was found to be no different from modern humans. X-rays showed he had suffered from arthritis, frostbite and broken ribs.

Not everybody was worried about these finer points, however. Several Austrian and Italian women contacted Innsbruck University shortly after the discovery and asked to be impregnated with Ötzi's frozen sperm, but the all-important part of his body was missing.

Ötzi was relinquished to the Italians to become the centrepiece of a museum in Bol-zano in 1998. In September 2010 the family of the late Helmut Simon were rewarded €175,000 for his groundbreaking discovery.

Romans

The Romans, who crossed the Alps in force in 15 BC and settled south of the Danube River, carved up regions of Austria into administrative areas and built *Limes* (fortresses) and towns such as Carnuntum, Vindobona (the forerunner of Vienna), Brigantium (Bregenz), Juvavum (Salzburg), Flavia Solva (Leibnitz in Styria), Aguntum and Virunum (north of Kla-genfurt). However, the Western Empire created by the Romans collapsed in the 5th century, leaving a vacuum that was filled by newly arriving tribes: the Germanic Alemanni in Vorarlberg, Slavs who pushed into Car-inthia and Styria, and Bavarians who settled south of the Danube in Up-per and Lower Austria, Tyrol and around Salzburg. The Bavarians proved to be the most successful, and by the 7th century they had most regions of Austria in their grip, creating a large German-speaking territory.

Carolingian Empire

Once the Roman Empire had collapsed in the 5th century, it was difficult to talk about fully fledged empires. This changed in Europe and in Aus-tria itself with the growth of the Carolingian Empire in the 6th century. This was Europe's most powerful empire in its day. It originated in west-ern France and Belgium, grew into a heavyweight under Charlemagne

15 BC–AD 600	AD 8	795	976 & 996
Romans establish relations with Celts and Nordic tribes. Roman occupation begins in the provinces of Rhaetia, Noricum and Pannonia. Slavic, Germanic and other tribes later overrun the territories.	Vindobona, the forerunner of Vienna's Innere Stadt, becomes part of the Roman province of Pannonia.	Charlemagne creates a buffer region in the Danube Valley, later dubbed Ostmark (Eastern March) by the Nazis; this shores up the eastern edge of his empire.	The Babenbergs are entrusted with the Ostmark in 976 and administer it as margraves; in 996 this appears for the first time in a document as Ostarrîchi.

(747–814) and took its inspiration from the Romans. Significantly for future Austria, Charlemagne created a buffer region in the Danube Valley, later dubbed Ostmark (Eastern March), which shored up the eastern edge of his empire, and in 800 he was crowned kaiser by the pope.

Babenberg Dynasty

Fate took a decisive turn in 976, when Ostmark landed in the hands of Leopold von Babenberg (940–94), a descendent of a noble Bavarian family. Leopold received territory as a gift from Otto II (955–83), a Holy Roman emperor whom Leopold had supported during an uprising in Bavaria. The Babenbergs were a skilful clan who in the 11th century expanded their small territory to include most of modern-day Lower Austria (with Vienna), and a century later Styria (1192) and much of Upper Austria. In 1156, under the Babenberg monarch Heinrich II 'Jasomirgott', the Ostmark (still a political fence until that time) was elevated to a duchy (ie with its own duke and special rights) and Vienna became its capital.

In 1246 Duke Friedrich II died (leaving no heirs) following a battle with the Hungarians over the border between Hungary and his lands in Austria. This allowed the ambitious Bohemian king Ottokar II to move in and assert his control. He bolstered his claim to the Babenberg lands by marrying Friedrich's widow, but he refused to swear allegiance to Rudolf von Habsburg, who had been elected ruler of the Holy Roman Empire in 1273. This caused one of the most celebrated clashes in Austrian history when in 1278 the House of Habsburg and its Bohemian arch-rival Ottokar II (who now controlled Styria and Carinthia) went to battle on the Marchfeld, 30km northeast of Vienna. Ottokar, held up while trying to penetrate Drosendorf's fortress en route to the battle, was killed, allowing the Habsburg family to reign uncontested over Austria and marking the beginning of the Habsburg's grip over the nebulous Holy Roman Empire until it finally collapsed in 1806.

The patron saint of Austria is Saint Leopold III of Babenberg (1096–1135).

Early Habsburg Monarchy

The rise of the Habsburgs to rule was shaky at first. The period directly leading up to the election of Rudolf I was known as the Interregnum, a time when the Holy Roman Empire failed to produce an unchallenged and enduring monarch. After Rudolf died in 1291, the crown slipped out of Habsburg hands for a few years until the non-Habsburgian successor was slain by the Hungarians, and Rudolf's eldest son, Albert I, was elected to head the empire in 1298.

The Habsburgs initially suffered some humiliating setbacks, including at the hands of the Swiss, who had begun forming political unions to help maintain peace following the death of Rudolf I. These unions sub-

1137	1156	1192	1246–78
Vienna is first documented as a city in the Treaty of Mautern between the Babenbergs and the Bishops of Passau.	As consolation for relinquishing Bavaria, Austria becomes a duchy (Privilegium Minus) and the Babenberg ruler Heinrich Jasomirgott (1107–77) becomes Austria's first duke, residing in Vienna.	Styria is given to Babenberg Leopold V (1157–94) on the condition that it stays part of Austria forever. Styria then includes chunks of Slovenia and Lower and Upper Austria.	The last Babenberg dies in 1246. Habsburg Rudolf I is elected king of the Holy Roman Empire in 1273; he defeats Bohemian Ottokar II in the 1278 Battle of Marchfeld.

sequently fought the Habsburgs on numerous occasions and created the basis for greater autonomy and, much later, Swiss independence from the Habsburgs.

In Austria itself, however, the Habsburgs managed to consolidate their position: Carinthia (as well as Carniola in Slovenia) lost its independence and was annexed in 1335, followed by Tyrol in 1363. These foundations allowed Duke of Austria Rudolf IV (1339–65) to forge ahead with developing his lands: he founded the University of Vienna in in 1365 and he created Vienna's most visible landmark today by ordering the building of Gothic Stephansdom in 1359, justifiably earning himself the moniker 'Rudolf the Founder'.

Keeping it Habsburg

Marriage, not muscle, was the historic key to Habsburg land gains. The Hungarian king Matthias Corvinus (1443–90) once adapted lines from Ovid when he wrote: 'Let others wage war but you, lucky Austria, marry! For the empires given to others by Mars are given to you by Venus.'

The age of the convenient wedding began in earnest with Maximilian I (1459–1519), whose moniker was the Last Knight because of his

Historic Palaces

Schloss Schönbrunn, Vienna

Schloss Belvedere, Vienna

Schloss Eggenberg, Graz

Festung Hohensalzburg, Salzburg

HISTORY EARLY HABSBURG MONARCHY

AUSTRIA & THE HOLY ROMAN EMPIRE

The Holy Roman Empire was Europe's oddest 'state'. Its foundations were laid when the Carolingian king, Pippin, rescued a beleaguered pope and became *Patricius Romanorum* (Protector of Rome), making him Caesar's successor. The title 'kaiser' is derived from 'Caesar'. Pippin, with Italian spoils on his hands (one being the present-day Vatican), gave these to the pope. Pippin's son, Charlemagne, continued this tradition as protector (which meant he had the title kaiser), and in 962, with the crowning of Otto I (912–73) as Holy Roman Emperor, the empire was officially born.

Kings in the empire were elected in political horse-trading by a handful of prince electors, but for a king to take the next step and become kaiser (and protector of the pope), he had to be crowned by the pope. Depending on how feisty the pope happened to be, this brought other troubles. In 1338 enough was enough and the electors threw the pope overboard, deciding they could elect their own kaiser.

In 972, just before Otto I died, borders of the empire included present-day Austria, Slovenia, Czech Republic, Germany, Holland, Belgium and much of the Italian peninsula. These borders ebbed and flowed with the times. When Rudolf I arrived in 1273, all – or what remained of it – belonged to the Habsburgs.

The empire was formally buried in 1806 when Napoleon Bonaparte tore through Europe, and by the time the Austro-Hungarian Empire (a dual monarchy of Austria and Hungary) took shape in 1867, it was little more than a dim and distant reminder of medieval times.

1335 & 1363	1420–21	1496	1517
Bavarian Ludwig IV (1314–47) gives Carinthia to the Habsburgs in 1335; territories include Austria (Ostarrîchi), Styria and Carinthia. In 1363 Margarethe Maultasch (1318–63) dies and Tyrol is added.	Under Duke Albrecht V, the first large-scale persecution of Jews (known as the *Wiener Geserah*) in Austria's capital takes place.	Habsburg Philipp der Schöne (Philip the Handsome) marries Juana la Loca (Johanna the Mad) in the 'Spanish Marriage': Spain and its resource-rich Central and South American territories become Habsburg.	Theology professor Martin Luther sparks the Reformation when he makes public his 95 theses that call into question corrupt practices of the church, and most of Austria becomes Lutheran (Protestant).

THE
HABSBURGS

outdated predilection for medieval tournaments. His other loves were Renaissance art, his own grave (which he commissioned during his lifetime) and Albrecht Dürer (1471–1528), whom Maximilian commissioned to work on the very same grave before he stepped into it. It is now in Innsbruck's Hofkirche.

But it was Maximilian's affection for Maria of Burgundy (1457–82) that had the greatest influence on the fortunes of the Habsburgs. The two married, and when Maria fell from a horse and died as a result of a miscarriage in 1482, Burgundy, Lorraine and the Low Countries fell into Habsburg hands. In their day, these regions were the last word in culture, economic prosperity and the arts. However, this began a difficult relationship with France that stuck to the Habsburg shoe for centuries.

The 'Spanish Marriage' in 1496 was another clever piece of royal bedding. When Maximilian's son Philipp der Schöne (Philip the Handsome) married Juana la Loca (Johanna the Mad; 1479–55), Spain and its resource-rich overseas territories in Central and South America became Habsburgian. When their son, Ferdinand I (1503–64) married Anna of Hungary and Bohemia (1503–47), fulfilling a deal his grandfather Maximilian I had negotiated with King Vladislav II (1456–1516), Bohemia was also in the Habsburg fold. In the same deal, Maria von Habsburg (1505–58) married into the Polish-Lithuanian Jagiellonen dynasty, which traditionally purveyed kings to Poland, Bohemia and Hungary at that time. By 1526, when her husband Ludwig II (1506–26) drowned in a tributary of the Danube during the Battle of Mohács against Turks, Silesia (in Poland), Bohemia (in the Czech Republic) and Hungary were all thoroughly Habsburg.

The distended lower jaw and lip, a family trait of the early Habsburgs, is discreetly down-played in official portraits.

Under Karl V (1500–58), the era of the universal monarch arrived, and the Habsburgs had added the kingdom of Naples (southern Italy, including Sicily). That was about as good as it got.

Reformation & the Thirty Years' War

The 16th century was a crucial period in Austria during which the country came to terms with religious reformation brought about by Martin Luther, Counter-Reformation aimed at turning back the clock on Luther's Church reforms, and a disastrous Thiry Years' War that saw the Habsburgs' German territories splinter and slip further from their grasp.

In the German town of Wittenberg in 1517, theology professor Martin Luther (1483–1546) made public his 95 theses that questioned the papal practice of selling indulgences to exonerate sins. Threatened with excommunication, Luther refused to recant, broke from the Catholic Church, was banned by the Reich, and whilst in hiding translated the New Testament into German. Except in Tyrol, almost the entire population of Austria had become Protestant. In 1555 Karl V signed the Peace of Augs-

1529	**1556**
The first Turkish siege of Vienna takes place, undertaken by Süleyman the Magnificent, but Süleyman's forces are not strong enough to take control of the city.	Abandoning the idea of uniting an empire under Catholicism, Karl V abdicates – the Spanish part goes to his son Philip II, and Ferdinand I gets Austria, Bohemia and largely Turkish-occupied Hungary.

➜ Naturhistorisches Museum (p70), Vienna

burg, which gave the Catholic and Protestant churches equal standing and allowed each local prince to decide the religion of their principality. The more secular northern principalities of the German lands adopted Lutheran teachings, while the clerical lords in the south, southwest and Austria remained Catholic or adopted Catholicism. Not only does this explain the patchwork of Protestant and Catholic religions today in many regions that used to be part of the Holy Roman Empire, but it also made a mess of one Habsburg vision: Emperor Karl V had dedicated his life to creating a so-called 'universal Catholic monarchy'. Seeing the writing clearly on the wall, he abdicated in 1556 and withdrew to a monastery in Spain to lick his wounds and die.

The spoils were divided up among Habsburgs. The brother of Karl V, Ferdinand I, inherited Austria as well as Hungary and Bohemia, and Karl V's only legitimate son, Philip II (1527–98) got Spain, Naples and Sicily, the Low Countries, and the overseas colonies. To bolster Catholicism in Austria, Ferdinand I invited the Jesuits to Vienna in 1556; in contrast, his successor Maximilian II was extremely tolerant of Protestantism and the ideas of the Reformation. When the fanatically Catholic Ferdinand II took the throne in 1619 and put his weight behind a Counter-Reformation movement, the Protestant nobles in Bohemia finally rebelled in an armed conflict that quickly spread and developed into the pan-European Thirty Years' War; Sweden and France had joined this by 1635. In 1645 a Protestant Swedish army marched to within sight of Vienna but did not attack.

> Really mad or really handsome? Johanna the Mad kissed the feet of husband Philip the Handsome when his coffin was opened five weeks after his death in 1506.

WHATEVER HAPPENED TO THE HABSBURGS?

They're still around – about 500 of them, some 280 of whom still live in Austria. The current family head is Karl Habsburg-Lothringen (b 1961). He recently took on the job of heading Europe's most famous family after the death of his father Otto von Habsburg (1912–2011). Famous for his bon mots, Otto von Habsburg renounced his claims to the Habsburg lands in 1961, a step that allowed him to re-enter Austria and launch a career in European politics.

Once asked why his name never surfaced in the tabloids, the aged 'monarch' had replied: 'I've not once attended a ball. I prefer to sleep at night. And if you don't go to nightclubs, you don't run into the gossip columnists'. He was something of a sporting man, too: when quizzed about who he thought would win an Austria–Hungary football match, Otto reportedly replied, 'Who are we playing?'

Most poignant is perhaps a comment by German President Paul von Hindenburg to Otto von Habsburg in 1933 (the year Hitler seized power in Germany): 'You know, your majesty, there's only one person with hostile feelings towards the Habsburgs, but he's an Austrian.'

1618–48	1670	1683	1740–48
Anti-reformer Ferdinand II challenges Bohemia's confessional freedom. Habsburg counsels are thrown out of a window (the Prague Defenestration), triggering the Thirty Years' War.	Leopold I drives the Jews out of Unterer Werd in Vienna and the quarter is renamed Leopoldstadt, the name it bears today.	Turkish siege of Vienna. Christian Europe is mobilised and the threat persists until 1718, after which the Ottoman Empire gradually wanes.	Maria Theresia inherits Habsburg possessions, Prussia seizes Silesia (in Poland today) and the Austrian War of Succession starts a power struggle between Prussia and Habsburg-controlled Austria-Hungary.

Calm was restored with the Peace of Westphalia (1648) but it left the Habsburgs' Reich – embracing more than 300 states and about 1000 smaller territories – a nominal, impotent state. Switzerland and the Netherlands gained formal independence, and the Habsburgs lost territory to France.

Turks & the Siege of Vienna

The Ottoman Empire viewed Vienna as 'the city of the golden apple', but it wasn't *Apfelstrüdel* they were after in their great sieges. The first, in 1529 during the reign of Karl V, was begun by Süleyman the Magnificent, who advanced into Hungary and took Budapest before beginning an 18-day siege to capture Vienna. This was the meeting of two powers almost at the peak of their power, but – for reasons that are unclear today – the Ottomans suddenly withdrew back to Hungary. The Turkish sultan died at the siege of Szigetvár, yet his death was kept secret for several days in an attempt to preserve the morale of his army. The subterfuge worked for a while. Messengers were led into the presence of the embalmed body, which was placed in a seated position on the throne. They then relayed their news to the corpse.

At the head of the second Turkish siege in 1683 was the general and grand vizier Kara Mustapha. Amid the 25,000 tents of the Ottoman army that surrounded Vienna's medieval centre, he installed 1500 concubines, guarded by 700 black eunuchs. Their luxurious quarters contained gushing fountains and regal baths, all set up in haste but with great effect.

Again, it was all to no avail, even though Vienna was only lightly defended by 10,000 men. Mustapha's overconfidence was his downfall; failing to put garrisons on Kahlenberg, he and his army were surprised by a swift attack from this famous hill. Mustapha was pursued from the battlefield and defeated once again, at Gran. At Belgrade he was met by the emissary of Sultan Mehmed IV. The price of failure was death, and Mustapha meekly accepted his fate. When the Austrian imperial army conquered Belgrade in 1718 the grand vizier's head was dug up and brought back to Vienna in triumph.

> Austria's greatest military hero, Prince Eugene of Savoy, was in fact French. Refused entry to the French army by Louis XIV, Eugene went on to humiliate him on the battlefield.

Maria Theresia & the Enlightenment

Maria Theresia (1717–80), whose plump figure in stone fills a regal stool on Maria-Theresian-Platz in Vienna today, was something of the mother of the nation. Thrust into the limelight when her father died with no male heirs, she ruled for 40 years while also managing to give birth to 16 children – among them Marie Antoinette, future wife of Louis XVI. Maria Theresia's fourth child, Joseph II, weighed a daunting 7kg at birth.

1751	1752	1764	1789–99
Tiergarten Schönbrunn is established in Vienna, making it the world's oldest zoological garden.	Maria Theresia introduces the short-lived Commission Against Immoral Conduct, which pillages homes and attempts to snatch men entertaining loose women.	Reformer Kaiser Joseph II (1741–90) takes the throne and the Age of Enlightenment that began under Maria Theresia is in full swing. The power of the church is curbed.	French Revolution takes place, bringing a new age of republicanism to Europe and challenging feudalistic establishments such as the Holy Roman Empire.

Although Maria Theresia is famous for her many enlightened reforms, she was remarkably prudish for a family that had married and bred its way to power. One of her less-popular measures was the introduction of the short-lived Commission Against Immoral Conduct in 1752, which raided private homes, trying to catch men entertaining loose women – the commission even tried to snare Casanova during his visit to Vienna, throwing him out of the city in 1767.

Maria Theresia's low take on fornication (and Casanova's womanising and proclivity for urinating in public) was no doubt coloured by the conduct of her husband, Francis I, who was apparently very adept and enthusiastic when it came to fornication. Yet despite her husband's philandering, Maria Theresia felt she should remain loyal to her spouse, and when he died suddenly in 1765 she stayed in mourning for the rest of her life. She retreated to Schloss Schönbrunn in Vienna, left the running of the state in the hands of Joseph II (of 7kg fame) as co-regent, and adopted a low profile and chaste existence.

The period of the Enlightenment began under Maria Theresia and continued during the co-reign of Joseph II in the late 18th century. Vienna was transformed from being a place in which the Habsburgs lived and ruled into an administrative capital. A functioning bureaucracy was established for the first time and this was directly responsible to the monarchy. Joseph was mostly of the same mettle as his mother. He ushered in a period of greater religious tolerance and in 1781 an edict ensured Protestants would enjoy equal rights with Catholics. While decrees gave Jews much more freedom, paving the way for a more active role in trade and education, paradoxically he promoted assimilation of Jews into the Austrian mainstream, banning whatever customs he thought hindered this.

Napoleon, Revolution & Empire

The French Revolution of 1789–99 was a political explosion that ushered in a new age of republicanism in Europe and challenged surviving feudalistic undertakings like the Holy Roman Empire. It also led to the rise of Napoleon Bonaparte (1769–1821), Europe's diminutive moderniser. His code of law, the Napoleonic Code, was the backbone of modern laws and was anathema to precisely those privileges of rank and birth that had allowed the Habsburgs to rule and govern for so long.

Austria played a role in virtually all the Napoleonic wars from 1803 to 1815, the year Napoleon was finally defeated at Waterloo. He occupied Vienna twice (in 1805 and 1809) and in April 1809, during occupation of Austrian regions, Tyrol – which had fallen into the hands of Bavaria – was the scene of discontent when innkeeper Andreas Hofer (1767–1810) led a rebellion for independence. For his troubles, Hofer was put on trial

1793	1804–05	1809	1813 & 1815
Following a marriage to French king Louis XVI (1754–93), Maria Theresia's 15th child, Marie Antoinette – who the French call 'L'Autrichienne' (the Austrian) – is beheaded during the French Revolution.	Napoleon (1769–1821) occupies Vienna in 1805. The Holy Roman Empire is abolished; Franz II reinvents himself as Austrian Kaiser Franz I. In 1809 the Frenchman returns to retake Vienna.	In the midst of the Napoleonic occupation, Tyrol – which has fallen under Bavarian control – is the scene of another rebellion when innkeeper Andreas Hofer leads a bid for independence.	Napoleon is defeated in Leipzig in 1813 and, in his final battle, at Waterloo in 1815.

and executed at Napoleon's behest. His body is entombed in Innsbruck's Hofkirche.

Despite ultimately being defeated, Napoleon's ventures triggered the collapse of the Holy Roman Empire. Its ruler Franz II reinvented himself as Franz I of Austria, and the man he appointed to help draw up a post-Napoleon Europe, the chief minister Klemenz von Metternich, rose to dominate Europe's biggest diplomatic party, the Congress of Vienna, held in 1814–15 to reshape the continent. The Habsburgs survived all this and in the post-Napoleon Vormärz (Pre-March) years, they dominated a loose Deutscher Bund (German Alliance) comprising hundreds of small 'states' cobbled together in an oppressive period of modest cultural flourish and reactionary politics called the Biedermeier period.

Revolutions of 1848

With citizens being kept on a short leash by their political masters in the first half of the 19th century, it's not surprising that they began to seek new freedoms. Klemenz von Metternich, who had become court and state chancellor, believed in absolute monarchy and his police took a ferocious approach to liberals and Austrian nationalists who demanded their freedom. Meanwhile, nationalism – one of the best chances of liberalising Austrian society at that time – was threatening to chip away the delicate edges of the Habsburg empire. On top of this, atrocious industrial conditions added fuel to the fires of discontent.

The sparks of the Paris revolution in February 1848 ignited Vienna in March 1848. Reflecting the city–country divide, however, the uprising failed to take hold elsewhere in Austria except in Styria. A similar revolution in Germany meant that some Austrian revolutionaries were now in favour of becoming part of a greater, unified and liberal Germany. This was the difficult Grossdeutsch-Kleindeutsch (Greater Germany–Lesser Germany) question – Germany with or without Austria – and reflects the unsettled relationship between the Austrian and German nations.

The rebels demanded a parliament, and in May and June 1848 Kaiser Ferdinand I issued manifestos which paved the way for a parliamentary assembly a month later. He packed his bags and his family and fled to Innsbruck. This should have been the end of the Habsburgs. It wasn't. Parliament passed a bill improving the lot of the peasants, and Ferdinand cleverly sanctioned this, overnight winning the support of rural folk in the regions. Meanwhile, the Habsburgs received a popular boost when General Radetzky (1766–1858) won back Lombardy (Italy) in successful military campaigns.

In October 1848, however, the revolution escalated and reached fever pitch in Vienna. Although this uprising could be quashed, the Habsburgs decided to dispense with Ferdinand I, replacing him with his nephew

Historic Sights

Vienna's Hofburg

Stift Melk in the Wachau

Neolithic Ötzi Dorf

1815–48	1818	1848	1850
The Metternich system, aimed at shoring up the monarchies of Austria, Russia and Prussia, ushers in the stifling Biedermeier period.	The Austrian tailor Josef Madersperger invents the world's first sewing machine.	Revolution topples Chancellor Klemens von Metternich, who flees disguised as a washerwoman. Franz Josef I abolishes many reforms. Austria's first parliament is formed.	Vienna's city limits are expanded, mostly to include the area within the Linienwall (today the Gürtel). Districts are numbered – the old city becoming the 1st, the Vorstädte (inner suburbs) the 2nd to 9th.

Franz Josef I, who introduced his own monarchical constitution and dissolved parliament in early 1849. It would only be revived properly in 1867.

By September 1849 it was time to weigh up the damage, count the dead and, most importantly, look at what had been won. Austria was not a democracy, because the kaiser retained absolute powers that allowed him to veto legislation and govern by decree if he wished. The revolutions, however, had swept away the last vestiges of feudalism and, by giving them a taste of parliamentary rule, made state citizens out of royal subjects.

Austro-Hungarian Empire

In 1867 a dual monarchy was created in Austria and Hungary. This was an attempt by the Habsburgs to hold onto support for the monarchy among Hungarians by giving them a large degree of autonomy. The Austro-Hungarian Empire would grow to include core regions of Austria, Hungary, the Czech Republic, Slovakia, Slovenia, Croatia and Bosnia-Herzegovina, as well as regions like the Voivodina in Serbia, and small chunks in northern Italy, Romania, Poland and Ukraine.

Generally it is known as the 'KuK' (*König und Kaiser*; king and kaiser) monarchy – the kaiser of Austria was also king of Hungary. In practice, the two countries increasingly went separate ways, united only by the dual monarch and a couple of high-level ministries like 'war' and 'foreign affairs'. This so-called 'Danube Monarchy' or Austro-Hungarian Empire was the last stage of development in the Habsburg empire and would endure until 1918, when it collapsed completely.

WWI & the First Republic

Fin-de-Siècle Austria

Austria in the late 19th century followed a similar pattern of industrialisation and growth of political parties based around workers' movements that occurred in other continental European countries. The country's oldest political party, the Sozialdemokratische Partei Österreichs (SPÖ; Social Democratic Party of Austria), was founded as the Social Democratic Workers' Party in 1889, based on German models. By the turn of the 20th century, Austria – and Vienna in particular – was experiencing one of its most culturally exciting periods. The capital's population had almost doubled between 1860 and 1890, growing to more than two million inhabitants.

This was the political and cultural hub of an empire that spanned Austria and Hungary, but also included 15 other countries, proving a magnet for artists, architects, the persecuted and plain hangers-on who wanted

Carl E Schorske magically interlinks seven essays on the intellectual history of Vienna in his seminal work *Fin-de-Siècle Vienna*.

1857

Vienna's city walls are demolished to make way for the creation of the monumental architecture today found along the Ringstrasse.

1866

Austria and its allied principalities in Germany fight the Austro-Prussian War, which leads to victory for Prussia and creates the groundwork for a unified Germany that excludes Austria.

PAUL BERNSEN / GETTY IMAGES ©

→ Neoclassical facade of Parlament (p73), Ringstrasse, Vienna

to try their luck in the capital of an empire. In this empire, however, Austrians and Hungarians enjoyed a higher status than Slavs, leading to exploitation and often tensions in the capital.

Architecturally, Austria's capital was transformed by a spate of building and infrastructure projects that, among other large projects, saw it receive a metro system. The Secession movement, the Austrian equivalent of art nouveau, sprang up and rejected historicism. Villas sprouted out of the ground in Vienna and across the country, and the coffee houses, especially in the capital, became the centre of literary activity and music. In 1913 Arnold Schöneberg began developing his 'atonal' style of musical composition when he conducted his famous Watschenkonzert (so-called 'clip-over-the-ear concert') in Vienna's Musikverein. For a public used to the primrose tones of Romanticism, it must have felt like an unmitigated aural assault.

Meanwhile, Sigmund Freud (1856–1939) had set up his practice in Vienna's Bergstrasse and was challenging the sexual and psycho-social mores of the previous century. He used the term 'psychoanalysis' and explained the role of sexuality in our lives. This was, in fact, a highly sexualised period, with writers such as Arthur Schnitzler and Expressionist artists like Egon Schiele, Gustav Klimt and Oskar Kokoschka taking sexuality as a major theme in their works. WWI brought all this to an end.

> 'The Viennese are neither more abstinent nor more nervous than anyone else in big cities.' Sigmund Freud

WWI

The assassination of Franz Ferdinand, the nephew of Franz Josef, in Sarajevo on 28 June 1914 triggered the first of Europe's two catastrophic wars in the 20th century. Overnight, the cultural explosion of fin-de-siècle Austria was replaced by the explosion of shells in the trenches. Austria responded to the assassination by declaring war on Serbia one month later, in what it believed would be a short, punitive campaign. Austria-Hungary was poorly equipped, however, and the war rapidly escalated into a pan-European affair in which Germany, Austria-Hungary and Turkey found themselves pitted against a European power coalition made up of Russia, Britain, France and Italy. Halfway through the war Franz Josef died and was replaced by Karl I. Ultimately, military revolt by troops in Italy spread and caused the rest of the army to lay down its arms, bringing defeat and collapse of the empire. WWI resulted in about 1.4 million military casualties for Austria-Hungary, and another 3.5 million Austro-Hungarians were wounded. In the rest of Europe, it was perceived as unprecedented in the scale of destruction and suffering it caused, and so horrific that it was dubbed 'the war to end all wars'.

> Vienna's population peaked at more than two million between 1910 and 1914. After WWI, Vienna was one of the world's five largest cities.

1867	1874	1878	1897
Weakened by loss against Prussia, Austria is now forced by Hungary to create a dual Austro-Hungarian monarchy (the Ausgleich). Austria establishes a democratic parliament.	Viennese privatier Jakob Zelzer is buried in Vienna Zentralfriedhof (Central Cemetery) as its first deceased resident; today there are about 2.5 million.	To prevent the Russians increasing their influence in the Balkans after they win the Russo-Turkish War of 1877–78, Austria-Hungary occupies Bosnia and Herzegovina.	The giant Ferris wheel (Riesenrad) is built in Vienna's Prater recreational area, which until 1766 had been a royal hunting ground for Habsburgs.

The First Republic

With defeat and the abdication of Karl I, Austria declared itself a republic on 12 November 1918, having been reduced to a small country of about 6.5 million inhabitants, most of whom spoke German. South Tyrol was carved off from the rest of Austria and given to Italy, and the perception at the time was that a country of Austria's size would have little chance of surviving. Austria was therefore caught between contrasting movements that either wanted to unite with Germany, return to a monarchical system, or simply break away and join another country, as was the case with Vorarlberg (which sought union with Switzerland). The loss of land caused severe economic difficulties. Whole industries collapsed and unemployment soared, fuelled by the return of ex-soldiers and the influx of refugees, but also by a huge number of bureaucrats who, with the collapse of the monarchy, now had no job to return to.

One of the most serious problems facing the new republic was the divide between the socialist-governed cities, especially 'Red Vienna', and the extremely conservative rural regions. The 30,000-strong army created to ensure the country's existence was an additional conservative force in the country. The weakness of this army was matched by a police force that was helpless in thwarting the creation of left- and right-wing paramilitary forces.

The Social Democratic Workers' Party created its Republican Defence League (Schutzbund), whereas on the other side of the political fence the Christlichsoziale Partei (Christian Social Party), a Catholic nationalist party that had emerged in the late 19th century and survived until 1934, fostered close ties with a number of ultra-conservative paramilitary groups.

By the mid-1920s armed paramilitary groups from both sides were roaming the streets of Vienna and elsewhere, engaging in bloody clashes. When in 1927 a court in Vienna acquitted members of the right-wing paramilitary Frontkämpfer (Front Fighters) on charges of killing two people during demonstrations, left-wing groups rose up and stormed the city's Justizpalast (Palace of Justice). The police moved in and regained control of the building, but about 90 people died in the revolt and more than 1000 were injured. Troubled times had come.

Women in Austria gained the right to vote in national elections in 1919.

Austria's Jews – at the Edge of the Abyss

As Austria entered the 1930s, the threat to its Jewish population intensified and would culminate in cultural, intellectual and, above all, human tragedy.

Austrian Jewry enjoys a long and rich history. The first mention of Jews in Vienna was in 1194, when a minter by the name of Schlom was

1900	1905	1908	1910
Vienna becomes the centre of the *Jugendstil* (art nouveau) movement through its association with Otto Wagner and related artists called Vienna's Secession.	Austrian writer and pacifist activist Bertha von Suttner becomes the first woman to win the Nobel Peace Prize.	Fatefully, Austria-Hungary is given a mandate to occupy and administer Bosnia and Herzegovina, with the expectation that it will later be annexed completely.	Vienna's population breaks the two million barrier, the largest it has ever been. The rise is mainly due to exceptionally high immigration numbers – the majority of immigrants are Czechs.

appointed by the crown. The very same man was subsequently murdered along with 16 other Viennese Jews by zealous crusaders on their way to the Holy Land. Gradually, a ghetto grew around today's Judenplatz in Vienna, where a large synagogue stood in the 13th century.

Historically, Jews could only work in some professions. They were seldom allowed into tradesmen's guilds or to engage in agriculture, and therefore earned a living through trading goods and selling, or through money lending, which explains many of the clichés of the past and present. Two 'libels' in the Middle Ages made life difficult for Jews. One of these was the 'host desecration libel', which accused Jews of desecrating Christ by acts such as sticking pins into communion wafers and making them weep or bleed. The second was the 'blood libel', which accused Jews of drinking the blood of Christians during rituals. In 1420 these libels culminated in one of Vienna's worst pogroms, during which many Jews committed collective suicide. The synagogue on Vienna's Judenplatz was destroyed and the stones of the synagogue were used to build the old university.

Take a virtual tour through Jewish history in Austria from the Middle Ages to the present in the Jewish Virtual Library at www.jewish-virtuallibrary.org/jsource/vjw/Austria.html.

Jews were officially banned from settling in Vienna until 1624, but this law was regularly relaxed. It did mean, however, that Vienna's Jews had a particularly rough time of it, and in 1670 when Leopold I (1640–1705) drove them out of Unterer Werd, the quarter was re-christened Leopoldstadt, the name it bears today. They returned, however, and this district remained Vienna's largest Jewish quarter until WWII.

When money was tight following the 1683 Turkish siege, Jews were encouraged to settle in town as money lenders. Interestingly, once the threat subsided from 1718, Sephardic Jews from Spain arrived and were allowed to establish their own religious community. An edict from Kaiser Joseph II (1741–90) improved conditions for Jews, and after Kaiser Franz I remodelled himself into Austria's kaiser and allowed Jews to establish schools, some of Vienna's Jewry rose into bourgeois and literary circles.

The revolution of 1848 brought the biggest changes, however. Vienna's Jews were at the forefront of the uprising, and it brought them freedom of religion, press and schooling. Indirectly, it also led to the founding of the Israelitische Kultusgemeinde (Jewish Religious Community), more than a century after the Sephardic Jews had founded their own. Today this is the largest body that represents religious Jews in Austria.

In 1878 Jewry in Austria was shaken up again by the arrival from Budapest of Theodor Herzl (1860–1904), who founded political Zionism, a concept that brought together the ideas of the workers' movement with support for a Jewish state. His book *Der Judenstaat* (The Jewish State; 1896) would later be crucial to the creation of Israel.

Beginning with Adolf Fischhof (1816–93), whose political speech on press freedom in 1848 helped trigger revolution, and continuing with

1914	1918	1920s	1934
Austrian archduke Franz Ferdinand is assassinated in Sarajevo by a Serbian nationalist, triggering WWI, which sees Austria-Hungary in alliance with Germany and the Ottoman Empire.	WWI ends and Karl I abdicates after the humiliating defeat; the First Republic is proclaimed in Vienna. The Habsburg empire is shaved of border nationalities; Austria keeps most German-speaking regions.	The Social Democratic Party of Austria controls 'Red Vienna', its heart set on Austro-Marxism, while the provinces are controlled by conservative forces.	Austrian politics is polarised, paralysed by paramilitary groups. In 1934 parliament is gridlocked and Austria collapses into civil war – hundreds die in three-day fighting culminating in Social Democrat defeat.

Herzl and with the founding father of Austrian social democracy, Viktor Adler (1852–1918), Jews drove reforms in Austria and played a key role during the 'Red Vienna' period of the 1920s and early 1930s.

Anschluss & WWII

Austria's role in WWII is one of the most controversial aspects of its modern history. Hitler was popular inside Austria, and Austria itself supplied a disproportionately large number of officers for the SS and the German army. What Hitler and the Nazis couldn't achieve through pressure, large numbers of Austrians themselves helped achieve through their active and passive support for Nazism and Hitler's war.

Austro-Marxism & Austro-Fascism

The worldwide economic depression triggered by the crash of stock exchanges in 1929 further fuelled the flames of discontent and division. About 25% of the working population was now unemployed. Austro-Marxism, which sought a third way between Russian Leninism and the revisionism cropping up in some European social democratic movements, enjoyed a strong following in the cities. Key figures behind it – today reading like a who's who of street names in Vienna – were Karl Renner (1870–1950), Otto Bauer (1881–1938), Friedrich Adler (1879–1960), Max Adler (1873–1937) and Rudolf Hilferding (1877–1941). In contrast to revolutionary Marxism, leaders were committed to 'winning over minds, not smashing in heads' as Otto Bauer so aptly put it.

The first government of the Austrian Republic was a coalition of left- and right-wing parties under Chancellor Karl Renner. A key figure of the right was Ignaz Seipl (1876–1932), who was chancellor twice during the 1920s and saw his calling in opposing the Marxists.

In 1930 right-wing conservatives forced through a constitutional change that gave more power to the president and weakened parliament. In a radicalisation of politics, paramilitary groups close to the right formally backed homegrown Austrian fascism, and when Engelbert Dollfuss (1892–1934) became chancellor in 1932, Austria moved a step closer to becoming a fascist state.

During the chaos in a parliamentary session in 1933 following strikes by workers and a harsh response by the government, Dollfuss declared his intention to rule without parliament. This marked the beginning of a period when socialists and social democrats were gradually being outlawed and the workers' movements weakened. In 1933, police forced their way into the headquarters of the (left-wing) paramilitary Schutzbund, triggering an uprising in Linz, Vienna and other industrial centres that virtually led to civil war. The army quashed the uprising. Leading social democrats were executed and the social democratic movement

The roots of Austria's Österreichische Volkspartei (ÖVP; Austrian People's Party) go back to 1887; a forerunner of the Sozialdemokratische Partei Österreichs (SPÖ; Social Democratic Party of Austria) was founded a year later.

1938

Nazi troops march into Vienna; Hitler visits his beloved Linz, and Vienna to address 200,000 ecstatic Viennese on Heldenplatz. After a rigged referendum, Austria becomes part of Hitler's Reich.

1938–9

In the Pogromnacht of November 1938, Jewish businesses and homes are plundered and destroyed across Austria. 120,000 Jews leave Vienna over the next six months.

➜ Heldenplatz, Hofburg Imperial Palace (p65), Vienna

declared illegal, turning the fight against fascism into an underground movement.

In 1934 Dollfuss – a deeply religious man who was backed by the Italian dictator Benito Mussolini – was murdered in a failed putsch staged by Austrian Nazis, who he had also banned.

While Hitler was seizing power in Germany in 1933 and subsequently closing down all opposition, across the border in Austria, an Austro-Fascist government lifted the ban on local chapters of Hitler's Nationalsozialistische Deutsche Arbeiterpartei (National Socialist Democratic Workers' Party; NSDAP), which was neither democratic, sympathetic to workers' nor socialist. This was done under pressure from Hitler, allowing Austrian Nazis to make a power grab at home. On 12 March 1938, Hitler's troops crossed the border and occupied Austria, in the so-called Anschluss (annexation), according to which Austria became part of a greater Germany. This ended a a period of contradiction in which Austria's leaders had virtually set themselves up as dictators, but did not like the idea of becoming part of Hitler's Nazi Germany. A few days later, Hitler held his famous speech to a cheering crowd of tens of thousands on Vienna's Heldenplatz, declaring Austria part of the German nation.

Hella Pick's *Guilty Victim: Austria from the Holocaust to Haider* is an excellent analysis of modern-day Austria.

The Holocaust

The events of the Nazi era, culminating in the Holocaust, are etched in the collective memory of Jews everywhere: the prohibitive Nuremberg Laws, the forced sale and theft of Jewish property, and Reichspogromnacht (also known as 'The Night of Broken Glass') on 9 and 10 November 1939 when synagogues and Jewish businesses were burnt and Jews were attacked openly on the streets.

The arrival of Hitler in Vienna in March 1938 raised the stakes among those Jews who had not yet managed to flee the country. Vienna's 'father' of modern psychoanalysis, Sigmund Freud, had not wanted to read the signs for a long time; in June that year, however, he fled to England. The 20th century's most innovative classical composer, Arnold Schönberg (1874–1951), lost his job as a lecturer in Berlin in 1933 and went to the US. They were just two of many prominent Austrian Jews forced into exile.

Others were not as fortunate. The Holocaust (or Schoa), Hitler's attempt to wipe out European Jewry, was a brutal and systematic act that saw some 65,000 Austrian Jews perish in concentration camps throughout Europe. It ruptured Jewish history in Austria dating back to the early Middle Ages, and even today it's not really possible to talk about a 'recovery' of Jewish culture in the country.

Because of atrocities perpetrated on the Jewish population by the Nazis, today the Jewish community is only a fraction of its former size. About 8000 religiously affiliated Jews live in Austria, and there are about

1939–45	1948	1955	1955–66
War and genocide in Austria. More than 100,000 of Vienna's 180,000 Jews escape, but 65,000 die. In 1945 the Red Army liberates Vienna. Austria and Vienna are divided among the Allied powers.	Graham Greene flies to Vienna for inspiration for a film which becomes *The Third Man*, starring Orson Wells and featuring an iconic scene on the city's Riesenrad (Ferris wheel).	Austrian *Staatsvertrag* (state treaty) is ratified. Austria declares sovereignty and neutral status, ending a decade of occupation. Post-WWII international bodies come to Vienna; the UN later sets up offices here.	'Grand coalitions' of major parties govern Austria based on a system of *Proporz* (proportion), whereby ministerial posts are divided among the major parties. This becomes a hallmark of Austrian politics.

CUCKOO-CLOCK STABILITY

In 1948 the British author Graham Greene flew to Vienna and roamed the bomb-damaged streets looking for inspiration for a film he had been commissioned to write about the occupation of post-WWII Vienna. As chance would have it, Greene penned the script for one of Europe's finest films about the era – *The Third Man*, starring Orson Wells as the penicillin racketeer Harry Lime. At one point in Vienna's Prater, Orson Wells as Lime waxes lyrical about how under the bloody reign of the Borgias Italy produced some of its finest art. 'In Switzerland they had brotherly love, 500 years of democracy and peace, and what did they produce? The cuckoo clock.' Never mind that the cuckoo clock comes from Germany's Black Forest – not exactly a model of stability over the centuries. But that's another matter.

another 3000 to 5000 who are not affiliated with a community. The number was boosted by the arrival of Jews from the former Soviet Union in the 1990s, and increasingly Jews from Hungary, where anti-Semitism is on the rise, are moving to Vienna.

Resistance & Liberation

With the annexation of Austria in 1938, opposition turned to resistance. As elsewhere, whenever Hitler's troops crossed a border, resistance from within was extremely difficult. Interestingly, Tyrolean resistance leaders often rallied opposition to Nazism by recalling the revolt of Andreas Hofer in 1809 when Tyrol's innkeeper led his rebellion for independence. An Österreichisches Freiheitsbataillon (Austrian Freedom Battalion) fought alongside the Yugoslav People's Liberation Army, and partisan groups in Styria and Carinthia maintained links with other partisans across the Yugoslavian border. Tellingly, unlike other countries, Austria had no government in exile.

Resistance increased once the war looked lost for Hitler. The Austrian Robert Bernardis (1908–44) was involved in the assassination attempt on Hitler by high-ranking officers on 20 July 1944 and was then executed by the Nazis. Another involved in that plot, Carl Szokoll (1915–2004), survived undetected. The most famous resistance group, however, was called 05, whose members included Austria's president from 1957 to 1965, Adolf Schärf (1890–1965).

With the Red Army approaching Vienna in 1945, the resistance group 05 worked closely with Carl Szokoll and other military figures in Operation Radetzky to liberate Vienna in the last days of the war. Although they were able to establish contact with the Red Army as it rolled towards the city, they were betrayed at the last moment and

1972–8	1979	1981	1986
Vienna's Donauinsel (Danube Island) is created to protect the city against flooding. Today it serves as one of the city's recreation areas, with parks, river beaches, trails and forest.	A third UN headquarters is opened in Austria's capital. It is the headquarters for the International Atomic Energy Agency, Drugs & Crime office, and other functions.	Hohe Tauern National Park is established as the first of seven national parks in Austria.	Presidential candidate Kurt Waldheim (1918–2007) is accused of war crimes. Waldheim wins a tough election but is stained. The Historians Commission finds Waldheim unhelpful, but no proof of crimes.

several members were strung up from street lanterns. The Red Army, not Austrians, would liberate the capital.

Austria after 1945

Soon after liberation, Austria declared its independence from Germany. A provisional federal government was established under Socialist Karl Renner, and the country was occupied by the Allies – the Americans, Russians, British and French. Vienna was itself divided into four zones; this was a time of 'four men in a jeep', so aptly depicted in Graham Greene's book and film *The Third Man*.

Delays caused by frosting relations between the superpowers ensured that the Allied occupation dragged on for 10 years. On 15 May 1955 the Austrian State Treaty was ratified, with Austria proclaiming its permanent neutrality. The Soviet Union insisted that Austria declare its neutrality as a condition for ending Soviet occupation in 1955. At the last minute, recognition of Austria's guilt for WWII was struck out of the state treaty.

The Allied forces withdrew, and in December 1955 Austria joined the UN. The economy took a turn for the better through the assistance granted under the Marshall Plan, and the cessation of the removal of industrial property by the Soviets. As the capital of a neutral country on the edge of the Cold War front line, Vienna attracted spies and diplomats: Kennedy and Khrushchev met here in 1961, Carter and Brezhnev in 1979; the UN set up shop in 1979.

The report of the Historical Commission's inquiry into Austria during the Nazi era can be found at www.historiker kommission. gv.at.

Kurt Waldheim Affair

Austria's international image suffered following the election in 1986 of President Kurt Waldheim who, it was revealed, had served in a German Wehrmacht (armed forces) unit implicated in WWII war crimes. Austria seriously confronted its Nazi past for the first time. Accusations that Waldheim had committed these crimes while a lieutenant serving with the German army in the Balkans could never be proved, but Austria's elected president was unwilling to fully explain himself or express misgivings about his wartime role.

In 1993 Chancellor Franz Vranitzky finally admitted that Austrians were 'willing servants of Nazism'. Since then, however, Austria has attempted to make amends for its part in atrocities against the Jews. In 1998 the Austrian Historical Commission, set up to investigate and report on expropriations during the Nazi era, came into being, and in 2001 Vienna's mayor Dr Michael Häupl poignantly noted that after having portrayed itself as the first victim of National Socialism for many years, Austria now had to admit to its own active participation in the regime's crimes. This marked a more critical approach to Austria's role during the Nazi dictatorship.

1986	1995	1999
Vienna ceases to be the capital of surrounding Bundesland of Niederösterreich (Lower Austria), replaced by St Pölten.	Austria joins the EU in 1995, but because of guarantees in 1955 to Moscow to remain neutral it forgoes NATO membership.	Austria introduces the euro and abolishes the Austrian schilling as its currency, having easily satisfied the criteria for the level of debt and the inflation rate.

WITOLD SKRYPCZAK / GETTY IMAGES ©

➡ St Pölten, Lower Austria

'Westernisation' of Austria

According to the Hungarian political historian Anton Pelinka, Austria spent the first few decades of the Second Republic defining and asserting its own homegrown political and social path, but since the mid-1980s has followed a course of 'Westernisation'. Two features of this are its membership of the EU since 1995 and adoption of the euro currency when it was introduced in 1999.

The political consensus that saw the two larger parties, the SPÖ and Österreichisches Volkspartei (ÖVP; Austrian People's Party), completely dominate politics has given way to a polarisation. In 1986 Die Grünen (The Greens) party was founded, with close links to a similar ecologically focused party in Germany. On the other side of the political spectrum is the Freiheitliche Partei Österreichs (FPÖ; Freedom Party of Austria), which was founded in 1955 and had a high proportion of former Nazis in its ranks. In 1986, however, its charismatic leader Jörg Haider reinvented the party as a populist right-wing party with a focus on immigration issues, asylum laws and integration – issues that today figure strongly in its policies.

In 2000 the FPÖ formed a federal coalition for the first time with the ÖVP, resulting in regular 'Thursday demonstrations' against the FPÖ within Austria to protest its participation in government, and in sanctions imposed on Austria by other EU members. Splintering has continued in recent years, best exemplified by the formation in 2012 of Team Stronach, founded by Austria's most powerful industrialist, Frank Stronach, with a political platform bearing many of the hallmarks of right-wing populism.

When Governor Schwarzenegger allowed an execution to go ahead in California in 2005, some Austrians wanted to revoke his Austrian citizenship. Austria first abolished capital punishment in 1787.

2003	2007	2008	2010
Styrian muscleman, actor and director Arnold 'Arnie' Schwarzenegger is elected governor of California after becoming a US citizen in 1983.	A grand coalition government of Social Democrats (SPÖ) and the Austrian People's Party (ÖVP) is formed under Alfred Gusenbauer.	Austria cohosts football's European Cup with Switzerland.	SPÖ preferred presidential candidate Heinz Fischer is re-elected with an overwhelming majority as an independent; populist right-wing candidate Barbara Rosenkranz is resoundingly defeated.

Architecture

Thanks to the Habsburg monarchy and its obsession with creating grand works, Austria is packed with high-calibre architecture. The earliest 'architectural' signs are ancient grave mounds from the Iron Age Hallstatt culture outside Grossklein, and the marginally more recent Roman ruins of Vienna and Carnuntum. In later centuries and millennia, Romanesque, Gothic, Renaissance and especially baroque buildings rose up all over Austria.

'Prose is architecture, not interior decoration, and the baroque is over.' Ernest Hemingway, inadvertently revealing to us what he thought of baroque architecture (and also why he wrote about bullfights and not, say, Austrian churches).

Baroque – Elegantly Feral

According to one 19th-century Swiss art historian, Jacob Burckhardt, the baroque period and the Renaissance period that preceded it speak roughly the same language. The difference, however, is that the baroque speaks a dialect that has gone feral. The height of the baroque era of building was in the late 17th and early 18th century in Austria. It only moved into full swing once the Ottoman Turks had been beaten back from the gates of Vienna during the Turkish siege of 1683. It took the graceful columns and symmetry of the Renaissance and added elements of the grotesque, the burlesque and the saccharine.

A good example of this 'feral dialect' spoken by baroque architecture is the Karlskirche (Church of St Charles) in Vienna. Here you find towering, decorative columns rising up on Karlsplatz and a stunning cupola painted with frescoes. The church was instigated by the Habsburg Charles VI following the plague of 1713, and it was dedicated to St Charles Borromeo, who succoured the victims of plague in Italy. It is arguably the most beautiful of the baroque masterpieces.

Johann Bernhard Fischer von Erlach

The architect who shaped the Karlskirche was Johann Bernhard Fischer von Erlach (1656–1723). Fischer von Erlach was Austria's first, and possibly the country's greatest, architect of the baroque era. He was born in Graz, the capital of Styria, and began working as a sculptor in his father's workshop before travelling to Rome in 1670 and spending well over a decade studying baroque styles in Italy. He returned to Austria in 1686 and in 1693 completed one of his earliest works in the capital, the magnificent Pestsäule, a swirling, golden, towering pillar commemorating the end of the plague.

Fischer von Erlach's greatest talent during these early years was his interior decorative work, and in Graz he was responsible for the baroque interior of the Mausoleum of Ferdinand II. In 1689 he began tutoring the future Kaiser Joseph I (1678–1711) in architecture, before being appointed court architect for Vienna in 1694. Despite his high standing and connections to the royal court, he found himself without commissions, however, and worked in Germany, Britain and Holland until his favourite student, Joseph I, elevated him in 1705 to head of imperial architecture in the Habsburg-ruled lands.

Although Fischer von Erlach's original plans for Schloss Schönbrunn in Vienna would be revised, the palace is one of his true masterpieces and was built from 1700. It counts among the world's finest baroque palaces and landscaped gardens, comprising the palace itself, perfectly laid-out gardens, baroque fountains, mythological figures inspired from classical epochs, and an area used for hunting game that today is Vienna's zoo.

Johann Lukas von Hildebrandt

Alongside Schloss Schönbrunn, Vienna's other baroque palace masterpiece, Schloss Belvedere, was designed by Austria's second great architect of the era, Johann Lukas von Hildebrandt (1668–1745).

In his day, Hildebrandt fell into the long shadow cast by Fischer von Erlach. Like his renowned fellow architect, Hildebrandt headed the Habsburgs' Hofbauamt (Imperial Construction Office). His great works were not churches – although he built several of these – or grand abodes for the royal court, but primarily palaces for the aristocracy. He became the architect of choice for the field marshal and statesman Prince Eugene of Savoy, and it was Prince Eugene who commissioned Hildebrandt to build for him a summer residence in Vienna. Today the magnificent ensemble of palaces and gardens comprising Schloss Belvedere is Hildebrandt's most important legacy.

Baroque Across Austria

The Viennese palaces and churches were a high point in the art of the baroque, but the style was of course prevalent right across Austria. In Salzburg, when fire completely destroyed the city's Romanesque cathedral, the new Salzburger Dom (Salzburg Cathedral) was completed in place of the former cathedral in the baroque style in 1628. Meanwhile, in Melk on the Danube River, Jakob Prandtauer (1660–1726) and his disciple Josef Munggenast (1660–1741) completed the monastery Stift Melk between 1702 and 1738. In Graz, Schloss Eggenberg was commissioned in 1625 to the Italian architect Giovanni Pietro de Pomis (1565–1633), giving Austria another fine baroque palace and gardens.

Baroque Conversions

It is said that the baroque was a leveller of styles. This is ironic, because its grandeur was also an over-the-top display of power and wealth. Once the fad caught on, churches almost everywhere were pimped up and brought into line with the style.

The baroque era in Austria, as elsewhere, had begun in architecture before gradually spreading into the fine arts. The fresco paintings of Paul Troger (1698–1762) would become a feature of the late baroque. Troger is Austria's master of the baroque fresco and he worked together with Munggenast on such buildings as Stift Melk, where he created the library and marble hall frescoes, using light cleverly to deliver a sense of space.

The Austrian kaisers Leopold I (1640–1705), Joseph I and Karl VI (1685–1740) loved the dramatic flourishes and total works of art of the early baroque. During the

AUSTRIAN ARCHITECTURE

c AD 40
Romans establish Carnuntum and build military outpost Vindobona, today's Vienna.

11th Century
Gurk's Romanesque Dom, and Benedictine abbey Stift Millstatt are built in Carinthia.

12th Century
Early versions of Vienna's Stephansdom rise up.

12th–15th Centuries
Gothic Stephansdom in Vienna, the Hofkirche in Innsbruck and the Domkirche in Graz are built.

16th Century
The Renaissance in Austria produces Burg Hochosterwitz and Burg Landskron in Carinthia, Schallaburg in Lower Austria, Schloss Ambras in Innsbruck and the Schweizer Tor in Vienna's Hofburg.

17th–Mid-18th Centuries
The baroque era results in masterpieces throughout Austria, among them Vienna's Schloss Belvedere and Schloss Schönbrunn.

Mid-18th–Mid-19th Centuries
Neoclassicism takes root and the Burgtor is built in Vienna and Schloss Grafenegg in Lower Austria.

1815–48
A Biedermeier style casts off the strictness of classicism, focusing on housing with simple yet elegant exteriors and on light, curved furnishings and interior decoration.

ARCHITECTURE BAROQUE – ELEGANTLY FERAL

late 17th century the influence of Italy and Italian masters such as Solari (of Salzburger Dom fame), de Pomis (Schloss Eggenberg) and other foreigners was typical of the movement. Vorarlberg, however, was an exception, as here Austrians, Germans and Swiss played the lead roles. While the zenith of baroque was reached during the era of Fischer von Erlach from the early 18th century, during the reign of Maria Theresia (1717–80) from the mid-18th century Austria experienced its largest wave of conversion of older buildings into a baroque style. This, however, brought little in the way of new or innovative buildings. A neoclassicist movement was gaining popularity, and in Austria as elsewhere the movement left behind the saccharine hype and adopted a new style of strict lines.

Neoclassicism & Revivalism – Back to the Future

Walk around the Ringstrasse of Vienna today, admire the Burgtor (Palace Gate) fronting the Hofburg on its southwest side and dating from the early 19th century, the Neue Burg (New Palace) from the late 19th century, or the parliament building designed by the Dane Theophil von Hansen (1813–91) and you may feel as though you have been cast into an idealised version of ancient Greece or Rome. In Innsbruck, the 1765 Triumphpforte (Triumphal Arch) is an early work of neoclassicism in Austria and creates a similar impression.

In Austria, the love of all things classical or revivalist moved into full swing from the mid-19th century. The catalyst locally was the tearing down of the old city walls that had run around the Innere Stadt (Inner City), offering the perfect opportunity to enrich the city's architecture with grand buildings.

OTTO WAGNER

No single architect personifies the dawning of Austria's modern age in architecture more than Vienna-born Otto Wagner. Wagner, who for many years headed the Hofbauamt (Imperial Construction Office), ushered in a new, functional direction around the turn of the 20th century. When he was finished with Austria's capital it had a subway transport system replete with attractive art nouveau stations, he had given the flood-prone Wien River a stone 'sarcophagus' that allowed the surrounding area to be landscaped and part of it to be given over to the Naschmarkt food market, and he had given us the Postsparkasse building and a sprinkling of other interesting designs in Vienna and its suburbs.

Wagner's style was much in keeping with the contours of his epoch. He was strongly influenced in his early years by the architects of the Ringstrasse buildings and the revivalist style (which entailed resurrecting mostly the styles of ancient Rome and Greece), and he even (unsuccessfully) submitted his own plans for the new Justizpalast (Palace of Justice) in Vienna in a Ringstrasse revivalist style. Gradually, though, Wagner grew sceptical of revivalism and spoke harshly about his early works, characterising revivalism as a stylistic, masked ball. His buildings dispensed with 19th-century classical ornamentation and his trademark became a creative use of modern materials like glass, steel, aluminium and reinforced concrete. The 'studs' on the Postsparkasse building are the perfect example of this. Those who venture out to his 1907 Kirche am Steinhof will find another unusual masterpiece: a functional, domed art nouveau church built in the grounds of a psychiatric institution.

One of Wagner's most functional pieces of design was the Vienna U-Bahn (subway) system. He developed the system between 1892 and 1901 during his long spell heading the construction office of Vienna and he was responsible for about 35 stations in all – stops like Josefstädter Strasse on the U6 and Karlsplatz on the U4 are superb examples. One interesting way to get a feel for Wagner's masterpieces is simply to get onto the U-Bahn and ride the U6 north from Westbahnhof. It's sometimes called Wagner's *Gesamtkunstwerk* (total work of art) – in this case, one you can literally sit on.

Ancient Greek Inspiration

The age of neoclassicism took root during the second half of the 18th century, and over the next 100 years buildings inspired by ancient civilisations would spring up across Austria and elsewhere in Europe. By the mid-19th century, an architectural revivalist fad had taken root that offered a potpourri of styles: neo-Gothic, neo-Renaissance, and even a 'neo' form of neoclassicism.

Since the early days of the Renaissance, architects had looked to the ancient Greeks for ideas. The architecture of Rome was well known, but from the 18th century, monarchs and their builders were attracted to the purer classicism of Greece, and some of these architects travelled there to experience this first-hand. One of the triggers for this newly found love of all things Greek was the discovery in 1740 of three Doric temples in southern Italy in a Greek-Roman settlement known as Paestum.

The Ringstrasse

Vienna's medieval fortress had become an anachronism by the mid-19th century and the clearings just beyond the wall had been turned into Glacis (exercise grounds and parkland). In stepped Emperor Franz Josef I. His idea was to replace the Glacis with grandiose public buildings that would reflect the power and the wealth of the Habsburg Empire. The Ringstrasse was the result. It was laid out between 1858 and 1865, and in the decade afterwards most of the impressive edifices that now line this busy thoroughfare were already being built. It is something of a shopping list of grand buildings: the Staatsoper (National Opera; built 1861–69), the Museum für Angewandte Kunst (MAK; Museum of Applied Arts; 1868–71), the Naturhistorisches Museum (Museum of Natural History; 1872–81), the Rathaus (Town Hall; 1872–83), Kunsthistorisches Museum (Museum of Art History; 1872–91), the Parlament (1873–83), Burgtheater (1874–88), and the Heldenplatz section of the Hofburg's Neue Burg (1881–1908).

Hansen's parliament, with its large statue of Athena out front, possibly best symbolises the spirit of the age and its love of all things classical, but also ancient Greece as a symbol of democracy. One of the finest of the Ringstrasse buildings, the Kunsthistorisches Museum, is not only a neo-Renaissance masterpiece but also a taste of movements to come. This museum, purpose-built by the Habsburgs as a repository for their finest collection of paintings, is replete with colourful lunettes, a circular ceiling recess that allows a glimpse into the cupola when you enter, and paintings by Gustav Klimt (1862–1918).

WWI intervened and the empire was lost before Franz Josef's grand scheme for the Ringstrasse could be fully realised. By then, however, Gustav Klimt and contemporaries of his generation were pushing Austria in new directions.

Secession & Art Nouveau

They called it a 'temple for bullfrogs' or a temple for an anarchic art movement. Other unflattering names for the Secession building were 'the mausoleum', 'the crematorium' or, because of the golden filigree dome perched on top, 'the cabbage head'. Others still, according to today's Secession association, thought it looked like a cross between a greenhouse and an industrial blast furnace.

Mid-19th Century Onward

Lingering neoclassicism spills over into other revivalist styles, giving 'neo' prefixes to Gothic, baroque, Renaissance and other architecture on Vienna's Ringstrasse and across the country.

Late 19th–Early 20th Century

Backward-looking historicism is cast aside for lighter, modern styles such as Vienna's Secession building.

20th Century

While the Secession can still be felt, the Rotes Wien (Red Vienna) period produces large-scale workers housing, and later postmodernist and contemporary buildings like Graz' Kunsthaus spring up.

Friedensreich Hundertwasser abhorred straight lines. He moved towards spiritual ecology, believing that cities should be in harmony with their natural environment, a philosophy that is represented metaphorically in his 'wobbly' KunstHausWien and Hundertwasserhaus in Vienna.

In 1897, 19 progressive artists broke away from the conservative artistic establishment of Vienna and formed the Vienna Secession (*Sezession*) movement. In Austria, the movement is synonymous with art nouveau, although its members had a habit of drawing upon a broad spectrum of styles. Its role models were taken from the contemporary scene in Berlin and Munich and its proponents' aim had been to shake off historicism – the revivalist trend that led to the historic throwbacks built along Vienna's Ringstrasse. At the time, the Kunstlerhaus (Artists' House) of Vienna was the last word in the arts establishment, and Secessionists, including Gustav Klimt, Josef Hoffman, Kolo Moser and Joseph M Olbrich, distanced themselves from this in order to form their association.

Olbrich, a former student of Otto Wagner, was given the honour of designing an exhibition centre for the newly formed Secessionists. The 'temple for bullfrogs' was completed in 1898 and combined sparse functionality with stylistic motifs.

Initially, Klimt, Olbrich and their various colleagues had wanted to build on the Ringstrasse, but the city authorities baulked at the idea of watering down their revivalist thoroughfare with Olbrich's daring design. They agreed, however, to the building being situated just off it – a temporary building where for 10 years the Secessionists could hold their exhibitions.

Because art nouveau was essentially an urban movement, the scenes of its greatest acts were played out in the capitals or large cities: Paris, Brussels, New York, Glasgow, Chicago and Vienna. Like the Renaissance and baroque movements before it, Secession broke down the boundaries between painting and architecture. But it was also a response to the industrial age (although it used a lot of metaphors from nature), and the new movement sought to integrate traditional craftsmanship into its philosophy. The British were its role models for the crafts, and in 1903 Josef Hoffmann and Kolo Moser founded the Wiener Werkstätte (Vienna Workshop), which worked together with Vienna's School of the Applied Arts and the Secession movement to promote their ideas.

Another feature of Secession is its international tone. Vienna was a magnet for artists from the Habsburg-ruled lands. The movement was also greatly influenced by Otto Wagner. The Secession building, for instance, may have been domed by a floral 'cabbage', but its form had the hallmarks of Otto Wagner's strictness of lines.

> 'Because ornamentation is no longer an organic part of our culture it no longer expresses our culture. An ornament created today has nothing to do with us, no connection to human beings and nothing to do with the world order. It's not capable of developing any further.'
> Adolf Loos

ADOLF LOOS

In 1922 a competition was held to build 'the most beautiful and distinctive office building in the world' for the Chicago *Tribune* newspaper. The greats of the architectural world vied for the project, and one of them was Czech-born Adolf Loos (1870–1933). As fate would have it, a neo-Gothic design trumped Loos' entry, which resembled a Doric column on top of what might easily have passed for a car factory.

Loos studied in Bohemia and later Dresden, then broke out for the US, where he was employed as a mason and also did stints washing dishes. He was influenced strongly by Otto Wagner, but it is said that his time as a mason (less so as a dishwasher) heightened his sensitivity to materials. He detested ornamentation, and that's why he also locked horns with the art nouveau crew, whose flowers and ornamental flourishes (the golden cabbage-head dome of the Secession building, for instance) were anathema to his functional, sleek designs. Space, materials and even the labour used to produce a building ('Ornament is wasted labour and therefore a waste of good health') had to be used as fully as possible. Today, anyone who squeezes into Loos' miniscule American Bar in Vienna, with its mirrors, glistening onyx-stone surfaces and illusion of space, will get not only a decent cocktail but a good idea of what the architect was about.

Contemporary Directions

Austria is known for its historic masterpieces, but recent years have also brought interesting new designs, some of these incorporating or complementing existing historic architecture. While many of these are office buildings in the large cities, some are museums or locations for events. Schloss Grafenegg near the Danube Valley in the lush, rolling hills of Lower Austria is a fine instance of a postmodern concert location. Here a Renaissance palace was set on the shores of a lake but rebuilt from the 1840s in its current neoclassical form. The castle and grounds have long been a venue for classical-music events, but in 2007 they were given a new component: a 15m open-air stage called the Wolkenturm (Cloud Tower), designed by Viennese architects nextENTERprise. Set in a cleft in manicured parkland, this shiny, jagged and sculpture-like stage is a natural amphitheatre and takes on the hue of the surrounding parkland.

A similar reflection of surroundings is incorporated into the postmodern Loisium Weinwelt in Langenlois. This brings together a modern, upmarket hotel complex, the world of wine, and tours through historic cellars with an aluminium cube designed by New York architect Steven Holl. Meanwhile, further along the Danube River in Linz, the capital of Upper Austria, the Lentos Kunstmuseum is a cubic, postmodern construction with a glass facade that also reflects its surroundings.

States of Flux

This idea of the modern building reflecting or absorbing the tones of its environment contrasts with another approach in modern Austrian architecture: a building that is in a state of flux. Also in Linz, the postmodern Ars Electronica Center received an addition alongside its original modern building in 2007. The added dimension of an LED facade encloses both buildings and lights up and changes colour at night. Another example of this style is the Kunsthaus in Graz, which quickly became a new trademark of Styria's capital. Situated alongside the Mur River, this slug-like construction – the work of British architects Peter Cook and Colin Fournier – has an exterior that changes colour through illumination. The building's modernity seeks to create an 'aesthetic dialogue' with the historic side of Graz rising up on a bluff on the other side of the river. This dialogue is literally linked by the Murinsel (Mur Island), a swirl-shaped pontoon bridge situated in the middle of the river with a cafe, a children's playground and an amphitheatre for performance.

MuseumsQuartier

One of the most innovative architectural works of recent years has been the MuseumsQuartier in Vienna. The MuseumsQuartier has retained an attractive ensemble of 18th-century buildings that once served as the royal stables for the Habsburgs, added cafes and shops, and augmented these with new buildings, such as the dark-basalt Museum Moderner Kunst (MUMOK) and the Leopold Museum. These two museums are separated by the Kunsthalle and a bold public space that has grown to become a favourite gathering place in the inner city.

ARCHITECTURE CONTEMPORARY DIRECTIONS

'People love everything that fulfils the desire for comfort. They hate everything that wishes to draw them out of the secure position they have earned. People therefore love houses and hate art.' Adolf Loos

---

Don't Miss...

Vienna: Hofburg, MuseumsQuartier, Karlskirche, Schloss Schönbrunn and Kunsthistorisches Museum

Graz: Kunsthaus and Schloss Eggenberg

Salzburg: Festung Hohensalzburg

Melk: Stift Melk

Innsbruck: Hofburg and Hofkirche

Visual Arts & Music

Austria is a relatively small country, but it has a grandiose past and excellent contemporary offerings in the visual arts and music. The reason is simple: Habsburg monarchs fostered and patronised the arts for much of the period from Rudolf I's rise in 1273 until the early 20th century. Although Vienna is the uncontested centre of the visual arts, many important works are housed in smaller museums and, notably, in churches or public buildings – the latter is especially true for baroque painting.

Visual Arts

The Great Fresco Artists

The tradition of fresco painting in Austria dates back to the mid-Romanesque era of the 11th century, when frescoes appeared for the first time in churches, depicting religious scenes. Around 1200 original Romanesque frescoes were painted inside the former Dom (cathedral) in Gurk in eastern Carinthia, and in 1270 these were revamped with a 'zigzag' style, giving naturalistic figures long, flowing robes with folds; you can see some of these in Gurk today.

In the Gothic era that followed from about the 14th century (as for instance in Vienna's Stephansdom), fresco painting reached spatial limits due to vaulted ceilings and large windows (this encouraged glass painting). The height of magnificent fresco painting was therefore achieved in the baroque period of the 17th and early-18th centuries, when fresco painting is associated with three major figures: Johann Michael Rottmayr (1654–1730), Daniel Gran (1694–1757) and Paul Troger (1698–1762). Today the works of these three greats predominate in Vienna and especially in Lower Austria.

Rottmayr and Gran were active during the high baroque, which spans the late 17th century and early 18th century. Paul Troger, however, produced most of his work during the late baroque or rococo period from the mid-18th century. Troger spent several years in Italy learning techniques there and worked in Salzburg before moving to Vienna, where Rottmayr had been setting the tone for fresco painting since 1696. Over time Troger became the painter of choice for churches and monasteries in Lower Austria, and fine examples of his work survive in Stift Melk, Stift Zwettl and Stift Altenburg, as well as in the Dom in Klagenfurt, where you can find a Troger altar painting. Schloss Schönbrunn in Vienna also has work by Troger.

Rottmayr was Austria's first and the country's foremost baroque painter. He spent his early years as a court painter to the Habsburgs in Salzburg before he moved to Vienna in 1696, dominating the scene there for the next three decades. He became the favoured fresco painter of the architect Johann Bernhard Fischer von Erlach and is often compared to the Flemish painter Peter Paul Rubens. His work brought together Italian and Flemish influences into a style that featured plenty of bouncy, joyous figures and bright colours. Fine frescoes from Rottmayr can be found in Vienna decorating the Karlskirche, where a glass lift ascends over 70m into the cupola for a close-up view. In Lower Austria his work adorns Stift Melk and Klosterneuburg.

Daniel Gran, the third in the triumvirate of baroque fresco greats, also studied in Italy, but unlike the works of Troger and Rottmayr his style reined in the most extravagant features and offered a foretaste of neoclassicism – perhaps best illustrated by his ceiling fresco in the Nationalbibliothek (National Library) in Vienna. As fate would have it, Gran was the son of a court chef for Leopold I. But it was his talent, not his connections, that made his fresco in the library above the apotheosis of Leopold's son, Kaiser Karl VI, one of his most important legacies to the style and age.

The Expressionists

Tulln is a sleepy town slaked by the waters of the Danube River. It has a couple of interesting churches and the Minoritenkloster (Minorite Seminary), which each year presents a new exhibition on modern art. Tulln was also the home of Austria's most important expressionist painter, Egon Schiele (1890–1918), and a museum there tells the story of his life through a large collection of his paintings and sketches. Other works are held in Austria's foremost museum for expressionist art, the Leopold in Vienna's MuseumsQuartier, where Schiele's art is hung alongside the expressionists Oskar Kokoschka, Klagenfurt-born Herbert Boeckl, as well as Gustav Klimt, who worked in a number of styles.

Egon Schiele

In his day, Schiele was one of the country's most controversial artists. He left Tulln in 1906 to attend the Vienna's Akademie der Bildenden Künste (Academy of Fine Arts), one of Europe's oldest academies – and famous, incidentally, for having turned down Adolf Hitler in 1907. Schiele cofounded a group in Vienna known as the Neukunstgruppe (New Art Group) and around that time his work began to resonate with the public. Although he was very strongly influenced by one of the leading forces behind the Secession movement and art nouveau in Austria, Gustav Klimt, he is much more closely associated with expressionism than Klimt. Indeed, much of Klimt's early work had revivalist flavours before he broke away from the conservative art establishment of the Künstlerhaus Wien in 1897 and moved into art nouveau.

Sigmund Frued, Vienna's famous psychologist, apparently felt no affinity with expressionists like Schiele, preferring classical art and its neoclassical incarnations, but both Freud and Schiele were bedfellows in one way: the concept of the erotic. While Freud was putting together his theories on Eros and the unconscious, Schiele was capturing the erotic on canvas, often taking death and lust as his explicit themes.

He had come a long way from the conservative, idyllic Tulln countryside – a little too far, some thought. In 1912 Schiele was held in custody for three weeks and

VISUAL ARTS

20 BC
Roman

With the building of the fortress of Carnuntum in Lower Austria, the Romans use decorative mosaics, some of which survive in Carnuntum's open-air museum.

8th–12th Century
Romanesque

Salzburg becomes the centre for frescoes, many of which have Byzantine influences.

13th Century
Early Gothic

A transition from Romanesque to Gothic occurs, exemplified by frescoes today found in the former cathedral of Gurk.

14th Century
High Gothic

Ribbed Gothic interiors and high windows leave little space for frescoes but create new opportunities for glass painting.

16th Century
Danube School

In the transition from late Gothic to the Renaissance, a Danube School of landscape painting arises from the early 16th century, later absorbed into the Renaissance.

1680–1740
High & Late
Baroque

Fresco painting reaches dizzying heights of achievement in the age of Johann Michael Rottmayr, Paul Troger and Daniel Gran.

Early 19th Century
Biedermeier

Amid a wave of neoclassical and revivalist painting, the Biedermeier painter Ferdinand Georg Waldmüller becomes Austria's best-known painter of the era.

later found guilty of corrupting minors by exposing them to pornography. His arrest and imprisonment were the culmination of a series of events that saw the painter and his 17-year-old lover and model 'Wally' Neuzil flee the Vienna scene and move to Bohemia (Česky Krumlov in the Czech Republic), from where the two soon fled again. Today the Tulln museum dedicated to Schiele has a reconstruction of the prison cell near St Pölten where he was imprisoned.

Oskar Kokoschka

Like Schiele, Oskar Kokoschka, the second of the great Austrian expressionists, was born on the Danube River. Kokoschka comes from Pochlarn, near Melk. Like Klimt, he studied at the Kunstgewerbeschule (School of Applied Arts) in Vienna. Like Schiele, he was strongly influenced by Klimt, but another of his influences was Dutch post-Impressionist Vincent van Gogh. From 1907 he worked in the Wiener Werkstatte (Vienna Workshop). His earliest work had features of the Secession and art nouveau movements, but later he moved into expressionism. The Österreichische Galerie in Schloss Belvedere (Oberes Belvedere) has a collection of about a dozen of his oil paintings; some of these portraits highlight Kokoschka's skill for depicting the subject's unsettled psyche without in any way resorting to bleak colours.

Kokoschka's long life was punctuated by exile and travel. He moved to Prague in 1934 to escape the extreme right-wing politics of the day; once the Nazis came to power and declared his works 'degenerate' in 1937, seizing over 400 of them in German museums, Kokoschka packed his bags for Britain and became a UK citizen.

If Kokoschka was 'degenerate' and shocked the Nazis, it was a good thing the 'brown' men and women of the Thousand Year Reich were not around to see what would come later. It was called Viennese Actionism – and now even the mainstream art establishment was being sent into a state of shock.

> The Habsburgs were avid supporters of the arts, commissioning fresco painters to lend colourful texture and new dimensions to their buildings and using music as an expression of their own power and pomp.

Actionism: Shocking the Republic

Art has always enjoyed a good scandal. The expressionist Egon Schiele and the architect Adolf Loos were – rightly or wrongly – embroiled in moral charges that resulted in partial convictions. Kokoschka and Klimt explored in their paintings themes of eroticism, homoeroticism, and adolescence and youth. One day in 1968, however, the stakes were raised significantly higher when a group of artists burst into a packed lecture hall of Vienna's university and began an action that became known as the Uni-Ferkelei (University Obscenity). According to reports, at least one member of the group began masturbating, smearing themselves with excrement, flagellating and vomiting. Lovely, but was it art? One member was probably singing the Austrian national anthem, another seemed to

WOULD IT HAVE CHANGED HISTORY?

Vienna's Academy of Fine Arts was famous not only for being a place Oskar Kokoschka unkindly described as 'a hotbed of conservatism and somewhere you went to become an artist in a velvet skirt and beret'. In 1907 an aspiring young Adolf Hitler sat the entry exam at the academy (the exam themes were Expulsion from Paradise, Hunting, Spring, Building Workers, Death – you get the idea). There were 128 applicants in Hitler's year and 28 were successful. Not Adolf. He desolately crawled back to Linz to lick his wounds and lived from his allowance as an orphan (his mother had died) before trying and failing a second time. Disillusioned, Hitler enlisted to fight on the Western Front in WWI. The rest is history.

be rambling on about computers. Court cases followed, and so too did a couple of convictions and a few months in prison for two of those involved. It was all about breaking down the taboos of society.

If some of the art of the 1960s, like the Fluxus style of happenings (picked up from a similar movement in the US), was theatrical and more like performance on an impromptu stage, Actionism took a more extreme form and covered a broad spectrum. Some of it was masochistic, self-abasing or employed blood rituals. At the hard-core end of the spectrum a picture might be produced in an orgy of dramatics with colour and materials being splashed and smeared collectively from various bodily cavities while the artists ascended into ever-higher states of frenzied ecstasy. At the more harmless end, a few people might get together and squirt some paint.

Actionism doesn't lend itself to the formal gallery environment. Some of it has been caught on video – salad-smeared bodies, close-ups of urinating penises, that sort of thing – and is often presented in Vienna's MUMOK (Museum Moderner Kunst). The Uni-Ferkelei action survives only in a few photographs and a couple of minutes of film footage. Günter Brus (b 1938), one of the participants, was convicted of 'denigrating an Austrian symbol of state'. His colleague of the day, Oswald Wiener (b 1935), is now an author and respected academic who went on to win one of the country's most prestigious literary prizes. Meanwhile, Hermann Nisch (b 1938), who staged theatrical events in the early 1960s based on music and painting and leaned heavily on sacrificial or religious rituals, has advanced to become Austria's best-known contemporary Viennese Actionist. His work can be found in Vienna's MUMOK, the Lentos Museum in Linz and in St Pölten's Landesmuseum.

Music

What other country can match the musical heritage of Austria or the creative force of its great composers? Even some of the Habsburgs were gifted musicians: Leopold I (1640–1705) composed, Karl VI (1685–1740) stroked a violin, his daughter Maria Theresia (1717–80) played a respectable double bass, while her son Joseph II was a deft hand at harpsichord and cello. But it's the greats we remember: Haydn, Mozart, Beethoven, Schönberg and – yes, even that contemporary great – Falco.

Vienna Classic

Wiener Klassik (Vienna Classic), which dates back to the mid- and late 18th century, very much defines the way we perceive classical music today. In its day, the epoch marked a move away from the celestial baroque music of the royal court and the church and brought forms of classical music such as opera and symphonies to the salons and theatres of the upper-middle classes of Vienna and Austria.

The earliest of the great composers was Joseph Haydn (1732–1809), who in his long career would tutor a budding young German-born

1900
Art Nouveau
Vienna becomes the world's art nouveau capital, with the likes of Gustav Klimt, Hans Makart and Kolo Moser working in the city.

1910–20
Expressionism
Seeking a new language of art, expressionists Egon Schiele and Oskar Kokoschka move to the forefront of Austrian painting.

1918–1939
New Objectivity
Postexpressionism takes root and international movements such as surrealism, futurism and cubism reach Austria, while from 1925 Neue Sachlichkeit (New Objectivity) moves away from the 'subjective' approach of expressionism.

1960s
Viennese
Actionism
After the Nazi era (when little of lasting significance was achieved), a period of post-WWII fantastic realism adopted esoteric themes; later Viennese Actionism brings 'happenings': pain, death, sex and abasement move to the fore.

21st Century
Contemporary
A neo-expressionist Neue Wilde (New Wild Ones) movement of the 1980s gives way to 21st-century explorations using digital graphics to complement conventional forms of painting.

composer by the name of Ludwig van Beethoven (1770–1827). Another well-known figure of the epoch was Franz Schubert (1797–1828), and one of the least known was the female 'blind virtuoso' Maria Theresia von Paradis (1759–1824). Von Paradis received voice training from the Italian composer Antonio Salieri (1750–1825), and this is where we get to the heart of the matter during this epoch: the much-discussed but possibly fictional rivalry between Antonio Salieri and Wolfgang Amadeus Mozart (1756–91).

Mozart & Salieri

Mozart was born in Salzburg. He tinkled out his first tunes on the piano at the age of four years, securing a dazzling reputation as Austria's Wunderkind. Salieri had been appointed by the Habsburgs in 1774 to head Italian opera at the royal court in the years following Mozart's meteoric rise. The stage was set for rivalries and intrigue, and this culminated in rumours that Salieri had murdered Mozart. We will never know whether he did or not (it's extremely unlikely that he did), but this is a moot point. The interesting thing is how much art has been born of the rumours. The most recent artistic masterpiece is the film *Amadeus* (1984), directed by Miloš Formann (b 1932). It won eight Academy awards and is widely considered to be the best of its ilk.

According to an interesting article published in the mid-1990s in the *Hong Kong Medical Journal*, even Mozart himself in his final year believed he had been poisoned, saying one day on a walk through a park with his wife that someone had slipped him aqua tofana. This happens to be a slow-acting concoction of arsenic and lead that was commonly used in Italy at the time. The same year, when an anonymous wealthy nobleman asked Mozart to compose a requiem, Mozart was convinced he had been commissioned by the devil to write one for his own Requiem Mass. The day of reckoning came. On New Year's Eve in 1791, Mozart died (the exact cause of death is unknown), causing the plot to thicken. One German newspaper remarked casually in an article on Mozart's demise that some people thought the great composer had been poisoned.

End of story for the time being. Then, some time in the 1820s, according to the *Hong Kong Medical Journal* article, a senile and crumbling Salieri allegedly confessed that he had poisoned Mozart. A couple of years later, he swore to someone else that he hadn't. By this time, though, Salieri was ready to shuffle off this mortal coil, having become a crumbling old man with dementia. The hapless Salieri only poured more fuel onto the fires of conspiracy when he sought to hasten his shuffle in an attempted suicide. This, the conspiracy theorists cried, was due to his being wracked by guilt.

Salieri died in 1825. Now the plot shifts to Russia. The Russian poet and playwright Alexander Pushkin wrote the original play *Mozart and Salieri* in 1830. The Russian connection grew stronger when Nikolay Rimsky-Korsakov created a short opera out of this. About 150 years later the British dramatist Peter Schaffer, inspired by Pushkin, penned his *Amadeus*, and this created the basis for the screenplay of Miloš Formann's film. The rumours had come a long way.

Vormärz & Revolutionary Eras

The epoch of Wiener Klassik was losing momentum in 19th-century Vienna and, with Mozart, Salieri, Haydn, Beethoven and the other great proponents dead or dying off, Austrian society and Europe as a whole experienced a period of repressive conservatism that culminated in revolutions across the continent in 1848 aimed at liberal reform. The prerevolutionary period was known as the Vormärz ('Pre-March' – the

---

Innovative composer Arnold Schönberg (1874–1951) stretched tonal conventions to snapping point with his 12-tone style of composition. The most influential of his pupils were Alban Berg (1885–1935) and Anton von Webern (1883–1945); both were born in Vienna and both continued the development of Schönberg's technique.

Indie Music & Artists

Kreisky

Ja Panik!

A Life, A Song, A Cigarette

Bunny Lake

Marilies Jagsch

Mika Vember

Garish

revolutions began in March 1848); the Vormärz sounded the final death knell for Wiener Klassik and produced a creative lull in music. It was only once the noise of the revolutions had died down that a new wave of composers – the likes of Franz Liszt (1811–86), Johannes Brahms (1833–97) and Anton Bruckner (1824–96) – arrived on the scene to take the legacy of Wiener Klassik and transform it into new and exciting forms.

Contemporary Music

Austria has some great musicians and contemporary acts. Although none so far has achieved the international fame of Falco (real name Hans Hölzel; 1957–98), whose 'Rock Me, Amadeus' topped the US charts in 1986, there are some great acts to check out.

Klagenfurt, the provincial capital of Carinthia, has brought forth some good musicians. While Penny McLean (born as Gertrude Wirschinger) gave the 1970s one of its iconic disco songs in the form of 'Lady Bump', the indisputable king is the crooner Udo Jürgens. He has been long seen as a *Schlager* singer (a broad genre of soft pop or even folk with a sentimental edge), but he composed hits for US greats such as Shirley Bassey and Frank Sinatra, and his style is comparable with Sinatra's. In the German-speaking world he is also as famous as Sinatra.

Naked Lunch (www.nakedlunch.de) is probably the best-known Austrian band since Falco. Going a bit deeper into the underground, the duo Attwenger (www.attwenger.at) has a large following for its music with flavours of folk, hip-hop and trance. Completing the triumvirate of relative old hands, Graz-based Rainer Binder-Krieglstein (b 1966; performs as binder & krieglstein, www.mikaella.org/bk) has gone from an eclectic blend of headz, hip-hop, groove and nujazz to concentrate on folk music today.

For pure hip-hop, Linz-based Texta (www.texta.at) is the most established in the art. The bizarre Bauchklang (www.bauchklang.com) is remarkable for using only voices – no instruments – for its reggae- and ethnic-influenced hip-hop and trance. This, of course, is absolutely normal compared to the equally remarkable Fuckhead (www.fuckhead.at), who, solely for a tendency to perform in plastic robes or gear that looks suspiciously like underwear, will obviously not be everyone's cup of tea. Afterwards you might be ready to tune into the saccharine flavours of popular rocker Christina Stürmer (b 1982; www.christinastuermer.de).

For more on what's happening in contemporary music (rock, jazz, pop, electronic, world music, classical and everything between and beyond) check out the Music Austria website www.music austria.at/en.

VISUAL ARTS & MUSIC MUSIC

Kaffeehäuser – Austria's Living Rooms

The Kaffeehäuser (coffee houses) of Austria, and especially its capital Vienna, are legendary. These are as much a part of social life and the cultural fabric of the country as the diner in the United States or the local pub in Britain and Australia.

The Noble Bean Reaches Europe

'The coffee house is a place where people have to go to kill time so that time doesn't end up killing them.' Alfred Polgar

The Dutch were probably the first to smuggle the coffee bean into Europe – in 1616, when they illegally carried back cultivable beans to Holland and began raising the plants in greenhouses. From Europe the coffee bean spread to the United States, where it was mentioned for the first time in 1668.

Back in Vienna in 1683, the Ottoman Turks were conducting their second great onslaught, the Second Turkish Siege, to wrest control of the Occident. The seige saw the Turkish general and grand vizier Kara Mustafa along with his eunuchs, concubines and 25,000 tents, huddle on the fringe of fortified central Vienna in the *Vorstadt* (inner suburbs; places like Josefstadt and Alsergrund today).

According to legend, a certain Georg Franz Koltschitzky dressed himself up as a Turk and brought a message behind Turkish lines from the field Marshal Karl I of Lothringen and was rewarded for his efforts with some war booty that included sacks of coffee beans. Legend also says that our clever Koltschitzky sniffed the beans and saw his chance to establish Vienna's first *Kaffeehaus*. Koltschitzky is also said to have been the first person to mix milk and sugar into the exotic elixir.

True connoisseurs of coffee history scorn this version and raise their hats to a spy by the name of Deodato, who because of his Armenian background was the perfect man to open up a *Kaffeehaus* with the sanction of the Habsburg monarchy. He did this in Vienna's central district at what today is Rotenturmstrasse 14. We will probably never know the truth about who did what, but we do know that *Kaffeehäuser* soon flourished in Vienna, and here coffee was served with a glass of water. *Kaffeehäuser* in the 17th century also had a billiard table, but playing cards in them wasn't allowed until the late 18th century.

Gradually, newspapers were introduced, and from the late 18th century the *Konzertcafe* (concert cafe) took hold – places where music was played. This cast the humble *Kaffeehaus* into a new role of being a place where the likes of Mozart, Beethoven and later Johann Strauss (the elder) could try out their works in the equivalent of open-stage or 'unplugged' performances.

When Austria adopted Napoleon's trade embargo against Britain in 1813 it lost almost its entire source of imported coffee beans. Although alternatives like chicory, rye and barley were tried, in the end the

COFFEE CONUNDRUMS

Ordering 'a coffee, please' won't go down well in most *Kaffeehäuser* (coffee houses). A quick glance at a menu will uncover a long list of choices, and a little time studying the options is advisable. A good coffee house will serve the cup of java on a silver platter accompanied by a glass of water and a small sweet. The selection of coffee includes the following:

➡ **Brauner** Black but served with a tiny splash of milk; comes in *Gross* (large) or *Klein* (small).

➡ **Einspänner** With whipped cream, served in a glass.

➡ **Fiaker** *Verlängerter* with rum and whipped cream.

➡ **Kapuziner** With a little milk and perhaps a sprinkling of grated chocolate.

➡ **Maria Theresia** With orange liqueur and whipped cream.

➡ **Masagran, Mazagran** Cold coffee with ice and Maraschino liqueur.

➡ **Melange** Viennese classic; served with milk, and maybe whipped cream too; similar to a cappuccino.

➡ **Mocca, Mokka, Schwarzer** Black coffee.

➡ **Pharisäer** Strong *Mocca* topped with whipped cream, served with a glass of rum.

➡ **Türkische** Comes in a copper pot with coffee grounds and sugar.

➡ **Verlängerter** *Brauner* weakened with hot water.

➡ **Wiener Eiskaffee** Cold coffee with vanilla ice cream and whipped cream.

Kaffeehäuser started serving food and wine, which is why today you can still get a light meal or a drink in a traditional *Kaffeehaus*.

Literary Kaffeehäuser

Come the late 19th century, elegant *Kaffeehäuser* sprang up along Vienna's Ringstrasse and everywhere a new 'literary coffee house' developed where writers could work in a warm room. Café Grienstedl was the first, but Café Central, the favourite of writers Peter Altenberg and Alfred Polgar, and architect Adolf Loos, is the best-known literary *Kaffeehaus*.

The writer Stefan Zweig saw them as an inimitable 'democratic club' bearing no likeness to the real world, but your average *Kaffeehaus* did have a clear pecking order. At the bottom of the heap was the *Piccolo* who set the tables and topped up the guests' water glass, while flirting like a gigolo with the grand ladies whenever a spare moment presented itself. The cashier (in the ideal case of coffee-house tradition, buxom, blonde and with jewellery dripping from her ears) wrote the bills and kept a watchful eye on the sugar.

At the top of the heap was the *Oberkellner* (*Herr Ober*, for short, or head waiter), who until 1800 used to be a ponytailed fellow with a dinner jacket, white tie, laced shoes, striped stockings and often a green apron. No *Herr Ober* dresses like this today (there are hints of the old garb, but none of the kinky stuff), but they do still rule the tables and the spaces between them in their dark attire.

Today you find more of a *Konditorei* (cake shop) atmosphere, and most continue to be the living rooms of the Viennese. These are places where you can drink coffee or wine, eat a goulash or light meal, read the newspapers or even enjoy a lounge vibe.

Vienna's Best...

Postmodern: Café Drechsler (p101)

Rustic: Café Leopold Hawelka (p99)

Views: Café Gloriette (p103)

Grand: Café Sacher (p99)

Quirky: Café Jelinek (p103)

The Austrian Alps

For many people, Austria *is* the Alps and no wonder. After all, these are the alpine pastures where Julie Andrews made her twirling debut in *The Sound of Music*; the mountains that inspired Mozart's symphonies; the slopes where Hannes Schneider revolutionised downhill skiing with his Arlberg technique. Olympic legends, Hollywood blockbusters and mountaineering marvels have been made and born here for decades.

Alpine Landscapes

www.naturschutz.at is a one-stop shop for info on Austria's landscape, flora and fauna. It's in German, but there are a few links to English sites.

The Alps engulf almost two-thirds of the 83,858 sq km that is Austria. It's almost as though someone chalked a line straight down the middle and asked all the Alps to shuffle to the west and all the flats to slide to the east, so stark is the contrast in this land of highs and lows. Over millenniums, elemental forces have dramatically shaped these mountain landscapes, etched with wondrous glaciers and forests, soaring peaks and gouged valleys.

The Austrian Alps divide neatly into three principal mountain ranges running in a west–east direction. The otherworldly karst landscapes of the Northern Limestone Alps, bordering Germany, reach nearly 3000m and extend almost as far east as the Wienerwald (Vienna Woods). The valley of the Inn River separates them from the granitic Central Alps, a chain which features the highest peaks in Austria dwarfed by the majestic summit of Grossglockner (3798m). The Southern Limestone Alps, which include the Karawanken Range, form a natural barrier with Italy and Slovenia.

From meltwater streams to misty falls, water is a major feature of the Austrian Alps. Mineral-rich rivers like the Enns, Salzach and Inn wend their way through broad valleys and provide a scenic backdrop for pursuits like rafting in summer. Lakes, too, come in all shapes and sizes, from glacially cold alpine tarns to the famously warm (around 28°C) waters of Wörthersee in Carinthia.

SEASON'S GREETINGS

Spring When the snow melts, the springtime eruption of colourful wildflowers sets senses on high alert. Look out for bell-shaped purple gentian and startlingly pink alpine roses.

Summer Stay overnight in a mountain hut, bathe in pristine alpine lakes and bring your walking boots for some highly scenic hiking on passes above 2000m.

Autumn The larch trees turn a beautiful shade of gold in late autumn and you might spot rutting stags. Come in late September for the *Almabtrieb*, where cows adorned with flowers and bells are brought down from the pastures for the winter.

Winter Snow, snow and more glorious snow. Enjoy first-class skiing, crisp mountain air and cheese-loaded alpine food. Your snug wood chalet on the mountainside awaits.

ALPINE PHOTO TIPS

Photo ops abound in the Austrian Alps, but capturing the moment can be tricky. Here are our tips for getting that mountain shot just right:

➡ Make the most of the diffused early-morning and evening light. Stay overnight in an alpine hut to get a head start.

➡ To get *really* white snow, you may need to increase the exposure.

➡ Get close-up wildlife photos with a telephoto zoom lens; moving too close unnerves animals. Stay calm and quiet.

➡ Think about composition: a hiker or a cyclist in the foreground gives your photo scale and highlights the immensity of the Alps.

➡ A polariser filter can help you capture that true blue sky.

Wildlife in the Austrian Alps

Nature reigns on an impressive scale in the Austrian Alps. The further you tiptoe away from civilisation and the higher you climb, the more likely you are to find rare animals and plant life in summer. Besides a decent pair of binoculars, bring patience and a sense of adventure.

Watching Wildlife

Dawn and dusk are the best times for a spot of wildlife-watching, though a lot boils down to luck. High on the must-see list is the ibex, a wild goat with curved horns, which was at one stage under threat but is fortunately now breeding again. It is the master of mountain climbing and migrates to 3000m or higher in the Austrian Alps come July. The chamois, a small antelope more common than the ibex, is equally at home scampering around on mountainsides. It can leap an astounding 4m vertically and its hooves have rubberlike soles and rigid outer rims – ideal for maintaining a good grip on loose rocks.

At heights of around 2000m, listen and look out for marmots, fluffy rodents related to the squirrel and native to the Alps. This sociable animal lives in colonies of about two dozen members. Like meerkats, marmots regularly post sentries, which stand around on their hind legs looking alert. They whistle once for a predator from the air (like an eagle) and twice when a predator from the ground (such as a fox) is approaching and the whole tribe scurries to safety down a network of burrows.

Ornithologists flock to the Austrian Alps for a chance to see golden eagles, falcons and vultures – both bearded and griffin.

Endangered Species

Austria's most endangered species is the *Bayerische Kurzohrmaus* (Bavarian pine vole), which is endemic to Tyrol and found only in six localities. Following close behind is the *Kaiseradler* (imperial eagle), at one time extinct in Austria but fortunately staging a comeback through re-immigration. The *Europäische Hornotter* (long-nosed viper) may be a venomous snake at home in Carinthia, but humans are a far greater threat to its survival than its bite will ever be to ours.

Teetering on the brink of extinction, the Austrian Alps' population of brown bears is very low (estimated at less than 10), boosted now and then by inquisitive souls arriving from Slovenia and Italy. They only really appear in the Karawanks (Karawanken), Karnisch Alps (Karnischen Alpen) and Gailtal Alps (Gailtaler Alpen) in Carinthia, as well as in Osttirol. The survival of local populations and safety of transitory bears very much depends on the efforts of organisations like Austria's Brown Bear

Best Places to (Maybe) See...

Marmots: Kaiser-Franz-Josefs-Höhe, Grossglockner Rd

Golden eagles: Hohe Tauern National Park

Lynx: Nationalpark Kalkalpen

Falcons: Nationalpark Gesäuse

Ibex: Northern Limestone Alps

FLORAL HIGH FIVE

➡ **Edelweiss** Star-shaped white flowers found on rocky crags and crevices.

➡ **Gentian** Bell-shaped blue flowers of the high Alps.

➡ **Alpine crowfoot** Early-flowering anemone-like blooms.

➡ **Arnica** Bright yellow daisylike flowers found in alpine meadows.

➡ **Alpine roses** Hot pink rhododendron-like flowers.

Life Project and the WWF, which have invested millions of euros into bringing the bear back to the Alps and fostering awareness.

For the low-down on endangered species, consult the **Rote Liste** (www.umweltbundesamt.at), collated by the Umweltbundesamt (Federal Environment Agency).

Alpine Flora

Below the treeline, much of the Austrian Alps is thickly forested. At low altitudes you can expect to find deciduous birch and beech forests, while coniferous trees such as pine, spruce and larch thrive at higher elevations. At around 2000m trees yield to *Almen* (alpine pastures) and dwarf pines; beyond 3000m only mosses and lichens cling to the stark crags.

A highlight of the Austrian Alps are its flowers, which bring a riot of scent and colour to the high pastures from May to September. The species here are hardy, with long roots to counter strong winds, bright colours to repel some insects, and petals to ward against frost and dehydration.

Spring brings crocuses, alpine snowbells and anemones; summer alpine roses and gentians; and autumn thistles, delphiniums and blue aconites. Tempting though it may be to pick them, these flowers really do look lovelier on the slopes and most are protected species.

Men once risked life and limb to pluck edelweiss from the highest crags of the Alps for their sweethearts. The woolly bloom is Austria's national flower, symbolising bravery, love and strength.

National Parks in the Austrian Alps

For an area of such mind-blowing natural beauty, it may come as a surprise to learn that there are just three national parks (Hohe Tauern, Kalkalpen and Gesäuse) as well as one major nature reserve (Nockberge) in the Austrian Alps. But statistics aren't everything, particularly when one of these national parks is the magnificent Hohe Tauern, the Alps' largest and Europe's second-largest national park, which is a tour de force of 3000m peaks, immense glaciers and waterfalls.

The national-park authorities have managed to strike a good balance between preserving the wildlife and keeping local economic endeavours such as farming, hunting and tourism alive. The website www.nationalparksaustria.at has links to all national parks and a brochure in English to download.

Aside from national parks, protected areas and nature reserves are dotted all over the Austrian Alps, from the mesmerising mountainscapes of Naturpark Zillertaler Alpen in Tyrol to the lakes of the Salzkammergut. See www.naturparke.at for the low-down on Austria's nature parks.

Austria's Extremes

Europe's highest waterfall: 380m-high Krimmler Wasserfälle

World's largest accessible ice caves: Eisriesenwelt, Werfen

Largest national park in the Alps: Hohe Tauern (1786 sq km)

Longest glacier in the Eastern Alps: the 8km Pasterze Glacier

Austria's highest peak: 3798m Grossglockner (literally 'Big Bell')

A right pair of lovebirds, golden eagles stay together for life. See www.birdlife.at to find out more about these elusive raptors and other Austrian bird life.

Austria's Alpine Environment

Given the fragile ecosystem of the Austrian Alps, conservation, renewable energy and sustainable tourism are red-hot topics. In the face of retreating glaciers, melting snow, dwindling animal numbers and erosion, the people of the Alps come face to face with global warming and human impact on the environment on a daily basis.

Measures have been in place for years to protect Austria's alpine regions, yet some forest degradation has taken place due to air and soil pollution caused by emissions from industrial plants, exhaust fumes and the use of agricultural chemicals.

The good news is that Austrians are, by and large, a green and nature-loving lot. Recently, everyone from top hoteliers in St Anton to farmers in Salzburgerland has been polishing their eco credentials by promoting recycling and solar power, clean energy and public transport.

The government has moved to minimise pollutants by banning leaded petrol, assisting businesses in waste avoidance and encouraging renewable energy, such as wind and solar power. Some buses are gas powered and environmentally friendly trams are a feature of many cities.

Global Warming

With global warming a sad reality, 'snow-sure' is becoming more wishful thinking in resorts at lower elevations in the Austrian Alps. Every year, the snowline seems to edge slightly higher and snow-making machines are constantly on standby.

A United Nations Environment Programme (UNEP) report on climate change warned that rising temperatures could mean that 75% of alpine glaciers will disappear within the next 45 years, and that dozens of low-lying ski resorts such as Kitzbühel (762m) will be completely cut off from their slopes by 2030. Forecasts suggest that the snowline will shift from 1200m to 1800m by 2100. As well as the impact on Austria's tourist industry, the melting snow is sure to have other knock-on effects, including erosion, floods and an increased risk of avalanches.

Melting ice is a hot topic in the Hohe Tauern National Park. The Pasterze Glacier has shrunk to half its size over the past 150 years and is predicted to disappear entirely within 100 years.

THE AUSTRIAN ALPS AUSTRIA'S ALPINE ENVIRONMENT

ALPINE NATIONAL PARKS

PARK (AREA)	FEATURES	FAUNA	ACTIVITIES	BEST TIME	WEBSITE
Gesäuse (110 sq km)	rivers, meadows, gorges, thick forest, limestone peaks	owls, eagles, falcons, deer, bats, woodpeckers	hiking, rafting, caving, mountain biking, rock climbing	spring, summer, autumn	www.nationalpark.co.at
Hohe Tauern (1786 sq km)	classic alpine scenery with 3000m mountains, glaciers, lakes, high alpine pastures	ibex, chamois, marmots, bearded vultures, golden eagles	hiking, rock climbing & mountaineering, skiing, canyoning, paragliding	year-round	www.hohetauern.at
Kalkalpen (210 sq km)	high moors, mixed forest, rugged limestone mountains	lynx, brown bears, golden eagles, owls, woodpeckers, butterflies	hiking, cycling, rock climbing, cross-country skiing	year-round	www.kalkalpen.at
Nockberge (184 sq km)	gentle rounded peaks, alpine pastures, woodlands	marmots, snow eagles, alpine salamanders, butterflies	walking, climbing, cross-country & downhill skiing	year-round	www.nationalparknockberge.at

ECO SNOW

In a bid to offset the impact of skiing, many Austrian resorts are taking the green run with ecofriendly policies. For more details on reducing your carbon snowprint, see www. saveoursnow.com.

➡ Lech in Vorarlberg scores top points for its biomass communal heating plant, the photovoltaic panels that operate its chairlifts and its strict recycling policies.

➡ Zell am See launched Austria's first ISO-certified cable car at the Kitzsteinhorn Glacier. It operates a free ski bus in winter and runs an ecological tree- and grass-planting scheme.

➡ Kitzbühel operates green building and climate policies, and is taking measures to reduce traffic and the use of nonrenewable energy sources.

➡ St Anton am Arlberg has created protected areas to reduce erosion and pumps out artificial snow without chemicals. Its excellent train connections mean fewer cars.

➡ Ischgl uses renewable energy; recycles in all hotels, lifts and restaurants; and has a night-time driving ban from 11pm to 6am.

➡ Mayrhofen operates its lifts on hydroelectricity, separates all waste and has free ski buses to reduce traffic in the village.

Skiing

Austria's highly lucrative ski industry is a double-edged sword. On the one hand, resorts face mounting pressure to develop and build higher up on the peaks to survive; on the other, their very survival is threatened by global warming. For many years, ski resorts have not done the planet many favours: mechanically grading pistes disturbs wildlife and causes erosion, artificial snow affects native flora and fauna, and trucking in snow increases emissions.

However, many Austrian resorts now realise that they are walking a thin tightrope and are mitigating their environmental impact with renewable hydroelectric power, biological wastewater treatment and ecological buildings.

Survival Guide

Directory A–Z

Accommodation

From simple mountain huts to five-star hotels fit for kings – you will find a wide choice of accommodation in Austria. Tourist offices invariably keep lists and details, and some arrange bookings for a small fee, while others will help free of charge.

Facilities

Most hotel rooms in Austria have their own shower, although hostels and some rock-bottom digs usually have an *Etagendousche* (corridor shower). The better rooms have bath-tubs. Very often a hotel won't have lifts; if this is important, always check ahead. Tea- and coffee-making facilities are the exception rather than the rule.

Reservations & Cancellations

It's wise to book ahead at all times. Often a day or two in advance is sufficient, but reserve at least one week ahead to increase the chances of getting into your hotel of choice on Friday and Saturday nights, during the high season in July and August, and much longer ahead at Christmas, Easter and between December and April in ski areas. Some places require email confirmation following a telephone reservation but many places are also bookable online. Confirmed reservations in writing are binding, and cancellations within several days of expected arrival often involve a fee or full payment.

Guest Cards

In some resorts (not often in cities) a *Gästekarte* (guest card) is issued if you stay overnight. This card may offer discounts on things such as cable cars and admission, so check with a tourist office if you're not offered one at your resort accommodation.

Websites

Here are some good international and local websites for scanning and booking accommodation. Locally, always check the city or region website listed in that section, as many (such as in Vienna, Salzburg and Graz) have an excellent booking function.

Austrian Hotelreservation (www.austrian-hotelreservation.at)

Austrian National Tourist Office (www.austria.info)

Booking.com (www.booking.com)

Camping in Österreich (www.campsite.at)

Expedia (www.expedia.com)

Hostelling International (HI; www.hihostels.com)

Hostelworld (www.hostelworld.com)

Hotel.de (www.hotel.de)

Alpine Huts

There are over 400 of these huts in the Austrian Alps maintained by the **Österreichischer Alpenverein** (ÖAV; Austrian Alpine Club; www.alpenverein.at) and the German Alpine Club (DAV). Huts are found at altitudes between 313m and 3277m, and may be used by anyone. Meals or cooking facilities are often available. Bed prices for nonmembers are from €20. Members of the ÖAV or affiliated clubs pay at least €10 less and have priority. Contact the ÖAV or a local tourist office for lists of huts and to make bookings.

Camping

Austria has some 500 camping grounds that offer users a range of facilities such as washing machines, electricity connections, on-site shops and, occasionally, cooking facilities. Camping

---

BOOK YOUR STAY ONLINE

For more accommodation reviews by Lonely Planet authors, check out http://lonelyplanet.com/hotels/. You'll find independent reviews, as well as recommendations on the best places to stay. Best of all, you can book online.

gas canisters are widely available. Camp sites are often scenically situated in an out-of-the-way place by a river or lake – fine if you're exploring the countryside but inconvenient if you want to sightsee in a town. For this reason, and because of the extra gear required, camping is more viable if you have your own transport. Prices can be as low as €5 per person or small tent and as high as €12.

A majority of the camp sites close in the winter. If demand is low in spring and autumn, some camp sites shut, even though their literature says they are open, so telephone ahead to check during these periods.

Free camping in camper vans is allowed in autobahn rest areas and alongside other roads, as long as you're not causing an obstruction. It's illegal to camp in tents in these areas.

While in the country, pick up camping guides in bookshops or from the **Österreichischer Camping Club** (Austrian Camping Club; Map p62; ☑01-713 61 51; www.campingclub.at; Schubertring 1-3, Vienna) and the useful *Camping* brochure-map from the national tourism authority **Österreich Werbung** (www.austria.info), with international representatives.

Eco-Hotels

So-called *Bio-* or *Öko-* ('eco') hotels are widespread in Austria. Most of them are located outside towns in picturesque settings. Not a few of the hotels have wellness facilities like saunas and steam baths, and because of their rural location they often have winter skiing and activities. Generally, you will need to have your own wheels – a car or a bicycle – to reach these. Tourist offices keep lists or have a special section in their accommodation listings and on websites. The website www.biohotels.info also has a brief list.

Farmstays

If you have your own transport and want to get away from the towns, staying on a farm is a nice way to get away from it all. You will find lots of conventional *Bauernhöfe* (farmhouses) in rural areas. Most rent out apartments for a minimum of three nights, but some also have rooms accepting guests for one night. Depending on the region and type of accommodation, the cheapest cost from about €35 per person, going up to about €100 or more per night for a slick apartment with all mod cons.

In mountainous regions you will find *Almhütten* (alpine meadow huts), usually part of a farmstead. Some of these can be accessed by cable car, some by road, and the more isolated ones only by foot or by mountain bike on forestry tracks. Most are closed from October to April or May. During the day these isolated huts or *Gasthöfe* (inns) serve snacks or meals to hikers and mountain bikers, and many offer simple rooms (usually with shared bathrooms) and full board in rustic rooms, usually in wooden buildings.

The websites www.urlaubaufderalm.com and www.farmholidays.com are good places to look for farmstays, whereas tourist offices can also help with local mountain-top *Almhütten*.

Hostels

Austria is dotted with *Jugendherberge* (youth hostels) or *Jugendgästehaus* (youth guesthouses). Facilities are often excellent: four- to six-bed dorms with shower/toilet are the norm in hostels, while many guesthouses have double rooms or family rooms; internet facilities, free wi-fi and a restaurant or cafe are commonplace.

Austria has over 100 hostels affiliated with **HI** (www.hihostels.com), plus a smattering of privately owned hostels.

Memberships cards are always required, except in a few private hostels, but nonmembers pay a surcharge of about €3.50 per night and after six nights the stamped Welcome Card counts as full membership. Most hostels accept reservations by telephone or email and are part of the worldwide computer reservations system through the HI website. Average dorm prices are about €22 per night.

HI hostels are run by two hostel organisations (either can provide information on all HI hostels). JUFA is a guesthouse organisation with a loose affiliation.

Österreichischer Jugendherbergsverband (ÖJHV; ☑01-533 53 53; www.oejhv.or.at; Zelinkagasse 12, Vienna; ☺11am-5pm Mon-Fri, to 3pm Fri Sep-Mar; ⓜSchottenring, ⓡ1, 31 Schottenring)

Österreichischer Jugendherbergswerk (ÖJHW; Map p76; ☎01-533 18 33; www.jungehotels.at; Mariahilfer Strasse 22-24, Vienna; ⏰10am-6pm Mon-Thu, to 5pm Fri; Ⓜ Museumsquartier)

JUFA (☎05 70 83; www.jufa.at; ⏰8am-8pm Mon-Fri, 9am-1pm Sat) There are 40 JUFA guesthouses scattered around Austria, any of which can be booked by telephone on a local number, through the central booking service or online. They generally offer a higher standard of facilities than youth hostels and specialise in singles, doubles and family rooms. An average price is about €40 to €60 for a single room with bathroom and toilet, and €35 to €40 per person in a double or family room. Prices usually vary by demand.

Hotels & Pensionen

The majority of travellers stay in either a hotel or a *Pension* or *Gasthof* (B&B or guesthouse). All are rated by the same criteria for stars (from one to five stars). Hotels invariably offer more services, including bars, restaurants and garage parking, whereas *Pensionen* and guesthouses tend to be smaller than hotels and have fewer standardised fixtures and fittings but sometimes larger rooms.

TWO STARS

Functional rooms with cheap furnishings. Most cost under €40/80 per single/double but in many cases you're better off booking a good hostel room. Often more central than a hostel and near the train station. Breakfast is unlikely to thrill. The shower is in the room, but might be a booth.

THREE STARS

Most accommodation is in this midrange category. The majority of singles cost about €60 to €70, doubles €120 to €130 (from about €70/140 for a single/double in Vienna). Expect good clean rooms and a decent buffet breakfast. Usually there will be a minibar and snacks; often you have a place to sit or a desk to write on. Internet and either wi-fi or cable LAN is available, often free or inexpensively. Some specialise in catering to seminar guests. Showers and TVs (often flat screens) are in rooms.

FOUR AND FIVE STARS

Rooms in a four-star hotel or *Pension* are generally larger than those in a three-star hotel and should have better sound insulation as well as contemporary or quality furnishings. Expect decent wellness facilities in a four-star option, premium facilities in five-star hotels.

Private Rooms

Rooms in private houses are cheap (about €50 per double) and in most towns you will see *Privat Zimmer* (private room) or *Zimmer Frei* (room free) signs. Most hosts are friendly; the level of service is lower than in hotels.

Rental Accommodation

Ferienwohnungen (self-catering holiday apartments) are very common in Austrian mountain resorts, though it is sometimes necessary to book these well in advance. The best idea is to contact a local tourist office for lists and prices or book online if possible using the local tourist-office website.

University Accommodation

Studentenheime (student residences) are available to tourists over university summer breaks (from the beginning of July to around the end of September). Some rooms have a private bathroom but often there's no access to the communal kitchen. The widest selection is in Vienna, but tourist

---

PRACTICALITIES

→ **Seasonal opening hours** Opening hours can vary significantly between the high season (April to October) and winter – many sights and tourist offices are on reduced hours from November to March. Opening hours we provide are for the high season, so outside those months it can be useful to check ahead.

→ **Seasonal prices** In mountain resorts, high-season prices can be up to double the prices charged in the low season (May and November, which fall between the summer and winter seasons in mountains). In other towns, the difference may be 10% or less.

→ **Concession prices** Many sights have concessions for families and for children (generally under 16 years). Some places also have reduced student and senior citizen admission prices, which are generally slightly higher than the child's price. Children under 12 years usually receive a substantial discount on rooms they share with parents. Ask when booking. Children also travel at reduced rates on public transport.

→ **Smoking** Unless a separate room has been set aside, smoking is not allowed in restaurants, wherever food is served or in all but the smallest, one-room drinking venues. That's the theory. In practice Austria is a smoker's paradise as controls are lax. Look for the stickers on doors saying whether smoking is allowed in all or part of a place. It's legal to smoke anywhere on outdoor terraces. Most hotels stick to the smoking ban.

offices in Graz, Salzburg, Krems an der Donau and Innsbruck can point you in the right direction. Prices per person are likely to range from €20 to €75 per night and sometimes include breakfast. **Academia Hotels** (Map p74; ☏01-401 76 55; www.academiahotels.at; 08, Pfeilgasse 3a, Vienna; ☉rooms Jul-Sep; ☲46 Strozzigasse) handles bookings for its residencies in Vienna, Graz and Salzburg. Prices given above are for Vienna.

Children

Practicalities

FACILITIES

Facilities for travellers with kids are good. Some museums (especially in Vienna) have a children's play area; restaurants offer child portions and have high chairs; and many hotels have rooms that are connected by a door, making them especially suitable for families. In most hotels and *Pensionen* children under 12 years receive substantial discounts. Midrange and better hotels have cots (but book ahead). Family- or child-friendly hotels are highlighted in reviews.

RESTAURANTS

Most midrange restaurants have a child's menu or will prepare smaller portions for children if you ask. A few have a play area.

TRAVELLING WITH BABIES

Breastfeeding in public won't cause eyelids to bat. Everything you need for babies, such as formula and disposable nappies, is widely available in *Drogerien* (drug stores).

GETTING AROUND

Rental-car companies can arrange safety seats. Newer public transport, such as trams and buses in Vienna, are easily accessible for buggies and prams, but the older

Climate

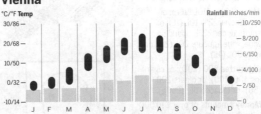

Innsbruck

Salzburg

Vienna

models can prove a nightmare. Children under six years usually travel free on public transport, or half-price until 15 years of age.

RESOURCES

Log on to www.kinderhotels.at for information on child-friendly hotels throughout the country.

Sights & Activities

Regional tourist offices often produce brochures aimed directly at families. Museums, parks and theatres often have programs for children over the summer holiday periods, and local councils occasionally put on special events and festivals for the little ones. Many museums in Vienna are free for those under 18 or 19 years. With its

parks, playgrounds and great outdoors, Austria has plenty to keep the kids amused.

Swimming Many lakes have a supervised beach area.

Hiking Lots of easy family walks as well as challenging ones in most places.

Cable cars and panoramic walkways Freak-out or tamer varieties, great rides and lookouts aplenty.

Museums and more Good ones include Zoom (p79), Haus der Musik (p65), FriDa & FreD (p179), Schlossberg Cave Railway (p179), Ars Electronica (p152), the Pöstlingbergbahn (p155), Minimundus miniature park (p263) and the Marionettentheater (p236).

Going underground Erzberg mine (p192) in Styria and the salt mines of Salzkammergut offer good experiences.

Customs Regulations

Austrian customs regulations are in line with all other EU countries. Items such as weapons, certain drugs (both legal and illegal), meat, certain plant materials and animal products are subject to strict customs control. All goods must be for personal use. The **Ministry of Finance** (http://english.bmf. gv.at) website has an overview of regulations. Below are some key guidelines for anyone 17 years or older importing items from an EU or non-EU country. The amounts in brackets are for items imported from outside the EU; if tobacco products don't have health warnings in the German language, these too are limited to the amounts given in brackets.

Alcohol Beer 110L (16L); or spirits over 22% 10L (1L); or spirits under 22%, sparkling wine, wine liqueurs 20L (2L); or wine 90L (4L).

Cigarettes 800 (200); or cigarillos 400 (100); or cigars 200 (50); or tobacco 1kg (250g).

Money Amounts of over €10,000 in cash or in travellers cheques (or the equivalent in cash in a foreign currency) must be declared on entering or leaving the EU. There is no limit within the EU, but authorities are entitled to request accurate information on the amount you are carrying.

Discount Cards

Various discount cards are available. Some are free with an overnight stay, some cost a few euros or, like the Kärnten Card in Carinthia, cards can cost €36 for one week but offer substantial benefits such as a 50% reduction on buses and trains.

SENIOR CARDS

In some cases senior travellers will be able to get discount admission to sights, but local proof is often required. It can't hurt to ask and show proof of age, though. The minimum qualifying age for Austrians is 60 or 65 for men and 60 for women.

STUDENT/YOUTH CARDS

International Student Identity Cards (ISIC) and European Youth Card (Euro<26; check www.euro26.org for discounts) will get you discounts at most museums, galleries and theatres. Admission is generally a little higher than the price for children.

Electricity

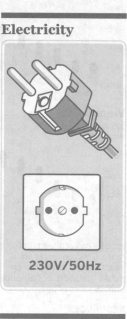

230V/50Hz

Food

See Eat & Drink Like a Local (p46) for information on Austrian cuisine and eating price ranges.

Gay & Lesbian Travellers

Vienna is reasonably tolerant towards gays and lesbians, more so than the rest of the country. Austria is these days close to Western European par on attitudes towards homosexuality.

Online information (in German) can be found at www.gayboy.at, www.rainbow.at, www.gayoesterreich. at and www.gaynet.at. The *Spartacus International Gay Guide,* published by Bruno Gmünder (Berlin), is a good international directory of gay entertainment venues worldwide (mainly for men).

Health

Travelling in Austria presents very few health risks. The water everywhere can be safely drunk from the tap, and the water in the lakes and streams is for the most part excellent and poses no risk of infection.

Recommended vaccinations The World Health Organization (WHO) recommends that all travellers should be covered for diphtheria, tetanus, measles, mumps, rubella and polio, as well as hepatitis B, regardless of their destination. A vaccination for tick-borne encephalitis is highly advisable.

Wasps and mosquitos Wasps can be a problem in midsummer but are only dangerous for those with an allergy or if you are stung in the throat. Look before you take a sip outdoors from a sweet drink. Mosquitoes can be a nuisance around lakes.

Tick-Borne Diseases

Ticks can carry lyme disease and encephalitis, and pose a serious outdoor hazard to health in many parts of Europe. They are usually found below 1200m in undergrowth at the forest edge or beside walking tracks.

Wearing long trousers tucked into walking boots or socks and using a DEET-based insect repellent is the best prevention against tick bites. If a tick is found attached, press down around the tick's head with tweezers, grab the tick as close as possible to the head and rotate continuously in one direction, without pulling, until the tick releases itself. Pharmacies sell plastic or metal tweezers especially for this purpose (highly recommended for hikers). Avoid pulling the rear of the body or smearing chemicals on the tick.

Lyme disease Also known as *Borreliose*, this is a bacterial infection caused by ticks and has serious long-term consequences if left untreated with antibiotics. It is often possible to recognise in the early stage (a rash or red infection around the bite). There is no vaccination against it.

Tickborne Eencephalitis This is called FSME in Austria. It is a serious infection of the brain and *vaccination is highly advised* for risk groups and in risk areas (especially campers, climbers and hikers). Austrians who are in risk groups or risk areas have usually been vaccinated. Distribution of tickborne encephalitis is uneven; the website www.zecken.at (go to FSME then Verbreitungsgebiete Österreich) has an interactive map showing dangerous areas. Local pharmacists always know whether FSME is a danger in their region and can advise if you're bitten.

Insurance

No matter how long or short your trip, make sure you have adequate travel insurance or are at least covered for the cost of emergency medical treatment. Worldwide travel insurance is available at www.lonelyplanet.com/travel_services. You can buy, extend and claim online anytime – even if you're already on the road.

HEALTH INSURANCE

If you are not an EU citizen and your country doesn't have a reciprocal arrangement with Austria for treatment costs, don't leave home without insurance. The USA, Canada, Australia and New Zealand don't have reciprocal agreements. Otherwise, expect to pay anything from €40 to €75 for a straightforward, nonurgent consultation with a doctor. Make sure you get a policy that covers you for

the worst possible scenario, such as an accident requiring an emergency flight home. Find out in advance if your insurance plan will make payments directly to providers or reimburse you later for overseas health expenditures, and whether it covers all activities (like skiing or climbing). If you're an EU citizen, a European Health Insurance Card (EHIC), available from your healthcare provider, covers you for most medical care. The cards will not cover you for nonemergencies or emergency repatriation home.

OTHER INSURANCE

Components of insurance worth considering include repatriation for medical treatment, burial or repatriation in the event of death, search and rescue, cost of returning home in case of illness or the death of a close relative, personal liability and legal expenses, loss of passport, luggage loss or delay, and expenses due to cancellations for a variety of reasons. For transport insurance see p393 and p397.

Internet Access

Wi-fi Available in most hotels of three-star quality or more. It's also free in many cafes and bars, and increasingly in public spaces like the MuseumsQuartier in Vienna and in town squares around Austria. Many tourist offices also have *WLAN* ('vee-lan') as it's called in German. Sometimes you need a password from staff. A wi-fi icon (🛜) in a listing in this book means a hotel has wi-fi access either in the room or in a public area for free. If it is not free, we've mentioned this in our reviews.

Internet terminals Many hotels have internet terminals that guests can use for free or for a small cost. In this book @ icons in reviews indicate these places.

Public access Prices in internet cafes vary from around €4 to €8 per hour. Small towns often won't have internet cafes but the

local library will probably have a terminal.

Smart Phones Make sure you turn off mobile data while roaming on your smart phone, otherwise you (and some of your apps) might run up a horrendous telephone bill. While there are sufficient free hotspots to rely on across the country if you have a mobile device with wi-fi capabilities. Otherwise you can buy prepaid SIM cards without formalities. This will allow you to surf with your tablet computer, surf stick or mobile phone (if there is no SIM lock).

Resources See www.freewave.at/en/hotspots for free hot spots in Vienna, and www.freewlan.at for Austria-wide hot spots.

Legal Matters

Carry your passport (or a copy) with you at all times, as police occasionally do checks. If you are arrested, the police must inform you of your rights in a language that you understand.

In Austria, legal offences are divided into two categories: *Gerichtsdelikt* (criminal) and *Verwaltungsübertretung* (administrative). If you are suspected of having committed a criminal offence (such as assault or theft) you can be detained for a maximum of 48 hours before you are committed for trial. If you are arrested for a less serious, administrative offence, such as being drunk and disorderly or committing a breach of the peace, you will be released within 24 hours.

Drunken driving is an administrative offence, even if you have an accident. If someone is hurt in the accident it becomes a criminal offence. Possession of a controlled drug is usually a criminal offence. Possession of a large amount of cannabis or dealing (especially to children) could result in a five-year prison term. Prostitution is legal provided prostitutes are registered and have a permit.

Legal Advice

If you are arrested, you have the right to make one phone call to 'a person in your confidence' within Austria, and another to inform legal counsel. If you can't afford legal representation, you can apply to the judge in writing for legal aid.

As a foreigner, your best bet when encountering legal problems is to contact your national consulate for advice.

Money

Like other members of the European Monetary Union (EMU), Austria's currency is the euro, which is divided into 100 cents. There are coins for one, two, five, 10, 20 and 50 cents, and for €1 and €2. Notes come in denominations of €5, €10, €20, €50, €100, €200 and €500. See Need to Know (p21) for exchange rates.

ATMs

Bankomaten (ATMs) are extremely common everywhere and accessible till midnight. Some are 24 hours. Most accept at the very least Maestro debit cards and Visa and MasterCard credit cards. There are English instructions and daily withdrawal limits of €400 with credit and debit cards. Check with your home bank before travelling for charges for using a *Bankomat*; there's usually no commission to pay at the Austrian end.

Cash & Emergency Transfers

ATMs mean that you don't need to carry large amounts of cash or use money-changing facilities. It is worth keeping a small amount in a safe place for emergencies. **Western Union** (www.western-union.com) money offices are available in larger towns for emergency transfers.

Credit Cards

Visa and MasterCard (Euro-Card) are accepted a little more widely than American Express (Amex) and Diners Club, although a surprising number of shops and restaurants refuse to accept any credit cards at all. Upmarket shops, hotels and restaurants will accept cards, though. Train tickets can be bought by credit card in main stations. Credit cards allow you to get cash advances at ATMs and over the counter at most banks.

For lost or stolen credit cards:

Amex (☑0810 910 940)

Diners Club (☑in Vienna 01-501 35 14)

MasterCard (☑0800 218 235)

Visa (☑0800 200 288, followed by 800 892 8134)

Taxes

Mehrwertsteuer (MWST; value-added tax) in Austria is set at 20% for most goods. Prices are always displayed inclusive of all taxes. Shops with a 'Global Refund Tax Free Shopping' sticker have the paperwork to reclaim about 13% of this tax on single purchases over €75 by non-EU citizens or residents. See www.globalrefund.com for more information. Refund desks are at the department stores **Gerngross** (Map p76; ☑01521 80; Mariahilfer Strasse 38-40) and **Steffl** (Map p62; ☑01514 31-0; Kärntner Strasse 19) in Vienna, and in Graz at **Kastner & Öhler** (Map p176; Sackstrasse 7-11; ☑9.30am-7pm Mon-Fri, to 6pm Sat). Vienna and Salzburg airports also have refund desks. It's easiest to claim this before leaving the country rather than at home.

Tipping

This is part of everyday life in Austria; in restaurants, bars and cafes and in taxis it's customary to give about 10%. Add the bill and the tip together and hand it over in one lump sum. It also doesn't hurt to tip hairdressers, hotel porters, cloak-room attendants, cleaning staff and tour guides one or two euros.

Opening Hours

Normal opening hours in Austria are as follows. For information on seasonal opening hours, see p384.

Banks From 8am or 9am until 3pm Monday to Friday, extended hours to 5.30pm on Thursdays. Many of the smaller branches close from 12.30pm to 1.30pm.

Cafes Hours vary considerably. Usually 7am or 8am to 11pm or midnight; some traditional coffee houses and cafes close at 7pm or 8pm.

Offices and government departments Usually from 8am to 3.30pm, 4pm or 5pm Monday to Friday.

Post offices Core hours are 8am to noon and 2pm to 6pm Monday to Friday; some also open 8am to noon Saturday, and many are open all day Monday to Friday.

Pubs and bars Close anywhere between midnight and about 4am.

Restaurants Generally 11am to 2.30pm or 3pm and 6pm to 11pm or midnight. The kitchen often closes an hour earlier in the evening and in some is open all day.

Shops Most open from 9am to 6.30pm Monday to Friday (often to 9pm Thursday or Friday in cities), from 9am to 5pm Saturday.

Public Holidays

Basically, everything shuts down on public holidays. The only establishments open are bars, cafes and restaurants, and even some of these don't open. Museums are usually – but not universally – open. The big school break is in July and August. This is a time when most families go on holiday so you'll find some places, like cities, a little quieter and others, such as popular holiday destinations, busier. Avoid ski breaks during much of February; school pupils have a week off during that time and invariably the ski slopes are full to overflowing with kids and parents. Plan bus trips more carefully on public holidays – services are usually reduced.

New Year's Day (Neujahr) 1 January

Epiphany (Heilige Drei Könige) 6 January

Easter Monday (Ostermontag) March/April

Labour Day (Tag der Arbeit) 1 May

Whit Monday (Pfingstmontag) 6th Monday after Easter

Ascension (Christi Himmelfahrt) 6th Thursday after Easter

Corpus Christi (Fronleichnam) 2nd Thursday after Whitsunday

Assumption (Maria Himmelfahrt) 15 August

National Day (Nationalfeiertag) 26 October

All Saints' Day (Allerheiligen) 1 November

Immaculate Conception (Mariä Empfängnis) 8 December

Christmas Day (Christfest) 25 December

St Stephen's Day (Stephanitag) 26 December

Telephone

Country code Austria's country code is 🖉0043.

Area codes Each town and region has its own area code beginning with '0' (eg '🖉01' for Vienna). Drop this when calling from outside Austria; use it for all landline calls inside Austria except for local calls or special toll and toll-free numbers.

Mobile, free and toll numbers Austrian *Handy* (mobile phone) numbers begin with 🖉0650 or higher up to 🖉0699 (eg 🖉0664/plus the rest of the number). All 🖉0800 numbers are free; 🖉0810 and 🖉0820 numbers cost €0.10 and €0. 20 respectively per minute; and 🖉0900 numbers are exorbitant and best avoided. Some large

organisations have '🖉050' numbers, which do not need an area code (a local call from a landline, but more expensive from a mobile phone).

Public telephones These take phonecards or coins. Thirty cents is the minimum for a local call and they are charged by length of call (and by distance rates if not local). Call centres for domestic and international calls are also widespread, and many internet cafes are geared for Skype calls.

Phonecards There's a wide range of local and international *Telefonwertkarte* (phonecards), which can save you money and help you avoid messing around with change. They are available from post offices, Telekom Austria shops, call shops and *Tabak* (tobacconist) kiosks.

International Calls

To direct-dial abroad, first telephone the overseas access code (🖉00), then the appropriate country code, then the relevant area code (minus the initial '0' if there is one), and finally the subscriber number. International directory assistance is available on 🖉0900 11 88 77.

Tariffs for making international calls depend on the zone. To reverse the charges (call collect), you have to call a free phone number to place the call. Some of the numbers are listed below (ask directory assistance for others):

Australia (🖉0800 200 202)

Ireland (🖉 800 200 213)

New Zealand (🖉0800 200 222)

South Africa (🖉0800 200 230)

UK (🖉0800 200 209)

USA (AT&T; 🖉0800 200 288)

Mobile Phones

ROAMING

The *Handy* (mobile phone) network works on GSM 1800 and is compatible with GSM 900 phones; it is not compatible with systems from the US unless the mobile phone is at least a tri-band

model that can receive one of these frequencies. Japanese mobile phones need to be quad-band (world phone) to work in Austria. Roaming can get very expensive if your provider is outside the EU.

PREPAID SIM CARDS

Phone shops sell prepaid SIM cards for making phone calls or SIM cards capable of being used on smart phones for data (ie surfing) as well as making calls. Typically, you pay about €15 for a SIM card and receive about €10 free credit. To use one, your mobile phone should be without a SIM lock.

WI-FI

Make sure your data transfer capability is deactivated while roaming. Austria has lots of wi-fi hot spots which can be used for surfing or making internet calls such as on Skype using smart phones with wi-fi capability.

Time

Austria has summer and winter time. *Sommerzeit* (daylight saving time) begins on the last Sunday in March and all clocks are put forward by one hour. On the last Sunday in October, normal Central European Time begins and clocks are put back one hour. Note that in German *halb* is used to indicate the half-hour before the hour, hence *halb acht* means 7.30, *not* 8.30.

Time Differences

When it's noon in Vienna (outside daylight saving time):

Berlin, Stockholm & Paris	noon
London	11am
Los Angeles & Vancouver	3am
Moscow	2pm
New York	6am
Perth	7pm
Sydney	9pm

Tourist Information

Any town or village that tourists are likely to visit will have a centrally situated tourist office and at least one of the staff will speak English. They go by various names – *Kurort*, *Fremdenverkehrsverband*, *Verkehrsamt*, *Kurverein*, *Tourismusbüro* or *Kurverwaltung* – but they can always be identified by a white 'i' on a green background.

Staff can answer enquiries, ranging from where and when to attend religious services for different denominations, to where to find vegetarian food or wi-fi. If you need a hotel with wi-fi in an isolated area, for instance, they can usually help you find one. Most offices have an accommodation-finding service, often free of charge. Maps, often also some great hiking and cycling maps, are available and usually free.

Some local tourist offices hold brochures on other localities, allowing you to stock up on information in advance. If you're empty-handed and arrive somewhere too late in the day to get to the tourist office, try asking at the railway ticket office, as staff there often have hotel lists or city maps. The tourist office may have a rack of brochures hung outside the door, or there may be an accommodation board you can access even when the office is closed. Top hotels usually have a supply of useful brochures in the foyer.

National & Regional Tourist Offices

Austria Info (www.austria.info)

Burgenland Tourismus (www.burgenland.info)

Kärnten Information (www.kaernten.at)

Niederösterreich Werbung (Map p62; www.niederoesterreich.at)

Oberösterreich Tourismus (www.oberoesterreich.at)

Salzburgerland Tourismus (www.salzburgerland.com)

Salzkammergut (www.salzkammergut.at)

Steirische Tourismus (www.steiermark.com)

Tirol Info (www.tirol.at)

Tourist Info Wien (www.wien.info)

Vorarlberg Tourismus (www.vorarlberg-tourism.at)

Travellers with Disabilities

The situation in Austria for travellers with disabilities is good in Vienna but outside the capital it is still by no means plain sailing. Ramps leading into buildings are common but not universal; most U-Bahn stations have wheelchair lifts but on buses and trams you'll often be negotiating gaps and one or more steps.

For distance travel, **Österreichische Bundesbahnen** (ÖBB, Austrian National Railways; ☑24hr hotline 05 1717; www.oebb.at) has a section for people with disabilities on its website. Change to the English-language option, then go to 'Planning your trip' and submenu 'Barrier-free travelling'. Use the ☑05 1717 number for special travel assistance (you can do this while booking your ticket by telephone). If you've already got a ticket, call the number and press '5' at the end of the recording for special services. Staff at stations will help with boarding and alighting. Order this at least 24 hours ahead of travel (48 hours ahead for international services). No special service is available at unstaffed stations.

The detailed pamphlet *Accessible Vienna* is available in German or English from **Tourist Info Wien** (www.wien.info). A comprehensive list of places in Vienna catering to visitors with special needs can be downloaded on www.wien.info/en/travel-info/accessible-vienna. In other cities, contact the tourist office directly for more information.

Some of the more expensive hotels (four stars or above, usually) have facilities tailored to travellers with disabilities; cheaper hotels invariably don't.

There is no national organisation for the disabled in Austria, but the regional tourist offices or any of the following can be contacted for more information:

Behinderten Selbsthilfe Gruppe (☑03332-65 405; www.bsgh.at; Sparkassenplatz 4, Hartberg, Styria) Maintains a database under www.barriere-freieurlaub.at with hotels and restaurants suitable for those with disabilities.

Bizeps (☑01-523 89 21; www.bizeps.at; Schönngasse 15-17, Vienna; Ⓜ︎Messe-Prater) A centre providing support and self-help for people with disabilities. Located two blocks north of Messe-Prater U-Bahn station.

Faktor i (Map p76; ☑01-274 92 74; www.faktori.wuk.at; 05, Rechte Wienzeile 81, Vienna; Ⓜ︎Pilgramgasse) Faktor i offers information to young people with disabilities. Located just north of the Pilgramgasse U-Bahn station.

Upper Austria Tourist Office (www.barrierefreies-oberoesterreich.at) Information and listings for people with disabilities tavelling in Upper Austria.

Visas

Visas for stays of up to three months are not required for citizens of the EU, the European Economic Area (EEA), much of Eastern Europe, Israel, USA, Canada, the majority of Central and South American nations, Japan, Korea, Malaysia, Singapore, Australia or New Zealand. All other nationalities, including Chinese and Russians, require a visa; the

Ministry of Foreign Affairs (www.bmaa.gv.at) website has a list of Austrian embassies where you can apply for one, and the Austrian embassy in Washington (www.austria. org/going-to-austria/entry-a-residence-permits) lists all visa-free nationalities. Apply at least three weeks in advance.

If you wish to stay longer than three months you should simply leave the country and re-enter. For those nationalities that require a visa, extensions cannot be organised within Austria; you'll need to leave and reapply. EU nationals can stay indefinitely but are required by law to register with the local *Magistratisches Bezirksamt* (magistrate's office) if the stay exceeds 60 days.

Austria is part of the Schengen Agreement, which includes all EU states (minus Britain and Ireland) and Switzerland. In practical terms this means a visa issued by one Schengen country is good for all the other member countries and a passport is not required to move from one to the other (a national identity card is required, though). Austrians are required to carry personal identification, and you too will need to be able to prove your identity.

Visa and passport requirements are subject to change, so always double-check before travelling. Lonely Planet's website, www.lonely-planet.com, has links to up-to-date visa information.

Volunteering

Voluntary work is a good way to meet people and do something for the country you're visiting. In Austria, maintaining hiking trails is popular, but other volunteer projects range from joining a performance group on social issues to repairing a school fence outside Vienna. Generally, there's something for everyone, young or senior, lasting anything from a week to 18 months or more.

The key to finding a volunteer position in Austria is to hook up with the networks in your home country and/or, if you speak German, approach an Austrian organisation directly.

Bergwald Projekt (www. bergwaldprojekt.at; Olympiastrasse 37, Innsbruck) Excellent volunteer work programs protecting and maintaining mountain forests in Austria, Germany and Switzerland. Generally, the Austrian programs last one week.

Freiwilligenweb (www. freiwilligenweb.at) Official Austrian government portal for volunteer work.

Service Civil International (SCI; www.sciint.org) Worldwide organisation with local networks.

International Voluntary Service Great Britain (IVS; http://ivsgb.org) The UK organisation networked with the SCI.

International Voluntary Service USA (www.sci-ivs. org) The US organisation networked with the SCI.

International Volunteers for Peace (www.ivp.org. au) An Australian organisation networked with the SCI.

Work

EU, EEA and Swiss nationals can work in Austria without a work permit or residency permit, though as intending residents they need to register with the police.

Non-EU nationals need both a work permit and a residency permit, and will find it pretty hard to get either unless they qualify for a Red-White-Red Card, which is aimed at attracting highly skilled workers. Your employer in Austria must apply for your work permit. You must apply for your residency permit via the Austrian embassy in your home country.

Teaching is a favourite of expats; look under '*Sprachschulen*' in the *Gelbe Seiten* (yellow pages) for a list of schools. Outside that profession (and barkeeping), you'll struggle to find employment if you don't speak German. There are some useful job websites:

Arbeitsmarktservice Österreich (www.ams.or.at) Austria's Labour Office.

Monster (www.monster.at)

StepStone (www.stepstone.at) Directed towards professionals.

Virtual Vienna Net (www. virtualvienna.net) Aimed at expats, with a variety of jobs, including UN listings.

Transport

GETTING THERE & AWAY

Austria is well connected to the rest of the world. Vienna and several regional capitals are served by no-frills airlines (plus regular services). Europe's extensive bus and train networks criss-cross the country and there are major highways from Germany and Italy. It's possible to enter Austria by boat from Hungary, Slovakia and Germany.

Flights, tours and rail tickets can be booked online at lonelyplanet.com/bookings.

Entering the Country

Passport

A valid passport is required when entering Austria. The only exception to this rule is when entering from another Schengen country (all EU states minus Britain and Ireland); in this case, only a national identity card is required.

Border Procedures

Formal border controls have been abolished for those entering from another EU country or Switzerland, but spot checks may be carried out at the border or inside Austria itself, or temporary border checks reinstated at short notice. See p390 for visa information.

Air

Vienna is the main transport hub for Austria, but Graz, Linz, Klagenfurt, Salzburg and Innsbruck all receive international flights. Flights to these cities are often cheaper option than those to the capital, as are flights to Airport Letisko (Bratislava Airport), which is only 60km east of Vienna, in Slovakia. Bregenz has no airport; your best bet is to fly into Friedrichshafen in Germany or Altenrhein in Switzerland.

Airports & Airlines

Austrian Airlines (www.austrian.com) is the national carrier based in Vienna; it's a member of **Star Alliance** (www.staralliance.com).

Among the low-cost airlines, Air Berlin and Niki fly to Graz, Air Berlin, Transavia, easyJet and Niki to Innsbruck, germanwings and Ryanair to Klagenfurt, Ryanair to Linz, Air Berlin and Ryanair to Salzburg, and Ryanair to Bratislava (for Vienna). Air Berlin, easyJet and germanwings fly to Vienna Airport.

Airport Bratislava (BTS; ☑421 2 3303 33 53; www.airportbratislava.sk) Airport Letisko Bratislava, serving Bratislava, is connected to Vienna International Airport and Südtiroler Platz in Vienna by almost hourly buses (one way/return valid 180 days €7.70/14.30). Book online at www.slovaklines.sk or at www.eurolines.com. You can also take the bus to the centre of Bratislava and pick up a frequent train from Bratislava train station to Vienna.

Blue Danube Airport (LNZ; ☑07221-600; www.flughafen-linz.at; Linz)

CLIMATE CHANGE & TRAVEL

Every form of transport that relies on carbon-based fuel generates CO_2, the main cause of human-induced climate change. Modern travel is dependent on aeroplanes, which might use less fuel per kilometre per person than most cars but travel much greater distances. The altitude at which aircraft emit gases (including CO_2) and particles also contributes to their climate change impact. Many websites offer 'carbon calculators' that allow people to estimate the carbon emissions generated by their journey and, for those who wish to do so, to offset the impact of the greenhouse gases emitted with contributions to portfolios of climate-friendly initiatives throughout the world. Lonely Planet offsets the carbon footprint of all staff and author travel.

Graz Airport (GRZ; ☑0316-29 020; www.flughafen-graz.at)

Innsbruck Airport (INN; ☑0512-22 525; www.innsbruck-airport.com; Fürstenweg 180)

Kärnten Airport (KLU; ☑0463-41 500; www.klagenfurt-airport.com; Klagenfurt)

Salzburg Airport (SZG; ☑0662-85 800; www.salzburg-airport.com)

Vienna Airport (VIE; ☑01-700 72 2233; www.viennaairport.com)

Land

Bus

Travelling by bus is a cheap but less comfortable way to reach Austria from other European countries. Some options are listed below.

EUROLINES

Eurolines (☑Graz 0316-67 11 55, Vienna 01-798 29 00; www.eurolines.at) buses pass through Vienna, stops in Austria include Graz, Linz, Salzburg, Klagenfurt, Villach and Innsbruck. A 15-day adult pass is €210 to €350, a 30-day pass is €315 to €460 (cheaper for those under 26 and over 60). Covers 42 cities across Europe, including Vienna, Italy, Germany, Czech Republic and Hungary

London Buses connect London (Victoria coach station) and Vienna (one way/return €108/148, 23 hours, six days per week); anyone under 26 or over 60 gets a 10% discount on most fares and passes.

Prague Buses (one way/return €22/44, four hours) run three times daily.

Bratislava From Vienna 10 buses run daily (one way/return €7.20/12, 80 minutes). Bratislava Airport one way/return is €10/18.

BUSABOUT

London-based **Busabout** (☑UK 08450 267 514; www.busabout.com; 1/2/3 loops €515/879/1069) offers hop-on, hop-off passes for travel

to about 50 European cities from May to late October. The Northern Loop includes Vienna and Salzburg, as well as Prague, Amsterdam, Paris and several German cities.

ÖBB INTERCITY BUS

An **Österreichische Bundesbahnen** (ÖBB, Austrian National Railways; ☑24hr hotline 05 1717; www.oebb.at) Intercity bus connects Klagenfurt via Villach and Udine with Venice (€25, 4¼ hours, four to five times daily).

Car & Motorcycle

BORDER CROSSINGS

There are numerous entry points by road from Germany, the Czech Republic, Slovakia, Hungary, Slovenia, Italy and Switzerland. Liechtenstein is so small that it has just one border-crossing point, near Feldkirch in Austria. The Alps limit the options for approaching Tyrol from the south (Switzerland and Italy). All border-crossing points are open 24 hours.

INSURANCE

Proof of ownership of a private vehicle and a driver's licence should always be carried while driving. EU licences are accepted in Austria; all other nationalities require a German translation or an International Driving Permit (IDP). Translations can be obtained on the spot for a small fee from Austrian automobile associations (see p397). Third-party insurance is a minimum requirement in Europe and you'll need to carry proof of this in the form of a Green Card. If you're a member of an automobile association, ask about free reciprocal benefits offered by affiliated organisations in Europe. The car must also display a sticker on the rear indicating the country of origin.

SAFETY

Carrying a warning triangle and first-aid kit in your vehicle is compulsory in Austria.

Train

Austria benefits from its central location within Europe by having excellent rail connections to all important destinations.

Vienna is one of the main rail hubs in Central Europe. Linz, Salzburg, Villach, Klagenfurt and Graz also have excellent connections with neighbouring countries.

➡ Express trains can be identified by the symbols EC (EuroCity, serving international routes) or IC (InterCity, serving national routes). Railjet national and international train services are faster than IC/EC trains, cost the same but are more luxurious. The French Train à Grande Vitesse (TGV) and the German InterCityExpress (ICE) trains are high-speed trains. Surcharges are levied for these.

➡ Overnight trains usually offer a choice between a *Liegewagen* (couchette) or a more expensive *Schlafwagen* (sleeping car). Long-distance trains have a dining car or snacks available.

TIMETABLES

ÖBB (☑24hr hotline 05 1717; www.oebb.at) With national and international connections. Only national connections have prices unless they are special deals to and from neighbouring countries. Online national train booking. It also shows Postbus services.

Deutsche Bahn (German Railways; www.bahn.de) Useful for finding special deals to/from Germany or to check connections (but not prices and bookings) in Austria.

Thomas Cook (www.thomascookpublishing.com) The *Thomas Cook European Timetable* contains all train schedules, supplements and reservations information. The monthly edition can be ordered from Thomas Cook.

TICKETS

Extra charges can apply on fast trains and international trains, and it is a good idea

VIENNA'S NEW HAUPTBAHNHOF

Vienna's new Hauptbahnhof (central train station) went partially into service in 2012 and should go into full service by early 2015. Services to/from Bratislava, the Czech Republic, Wiener Neustadt and a few other regions of Lower Austria and Burgenland have been using a new section of the station since late 2012. Until Hauptbahnhof goes into full service, trains mostly servicing western Austria and international trains to/from European neighbours west of Austria's borders will continue to use Westbahnhof. (This will eventually get only minor regional trains.) Wien-Meidling (Meidling-Philadelphiabrücke U-Bahn, *not* Meidling Hauptstrasse) is for an interim period being used for trains mostly serving southern cities. For the current situation, always consult the timetables on www.oebb.at – and look at your ticket closely.

(sometimes obligatory) to make seat reservations for peak times and on certain lines. Prices we give for national and international trains can vary slightly according to the route and type of train.

The **Rail Europe Travel Centre** (✆0844 848 4078; www.raileurope.co.uk; 193 Piccadilly, London; ⊙10am-6pm Mon-Fri, to 5pm Sat) handles bookings for a UK£8 surcharge walk-in or by telephone, and also online; tickets from many different countries can be booked through the website. It's often cheapest to book the continental Europe leg, then find the best Eurostar deal. **Deutsche Bahn** (✆UK 08718 8080 66; www.bahn.de; ⊙call centre 9am-8pm Mon-Fri, 9am-1pm Sat & Sun) in London is also useful, especially for taking advantage of savings through early booking.

FROM LONDON

There are several good options. The fastest is by Eurostar to Brussels, then to Frankfurt, then Vienna, which can be done during the day (13¼ hours) or overnight (17 hours). An alternative is to take the Eurostar to Brussels, change there for Cologne, and take the overnight train from Cologne to Vienna (total trip 17 hours). There are also connections

via Paris. See www.eurostar.com for the best deals and for booking the leg from London. This starts at €39 one way. Expect to pay €69 to €116 one way for Cologne to Vienna, or €69 to €136 for Brussels to Vienna via Frankfurt. The website www.seat61.com also has helpful tips and details on booking.

River

The **Danube Tourist Commission** (www.danube-river.org) has a country-by-country list of operators and agents who can book canal tours, including companies in Australia, New Zealand, the US, Canada and various European countries.

Danube Cruises

Avalon Waterways (www.avaloncruises.co.uk) is an international cruise operator with a branch in the UK, as well as **Australia** (www.avalonwaterways.com.au), **Canada** (www.avalonwaterways.ca), **New Zealand** (www.avalonwaterways.co.nz) and **USA** (www.avalonwaterways.com). It can also handle bookings from other regions. Typical cruises include eight days from Budapest to Vienna (US$1839), nine days Vienna to Munich (US$2739) and 15 days Amsterdam to Bu-

dapest (US$4149); all prices exclude air connections.

Excursion Services

Twin City Liner (Map p62; ✆Vienna 01-588 80; www.twincityliner.com; Schwedenplatz, 01, Vienna; 1 way adult €20-35; ⊙late Mar-early Nov) Vienna to/from Bratislava, 1¼ hours, three to five times daily from late March to early November. Ships dock at the Wien-City Twin City Liner terminal on the Danube Canal.

LOD (✆in Bratislava 2 529 32 226; www.lod.sk; Quai 6, Reichsbrücke, departure point; 1 way/return €23/38) Slovakian ferry company with hydrofoils between Bratislava and Vienna, 1½ hours, five to seven days per week from late April to early October. Best value on weekends and for return trips. Booking is online unless you call Bratislava to reserve and then pay cash on the ship.

DDSG Blue Danube (Budapest service; ✆in Vienna 01-58 880; www.donauschiffahrtwien.at; Handelskai 265; 1 way €99-109, return €125) Hydrofoil Vienna to/from Budapest, 5½–6½ hours, three to seven times a week late April to late September.

GETTING AROUND

Transport systems in Austria are highly developed and generally very efficient, and reliable information is usually available in English. Individual bus and train *Fahrplan* (timetables) are readily available, as are helpful annual timetables.

Austria's main rail provider is the **ÖBB** (✆24hr hotline 05 1717; www.oebb.at), which has an extensive countrywide rail network. This is supplemented by a handful of private railways. Wherever trains don't run, a **Postbus** (✆24 hr 05 17 17; www.postbus.at) usually does. Sometimes there's an overlap of services and you have a choice of bus or train. Timetables and prices for most train and bus connections can be found online at www.oebb.at.

Most provinces have an integrated transport system offering day passes covering regional zones for both bus and train travel.

Air

Flying within a country the size of Austria is rarely necessary. The main exception is Innsbruck in the far west of Austria.

Austrian Airlines (www.austrian.com) The national carrier and its subsidiaries Tyrolean Airways and Austrian Arrows offer several flights daily between Vienna and Graz, Innsbruck, Klagenfurt, Linz and Salzburg.

Bicycle

Tours

Most regional tourist boards have brochures on cycling facilities and routes within their region. Separate bike tracks are common in cities, and long-distance tracks and routes also run along many of the major valleys such as the Danube, Enns and Mur. Others follow lakes, such as the bike tracks around the Neusiedler See in Burgenland and the Wörthersee in Carinthia. *Landstrassen* (L) roads (see p396) are usually good for cyclists. The Danube cycling trail is like a Holy Grail for cyclists, following the entire length of the river in Austria between the borders with Germany and Slovakia. The Tauern Radweg is a 310km trail through the mountain landscapes of Hohe Tauern National Park.

Mountain Biking

Austria's regions are well equipped for mountain biking of various levels of difficulty. Carinthia (around Hermagor) and northern Styria (the Gesäuse, Schladming and Mariazell) are excellent

places. The Dachstein Tour can be done over three days, whereas the Nordkette Single Trail in Innsbruck is one of the toughest and most exhilarating downhill rides in the country.

Bike Transport

It's possible to take bicycles on trains with a bicycle symbol at the top of its timetable. You can't take bicycles on bus services.

Regional A ticket for a day/week on a Regionalzug (R; regional train), Regionalexpress (REX; regional express), S-Bahn (S) or RegionalS-Bahn (RB; regional S-Bahn) costs €5/10. The exception is when you buy a EURegio ticket, for which bicycle transport is free on trains with capacity and with the bicycle symbol.

Intercity and international On these trains with bicycle facilities you need to reserve ahead and place the bike in one of the special racks on board. National tickets cost €10 (€5 discounted) and international tickets €12.

Hire

All large cities have at least one bike shop that doubles as a rental centre. In

places where cycling is a popular pastime, such as the Wachau in Lower Austria and the Neusiedler See in Burgenland, almost all small towns have rental facilities. Rates vary but expect to pay around €15 to €25 per day.

HIRE STATIONS

Some regions have summer bicycle-rental stations where you can rent and drop off a bicycle at different stations, often using a credit card. In Lower Austria and Burgenland the system is very well established. A similar network is also located around the Wörthersee in Carinthia. Vienna also has a pick-up and drop-off service using credit cards.

E-BIKES & E-MBS

Touring electric bikes (e-bikes) are available in most regions. Pedal cleverly using energy-saving options and you can get well over 100km out of some models. A few places also rent e-mountain bikes (e-MBs) which cope with the hills and distances remarkably well. Taking advantage of energy options

INTERNATIONAL TRAINS

TRAIN CONNECTION	PRICE (€)	DURATION (HR)
Belgrade–Villach	82	11
Budapest–Graz	46	5½
Dortmund–Linz	163	9 (departs Vienna, change in Würzburg for northern Germany)
Frankfurt Main–Villach	147	8½
Ljubljana–Graz	41	3½ (some continue to Zagreb & Belgrade)
Ljubljana–Villach	23	1¾
Munich–Graz	87	6 (via Salzburg)
Munich–Innsbruck	41	2
Munich–Salzburg	35	2
Munich–Villach	70	4½
Prague–Linz	47	5
Verona–Innsbruck	37	3½
Zagreb–Villach	45	4
Zürich–Innsbruck	61	3¾

TRANSPORT BOAT

and the terrain on a good model, it's even possible to return an e-MB with almost as much juice as you set out with.

Movelo (www.movelo.com) This e-bike operator has a network of partner outlets for hire and/or battery change in holiday regions of Austria. Typically, an e-bike costs €20 to €25 per day or 24 hours, depending on the station. You book the bikes directly through the stations (see the website for a list).

Boat

The Danube serves as a thoroughfare between Vienna and Lower and Upper Austria. Services are generally slow, scenic excursions rather than functional means of transport. Some of the country's larger lakes, such as Bodensee and Wörthersee, have boat services.

Bus

Rail routes are often complemented by **Postbus** (☏24hr 05 17 17; www.postbus.at) services, which really come into their own in the more inaccessible mountainous regions. Buses are fairly reliable, and usually depart from outside train stations.

Remote regions Plan a day or two ahead and travel on a weekday; services are reduced or nonexistent on Saturday, and often nonexistent on Sunday. Pay attention to timetables on school buses in remote regions. These are excellent during the term but don't operate outside school term.

Telephone information Inside Austria, call ☏05 1717. From outside Austria, call ☏+43 5 17 17.

Online information Consult www.postbus.at or www.oebb. at. Local bus stations or tourist offices usually stock free timetables for specific bus routes.

Reservations Usually unnecessary. It's possible to buy tickets in advance on some routes, but on others you can only buy tickets from the drivers.

Costs and duration Oddly, travel by Postbus can work out to be more expensive than train, especially if you have a Vorteilscard for train discounts (only family Vorteilscards are valid on buses). The ÖBB intercity bus between Graz and Klagenfurt (€26) is cheaper, direct and slightly faster than the train. Mostly, though, buses are slower.

Car & Motorcycle

Roads Autobahns are marked 'A', some are pan-European 'E' roads. You can only drive on them with a *Vignette* (motorway tax). *Bundesstrassen* or 'B' roads are major roads, while *Landstrassen* (L) are places to enjoy the ride rather than get quickly from one place to another.

ROAD DISTANCES (KM)

	Bad Ischl	Bregenz	Bruck an der Mur	Eisenstadt	Graz	Innsbruck	Kitzbühel	Klagenfurt	Krems	Kufstein	Landeck	Lienz	Linz	Salzburg	St Pölten	Vienna	Villach
Bregenz	432																
Bruck an der Mur	170	577															
Eisenstadt	297	704	127														
Graz	193	600	54	175													
Innsbruck	239	193	384	511	407												
Kitzbühel	191	300	275	469	400	113											
Klagenfurt	245	510	145	298	133	322	264										
Krems	222	626	175	132	229	433	372	320									
Kufstein	161	271	331	460	356	78	37	286	355								
Landeck	316	117	461	588	484	77	186	394	510	155							
Lienz	232	424	266	393	277	178	94	144	432	142	248						
Linz	103	507	190	246	237	314	247	253	145	236	391	359					
Salzburg	58	374	228	362	264	181	129	223	257	103	258	180	138				
St Pölten	206	610	140	123	194	417	356	285	32	339	494	416	129	241			
Vienna	266	670	145	50	191	477	420	316	79	399	554	411	189	301	66		
Villach	250	486	178	335	170	287	226	37	353	251	370	109	330	188	318	353	
Wiener Neustadt	268	675	98	31	146	482	441	267	137	431	559	364	237	339	114	53	316

Seasonal closures Some minor passes are blocked by snow from November to May. Carrying snow chains in winter is highly recommended and is compulsory in some areas.

All-weather tyres Compulsory from 1 November to 15 April.

Navigation systems These work well in Austria, but use your eyes and don't rely 100% on them.

Motorcycles Motorcyclists and passengers must wear a helmet. Dipped lights must be used in daytime. You must carry a first-aid kit. The **National Austrian Tourist Office** (www. austria.info) has an *Austrian Classic Tour* brochure, which covers 3000km of the best roads for motorcyclists in the country.

Motorail trains A number of train services allow you to transport a car with you (see p398).

Automobile Associations

Two automobile associations serve Austria. Both provide free 24-hour breakdown service to members and have reciprocal agreements with motoring clubs in other countries; check with your local club before leaving. Both have offices throughout Austria, and it is possible to become a member, but you must join for six months or a year; expect to pay around €38 or €75 respectively. For a small fee, the associations also translate non-German-language driving licences.

If you're not entitled to free assistance, you'll incur a fee for call-outs, which varies depending on the time of day.

ARBÖ (☑24hr emergency assistance 123, office 050-123 123; www.arboe.at; Mariahilfer Strasse 180, Vienna; ☺office telephone 6am-7pm daily)

ÖAMTC (☑24hr emergency assistance 120, office 01-711 99-0; www.oeamtc.at; Schubertring 1-3, Vienna; ☺8am-6pm Mon-Fri, 9am-1pm Sat)

Bring Your Own Vehicle

You need to have proof of ownership papers and third-party insurance. The car must display a sticker on the rear indicating the country of origin.

Driving Licence

A licence should always be carried. If it's not an EU licence or in German, you need to carry a translation or International Driving Permit (IDP) as well. Automobile associations can translate licences for a fee.

Hire

MINIMUM REQUIREMENTS

Minimum age for hiring small cars is 19 years, for prestige models 25 years. A valid licence issued at least a year ago is necessary. If taking the car across the border, especially into Eastern Europe, let the rental company know beforehand and check for any add-on fees and possible age requirements. Although companies accept any licence that is written in Latin letters, a translation or International Driving Permit (IDP) is required for any non-EU licence not in German.

WHERE TO HIRE

It is much easier to hire in large cities. Small towns either have no hire companies or a limited number of vehicles that can be expensive or booked out. If you have time, shop around for small companies as they can be cheaper (but more restrictions often apply).

INSURANCE

Third-party insurance is a minimum requirement. All companies offer personal accident insurance (PAI) for occupants and collision damage waiver (CDW) for an additional charge. PAI may not be necessary if you or your passengers hold personal travel insurance.

COMPANIES

Auto Europe (☑0800 56 00 333; www.autoeurope.de) Can be at a lower rate than by going directly through a company.

Avis (☑0800 0800 87 57, in Vienna 01-60187-0; www.avis.at)

EasyMotion (☑0900 240 120; www.easymotion.at) Expensive 0900 telephone. Use the web.

Europcar (www.europcar. co.at)

Hertz (www.hertz.at)

Holiday Autos (☑0810 000 999; www.holidayautos.com) By booking early, prices can be about 60% of those charged by the international companies.

Megadrive (☑05 01 05-4124; www.megadrive.at) Formerly Denzeldrive. Good network in major cities, often cheaper.

Sixt (☑0810 977 424; www.sixt.at)

Autobahn Tax & Tunnel Tolls

A *Vignette* (motorway tax) is imposed on all autobahns; charges for cars below 3.5 tonnes are €8.30 for 10 days, €24.20 for two months and €80.60 for one year. For motorbikes expect to pay €4.80 for 10 days, €12.10 for two months and €32.10 for one year. *Vignette* can be purchased from motoring organisations, border crossings, petrol stations, post offices and *Tabak* (tobacconist) shops.

Anything above 3.5 tonnes is charged per kilometre. The system uses a GO-Box, available from petrol stations along the autobahn for €5, which records the kilometres you travel via an electronic tolling system. A minimum of €75 must be loaded onto the box (plus a €5 fee the first time you load), with a maximum amount of €500. Information on the system and prices can be found online at www.asfinag.at

A toll (*not* covered by the motorway tax) is levied on some mountain roads and tunnels. For a full list of toll roads, consult one of the automobile organisations.

Road & Parking Rules

Drive on the right-hand side of the road. The minimum driving age is 18.

Alcohol The penalty for drink-driving – driving with over 0.05% blood-alcohol concentration (BAC) – is a hefty on-the-spot fine and confiscation of your licence.

Children Those under the age of 14 who are shorter than 1.5m must have a special seat or restraint.

Fines Can be paid on the spot, but ask for a receipt.

Giving way Give way to the right at all times except when a priority road sign indicates otherwise or one street has a raised border running across it (the vehicle entering from such a street must give way). Note: the give way to the right rule also applies at T-junctions.

Helmets Compulsory for motorcyclists and their passengers as well as for children under 13 years on bicycles.

Parking Most town centres have a designated *Kurzparkzone* (short-term parking zone), where on-street parking is limited to a maximum of 1½ or three hours (depending upon the place) between certain specified times. *Parkschein* (parking vouchers) for such zones can be purchased from *Tabak* shops or pavement dispensers and then displayed on the windscreen. Outside the specified time, parking in the *Kurzparkzone* is free.

Seat belts Compulsory.

Speed limits Fifty kilometres per hour in built-up areas, 130km/h on autobahns and 100km/h on other roads. In some places,

the speed on country roads is restricted to 70km/h.

Speed limits at night Except for the A1 between Vienna and Salzburg and the A2 between Vienna and Villach, the speed limit on autobahns from 10pm to 5am is 110km/h.

Trams These always have priority. Vehicles should wait behind while trams slow down and stop for passengers.

Local Transport

Austria's local transport infrastructure is excellent, inexpensive and safe.

Buses and trams Bus services operate in most cities and are complemented by a few night bus lines. Tram and bus services in most places run from about 5am to 11pm or midnight. You usually need to press the stop button, often even in trams.

Metro In Vienna, the metro runs all night on Friday and Saturday nights. From Sunday night to Thursday night it stops around midnight or 12.30am. No other towns have metro systems.

Taxis Austrians mostly call ahead or use taxi ranks. Flagging down a taxi usually works, though. Drivers expect a 10% tip.

Tickets

Ticketing systems and prices vary from region to region. Often they're sold from machines at stops. In Graz you buy them on machines in trams, in Salzburg you can buy them from the driver. Universally, tickets are cheaper from any *Tabak* shop, also known as a *Trafik*.

Passes for single trips, 24 hours and several days or a week are usually available.

Fines are stiff if you don't have a ticket – about €60 to €100 is common, and controls are frequent, especially in the provincial capitals.

Train

While the country bemoans the state of its 'rundown' rail system, travellers praise it to the heavens. It's good by any standard, and with a discount card it's inexpensive.

The **Österreichische Bundesbahnen** (☑24hr hotline 05 1717; www.oebb.at) is the main operator, supplemented by a handful of private lines. Call to book a ticket or get information 24 hours.

Buying tickets Tickets can be purchased by telephone (in which case you are given a 12-digit collection code for printing the ticket at a machine or at the service desk). The other options are online (with registration and self-printing), from staffed counters at stations and from machines at stations.

Reservations Cost €3.50 for most 2nd-class express services within Austria. If you haven't reserved ahead, check (before you sit) whether your intended seat has been reserved by someone else. Reservations are recommended for weekend travel.

Disabled passengers Use the ☑05 1717 number for special travel assistance (you can do this while booking your ticket by telephone). If you've already got a ticket, call the number and press '5' at the end of the recording for special services. Staff at stations will help with boarding and alighting. Order this at least 24 hours ahead of travel (48 hours ahead for international services).

Smoking Not allowed on trains.

Etiquette The ÖBB takes a strong stand on putting your feet on the seats. You can be fined for it.

MOTORAIL TRAINS

ROUTE	PRICE (€)	TIME (HR)
Graz–Feldkirch	86	9
Vienna–Feldkirch	96	7½
Vienna–Innsbruck	76	5¼
Vienna–Lienz	70	5¾
Vienna–Villach	62	4¼
Villach–Feldkirch	79	8¾

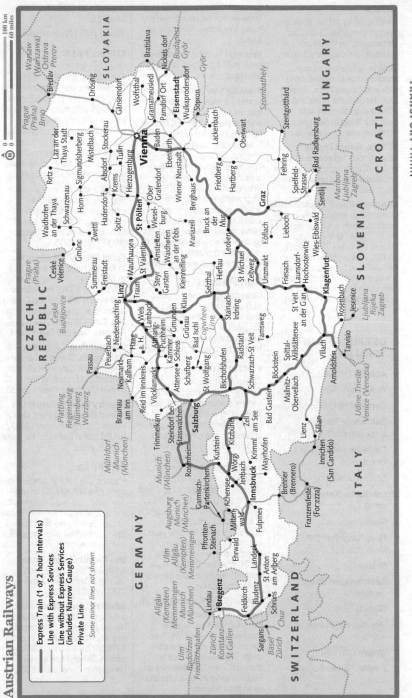

Austrian Railways

100 km
60 miles

Express Train (1 or 2 hour intervals)

Line with Express Services

Line without Express Services
(includes Narrow Gauge)

Private Line

Some minor lines not shown

SLOVAKIA

CZECH REPUBLIC

HUNGARY

CROATIA

SLOVENIA

ITALY

GERMANY

SWITZERLAND

Warsaw (Warszawa)
Ostrava
Přerov
Breclav
Brno
Prague (Praha)
Bratislava
Nickelsdorf
Drösing
Wolfsthal
Gänserndorf
Gramatneusiedl
Pamdorf Ort
Eisenstadt
Wulkaprodersdorf
Sopron
Szombathely

Laa an der Thaya Stadt
Retz
Stockerau
Mistelbach
Absdorf
Sigmundsherberg
Tulln
Vienna
Ebenfurth
Wiener Neustadt
Friedberg
Lackenbach
Oberwart
Szentgotthárd

Waidhofen an der Thaya
Schwarzenau
Hadersdorf
Horn
Krems
Herzogenburg
Ober-Grafendorf
Wiesel-burg
St Pölten
Baden
Bruck an der Mur
Berghaus
Hartberg
Fehring
Spielfeld-Strasse
Bad Radkersburg
Graz
Maribor
Ljubljana
Zagreb
Sentilj

Prague (Praha)
České Velenice
Summerau
Freistadt
Gmünd
Zwettl
Spitz
Amstetten
Waidhofen an der Ybbs
Mariazell
Kleinreifling
Leoben
Köflach
Lieboch
Wies-Eibiswald

Passau
Peuerbach
Linz
Mauthausen
St Valentin
Steyr
Garsten
Klaus
Selzthal
Hieflau
St Michael
Zeltweg
Unzmarkt
Friesach
Launsdorf-Hochosterwitz

Plattling
Regensburg
Nürnberg
Würzburg
Neumarkt Kallham
Wels
Lambach
Haag a. H.
Niederspaching
Attnang-Puchheim
Kammer Schloss
Gmunden
Grünau
Bad Ischl
Cogwheel Line
Stainach Irdning
Radstadt
Tamsweg
St Veit an der Glan
Klagenfurt
Rosenbach
Jesenice
Ljubljana
Rijeka
Zagreb

Braunau am Inn
Reid im Innkreis
Vöcklamarkt
Attersee
Schafberg
St Wolfgang
Schwarzach-St Veit
Böckstein
Spittal-Millstättersee
Villach
Tarvisio
Arnoldstein

Mühldorf
Munich (München)
Trimmelkam
Steindorf bei Stasswalchen
Salzburg
Bischofshofen
Bad Gastein
Mallnitz-Obervellach
Udine Trieste
Venice (Venezia)

Munich (München)
Augsburg
Munich (München)
Rosenheim
Kufstein
Wörgl
Jenbach
Kitzbühel
Zell am See
Krimml
Mayrhofen
Lienz
Sillian
Innichen (San Candido)

Allgäu (Kempten)
Memmingen
Munich (München)
Garmisch-Partenkirchen
Achensee
Mittenwald
Innsbruck
Brenner (Brennero)
Franzensfeste (Forezza)

Ulm
Radolfzell
Friedrichshafen
Lindau
Bregenz
Feldkirch
Bludenz
Schruns
Fulpmes
Ehrwald
Pfronten-Steinach

Zürich
Konstanz
St Gallen
Sargans
Basel
Zürich
Chur
Landeck
St Anton am Arlberg

Costs

Fares quoted in this book are always those for 2nd class. Depending on the exact route, a fare can vary slightly.

Tickets Tickets can be purchased online or by telephone with credit cards (Visa, Diners Club, MasterCard, Amex and JCB), and additionally with cash or a Maestro debit card at machines and service desks.

EURegio tickets These discount return tickets between Austria and the Czech Republic, Hungary or Slovakia can be great value for short visits.

Boarding without a ticket If you board and go immediately to the conductor, only a €3 surcharge will be applied to the normal price of the ticket. If you don't do this, a fee and fine totalling €95 will have to be paid (unless you board at an unstaffed station without a ticket machine or the ticket machine is out of order).

USEFUL TRAIN TERMS

Abfahrt Departure

Ankunft Arrival

Bahnhof (Bf) Station

Bahnsteig Track (the track number)

Einfache Fahrt ('hin') One way

Erste Klasse First class

Fahrkarte (Fahrausweis) Ticket

Gleis Platform

Hauptbahnhof (Hbf) Main station

Retour Return

Speisewagen Dining carriage

Täglich Daily

Umsteigen Change of trains

Wagen Carriage

Zweite Klasse Second class

Children Children aged six to 15 travel half-price; younger kids travel free if they don't take up a seat.

Pets Kept in suitable containers, small pets travel free; larger pets travel half-price.

Breaking your journey One-way tickets for journeys of 100km or less are valid for only one day and the journey can't be broken. For trips of 101km or more, the ticket is valid for one month and you can alight en route. This is worth doing, as longer trips cost less per kilometre. Return tickets of up to 100km each way are valid for one day; tickets for longer journeys are valid for one month, though the initial outward journey must still be completed within six days. A return fare is usually the equivalent price of two one-way tickets.

Rail Passes

Depending on the amount of travelling you intend to do and your residency status, rail passes can be a good deal and can be purchased from any major train station.

VORTEILSCARD

These Austrian National Railways discount tickets can be purchased by anyone. They offer a 45% discount on inland trains for tickets purchased at the counter and 50% if you buy at a ticket machine. After purchasing one (bring a photo and your passport or other ID), you receive a temporary card and can begin using it right away. The plastic permanent card is posted to your home address. It's valid for one year, but not on buses. For more information visit the **ÖBB** (☎24hr hotline 05 1717; www. oebb.at) website, and click on Customer cards.

Classic (€100) For those over 26.

Family (€20) Valid for up to two adults and any number of children. The children must be travelling with you. Children under 14 years travel free on this card. Also 50% discount on Postbus services for adults and up to two children.

Jugend <26 (€20) For those under 26.

Senior (€27) For those over 60.

EURAIL PASS

Only available to non-European residents, Eurail passes are valid for unlimited 2nd-class travel on national railways and some private lines in 24 countries. You can also pay a supplement if you want to travel 1st class. Those under 26 receive substantial discounts. See www. eurail.com for all options.

Global Pass Options for travelling 10/15 days within two months (US$908/1191), or continuous travel for a period from 15 days to three months (US$771 to $2127).

Eurail Select Pass Allows you to tailor a rail trip in three, four or five of 24 bordering countries (US$318 to $391). For Austria, that means Slovenia and Croatia (classed as one Eurail Pass country), Czech Republic, Germany, Hungary, Italy and Switzerland.

Regional Pass Combine Austria with Croatia/Slovenia, Germany, Hungary, the Czech Republic or Switzerland for four or five to 10 days within a two-month period.

Country Pass For Austria this is valid for three to eight days within one month; from US$172 to US$269 in 2nd class for those over 26 years.

INTERRAIL

Passes are for European citizens (including UK) or anyone who has lived in Europe for at least six months. Those under 26 receive substantial discounts. See www.interrail-net.com for all options.

One Country Pass Austria Adult 2nd class three/four/six/eight days within a month €187/212/276/321.

InterRail Global Flexi Valid for a certain number of days or continuously in up to 30 countries; five days' travel in 10 days costs €276, 10 days' travel in 22 days costs €393 and one month's continuous travel costs €658.

Language

The national language of Austria is German, though there are a few regional dialects. For example, the dialect spoken in Vorarlberg is much closer to Swiss German (Schwyzer- tütsch) – a language all but incomprehen- sible to most non-Swiss – than it is to the standard High German (Hochdeutsch) dialect. Nevertheless, Austrians can easily switch from their dialect to High German.

There are many words and expressions in German that are used only by Austrians, some throughout the country and others only in particular regions, although they'll prob- ably be understood elsewhere. Most of these would not automatically be understood by non-Austrian German speakers. On the other hand, the 'standard' German equivalents would be understood by all Austrians. The greetings and farewells included in this chap- ter are specific to Austria.

Pronunciation

It's easy to pronounce German because almost all sounds are also found in English. If you read our coloured pronunciation guides as if they were English, you'll be understood.

Note that the vowel ü sounds like the 'ee' in 'see' but with rounded lips. As for the conso- nants, the kh sound is pronounced like a hiss from the back of the throat (as in the Scottish *loch*). The r sound is pronounced at the back of the throat, almost like saying a g sound, but with some friction – a bit like gargling.

WANT MORE?

For in-depth language information and handy phrases, check out Lonely Planet's *German Phrasebook*. You'll find it at **shop.lonelyplanet.com**, or you can buy Lonely Planet's iPhone phrase- books at the Apple App Store.

As a general rule, word stress in German falls mostly on the first syllable. In our pro- nunciation guides the stressed syllable is indicated with italics.

BASICS

German has polite and informal forms for 'you' (*Sie* and *du* respectively). When ad- dressing people you don't know well, use the polite form (though younger people will be less inclined to expect it). In this language guide the polite form is used unless indicated with 'inf' (for 'informal') in brackets.

Hello.	*Servus.*	zer·vus
Goodbye.	*Auf Wiedersehen.*	owf vee·der·zay·en
Yes.	*Ja.*	yah
No.	*Nein.*	nain
Please.	*Bitte.*	bi·te
Thank you.	*Danke.*	dang·ke
You're welcome.	*Bitte sehr.*	bi·te zair
Excuse me.	*Entschuldigung.*	ent·shul·di·gung
Sorry.	*Entschuldigung.*	ent·shul·di·gung

How are you?
Wie geht es Ihnen/ dir?   vee gayt es ee·nen/ deer (pol/inf)

Fine, thanks. And you?
Danke, gut. Und Ihnen/dir?   dang·ke goot unt ee·nen/deer (pol/inf)

What's your name?
Wie ist Ihr Name?   vee ist eer nah·me (pol)
Wie heißt du?   vee haist doo (inf)

My name is ...
Mein Name ist ...   main nah·me ist ... (pol)
Ich heiße ...   ikh hai·se ... (inf)

Do you speak English?
Sprechen Sie Englisch? shpre·khen zee eng·lish

I don't understand.
Ich verstehe nicht. ikh fer·shtay·e nikht

ACCOMMODATION

Do you have a room?
Haben Sie ein Zimmer? hah·ben zee ain tsi·mer

How much is it per night/person?
Wie viel kostet es vee feel kos·tet es
pro Nacht/Person? praw nakht/per·zawn

air-con	*Klimaanlage*	klee·ma·an·lah·ge
bathroom	*Badezimmer*	bah·de·tsi·mer
campsite	*Campingplatz*	kem·ping·plats
double room	*Doppelzimmer*	do·pel·tsi·mer
guesthouse	*Pension*	pahng·zyawn
hotel	*Hotel*	ho·tel
inn	*Gasthof*	gast·hawf

KEY PATTERNS

To get by in German, mix and match these simple patterns with words of your choice:

When's (the next flight)?
Wann ist (der van ist (dair
nächste Flug)? naykhs·te flook)

Where's (the station)?
Wo ist (der vaw ist (dair
Bahnhof)? bahn·hawf)

Where can I (buy a ticket)?
Wo kann ich (eine vaw kan ikh (ai·ne
Fahrkarte kaufen)? fahr·kar·te kow·fen)

Do you have (a map)?
Haben Sie (eine hah·ben zee (ai·ne
Karte)? kar·te)

Is there (a toilet)?
Gibt es (eine gipt es (ai·ne
Toilette)? to·a·le·te)

I'd like (a coffee).
Ich möchte ikh merkh·te
(einen Kaffee). (ai·nen ka·fay)

I'd like (to hire a car).
Ich möchte ikh merkh·te
(ein Auto mieten). (ain ow·to mee·ten)

Can I (enter)?
Darf ich darf ikh
(hereinkommen)? (her·ein·ko·men)

Could you please (help me)?
Könnten Sie (mir kern·ten zee (meer
helfen)? hel·fen)

Do I have to (book a seat)?
Muss ich (einen Platz mus ikh (ai·nen plats
reservieren lassen)? re·zer·vee·ren la·sen)

---

single room	*Einzelzimmer*	ain·tsel·tsi·mer
window	*Fenster*	fens·ter
youth hostel	*Jugend-*	yoo·gent·
	herberge	her·ber·ge

DIRECTIONS

Where's (a bank)?
Wo ist (eine Bank)? vaw ist (ai·ne bangk)

What's the address?
Wie ist die Adresse? vee ist dee a·dre·se

Can you please write it down?
Könnten Sie das bitte kern·ten zee das bi·te
aufschreiben? owf·shrai·ben

Can you show me (on the map)?
Können Sie es mir ker·nen zee es meer
(auf der Karte) zeigen? (owf dair kar·te) tsai·gen

at the corner	*an der Ecke*	an dair e·ke
at the traffic lights	*bei der Ampel*	bai dair am·pel
behind ...	*hinter ...*	hin·ter ...
far away	*weit weg*	vait vek
in front of ...	*vor ...*	fawr ...
left/right	*links/rechts*	lingks/rekhts
near	*nahe*	nah·e
next to ...	*neben ...*	nay·ben ...
opposite ...	*gegenüber ...*	gay·gen·ü·ber ...
straight ahead	*geradeaus*	ge·rah·de·ows

EATING & DRINKING

A table for (two) people, please.
Einen Tisch für (zwei) ai·nen tish für (tsvai)
Personen, bitte. per·zaw·nen bi·te

What would you recommend?
Was empfehlen Sie? vas emp·fay·len zee

What's in that dish?
Was ist in diesem vas ist in dee·zem
Gericht? ge·rikht

I don't eat ...
Ich esse kein ... ikh e·se kain ...

Cheers!
Prost! prawst

That was delicious.
Das war sehr lecker. das vahr zair le·ker

The bill, please.
Die Rechnung, bitte. dee rekh·nung bi·te

Key Words

appetisers	*Vorspeisen*	fawr·shpai·zen
ashtray	*Aschenbecher*	a·shen·be·kher
bar	*Kneipe*	knai·pe
bottle	*Flasche*	fla·she

bowl	Schüssel	shü·sel
breakfast	Frühstück	frü·shtük
cold	kalt	kalt
cup	Tasse	ta·se
dinner	Abendessen	ah·bent·e·sen
drink list	Getränke-karte	ge·treng·ke·kar·te
food	Essen	e·sen
fork	Gabel	gah·bel
glass	Glas	glahs
grocery store	Lebensmittel-laden	lay·bens·mi·tel·lah·den
hot (warm)	heiß	hais
knife	Messer	me·ser
local speciality	örtliche Spezialität	ert·li·khe shpe·tsya·li·tayt
lunch	Mittagessen	mi·tahk·e·sen
main courses	Hauptgerichte	howpt·ge·rikh·te
menu	Speisekarte	shpai·ze·kar·te
market	Markt	markt
plate	Teller	te·ler
restaurant	Restaurant	res·to·rang
spicy	würzig	vür·tsikh
spoon	Löffel	ler·fel
vegetarian food	vegetarisches Essen	ve·ge·tah·ri·shes e·sen
with/without	mit/ohne	mit/aw·ne

Meat & Fish

bacon	Speck	shpek
beef	Rindfleisch	rint·flaish
brains	Hirn	heern
carp	Karpfen	karp·fen
chicken	Huhn	hoon
duck	Ente	en·te
eel	Aal	ahl
fish	Fisch	fish
goose	Gans	gans
ham	Schinken	shing·ken
hare	Hase	hah·ze
lamb	Lamm	lam
liver	Leber	lay·ber
minced meat	Hackfleisch	hak·flaish
plaice	Scholle	sho·le
pork	Schweinfleisch	shvai·n·flaish
salmon	Lachs	laks
tongue	Zunge	tsung·e
trout	Forelle	fo·re·le
tuna	Thunfisch	toon·fish

Signs

Ausgang	Exit
Damen	Women
Eingang	Entrance
Geschlossen	Closed
Herren	Men
Offen	Open
Toiletten	Toilets
Verboten	Prohibited

turkey	Puter	poo·ter
veal	Kalbfleisch	kalp·flaish
venison	Hirsch	hirsh

Fruit & Vegetables

apple	Apfel	ap·fel
apricot	Aprikose	a·pri·ko·ze
asparagus	Spargel	shpar·gel
banana	Banane	ba·nah·ne
beans	Bohnen	baw·nen
beetroot	Rote Rübe	raw·te rü·be
cabbage	Kohl	hawl
carrots	Karotten	ka·ro·ten
cherries	Kirschen	kir·shen
corn	Mais	mais
cucumber	Gurke	gur·ke
garlic	Knoblauch	knawp·lowkh
grapes	Trauben	trow·ben
green beans	Fisolen	fee·zo·len
mushrooms	Pilze	pil·tse
onions	Zwiebeln	tsvee·beln
pear	Birne	bir·ne
peas	Erbsen	erp·sen
peppers	Paprika	pap·ri·kah
pineapple	Ananas	a·na·nas
plums	Zwetschgen	tsvech·gen
potatoes	Kartoffeln	kar·to·feln
raspberries	Himbeeren	him·bee·ren
spinach	Spinat	shpi·naht
strawberries	Erdbeeren	ert·bee·ren
tomatoes	Tomaten	to·mah·ten

Other

bread	Brot	brawt
butter	Butter	bu·ter
cheese	Käse	kay·ze
chocolate	Schokolade	sho·ko·lah·de

cream	Sahne	zah·ne
dumplings	Knödel	kner·del
eggs	Eier	ai·er
honey	Honig	haw·nikh
jam	Marmelade	mar·me·lah·de
mustard	Senf	zenf
nut	Nuss	nus
oil	Öl	erl
pasta	Nudeln	noo·deln
pepper	Pfeffer	pfe·fer
rice	Reis	rais
salad	Salat	za·laht
salt	Salz	zalts
sugar	Zucker	tsu·ker

Drinks

beer	Bier	beer
coffee	Kaffee	ka·fay
(orange) juice	(Orangen-) saft	(o·rahng·zhen·) zaft
milk	Milch	milkh
red wine	Rotwein	rawt·vain
tea	Tee	tay
(mineral) water	(Mineral-) wasser	(mi·ne·rahl·) va·ser
white wine	Weißwein	vais·vain

EMERGENCIES

Help!
Hilfe! — hil·fe

Leave me alone!
Lassen Sie mich in Ruhe! la·sen zee mikh in roo·e

I'm lost.
Ich habe mich verirrt. ikh hah·be mikh fer·irt

Call the police!
Rufen Sie die Polizei! roo·fen zee dee po·li·tsai

Call a doctor!
Rufen Sie einen Arzt! roo·fen zee ai·nen artst

I'm sick.
Ich bin krank. ikh bin krangk

It hurts here.
Es tut hier weh. es toot heer vay

Question Words
How?	Wie?	vee
What?	Was?	vas
When?	Wann?	van
Where?	Wo?	vaw
Who?	Wer?	vair
Why?	Warum?	va·rum

I'm allergic to (antibiotics).
Ich bin allergisch gegen (Antibiotika). ikh bin a·lair·gish gay·gen (an·ti·bi·aw·ti·ka)

Where is the toilet?
Wo ist die Toilette? vaw ist dee to·a·le·te

SHOPPING & SERVICES

I'd like to buy ...
Ich möchte ... kaufen. ikh merkh·te ... kow·fen

I'm just looking.
Ich schaue mich nur um. ikh show·e mikh noor um

Can I look at it?
Können Sie es mir zeigen? ker·nen zee es meer tsai·gen

How much is this?
Wie viel kostet das? vee feel kos·tet das

That's too expensive.
Das ist zu teuer. das ist tsoo toy·er

Can you lower the price?
Können Sie mit dem Preis heruntergehen? ker·nen zee mit dem prais he·run·ter·gay·en

There's a mistake in the bill.
Da ist ein Fehler in der Rechnung. dah ist ain fay·ler in dair rekh·nung

ATM	Geldautomat	gelt·ow·to·maht
PIN	Geheimnummer	ge·haim·nu·mer
post office	Postamt	post·amt
tourist office	Fremdenverkehrsbüro	frem·den·fer·kairs·bü·raw

TIME & DATES

What time is it?
Wie spät ist es? vee shpayt ist es

It's (one) o'clock.
Es ist (ein) Uhr. es ist (ain) oor

Half past one.
Halb zwei. (lit: 'half two') halp tsvai

morning	Morgen	mor·gen
afternoon	Nachmittag	nahkh·mi·tahk
evening	Abend	ah·bent
yesterday	gestern	ges·tern
today	heute	hoy·te
tomorrow	morgen	mor·gen

Monday	Montag	mawn·tahk
Tuesday	Dienstag	deens·tahk
Wednesday	Mittwoch	mit·vokh
Thursday	Donnerstag	do·ners·tahk
Friday	Freitag	frai·tahk
Saturday	Samstag	zams·tahk
Sunday	Sonntag	zon·tahk

January	Januar	yan·u·ahr
February	Februar	fay·bru·ahr
March	März	merts
April	April	a·pril
May	Mai	mai
June	Juni	yoo·ni
July	Juli	yoo·li
August	August	ow·gust
September	September	zep·tem·ber
October	Oktober	ok·taw·ber
November	November	no·vem·ber
December	Dezember	de·tsem·ber

TRANSPORT

Public Transport

boat	Boot	bawt
bus	Bus	bus
plane	Flugzeug	flook·tsoyk
train	Zug	tsook

At what time does it leave?
Wann fährt es ab?   van fairt es ap

At what time does it arrive?
Wann kommt es an?   van komt es an

I want to go to ...
Ich mochte nach ...   ikh merkh·te nahkh ...
fahren.   fah·ren

Does it stop at ...?
Hält es in ...?   helt es in ...

I want to get off here.
Ich mochte hier   ikh merkh·te heer
aussteigen.   ows·shtai·gen

| one-way ticket | einfache Falırkarte | ain·fa·khe fahr·kar·te |
| return ticket | Rückfahrkarte | rük·fahr·kar·te |

first	erste	ers·te
last	letzte	lets·te
next	nächste	naykhs·te

aisle seat	Platz am Gang	plats am gang
platform	Bahnsteig	bahn·shtaik
ticket office	Fahrkarten- verkauf	fahr·kar·ten- fer·kowf
timetable	Fahrplan	fahr·plahn
train station	Bahnhof	bahn·hawf
window seat	Fensterplatz	fens·ter·plats

Numbers

1	eins	ains
2	zwei	tsvai
3	drei	drai
4	vier	feer
5	fünf	fünf
6	sechs	zeks
7	sieben	zee·ben
8	acht	akht
9	neun	noyn
10	zehn	tsayn
20	zwanzig	tsvan·tsikh
30	dreißig	drai·sikh
40	vierzig	feer·tsikh
50	fünfzig	fünf·tsikh
60	sechzig	zekh·tsikh
70	slebzig	zeep·tsikh
80	achtzig	akht·tsikh
90	neunzig	noyn·tsikh
100	hundert	hun·dert
1000	tausend	tow·sent

Driving & Cycling

I'd like to hire a ...	Ich möchte ein ... mieten.	ikh merkh·te ain ... mee·ten
bicycle	Fahrrad	fahr·raht
car	Auto	ain ow·to
motorcycle	Motorrad	maw·tor·raht

child seat	Kindersitz	kin·der·zits
helmet	Helm	helm
mechanic	Mechaniker	me·khah·ni·ker
petrol/gas	Benzin	ben·tseen
pump	Luftpumpe	luft·pum·pe
service station	Tankstelle	tangk·shte·le

Does this road go to ...?
Führt diese Strasse   fürt dee·ze shtrah·se
nach ...?   nahkh ...

Can I park here?
Kann ich hier parken?   kan ikh heer par·ken

The car has broken down (at ...).
Ich habe (in ...) eine   ikh hah·be (in ...) ai·ne
Panne mit meinem Auto.   pa·ne mit mai·nem ow·to

I have a flat tyre.
Ich habe eine   ikh hah·be ai·ne
Reifenpanne.   rai·fen·pa·ne

I've run out of petrol.
Ich habe kein Benzin   ikh hah·be kain ben·tseen
mehr.   mair

Behind the Scenes

SEND US YOUR FEEDBACK

We love to hear from travellers – your comments keep us on our toes and help make our books better. Our well-travelled team reads every word on what you loved or loathed about this book. Although we cannot reply individually to postal submissions, we always guarantee that your feedback goes straight to the appropriate authors, in time for the next edition. Each person who sends us information is thanked in the next edition – the most useful submissions are rewarded with a selection of digital PDF chapters.

Visit **lonelyplanet.com/contact** to submit your updates and suggestions or to ask for help. Our award-winning website also features inspirational travel stories, news and discussions.

Note: We may edit, reproduce and incorporate your comments in Lonely Planet products such as guidebooks, websites and digital products, so let us know if you don't want your comments reproduced or your name acknowledged. For a copy of our privacy policy visit lonelyplanet.com/privacy.

OUR READERS

Many thanks to the travellers who used the last edition and wrote to us with helpful hints, useful advice and interesting anecdotes:
Bill Evans, Ciska Tillema, George MacDonald, Katrin Flatscher, Laurent Candelon, Markus Deutsch, Martin Hellwagner, Natalie Walker, Nikki Buran, Sain Alizada, Sebastian Cosgrove, Sheri Hendsbee, Torben Retboll, Wilfried Nutz.

AUTHOR THANKS

Anthony Haywood

Many thanks to the many Viennese who helped with expert knowledge and advice for that chapter – including staff at the Vienna Tourist Board, Ishimitsu Takako for her interview, Reini Weissensteiner for offering tips in Vienna and the Gesäuse, Andreas Hollinger in the Gesäuse, and to those who provided information at the various stops along the way. Many thanks to coauthors Kerry Christiani and Marc Di Duca for their great work on the book, commissioning editor Dora Whitaker, Annelies Mertens and the rest of the LP team.

Kerry Christiani

A big thank you to Monika Christiani for her company on the trails in Tyrol and Salzburg. A heartfelt *dankeschön*, too, goes to Salzburg tour guide Christiana Schneeweis and the après-ski instructors in St Anton including Maggie Ritson and Shane Pearce for their invaluable local knowledge. Thanks to all the tourism professionals who made the road to research smooth, especially Sabine Günterseder (Upper Austria Tourism), Birgit Weszelka (Salzburg Information) and Colette Spiss-Verra (Innsbruck Tourism). Last but not least, thanks to Dora Whitaker, coauthors Anthony and Marc and the entire Lonely Planet production team.

Marc Di Duca

Many thanks go to staff at tourist offices across Lower Austria and Burgenland for their invaluable assistance throughout, especially those in Krems, Melk and Eisenstadt, and to the Austrian National Tourist Office in London. Huge thanks to my parents-in-law in Kyiv for looking after the boys while I was on the road and to my wife, Tanya, for the patience she shows during all the days we spend apart.

ACKNOWLEDGMENTS

Climate map data adapted from Peel MC, Finlayson BL & McMahon TA (2007) 'Updated World Map of the Köppen-Geiger Climate Classification', Hydrology and Earth System Sciences, 11, 1633¬44.

Vienna U- & S-Bahn map © 2013 Wiener Linien

Cover photograph: Schloss Schönbühel, The Danube Valley, Lower Austria, Giovanni Simeone/4Corners

THIS BOOK

This 7th edition of Lonely Planet's *Austria* guidebook was researched and written by Anthony Haywood, Kerry Christiani and Marc Di Duca. Anthony and Kerry also worked on the 5th and 6th editions and on the latter with Caroline Sieg. The 4th edition was written by Neal Bedford and Gemma Pitcher. The first three editions were written by Mark Honan. This guidebook was commissioned in Lonely Planet's London office, and produced by the following:

Commissioning Editor
Dora Whitaker
Coordinating Editors
Penny Cordner, Monique Perrin
Senior Cartographer
Corey Hutchison
Book Designer Mazzy Prinsep
Managing Editors Annelies Mertens, Angela Tinson, Sasha Baskett
Senior Editors Karyn Noble, Catherine Naghten
Assisting Editors Carolyn Bain, Charlotte Orr, Susan Paterson

Assisting Cartographers
Jennifer Johnston, Eve Kelly, Gabriel Lindquist, James Leversha
Cover Research Naomi Parker
Language Content
Branislava Vladisavljevic
Thanks to Anita Banh, Ryan Evans, Samantha Forge, Larissa Frost, Mark Griffiths, Genesys India, Jouve India, Indra Kilfoyle, Alison Lyall, Korina Miller, Virginia Moreno, Trent Paton, Dianne Schallmeiner, John Taufa, Juan Winata

Index

NOTES

Map Legend

Sights

- Beach
- Bird Sanctuary
- Buddhist
- Castle/Palace
- Christian
- Confucian
- Hindu
- Islamic
- Jain
- Jewish
- Monument
- Museum/Gallery/Historic Building
- Ruin
- Sento Hot Baths/Onsen
- Shinto
- Sikh
- Taoist
- Winery/Vineyard
- Zoo/Wildlife Sanctuary
- Other Sight

Activities, Courses & Tours

- Bodysurfing
- Diving
- Canoeing/Kayaking
- Course/Tour
- Skiing
- Snorkelling
- Surfing
- Swimming/Pool
- Walking
- Windsurfing
- Other Activity

Sleeping

- Sleeping
- Camping

Eating

- Eating

Drinking & Nightlife

- Drinking & Nightlife
- Cafe

Entertainment

- Entertainment

Shopping

- Shopping

Information

- Bank
- Embassy/Consulate
- Hospital/Medical
- Internet
- Police
- Post Office
- Telephone
- Toilet
- Tourist Information
- Other Information

Geographic

- Beach
- Hut/Shelter
- Lighthouse
- Lookout
- Mountain/Volcano
- Oasis
- Park
- Pass
- Picnic Area
- Waterfall

Population

- Capital (National)
- Capital (State/Province)
- City/Large Town
- Town/Village

Transport

- Airport
- Border crossing
- Bus
- Cable car/Funicular
- Cycling
- Ferry
- Metro station
- Monorail
- Parking
- Petrol station
- S-Bahn/S-train/Subway station
- Taxi
- T-bane/Tunnelbana station
- Train station/Railway
- Tram
- Tube station
- U-Bahn/Underground station
- Other Transport

Note: Not all symbols displayed above appear on the maps in this book

Routes

- Tollway
- Freeway
- Primary
- Secondary
- Tertiary
- Lane
- Unsealed road
- Road under construction
- Plaza/Mall
- Steps
- Tunnel
- Pedestrian overpass
- Walking Tour
- Walking Tour detour
- Path/Walking Trail

Boundaries

- International
- State/Province
- Disputed
- Regional/Suburb
- Marine Park
- Cliff
- Wall

Hydrography

- River, Creek
- Intermittent River
- Canal
- Water
- Dry/Salt/Intermittent Lake
- Reef

Areas

- Airport/Runway
- Beach/Desert
- Cemetery (Christian)
- Cemetery (Other)
- Glacier
- Mudflat
- Park/Forest
- Sight (Building)
- Sportsground
- Swamp/Mangrove

OUR STORY

A beat-up old car, a few dollars in the pocket and a sense of adventure. In 1972 that's all Tony and Maureen Wheeler needed for the trip of a lifetime – across Europe and Asia overland to Australia. It took several months, and at the end – broke but inspired – they sat at their kitchen table writing and stapling together their first travel guide, *Across Asia on the Cheap*. Within a week they'd sold 1500 copies. Lonely Planet was born.

Today, Lonely Planet has offices in Melbourne, London and Oakland, with more than 600 staff and writers. We share Tony's belief that 'a great guidebook should do three things: inform, educate and amuse'.

OUR WRITERS

Anthony Haywood

Coordinating Author, Vienna, Styria, The Salzkammergut, Carinthia Born in Fremantle, Western Australia, Anthony pulled anchor early on to hitchhike in Europe, the US and North Africa. Aberystwyth in Wales and Ealing in London were his wintering grounds in those days. He later studied comparative literature and Russian. In the 1990s, fresh from a spell in post-Soviet, pre-anything Moscow, Anthony moved to Germany and became a frequent traveller to Austria. Expeditions along the urban rifts of Vienna later gave way to long journeys into the other cities and regions of Austria. Some of those were to update earlier editions of this book. Anthony is a freelance journalist and writer. His publications include numerous Lonely Planet guidebooks, a cultural history of Siberia, travel articles, short stories and translations.

Anthony also wrote the Understand and Survival Guide sections, and most of the Plan Your Trip section of this guide.

Read more about Anthony at:
lonelyplanet.com/members/anthonyhaywood

Kerry Christiani

Upper Austria, Salzburg & Salzburgerland, Tyrol & Vorarlberg Kerry's first encounter with real snow in Tyrol 15 years ago sparked her enduring love affair with the Austrian Alps, and she's been coming back ever since. For this edition, she road-tested Mozart and Maria trails in Salzburg, sweated out rare 40°C temperatures in the Alps and climbed (almost) every mountain. Kerry is an award-winning travel writer, and has authored/coauthored some 20 guidebooks, including Lonely Planet's *Switzerland*, *Germany* and *France*.

Kerry also wrote the Eat & Drink Like a Local and Austria Outdoors chapters for this edition. She tweets @kerrychristiani and lists her latest work at www.kerrychristiani.com.

Read more about Kerry at:
lonelyplanet.com/members/kerrychristiani

Marc Di Duca

Lower Austria & Burgenland An exchange visit in the mid-1980s provided Marc's first taste of Austria and he's been dipping into the land of Mozart and schnitzel ever since. However, with no head for heights, it's the often-overlooked flatlands around Vienna and the gentle hills of the Danube Valley that Marc returns to most gladly.

Read more about Marc at:
lonelyplanet.com/members/Madidu

Published by Lonely Planet Publications Pty Ltd
ABN 36 005 607 983
7th edition – May 2014
ISBN 978 1 74220 047 7
© Lonely Planet 2014 Photographs © as indicated 2014
10 9 8 7 6 5 4 3 2 1
Printed in China

Although the authors and Lonely Planet have taken all reasonable care in preparing this book, we make no warranty about the accuracy or completeness of its content and, to the maximum extent permitted, disclaim all liability arising from its use.